Fairmount Park, Philadelphia.

Centennial Newspaper Exhibition, 1876.

A Complete List of American Newspapers,
A Statement of the Industries, Characteristics, Population and Location of Towns in which they are published; also,
A Descriptive account of some of the Great Newspapers of the day.

Compiled by Geo. P. Rowell & Co.,
New York.
1876.

AMERICAN

Newspaper Directory,

EDITION FOR 1876,

CONTAINS:

A complete list of Newspapers and other Periodicals in the United States, Territories, and Dominion of Canada, arranged alphabetically by towns, giving name, days of issue, politics or general character, form, size, subscription price per year, date of establishment, editors' and publishers' names, and circulation.

ALSO THE FOLLOWING CLASSIFIED LISTS:

Periodicals publishing over 5,000 copies each issue; Religious Newspapers and Periodicals; Newspapers and Periodicals devoted to Agriculture, Horticulture, and Stock Raising; Medicine and Surgery; Educational Institutions or devoted to Educational Matters; Amusement and Instruction of children; Freemasonry, Oddfellowship, Temperance, and Knights of Pythias; Commerce and Finance, Insurance, Real Estate, Science and Mechanics, Law, Printers and Publishers, Sporting, Music, Fashions, and Woman's Suffrage; also, Newspapers and Periodicals printed wholly or in part in the German, French, Scandinavian, Spanish, Hollandish, Italian, Welsh, Bohemian, Portuguese, Polish and Hebrew languages.

The object of the American Newspaper Directory is not very different from that of the well-known mercantile agencies which exist in all our leading cities. The latter keep their subscribers informed of the character, habits, reputation, business ability, and financial strength of persons with whom they are likely to have business transactions, enabling them thereby to so regulate those transactions as to secure probably profitable dealings, or to avoid such as will be likely to result in ultimate annoyance or loss.

The Directory conveys the best obtainable information concerning the character and value of newspapers. Its patrons are the men who expend money in advertising (a large and important class), and it is from them that the publishers of the Directory, in their capacity of Advertising Agents, derive their profit and support.

As the most important portion of the information supplied by a mercantile agency consists of a report of the financial strength of the person about whom information is asked, so is the *circulation* of a newspaper generally considered the point upon which information will be of most value to the advertiser.

The greatest possible care is taken to make the Directory reports correct. Every publisher is applied to very systematically. All information is taken in a form which excludes any but definite statements which cannot be misunderstood; while every effort is made to protect honest publishers against such as would resort to lying or perjured reports to gain an unfair advantage.

ONE THOUSAND PAGES. PRICE, FIVE DOLLARS

PUBLISHED BY

GEO. P. ROWELL & CO., ADVERTISING AGENTS,

(Newspaper Pavilion, Centennial Grounds, Philadelphia.)

PRINCIPAL OFFICE: 41 PARK ROW, NEW YORK.

Fairmount Park, Philadelphia.

(FOUNTAIN AVE., OPPOSITE U. S. GOV'T BUILDING.)

CENTENNIAL

Newspaper Exhibition,

1876.

A Complete List of American Newspapers.

A Statement of the Industries, Characteristics, Population and Location of Towns in which they are published; also,

A Descriptive account of some of the Great Newspapers of the day.

NEW YORK:

COMPILED BY GEO. P. ROWELL & CO.,

1876

(*Licensed by the Catalogue Co.*)

WHEAT & CORNETT,
BOOK, JOB AND NEWSPAPER PRINTERS,
8 SPRUCE STREET, N. Y.

CRUM & RINGLER,
MANHATTAN ELECTROTYPE
1.3 NASSAU STREET, N.

PREFACE.

The early proposition for the celebration of the first century of American nationality was simply patriotic, but it took on no definite form. As the people grew familiar with the idea this vagueness drifted into the shape which it has since assumed. Its present form seemed the best, as it utilized the world's selfishness and made it give eclat to the occasion. We invited all peoples to exhibit their handiwork and products here among our millions of customers and consumers, and they accepted our proposition and did come, bringing with them their inventions and their works.

[illegible]ventions which have benefited mankind in all ages had their origin in man's lo[illegible]r comforts. As the forests fell before the axe of civilization, the pick and shovel, aided by steam, upheaved the coal from its beds where nature had stored it away cycles of ages before; as wheat fields replaced the felled forests, the invention of steam-plows and agricultural implements to garner the fruits of the earth appeared; as man craved intercourse with his fellow the world around, correspondence became a necessity, and the lightnings were laid under contribution to unite them; and as civilization advanced, bringing in its train a taste for luxuries unknown in ruder days, the heavens, earth and seas were ransacked by the scientific and plodding to gratify it. The first great Exposition of the world's industry simply developed the extent to which man had advanced in economics a quarter of a century ago, and incited other nations to emulate the English in their adventure. The displays in other lands which followed rapidly, testified to the same desire for comforts and luxuries; and this, the latest Exposition, telling the same story in the Western Hemisphere, is a fitting memorial of the first century which has passed over these United States. In the various buildings dotting the Park at Fairmount may be seen the works of art and usefulness which sprang from the necessities of mankind, and taxed inventive genius and mechanical knowledge to contribute to their enjoyment. Necessity, like the great central engine, which the hand of our President sent wheeling on its course, moving the machinery through all the extent of that huge hall, has brought together the wise men of the world with their offerings of "gold and frankincense," to lay them before the new dispensation of "peace on earth, good will to men." Our mechanic, as he wanders through the corridors of the buildings, may learn to estimate properly his works, by comparing them with those of other lands. While it was most proper and will be profitable that the works of the world's busy artificers and artists should be here displayed, the initiatory steps for a fitting representation of the unity, extent and progress of the 'Press" were not taken until long after the inception of the idea of a suitable commemoration of our Nation's natal day. All agree that the Press is potential and useful, and it was believed to have kept pace with other industries, but none thought of specially exhibiting it in its entirety. Its scientific magazines supplied the mental pabulum which fed the genius of our inventors; its records of victories in mechanics and useful arts have inspired others to experiment and effort; its illustrated journals presented to every citizen at most moderate prices the models of buildings, tools, machinery, and whatever else was deemed desirable in this direction. It was elevating in this land the standard of taste and work, and building up as its reflex the schools which abound in our country. As an evidence of what we might have been without this instrumentality, it may be well to point to nations where the press has no existence. In Egypt there is not one paper printed in the Arabic language; some few there are in French and German, but not for the Egyptians, and the rudeness of the work of the general people testifies to the lack of popular instruction through the power of newspapers. Track the globe around, and those lands will be found most highly civilized and forward in catering to their people's comfort where the press is most plentiful, free and powerful. On the banks of a beautiful lake glistening between the Machinery Hall and the United States buildings stands a modest house, costing but little in money and small in extent, yet in it are gathered every newspaper and magazine published in this country.

There are eight thousand one hundred and twenty-nine newspapers published regularly in the United States. The combined issues of all the other nations of the earth do not equal this number. An exhibition of a sample copy of each of all these thousands of periodicals would hardly convey an adequate idea of the importance of journalism in this country, yet it would do something towards that end; and believing that it would not be practical to attempt more, Messrs. Geo. P. Rowell & Co., in the early spring of 1875, addressed the Centennial Commission, making application for space in the main building, estimating that room would be required for fifty volumes of two thousand pages each. This was before the departments were thoroughly organized, and no response having been made to their formal application, the matter waited in abeyance until September, when it was again brought up by General Joseph R. Hawley, President of the Commission, and an exhibition was finally arranged, as set forth in the following correspondence:

GEO. P. ROWELL & CO., New York City, PHILADELPHIA, Sept. 17, 1875.
Gentlemen:—Some time ago I made a memorandum that I must write you concerning an exhibit of the American newspaper, that wonderful feature in American civilization. It seems to me that an exhibit of its progress during the century and its present condition would be exceedingly interesting. Could every existing American periodical from semi-annual down to daily be shown? How and where? Have you any scheme in mind? Can you submit a plan? Can you come here and talk it over? Respectfully yours,
J. R. HAWLEY, President U. S. C. C

GEO. P. ROWELL & CO., New York, PHILADELPHIA, Sept. 20, 1875
Gentlemen:—I have just read your note of the 18th. By all means develop the project. There ought to be a presentation of the periodical press of 1776 and 1876. * * * Do not forget this matter. Hastily yours, JOSEPH R. HAWLEY.

GEO. P. ROWELL, 41 Park Row, New York, PHILADELPHIA, Nov. 15, 1875.
Dear Sir:—Did I answer your letter? I'm not sure. * * * * I shall be glad to see you, for your exhibition *ought to be made.* The American newspaper is a peculiar institution—a special feature of American political and general education.
Hastily yours, J. R. HAWLEY.

GEO. P. ROWELL, ESQ., PHILADELPHIA, Nov. 20, 1875.
Dear Sir:—Your application for space in the International Exhibition for a display of sample copies of every periodical in the United States has been placed before me for consideration. It has been suggested that such an exhibition would be very much more attractive and interesting if an outside pavilion were provided for that purpose. * * * * I most cordially commend this suggestion to you, with the hope that the newspaper interest of the country will join in providing such a pavilion, which would be a distinctive feature of the Exhibition. * * * * *
Yours very respectfully, A. T. GOSHORN, Director-General.

GEO. P. ROWELL, ESQ., PHILADELPHIA, Jan. 12th, 1876.
Dear Sir:—We have a number of applications similar. * * * * It is not my intention to grant any other privilege of this kind. Yours very respectfully,
A. T. GOSHORN, Director-General.

MR. GEO. P. ROWELL, FAIRMOUNT PARK, PHILADELPHIA, 1876.
Dear Sir:—I have made a new design for your building, and will send the drawings to you in a few days. Yours respectfully, W. J. SCHWARZMANN, Architect.

MESSRS. GEO. P. ROWELL & CO., PHILADELPHIA, Jan. 15, 1876.
Gentlemen:— * * * * I called Mr. Schwarzmann's attention to the subject of your letter yesterday, and he will transmit to-day or Monday the plans for your proposed building. I hope very soon to be advised definitely of your success in securing the Exhibition. Yours very respectfully,
A. T. GOSHORN, Director-General.

GEO. P. ROWELL, ESQ., FAIRMOUNT PARK, PHILADELPHIA, 1876.
Dear Sir:—I sent you to-day by Adams' Express the drawings for your building. The general arrangement and construction remain the same.
Yours respectfully, W. J. SCHWARZMANN.

GEO. P. ROWELL, ESQ., 41 Park Row, PHILADELPHIA, Jan. 29, 1876.
Dear Sir:—I am right glad you are going ahead with your work. It will be as distinctive and interesting an American exhibit as we shall have on the grounds. * * * *
Yours truly, J. R. HAWLEY.

It was now decided to attempt a much more comprehensive display than had first been thought of. Instead of a sample copy of a paper, every publisher was to be allowed to exhibit a file for several weeks or months, and in place of being bound up in heavy volumes it was arranged that every paper should be made instantly accessible, and the exhibition thus serve the additional purpose of a monster reading room and an exchange for newspaper men.

About this time Messrs. Rowell & Co. received a communication from a well known printer (Peter C. Baker, Esq., of New York), who has devoted much time to the interests of the craft. He writes as follows:

"The pamphlet, job and ornamental printers will, I believe, very generally present the best specimens of their work; and many of these beautiful productions of typographical skill will show what rapid advances the printer is making toward placing himself by the side of the artist and engraver.

"But what is the Newspaper and Periodical Press doing to show that in this department especially our country surpasses all other nations of the world? I have not yet learned that any positive arrangements have been made to give tangible evidence of the immensity of the newspaper and periodical interests of our country, and therefore I very respectfully and earnestly suggest that immediate steps be taken to take this important matter in charge, and prepare a plan by which a copy of every newspaper and periodical published in the United States be collected and shown at the Centennial. No feature of the exhibition would be more effective than this to show the world the general intelligence of our people, and make plain the secret of the success of our republican experiment."

Other communications of a kindred tenor came from unexpected sources.

Being thus encouraged, plans were perfected and adopted. A prominent position was assigned the Newspaper Pavilion by Director-General Goshorn on Fountain Avenue.

The above engraving represents the exterior. The following description first appeared in the New York *Sun* of February 14th:

"The plan of exhibition is an alphabetical arrangement of partial files of each newspaper or periodical in such a manner as makes them instantly accessible, the space devoted to each bearing a label with the name of the publication printed thereon, and further designated by a number, by means of which a stranger, upon reference to his catalogue, is able at once to approach the section of the building where the particular journal which he desires to examine or refer to may be found.

"The cases containing these files form alcoves similar to those in public libraries for the arrangement of books, these alcoves forming long tiers, one on each side of the building, throughout its entire length, a portion of the space between being reserved for the accommodation of attendants, leaving a passage-way for the public eighteen feet in width, extending from one end of the structure to the other.

"The second story, approached by four flights of stairs, is devoted to reading rooms for the accommodation more especially of newspaper men, and supplied with conveniences for correspondents."

A better impression of the interior architecture may be obtained from the following written after an examination of the plans by GAR, the accomplished (but decidedly critical) correspondent of the New York *Times*, in its issue of February 20th:

"The building is of timber and very neat. It has a length of sixty-seven feet, with a width of forty-six feet, and a total height of thirty-three feet. From the exterior it appears to be in two stories, but the centre of the building is only one story, and is a very fine chamber, with ample light and space. The whole is arranged with that precision and mastery over details which have gained for Mr. Rowell his celebrity as a business man. The alcoves are fairly lighted by windows which occupy the entire space between them, so that there is no difficulty in obtaining the wished-for file if the directions furnished are followed. The height of the side chambers where these alcoves are placed is eight feet, and over them are the writing galleries, where numerous desks are placed. Nothing can be simpler or more efficacious than this system, which, undoubtedly, is the very best that could have been devised. The galleries are lighted by rows of windows corresponding to those in the alcoves below, and by the large transom windows at each end. In the facade this window is set back from the gable roof about five feet, and a very effective ornamentation of radiating, incised planking is introduced, which relieves very pleasantly the simplicity of the structure. The interior is perfectly ventilated by a large lantern roof, and therefore the building deserves the praise of being thoroughly lighted, thoroughly ventilated, and of being admirably arranged for the desired purpose."

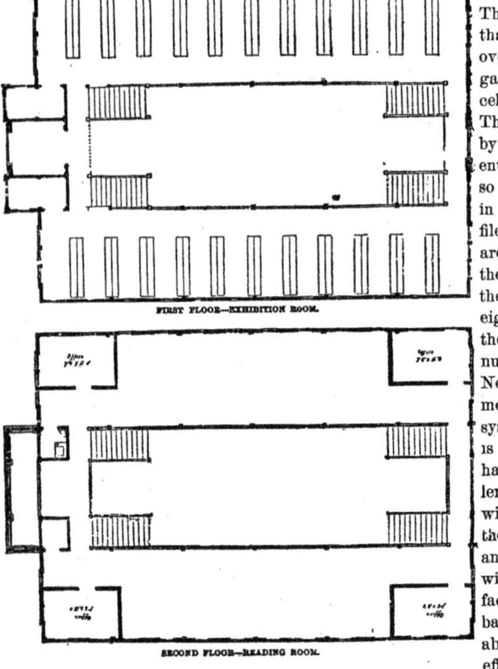

FIRST FLOOR—EXHIBITION ROOM.

SECOND FLOOR—READING ROOM.

The cost of the structure, with its fittings and furniture, has not fallen short of ten thousand dollars, while the necessary attendants, books, blanks, together with the compilation and distribution of a large edition of a three hundred page catalogue, require another allowance of a similar amount. In the mere item of postage more than twelve hundred dollars was expended before the opening day of the exhibition. When it is remembered that no less than two hundred and fifty dollars' worth of stamps are required to communicate once with all the publishers, the rapidity with which these items count up is readily comprehended.

But with all these matters Messrs. Rowell & Co. had abundant experience. Furthermore, through intimate relations with the press of the country, extending over a period of more than ten years, they had always been seconded in a most generous manner. They were therefore fully convinced of two things: First, that their efforts would be appreciated by publishers to such an extent that the entire expense of the exhibition would be returned to them in the form of voluntary subscriptions. Second, that should this fail entirely, the exhibition would be worth its full cost as an advertisement of their own business, as conductors of the most complete newspaper advertising agency in the world.

In their application to publishers to send their papers and contribute towards the enterprise they made the following pledge:

"The Exhibition will be made precisely as set forth, even if there should not be a single subscription offered."

Events have shown that their faith in the good-will and intelligent co-operation of publishers was not misplaced.

The proprietors of leading journals responded with such promptness and generosity that they may be said to have themselves assumed the cost of the exhibition.

An opportunity to contribute to the money expense was offered only to Representative Newspapers, and it is believed that among those of prominence which have neglected to respond not one has done so from an unfriendly feeling towards the enterprise, but mainly or solely from the pressing call for an economical management of expenditures which the stagnation of business for two years just past has made so loud in many establishments deemed prosperous.

Nothing but good-will has been evinced from the beginning. No disparaging word has appeared in any respectable journal, while favorable comments have filled the columns of the press from Maine to Oregon, from Florida to Texas.

One of the most pleasing features has been the handsome manner in which Messrs. Rowell & Co. have been encouraged by their brother advertising agents, as evinced by the following extracts from letters received:

Offices, 37 Park Row, N. Y.; 10 State St., Boston; 701 Chestnut St., Philadelphia, February 22, 1876.

We are pleased to learn that you have made arrangements to erect a building on the Centennial Exhibition grounds, in which to keep complete files of the newspapers of our country for the use of the public, and that you will also have good accommodations for editors, reporters, publishers, and others connected with the press. The enterprise could not be in better hands, and we hope and believe it will prove a great success.

Yours truly, S. M. PETTENGILL & Co.

S. R. NILES' NEWSPAPER ADVERTISING AGENCY, BOSTON, Feb. 14, 1876.

Permit me to express my gratification that to you has been delegated the important task of making a complete exhibition of the newspapers and periodicals of the country at the forthcoming Centennial. From your extensive business connections and personal popularity with the press in all parts of the country, and your well-known experience and ability, no one, I am sure, could be selected who would manage it more satisfactorily. The whole newspaper fraternity are to be congratulated that this attractive and interesting exhibition is in such able hands. It will afford me pleasure to co-operate with you or assist you in any way in my power.

Very truly yours, S. R. NILES.

S. H. PARVIN, PIONEER ADVERTISING AGENCY, CINCINNATI, Feb. 14, 1876.

I am more than gratified that such an exhibition is to be made. * *

Yours truly, S. H. PARVIN.

BOSTON, Feb. 15, 1876.

* * * * I can but commend the enterprising spirit manifested in such an undertaking. Notwithstanding the immense number of the exhibitions of skill and enterprise, such a building as you propose and such an array of newspapers as you suggest, will attract a large number of visitors. * * * * No one, I think, can do this thing better.

Truly yours, U. L. PETTENGILL.

C. A. COOK & CO'S. NEWSPAPER ADVERTISING AGENCY, CHICAGO, Feb. 15, 1876.

* * * * We know of no agency—*in the East*—better calculated to conduct and insure success in such an enterprise. * * * *

Yours truly, C. A. COOK.

T. C. EVANS' ADVERTISING AGENCY, 252 WASHINGTON ST., BOSTON, Feb. 11 1876.

I cannot refrain from expressing my gratification at the prospect of there being at the Centennial such an exhibition as you contemplate. It deserves to be, and I feel sure under your management it *cannot help being* a success. I should be glad if I could do anything to help you make it so. * * * *

Yours very truly, T. C. EVANS.

CINCINNATI, Feb. 6, 1876.

In congratulating you on your appointment to the management of the newspaper department in connection with the Centennial Exposition, we express not only our own conviction, but we believe also that of the entire fraternity, when we say that the Commission have done well in selecting you for this responsible position. Your well known ability as a manager is a sure guarantee of a successful exhibition.

Yours truly, E. N. FRESHMAN & BROS.

CHICAGO, Feb. 14, 1876.

Allow us to express our gratification that you have been selected to carry out the plan.

Yours truly, CHANDLER, LORD & CO.

DODD'S NEWSPAPER ADVERTISING AGENCY,
265 WASHINGTON STREET, BOSTON, Feb. 14, 1876.

I know of no one more competent to carry out the arrangement than yourself, and it assures me at once of its success. I will render all aid possible.

Yours very truly, HORACE DODD.

BATES & LOCKE'S NEWSPAPER ADVERTISING AGENCY,
NEW YORK, Feb. 28, 1876.

Your proposed exhibition of American newspapers at the Centennial not only deserves to succeed but will certainly do so, because you are a good man to have it in charge, and because you will surely have the cordial co-operation and good wishes of all persons in any wise connected with the newspaper press.

Yours truly, J. H. BATES.

That Philadelphia agents were the only ones not joining in these expressions is doubtless of greater apparent than real significance.

Americans are a nation of newspaper readers. There are papers for girls and boys, for teachers and taught, for trades, arts and sciences, for the lovers of the wonderful, the religious, the agriculturists, the metallurgists—in a word, the physician, as he rides to the expected birthplace of some young patient, and the undertaker, as he drives to the house of mourning, must each have his paper to while away his time. The opening exercises of the 10th of May were read by millions in every part of this land, and carried to distant countries by the press and the aid of the telegram it called to its use.

Good men are not afraid of criticism by the press. It makes statesmen and unmasks hypocrites; it incites to great deeds; it brings to every man's door the record of progress made in every department of learning and activity; it develops science, and whiles away the tedium of heavily hanging hours It fits out exploring expeditions to discover new fields for civilization; it lays before its readers the doings of the world's busy multitudes, the fall of empires, the uprisings of nationalities, the record of the Storm-king's progress around the world, the decisions of the forum, the acts of governors and legislators; it tells the farmer what to plant and when; it develops the latest inventions; it weighs in the nice balance of purity of motive the deeds of the ruling powers; before it the unjust tremble, and on its pages, as on the walls of the ancient banqueting hall, the wicked rulers may read, "weighed in the balance and found wanting"; it stirs the heart of benevolence to greater deeds of charity, it inspires the desponding, deters the plotters, and from the ruler to the humblest citizen, it throws its Minervian aegis around all alike. It is the voltaic pile, where is contained the vitalizing power of a universe. In this little Newspaper Pavilion, which may not be visited by all who go to the Centennial, are deposited the thousands of papers which mould American sentiment. At Virginia City one may go down the shaft of a mine which, in the dark and dismal rocks, is pouring out constantly a stream of molten silver to enrich man. Few will venture into those profound depths from curiosity alone, but the men at work keep right along turning out the precious metal for man's delectation and their own profit.

In these grounds is exhibited a nugget of silver said to weigh two tons, the product of one of those mines. Thousands of curious men and women are drawn about it, and look wonderingly and wistfully upon its huge form. It represents to man's cupidity just so much of life's happiness. But thieves may break through and steal such treasures. A short distance from this mass of metal stands the modest house where are clustered the fruits of ten thousand minds, printed so plainly that a wayfaring man, though a fool, need not err therein. Who thinks of the toiling thousands of earnest literary men and women, scattered over our states and territories, who waste midnight oil in preparing that mental food which, enduring when silver and gold have taken to them wings and departed never to return, proves to be a lasting comfort?

Newspapers are the synonym of goodness and virtue, however much some men may affect to despise them. It was a labor of almost infinite trouble to gather these papers from all quarters, but the work is a great success, and there is no worthier place to visit than the

NEWSPAPER PAVILION.

TABLES

OF NEWSPAPER STATISTICS, COMPLIED BY GEO. P. ROWELL & CO. FOR THE CENTENNIAL NEWSPAPER EXHIBITION; BASED UPON THE AMERICAN NEWSPAPER DIRECTORY FOR THE CURRENT YEAR AND THE UNITED STATES CENSUS FOR 1870.

1876.

A TABLE SHOWING THE NUMBER OF NEWSPAPERS AND PERIODICALS PUBLISHED IN THE UNITED STATES AND TERRITORIES. COMPILED BY GEO. P. ROWELL & CO., NEW YORK.

STATES.	*Daily.*	*Tri-Weekly.*	*Semi-Weekly.*	*Weekly.*	*Bi-Weekly.*	*Semi-Monthly.*	*Monthly.*	*Bi-Monthly.*	*Quarterly.*	*Total.*
Alabama	8	2	..	79	..	1	1	..	..	91
Arkansas	6	..	2	58	..	..	2	..	..	68
California	47	1	6	163	..	1	21	..	..	239
Connecticut	17	..	5	68	1	2	6	..	3	102
Delaware	5	..	..	16	2	..	..	..	1	24
District of Columbia	8	..	..	17	..	2	7	..	1	35
Florida	1	1	1	26	..	..	1	..	..	30
Georgia	11	4	2	118	..	1	17	..	..	153
Illinois	50	7	5	553	2	4	77	3	6	707
Indiana	35	3	3	307	1	2	23	..	1	375
Iowa	24	3	3	352	..	4	14	..	1	401
Kansas	14	1	..	139	..	..	4	..	..	158
Kentucky	10	3	3	109	..	5	8	1	..	139
Louisiana	9	..	1	84	2	..	1	1	..	98
Maine	8	1	..	64	1	..	8	..	1	83
Maryland	10	..	1	92	..	2	12	..	..	117
Massachusetts	27	1	11	236	4	3	55	..	9	346
Michigan	22	3	5	254	2	1	18	..	2	307
Minnesota	5	3	2	128	..	1	2	..	..	141
Mississippi	3	2	..	101	..	..	3	..	..	109
Missouri	27	4	2	305	1	3	32	1	3	378
Nebraska	8	..	..	91	..	..	6	..	..	105
Nevada	14	..	..	10	..	..	..	..	..	24
New Hampshire	9	..	..	49	..	..	6	..	1	65
New Jersey	23	..	3	139	1	1	8	1	1	177
New York	104	3	16	726	6	26	183	4	20	1,088
North Carolina	8	1	4	86	..	3	5	..	..	107
Ohio	33	12	8	436	4	12	58	1	4	568
Oregon	5	..	..	37	..	..	2	..	..	44
Pennsylvania	73	2	5	533	1	15	102	1	6	738
Rhode Island	6	..	1	18	..	..	2	..	..	27
South Carolina	4	2	1	61	1	1	5	..	2	77
Tennessee	10	..	2	106	1	2	14	..	1	136
Texas	23	1	5	152	..	..	5	..	..	186
Vermont	6	..	1	52	..	..	4	..	..	63
Virginia	20	3	8	95	..	9	12	.	..	147
West Virginia	5	2	1	63	..	1	2	..	1	75
Wisconsin	18	2	3	216	1	2	17	..	2	261
	716	67	110	6,139	31	104	743	13	66	7,989
Territories	22	3	11	96	2	1	4	..	1	140
Totals	738	70	121	6,235	33	105	747	13	67	8,129

A TABLE SHOWING THE AVERAGE CIRCULATION OF THE NEWSPAPERS AND PERIODICALS PRINTED IN THE UNITED STATES AND TERRITORIES. COMPILED FROM THE AMERICAN NEWSPAPER DICECTORY.

	Daily.	*Tri-Weekly.*	*Semi-Weekly.*	*Weekly.*	*Bi-Weekly.*	*Semi-Mon'ly.*	*Mon'ly.*	*Bi-Mon'ly.*	*Quarterly.*	*Total.*
Alabama.........	1,197	300	......	777	......	1,200	......	......	......	798
Arkansas.........	875	......	2,234	577	......	......	500	......	......	636
California.........	3,808	......	2.280	1,578	......	400	2,191	......	......	2,035
Connecticut.......	2,292	......	832	1,496	550	425	949	......	1,262	1,518
Delaware	2,211	......	......	984	......	......	......	......	......	1,257
Dist. of Columbia.	5,223	......	......	3,375	......	600	3,370	......	......	3,697
Florida...........	......	......	300	478	......	......	......	......	......	470
Georgia...........	1,590	392	325	1,262	......	25,000	1,886	......	......	1,496
Illinois............	2.835	650	1.480	1,536	1,500	1,942	3,607	1,200	1,800	1,819
Indiana	1,691	611	652	1,044	......	1,400	3,751	......	......	1,197
Iowa.............	828	290	545	919	......	1,492	1,041	......	......	912
Kansas.	1,336	200	......	900	......	......	3,500	......	......	970
Kentucky	3.109	812	767	1,644	......	4,000	1,734	334	......	1,691
Louisiana	3,114	......	8,000	903	2,250	......	500	......	......	1,229
Maine.............	1,511	456	......	2,407	525	......	14,474	......	1,568	3,062
Maryland	11,336	......	1,000	2,280	......	......	3,075	......	......	3,077
Massachusetts.....	9,942	664	1,747	3,777	1,263	4,480	8,258	......	2,336	4,582
Michigan.........	2,423	767	770	1,198	400	200	2,556	......	......	1,327
Minnesota.........	2,657	500	400	945	......	......	1,273	......	......	994
Mississippi	734	360	......	811	......	......	......	......	......	802
Missouri..........	3,590	750	1,000	1.368	2,267	500	3,029	......	1,056	1,647
Nebraska.........	782	......	......	730	......	......	562	......	......	728
Nevada	795	......	......	400	......	......	......	......	......	690
New Hampshire..	919	......	......	2,051	......	......	4,167	......	......	1,982
New Jersey......	2,137	......	1,050	1,065	......	......	2,234	......	1,000	1,256
New York........	8,402	1,316	2,976	4,120	4,459	4,512	7,379	1,884	4.078	4,991
North Carolina...	1,063	100	475	829	......	1,496	350	......	......	831
Ohio.............	3,684	754	1,112	1,866	4,742	3,193	3,693	900	1,117	2,116
Oregon	1,739	......	......	888	......	......	......	......	......	936
Pennsylvania.....	5.038	1,400	1,839	2,125	1,000	2,009	7,562	......	700	2,919
Rhode Island.....	4,159	......	700	1,791	......	......	1,100	......	......	2,301
South Carolina....	2,097	424	400	804	500	......	694	......	600	835
Tennessee........	1,969	......	516	1,321	......	800	2,323	......	......	1,419
Texas............	855	......	389	782	......	......	......	......	......	785
Vermont..........	1,222	......	950	1,470	......	......	11,103	......	......	2,168
Virginia..........	858	350	482	940	......	594	1,945	......	......	927
West Virginia....	1,172	300	200	685	......	400	867	......	......	703
Wisconsin.........	1.324	700	444	992	417	350	2,967	......	......	1,098
Territories	787	564	1,196	822	1,000	......	3,275	......	......	914
Total averages..	3,877	650	1,400	1,768	2,144	2,994	5,144	1,347	2,399	2,196

A TABLE SHOWING THE AREA, POPULATION, ANNUAL CIRCULATION OF ALL NEWSPAPERS AND PERIODICALS PRINTED IN THE UNITED STATES AND TERRITORIES, AND THE NUMBER OF COPIES PRINTED PER YEAR FOR EACH INHABITANT, BASED UPON THE U. S. CENSUS FOR 1870, AND THE AMERICAN NEWSPAPER DIRECTORY FOR 1876.

	Area in Square Miles.	*Population, Census of 1870.*	*Total No. of Copies Printed Annually.*	*Average No. of Copies Printed Yearly for each inhabitant.*	*Average Area for each Publication, Sq. Miles.*
Alabama	50,722	996,992	5,132,980	5	557
Arkansas	52,198	484,471	1,787,844	4	768
California	188,981	582,031	52,596,100	90	791
Connecticut	4,750	537,454	14,020,376	26	47
Delaware	2,120	125,015	3,545,696	28	88
District of Columbia	64	131,700	10,152,000	77	2
Florida	59,268	188,248	577,148	3	1,976
Georgia	58,000	1,184,109	11,850,528	10	379
Illinois	55,410	.2,539,891	65,402,256	26	78
Indiana	33,809	1,680,637	28,666,132	11	90
Iowa	55,045	1,194,320	18,387,488	15	137
Kansas	81,318	373,299	9,670,252	26	515
Kentucky	37,680	1,321,011	14,585.996	11	271
Louisiana	41,346	726,915	12,116,124	17	422
Maine	35,000	626,915	12,084,526	19	422
Maryland	11,124	780,894	38,764,896	50	95
Massachusetts	7,800	1,457,351	115,853,116	79	23
Michigan	56,451	1,187,234	29,554,260	24	184
Minnesota	83,531	446,056	8,731,924	20	593
Mississippi	47,156	827,922	3,794,984	5	433
Missouri	65,350	1,721,295	43,441,738	25	173
Nebraska	75,995	129,322	4,063,720	31	724
Nevada	104,125	58,711	2,881,600	49	4,339
New Hampshire	9,280	318,300	7,485,920	24	143
New Jersey	8,320	906,096	21,005,944	23	47
New York	47,000	4,387,464	390,529,912	89	43
North Carolina	50,704	1,071,361	5,346,144	5	474
Ohio	39,964	2,665,260	74,404,936	28	70
Oregon	95,274	101,883	2,634,836	26	2,165
Pennsylvania	46,000	3,522,050	162,507,048	46	62
Rhode Island	1,306	217,353	9,387,272	43	48
South Carolina	34,000	705,606	4,315,844	6	442
Tennessee	45,600	1,258,520	11,127,384	9	335
Texas	274,356	818,899	10,339,020	13	1,475
Vermont	10,212	330,551	5,557,372	17	162
Virginia	38,348	1,225,163	8,997,000	7	261
West Virginia	23,000	442,014	3,826,328	9	307
Wisconsin	53,924	1,064,985	16,181,174	15	207
Territories	1,041,963	517,839	8,716,772	17	7,743
Totals	3,026,494	38,855,137	1,250,024,590	32	372

SUBSCRIBERS.

THE PROPRIETORS OF THE PROMINENT NEWSPAPERS ENUMERATED ON THE FOLLOWING PAGES RESPONDED WITH SUCH PROMPTNESS AND GENEROSITY TO THE CALL FOR SUBSCRIPTIONS TOWARDS DEFRAYING THE EXPENSE OF THE CENTENNIAL NEWSPAPER EXHIBITION, THAT MESSRS. GEO. P. ROWELL & CO. HAVE THE SATISFACTION OF SEEING THE ENTERPRISE A SUCCESS WITHOUT ANY ACTUAL COST TO THEMSELVES BEYOND THE CARE AND RESPONSIBILITY OF ITS SUPERVISION. IT IS TO THE PUBLISHERS OF THESE PAPERS, THEREFORE, THAT JOURNALISTS AND THE PUBLIC ARE MAINLY INDEBTED FOR THE MAGNIFICENT DISPLAY OF THE NEWSPAPER INTEREST OF THE UNITED STATES OF AMERICA.

THE PROPRIETORS OF THE FOLLOWING JOURNALS MAY BE SAID TO HAVE ASSUMED THE ENTIRE COST OF THE CENTENNIAL NEWSPAPER EXHIBITION:

NEW YORK.

THE ARGUS, Albany.
THE BROOKLYN EAGLE.
TIMES, Troy.

NEW YORK CITY.

THE COURRIER DES ETATS UNIS.
THE SUN.
THE NEW YORKER STAATS ZEITUNG.
AMERICAN AGRICULTURIST.
THE NEW YORK TIMES.
THE EVENING POST.
THE NEW YORK EVENING EXPRESS.
THE SCIENTIFIC AMERICAN.
SPIRIT OF THE TIMES.
THE NEW YORK LEDGER.
THE SHOE AND LEATHER REPORTER.
THE NEW YORK EVANGELIST.
THE NEW YORK WEEKLY.
THE NEW YORK CLIPPER.
THE CHURCHMAN.
THE IRON AGE.
THE CHRISTIAN UNION.
THE WORLD.

PENNSYLVANIA.

THE PHILADELPHIA DEMOCRAT.
THE PUBLIC LEDGER, Philadelphia.
THE PHILADELPHIA PRESS.
THE PRESBYTERIAN, Philadelphia.

DIST. OF COLUMBIA.

THE EVENING STAR, Washington.

OHIO.

THE CINCINNATI GAZETTE.
CLEVELAND HERALD.

KENTUCKY.

THE COURIER-JOURNAL, Louisville.

NEW JERSEY.

THE EVENING JOURNAL, Jersey City.

MICHIGAN.

THE EVENING NEWS, Detroit.

GEORGIA.

The Morning News, Savannah.

CALIFORNIA.

The Evening Bulletin, San Francisco.
The Morning Call, San Francisco.
Sacramento Record—Union.

NEBRASKA.

The Bee, Omaha.

TENNESSEE.

The Nashville American.
The Avalanche, Memphis.

MASSACHUSETTS.

The Watchman, Boston.
The Youth's Companion, Boston.
The Congregationalist, Boston.
Boston Advertiser.
Springfield Republican.

ILLINOIS.

The Staats Zeitung, Chicago.
The Inter-Ocean, Chicago.

MISSOURI.

Westleche Post, St. Louis.
The Kansas City Times.

MINNESOTA.

Pioneer Press and Tribune, St. Paul and Minneapolis.

IOWA.

The State Register, Des Moines.

MAINE.

Portland Transcript.

NEW HAMPSHIRE.

Independent Statesman, Concord.
Manchester Mirror.

VERMONT.

The Household, Brattleboro.

MARYLAND.

The Baltimore American.

Extract from *NEW YORK TIMES*, June 14, 1875.

Ten years ago Messrs. Geo. P. Rowell & Co. established their Advertising Agency in New York City. Five years ago they absorbed the business conducted by Mr. John Hooper, who was the first to go into this kind of enterprise. Now they have the satisfaction of controlling the most extensive and complete advertising connection which has ever been secured, and one which would be hardly possible in any other country but this. They have succeeded in working down a complex business into so thoroughly a systematic method that no change in the newspaper system of America can escape notice, while the widest information upon all topics interesting to advertisers is placed readily at the disposal of the public.

A COMPLETE LIST OF NEWSPAPERS PRINTED IN THE UNITED STATES,

AND A STATEMENT OF THE LOCATION, POPULATION AND CHARACTERISTICS OF THE TOWNS IN WHICH THEY ARE PUBLISHED.

ALABAMA.

ABBEVILLE, c. h., Henry Co., 500† p., 90 m. S. E. of Montgomery, and 15 W. of Fort Gaines, Georgia.
Henry Co. Register...........W. **1**

ASHVILLE, c. h., St. Clair Co., on A & C. Rd.
Southern Ægis................W. **2**

ATHENS, c. h., Limestone Co., 1,500† p., on Nashville & Decatur line of Louisville & Nashville & Great Southern Rd., 107 m. S. of Nashville and 195 N. of Montgomery.
Limestone News..............W. **3**
Post.

BANGOR, Blount Co.
Broad-Axe...................W. **5**

BIRMINGHAM, Jefferson Co., 1,200 p., at junction of Alabama & Chattanooga and S. & N. Alabama Rds., 90 m. from Alabama and 54 from Tuscaloosa; centre of iron and coal trade.
Jefferson Independent.........D. **6**
" " ....W. **7**
Iron Age.....................W. **8**

BUTLER, c. h., Choctaw Co.
Choctaw Herald.

CAMDEN, c. h., Wilcox Co., 2,000 p., near Alabama r., 30 m. S. by W. of Selma. A place of considerable trade, and an important shipping point.
Wilcox Vindicator...........W. **10**

CARROLLTON, c. h., Pickens Co., 600† p., about 30 m. W. of Tuscaloosa; about the same distance S. E. of Columbus, Miss. Surrounded by a cotton-growing district.
West Alabamian.............W. **11**

CENTRE, c. h., Cherokee Co., 2,500 p., on Coosa r., 140 m. N. by E. of Montgomery and 20 N. of Jacksonville.
Cherokee Advertiser.........W. **12**

CLANTON, c. h., Chilton Co.
Chilton Co. Courier.........W. **13**

CLAYTON, c. h., Barbour Co., 800 p., near centre of county, 20 m. W. of Eufaula and 75 S. E. of Montgomery.
Courier & Agricultural Journal.W. **14**

COLUMBIANA, c. h., Shelby Co., 1,040 p., on Selma, Rome & Dalton Rd., 72 m. from Selma.
Shelby Sentinel..............W. **15**

DADEVILLE, c. h., Tallapoosa Co., 1,266 p., on the Savannah & Memphis Rd., 30 m. from Opelika and 45 N. E. of Montgomery.
Head-Light and News.......W. **16**

DECATUR, Morgan Co., 2,500† p., on Tennessee r. and the Memphis & Charleston Rd., 43 m. E. of Tuscumbia and 24 W. of Huntsville.
News.........................W. **17**

DEMOPOLIS, Marengo Co., 1,539 p., on the Tombigbee r. and Alabama Central Rd., 52 m. W. of Selma. Surrounded by a cotton-growing district; principal shipping point in the county.
Marengo News-Journal.....W. **18**

EUFAULA, Barbour Co., 4,800† p., on Chattahoochee r., at junction of Montgomery & Eufaula with Southwestern Rd. A cotton-shipping point, 142 m. from Macon, Ga., and 80 from Montgomery.
News....................T. W. **19**
" ....W. **20**
Times...................T. W. **21**
" ....W. **22**

EUTAW, c. h., Greene Co., 1,920 p., on the Alabama & Chattanooga Rd., 35 m. from Tuscaloosa and 60 W. from Selma, in a cotton-growing district.
Whig and Observer..........W. **23**

EVERGREEN, c. h., Conecuh Co., 1,700 p., on Mobile & Montgomery Rd., 82 m. from Montgomery and 104 from Mobile.
Conecuh-Escambia Star.....W. **24**

FAYETTE, c. h., Fayette Co., 500† p., near Sipsey r., 140 m. N. W. of Montgomery, and 40 N. E. of Columbus, Miss.
Gazette........................W. **25**
Luxapalilan.................W. **26**

FLORENCE, c. h., Lauderdale Co., 2,003 p., on Tennessee r., at head of navigation; principal shipping point for the county and adjoining towns in Tennessee; a branch railroad crosses the river, connecting with Memphis & Charleston Rd. at Tuscumbia.
Gazette.......................W. **27**

GADSDEN, c. h., Etowah Co., 2,203 p., on Coosa r., and E. Alabama and Cincinnati Rd., in the midst of iron and coal fields. Cotton and grain-growing district; considerable trade in lumber.
Times.........................W. **28**

GAINESVILLE, Sumter Co., 3,916 p., on Tombigbee r., eastern terminus of a branch of the Mobile & Ohio Rd., 15 m. W. of Eutaw, 54 from Tuscaloosa. A trade centre; one of the principal shipping points in the county.
Dispatch.....................W. **29**

GREENSBORO, c. h., Hale Co., 1,760 p., the centre of considerable trade, sur-

EXPLANATORY NOTE—The population is from census of 1870, or estimate of resident postmasters—the latter case indicated by a dagger—c. h. stands for court house, county seat—m. for miles—p. for population—r. for river and Rd. for railroad.

ALABAMA.

rounded by cotton plantations; 18 m. E. of Eutaw, and 40 N.W. of Selma.
Alabama Beacon............W. **30**

GREENVILLE, c. h., Butler Co., 3,000† p., on Mobile & Montgomery Rd., 45 m. from Montgomery. Centre of a cotton trade.
Advocate....................W. **31**
South Alabamian...........W. **32**

GROVE HILL, c. h., Clark Co.
Clark Co. Democrat.........W. **33**

GUNTERSVILLE, c. h., Marshall Co.
Marshall Tribune............W. **34**

HARTSELLE, c. h., Morgan Co.
Hawkeye....................W. **35**

HAYNEVILLE, c. h., Lowndes Co. 3,484 p., 23 m. S. W. of Montgomery.
Examiner...................W. **36**

HUNTSVILLE, c. h., Madison Co., 6,000† p., 10 m. N. of Tennessee on the Memphis & Charleston Rd., 24 m. E. of Decatur and 59 W. of Stevenson. Centre of trade; surrounded by a farming district; actively engaged in manufactures of various kinds.
Advocate....................W. **37**
Democrat...................W. **38**
Independent.................W. **39**
New South..................W. **40**

JACKSONVILLE, c. h., Calhoun Co. 1,200† p., on Selma, Rome & Dalton Rd., 145 m. from Selma. The trading point for an agricultural section. Has good educational advantages, and is visited during summer for the mineral waters found near.
Republican..................W. **41**

JASPER, c. h., Walker Co., 1,500 p., 50 m. N. N. E. of Tuscaloosa, and 60 S. of Decatur. An agricultural and cotton-growing district.
Mountain Eagle.............W. **42**

LAFAYETTE, c. h., Chambers Co., 1,382 p., on E. Alabama & Cincinnati Rd. 18 m. from Opelika and 84 from Montg mery. Cotton market, and headquarters for supplies for surrounding country.
Clipper......................W. **43**

LIVINGSTON, c. h., Sumter Co., 2,320 p., on Alabama and Chattanooga Rd., 10 m. from its junction with Alabama Central Rd., 26 m. from Eutaw and 80, W. of Selma.
Journal.....................W. **44**

MARION, c. h., Perry Co., 3,476† p., 30 m. N. W. of Selma, on Selma, Marion & Memphis Rd. Engaged in agriculture. Several educational institutions are located here.
Alabama Baptist............W. **45**
Commonwealth........ .....W. **46**

MOBILE, c. h., Mobile Co., 32,084 p., on Mobile r., near its entrance into Mobile Bay, engaged in foreign and domestic commerce and manufactures, and, next to New Orleans, the largest cotton market in the United States. Regular lines of steamboats run to various points on Alabama and Tombigbee rs., and to New Orleans. Southern terminus of Mobile & Ohio Rd., which connects with Illinois Central Rd. at Cairo, forming a continuous line from the Gulf to the Lakes. Mobile & Great Northern Rd. connects with Montgomery and other points N. and E.
Register.....................D. **47**

ALABAMA.

Register.....................W. **48**
Tribune......................D. **49**
Cycle.........................W. **50**
Progressive Farmer..........M. **51**

MONROEVILLE, c. h., Monroe Co., 300† p., 10 m. from Claiborne, on Alabama r., 100 from Mobile and 90 S. of Selma. Surrounded by a cotton-growing country.
Monroe Journal.............W. **52**

MONTEVALLO, Shelby Co.
Shelby Guide.................W. **53**

MONTGOMERY, c. h., Montgomery Co., State capital, 15,000† p., on Alabama r., 197 m. N. E. of Mobile, at centering point of four railroads; engaged in cotton trade, shipping by steamboat to Mobile.
Advertiser and Mail.........D. **54**
" " " ....W. **55**
Alabama State Journal......D. **56**
" " " .....W. **57**
Evening Bulletin.............D. **58**
Sunday Bulletin...........Sund. **59**
Southern Plantation.........W. **60**

MOULTON, c. h., Lawrence Co., 2,006 p., 15 m. S. of Memphis & Charleston Rd. at Courtland, and 165 N. by W. of Montgomery.
Advertiser....................W. **61**

NOTASULGA, Macon Co., 1,691 p., on Montgomery & West Point Rd., 48 m. from Montgomery.
Universalist Herald.......S. M. **62**

OPELIKA, c. h., Lee Co., 5,085 p., on Western Alabama Rd., at junction of Savannah & Memphis and E. Alabama & Cincinnati Rds., 64 m. E. of Montgomery, 28 from Columbus, 113 from Atlanta. Centre of a cotton and grain-growing country.
Times.........................D. **63**
" ....W. **64**
Observer and Locomotive....W. **65**
Southern Reformer...........W. **66**

OXFORD, Calhoun Co., 1,147 p., on Selma, Rome & Dalton Rd.. 10 m. from Jacksonville and 21 from Talladega.
Tribune.......................W. **67**

OZARK, Dale Co., 720† p., 40 m. S. E. of Troy. Most important place in the county.
Southern Star.

PRATTSVILLE, c. h., Autauga Co., 1,346 p., 14 m. N. W. of Montgomery.
Autauga Citizen.

SCOTTSBORO, c. h., Jackson Co., 1,000† p., on Memphis & Charleston Rd., 42 m. from Huntsville and 55 from Chattanooga.
Alabama Herald..............W. **70**
North Alabama Observer....W. **71**

SEALE, c. h., Russell Co.
Russell Register..............W. **72**

SELMA, c. h., Dallas Co., 6,484 p., on Alabama r, 300 m. from its mouth. Surrounded by a cotton-growing district, centre of trade in cotton, lumber, iron and coal. Terminus of Selma, Rome & Dalton, Selma & Meridian and Selma & Montgomery Rds.
Times.........................D. **73**
Dallas Times.................W. **74**
National Republican........W. **75**
Southern Argus..............W. **76**

TALLADEGA, c. h., Talladega Co., 2,640

ALABAMA.

p., on Selma, Rome & Dalton Rd., 109 m. from Selma and 36 from Jacksonville. State Institution for the Deaf, Dumb and Blind is located in this city.
Alabama Templar............W. 77
Our Mountain Home.........W. 78
Reporter and Watch Tower..W. 79

TROY, c. h., Pike Co., 2,000† p., terminus of Mobile & Girard Rd., 32 m. from Union Springs and 50 from Montgomery. Centre of a cotton trade.
Enquirer.......................W. 80
Messenger.....................W. 81

TUSCALOOSA, c. h., Tuscaloosa Co., 1,689 p., on Black Warrior r., at head of steamboat navigation and Alabama & Chattanooga Rd., 71 m. from its junction with Alabama Central. Surrounded by a cotton-growing district. Cotton is shipped from this point. State University, Agricultural College and other institutions located here.
Gazette........................W. 82
Times..........................W. 83

TUSCUMBIA,, c. h., Colbert Co., 1,214 p., near Tennessee r. and on Memphis & Charleston Rd., 43 m. from Decatur and 67 from Huntsville. Surrounded by an agricultural district. A branch railroad extends to Florence, on Tennessee r. Business centre.
North Alabamian............W. 84

TUSKEGEE, c. h., Macon Co., 4,392 p., 40 m. from Montgomery.
News...........................W. 85

UNION SPRINGS, c. h., Bullock Co., 1,455 p., on Montgomery & Eufaula Rd., at intersection of Mobile & Girard Rd., 40 m. from Montgomery and 54 from Columbus, Ga.
Herald.........................W. 86

VERNON, c. h., Sanford Co.
Pioneer........................W. 87

WARRIOR, Jefferson Co.
Alabama Staats Zeitung.....W. 88
Alabama Tribune............W. 89

WEDOWEE, c. h., Randolph Co., 200† p., near centre of county, and 50 m. N. of Opelika and 40 S. by E. of Jacksonville.
Randolph Enterprise.........W. 90

WETUMPKA, c. h., Elmore Co., 1,137 p., on Coosa r., at head of navigation, 14 m. from Montgomery, 6 E. of Elmore Station, on S. & N. Alabama Rd., in centre of State. A cotton-growing district.
People's Banner..............W. 91

ARKANSAS.

ARKADELPHIA, c. h., Clark Co., 948 p., on Ouachita r., 75 m. S. by W. of Little Rock. Surrounded by an agricultural and cotton-producing country; possesses water power; centre of trade for eight counties.
Southern Standard..........W. 92

ARKANSAS CITY, Chicot Co.
Post............................W. 93

AUGUSTA, c. h., Woodruff Co.
Bulletin........................W. 94

BATESVILLE, c. h., Independence Co., 881 p., on White r., 90 m. N. by E. of Little Rock. Steamboats ascend the river to this point. An agricultural and mineral country. Cotton, tobacco, corn, wheat, oats, fruit and vegetables are cultivated.
North Arkansas Times.......W. 95
Republican...................W. 96

BEEBE STATION, White Co.
Magnet.......................W. 97

BELLEFONTE, Boone Co., 1,000† p., in the northern tier of counties, about 50 m. from Bentonville. An agricultural and stock-raising district.
Record........................W. 98

BENTONVILLE, c. h., Benton Co., 2,000 p., in the N. W. corner of the State, 180 m. from Little Rock. An agricultural district and tobacco mart. Several manufactories in operation.
Advance......................W. 99

BERRYVILLE, Carroll Co.
Advocate.....................W. 100

BOONEVILLE, Sarber Co.
Enterprise...................W. 101

CAMDEN, c. h., Ouachita Co., 1,612 p., on Ouachita r., 110 m. S. by W. of Little Rock, 70 S. W. of Pine Bluff. Steamboats ascend the river to this point, making it an active trade centre. A cotton-growing section, and the principal shipping point for that product in the southern portions of the State.
Beacon.......................W. 102
Tribune.......................

CARROLLTON, c. h., Carroll Co.
Bowlder.....................W. 104

CLARENDON, c. h., Monroe Co.
Age...........................W. 105

CONWAY, c. h., Faulkner Co.
Arkansas Traveler..........W. 106

CORNING, c. h., Clayton Co.
Express......................W. 107

DARDANELLE, Yell Co., 1,838 p., on Arkansas r., 72 m. N. W. of Little Rock. A shipping point and trade centre.
Arkansas Independent....W. 108

DES ARC, Prairie Co., 1,000 p., on White r., 50 m. N. E. of Little Rock and 15 N. of the line of Memphis & Little Rock Rd.
Citizen.......................W. 109

DEWITT, c. h., Arkansas Co., 500 p., 15 m. from Arkansas r. and 70 S. E. of Little Rock, 30 m. from Mississippi r. Surrounded by an agricultural district.
Indicator....................W. 110

FAYETTEVILLE, c. h., Washington Co., 1,800† p., 60 m. N. of Arkansas r., and 170 N. W. of Little Rock. An agricultural, coal, lead, iron-producing region.
Arkansas Sentinel..........W. 111
Democrat....................W. 112

FOREST CITY, St. Francis Co.
Times.........................W. 113

FORT SMITH, Sebastin Co., 2,800† p., on Arkansas r., 163 m. W. by N. of Little Rock. Beef packing carried on; also the centre of trade in agricultural products, stock, lumber, hides, etc.; most important town in western Arkansas. Western terminus of Little Rock & Ft. Smith Rd.
Herald........................W. 114
New Era.....................W. 115
Western Independent......W. 116

GAINESVILLE, c. h., Greene Co.
Times.........................W. 117

ARKANSAS.

HAMBURGH, c. h., Ashley Co., 2,000 p., 110 m. S. by E. of Little Rock, about 45 from the Mississippi r.
Monitor....................W. **118**

HARRISON, c. h., Boone Co.
Highlander....................W. **119**

HELENA, c. h., Phillips Co., 2,249 p., on Mississippi r., 80 m. below Memphis, 8 below the mouth of St. Francis r. The river steamers touch here, making it a trade centre.
Mail....................D. **120**
" ....W. **121**
World....................D. **122**
" ....W. **123**

HOPE, Hempstead Co.
City Times....................W. **124**
Star of Hope....................W. **125**

HOT SPRINGS, Hot Springs Co., 1,276 p., 55 m. from Little Rock and 7 from Washita r.
Advertiser....................D. **126**
Telegraph....................D. **127**
" ....W. **128**

JACKSONPORT, c. h., Jackson Co., 769 p., at confluence of Black and White rs., about 25 m. N. of Augusta. Head of navigation for large boats. A cotton shipping point.
Herald....................W. **129**

LA CROSSE, Izard Co.
Post.

LAKE VILLAGE, c. h., Chicot Co.
Lake Shore Sentinel........W. **131**

LEWISBURG, Conway Co., 800† p., on Arkansas r. and Little Rock & Fort Smith Rd., 49 m. from Little Rock. Trade centre and shipping point. Engaged in raising cotton, corn, wheat, potatoes and stock.
State....................W. **132**

LITTLE ROCK, Pulaski Co., State capital, 20,270† p., on Arkansas r., 300 m. from its mouth. Steamboats connect with various points on Arkansas and Mississippi rs. Terminus of Memphis & Little Rock and Little Rock & Fort Smith Rds.
Arkansas Gazette...........D. **133**
" " ....S. W. **134**
" " ....W. **135**
Evening Star................D. **136**
Herald....................D. **137**
Arkansas Herald..........W. **138**
Arkansas Freie Presse...S. W. **139**
Western Baptist...........W. **140**
St. John's College Record...M. **141**
Spirit of Arkansas.........M. **142**

LONOKE, c. h., Lonoke Co.
Democrat....................W. **143**

MARIANNA, c. h., Lee Co.
Index....................W. **144**

MONTICELLO, c. h., Drew Co., 1,000 p., 85 m. S. by E. of Little Rock, and about 35 from Mississippi r.
Monticellonian.............W. **145**

NEWPORT, Jackson Co.
News....................W. **146**

OSCEOLA, c. h., Mississippi Co., on Mississippi r., 87 m. above Memphis. A shipping point and trade centre.
Times....................W. **147**

OZARK, c. h., Franklin Co.
Banner....................W. **148**

PINE BLUFF, c. h., Jefferson Co., 4,000† p., on Arkansas r. at head of low water navigation, 45 m. from Little Rock. Centre of an agricultural region, cotton being the principal staple.
Jefferson Republican.......W. **149**
Press....................W. **150**

PRESCOTT, Nevada Co.
Banner....................W. **151**

RUSSELLVILLE, Pope Co., 1,000† p., on Little Rock & Fort Smith Rd., about 75 m. from Little Rock.
Democrat....................W. **152**

SEARCY, c. h., White Co., 874 p., on Little Red r., 3 m. from Cairo & Fulton Rd., about 55 m. N. E. of Little Rock. Centre of trade for several counties. Shipping point for pork and cotton. Sulphur Springs are located at this place.
Arkansas Tribune.
White Co. Record..........W. **154**

TEXARKANA, Miller Co.
Democrat....................W. **155**

VAN BUREN, c. h., Crawford Co., 1,200† p., on Arkansas r., 160 m. W. by N. of Little Rock. Centre of trade. Near Fort Smith, Ark.
Argus....................W. **156**
Press....................W. **157**

WASHINGTON, c. h., Hempstead Co., 600† p., 125 m. S. W. of Little Rock and 14 N. of Red r.
Telegraph....................W. **158**

WITTSBURG, c. h., Cross Co.
Phœnix....................W. **159**

CALIFORNIA.

ALAMEDA, Alameda Co., 3,500† p., on the eastern shore of San Francisco Bay, on a peninsula about four miles in length and one and a half miles in width, comprising an area of nearly 22,000 acres, distant two miles from Oakland and eleven miles from San Francisco. It is ornamented by nature with a profusion of majestic oaks, and is one continuous park of fine streets, trees, shrubbery and grass-plats, interspersed with fine cultivated gardens of semi-tropical plants and rare flowers, sending forth their rich blossoms every month during the year.
Encinal....................W. **160**

ANAHEIM, Los Angeles Co., 1,500† p., 28 m. S. of Los Angeles and in the Valley of Santa Anna, 12 m. from Pacific Ocean. Wine making the principal branch of industry.
Gazette....................W. **161**

ANTIOCH, Contra Costa Co., 600 p., on San Joaquin r., 60 m. from San Francisco; surrounded by a farming district, and a shipping point for coal. Some manufacturing done here.
Ledger....................W. **162**

AUBURN, c. h., Placer Co., 1,500 p., in a mining district, near Central Pacific Rd., 35 m. N. E. of Sacramento. Engaged in fruit growing and production of wine and brandy.
Placer Argus..............W. **163**
Placer Herald.............W. **164**

BAKERSFIELD, Kern Co., 800 p., on Kern r., 95 m. from Visalia. An agricultural region surrounding.

CALIFORNIA.

Kern Co. Courier..........W. **165**
Kern Co. Gazette..........W. **166**
Southern Californian......W. **167**

CASTROVILLE, Monterey Co., 800 p., on Monterey Bay, near mouth of Salinas r., 30 m. from Gilroy. Centre of an agricultural district and a place of considerable commercial importance.
Argus......................W. **168**

CHICO, Butte Co., 3,714 p., on Chico Creek and Oregon division of Central Pacific Rd., 96 m. N. of Sacramento; centre of a farming community, and trade centre for the mining districts.
Butte Record................W. **169**
Enterprise..................W. **170**

COLUSA, c. h., Colusa Co., 2,500† p., on Sacramento r., 60 m. N. by W. of Sacramento. Engaged in agriculture and stock raising. The river navigation is quite important.
Independent................W. **171**
Sun........................W. **172**

CRESCENT CITY, c. h., Del Norte Co.
Courier.....................W. **173**

DARWIN, Inyo Co.
Coso Mining News........W. **174**

DIXON, Solano Co.
Tribune....................W. **175**

DORRIS BRIDGE, c. h., Modoc Co.
Modoc Independent........W. **176**

DOWNEY CITY, Los Angeles Co.
Courier.....................W. **177**

DOWNIEVILLE, c. h., Sierra Co., 1,200 p., on North Yuba r., 90 m. N. E. of Sacramento. Quartz and gravel mining the chief industries.
Mountain Messenger......W. **178**

DUTCH FLAT, Placer Co.
Forum......................W. **179**

EUREKA, c. h., Humboldt Co., 3,000 p., engaged in agriculture and lumbering, situated on Humboldt Bay, 7 m. from the sea and 225 N. of San Francisco. Redwood shipping point for San Francisco. Commerce and lumber trade are carried on.
Humboldt Times...........D. **180**
" " ....W. **181**
West Coast Signal........W. **182**

FOLSOM, Sacramento Co., 2,500 p., on Sacramento Valley Rd., 23 m. from Sacramento, in an agricultural and mining district, on American r., which furnishes extensive water power, which is partially employed in manufacturing.
Telegraph...................W. **183**

FRESNO, Fresno Co.
Expositor..................W. **184**

GILROY, Santa Clara Co., 2,000 p., on Southern Pacific Rd., 80 m. from San Francisco, in an agricultural valley, the centre of a considerable trade.
Advocate and Leader....... **185**

GRASS VALLEY, Nevada Co., 6,000† p., 12 m. from Central Pacific Rd., in a quartz mining district, about 60 m. N. E. of Sacramento; surrounded by an agricultural and fruit-growing district.
Union......................D. **186**
Foot-Hill Tidings..........W. **187**

GUADALUPE, Santa Barbara Co.
Telegraph..................W. **188**

HEALDSBURGH, Sonoma Co., 1,800† p., on Russian r. and San Francisco & North Pacific Rd., 72 m. from San Francisco. Surrounded by an agricultural, stock-raising and wine-producing district.
Russian River Flag........W. **189**

HOLLISTER, c. h., San Benito Co., 2,000 p., about 15 m. from Gilroy and 58 N. E. of Monterey, on a branch of the Southern Pacific Rd. A place of trade, and centre of an agricultural and stock-raising district.
San Benito Advance.......W. **190**

INDEPENDENCE, c. h., Inyo Co., 400 p., 500 m. E. by S. from San Francisco; the principal point in an agricultural valley, surrounded by a mining region.
Inyo Independent.........W. **191**

JACKSON, c. h., Amador Co., 2,000 p., in a mining, agricultural, stock-raising district, about 40 m. S. E. of Sacramento.
Amador Dispatch.........W. **192**
Amador Ledger...........W. **193**

LAKEPORT, c. h., Lake Co.
Lake Co. Bee..............W. **194**
Lake Democrat............W. **195**

LIVERMORE, Alameda Co.
Enterprise..................W. **196**

LOMPOC, Santa Barbara Co.
Record......................W. **197**

LOS ANGELES, c. h., Los Angeles Co., 20,000† p., on Los Angeles r. and Southern Pacific Rd., 400 S. E. of San Francisco. An agricultural county producing the principal grains, wines, fruit, brandy, wool and hides; also having gold, silver and lead mines.
Evening Republican........D. **198**
Express......................D. **199**
" ....W. **200**
Herald.......................D. **201**
" ....W. **202**
Star..........................D. **203**
" ....W. **204**
La Cronica..............S. W. **205**
Mirror......................W. **206**
Semi-Tropical Farmer.....W. **207**
Sued-Californische Post...W. **208**

MARIPOSA, c. h., Mariposa Co., 900 p., on Mariposa r. Engaged in mining; situated 91 m. S. E. of Stockton, on the route to the Yosemite Valley.
Mariposa Co. Gazette......W. **209**

MARTINEZ, c. h., Contra Costa Co.
Contra Costa Gazette......W. **210**

MARYSVILLE, c. h., Yuba Co., 6,000 p., on Feather r., at head of navigation, and on Marysville branch of the California Pacific, at the intersection of the Oregon division of the Central Pacific Rd., 57 m. N. of Sacramento and 116 from San Francisco. Engaged in manufacturing and centre of trade. Surrounded by a large, fertile agricultural district.
Appeal....................D. **211**
" ....W. **212**

MENDOCINO, Mendocino Co., a shipping point for large vessels, at mouth of Big r., 130 m. N. of San Francisco. Centre of considerable trade.
West Coast Star ....W. **213**

MERCED, c. h., Merced Co., 500 p., on Central Pacific Rd. Agriculture is the chief industry.
Express....................W. **214**
San Joaquin Valley Argus.W. **215**

CALIFORNIA.

MODESTO, c. h., Stanislaus Co., 1,800† p., on Visalia division of Central Pacific Rd., 20 m. from Lathrop and 29 from Stockton. Engaged in agriculture and manufactures.
Herald....................W. **216**
Stanislaus Co. News.......W. **217**

MOKELUMNE HILL, c. h., Calaveras Co., 1,000 p., 50 m. from Stockton, 60 from Sacramento. Industries are mining, agriculture and stock raising.
Calaveras Chronicle.......W. **218**

MONTEREY, c. h., Monterey Co., 1,150 p., engaged in sheep and stock raising, situated on Monterey Bay, 94 m. S. by E. of San Francisco, to which it is connected by steamers and sailing vessels. It has a well protected harbor and considerable commerce.
Herald....................W. **219**

NAPA CITY, c. h., Napa Co., 6,000† p., on Napa r. and Napa Valley Rd., 37 m. N. E. of San Francisco, to which it is connected by a line of steamers, and 65 from Sacramento City by rail. Surrounded by an agricultural and wine-producing district; a trade centre.
Register....................D. **220**
" ....W. **221**
Napa Co. Reporter........W. **222**
Classic....................M. **223**

NEVADA, c. h., Nevada Co., 3,986 p., on Deer Creek, 65 m. N. by E. of Sacramento. Is surrounded by a mining region, and engaged in cultivating fruit and vines.
Transcript.................D. **224**

NORTH SAN JUAN, Nevada Co.
• *Times*....................W. **225**

OAKLAND, Alameda Co., 25,000† p., on San Francisco Bay, opposite and 7 m. from San Francisco, in an agricultural district; residence of a large number of persons doing business in San Francisco. Terminus of Pacific Rd. State University and Deaf, Dumb and Blind Asylums are located here. Called the Athens of the Pacific.
News....................D. **226**
Transcript.................D. **227**
Alameda Co. Gazette.......W. **228**
Tribune....................D. **229**
Berkeleyan.................M. **230**

OROVILLE, c. h., Butte Co., 1,500 p., on Feather r. and California Pacific Rd., 26 m. from Marysville and 152 from San Francisco.
Mercury....................W. **231**

PACHECO, Contra Costa Co., 800 p., 5 m. E. of Martinez, at head of navigation on Pacheco Slough. In an agricultural district. Tobacco raised.
Contra Costa News........W. **232**

PETALUMA, Sonoma Co., 5,400 p., on Petaluma Creek, 10 m. from San Pablo Bay, and on San Francisco and North Pacific Rd., 42 m. from San Francisco. A daily line of steamers also ply between this point and San Francisco. Engaged in manufacturing, agriculture and stock raising. The cultivation of fruits, grapes, and the making of wine carried on.
Argus....................W. **233**

PLACERVILLE, c. h., El Dorado Co., 1,800† p., 12 m. from Shingle Springs, 60 E. by N. E. of Sacramento, to which it is connected by railroad. Centre of a gold mining and agricultural region.
El Dorado Co. Republican.W. **234**
Mountain Democrat.......W. **235**

QUINCY, c. h., Plumas Co., 900 p., on Spanish Creek; engaged in agriculture, mining and lumbering: situated 250 m. N. E. of San Francisco and 80 N. W. of Virginia City, Nev.
Plumas National..........W. **236**

RED BLUFF, c. h., Tehama Co., 3,000† p., on Oregon division of Central Pacific Rd. and Sacramento r., at head of navigation, 145 m. from Sacramento. Centre of trade; lumbering, farming, and stock and wool raising largely carried on; a glove manufactory is also located here.
Peoples' Cause..............W. **237**
Sentinel....................W. **238**

REDWOOD CITY, c. h., San Mateo Co., 1,500† p., on the Southern Pacific Rd., 28 m. from San Francisco, and on Redwood Creek, which is navigable to this point by vessels of light draught. Engaged in agriculture and lumbering.
Times and Gazette.........W. **239**

RIVERSIDE, San Bernandino Co.
News....................W. **240**

SACRAMENTO, c. h., Sacramento Co., 20,000 p., State capital, on Sacramento r., 120 m. N. E. of San Francisco, on Central Pacific Rd. and at junction of four other railroads. Accessible for steamers and sailing vessels, and the centre of trade and commerce. Largely engaged in various manufactures.
Bee....................D. **241**
Evening Herald............D. **242**
Evening Leader............D. **243**
Leader....................W. **244**
Record Union..............D. **245**
" " ....S. W. **246**
Journal..................S. W. **247**
Enterprise................W. **248**
Sacramento Valley Agriculturist..................W. **249**
California Teacher.........M. **250**

ST. HELENA, Napa Co.
Star....................W. **251**

SALINAS, c. h., Monterey Co., 1,150 p., engaged in sheep and stock raising, situated on Monterey Bay, 94 m. S. by E. of San Francisco, to which it is connected by steamers and sailing vessels. It has a well protected harbor and considerable commerce.
Recorder.................D. **252**,
" ....W. **253**
Monterey Democrat.......W. **254**

SAN ANDREAS, Calaveras Co., 1,000 p., 42 m. N. E. of Stockton. Engaged in agriculture, horticulture and gold mining, the latter being still an important branch of industry.
Calaveras Citizen..........W. **255**
Foothill Democrat.........W. **256**

SAN BERNARDINO, c. h., San Bernardino Co., 2,500 p., 5 m. N. of Santa Anna r., about 60 E. of Los Angeles, and 480 S. by E. of San Francisco. Agriculture and horticulture are the chief industries.
Argus....................D. **257**
" ....W. **258**
Times....................D. **259**
" ....W. **260**
Guardian..................W. **261**

SAN BUENAVENTURA, Santa Bar-

CALIFORNIA.

bara Co., 2,491 p., on the coast, about 30 m. S. E. of Santa Barbara. Trade with the interior centre here.

Free Press..................D. **262**
Ventura Free Press........W. **263**
Ventura Signal...........W. **264**

SAN DIEGO, c. h., San Diego Co., 4,000† p., on San Diego Bay, about 450 m. from San Francisco. The seaport town of southern California, having a good harbor. The centre of trade for a large country, and rapidly growing in commerce, wealth and business importance.

Union......................D. **265**
" ....W. **266**
World......................D. **267**
" ....W. **268**

SAN FRANCISCO, c. h., San Francisco Co., 170,000† p., the great metropolis of Pacific Coast, situated on San Francisco Bay 7 m. from ocean, at entrance through Golden Gate. It has one of the finest harbors in the world, and is engaged in foreign and domestic commerce. Depot for all imports and exports, the railroads from different parts of the State centering here; largest city west of Rocky Mountains.

Abend Post................D. **269**
" " ....W. **270**
Alta California............D. **271**
" " ....W. **272**
California Demokrat.......D. **273**
California Staats Zeitung .W. **274**
California Cronick......Sund. **275**
Chronicle...................D. **276**
" ....W. **277**
Sunday Chronicle.......Sund. **278**
Commercial News..........D. **279**
Courrier de San Francisco..D. **280**
" " " " ..W. **281**
El Tecolote.................D. **282**
Evening Bulletin...........D. **283**
Bulletin....................W. **284**
Evening Post...............D. **285**
Examiner...................D. **286**
" ....W. **287**
Figaro......................D. **288**
Morning Call...............D. **289**
Stock Exchange.............D. **290**
Stock Report and California Street Journal........... D. **291**
Stock Report and California Street Journal...........W. **292**
Guide.
La Sociedad.............S.W. **294**
La Voz del Nuevo Mundo.
California Christian Advocate.........................W. **296**
California Farmer.........W. **297**
California Journal and Sonntags Gast.................W. **298**
California Posten.........W. **299**
California Spirit of the Times & Underwriters' Journal.W. **300**
Commercial Herald and Market Review...........W. **301**
Elevator....................W. **302**
Evangel.....................W. **303**
Golden Era.................W. **304**
Hebrew.....................W. **305**
Hebrew Observer...........W. **306**
Journalist and Humorist..W.
Journal of Commerce and Price Current...........W. **308**
La Voce del Popolo and L'Eco della patria........W. **309**
Le Petit Journal...........W. **310**
Mining and Scientific Press.W. **311**
Monitor....................W. **312**
New Age....................W. **313**
News Letter and California Advertiser...............W. **314**
Occident....................W. **315**
Pacific......................W. **316**
Pacific Appeal ....W. **317**
Pacific Churchman.........W. **318**
Pacific Coast Wine and Liquor Herald.............W. **319**
Pacific Grocer..............W. **320**
Pacific Law Reporter......W. **321**
Pacific Methodist...........W. **322**
Pacific Rural Press........W. **323**
Rescue......................W. **324**
Sunday Ledger.............W. **325**
Thistleton's Illustrated Jolly Giant.......................W. **326**
Voice of Israel.
Alaska Herald..........S. M. **328**
California China Mail and Flying Dragoon.... .....M. **329**
California Horticulturist and Floral Magazine....M. **330**
California Mail Bag.......M. **331**
Coast Review...............M. **332**
Golden Dawn...............M. **333**
Herald's College Journal...M. **334**
Irish News..................M. **335**
Pacific Liberal.............M. **336**
Pacific Medical and Surgical Journal..............M. **337**
Railroad Gazetteer..........M. **338**
Real Estate Circular.......M. **339**
Resources of California.
Sherman & Hyde's Musical Review.....................M. **341**
Union Christian Worker..M. **342**
Watchmaker's Guide.......M. **343**
Western Lancet.
Wine Dealer's Gazette......M. **345**

SAN JOSE, c. h., Santa Clara Co., 14,000† p., situated on Guadalupe r., 51 m. from San Francisco Bay, and on Southern Pacific Rd., 51 m. S. by E. of San Francisco. Engaged in fruit and grain growing. State Normal School located here.

Mercury....................D. **346**
" ....W. **347**
Patriot......................D. **348**
Argus.......................W. **349**
California Agriculturist and Live Stock Journal......M. **350**

SAN LEANDRO, c. h., Alameda Co., 2,300 p., on San Jose branch of Central Pacific Rd., about 7 m. S. of Oakland, in an agricultural district.

Record.....................W. **351**

SAN LUIS OBISPO, c. h., San Luis Obispo Co., 2,000† p., engaged in stock raising; situated 9 m. from San Luis Obispo Bay and 250 S. E. of San Francisco, and on the stage route from Gilroy to Los Angeles.

Tribune.....................W. **352**

SAN RAFAEL, c. h., Marin Co., 1,200 p., in an agricultural and stock-raising district on W. side of San Pablo Straits, 15 m. N. of San Francisco.

Herald.....................W. **353**
Marin Co. Journal........W. **354**

SANTA BARBARA, c. h., Santa Barbara Co., 2,672 p., engaged in agriculture and stock-raising, situated near the coast, on the Santa Barbara Channel, and between

CALIFORNIA.

San Luis Obispo and Los Angeles, 362 m. S. E. of San Francisco.
Morning Republican........D. **355**
News........................D. **356**
" ....W. **357**
Press........................D. **358**
" ....W. **359**
Index........................W. **360**

SANTA CLARA, Santa Clara Co., 4,000 p., on Southern Pacific Rd., 3 m. from San Jose and 47 from San Francisco. Surrounded by an agricultural district, and engaged in manufacturing and general trade. Several institutions of learning are located here.
Echo........................W. **361**

SANTA CRUZ, c. h., Santa Cruz Co., 3,000 p., on N. side of Bay of Monterey, 59 m. S. by E. of San Francisco. Engaged in agriculture, stock-raising and manufacturing. A place of summer resort.
Local Item................W. **362**
Sentinel....................W. **363**

SANTA MONICA, Los Angeles Co.
Outlook....................W. **364**

SANTA ROSA, c. h., Sonoma Co., 5,000† p., on Santa Rosa Creek and North Pacific Rd., 67 m. N. of San Francisco; actively engaged in wine-making, agriculture and stock raising.
Democrat....................D. **365**
Sonoma Democrat.........W. **366**

SHASTA, c. h., Shasta Co., 1,200 p., engaged in manufacturing; supply point for a mining district; 180 m. from Sacramento and 45 N. of Red Bluff.
Courier......................W. **367**

SILVER MOUNTAIN, Alpine Co., 300 p., in a mining district, about 120 m. E. of Sacramento, and 50 from Carson City, Nevada, to which it is connected by a stage route.
Alpine Chronicle...........W. **368**

SONORA, c. h., Tuolumne Co., 1,650 p., on Woods Creek, 60 m. E. of Stockton, 38 from both the Stockton, Visalia, and Stockton & Copperopolis Rds. Centre of a mining and lumber trade. A fruit-growing district. Marble, slate and soapstone quarries located here; 130 m. E. of San Francisco.
Union Democrat...........W. **369**

STOCKTON, c. h., San Joaquin Co., 14,000† p., on Central Pacific Rd., 87 m. from San Francisco and 48 from Sacramento, and at the junction of Stockton & Copperopolis Rd., in an agricultural district, situated 3 m. from San Joaquin r., to which it is connected by a navigable creek. Engaged in various manufactures.
Evening Herald..............D. **370**
" " ....W. **371**
Independent.................D. **372**
" ....W. **373**
Courier......................W. **374**

SUISUN, c. h., Solano Co., 800† p., on Suisun Bay, 54 m. N. E. of San Francisco, a shipping point, and a place of considerable trade.
Solano......................W. **375**

SUSANVILLE, c. h., Lassen Co., 638 p., on Susan r., 80 m. from Central Pacific Rd., at Virginia City, Nev., and 150 from Sacramento. Farming and grazing the principal branches of industry.
Lassen Advocate...........W. **376**
Lassen Co. Farmer........W. **377**
Lassen Co. Journal........W. **378**

SUTTER CREEK, Amador Co.
Foothills Ensign...........W. **379**

TEHAMA, Tehama Co., 881 p., on Sacramento r. and Oregon division of Central Pacific Rd., 123 m. from Sacramento; surrounded by an agricultural district.
Tocsin.......................W. **380**

TRUCKEE, Nevada Co., 750 p., on Truckee r. and Central Pacific Rd., 120 m. from Sacramento. Engaged in cutting and manufacturing lumber. Surrounded by some of the finest scenery in the Sierra Nevada Mountains.
Republican..............S. W. **381**

UKIAH, c. h., Mendocino Co., 1,200 p., on Russian r., 121 m. N. by W. of San Francisco. Engaged in farming, stock raising and lumbering.
Democratic Dispatch.......W. **382**
Mendocino Democrat.......W. **383**

VALLEJO, Solano Co., 5,000 p., on San Pablo Bay, at terminus of California Pacific Rd., 24 m. N. E. of San Francisco. It has a fine harbor, accessible for the largest ships. Engaged in agriculture and manufacturing. U. S. Navy Yard is located on Mare Island, directly opposite.
Chronicle.....................D. **384**
" ....W. **385**
Solano Times...............D. **386**

VISALIA, c. h., Tulare Co., 2,800† p., on Kaweath r., in an agricultural and stock-raising district, 18 m. N. E. of Tulare Lake, and about 200 S. by E. of Sacramento.
Delta........................W. **387**
Tulare Times...............W. **388**

WASHINGTON, Nevada Co.
Alameda Independent.....W. **389**

WATSONVILLE, Santa Cruz Co., 2,000† p., on Pajaro r., 5 m. from Monterey Bay, 19 S. E. of Santa Cruz and 20 from Gilroy. In an agricultural district, and a place of considerable trade.
Pajaronian.................W. **390**

WEAVERVILLE, c. h., Trinity Co., 1,000 p., on Weaver Creek, in a mining district, 180 m. N. by W. of Sacramento, and about 60 m. E. of Eureka. Centre of a large traffic with various mining camps. The mines in this section are rich.
Trinity Journal.............W. **391**

WEST OAKLAND, Alameda Co.
Oakland Semi-Tropical Press.W. **392**

WHEATLAND, Yuba Co.
Free Press..................W. **393**

WOODLAND, c. h., Yolo Co., 3,500† p., on the California Pacific Rd., 20 m. from Sacramento and 50 from Vallejo, in an agricultural district. Chief production wheat and grapes. Engaged in manufacturing.
Yolo Democrat..............W. **394**
Yolo Mail....................W. **395**

YREKA, c. h., Siskiyou Co., 1,500 p., on Yreka Creek. Engaged in agriculture and mining; situated about 300 m. N. of Sacramento, and about 25 S. of Oregon State line. A trade centre for the northern part of the State.
Journal......................W. **396**
Union........................W. **397**

YUBA CITY, c. h., Sutter Co., 1,000 p., in

CALIFORNIA.

an agricultural district on Feather r., nearly opposite Marysville, and 57 m. N. of Sacramento.
Sutter Banner..............W. **398**

CONNECTICUT.

ANSONIA, New Haven Co., 5,500† p., on Naugatuck Rd. and r., 2 m. N. of Derby and 16 N. of Bridgeport. Engaged in manufactures.
Naugatuck Valley Sentinel. W. **399**

BIRMINGHAM, New Haven Co., 2,103 p., in Derby township, at junction of Naugatuck and Housatonic rs., 10 m. W. of New Haven.
Derby Transcript..........W. **400**

BRIDGEPORT, Fairfield Co., 25,000 p., on Long Island Sound and New York & New Haven Rd., 59 m. from New York City and at the junction of Housatonic and Naugatuck Rds. Engaged in sewing machine, carriage, furniture, fire-arms, and other manufactures and coast trade.
Evening Farmer............D. **401**
Republican "............W. **402**
Standard...................D. **403**
Republican Standard......W. **404**
Bridgeporter Zeitung....S. W. **405**
Journal..................S. W. **406**
Leader...................S. W. **407**

BRISTOL, Hartford Co.
Pequabuck Valley Gazette..W. **408**
Press.....................W. **409**

CHESTER, Middlesex Co.
New Era...................M. **410**

DANBURY, c. h., Fairfield Co., 10,000† p., at terminus of Danbury & Norwalk Rd., 68 m. from New York; a branch railroad also connects with Housatonic at Brookfield. Engaged in manufactures, the principal of which is hats.
Globe.....................W. **411**
News......................W. **412**

DANIELSONVILLE, Windham Co., 3,500 p., in Killingly township, on Quinnebaug r. and Norwich & Worcester Rd., 30 m. from Norwich. Engaged in cotton and woolen manufacture.
Windham Co. Press........W. **413**
Windham Co. Transcript..W. **414**

EAST HARTFORD, Hartford Co.
Elm Leaf..................W. **415**

HARTFORD, c. h., Hartford Co., State capital, 40,000† p., on Connecticut r. and on New Haven & Hartford Rd. Engaged in commerce and manufactures.
Courant...................D. **416**
Connecticut Courant.......W. **417**
Post......................D. **418**
Connecticut Post..........W. **419**
Times.....................D. **420**
"......................W. **421**
Advertiser................W. **422**
Christian Secretary.......W. **423**
Clarion...................W. **424**
Religious Herald..........W. **425**
Sunday Journal...........W. **426**
Trinity Tablet.
Poultry World.............M. **428**
American Journal of Education...................Qr. **429**

LITCHFIELD, c. h., Litchfield Co., 3,850 p., on the Shepaug branch of Danbury & Norwalk Rd., and about 4 m. W. of the line of the Naugatuck Rd. Engaged in manufactures, and centre of considerable trade.
Enquirer..................W. **430**

MANCHESTER, Hartford Co.,
Times.....................W. **431**

MIDDLETOWN, c. h., Middlesex Co., 11,143 p., on Connecticut r. and New Haven, Middletown & Willimantic Rd., at an equal distance from New York and Boston, and 35 m. from Long Island Sound. Engaged in various manufactures. Centre of a large trade.
Constitution..............D. **432**
"..............W. **433**
Sentinel..................D. **434**
Sentinel and Witness......W. **435**
College Argus...........B. W. **436**

MILFORD, New Haven Co.
Sentinel..................W. **437**

MOODUS, Middlesex Co., in East Haddam township, on Moodus r. near its entrance into the Connecticut, and about 12 m. S. E. of Middletown.
Connecticut Valley Advertiser.....................W. **438**

MYSTIC RIVER, New London Co.
Mystic Journal............W. **439**
Mystic Press..............W. **440**

NEW BRITAIN, Hartford Co., 11,000† p., 10 m. from Hartford, on Hartford, Providence & Fishkill Rds. Engaged in manufacturing hardware, jewelry and other articles.
Observer..................W. **441**
Record....................W. **442**

NEW HAVEN, New Haven Co., 55,000† p., at head of New Haven Bay, 4 m. from Long Island Sound. Several railroads centre here. Seat of Yale College. Engaged in commerce, and in carriage and other manufactures.
Journal and Courier........D **443**
Connecticut Herald and Journal.....................W. **444**
Palladium.................D. **445**
"..................W. **446**
Register..................D. **447**
Columbian Register........W. **448**
Union.....................D. **449**
"......................W. **450**
"......................Sund. **451**
Connecticut Republikaner.S.W. **452**
Commonwealth..............W. **453**
Yale Courant..............W. **454**
Yale Record...............W. **455**
American Journal of Science and Arts...................M. **456**
Hubbard's Newspaper Advertiser...................M. **457**
Loomis' Musical and Masonic Journal..............M. **458**
Yale Literary Magazine....M. **459**
New Englander.............Qr. **460**

NEW LONDON, c. h., New London Co., 11,000† p., on Thames r., having a good harbor. Engaged in commerce and manufacturing.
Evening Telegram..........D. **461**
Connecticut Gazette........W. **462**

NEW MILFORD, Litchfield Co., 3,700† p., on Housatonic r. and Rd., 35 m. from Bridgeport. Engaged in manufactures.
Housatonic Ray............W. **463**

CONNECTICUT.

NORWALK, Fairfield Co., 15,000† p., on Norwalk r. and New York & New Haven Rd., 45 m. from New York, and at junction of Norwalk & Danbury Rd. Engaged in manufactures.

Gazette....................W. **464**

Hour and Westport Advertiser....................W. **465**

NORWICH, c. h., New London Co., 16,653 p., at head of navigation on Thames r., 13 m. from New London, and midway between New York and Boston, on Norwich & Worcester and New London Northern Rd. A line of steamers make daily trips between here and New York. Engaged in commerce and manufactures.

Argus....................D. **466**

" ....W. **467**

Morning Bulletin..........D. **468**

Courier....................W. **469**

Aurora....................W. **470**

PLAINVILLE, Hartford Co.

News....................W. **471**

PUTNAM, Windham Co., 6,000† p., on Quinnebaug r. and Boston, Hartford & Erie Rd., at intersection of Norwich & Worcester Rd., 26 m. from Worcester and 34 from Norwich. Engaged in the manufacture of cotton and boots and shoes.

Patriot....................W. **472**

Putnam Co. News.........W. **473**

ROCKVILLE, Tolland Co., 6,000† p., in Vernon township, 17 m. from Hartford, on Rockville branch of Hartford, Providence & Fishkill Rd. Principally engaged in manufacture of woolen and silk goods.

Tolland Co. Journal.......W. **474**

SALISBURY, Litchfield Co., 3,320 p., on Connecticut Western Rd., 71 m. from Bridgeport. Engaged in manufacturing and iron mining.

Connecticut Western News..W. **475**

SEYMOUR, New Haven Co.

Record....................W. **476**

SOUTH COVENTRY, Tolland Co., 4,000† p., on Willimantic r. and New London Northern Rd., 35 m. from New London. Engaged in manufactures.

Coventry Local Register....W. **477**

SOUTHINGTON, Hartford Co.

Reporter....................W. **478**

SOUTH NORWALK, Fairfield Co.

Sentinel....................W. **479**

SOUTH WILTON, Fairfield Co.

School Festival.............Qr. **480**

STAFFORD SPRINGS, Tolland Co., 3,500 p., in Stafford township, on Willimantic r. and New London Northern Rd., 50 m. from New London. Engaged in woolen, cotton and iron manufactures. Mineral springs located here.

Tolland Co. Press..........W. **481**

STAMFORD, Fairfield Co., 9,714 p., on Long Island Sound and New York & New Haven Rd., 37 m. from New York. Engaged in manufactures and coast trade, and is a summer resort.

Advocate....................W. **482**

Herald....................W **483**

STONINGTON, New London Co., 6,313 p., and port of entry on the sea-coast at eastern extremity of Long Island Sound, 12 m. E. of New London, with which it is connected by the Stonington & Providence Rd.; New York & Stonington Steamboat line connects with New York city daily. Has a good harbor, and is engaged in coast trade and manufactures.

Mirror....................W. **484**

THOMPSONVILLE, Hartford Co.

Gazette....................W. **485**

WATERBURY, New Haven Co., 15,000† p., on Naugatuck Rd., 32 m. from New Haven and 33 from Hartford, at intersection of Hartford, Providence & Fishkill Rd. Engaged in manufacturing brass, German silver, buttons, and various other articles.

American....................D. **486**

" ....W. **487**

Valley Index...............W. **488**

WEST HAVEN, New Haven Co.

Journal..................S. M. **489**

WEST MERIDEN, New Haven Co., 10,495 p., on Hartford & New Haven Rd., 18 m. from New Haven and same distance from Hartford. Engaged in manufacture of hardware in all its branches. Several manufacturing establishments are located here.

Meriden Recorder...........D. **490**

Meriden Literary Recorder.W. **491**

Meriden Republican........D. **492**

" " ....W. **493**

Morning Call.............S. W. **494**

Meriden Citizen............W. **495**

WEST WINSTED, Litchfield Co.

Winsted Herald.............W. **496**

WILLIMANTIC, Windham Co., 5,000 p., in Windham township, on Willimantic r. and New London Northern Rd., at intersection of Hartford, Providence & Fishkill Rd., 30 m. from Hartford and 50 from Providence. Engaged in silk, cotton and other manufactures.

Journal....................W. **497**

WINSTED, Litchfield Co., 6,500 p., at terminus of Naugatuck Rd., 26 m. from Hartford and 62 from Bridgeport. Extensively engaged in manufacturing. Centre of trade.

News....................W. **498**

Press....................W. **499**

WOLCOTTVILLE, Litchfield Co.

Register....................W. **500**

DELAWARE.

DOVER, c. h., Kent Co., State capital. 2,332† p., on Jones Creek, 5 m. from Delaware Bay, and on Delaware Rd., 48 m. from Wilmington and 77 from Philadelphia. Surrounded by a peach-growing and agricultural district.

Delawarean..................W. **501**

State Sentinel...............W. **502**

GEORGETOWN, c. h., Sussex Co., 850† p., on Junction & Breakwater Rd., 40 m. from Dover and 89 from Wilmington.

Sussex Journal............W. **503**

HARRINGTON, Kent Co.

Record....................W. **504**

LEWES, Sussex Co., 1,350† p., on Delaware Bay, opposite the Breakwater, and at terminus of Junction & Breakwater Rd., 104 m. from Wilmington and 56 from Dover.

Breakwater Light..........W. **505**

MIDDLETOWN, New Castle Co., 1,200†

DELAWARE.

p., on Delaware Rd., 25 m. from Wilmington. Engaged in the manufacture of carriages.
Transcript..................W. **506**

MILFORD, Kent Co., 3,100 p., on Mispillian r. and Junction & Breakwater Rd., 68 m. from Wilmington, 90 from Philadelphia. Centre of an agricultural and fruit-growing section.
Peninsula News and Advertiser..................W. **507**

NEWARK, New Castle Co.
Saturday Visitor..........W. **508**

SEAFORD, Sussex Co., 1,304 p., on Nanticoke r. and Delaware Rd., at junction and terminus of Dorchester & Delaware Rd., 36 m. from Dover and 33 from Cambridge, Md. Actively engaged in trade and oyster canning.
Citizen.

SMYRNA, Kent Co., 2,110 p., on Smyrna branch of Delaware Rd., 36 m. from Wilmington and 60 from Philadelphia. Engaged in the peach trade, and has several manufactories.
Times..................W. **510**

WILMINGTON, New Castle Co., 3,500† p., on Delaware Bay, near junction of Delaware and Brandywine rs. The Philadelphia, Wilmington & Baltimore Rd. connects with all the important cities North and South, and Delaware Rd. extends from here through the State to Salisbury, Maryland. The Wilmington & Reading, also the Wilmington & Western Rds., have their terminus here. Engaged in the building of steamboats and cars and manufacturing machinery, cotton and woolen goods, and various other articles.
Commercial..................D. **511**
Delaware Tribune..........W. **512**
Delaware Gazette..........D. **513**
" " ....W. **514**
Every Evening..............D. **515**
Morning Herald.............D. **516**
Republican..................D. **517**
Delaware Republican......W. **518**
Chronicle....................W. **519**
Delaware Pioneer..........W. **520**
Rescue........................W. **521**
Delaware Farmer.......B. W. **522**
Sunday School Worker..B. W. **523**
Harkness' Magazine........Qr. **524**

DISTRICT OF COLUMBIA.

GEORGETOWN, 15,000 p., on Potomac r. Terminus of Chesapeake and Ohio Canal. Just above Washington, and separated from it by Rock Creek. Engaged in manufacturing and Cumberland coal trade.
Courier......................W. **525**
College Journal..............W. **526**

WASHINGTON, c. h., Capital of the United States, 109,204 p., on Potomac r. The political centre of the United States, containing the Capitol and department buildings.
Chronicle....................D. **527**
" ....W. **528**
Critic..........................D. **529**
Evening Star...............D. **530**
Star...........................W. **531**
Morning News..............D. **532**
National Republican........D. **533**
Telegram.....................D. **534**
Tribune.......................D. **535**
Washingtoner Journal......D. **536**
Capital........................W. **357**
Card Basket.................W. **538**
Commoner....................W. **539**
Der Volks-Tribune..........W. **540**
Forney's Sunday Morning Chronicle.................W. **541**
Gazette........................W. **542**
Index..........................W. **543**
Law Reporter...............W. **544**
National Intelligencer......W. **545**
New National Era & Citizen.
Official Gazette.............W. **547**
Sentinel......................W. **548**
Sportsman...................W. **549**
Sunday Herald.............W. **550**
Real Estate Record.......S. M. **551**
Silent World..............S. M. **552**
Copp's Land Owner........M. **553**
Field and Forest............M. **554**
Mackey's National Free Mason.
Post Office Gazette..........M. **556**
Republic......................M. **557**
United States Record and Gazette....................M. **558**
African Repository.........Qr. **559**

FLORIDA.

CEDAR KEYS, Levy Co.
Florida State Journal....W. **560**

FERNANDINA, c. h., Nassau Co., 2,000 p., on Amelia Island and St. Mary's Bay, having a fine harbor and considerable trade. Eastern terminus of Florida Rd.
Observer.....................W. **561**

GAINESVILLE, c. h., Alachua Co., 1,444 p., on Florida Rd., 98 m. from Fernandina and 60 from Jacksonville. Engaged in agricultural pursuits.
Alachua Citizen and New Era..........................W. **562**

JACKSONVILLE, c. h., Duval Co., 6,912 p., on St. John's r., at terminus of Jacksonville, Pensacola & Mobile Rd. Engaged in commerce, and centre of trade. Lumbering carried on, exporting annually from 60,000,000 to 100,000,000 feet.
Florida Union...............D. **563**
" " ....W. **564**
Florida Sun.................D. **565**
" " ....W. **566**
Press.....................S. W. **567**
" ....W. **568**
Florida Agriculturist......W. **569**
Semi-Tropical...............M. **570**

KEY WEST, c. h., Monroe Co., 11,000† p., on the Gulf of Mexico. Interested in shipping and the manufacture of salt. The Charleston and Havana steamer touches at this port once a week.
Dispatch......................W. **571**
Key of the Gulf.............W. **572**

LAKE CITY, c. h., Columbia Co., 964 p., on Jacksonville, Pensacola & Mobile Rd., 106 m. from Tallahassee and 60 from Jacksonville. Centre of a large mercantile trade.
Reporter.....................W. **573**

LIVE OAK, Suwanee Co., 396 p., on Jacksonville, Pensacola & Mobile Rd., 83

FLORIDA.

m. E. of Tallahassee. A railroad connects with Jesup, on Atlantic & Gulf Rd. Engaged in the production of sugar cane, cotton and sweet potatoes.

Times......................W. **574**

MADISON, c. h., Madison Co.

Recorder...................W. **575**

MARIANNA, c. h., Jackson Co., 1,000 p., 72 m. W. by N. of Tallahassee. Surrounded by a cotton-producing region. Centre of trade.

Courier....................W. **576**

MELLONVILLE, Orange Co.

Advertiser.................W. **577**

MONTICELLO, c. h., Jefferson Co., 1,082 p., on a branch of Jacksonville, Pensacola & Mobile Rd., 31 m. from Tallahassee. In an agricultural and cotton-producing section.

Constitution...............W. **578**

OCALA, c. h., Marion Co., 700 p., about 35 m. S. by E. of Gainesville. In an agricultural section. Sugar cane and sweet potatoes are the chief products. 5½ m. from the famous Silver Spring. Steamboats landing at the spring gives water communication to the town.

Banner.....................W. **579**

PALATKA, c. h., Putnam Co., 1,200† p., on St. John's r., 200 m. from Tallahassee and 30 S. W. of St. Augustine. Surrounded by an agricultural section, and interested in the cotton and sugar trade.

Eastern Herald.............W. **580**

PENSACOLA, c. h., Escambia Co., 5,500† p., on Pensacola Bay, and at the southern terminus of the Pensacola & Louisville Rd., 10 m. from the Gulf of Mexico and 64 E. of Mobile. Has a fine harbor, and is engaged in commerce and lumber trade.

Florida Express.

Gazette....................W. **582**

QUINCY, c. h., Gadsden Co., 800 p., on Jacksonville, Pensacola & Mobile Rd., 24 m. from Tallahassee. One of the best agricultural sections of the State.

Journal....................W. **583**

ST. AUGUSTINE, c. h., St. John's Co., 2,500 p., on Matanzas Sound. One of the largest cities in the State, having considerable trade, and a place of resort for travelers in winter. 16 m. E. of St. John's r., and on St. John's Rd.

Examiner...................W. **584**

Florida Press..............W. **585**

SANFORD, Orange Co.

South Florida Journal......W. **586**

TALLAHASSEE, c. h., Leon Co., State capital, 3,000† p., on the Jacksonville, Pensacola & Mobile Rd.

Floridian..................W. **587**

Sentinel...................W. **588**

TAMPA, c. h., Hillsborough Co., 1,500 p., on Tampa Bay. It has a good harbor. One of the most important places in southern Florida.

Guardian...................W. **589**

GEORGIA.

ALAPAHA, Berrien Co.

Berrien Co. News...........W. **590**

ALBANY, c. h., Dougherty Co., 3,000† p., on Flint r. and Albany branch of Atlantic & Gulf Rd. Southwestern and Brunswick & Albany Rds. terminate here. 260 m. W. of Savannah. An agricultural county, which produces cotton and corn.

News.......................W. **591**

Way of Holiness............M. **592**

AMERICUS, c. h., Sumter Co., 5,000† p., on Muckalee Creek and the Southwestern Rd., 70 m. from Macon. In an extensive cotton and sugar cane producing region, and the centre of a large trade. Several institutions of learning located here.

Sumter Republican......S. W. **593**

" " ....W. **594**

ATHENS, c. h., Clarke Co., 5,050† p., on Oconee r. and Athens branch of Georgia Rd., about 100 miles W. by N. of Augusta. Centre of a cotton-growing district. Considerable manufacturing carried on.

Georgian...................W. **595**

Southern Watchman..........W. **596**

" *Cultivator*..........M. **597**

ATLANTA, c. h., State capital, Fulton Co., 40,000† p., at junction of five important railroads. Cotton is brought here from the surrounding counties for shipment. A trade centre, and one of the most important cities in the State.

Constitution...............D. **598**

" ....W. **599**

Courier....................D. **600**

Evening Commonwealth....D. **601**

Georgia " ...W. **602**

Christian Index............W **603**

Georgia Grange.............W. **604**

Methodist Advocate.........W. **605**

Republican.................W. **606**

Sunny South................W. **607**

Georgia Musical Eclectic.

Homeward Star..............M. **609**

Kennesaw Route Gazette....M. **610**

Masonic Signet and Journal.

Medical & Surgical Journal.M. **612**

Rural Southerner and Plantation.....................M. **613**

Southern Medical Record...M. **614**

Southern Policy Holder.....M. **615**

AUGUSTA, c. h., Richmond Co., 21,000† p., on Savannah r., at the head of navigation and at terminus of Georgia Rd. Five important railroads connect at this point. Engaged in manufacturing. Principal trade derived from cotton. There is a cotton factory and five flour mills located here.

Chronicle and Sentinel......D. **616**

" " " ..T. W. **617**

" " " .....W. **618**

Constitutionalist...........D. **619**

" ....T. W. **620**

" ....W. **621**

BAINBRIDGE, c. h., Decatur Co., 1,351 p., on Flint r., near S. W. corner of the State. Terminus of Atlantic & Gulf Rd. 236 m. from Savannah. Important as a shipping point. Has one cotton manufactory.

Democrat...................W. **622**

BARNESVILLE, Pike Co., 754 p., on Macon & Western Rd., 40 m. from Macon, and at junction of Barnesville Rd.

Gazette....................W. **623**

BELTON, Hall Co.

Courier....................W. **624**

BLACKSHEAR, c. h., Pierce Co., 1,000

GEORGIA.

p., on the Atlantic & Gulf Rd., 85 m. from Savannah. In an agricultural district. Sweet potatoes and sugar cane largely cultivated.
Southern Georgian.........W. 625

BLAKELEY, c. h., Early Co., 1,000 p., about 10 m. from Chattahoochee r. and 35 N. W. of Bainbridge. Surrounded by an agricultural district. Chief products, sugar cane, sweet potatoes, cotton and corn.
Early Co. News............W. 626

BRUNSWICK, c. h., Glynn Co., 2,348 p., on St. Simon's Sound, terminus of Macon & Brunswick and Brunswick & Albany Rds., 186 m. S. E. of Macon. It has a spacious harbor, and is the centre of considerable trade and commerce. Large yellow pine lumber market. Has a weekly line of steamers to New York.
Advertiser..................W. 627
Seaport Appeal............W. 628

BUENA VISTA, c. h., Marion Co.
Argus ....W. 629

BUTLER, c. h., Taylor Co.
Herald......................W. 630

CALHOUN, c. h., Gordon Co., 600 p., on Western & Atlantic Rd., 80 m. from Atlanta and 21 from Dalton. Surrounded by an agricultural district, and centre of trade. Chief products, tobacco, potatoes and corn
Times........................W. 631

CAMILLA, c. h., Mitchell Co., 750† p., on Albany branch of Atlantic & Gulf Rd., 26 m. from Albany. A fine agricultural section, with rich soil. Cotton, corn, sugar cane and sweet potatoes are among the principal products.
Enterprise..................W. 632

CANTON, c. h., Cherokee Co.
Cherokee Georgian.........W. 633

CARNESVILLE, c. h., Franklin Co.
Franklin Co. Register......W. 634

CARROLLTON, c. h., Carroll Co., 950† p., about 20 m. N. W. of Newnan, in an agricultural and stock-raising section.
Carroll Co. Register........W. 635
" " *Times*.........W. 636

CARTERSVILLE, c. h., Bartow Co., 2,500† p., on Western & Atlantic Rd., 48 m. from Atlanta and at junction of Cherokee Rd.
Express......................W. 637
Planters' Advocate..........W. 638
Sentinel.

CAVE SPRING, Floyd Co.
Enterprise...................W. 640

CEDARTOWN, c. h., Polk Co.
Express......................W. 641
Record.......................W. 642

CLAYTON, c. h., Raybun Co.
Baker Co. Record...........W.

COLUMBUS, c. h., Muscogee Co., 10,800 p., on Chattahoochee r. The Muscogee Rd. connects with the Southwestern Rd. at Fort Valley, and a railroad from the opposite side of the river connects it with Mobile. The river is navigable to this point a large portion of the year. Cotton is shipped from here by steamboat and railroad.
Enquirer.....................D. 644
" ....W. 645

GEORGIA.

Enquirer....................Sund. 646
Times..........................D 647
" ....W. 648

CONYERS, Newton Co., 637 p., on Georgia Rd., 141 m. W. of Augusta.
Rockdale Register..........W. 649

COVINGTON, c. h., Newton Co., 1,500 p., on Georgia Rd., 130 m. from Augusta, 40 m. from Atlanta, in an agricultural district.
Georgia Enterprise.........W. 650
Star...........................W. 651

CRAWFORD, Oglethorpe Co.
Oglethorpe Echo.
Gazette.

CUMMING, c. h., Forsyth Co.
Clarion.......................W. 654

CUTHBERT, c. h., Randolph Co., 2,600† p., on Southwestern Rd., 118 m. from Macon and 26 from Eufaula. A cotton factory and several institutions of learning are located here.
Appeal........................W. 655
Messenger...................W. 656

DAHLONEGA, c. h., Lumpkin Co., 1,000† p., on Chestaee r., 70 m. N. by E. of Atlanta. A good agricultural district.
Mountain Signal............W. 657

DALTON, c. h., Whitfield Co., 3,000† p., on Western & Atlantic Rd., at junction of East Tennessee Rd., 100 m. from Atlanta and 36 from Chattanooga, Tenn. Engaged in agriculture and stock raising. Tobacco and corn are the chief products.
Enterprise...................W. 658
North Georgia Citizen......W. 659
Cherokee Agriculturist......M. 660

DARIEN, c. h., McIntosh Co.
Timber Gazette..............W. 661

DAWSON, c. h., Terrell Co., 1,500† p., on the Southwestern Rd., 98 m. from Macon. The centre of trade for a large cotton and sugar cane producing section.
Journal.......................W. 662

EASTMAN, c. h., Dodge Co.
Times.........................W. 663

EATONTON, c. h., Putnam Co., 1,200† p., at terminus of branch of Macon & Augusta Rd., 28 m. from Gordon and 18 from Milledgeville. In a cotton-growing district.
Messenger...................W. 664

ELBERTON, c. h., Elbert Co., 500† p., about 10 m. from Savannah r. and 72 from Augusta. Engaged in the cultivation of cotton, corn and other grain.
Gazette......................W. 665

ELLIJAY, c. h., Gilmer Co.
Courier.......................W. 666

FORSYTH, c. h., Monroe Co., 1,500 p., on Macon & Western Rd., 26 m. from Macon; in an extensive cotton-growing section.
Monroe Advertiser..........W. 667

FORT VALLEY, Houston Co., 1,500† p., on Southwestern Rd., 29 m. from Macon. A growing place and centre of business in agricultural products. Various manufactures carried on.
Mirror........................W. 668

GAINESVILLE, c. h., Hall Co., 2,000 p., at the northern terminus of Atlanta & Richmond Air Line Rd., 53 m. from Atlanta, surrounded by an agricultural dis-

trict. Fine climate, which renders it a place of resort in summer.
Eagle......................W. **669**
Southron..................W. **670**

GREENSBORO, c. h., Greene Co., 1,100 p., on Georgia Rd., 84 m. from Augusta. Engaged in the cultivation of cotton and corn.
Georgia Home Journal.....W. **671**
Herald......................W. **672**

GREENVILLE, c. h., Meriwether Co.
Meriwether Co. Vindicator..W. **673**

GRIFFIN, c. h., Spalding Co., 5,000† p. on Macon & Western Rd., at junction of Savannah, Griffin & North Alabama Rd., 43 m. from Atlanta. A place of active trade, surrounded by a cotton-growing district.
News........................D. **674**
" ....W. **675**
Farmers' Friend...........W. **676**
Press and Cultivator.......W. **677**
Georgia Advertiser.........M. **678**

HAMILTON, c. h., Harris Co.
Journal......................W. **679**

HAMPTON, Henry Co.
Henry Co. Ledger..........W. **680**

HAWKINSVILLE, c. h., Pulaski Co., 813 p., on Ochmulgee r., at head of navigation, and on Hawkinsville branch of Macon & Brunswick Rd., about 35 m. from Macon. Surrounded by a cotton-raising district.
Dispatch....................W. **681**

HINESVILLE, c. h., Liberty Co., 350† p., near Atlantic & Gulf Rd., midway between Altamaha and Ogeechee rs. Located within the great timber, cotton and rice regions of east Georgia.
Gazette......................W. **682**

IRWINTON, c. h., Wilkinson Co.
Southerner and Appeal....W. **683**

JEFFERSON, c. h., Jackson Co.
Forest News................W. **684**

JESUP, c. h., Wayne Co.
Georgian.

JONESBORO, c. h., Clayton Co., 1,775† p., on Macon & Western Rd., 80 m. from Macon, 20 from Atlanta. An agricultural section. Good cotton market.
News........................W. **686**

LA GRANGE, c. h., Troup Co., 2,053 p., on Atlanta & West Point Rd., 72 m. from Atlanta and 15 from West Point. Cotton, potatoes and field peas are largely cultivated.
Reporter....................W. **687**

LAWRENCEVILLE, Gwinnett Co., 1,200 p., 20 m. N. of the line of Georgia Rd., and about 40 W. of Athens. In an agricultural section. Cotton, corn and sorghum are the chief products. Site elevated and healthy.
Gwinnett Herald...........W. **688**

LOUISVILLE, c. h., Jefferson Co., 500 p., on Rocky Comfort Creek, 10½ m. from the line of Central Rd. of Georgia and 54 E. of Milledgeville. In an agricultural section; cotton, corn and sweet potatoes the chief products.
Jefferson News and Farmer.W. **689**

LUMPKIN, c. h., Stewart Co., 1,200 p., about 15 m. E. of Chattahoochee r. and 25 W. of Americus; in a mineral region.
Independent................W. **690**

MACON, c. h., Bibb Co., 12,500† p., on Ocmulgee r., at junction of five important railroads. 100 m. from Atlanta, 100 from Columbus, 100 from Augusta, and 192 from Savannah. An extensive cotton market, and centre of a large and flourishing trade.
Telegraph and Messenger....D. **691**
" " " S. W. **692**
" " " ...W. **693**
Kind Words................W. **694**
" " ....S. M. **695**
" " ....M. **696**
Southern Christian Advocate.....................W. **697**

MADISON, c. h., Morgan Co., 1,710 p., on Georgia Rd., 104 m. from Augusta and 68 from Atlanta. A place of active trade and shipping point for cotton.
Home Journal..............W. **698**
Southern Farmer and Stock Journal...................M. **699**

MARIETTA, c. h., Cobb Co., 2,680 p., on Western & Atlantic Rd., 20 m. from Atlanta, in an agricultural and stock-raising section.
Journal......................W. **700**

MILLEDGEVILLE, c. h., Baldwin Co., 3,000 p., on Oconee r. and on Milledgeville and Eatonton branch of Central Rd., 30 m. from Macon. In an agricultural district. Cotton is the chief product. The river furnishes water power for milling and manufacturing.
Every Saturday.
Union and Recorder........W. **702**

MONTEZUMA, Macon Co.
Weekly.......................W. **703**

MONTICELLO, c. h., Jasper Co.
Jasper Co. Banner.........W. **704**

NEWNAN, c. h., Coweta Co., 3,000† p., on Atlanta & West Point Rd., 40 m. from Atlanta. Present terminus of Savannah, Griffin & North Alabama Rd. Possesses water power, which is employed in manufactures of various kinds.
Blade........................W. **705**
Herald.......................W. **706**

PEARSON, Coffee Co.
Pioneer......................W. **707**

PERRY, c. h., Houston Co., 1,500 p., on Big Indian Creek, in the central part of the county, 28 m. from Macon. It is surrounded by cotton plantations.
Home Journal..............W. **708**

QUITMAN, c. h., Brooks Co., 1,500† p., on Atlantic & Gulf Rd., 176 m. S. W. of Savannah. Centre of a fertile agricultural district.
Reporter....................W. **709**

RINGGOLD, c. h., Catoosa Co., 450 p., on the Western & Atlantic Rd., 115 m. from Atlanta and 23 from Chattanooga, Tenn. Engaged in agriculture and manufacturing, and a place of active business.
Catoosa Courier............W. **710**

ROME, c. h., Floyd Co., 3,000† p., on Coosa r. and Selma, Rome & Dalton Rd., at junction of Rome Rd. Surrounded by an agricultural community, and the centre of trade for this part of the State.
Commercial................D. **711**

GEORGIA.

Commercial.................W. **712**
Courier..................T. W. **713**
" ....W. **714**
Bulletin...................W. **715**
People's Friend............W. **716**
Moon's Bee World.........M. **717**
Southern Printers' Journal..M. **718**

SANDERSVILLE, c. h., Washington Co., 1,500 p., about 5 m. from line of Central Rd. and 58 from Macon. The centre of trade for a cotton-growing country.
Herald and Georgian.......W. **719**

SAVANNAH, c. h., Chatham Co., 28,235 p., on Savannah r. 18 m. from its mouth, eastern terminus of Georgia Central, southern terminus of Savannah & Charleston, and northern terminus of Atlantic & Gulf Rds., and is engaged in foreign and domestic commerce. Cotton is brought here for shipment.
Morning News...............D. **720**
" " ....T. W. **721**
" " ....W. **722**
Abend Zeitung..............W. **723**
Georgia Expositor...........W. **724**
Southern Cross.............W. **725**
Southern Musical Journal..M. **726**

SENOIA, Coweta Co., 900† p., on Savannah, Griffin & North Alabama Rd., about 18 m. from Newnan. In a cotton-growing section.
Enterprise..................W. **727**

SPARTA, c. h., Hancock Co., 1,500† p., on Macon branch of the Georgia Rd., about midway between Macon and Augusta. Centre of an agricultural region.
Times and Planter.........W. **728**

SUMMERVILLE, c. h., Chattooga Co., 350 p., on Chattooga r., 93 m. N. W. of Atlanta. An agricultural district and centre of trade.
Gazette.....................W. **729**

TALBOTTON, c. h., Talbot Co., 1,000 p., 30 m. N. E. of Columbus, Ga., and 7 from Southwestern Rd. Population principally farmers, producing cotton.
Standard...................W. **730**

THOMASTON, c. h., Upson Co., 1,200† p., terminus of Thomaston & Barnesville Rd., a branch of Macon & Western Rd., about 80 m. S. of Atlanta and 55 from Macon.
Herald.....................W. **731**

THOMASVILLE, c. h., Thomas Co., 3,000 p., on Atlantic & Gulf Rd., 200 m. from Savannah. The Albany branch connects with the main line at this point. In one of the largest cotton. wool and sugar cane producing sections of the State.
Southern Enterprise........W. **732**
Times.......................W. **733**

THOMSON, McDuffie Co., 1,000 p., on Georgia Rd., 37 m. from Augusta. Cotton, corn, wheat and sweet potatoes are the chief products.
McDuffie Journal..........W. **734**

TOCCOA CITY, Habersham Co.
North Georgia Herald......W. **735**

VALDOSTA, c. h., Lowndes Co., 1,500† p., on Atlantic & Gulf Rd., 157 m. from Savannah. Cotton, sweet potatoes, sugar cane, rice and corn are the chief products.
Times.......................W. **736**

WADLEY, (station No. 10½, Georgia Central Rd.)
Enterprise..................W. **737**

WARRENTON, c. h., Warren Co., 900 p., on Macon & Augusta Rd., 52 m. from Augusta. Agriculture is the chief occupation.
Clipper.....................W. **738**

WASHINGTON, c. h., Wilkes Co., 1,800† p., terminus of a branch of Georgia Rd., about 50 m. from Augusta. Centre of a cotton and grain country.
Gazette.....................W. **739**

WAYNESBORO, c. h., Burke Co., 1,000† p., on Augusta branch of Georgia Central Rd., 32 m. S. of Augusta and 100 N. W. of Savannah.
Expositor...................W. **740**

WEST POINT, Troup Co., 2,000† p., on Chattahoochee r., at junction of Atlanta & West Point with West Point & Montgomery Rd., 87 m. from Atlanta, and an equal distance from Montgomery, Ala. Does a fine agricultural trade. Has two cotton factories and one iron foundry in operation.
State Line Press............W. **741**

WRIGHTSVILLE, c. h., Johnson Co.
Johnson Reporter.

ILLINOIS.

ABINGDON, Knox Co., 2,000† p., on Chicago, Burlington & Quincy Rd., 10 m. from Galesburg. The seat of Abingdon and Hedding Colleges.
Knox Co. Democrat........W. **743**
Knoxonian...................W. **744**

ALBION, c. h., Edwards Co., 1,200† p., 170 m. S. E. of Springfield and 15 E. of Fairfield. Pork packing and wagon making carried on.
Independent................W. **745**
Journal.....................W. **746**

ALEDO, c. h., Mercer Co., 1,200 p., on Galva, New Boston & Keithsburg branch of Chicago, Burlington & Quincy Rd., 15 m. from Mississippi r. and 22 from Rock Island. Located in a rich farming district. Stock and grain the principal shipments. Coal is found in the vicinity.
Banner......................W. **747**
Record......................W. **748**

ALEXIS, Warren Co.
Journal.....................W. **749**

ALTAMONT, Effingham Co.
Telegram...................W. **750**

ALTON, Madison Co., 10,000 p., on Mississippi r., 25 m. from St. Louis and 4 above the mouth of the Missouri r., and on Chicago, Alton & St. Louis, and branch of Indianapolis, Terre Haute & St. Louis Rds. Extensively engaged in river trade and manufactures, and the great depot for shipment of the produce of a large section of country.
Telegraph...................D. **751**
" ....W. **752**
Banner......................W. **753**
Democrat...................W. **754**
Our Faith...................M. **755**

AMBOY, Lee Co., 3,562† p., on Illinois Central Rd., 62 miles from Amboy. Large quantities of produce are shipped from this point.
Journal.....................W. **756**

ILLINOIS.

ANNA, Union Co., 2,000† p., on Illinois Central Rd., 37 m. from Cairo and about 1 E. of Jonesboro.
Union....................W. **757**
Medical Register and Advertiser....................M. **758**

ARCOLA, Douglas Co., 2,700† p., at junction of Illinois Central and Paris & Decatur Rds., 158 m. from Chicago. Shipping point for stock and grain.
Douglas Co. Democrat.....W. **759**
Record....................W. **760**

ARLINGTON HEIGHTS, Cook Co.
Cook Co. Chronicle.........W. **761**

ASHKUM, Iroquois Co.
Gazette....................W. **762**

ASHLAND, Cass Co.
Eagle....................W. **763**

ATLANTA, Logan Co., 2,339 p., on Chicago & Alton Rd., 11 m. N. E. of Lincoln. Supported by the agriculture of adjacent country.
Argus....................W. **764**

AUBURN, Sangamon Co.
Citizen....................W. **765**

AURORA, Kane Co., 12,000 p., on Fox r., and Chicago, Burlington & Quincy and Chicago & Iowa Rds., 40 m. from Chicago. Engaged in manufacturing. Centre of a large trade. The railroad repair shops are located here.
News....................D. **766**
Beacon....................S. W. **767**
" ....W. **768**
Herald....................W. **769**
Volksfreund....................W. **770**

BARRY, Pike Co., 2,000† p., on Hannibal and Naples division of Toledo, Wabash & Western Rd., 18 m. from Mississippi r.
Adage....................W. **771**

BATAVIA, Kane Co., 4,000† p., on Batavia branch of Chicago, Burlington & Quincy Rd. and Batavia branch of Chicago & Northwestern Rd., and on Fox r., 7 m. N. of Aurora, 35 from Chicago. Extensively engaged in various manufactures. Several large stone quarries are located here.
News....................W. **772**

BEARDSTOWN, c. h., Cass Co., 4,100† p., on Illinois r. and Rockford Rock Island & St. Louis Rd., 111 m. from St. Louis, 128 from Rock Island and 46 from Springfield. The Springfield & Illinois Southeastern Rd. has its northern terminus here. Surrounded by an agricultural district. Engaged in manufacturing.
Central Illinoian............W. **773**
Champion....................W. **774**

BELLEVILLE, c. h., Saint Clair Co., 8,146 p., 14 m. from St. Louis, to which it is connected by the St. Louis, Belleville & Southern Illinois and St. Louis & Southeastern Rds. A rich and highly productive district, extensively engaged in various manufactures. Extensive beds of coal are found in the vicinity.
Stern des Westens...........D. **775**
" " " ....W. **776**
Advocate....................W. **777**
Democrat....................W. **778**
Treu Bund....................W. **779**
Zeitung....................W. **780**

BELVIDERE, c. h., Boone Co., 3,500 p., on Galena division of Chicago & Northwestern Rd., 78 m. from Chicago.
North Western..............W. **781**
Standard....................W. **782**

ILLINOIS.

BEMENT, Piatt Co.
Register....................W. **783**

BENSON, Woodford Co.
Journal....................W. **784**

BENTON, c. h., Franklin Co., 700† p., near Big Muddy r., about 85 m. from Cairo. Surrounded by an agricultural district. Corn, tobacco and sorghum are the chief products.
Franklin Co. Courier.......W. **785**
Standard....................W. **786**

BIGGSVILLE, Henderson Co.
Clipper....................W. **787**

BLANDINSVILLE, McDonough Co.
Era....................W. **788**

BLOOMINGTON, c. h., McLean Co., 18,000 p., on Illinois Central Rd.; a number of railroads intersect here; 126 m. from Chicago and 50 from Springfield. Extensively engaged in manufacturing. Centre of a large wholesale and retail trade. Seat of several institutions of learning. Farming, fruit-growing and the nursery business extensively carried on.
Leader....................D. **789**
" ....W **790**
Pantagraph..................D. **791**
" ....W. **792**
Appeal....................W. **793**
Banner of Holiness.........W. **794**
McLean Co. Deutsche Presse.W. **795**
Post....................W. **796**
Alumni Journal.............M. **797**

BLUE ISLAND, Cook Co.
Press....................D. **798**
Herald....................W. **799**

BRAIDWOOD, Will Co., on Chicago & Alton Rd., 57 m. from Chicago. Situated in a rich farming country.
Journal....................W. **800**
Republican..................W. **801**

BRIGHTON, Macoupin Co., 1,430 p., on Chicago & Alton Rd., at the intersection of Rockford, Rock Island & St. Louis Rd., 12 m. from Alton.
Advance....................W. **802**

BRIMFIELD, Peoria Co.
Gazette....................W. **803**

BUCKLEY, Iroquois Co.
Inquirer....................W. **804**

BUNKER HILL, Macoupin Co., 1,600† p., on Indianapolis & St. Louis Rd., 36 m. from St. Louis. Centre of large fruit and stock-raising section.
Gazette....................W. **805**

BUSHNELL, McDonough Co., 2,800† p., on Chicago, Burlington & Quincy Rd., at the crossing of Toledo, Peoria & Warsaw, and Rockford, Rock Island & St. Louis Rds., 12 m. N. E. of Macomb, 192 S. W. of Chicago. Engaged in manufacturing and an active trade centre.
Gleaner....................W. **806**
Record....................W. **807**

BYRON, Ogle Co.
News....................W. **808**

CAIRO, c. h., Alexander Co., 6,267 p., at junction of Ohio and Mississippi rs., 175 m. below St. Louis. Terminus of Illinois Cen-

ILLINOIS.

tral, Cairo & Fulton, Cairo & St. Louis and Cairo & Vincennes Rds. Has considerable trade and some manufacturing. Source of supply for southern Illinois, southwest Missouri and western Kentucky.

Bulletin....................D. **809**
" ....W. **810**
Evening Sun..............D. **811**
Sun and Commercial.......W. **812**
Argus and Mound City Journal.....................W. **813**
Gazette....................W. **814**

CAMBRIDGE, c. h., Henry Co., 2,500† p., on Peoria & Rock Island Rd. Centre of agricultural region. Depot for the shipment of produce from the surrounding country. Coal is found in this vicinity.

Henry Co. Chronicle.......W. **815**
Prairie Chief..............W. **816**

CAMP POINT, Adams Co., 1,500 p., at junction of Chicago, Burlington & Quincy Rd. with Toledo, Wabash & Western Rd., 22 m. from Quincy.

Journal....................W. **817**

CANTON, Fulton Co., 3,308 p., on Chicago, Burlington & Quincy and Toledo, Peoria & Warsaw Rds., 14 m. from Lewiston, 210 from Chicago, and 28 from Peoria. Engaged in manufacturing and coal mining.

Fulton Co. Ledger.........W. **818**
Register....................W. **819**

CARBONDALE, Jackson Co., 3,370 p., on Illinois Central Rd., 50 m. from Cairo. A branch railroad extends from this point to Grand Tower on the Mississippi r. Centre of a fruit-growing and coal region. State Normal University located here.

Jackson Co. Era and Southern Illinoisan...........W. **820**
Observer....................W. **821**

CARLINVILLE, c. h., Macoupin Co., 5,808 p., on Chicago & Alton Rd., 39 m. from Springfield, 33 from Alton, and 57 from St. Louis. The centre of a thriving trade.

Democrat................S. W. **822**
" ....W. **823**
Macoupin Enquirer........W. **824**

CARLYLE, c. h., Clinton Co., 1,364 p., on Kaskaskia r., and Ohio & Mississippi Rd., 47 m. from St. Louis. Centre of an agricultural region. Shipping point for lumber.

Clinton Co. Pioneer..........W. **825**
Constitution and Union....W. **826**
Union Banner..............W. **827**

CARMI, c. h., White Co., 2,480 p., at head of navigation, on little Wabash r., on St. Louis, Evansville, Henderson & Nashville Rd., 45 m. from Evansville, Ind. It is situated in the centre of the county and southern portion of Illinois, called Egypt, because of the abundance of corn raised in it every year. There are several manufactories at this place.

Courier....................W. **828**
Times......................W. **829**

CARROLLTON, c. h., Greene Co., 2,700 p., on Jacksonville, Alton & St. Louis Rd., 34 m. from Jacksonville, in an agricultural district. Engaged in lumber trade. Coal found in abundance in the vicinity.

Gazette....................W. **830**
Patriot....................W. **831**

CARTHAGE, c. h., Hancock Co., 2,500† p. on Toledo, Wabash & Western, Carthage & Burlington, and Quincy & Carthage Rds., 38 m. from Quincy, 180 from Chicago, 200 from St. Louis, and 12 from Mississippi r. Surrounded by a farming country. Seat of the Carthage College.

Gazette....................W. **832**
Republican..................W. **833**

CASEY, Clark Co., 1,000† p., on St. Louis, Vandalia, Terre Haute & Indianapolis Rd., 36 m. from Terre Haute.

Times......................W. **834**

CENTRALIA, Marion Co., 3,190 p., on Illinois Central Rd., at the junction of the Chicago branch with the main line, 112 m. from Cairo and 136 from Bloomington, 255 from Chicago. The railroad repair shops are located here, giving employment to a large number of men.

Democrat....................W. **835**
Sentinel....................W. **836**

CHAMPAIGN, Champaign Co., 6,000† p., on Illinois Central Rd., at intersection of Indianapolis, Bloomington & Western Rd., 128 m. from Chicago, and 48 from Bloomington. The eastern terminus of Monticello Rd. County devoted to agriculture. State Industrial University located here.

Champaign Co. Gazette.....W. **837**
Times......................W. **838**
Union......................W. **839**
Illini......................M. **840**

CHARLESTON, c. h., Coles Co., 3,500† p., on St. Louis & Indianapolis Rd., 46 m. from Terre Haute. Centre of an agricultural county. Does a thriving trade.

Courier....................W. **841**
Plaindealer..................W. **842**

CHATSWORTH, Livingston Co.

Plaindealer..................W. **843**

CHEBANSE, Iroquois Co., 974 p., on Central Rd., 64 m. S. by W. of Chicago.

Herald......................W. **844**
Independent................W. **845**

CHENOA, McLean Co., 1,500 p., on Chicago & Alton Rd., at intersection of the Toledo, Peoria & Warsaw Rd., 17 m. from Bloomington.

Monitor....................W. **846**

CHESTER, c. h., Randolph Co. 1,615 p., on Mississippi r., just below mouth of Kaskaskia r., and at terminus of Chester & Tamaroa Rd., about 83 m. below St. Louis. It has a large river commerce, and is a place of active business in coal, iron, lead and agricultural products.

Tribune....................W. **847**
Valley Clarion.............W. **848**

CHICAGO, c. h., Cook Co., 450,000† p., on Lake Michigan and Chicago r. Metropolis of the Northwestern States. Railroads centre here from all points. Central depot for the shipment of the various products of the West to the Eastern markets, by way of the Lakes and through lines of railroad. Largest grain, provision and lumber market in the world. Lake commerce is extensive. Largest city in the State.

Freie Presse...................D. **849**
" " ....W. **850**
Daheim..................Sund. **851**
Illinois Staats Zeitung......D. **852**
" " " .....W. **853**
Der Westen..............Sund. **854**
Inter Ocean.................D. **855**
" " ....S. W. **856**

ILLINOIS.

Inter Ocean..............W. **857**
Journal..................D. **858**
" ....T. W. **859**
" ....W. **860**
Mercantile Price Current...D. **861**
" " " ..W. **862**
Morning Courier...........D. **863**
" " ....W. **864**
National Hotel Reporter.....D. **865**
News.....................D. **866**
Post and Mail..............D. **867**
" " " ....W. **868**
Skandinaven...............D. **869**
" ....W. **870**
Svornost..................D. **871**
Amerikan..................W. **872**
Times.....................D. **873**
" ....T. W. **874**
" ....W. **875**
Tribune...................D. **876**
" ....T. W. **877**
" ....W. **878**
Union.....................D. **879**
" ....W. **880**
Belletristische Zeitung...Sund. **881**
Advance...................W. **882**
Advent Christian Times....W. **883**
Alliance...................W. **884**
Carl Pretzel's Weekly.......W. **885**
Christian Cynosure.........W. **886**
Commercial Advertiser. ...W **887**
Cook Co. Sun..............W. **888**
Democrat..................W. **889**
Dollar Sun.................W. **890**
Drovers' Journal...........W. **891**
Engineering News..........W. **892**
Enterprise and Times......W. **893**
Eulenspiegel...............W. **894**
Field......................W. **895**
Gamla och Nya Hemlandet W. **896**
Gazeta Polska..............W. **897**
Gazeta Polska Katolicka....W. **898**
Handels und Industrie Zeitung..................W. **899**
Hejmdal...................W. **900**
Hotel World................W **901**
Industrial Age.............W. **902**
Interior...................W. **903**
Journal of Commerce.......W. **904**
Katholisches Wochenblatt...W. **905**
Ledger....................W. **906**
Legal News................W. **907**
New Covenant..............W. **908**
Norden....................W. **909**
North-Western Christian Advocate...................W. **910**
North-Western Lumberman.W. **911**
Nya Svenska Amerikanaren.W. **912**
Nya Verlden...............W. **913**
Occident...................W. **914**
Pilot......................W. **915**
Pomeroy's Democrat.......W. **916**
Prairie Farmer.............W. **917**
Railway Review............W. **918**
Real Estate and Building Journal..................W. **919**
Religio-Philosophical Journal.....................W. **920**
Sandebudet................W. **921**
Saturday Evening Herald..W. **922**
Standard..................W. **923**
Sun.......................W. **924**
Union Park Advocate......W. **925**
Vorbote...................W. **926**
Western Age...............W. **927**
Western Catholic...........W. **928**
Western Farm Journal.....W. **929**
Western Rural.............W. **930**

ILLINOIS.

Workingman's Advocate....W. **931**
Lakeside Library.......T. M. **932**
Bridal Veil............B. W. **933**
Lutherischer Kirchenfreund...............S. M. **934**
United States Medical Investigator...........S. M. **935**
Advocate..................M. **936**
Agent's Guide..............M. **937**
American Aspirant........
American Bee Journal.....M. **939**
American Miller...........M. **940**
American Poultry Journal and Record...............M. **941**
Balance...................M. **942**
Crusader..................M. **943**
Everybody's Paper.........M. **944**
Furniture Trade...........M. **945**
Gem of the West and Soldier's Friend..................M. **946**
Goldbeck's Journal of Music.M.
Guardian..................M. **948**
Herald....................M. **949**
Home Visitor..............M
Humane Journal...........M. **951**
Illustrated Bible Studies....M. **952**
Illustrated Press...........M. **953**
In Door and Out...........M. **954**
Insurance Critic...........M. **955**
Investigator...............M. **956**
Lady's Friend..............M.
Land Owner...............M. **958**
Legal Adviser.............M. **959**
Little Bouquet.............M. **960**
Little Folks...............M. **961**
Magazine..................M. **962**
Manford's Magazine........M. **963**
Matrimonial Bazar.........M. **964**
Medical Journal and Examiner...................M. **965**
Medical Times.............M. **966**
Naer och Fjerran..........M. **967**
National Live Stock Journal M. **968**
National Sunday School Teacher.................M. **969**
New Church Independent...M. **970**
Old Oaken Bucket..........M. **971**
Pharmacist................M. **972**
Railway Guide.............M. **973**
Reporter..................M. **974**
School World..............M. **975**
Temperance Monthly.......M.
Voice of Masonry and Family Magazine.............M. **977**
Volante...................M. **978**
Watchman.................M. **979**
Western Home.............M.
Western Journal of Education.....................M. **981**
Western Manufacturer......M. **982**
Western Paper Trade.......M. **983**
Western Postal Record......M. **984**
Wilson's Reflector..........M. **985**
Workers' Lamp............M. **986**
Young Folks' Monthly......M. **987**
Rapid Writer...........B. M. **988**
Tachygrapher...........B. M. **989**
Watch..................B. M. **990**
Electrotype Journal........Qr. **991**
Electrotyper...............Qr. **992**
Printing Press.............Qr. **993**
Round's Printers' Cabinet..Qr. **994**
Specimen..................Qr. **995**

CHILLICOTHE, Peoria Co., 960 p., on Illinois r., at the head of Peoria Lake, and on Peoria branch of Chicago & Rock Island Rd., 13 m. from Peoria.

Reporter...................W. **996**

ILLINOIS.

CHRISMAN, Edgar Co.
Enterprise..................W. 997

CLEMENT, Clinton Co.
Register....................W. 998

CLIFTON, Iroquois Co.
Reporter....................W. 999

CLINTON, c. h., Dewitt Co., 3,500† p., on Illinois Central Rd., at intersection of Gilman, Clinton & Springfield Rd., 22 m. from Bloomington. A farming district. Has a good general trade. The railroad machine shops are located here.
Public....................W. 1,000
Register..................W. 1,001

COLLINSVILLE, Madison Co., 1,800† p., on the St. Louis, Vandalia, Terre Haute & Indianapolis Rd., 11 m. from St. Louis.
Argus....................W. 1,002
Liberal Democrat.........W. 1,003

COWDEN, Shelby Co.
Herald...................W. 1,004

CRESTON, Ogle Co., 540 p., on Chicago & Northwestern Rd., 79 m. from Chicago and 5 from Rochelle.
Times....................W. 1,005

CRETE, Will Co.
Enterprise...............W. 1,006

DAKOTA, Stephenson Co.
Farmers' Advocate.

DALLAS CITY, Hancock Co., 1,500† p., on Mississippi r., 15 m. below Burlington, Iowa, and 18 N. of Carthage.
Advocate.................W. 1,008

DANA, La Salle Co.
Local Times..............W. 1,009

DANVILLE ,c. h., Vermillion Co., 8,000† p., on Vermillion r. and Toledo, Wabash & Western Rd., at intersection of Chicago, Danville & Vincennes and Indianapolis, Bloomington & Western Rds., 112 m. from Springfield, 125 from Chicago. Actively engaged in coal mining, manufacturing and agriculture.
Times....................D. 1,010
" ....W. 1,011
Commercial...............W. 1,012
News.....................W. 1,013

DAVIS, Stephenson Co., 800 p., on Western Union Rd., 14 m. from Freeport, in a thickly settled agricultural district.
Budget...................W. 1,014

DAVIS JUNCTION, Ogle Co.
Enterprise...............W. 1,015

DECATUR, c. h., Macon Co., 10,000† p., on Sangamon r. and on the Illinois Central Rd., at the intersection of Toledo, Wabash & Western Rd., 38 m. from Springfield, 108 from St. Louis and 160 from Chicago. Surrounded by an agricultural district. Engaged in manufacturing, and a place of active trade.
Republican...............D. 1,016
" ....W. 1,017
Times....................D. 1,018
" ....W. 1,019
Local Review.............W. 1,020

DE KALB, De Kalb Co., 2,164 p., on Chicago & Northwestern Rd., 58 m. from Chicago.
De Kalb Co. News.......W. 1,021

DELAVAN, Tazewell Co., 2,500† p., on main line of Chicago & Kansas City through route, Jacksonville division of Chicago & Alton and Toledo, Wabash & Western Rds., 31 m. S. W. of Bloomington and 15 S. of Pekin. The best grain-growing and stock producing district in the county.
Advertiser...............W. 1,022
Times....................W. 1,023

DIXON, c. h., Lee Co., 4,500 p., on Rock r. and Illinois Central Rd., at intersection of Chicago & Northwestern Rd., 86 m. from Galena. The river furnishes power, which is employed in a number of mills.
Sun......................W. 1,024
Telegraph................W. 1,025
Western Farmer..........M. 1,026

DOLTON-RIVERDALE, Cook Co.
Review...................W. 1,027

DU QUOIN, Perry Co., 3,000† p., on Illinois Central, at junction of St. Louis, Belleville & Southern Rds., 70 m. from St. Louis and 290 from Chicago. Surrounded by rich coal fields, and produces and ships large quantities of tobacco, wool, castor beans, corn, oats and wheat, apples, peaches and plums, etc.
Tribune..................W. 1,028

DURAND, Winnebago Co.
Patriot..................W. 1,029

DWIGHT, Livingston Co., 2,400† p., on Chicago & Alton Rd., at the junction of the Dwight & Washington Rd., 74 m. from Chicago. Farming and stock raising the principal branch of industry.
Star.....................W. 1,030
Western Postal Review..M. 1,031

EARLVILLE, La Salle Co., 1,000 p., on Chicago, Burlington & Quincy Rd., 35 m. W. S. W. of Aurora.
Gazette..................W. 1,032

EAST ST. LOUIS, Saint Clair Co., 7,500† p., on Mississippi r., directly opposite St. Louis, Mo.
Press....................D. 1,033
" ....W. 1,034
Gazette..................W. 1,035
St. Clair Tribune........W. 1,036
Stock Yard Reporter.....W. 1,037

EDWARDSVILLE, c. h., Madison Co., 2,200† p., on St. Louis branch of the Toledo, Wabash & Western Rd., at the junction of the Madison Co. Rd., 12 m. from Alton, in a rich and populous agricultural district, and centre of an active trade.
Intelligencer............W. 1,038
Madison Co. Anzeiger...W. 1,039
Republican...............W. 1,040

EFFINGHAM, c. h., Effingham Co., 3,000† p., at intersection of Illinois Central Rd. with St. Louis & Terre Haute Rd., 98 m. from St. Louis. Engaged in manufacturing; the centre of considerable trade.
Democrat.................W. 1,041
Republican...............W. 1,042

ELGIN, Kane Co., 5,441 p., on Fox r. and Fox River and Chicago & Northwestern Rds., 52 m. from Chicago. The river furnishes power, which is employed in various manufactures. The Elgin National Watch Company located here. Centre of a fine agricultural district.
Bluff City...............D. 1,043
Advocate.................W. 1,044
Citizen..................W. 1,045

Times............... ....W. **1,046**
Informer... ....M. **1,047**
Lady Elgin...............M. **1,048**

ELIZABETHTOWN, c. h., Hardin Co., 850 p., on Ohio r., midway between Evansville and Cairo. Industries, mining iron, coal, lead and copper, and agriculture.
Hardin Gazette..........W. **1,049**

ELMWOOD, Peoria Co., 1,750† p., at junction of Salisbury & Peoria and Buda & Rushville branches of Chicago, Burlington & Quincy Rds., 26 m. from Peoria. Centre of a thriving trade, having various manufactories.
Messenger...............W. **1,050**

EL PASO, Woodford Co., 1,564 p., on Illinois Central Rd., at intersection of Toledo, Peoria & Warsaw Rd., 33 m. from Peoria and 17 from Bloomington. Engaged in merchandise, agriculture and stock raising.
Journal.................W. **1,051**

ERIE, Weld Co.
Bulletin.................W. **1,052**

EUREKA, Woodford Co., 1,800† p., on Toledo, Peoria & Warsaw Rd., 20 m. from Peoria. Grain and stock trade carried on.
Woodford Journal......W. **1,053**

EVANSTON, Cook Co.
Herald...................W. **1,054**
Index....................W. **1,055**

EWING, Franklin Co.
Baptist Banner.........W. **1,056**

FAIRBURY, Livingston Co., 3,000† p., on Toledo, Peoria & Warsaw Rd., 59 m. from Peoria; a prominent point for manufactures. The principal market for a large agricultural community; two coal shafts are in constant operation in the vicinity, furnishing the county with an abundance of fuel.
Independent.............W. **1,057**
Livingston Co. Blade....W. **1,058**

FAIRFIELD, c. h., Wayne Co., 975 p., on Springfield & Illinois Southeastern Rd., 129 m. from Springfield. Surrounded by an excellent fruit-growing district, and a shipping point for valuable lumber.
Democrat................W. **1,059**
Wayne Co. Press........W. **1,060**
Wayne Co. Republican..W. **1,061**

FARMER CITY, De Witt Co., 1,500† p., on Indianapolis, Bloomington & Western Rd., at intersection of Gilman, Clinton & Springfield Rd., 25 m. from Bloomington and 18 from Clinton. A place of active trade.
Journal....... ....W. **1,062**

FARMINGTON, Fulton Co.
News.....................W. **1,063**

FLORA, Clay Co., 2,000† p., on Ohio and Mississippi Rd. Engaged in agriculture and manufactures.
Southern Illinois Journal.W. **1,064**

FORRESTON, Ogle Co., 1,200† p., on northern division of Illinois Central Rd., at intersection of Chicago & Iowa Rd., 13 m. from Freepo t. Surrounded by an agricultural and stock-raising district.
Herald...................W. **1,065**

FRANKLIN GROVE, Lee Co., 1,200† p., on Chicago & Northwestern Rd. Centre of a rich agricultural region Large amounts of grain shipped from here.
Franklin Reporter.......W. **1,066**

FREEPORT, c. h., Stephenson Co., 10,000† p., on Illinois Central, Chicago & Northwestern and Western Union Rds., 121 m. W. of Chicago and 50 from Galena. An active business place, located in a farming district.
Times...................D. **1,067**
Bulletin.................W. **1,068**
Deutscher Anzeiger......W. **1,069**
Illinois Monitor.........W. **1,070**
Journal..................W. **1,071**
Nordwestliche Post......W. **1,072**
True Mission............W. **1,073**
News.....................M. **1,074**
Soldiers' Advocate........M. **1,075**

FULTON, Whitesides Co., 2,270† p., on Mississippi r., about 40 m. above Davenport and 136 W. of Chicago, on Chicago & Northwestern Rd. Located in a fine farming district. One of the best shipping points in the West.
Journal.......... .....W. **1,076**

GALENA, c. h., Jo. Daviess Co., 8,000† p., on Fevre r., 6 m. from its entrance into the Mississippi. Very extensive lead mines are found in this vicinity. The Fevre r. is navigable to this point, and steamboats make regular trips from here to various points up and down the Mississippi. Connected with Chicago by Western Union Rd.
Gazette..................D. **1,077**
" ....T. W. **1,078**
" ....W. **1,079**
Commercial Advertiser..W. **1,080**
Industrial Press.........W. **1,081**
Volksfreund..............W. **1,082**

GALESBURG, Knox Co., 12,000† p., on Chicago, Burlington & Quincy Rd., at junction of Peoria Rd., 165 m. from Chicago and 53 from Peoria. Engaged in manufacturing and centre of an active trade. Knox and Lombard Colleges are located here.
Press....................D. **1,083**
" ....W. **1,084**
Republican Register......D. **1,085**
" " ......W. **1,086**
Plain Dealer............W. **1,087**

GALVA, Henry Co., 3,000† p., on Chicago, Burlington & Quincy Rd., 23 m. from Galesburg.
Journal..................W. **1,088**

GENESEO, Henry Co., 4,584† p., on Chicago, Rock Island & Pacific Rd., 23 m. from Rock Island. Centre of an agricultural district.
Henry Co. News.........W. **1,089**
Republic.................W. **1,090**

GENEVA, c. h., Kane Co., 2,000† p., on Fox r., and Burlington, Quincy & Northwestern Rd., 36 m. from Chicago. Engaged in manufacturing farming tools and other implements.
Kane Co. Republican...W. **1,091**

GIBSON CITY, Ford Co.
Courier..................W. **1,092**

GILMAN, Iroquois Co., 952 p., on Illinois Central, Toledo & Peoria, and Gilman & Springfield Rds. Surrounded by a fruit-growing district; 81 m. S. by W. of Chicago.
Saturday Star...........W. **1,093**

ILLINOIS.

GIRARD, Macoupin Co.
Review..................W. **1,094**

GOLCONDA, c. h., Pope Co., 1,600 p., on Ohio r., at mouth of Lusk Creek and 20 m. above the mouth of Cumberland r., 80 from Cairo, 120 from Evansville, Ind. Principal shipping point for a large agricultural and mineral country. Has several manufactures.
Herald..................W. **1,095**

GRAND TOWER, Jackson Co.
Item..................W. **1,096**

GRAYVILLE, White Co., 1,925 p., on Wabash r., 35 m. from Evansville, Ind. It has an active trade and is rapidly increasing in population. Engaged in manufacturing, and an important shipping point.
Independent.............W. **1,097**

GREENFIELD, Greene Co., 1,200† p., on Rockford, Rock Island & St. Louis Rd., 12 m. S. of Whitehall. Agricultural and stock-raising county.
News....................W. **1,098**

GREENVILLE, c. h., Bond Co., 2,000† p., on St. Louis, Vandalia, Terre Haute & Indianapolis Rd., 50 m. from St. Louis. In an agricultural district. Corn is the chief product.
Advocate................W. **1,099**

GRIDLEY, McLean Co.
Journal..................W. **1,100**
Monitor..................W. **1,101**

GRIGGSVILLE, Pike Co., 2,100 p., on Hannibal and Naples division of Toledo, Wabash & Western Rd., 50 m. from Quincy, 4 W. of Illinois r., 30 E. of Mississippi r. A thriving agricultural district. Extensively engaged in various manufactures.
Reflector................W. **1,102**

HAMILTON, Hancock Co.
Dollar Rural Messenger..W. **1,103**

HARDIN, c. h., Calhoun Co., 200† p., on Illinois r., opposite the mouth of Macoupin Creek, about 28 m. above Alton.
Calhoun Co. Democrat...W. **1,104**
Calhoun Herald.........W. **1,105**

HARRISBURG, c. h., Saline Co., 1,500† p., on Cairo & Vincennes Rd., 100 m. from St. Louis, about 63 from Cairo, and 30 from Ohio r. Surrounding country prolific in coal, iron and salt. Has a fine trade.
Chronicle................W. **1,106**

HARVARD, McHenry Co., 1,800† p., on Chicago & Northwestern Rd., at the intersection of the Rockford & Kenosha Rd., 63 m. from Chicago. Agriculture and manufacturing the principal branches of industry.
Independent.............W. **1,107**

HAVANA, c. h., Mason Co., 1,987 p., on Illinois r., and Peoria, Pekin & Jacksonville Rd., at intersection of Springfield & Northwestern Rd., 31 m. from Pekin.
Democratic Clarion......W. **1,108**
Mason Co. Republican....W. **1,109**

HENNEPIN, Putnam Co., 2,144 p., on Illinois r., 50 m. above Peoria. River navigable for small boats. Considerable produce shipped here.
Putnam Record..........W. **1,110**

HENRY, Marshall Co., 2,162 p., on Illinois r., and Peoria branch of Chicago, Rock Island & Pacific Rd., 33 m. from Peoria. Extensively engaged in the shipping of grain and manufactures.
Republican..............W. **1,111**

HIGHLAND, Madison Co., 2,057† p., on St. Louis, Vandalia, Terre Haute & Indianapolis Rd., 30 m. from St. Louis. An active business centre. Engaged in agriculture and manufactures.
Union...................W. **1,112**

HILLSBORO, c. h., Montgomery Co., 2,000† p., on Indianapolis & St. Louis Rd., 66 m. from St. Louis. Engaged in agriculture and manufactures.
Blade....................W. **1,113**
Montgomery News........W. **1,114**

HOMER, Champaign Co.
Press....................W. **1,115**

HOOPESTON, Vermillion Co.
Chronicle................W. **1,116**

IPAVA, Fulton Co.
Fulton Phœnix...........W. **1,117**

JACKSONVILLE, c. h., Morgan Co., 12,000† p., on Toledo, Wabash & Western Rd., 34 m. from Springfield, connected by railroads with St. Louis and Chicago. Pleasantly situated, and surrounded by a rich and populous agricultural district. Large amount of produce shipped from here. Has several manufactories of importance.
Evening Enterprise.......D. **1,118**
Enterprise...............W. **1,119**
Journal..................D. **1,120**
"..........................W. **1,121**
Deaf Mute Advance......W. **1,122**
Illinois Sentinel..........W. **1,123**

JERSEYVILLE, c. h., Jersey Co., 3,500† p., on St. Louis, Jacksonville & Chicago Rd., 19 m. from Alton, and midway between Jacksonville & St. Louis. Centre of good farming region. Engaged in various manufactures.
Jersey Co. Democrat.....W. **1,124**
Republican...............W. **1,125**

JOLIET, c. h., Will Co., 9,450 p., on Des Plaines r., and on Chicago & Rock Island Rd., at the intersection of Chicago & Alton Rd., 40 m. from Chicago. The Michigan Canal passes through here and furnishes extensive water power. Centre of a rich and populous agricultural district, and depot for the shipment of large quantities of grain and produce. Considerable manufacturing done here.
Sun......................D. **1,126**
"..........................W. **1,127**
Republican............S. W. **1,128**
"..........................W. **1,129**
Herold...................W. **1,130**
Record...................W. **1,131**
Signal....................W. **1,132**
Will Co. Courier.........W. **1,133**

JONESBORO, c. h., Union Co., 2,000† p., near Illinois Central Rd., 37 m. from Cairo.
Advertiser...............W. **1,134**
Gazette...................W. **1,135**

KANE, Greene Co.
Express..................W. **1,136**

KANKAKEE, c. h., Kankakee Co., 5,189 p., on Kankakee r. and Chicago branch of Illinois Central Rd., 56 m. from Chicago. A general trading and manufac-

ILLINOIS.

turing town. One of the finest water powers in the State.
Courrier de L'Illinois....W. **1,137**
Gazette..................W. **1,138**
Herald..................W. **1,139**
Times...................W. **1,140**

KANSAS, Edgar Co., on St. Louis, Alton & Terre Haute Rd., 14 m. W. of Paris.
News....................W. **1,141**

KEITHSBURG, Mercer Co., 1,179 p., on Mississippi r., and Galva, New Boston & Keithsburg branch of Chicago, Burlington & Quincy Rd., and at northern terminus of Rockford, Rock Island & St. Louis Rd., 18 m. from Sagetown, 150 from Springfield.
News....................W. **1,142**

KENNEY, De Witt Co.
Register..................W. **1,143**

KEWANEE, Henry Co., 4,225 p., on Chicago, Burlington & Quincy Rd., 32 m. from Galesburg, 132 from Chicago. Coal mining and manufacturing are its industries.
Independent.............W. **1,144**

KINMUNDY, Marion Co., 1,032† p., on Illinois Central Rd., 24 m. N. E. of Centralia.
Bulletin.................W. **1,145**
Independent.............W. **1,146**

KIRKWOOD, Warren Co., 1,245 p., on Chicago, Burlington & Quincy Rd., 7 m. from Monmouth. Situated in a farming community.
News....................W. **1,147**

KNOXVILLE, Knox Co., 2,500† p., on Peoria Rd., 41 m. from Peoria; is engaged in carriage manufacture, and also woolen goods.
Knox Co. Republican....W. **1,148**
Diocese.................M. **1,149**
Zion's Banner............M. **1,150**

LACON, c. h., Marshall Co., 2,500 p., on Illinois r. and Lacon branch of western division of Chicago & Alton Rd., 26 m. from Peoria. Steamboats run up the river to this point, excepting in very low water. Large quantities of grain and produce are shipped from this point.
Farmers' Advocate.......W. **1,151**
Home Journal...........W. **1,152**

LA HARPE, Hancock Co.
La Harper..............W. **1,153**

LANARK, Carroll Co., 1,200† p., on Western Union Rd., 20 m. from Freeport, 140 from Chicago and Milwaukee. A shipping point for grain.
Carroll Co. Gazette......W. **1,154**

LA ROSE, Marshall Co.
Vidette..................W. **1,155**

LA SALLE, La Salle Co., 7,000† p., on Illinois r., at intersection of Illinois Central Rd. with Chicago & Rock Island Rd., and at the terminus of Chicago, Rock Isl and Canal, 99 m. from Chicago. Centre of a very large trade. Coal is found in abundance in the vicinity.
Independent............W, **1,156**
La Salle Co. Press.......W. **1,157**
Reporter.................W. **1,158**

LAWRENCEVILLE, c. h., Lawrence Co., 800† p., on Embarras r., and Ohio & Mississippi Rd., 10 m. from Vincennes. Agriculture and manufacturing carried on.

ILLINOIS.

Democratic Herald......W. **1,159**
Rural Republican........W. **1,160**

LEBANON, Saint Clair Co., 2,117 p., on Ohio & Mississippi Rd., 22 m. from St. Louis. Engaged in farming and coal mining. A place of active trade, and seat of McKendree College.
Courier..................W. **1,161**
Journal..................W. **1,162**
McKendree Repository....M. **1,163**

LENA, Stephenson Co., 1,294 p., on Galena division of Illinois Central Rd., 12 m. from Freeport. The centre of an extensive grain and stock trade.
Star......................W. **1,164**

LE ROY, McLean Co., 1,800† p., on Indianapolis, Bloomington & Western Rd., 15 m. E. of Bloomington. Centre of an agricultural country.
Enterprise...............W. **1,165**

LEWISTON, c. h., Fulton Co., 2,952 p., on Galesburg, Peoria & Lewiston Rd., 53 m. from Galesburg. Engaged in manufacturing and a trade centre.
Fulton Democrat........W. **1,166**

LINCOLN, c. h., Logan Co., 7,000† p., on Salt r., Chicago & Alton and Pekin, Lincoln & Decatur and Urbana Rds., 28 m. from Springfield and 157 from Chicago. Great agricultural region. Largest grain shipping point between Chicago and St. Louis. Manufacturing carried on to a considerable extent.
Sharp's Statesman........D. **1,167**
" " ....W. **1,168**
Herald...................W. **1,169**
Illinois Volksfreund......W. **1,170**
Times....................W. **1,171**
Alumni Journal.........M. **1,172**

LITCHFIELD, Montgomery Co., 3,000† p., on Toledo, Wabash & Western and Indianapolis & St. Louis Rds., 43 m. from St. Louis. The best grain market within a radius of 50 m.
Montgomery Co. Democrat....................W. **1,173**
Union Monitor..........W. **1,174**

LOCKPORT, Will Co.
Phœnix...................W. **1,175**

LODA, Iroquois Co., 1,200† p., on Chicago division of Illinois Central Rd., 100 m. from Chicago. A grain and produce market for a large tract of country.
Register..................W. **1,176**

LOUISVILLE, c. h., Clay Co., 1,000† p., on Little Wabash r., and Springfield division of O. & M. Rd., 96 m. from St. Louis and 244 from Cincinnati. Surrounded by a rich farming district.
Clay Co. Tribune.........W. **1,177**
Ledger...................W. **1,178**

LOVINGTON, Moultrie Co.
Index.....................W. **1,179**

McHENRY, McHenry Co.
Plaindealer..............W. **1,180**

McLEANSBORO, c. h., Hamilton Co., 1,086† p., on St. Louis & Southeastern Rd., at junction of St. Louis, Evansville and Shawneetown divisions, 101 m. from St. Louis, 61 from Evansville, 40 from Shawneetown. A well-timbered agricultural district. Seat of Hamilton College.
Golden Era...............W. **1,181**
Times....................W. **1,182**

ILLINOIS.

MACOMB, c. h., McDonough Co., 3,500† p., on Chicago, Burlington & Quincy Rd., 58 m. from Quincy and 206 W. of Chicago, in an agricultural district; largest business point in the county.
Eagle....................W. **1,183**
Illinois Granger.........W. **1,184**
Journal...................W. **1,185**

MAGNOLIA, Putnam Co., 1,667 p., about 12 m. from Illinois r. and about 15 S. E. of Hennepin.
News.....................W. **1,186**

MAJORITY POINT, c. h., Cumberland Co., 1,600 p., 134 m. S. E. of Springfield, and near line of Illinois Central Rd.
Cumberland Democrat...W. **1,187**
Republican Mail.........W. **1,188**

MARENGO, McHenry Co., 1,500† p., on Galena division of the Chicago & Northwestern Rd., 66 m. from Chicago and 27 from Rockford.
Republican..............W. **1,189**

MARION, c. h., Williamson Co., 1,200 p., on the Carbondale & Marion Rd., 18 m. from Carbondale and 172 from Springfield.
Democrat...............
Egyptian Press..........W. **1,191**
Monitor..................W. **1,192**

MAROA, Macon Co., 1,200† p., at junction of the Illinois Central and Illinois Midland Rd., 13 m. N. of Decatur. A shipping town, and in the midst of an agricultural region.
News.....................W. **1,193**

MARSEILLES, La Salle Co., 3,000† p., on Chicago, Rock Island & Pacific Rd., 8 m. from Ottawa. A manufacturing place, contains numerous stone quarries.
Herald...................W. **1,194**

MARSHALL, c. h., Clark Co., 2,541 p., on Vandalia, Terre Haute & Indianapolis and Paris, Danville & Vincennes Rds., 147 m. from St. Louis and 20 from Terre Haute.
Clark Co. Herald........W. **1,195**
Messenger...............W. **1,196**

MARTINSVILLE, Clark Co., 1,572 p., on St. Louis, Vandalia, Terre Haute & Indianapolis Rd., 29 m. from Terre Haute.
Express..................W. **1,197**

MASCOUTAH, St. Clair Co.
Enterprise...............W. **1,198**

MASON CITY, Mason Co., 1,615 p., about 20 m. from Havana, on Jacksonville branch of Chicago, Alton & St. Louis Rd., 40 m. N. of Springfield. Extensively engaged in agricultural pursuits.
Independent.............W. **1,199**
Journal..................W. **1,200**

MATTOON, Coles Co., 6,251† p., on St. Louis, Alton & Terre Haute Rd., at intersection of Illinois Central Rd., 173 m. from Chicago and 56 from Terre Haute. A corn-growing and shipping point.
Journal..................D. **1,201**
" ....W. **1,202**
Commercial..............W. **1,203**
Gazette..................W. **1,204**

MENDOTA, La Salle Co., 4,000 p., on Illinois Central Rd., at intersection of Chicago, Burlington & Quincy Rd., 85 m. from Chicago.
Bulletin..................W. **1,205**
News.....................W. **1,206**

METAMORA, c. h., Woodford Co., 1,167 p., on western division of Chicago & Alton Rd., 30 m. from Bloomington. Engaged in manufactures.
Woodford Sentinel.......W. **1,207**

METROPOLIS, c. h., Massac Co., 4,000† p., on Ohio r., 40 m. from Cairo. One of the largest manufacturing places in southern Illinois.
Massac Journal..........W. **1,208**
Times.....................W. **1,209**

MILFORD, Iroquois Co.
Gazette...................W. **1,210**

MILLINGTON, Kendall Co.
Enterprise...............W. **1,211**

MILTON, Pike Co.
Beacon...................W. **1,212**

MINIER, Tazewell Co., 525 p., on Chicago & Alton Rd., 17 m. from Bloomington.
News.....................W. **1,213**

MINONK, Woodford Co., 2,200† p., on Illinois Central Rd., 30 m. from Bloomington.
Index.....................W. **1,214**
Journal...................W. **1,215**
Times.....................W. **1,216**

MOAWEQUA, Shelby Co.
Register..................W. **1,217**

MOLINE, Rock Island Co., 7,700† p., on Mississippi r., and Pacific, Western Union, Rockford, Rock Island & St. Louis, Peoria & Rock Island Rds., 180 m. from Chicago. The rapids afford abundant water-power, which is used in mills and factories.
Review...................W. **1,218**

MOMENCE, Kankakee Co., 1,100† p., at intersection of Chicago, Danville & Vincennes Rd., 54 m. from Chicago. Extensively engaged in manufactures. Stone quarries, iron ore and coal mines in the vicinity.
Reporter.................W. **1,219**

MONMOUTH, c. h., Warren Co., 4,662 p., on Chicago, Burlington & Quincy and Rockford, Rock Island & St. Louis Rds., 26 m. from Mississippi r. Surrounded by a rich agricultural district. Engaged in manufacturing agricultural implements and various other articles. The seat of Monmouth College.
Atlas.....................W. **1,220**
Review...................W. **1,221**
College Courier..........M. **1,222**

MONTICELLO, c. h., Piatt Co., 2,000† p., on Sangamon r. and on Monticello Rd., about midway between Champaign and Decatur. Noted for stock raising.
Piatt Co. Herald.........W. **1,223**
Piatt Republican........W. **1,224**

MORRIS, c. h., Grundy Co., 3,875† p., on Illinois & Michigan Canal and Chicago, Rock Island & Pacific Rd,. 62 m. from Chicago. Depot for the shipment of grain, cattle, pork, coal, etc. Several factories are located here.
Herald...................W. **1,225**
Liberal Reformer........W. **1,226**

MORRISON, c. h., Whitesides Co., 3,500 p., on Chicago & Northwestern Rd., 124 m. from Chicago. Derives its importance mainly from the rich agricultural and stock raising country surrounding it.
Times.....................W. **1,227**
Whiteside Sentinel......W. **1,228**

MORRISONVILLE, Christian Co.
Times.....................W. **1,229**

ILLINOIS.

MOUND CITY, Pulaski Co., 2,300 p., on Ohio r., 7 m. above Cairo, on Mound City Rd. The Western Naval Station is located here. Does extensive business in lumber and ship-building, and various manufactures.
Pulaski Patriot..........W. **1,230**

MOUNT CARMEL, Wabash Co., 3,000† p., on Wabash r. about 24 m. below Vincennes, and on Louisville, New Albany & St. Louis Air Line Rd. Is extensively employed in manufactures.
Democrat...............W. **1,231**
Register...............W **1,232**

MOUNT CARROLL, c. h., Carroll Co., 2,000† p., on Western Union Rd., 27 m from Freeport, 130 from Chicago. Several institutions of learning are located here.
Carroll Co. Mirror......W. **1,233**
Oread...................Qr **1,234**

MOUNT PULASKI, Logan Co.
Star....................W. **1,235**

MOUNT STERLING, c. h., Brown Co., 1,800† p., on Toledo, Wabash & Western Rd., 75 m. from Springfield and 39 from Quincy.
Brown Co Democrat....W. **1,236**
Illinois Message.........W. **1,237**

MOUNT VERNON, c. h., Jefferson Co., 3,000† p., on St. Louis & Southeastern Rd., 76 m. from St. Louis.
Free Press..............W. **1,238**
News....................W. **1,239**

MURPHYSBORO, c. h., Jackson Co., 1,750 p., on Big Muddy r., 15 m. E. of Mississippi r., and about 8 from Carbondale.
Independent.............W **1,240**

NAPERVILLE, Du Page Co., 3,000† p., on Dupage r. and Chicago, Burlington & Quincy Rd., 30 m. from Chicago.
Clarion.................W. **1,241**

NASHVILLE, c. h., Washington Co., 2,500† p., on St. Louis & Southeastern Rd., 120 m. from Springfield, 15 from Illinois Central Rd., 50 from St. Louis Surrounded by a fertile prairie.
Democrat................W. **1,242**
Journal.................W. **1,243**
Washington Co. Zeitung.W. **1,244**

NAUVOO, Hancock Co., 1,578 p., on Mississippi r., at head of lower rapids, and about 15 m. above Keokuk. Engaged in grape culture and general agriculture.
Hancock Co. Journal...
Independent.............W. **1,246**

NEOGA, Cumberland Co.
News....................W. **1,247**

NEW BURNSIDE, Johnson Co.
Journal.................W. **1,248**

NEWMAN, Douglas Co.
Independent.............W. **1,249**

NEW RUTLAND, La Salle Co.
Journal.................W. **1,250**
Times...................W. **1,251**

NEWTON, c. h., Jasper Co., 650† p., on the Embarras r., about 20 m. N. of Ohio and Mississippi Rd., at Olney, on St. Louis, Vandalia & Terre Haute Rd.
Jasper Co. Clipper.......W. **1,252**
Press....................W. **1,253**

NEW WINDSOR, Mercer Co., 650† p., on Rockford, Rock Island & St. Louis Rd., at intersection of Galva, New Boston & Keithsburg branch of Chicago, Burlington & Quincy Rd., 21 m. from Galva.
Press....................W. **1,254**

NIANTIC, Macon Co.
Herald.

NILWOOD, Macoupin Co.
Journal..................W. **1,256**

NOKOMIS, Montgomery Co., 1,500† p., on Indianapolis & St. Louis Rd., 16 m. N. E. of Hillsboro and 81 from St. Louis. An agricultural region. The centre of a large trade.
Gazette..................W. **1,257**

NORMAL, McLean Co.
Illinois School Master....M. **1,258**

OAKLAND, Coles Co.
Herald...................W. **1,259**

ODELL, Livingston Co., 2,185 p., on Chicago & Alton Rd., 8 m. from Dwight.
Centennial...............W. **1,260**

O'FALLON, St. Clair Co.
Advance.

OLNEY, c. h., Richland Co., 4,000† p., on Ohio & Mississippi Rd., 31 m. from Vincennes, Ind., 117 from St. Louis. An important shipping point and trade centre. Extensively engaged in various manufactures.
Ledger...................D. **1,262**
" ....W **1,263**
News.....................W **1,264**
Times....................W **1,265**

ONARGA, Iroquois Co., 3,500† p., on Illinois Central Rd., 85 m. from Chicago, in an agricultural district.
Review...................W. **1,266**

OQUAWKA, c. h., Henderson Co., 1,250† p., on Mississippi r. and Rockford, Rock Island & St. Louis Rd., 132 m. N. W. of Springfield. Surrounded by an agricultural country.
Spectator................W. **1,267**

OREGON, c. h., Ogle Co., 2,000† p., on Rock r., Chicago & Iowa Rd., 18 m. from Dixon, 85 from Chicago. Engaged in manufacturing, farming and grain raising.
Courier..................W. **1,268**
Ogle Co. Reporter........W. **1,269**

ORION, Henry Co.
Chief....................W. **1,270**

OTTAWA, c. h., La Salle Co., 10,000† p., on Illinois r., at mouth of Fox r., on Illinois & Michigan Canal, and Chicago, Rock Island & Pacific Rd., and on Fox r. branch of Chicago, Burlington & Quincy Rd., 84 m. from Chicago. The fall in the river at this point furnishes abundance of water power, which is employed in various manufactures. Immense quantities of grain are shipped from this point. Located in the centre of an extensive coal region.
Central Ill. Wochenblatt..W. **1,271**
Free Trader...............W. **1,272**
Republican...............W. **1,273**

PALATINE, Cook Co.
Herald...................W **1,274**
Enterprise...............M **1,275**

PANA, Christian Co., 4,000† p., on Illinois Central, at intersection of Indianapolis, St. Louis, and Springfield & Illinois Southeastern Rds., 95 m. from St. Louis and 42 from Springfield.
Gazette..................W. **1,276**
Palladium................W **1,277**

PARIS, c. h., Edgar Co., 4,900† p., on Indianapolis & St. Louis Rd., 19 m. from Terre Haute. Engaged in manufacturing; railroad and trade centre.

Edgar Co. Gazette.......W. **1,278**
Edgar Co. Times........W. **1,279**
Prarie Beacon and Valley Blade..............W. **1,280**

PARK RIDGE, Cook Co.

Normal Herald..........W. **1,281**

PAW PAW, Lee Co.

News....................W. **1,282**

PAXTON, c. h., Ford Co., 2,056† p., on Chicago division of Illinois Central Rd., 103 m. from Chicago and 25 from Champaign. In an agricultural county.

Record..................W. **1,283**

PECATONICA, Winnebago Co.

News....................W. **1,284**

PEKIN, c. h., Tazewell Co., 10,000† p., on Illinois r., 12 m. below Peoria, on the Peoria, Pekin & Jacksonville Rd. Steamboats connect with various points on Illinois and Mississippi rs.

Bulletin.................D. **1,285**
Tazewell Co. Republican.W. **1,286**
Times...................W. **1,287**

PEORIA, c. h., Peoria Co., 30,639† p., on Illinois r., at the outlet of Peoria Lake. The river is navigable for steamboats to this point. Railroads connect with the principal cities in all directions. Surrounded by coal mines, and one of the most extensive grain-growing sections of the State. It also connects with Chicago by means of the Michigan Canal. Its central position makes it one of the most important manufacturing and commercial points in the State.

Demokrat................D. **1,288**
" ....W. **1,289**
Deutsche Zeitung.........D. **1,290**
" " ....W. **1,291**
National Democrat.......D. **1,292**
" " ......W. **1,293**
Review..................D. **1,294**
Transcript...............D. **1,295**
" ....T. W. **1,296**
" ....W. **1,297**
Advertiser...............W. **1,298**

PERU, La Salle Co., 3,650 p., on Illinois r., at mouth of Illinois & Michigan Canal and Chicago & Rock Island Rd., 100 m. from Chicago. Coal is found in abundance here and mining is carried on extensively.

Herald..................W. **1,299**

PETERSBURG, Menard Co., 1,792 p., on Sangamon r., and Chicago & Alton and Springfield & Northwestern Rds., 30 m. N. W. of Springfield. The trading point for 30 square miles.

Democrat................W. **1,300**
Menard Co. Times.......W. **1,301**

PINCKNEYVILLE, c. h., Perry Co. 1,100† p., on Beaucoup Creek and St. Louis, Belleville & Southern Illinois Rd., 10 m. from Du Quoin, 61 m. from St. Louis, and at the intersection of the Chester & Tamaroa Rd.

Independent.............W. **1,302**

PITTSFIELD, c. h., Pike Co., 4,500† p., on branch of Hannibal and Naples division of Toledo, Wabash & Western Rd., about 12 m. from Illinois r. and 30 from Jacksonville. Centre of trade of a wealthy county and engaged in manufactures.

Old Flag................W. **1,303**
Pike Co. Democrat.......W. **1,304**

PLANO, Kendall Co., 1,600 p., on Chicago, Burlington & Quincy Rd., about 50 m. from Chicago.

Mirror..................W. **1,305**
True Latter Day Saints' Herald..............S. M. **1,306**
Zion's Hope...........S. M. **1,307**

POLO, Ogle Co., 2,500† p., on Illinois Central Rd., 23 m. from Freeport.

Ogle Co. Press...........W. **1,308**
Christian Radical........W. **1,309**
Poultry Argus...........W. **1,310**

PONTIAC, c. h., Livingston Co., 3,300† p., on Vermillion r. and Chicago & Alton Rd., 92 m. from Chicago. Coal is found in this vicinity in abundance.

Free Trader..............W. **1,311**
Sentinel.................W. **1,312**

PRAIRIE CITY, McDonough Co., 1,250† p., on Chicago, Burlington & Quincy Rd., 23 m. S. by E. of Galesburg, 70 from Quincy, in the midst of a rich tract of agricultural country. Some manufacturing carried on.

Herald..................W. **1,313**

PRINCETON, c. h., Bureau Co., 5,400† p., on Chicago, Burlington & Quincy Rd., 105 m. from Chicago, in a fertile district, having an active trade. Some manufacturing done here. Superior coal found in abundance.

Bureau Co. Republican..W. **1,314**
Bureau Co. Tribune......W. **1,315**
Bureau Co. Repertory....M. **1,316**

PROPHETSTOWN, Whitesides Co., 1,500† p., on Rock r., about midway between Dixon and Rock Island.

Spike....................W. **1,317**

QUINCY, c. h., Adams Co., 24,050 p., on Mississippi r., 170 m. above St. Louis, at terminus of five important railroads. The centering point of a thickly populated agricultural district. Engaged in river trade. Considerable manufacturing carried on.

Germania................D. **1,318**
" ....W. **1,319**
Herald..................D. **1,320**
" ....T. W. **1,321**
" ....W. **1,322**
Whig....................D. **1,323**
" ....W. **1,324**
Commercial Review......W. **1,325**
Der Erz-Druide..........M. **1,326**
Druidic Record.........W. **1,327**
Western Agriculturist....M. **1,328**

RANTOUL, Champaign Co.

News....................W. **1,329**

RIVERTON, Sangamon Co.

Gazette..................

ROANOKE, Woodford Co.

Times.................. W. **1,331**

ROBERTS, Ford Co.

Advocate................

ROBINSON, c. h., Crawford Co., 1,851 p., about 12 m. from Wabash r. and 40 from Terre Haute, Ind. A corn and wheat-growing and wool-producing county.

Argus...................W. **1,333**
Constitution............W. **1,334**

ROCHELLE, Ogle Co., 1,900 p., on Ga-

lena division of Chicago & Northwestern Rd., 23 m. E. of Dixon. Centre of a thriving trade. One of the best grain markets in northern Illinois.
Register..................W. **1,335**

ROCK FALLS, Whitesides Co., 877 p., on Rock r., opposite Sterling, 110 m. from Chicago. Has large water power and several manufacturing establishments.
Progress..................W. **1,336**

ROCKFORD, c. h., Winnebago Co., 14,000† p., on Rock r., on the Galena division of the Chicago & Northwestern Rd., 92 m. from Chicago. A branch railroad connects with Kenosha on Lake Michigan. It has abundant water power, and is extensively engaged in manufacturing agricultural implements and various articles.
Gazette..................W. **1,337**
Journal..................W. **1,338**
Nya Sverige.
Register..................W. **1,340**
Times..................W. **1,341**

ROCK ISLAND, c. h., Rock Island Co., 12,000† p., on Mississippi r., opposite Davenport, Iowa, to which it is connected by a bridge. The Chicago, Rock Island & Pacific, Western Union, Rock Island & St. Louis, Peoria & Rock Island and Rockford Rds. all terminate here, excepting the first named. The Government Island United States Arsenal and workshops are situated here. Extensively engaged in manufactures, coal mining and river trade.
Argus..................D. **1,342**
"..................W. **1,343**
Union..................D. **1,344**
"..................W. **1,345**
Neue Volks Zeitung....S. W. **1,346**

ROCKTON, Winnebago Co.
Herald..................W. **1,347**

ROODHOUSE, Greene Co., 1,100† p., on Chicago & Alton Rd., 21 m. from Jacksonville.
Independent..................W. **1,348**
Signal..................W. **1,349**

ROSSVILLE, Vermillion Co.
Observer..................W. **1,350**

RUSHVILLE, c. h., Schuyler Co., 1,800 p., terminus of Rushville branch of Chicago, Burlington & Quincy Rd., 226 m. from Chicago and 9 from Illinois r. Engaged in manufacturing to some extent. Centre of a large grain and fruit-growing region.
Schuyler Citizen..................W. **1,351**
Times..................W. **1,352**

ST. CHARLES, Kane Co., 2,281 p., on Fox r. branch of Chicago & Northwestern Rd., 35 m. from Chicago. The extensive water power gives motion to numerous mills.
Leader..................W. **1,353**

SALEM, c. h., Marion Co., 3,132 p., on Ohio & Mississippi Rd., 16 m. N. E. of Centralia and 69 from St. Louis.
Advocate..................W. **1,354**
Industrial..................W. **1,355**

SANDWICH, De Kalb Co., 1,400 p., on Chicago, Burlington & Quincy Rd., 57 m. S. W. of Chicago.
Free Press..................W. **1,356**
Gazette..................W. **1,357**

SAVANNA, Carroll Co.
Times..................W. **1,358**

ILLINOIS.

SAYBROOK, McLean Co.
Herald..................W. **1,359**

SHAWNEETOWN, c. h., Gallatin Co., 2,500† p., on Ohio r., 9 m. from mouth of Wabash. Terminus of St. Louis & Southeastern and Springfield & Illinois Southeastern Rds. It has a steamboat landing, and is a shipping point for a farming and mining region. Engaged in manufacturing, milling and pork packing.
Gazette..................W. **1,360**
Shawnee Herald..................W. **1,361**
Shawnee News..................W. **1,362**

SHELBYVILLE, c. h., Shelby Co., 3,500† p., on Kaskaskia r. and the Indianapolis & St. Louis Rd., 79 m. from Terre Haute, 109 from St. Louis. Surrounded by an agricultural district. Also extensively engaged in manufacturing.
Shelby Co. Independent..W. **1,363**
Shelby Co. Leader..................W. **1,364**
Union..................W. **1,365**

SHELDON, Iroquois Co.
Enterprise..................W. **1,366**

SHERIDAN, La Salle Co., 550† p., on Fox r. branch of Chicago, Burlington & Quincy Rd., 16 m. from Ottawa.
News Letter..................W. **1,367**

SHIPMAN, Macoupin Co.
True Flag..................W. **1,368**

SOMONAUK, De Kalb Co.
Free Press..................W. **1,369**
Reveille..................W. **1,370**

SPARLAND, Marshall Co., 700† p., on Peoria branch of Chicago, Rock Island & Pacific Rd., 26 m. N. of Peoria and near Lacon, 134 from Chicago. Business, coal mining and distilling.
Chronicle..................W. **1,371**

SPARTA, Randolph Co., 2,500† p., about 20 m. from Chester, and about 8 from the line of St. Louis & Southeastern Rd., and 50 from St. Louis.
Plaindealer..................W. **1,372**

SPRINGFIELD, c. h., Sangamon Co., State capital, 25,000† p., on Sangamon r. The Chicago, Alton & St. Louis Rd. intersects the Toledo, Wabash & Western at this point. The Springfield & Southeastern, Springfield & Northwestern and Gilman & Clinton Rds. also centre here. A rich and populous agricultural district. Coal is found in abundance in the vicinity. Engaged in manufactures and inland commerce.
Illinois State Journal....D. **1,373**
" " " .T. W. **1,374**
" " " ....W. **1,375**
Illinois State Register....D. **1,376**
" " " ....W. **1,377**
Illinois Freie Presse......W. **1,378**
Sangamo Monitor..........W. **1,379**
Labor of Love..........M. **1,380**

STEELEVILLE, Randolph Co.
Times..................W. **1,381**

STERLING, Whitesides Co., 4,000 p., on Rock r., Rockford, Rock Island & St. Louis and Chicago & Northwestern Rds., 110 m. from Chicago. Has good water-power, which is being rapidly developed. Surrounded by a fine agricultural district.
Gazette..................W. **1,382**
Standard..................W. **1,383**

ILLINOIS.

STONEFORT, Saline Co.
Journal..................W. **1,384**

STREATOR, La Salle Co., 1,486 p., on Vermillion r. and western division of Chicago, Alton & St. Louis, and Oswego & Fox River Valley Rds., the latter being under construction, and 100 m. W. of Chicago; surrounded by the Vermillion coal fields 10,000 tons being mined per day by the company. Centre of business; 15 m. S. of Ottawa.
Free Press..............W. **1,385**
Monitor..................W. **1,386**
Pioneer..................W. **1,387**

SULLIVAN, c. h., Moultrie Co., 2,000† p., 24 m. from Decatur, at intersection of Chicago & Illinois Southern Rd. with the Chicago & Paducah Rd., 14 m. from Mattoon. Rich agricultural region. Grain and stock-raising the principal branches of industry.
Journal..................W. **1,388**
Progress..................W. **1,389**

SUMNER, Lawrence Co.
Lawrence Co. Press.....W. **1,390**

SYCAMORE, c. h., De Kalb Co., 4,000† p., surrounded by an agricultural district about 5 m. from Cortlandt, on Chicago & Northwestern Rd. Engaged in manufactures.
City Weekly.............W. **1,391**
Free Methodist...........W. **1,392**
Reformer and Free Press.W. **1,393**
True Republican.........W. **1,394**
Christian Pilgrim.......W. **1,395**

TALLULA, Menard Co.
Enterprise...............W. **1,396**

TAMAROA, Perry Co.
Perry Co. Watchman....W. **1,397**

TAYLORVILLE, c. h., Christian Co., 2,180 p., at crossing of Toledo, Wabash & Western and Springfield, Illinois & Southeastern Rds., 25 m. from Springfield and 90 from St. Louis. In an agricultural district. Coal found in the vicinity. Engaged in manufactures.
Christian Co. Farmer's Journal...............W. **1,398**
Democrat...............W. **1,399**
Illinois Republican......W. **1,400**

THOMSON, Carroll Co., 1,500 p., on Mississippi r., and Western Union Rd., 7 m. above Fulton.
Journal.................
Village Echo....... ....W. **1,402**

TOLONO, Champaign Co.
Herald.................. W. **1,403**

TONICA, La Salle Co., 1,000 p., on Illinois Central Rd., 9 m. S. of La Salle.
Local....................W. **1,404**
News....................W. **1,405**

TOULON, c. h., Stark Co., 1,200 p., on Peoria & Rock Island Rd., 37 m. from Peoria, in an enterprising and thrifty farming district.
Stark Co. News..........W. **1,406**

TROY, Madison Co.
Bulletin.................W. **1,407**

TURNER JUNCTION, Du Page Co., 1,000† p., on Chicago & Northwestern Rd., 30 m. from Chicago.
News....................W. **1,408**

TUSCOLA, Douglas Co., 2,000 p., on Illinois Central Rd., 150 m. from Chicago, in a farming district.
Douglas Co. Review.....W. **1,409**
Journal.................W. **1,410**

UPPER ALTON, Madison Co., 1,000 p., about 2 m. from Alton City. Seat of Shurtleff College.
Qui Vive................W. **1,411**

URBANA, c. h., Champaign Co., 5,000† p., on Indianapolis, Bloomington & Western Rd., 92 m. from Springfield and 1½ from Champaign. A place of active trade. Surrounded by an agricultural and mineral district.
Republican.............W. **1, 412**

VANDALIA, c. h., Fayette Co., 1,999 p., on Kaskaskia r. and Illinois Central Rd., at intersection of St. Louis, Vandalia, Terre Haute & Indianapolis Rd., 106 m. from Bloomington and 77 from St. Louis. A shipping point and trade centre for a large agricultural section.
Fayette Democrat.......W. **1,413**
Union...................W. **1,414**

VERMONT, Fulton Co., 2,300 p., on Chicago, Burlington & Quincy and Rockford, Rock Island & St. Louis Rds., 16 m. S. W. of Lewistown. Engaged largely in agriculture.
Chronicle................W. **1,415**

VIENNA, c. h., Johnson Co., 900† p., 190 m. from Springfield, about 34 from Cairo, on Cairo & Vincennes Rd., has an extensive trade in tobacco, grain, hay, fruit and lumber
Johnson Co. Journal ...W. **1,416**
Johnson Co. Yeoman....W. **1,417**

VIRDEN, Macoupin Co., 2,500† p., on Chicago & Alton Rd., 17 m. from Carlinville and 22 from Springfield. Centre of a thriving trade. Extensively engaged in the shipping of grain.
Record...................W. **1,418**

VIRGINIA, c. h., Cass Co., 1,500† p., at intersection of Peoria, Pekin & Jacksonville Rd. with Ohio & Mississippi Rd. In centre of county; in a fine agricultural district.
Enquirer.................W. **1,419**
Gazette...................W. **1,420**

WARREN, Jo. Daviess Co., 1,666 p., on Illinois Central Rd., at junction of Mineral Point Rd., 26 m. from Galena, 25 W. of Frankfort and 145 W. of Chicago. Manufacturing, lead mining and agriculture is carried on. Is in the midst of a large farming district.
Sentinel.................W **1,421**

WARSAW, Hancock Co., 3,750 p., on Mississippi r., 5 m. below Keokuk, at terminus of Toledo, Peoria, Wabash & Western Rd. Large river steamboats run to this point. Engaged in shipping produce and a place of active trade.
Bulletin.................W. **1,422**

WASHBURN, Woodford Co., 1,000 p., on western division of Chicago & Alton Rd., 125 m. from Chicago.
Reveille..................W. **1,423**

WASHINGTON, Tazewell Co., 2,000† p., on Toledo, Peoria & Warsaw and western division of Chicago & Alton Rds., 13 m. E. of Peoria. It is an extensive shipping point for grain and hogs. Actively engaged in manufactures.
Herald..................W. **1,424**

ILLINOIS.

WASHINGTON HEIGHTS, Cook Co.
Home Journal..........W. **1,425**

WATERLOO, c. h., Monroe Co., 1,700† p., 12 m. from Mississippi r. and 22 S. E. of St. Louis. Surrounded by a wheat and corn country.
Advocate................W. **1,426**
Times....................W. **1,427**

WATERMAN, De Kalb Co.
Free Press..............W. **1,428**

WATSEKA, c. h., Iroquois Co., 2,500† p., on Iroquois r., at intersection of Toledo, Peoria & Warsaw with Chicago, Danville & Vincennes Rd., 80 m. from Chicago, in a farming district. The centre of a vast region of fertile country. 40 Artesian wells within the corporative limits; known as the "Artesian City."
Iroquois Times..........W. **1,429**
Republican..............W. **1,430**

WAUKEGAN, c. h., Lake Co., 6,000† p., on Lake Michigan and Chicago & Northwestern Rd., 35 m. from Chicago and 50 from Milwaukee. A place of active trade, having considerable lake commerce.
Gazette................. W. **1,431**
Lake Co. Patriot.........W. **1,432**

WAVERLY, Morgan Co., 2,463 p., on Illinois Farmers' Rd., about 25 m. from Jacksonville.
Temperance Banner.....

WENONA, Marshall Co., 1,500† p., at intersection of Illinois Central with Lacon branch of western division of Chicago & Alton Rd., 19 m. from Lacon, 39 from Bloomington. Centre of a large grain trade. Some manufacturing carried on.
Index...................W. **1,434**

WESTON, McLean Co.
Monitor.................W.

WHEATON, Du Page Co., 1,300† p., on Galena division of Chicago & Northwestern Rd., 25 m. from Chicago. An agricultural and stock-growing county.
Illinoian................W. **1,436**
College Record...........W. **1,437**

WHITE HALL, Greene Co., 1,600† p., on Rockford, Rock Island & St. Louis and Chicago & Alton Rds., 24 m. from Jacksonville and 60 from St. Louis. Centre of an agricultural county. Potters' clay and coal are found in the vicinity. Engaged in the manufacture of pottery.
Greene Co. Democrat.....W. **1,438**
Register.................W. **1,439**

WILMINGTON, Will Co., 3,150 p., on Kankakee r. and Chicago & Alton Rd., 53 m. from Chicago. Some manufacturing done here.
Advocate................W. **1,440**

WINCHESTER, c. h., Scott Co., 1,771† p., on Big Sandy Creek and the Rockford, Rock Island & St. Louis Rd., 10 m. from Illinois r., 18 from Jacksonville, 82 from St. Louis and 319 from Chicago. Engaged in various manufactures. Coal is found here. The centre of a fine agricultural district.
Independent.............W. **1,441**
Times...................W. **1,442**

WOODSTOCK, c. h., McHenry Co., 2,500 p., on Chicago & Northwestern Rd., 51 m. from Chicago.
New Era.................W. **1,443**
Sentinel................W. **1,444**

WYOMING, Stark Co., 1,200† p., on Spoon r., at intersection of Peoria & Rock Island Rd. with Buda & Rushville branch of Chicago, Burlington & Quincy Rd., 6 m. from Toulon.
Post....................W. **1,445**
Stark Co. Bee............W. **1,446**

YATES CITY, Knox Co., 900 p., on Peoria Rd., 23 m. S. S. E. of Galesburg.
East Knox News........W. **1,447**

YORKVILLE, c. h., Kendall Co., 1,400 p., on Fox r. and Fox River Valley Rd., 52 m. from Chicago. Engaged in agriculture and manufactures. Centre of trade for the county.
Kendall Co. Record......W. **1,448**
News....................W. **1,449**

INDIANA.

ALBION, c. h., Noble Co.
New Era.................W. **1,450**

ANDERSON, c. h., Madison Co., 4,000† p., on White River and Pittsburgh, Cincinnati & St. Louis Rd., at intersection of C., C., C. & I. Rd., also terminus of Cincinnati, Wabash & Michigan and Anderson, Lebanon & St. Louis Rds., 36 m. from Indianapolis and 48 from Logansport. A thriving town, carrying on manufacturing and a general trade.
Democrat................W. **1,451**
Herald..................W. **1,452**
Witness.................W. **1,453**

ANGOLA, c. h., Steuben Co., 1,075 p., near N. E. corner of State, 42 m. from Fort Wayne, on Fort Wayne, Jackson & Saginaw Rd. Engaged in agriculture and stock raising.
Herald..................W. **1,454**
Steuben Co. Republican..W. **1,455**

ATTICA, Fountain Co., 2,700† p., on Wabash r. and Wabash & Erie Canal, and the Toledo, Wabash & Western and Indiana North & South Rds., 22 m. from Lafayette. It has a large and flourishing trade. Engaged in general manufactures.
Ledger..................W. **1,456**

AUBURN, c. h., De Kalb Co., 2,000† p., on Baltimore & Chicago and Fort Wayne, Jackson & Saginaw Rds., at the intersection of the Detroit, Eel r. & Illinois Rd., 22 m. from Fort Wayne. A thriving place; rapidly building up; considerable manufacturing carried on.
Courier.................W. **1,457**
De Kalb Co. Republican.W. **1,458**

AURORA, Dearborn Co., 4,500† p., on Ohio r. and Louisville branch of Ohio & Mississippi Rd., 25 m. below Cincinnati. Steamboats run to Cincinnati and other points on the river. Engaged in milling, distilling, coopering, and exporting hay and grain.
Dearborn Independent...W. **1,459**

BEDFORD, c. h., Lawrence Co., 1,954 p., on Louisville, New Albany & Chicago Rd., 71 m. from New Albany, 255 from Chicago. County seat and place of active trade.
Banner..................W. **1,460**
Independent.............W. **1,461**

INDIANA.

Lawrence Gazette........W. **1,462**
Common School Teacher..M. **1,463**

BLOOMFIELD, c. h., Greene Co., 2,000 p., near W. fork of White r., 80 m. from Indianapolis. A place of active trade, in a rich and fertile valley.
Democrat................W. **1,464**
Tribune.................W. **1,465**

BLOOMINGTON, c. h., Monroe Co., 3,200† p., on Louisville, New Albany & Chicago Rd., 97 m. from New Albany and 60 from Indianapolis. Engaged in manufacturing, farming and quarrying limestone. Location of the Indiana State University.
Courier.................W. **1,466**
Progress................W. **1,467**
Times...................W. **1,468**

BLUFFTON, c. h., Wells Co., 2,131† p., on Wabash r., and Fort Wayne, Muncie & Cincinnati Rd., 25 m. S. of Fort Wayne. Engaged in lumbering and manufactures.
Banner..................W. **1,469**
Chronicle...............W. **1,470**

BOONVILLE, c. h., Warrick Co., 1,039 p., 10 m. from the Ohio r. and 17 from Evansville. Engaged in raising and manufacturing tobacco, and a place of active trade.
Enquirer................W. **1,471**
Standard................W. **1,472**

BOSWELL, Benton Co.
Leader..................W. **1,473**

BOURBON, Marshall Co., 1,500† p., on Pittsburgh, Fort Wayne & Chicago Rd., 53 m. N. W. of Fort Wayne, 96 E. of Chicago. Surrounded by a fertile country. Actively engaged in manufactures.
Mirror..................W. **1,474**

BOWLING GREEN, c. h., Clay Co., 1,500 p., on Eel r., about 20 m. E. of Terre Haute.
Clay Co. Deutsche Zeitung...............W. **1,475**
Clay Co. Herald.........W. **1,476**

BRAZIL, Clay Co., 3,500† p., on St. Louis, Vandalia, Terre Haute & Indianapolis Rd., 16 m. from Terre Haute and 55 W. of Indianapolis. In the Indiana Block Coal Region. Largely engaged in mining and manufacturing.
Clay Co. Enterprise......W. **1,477**
Echo.....................W. **1,478**
Manufacturer and Miner.W. **1,479**

BREMEN, Marshall Co.
Gazette..................W. **1,480**

BROOKSTON, White Co.
Reporter.................W. **1,481**

BROOKVILLE, c. h., Franklin Co., 2,463 p., on White Water r. and Canal, and White Water Valley Rd., 43 m. from Cincinnati. A place of considerable trade.
American................W. **1,482**
Der Leucht Thurm.......W. **1,483**
Franklin Democrat......W. **1,484**

BROWNSTOWN, c. h., Jackson Co., 925† p., on Ohio & Mississippi Rd., 1 m. S. E. of the E. fork of the White r., 10 S. W. of Seymour and 98 W. of Cincinnati. It is surrounded by a fertile country, which contains iron ore and valuable timber forests.
Banner..................W. **1,485**

BUNKER HILL, Miami Co.
Independent Press........W. **1,486**

INDIANA.

BUTLER, De Kalb Co.
Review..................W. **1,487**

CAMBRIDGE CITY, Wayne Co., 2,700† p., on the White Water Canal. The Pittsburgh, Cincinnati & St. Louis, Fort Wayne, Muncie & Cincinnati and White Water Valley Rds. pass through here; 53 m. from Indianapolis, and 75 from Cincinnati. The centre of a trade. Surrounded by a farming country. Extensively engaged in manufactures.
Review..................W. **1,488**
Tribune.................W. **1,489**

CANNELTON, c. h., Perry Co., 2,481 p., on Ohio r., 70 m. above Evansville and 125 below Louisville, Ky. Coal is found here in large quantities. The coal mines of Cannelton are noted as the largest below Pittsburgh. Engaged in cotton and other manufactures.
Enquirer................W. **1,490**
Reporter................W. **1,491**

CENTREVILLE, Wayne Co.
Odd Fellows' Chronicle..W. **1,492**
Wayne Co. Chronicle....W. **1,493**

CHARLESTOWN, c. h., Clarke Co., 2,204 p., 2½ m. from the Ohio r., and the Louisville branch of the Ohio & Mississippi Rd., and 12 from Louisville, Ky. It is surrounded by excellent land and has an active business.
Clarke Co. Record.......W. **1,494**
Herald..................W. **1,495**

CICERO, Hamilton Co., 800† p., on the Indianapolis, Peru and Chicago Rd., 27 m. from Indianapolis.
Gazette.................W. **1,496**

CLINTON, Vermillion Co.
Exponent................W. **1,497**

CLOVERDALE, Putnam Co.
Thursday Morning Bee..W. **1,498**

COLLEGE CORNER, Union Co.
Corner Stone............W. **1,499**

COLUMBIA CITY, c. h., Whitley Co., 3,100† p., on Pittsburgh, Fort Wayne & Chicago Rd., at the intersection of Detroit, Eel r. & Illinois Rd., 19 m. from Fort Wayne. It has a fine trade, and is located in the centre of a rich agricultural district.
Post....................W. **1,500**
Whitley Co. Commercial.W. **1,501**

COLUMBUS, c. h., Bartholomew Co., 6,000† p., on White r., 41 m. from Indianapolis, on the Jeffersonville, Madison & Indianapolis Rd., at the junction of the Cambridge City & Madison branch. In an agricultural district.
Bartholomew Democrat..W. **1,502**
Republican..............W. **1,503**

CONNERSVILLE, c. h., Fayette Co., 3,707 p., on White Water r. and the White Water Valley Rd., at the intersection of the Cincinnati & Indianapolis Junction Rd. with the Fort Wayne, Muncie & Cincinnati Rd., 42 m. from Hamilton, 65 from Cincinnati and 56 from Indianapolis. Engaged in manufactures and the centre of a large trade.
Examiner................W. **1,504**
Times...................W. **1,505**

CORYDON, c. h., Harrison Co., 1,000† p., on Indian Creek, 9 m. from the Ohio r. and 21 from Louisville, Ky. Noted for its great quantity of valuable building and

INDIANA.

lithographic stone, marble, timber, &c. Also as an agricultural region, being one of the finest wheat and grain producing counties in the State. It also contains some valuable sulphur springs.

Democrat................W. **1,506**
Republican..............W. **1,507**

COVINGTON, c. h., Fountain Co., 2,273† p., on Wabash r., Wabash & Erie Canal, and Indianapolis, Bloomington & Western Rd., 73 m. from Indianapolis. Large quantities of coal, live stock and produce are shipped from here.

People's Friend..........W. **1,508**
Spence's People's Paper..W. **1,509**

CRAWFORDSVILLE, c. h., Montgomery Co., 4,600† p., on Sugar Creek. The Louisville, New Albany & Chicago, Indianapolis, Bloomington & Western and Logansport, Crawfordsville & Southwestern Rds. all pass through here; 28 m. from Lafayette and 44 from Indianapolis. A fine agricultural and well-timbered district. Seat of Wabash College.

Journal..................W. **1,510**
Review...................W. **1,511**
Saturday Mercury..........W. **1,512**
Star......................W. **1,513**

CROWN POINT, c. h., Lake Co., 2,500† p., on Pittsburgh, Cincinnati & St. Louis Rd., 43 m. from Chicago. Extensively engaged in agriculture and stock raising.

Freie Presse.............W. **1,514**
Register.................W. **1,515**

DANVILLE, c. h., Hendricks Co., 1,040 p., on the Indianapolis & St. Louis Rd., 20 m. from Indianapolis. The county seminary is located here.

Hendricks Co. Union....W. **1,516**
Indianian...............W. **1,517**

DECATUR, c. h., Adams Co., 2,000† p., on St. Mary's r., 21 m. from Fort Wayne and on the Cincinnati, Richmond & Fort Wayne Rd., in the midst of an agricultural district. Extensively engaged in the lumber trade.

Democrat...............W. **1,518**

DELPHI, c. h., Carroll Co., 2,000† p., on Wabash & Erie River Canal, and Toledo, Wabash & Western Rd., 17 m. from Lafayette. The greatest lime region in the west. Extensively engaged in paper manufacture.

Journal.................W. **1,519**
Times...................W. **1,520**

DUBLIN, Wayne Co.

Wayne Register.........W. **1,521**

DUNKIRK, Jay Co.

Courier.................W. **1,522**

EDINBURG, Johnson Co., 2,000 p., on E. fork of White r., which furnishes good water-power, and on Jeffersonville, Madison & Indianapolis Rd., 30 m. S. E. of Indianapolis.

Courier.................W. **1,523**

ELKHART, Elkhart Co., 8,000† p., on St. Joseph's r., at the junction of the Northern Indiana Air Line and the Lake Shore & Michigan Southern Rds., 100 m. from Chicago. Has good water power, which is partly developed for manufacturing. Three rivers converge here—the St. Joseph's, Elkhart and Christiana.

Evening Review..........D. **1,524**
" "..........W. **1,525**
Observer................D. **1,526**

INDIANA.

Review..................W. **1,527**
Democratic Union........W. **1,528**
Herald of Truth..........M. **1,529**
Herold de Wahrheit......M. **1,530**

ELLETTSVILLE, Monroe Co., 1,000† p., on Louisville, New Albany & Chicago Rd., 7 m. from Bloomington and 104 from New Albany.

Republican..............W. **1,531**

EVANSVILLE, c. h., Vanderburgh Co., 40,000† p., on Ohio r., 195 m. below Louisville, and at terminus of Evansville, Crawfordsville & St. Louis, and Southeastern and Evansville, Henderson & Nashville Rds. The Wabash & Erie Canal terminates here, which, with the river commerce, makes it one of the most important commercial cities in the State. Considerable manufacturing done here, and large quantities of grain, pork, tobacco and cotton are shipped to other markets.

Courier..................D. **1,532**
"..................W. **1,533**
Demokrat................D. **1,534**
"................W. **1,535**
"............Sund. **1,536**
Herald.
Journal..................D. **1,538**
"...............T. W. **1,539**
Dollar Journal..........W. **1,540**
Union....................D. **1,541**
"....................W. **1,542**
Sunday Argus............W. **1,543**

FORT WAYNE, c. h., Allen Co., 25,327† p., at the confluence of St. Joseph and St. Mary's rs., which form the Maumee. The Toledo & Wabash Rd. here intersects the Pittsburgh, Fort Wayne & Chicago Rd. Four other important railroads centre here. One of the most important places in the State. Extensively engaged in manufactures of various kinds. Surrounded by a fine agricultural district.

Gazette..................D. **1,544**
"..................W. **1,545**
News.....................D. **1,546**
Sentinel.................D. **1,547**
".................W. **1,548**
Tagblatt.................D. **1,549**
Indiana Volksfreund....W. **1,550**
*Indiana Staats Zeitung*T.W. **1,551**
" " "..W. **1,552**
Journal.................W. **1,553**
Gem.....................M. **1,554**

FOWLER, c. h., Benton Co.

Benton Co. Herald.......W. **1,555**
Benton Democrat.........W. **1,556**

FRANKFORT, c. h., Clinton Co., 2,000 p., on Logansport, Crawfordsville & Southwestern Rd., 36 m. from Logansport and 79 from Terre Haute. In a fine farming district.

Banner..................W. **1,557**
Crescent................W. **1,558**

FRANKLIN, c. h., Johnson Co., 2,707 p., on Jeffersonville, Madison & Indianapolis Rd., at intersection of Martinsville division of Indianapolis, Cincinnati & Lafayette Rd., 20 m. from Indianapolis. Surrounded by a rich agricultural district. A place of active business.

Democratic Herald.......W. **1,559**
Jeffersonian............W. **1,560**

GARRETT, De Kalb Co.

News....................W. **1,561**

INDIANA.

GOODLAND, Newton Co.
Courier..................W. **1,562**

GOSHEN, c. h., Elkhart Co., 4,000† p., on the Elkhart r., at the intersection of the Northern Indiana Air Line with the Cincinnati, Wabash & Michigan Rd. The centre of a rich agricultural district, possessing good water power, which is extensively employed in manufacturing.
Democrat...............W. **1,563**
Times....................W. **1,564**

GOSPORT, Owen Co., 1,300 p., on banks of White r., at crossing of Louisville, New Albany & Chicago and Indianapolis & Vincennes Rds., 44 m. S. W. of Indianapolis. A shipping point for produce of the surrounding country. A place of active trade.
Gazette..................W. **1,565**

GRAND VIEW, Spencer Co., 900† p., on Ohio r., 6 m. above Rockport and 145 below Louisville.
Monitor..................W. **1,566**

GREENCASTLE, c. h., Putnam Co., 4,000 p., on Indianapolis & St. Louis and St. Louis, Vandalia, Terre Haute & Indianapolis Rds., at intersection of Louisville, New Albany & Chicago Rd., 39 m. W. of Indianapolis and 200 S. of Chicago. A rich and populous agricultural district and centre of a large trade.
Banner..................W. **1,567**
Indiana Press...........W. **1,568**
Star.....................W. **1,569**

GREENFIELD, c. h., Hancock Co., 1,203 p., on the Pittsburgh, Indianapolis & St. Louis Rd., 20 m. E. of Indianapolis. Engaged in manufacturing furniture and various other articles. The centre of a good farming district.
Hancock Democrat......W. **1,570**
News.....................W. **1,571**

GREENSBURG, c. h., Decatur Co., 3,000 p., on Indianapolis & Cincinnati Rd., 46 m. from Indianapolis. Engaged in milling and manufacturing, and surrounded by an extensive agricultural region. Extensive stone quarries are located here.
Decatur Press..........W. **1,572**
Standard................W. **1,573**

HARTFORD CITY, c. h., Blackford Co., 1,500 p., at crossing of Pittsburgh, Cincinnati & St. Louis and Fort Wayne, Muncie & Cincinnati Rds., 75 m. from Indianapolis, 175 from Chicago, 130 from Cincinnati, 47 from Fort Wayne. A large hub and spoke factory is here, also several other manufactories.
Courier.
News.....................W. **1,575**

HARTSVILLE, Bartholomew Co.
Literary Ensign.........W. **1,576**

HOPE, Bartholomew Co.
Independent.............W. **1,577**

HUNTINGBURG, Dubois Co., 2,663 p., 7 m. S. W. of Jasper. Engaged in agriculture and coal mining.
Signal....................W. **1,578**

HUNTINGTON, c. h., Huntington Co., 2,925 p., on Wabash r., and the Toledo, Wabash & Western Rd. and the Wabash & Erie Canal, 24 m. from Fort Wayne. Actively engaged in manufactures; has several factories, iron and wood. Makes immense quantities of lime.
Indiana Herald.........W. **1,579**

INDIANA.

INDIANAPOLIS, Marion Co., State capital, 114,000† p., on White r., near centre of State, 115 m. from Cincinnati, 110 m. from Louisville, 240 from St. Louis and 194 from Chicago. The centering point of eleven important railroads, and in a rich and fertile district, having an immense trade.
Evening News............D. **1,580**
News......................W. **1,581**
Journal....................D. **1,582**
Indiana State Journal..W. **1,583**
Sentinel...................D. **1,584**
State Sentinel............W. **1,585**
Telegraph.................D. **1,586**
Indiana Volksblatt and Telegraph..............W. **1,587**
Central Catholic.........W. **1,588**
Hoosier Patron and Lady Granger...............W. **1,589**
*Indiana Deutsche Zeitung*W. **1,590**
Indiana Deutsche Zeitung................Sund. **1,591**
Indiana Farmer........W. **1,592**
Journal of Commerce and Price Current.........W. **1,593**
People....................W. **1,594**
Saturday Herald.........W. **1,595**
Spootvogel...............W. **1,596**
Sun........................W. **1,597**
Zukunft....................W. **1,598**
Beham's Musical Review.M. **1,599**
Christian Monitor.......M. **1,600**
Indiana Official Railway and Business Guide...M. **1,601**
Indiana School Journal..M. **1,602**
Little Sower..............M. **1,603**
Masonic Advocate.......M. **1,604**
Mechanical Journal......M. **1,605**
Medical Review...........M. **1, 06**
Morning Watch...........M. **1,607**
Odd Fellow's Talisman...M. **1,608**
Our Monthly...............M. **1,609**
Pythian Journal..........M **1,610**
Laurel Wreath...........Qr. **1,611**

JASPER, c. h., Dubois Co., 750 p., on Patoka Creek, 120 m. from Indianapolis. Centre of trade. Engaged principally in agricultural pursuits. Flint, iron and coal found in vicinity.
Courier...................W. **1,612**

JEFFERSONVILLE, Clarke Co., 7,254 p., on Ohio r. opposite Louisville, Ky., and at the terminus of Indianapolis & Jeffersonville Rd. Extensively engaged in manufactures.
Evening News............D. **1,613**
National Democrat......W. **1,614**

JONESBORO, Grant Co., 800† p., on Mississinewa r. and Pittsburgh, Cincinnati & St. Louis Rd., 46 m. E. of Logansport.
Herald....................W. **1,615**

KENDALLVILLE, Noble Co., 2,800† p., on Air Line division of Lake Shore & Michigan Rd., at intersection of Grand Rapids & Indiana Rd., 26 m. from Fort Wayne and 91 from Toledo.
Standard.................W. **1,616**

KENTLAND, c. h., Newton Co., 802 p., on third division of Pittsburgh, Cincinnati & St. Louis Rd., 57 m. W. of Logansport, 4 E. of Illinois State line, 90 from Chicago and 80 from Indianapolis. Surrounded by a rich agricultural district and extensively engaged in manufactures of various kinds.

Gazette..................W. **1,617**
People's Press..............W. **1,618**

KNIGHTSTOWN, Henry Co., 1,528 p., on Blue r. and the Pittsburgh, Indianapolis & St. Louis Rd., 32 m. from Indianapolis. Engaged in agriculture and manufactures. Does a thriving trade.

Banner....................W. **1,619**
City Chronicle...............W. **1,620**

KNOX, Starke Co., 1,500† p., on Yellow r., about 10 m. from English Lake, about 10 E. of Kankakee r., at crossing of Pittsburgh, Chicago & St. Louis Rd. A new county and rich in mineral wealth, in the shape of iron ore. One of the finest districts for the cultivation of corn, tobacco and the raising of stock in the State.

Stark Co. Ledger........W. **1,621**

KOKOMO, c. h., Howard Co., 6,000† p., on Wildcat r., at the intersection of the Indianapolis, Penn. & Chicago with the Pittsburgh, Cincinnati & St. Louis Rd., 54 m. from Indianapolis. Engaged in agriculture and stock raising; lumbering and manufactures carried on.

Dispatch..................W. **1,622**
Saturday Evening Tribune...............W. **1,623**

LADOGA, Montgomery Co., 1,500 p., on Louisville, New Albany & Chicago Rd., 11 m. S. E. of Crawfordsville, 40 from Indianapolis and Lafayette. Mercantile and manufacturing interests well represented.

Journal..................W. **1,624**

LAFAYETTE, c. h., Tippecanoe Co., 21,000† p., on Wabash r., and Wabash & Erie Canal, and Toledo, Wabash & Western Rd., at intersection of Louisville, New Albany & Chicago Rd. The Cincinnati, Lafayette & Chicago, the Indianapolis, Cincinnati & Lafayette and Lafayette, Muncie & Bloomington Rds. terminate here. The railroad connections make it a centering point for the rich and populous agricultural districts surrounding it. Has fine steam and water power, which is extensively employed in manufactories.

Bee......................D. **1,625**
Bee and Tippecanoe Teacher..............W. **1,626**
Courier...................D. **1,627**
" ....W. **1,628**
Dispatch..................D. **1,629**
" ....W. **1,630**
Journal...................D. **1,631**
" ....W. **1,632**
Sunday Morning Leader.W. **1,633**
Western Granger and Home Journal.........W. **1,634**

LA GRANGE, c. h., La Grange Co., 1,500† p., on Grand Rapids & Indiana Rd., 46 m. N. of Fort Wayne and 100 W. of Toledo, 94 S. of Grand Rapids and 130 E. of Chicago. Engaged in agriculture and manufacturing.

Standard..................W. **1,635**

LA PORTE, c. h., La Porte Co., 9,015† p., on Lake Shore & Michigan Southern, at crossing of Cincinnati, Peru & Chicago Rd., 58 m. from Chicago. Extensively engaged in manufactures. Railroad repair shops located here.

Argus....................W. **1,636**
Chronicle.................W. **1,637**
Herald...................W. **1,638**

LAUREL, Franklin Co., 1,000† p., on the White Water Valley Rd., 10 m. from Connersville and 58 from Cincinnati. A limestone mart.

Times....................W. **1,639**

LAWRENCEBURGH, c. h., Dearborn Co., 3,159 p., on Ohio r., 22 m. from Cincinnati. The Ohio & Mississippi and the Indianapolis & Cincinnati Rds. pass through here. The terminus of the White Water Canal, which furnishes abundant water power, which is largely employed in manufacturing, particularly furniture.

Democratic Register......W. **1,640**
Press.....................W. **1,641**

LEAVENWORTH, c. h., Crawford Co., 1,000 p., on Ohio r., about 60 m. below Louisville, Ky. It is the shipping point for considerable country. Coal mines are under operation in the vicinity.

Crawford Co. Democrat..W. **1,642**

LEBANON, c. h., Boone Co., 3,100† p., on Indianapolis, Cincinnati & Lafayette Rd., 28 m. from Indianapolis.

Patriot...................W. **1,643**
Pioneer...................W. **1,644**

LIBERTY, c. h., Union Co., 1,095 p., on Cincinnati & Indianapolis Junction Rd., 50 m. from Cincinnati, 70 from Indianapolis and 15 from Richmond. Manufacturing, trading, agriculture and stock raising extensively carried on.

Herald...................W. **1,645**

LIGONIER, Noble Co., 2,160† p., on Elkhart r. and Air Line division of Lake Shore & Michigan Southern Rd., 25 m. from Elkhart and 108 from Toledo. Engaged in agriculture and various manufactures. An excellent shipping point for wheat and produce.

National Banner.........W. **1,646**

LOGANSPORT, c. h., Cass Co., 15,000† p., on Wabash r. and Wabash & Erie Canal, at the junction of the Middleport, Peoria & Burlington with the Toledo, Wabash & Western Rd. Cincinnati & Chicago Rd. intersects the Toledo, Wabash & Western at this place, making it an important railroad centre and a place of large and active trade.

Journal...................D. **1,647**
" ....W. **1,648**
Pharos...................D. **1,649**
" ....W. **1,650**
Star......................D. **1,651**
" ....W. **1,652**
" ....Sund. **1,653**
Post......................W. **1,654**
Sunday Chronicle........W. **1,655**
Harbinger..............S. M. **1,656**

LOOGOOTEE, Martin Co., 875 p., near E. fork of White r., and on Ohio & Mississippi Rd., 34 m. E. of Vincennes. Surrounded by a fine agricultural district, from which large quantities of wheat are exported.

Times....................W. **1,657**

LOWELL, Lake Co., 640 p., about 10 m. S. of Crown Point.

Star......................W. **1,658**

MADISON, c. h., Jefferson Co., 14,560† p., on Ohio r., at terminus of Jeffersonville, Madison & Indianapolis Rd., midway be-

INDIANA.

tween Cincinnati and Louisville. Steamboats make regular trips from here to Cincinnati, Louisville, and other ports on the Ohio and Mississippi rs. Engaged in manufacturing, and a shipping point for immense quantities of farm produce. Centre of a large and increasing trade.
Courier..................D. **1,659**
" ....W. **1,660**
Herald..................S. W. **1,661**
" ....W. **1,662**
City Commercial.
Spirit of the Age........W. **1,664**
Household Treasures.

MARION, c. h., Grant Co., 1,658 p., on Mississinewa r. and Pittsburgh, Cincinnati & St. Louis Rd., 41 m. from Logansport. A great agricultural and fruit-growing county.
Chronicle................W. **1,666**
Monitor..................W. **1,667**

MARTINSVILLE, c. h., Morgan Co., 2,500† p., on White r., and Indianapolis & Vincennes and Cincinnati Rds., 30 m. from Indianapolis. Surrounded by a fine agricultural country. Engaged in manufacturing.
Gazette..................W. **1,668**
Republican..............W. **1,669**

MARTZ, Clay Co.
Eaglet....................W. **1,670**

MICHIGAN CITY, La Porte Co., 6,000† p., on Lake Michigan and Michigan Central Rd., at northern terminus of Louisville, New Albany & Chicago Rd., 91 m. from Lafayette. Extensively engaged in lake commerce and the lumber trade.
Enterprise................W. **1,671**
News......................D. **1,672**

MILFORD, Kosciusko Co.
News......................W. **1,673**

MISHAWAKA, St. Joseph Co., 3,500† p., on St. Joseph r., and Lake Shore & Michigan Southern and Peninsula Rds., 4 m. from South Bend and 89 from Chicago. Engaged in manufacturing.
Enterprise..............W. **1,674**

MITCHELL, Lawrence Co., 1,500† p., at intersection of Ohio & Mississippi Rd. with Louisville, New Albany & Chicago Rd., 61 m. from New Albany, 127 W. of Cincinnati.
Commercial..............W. **1,675**
Enterprise.

MONROEVILLE, Allen Co., 1,050† p., on Pittsburgh, Fort Wayne & Chicago Rd., 14 m. S. E. of Fort Wayne.
Democrat..................W. **1,677**

MONTICELLO, c. h., White Co., 887 p., on Pittsburgh, Cincinnati & St. Louis Rd. and Tippecanoe r., 25 m. N. of Lafayette and 21 W. of Logansport. Has fine water power, which is extensively employed in manufactures.
Constitutionalist.........W. **1,678**
Herald....................W. **1,679**

MOORESVILLE, Morgan Co., 1,000 p., on Indianapolis & Vincennes Rd., 16 m. from Indianapolis. In a fertile agricultural section.
Herald....................W. **1,680**

MOUNT VERNON, c. h., Posey Co., 4,500 p., on Ohio r., 12 m. above the mouth of Wabash r. and about 23 below Evansville. A place of considerable trade and river commerce.
Democrat.................W. **1,681**
Republican...............W.
Wochenblatt.............W. **1,683**

MUNCIE, c. h., Delaware Co., 4,754† p., on White r., at the intersection of the Indianapolis division of the Cleveland, Columbus, Cincinnati & Indianapolis Rd. with the Fort Wayne, Muncie & Cincinnati Rd., 54 m. from Indianapolis, 100 from Cincinnati and 65 from Fort Wayne. Engaged in milling, pork packing and agricultural produce. An excellent point for all kinds of manufactures.
Courier-Democrat.......W. **1,684**
News......................W. **1,685**
Times.....................W. **1,686**

NASHVILLE, c. h., Brown Co., 500 p., about 35 m. S. of Indianapolis and 20 W. of Columbus.
Jacksonian..............W. **1,687**

NEW ALBANY, c. h., Floyd Co., 18,205 p., on Ohio r., 3 m. below Louisville, at the terminus of the Louisville, New Albany & Chicago Rd. One of the leading commercial towns in the State. Extensively engaged in manufactures. The largest plate glass factory in the U. S. located here.
Deutsche Zeitung.........D. **1,688**
Ledger-Standard.........D. **1,689**
" " ....W. **1,690**

NEW CASTLE, c. h., Henry Co., 2,000† p., on Pittsburgh, Cincinnati & St. Louis Rd., at the intersection of the Fort Wayne, Muncie & Cincinnati Rd., 83 m. from Fort Wayne and 26 from Connersville. Engaged in agriculture and manufacturing.
Courier....................W. **1,691**
Mercury...................W. **1,692**
Clipper....................S. M. **1,693**
Knights of Pythias Record....................M. **1,694**

NEW HARMONY, Posey Co., 1,000 p., on Wabash r., 15 m. from Mount Vernon.
Register...................W. **1,695**

NEW HAVEN, Allen Co.
Palladium.................W. **1,696**

NEWPORT, c. h., Vermillion Co., 600† p., 2 m. from the Wabash r. and on the Evansville, Terre Haute & Chicago Rd., 30 m. N. of Terre Haute, 75 W. of Indianapolis. Coal in abundance and of fine quality. Surrounded by a well-timbered district.
Hoosier State............W. **1,697**

NOBLESVILLE, c. h., Hamilton Co., 1,435 p., on White r. and the Indianapolis, Peru & Chicago Rd., 22 m. from Indianapolis. Surrounded by an agricultural district and the centre of considerable trade.
Independent.............W. **1,698**
Ledger....................W. **1,699**

NORTH JUDSON, Starke Co.
Courier....................W. **1,700**

NORTH MANCHESTER, Wabash Co., 1,869† p., on Eel r. and Detroit, Eel r. & Illinois Rd., at the intersection of the Cincinnati, Wabash & Michigan Rd., 15 m. from Wabash and 19 from Columbia City. Engaged in manufacturing and farming.
Journal....................W. **1,701**
Manchester Republican...W. **1,702**

NORTH VERNON, Jennings Co., 2,441† p., on Ohio & Mississippi Rd., at junction of Louisville branch; also at intersection of Madison division of Jeffersonville, Madison & Indianapolis Rd., 73 m. from Cin-

INDIANA.

cinnati, 53 N. of Louisville, 61 S. of Indianapolis. Stone quarries of dolomite and limestone are located here.
Plain Dealer............W. **1,703**
Sun....................W. **1,704**

NOTRE DAME, St. Joseph Co.
Ave Maria..............W. **1,705**
Scholastic..............W. **1,706**

OSGOOD, Ripley Co,
Item....................W. **1,707**
Ripley Co. Journal......W. **1,708**

OWENSBURG, Greene Co.
Register................W. **1,709**

OXFORD, c. h., Benton Co., 1,300† p., 70 m. N. W. of Indianapolis, on the Lafayette & Bloomington branch of the Toledo, Wabash & Western Rd. Centre of a fine agricultural and stock-raising region. Rapidly filling up with settlers. The great centre of trade for a radius of 80 m.
Tribune.................W. **1,710**

PAOLI, c. h., Orange Co., 2,207 p., 40 m. N. W. of New Albany and 8 from Louisville, New Albany & Chicago Rd.
News....................W. **1,711**
Republican..............W. **1,712**

PENDLETON, Madison Co., 900† p., on C., C., C. & I. Rd., 28 m. from Indian Rapids and 7 from Anderson.
Dollar Register..........W. **1,713**

PERU, c. h., Miami Co., 3,617 p., on Wabash r., Wabash & Erie Canal, and Toledo, Wabash & Western Rd., at intersection of Indianapolis, Peru & Chicago Rd., 75 m. from Indianapolis and 56 from Fort Wayne. Surrounded by an agricultural district, and a trade centre. Engaged extensively in manufacturing.
Miami Co. Sentinel......W. **1,714**
Republican..............W. **1,715**
Times...................W. **1,716**

PETERSBURGH, c. h., Pike Co., 1,200† p., near White r., and on Wabash and Erie Canal, 35 m. from Evansville. Flour, pork, stock raising, tobacco, coal mining, and the manufacture of woolen goods are the principal branches of industry.
Pike Co. Democrat.......W. **1,717**
Press...................W. **1,718**

PLAINFIELD, Hendricks Co.
Citizen.................W. **1,719**
Reform School Record....M. **1,720**

PORTLAND, c. h., Jay Co., 1,700† p., on Sallamonie r. and Cincinnati, Richmond & Fort Wayne Rd., 49 m. from Fort Wayne. Engaged in manufacturing. Does a large lumber trade.
Democrat................W. **1,721**
Marshall Co. Republican.W. **1,722**
Restitution..............W. **1,723**
Commercial..............W. **1,724**
Jay Co. Granger.........W. **1,725**

PRINCETON, c. h., Gibson Co., 2,700 p., on the Evansville & Crawfordsville Rd., 27 m. from Evansville and 24 from Vincennes. In a rich and populous agricultural district.
Clarion.................W. **1,726**
Democrat................W. **1,727**

REMINGTON, Jasper Co., 1,200† p., on Indianapolis and Chicago division of Pittsburgh, Cincinnati & St. Louis Rd., 40 m. from Logansport. In an agricultural section.
Record..................W. **1,728**

INDIANA.

RENSSELAER, c. h., Jasper Co., 650 p., on Iroquois r., 100 m. from Indianapolis and 40 N. by W. of Lafayette.
Union and Jasper Republican....................W. **1,729**

REYNOLDS, White Co., 580 p., on Louisville, New Albany & Chicago Rd., at the intersection of Pittsburgh, Cincinnati & St. Louis Rd., 27 m. from Logansport and 23 from Lafayette.
White Co. Register.......W. **1,730**

RICHMOND, Wayne Co., 15,000† p., on Pittsburgh, Cincinnati & St. Louis Rd., at the junction of several other railroads, 69 m. from Indianapolis and 15 from Cambridge City. Extensively engaged in various kinds of manufactures and a place of active trade.
Free Press...............D. **1,731**
" " ....W. **1,732**
Independent..............D. **1,733**
" ....W. **1,734**
Palladium...............D. **1,735**
" ....W. **1,736**
Volkszeitung..........S. W. **1,737**
Telegram................W. **1,738**
Earlhamite...............M. **1,739**
Mill Stone...............M. **1,740**

RISING SUN, c. h., Ohio Co., 1,760 p., on Ohio r., 36 m. below Cincinnati, 65 above Louisville, Ky. Engaged in various manufactures and a place of active trade. Surrounded by an agricultural country.
Recorder................W. **1,741**
Saturday News..........W. **1,742**

ROANOKE, Huntington Co.
Register................W. **1,743**

ROCHESTER, c. h., Fulton Co., 2,500† p., on the Indianapolis, Peru & Chicago Rd., 98 m. from Indianapolis and 20 from Plymouth.
Sentinel.................W. **1,744**
Union Spy...............W. **1,745**

ROCKPORT, c. h., Spencer Co., 2,900† p., on Ohio r., 50 m. above Evansville and 150 below Louisville. A market for the tobacco, pork and produce of the surrounding district.
Democrat................W. **1,746**
Republican Journal......W. **1,747**

ROCKVILLE, c. h., Parke Co., 1,187 p., on Logansport, Crawfordsville & Southwestern Rd., 23 m. from Terre Haute and 30 from Crawfordsville. A rich farming district.
Indiana Patriot.........W. **1,748**
Republican..............W. **1,749**

RUSHVILLE, c. h., Rush Co., 1,800 p., on Cincinnati & Indianapolis Junction Rd., at intersection of Cambridge City branch of Jeffersonville, Madison & Indianapolis Rd., 39 m. from Indianapolis. A fertile district and has considerable trade.
Jacksonian..............W. **1,750**
Republican..............W. **1,751**

SALEM, c. h., Washington Co., 2,000 p., on Great Blue r., Louisville, New Albany and Chicago Rd., 35 m. from New Albany, in an agricultural district. One of the most important manufacturing points in Southern Indiana. Has a large and thrifty trade.
Democrat................W. **1,752**
Independent.............W. **1,753**

INDIANA.

SCOTTSBURG, c. h., Scott Co.
Scott Co. Democrat.......W. 1,754

SEYMOUR, Jackson Co., 4,000† p., at intersection of Ohio & Mississippi with Jeffersonville & Indianapolis Rd., 50 m. from Louisville.
Democrat...............W. 1,755
Times...................W. 1,756

SHELBYVILLE, c. h., Shelby Co., 3,500 p., on Blue r., and Indianapolis, Cincinnati & Lafayette Rd., at intersection of Cambridge City branch of Jeffersonville, Madison & Indianapolis Rd., 26 m. from Indianapolis.
Shelby Republican.......W. 1,757
Volunteer...............W. 1,758

SHOALS, Martin Co.
Martin Co. Herald.......W. 1,759

SOUTH BEND, c. h., St. Joseph Co., 10,706† p., on St. Joseph r., and Lake Shore & Michigan Southern Rd., 85 m. from Chicago. The river furnishes water power, which is employed in various manufactures. Agricultural implements and wagons are manufactured on a large scale.
Morning Herald.........D. 1,760
Herald.................W. 1,761
Register................D. 1,762
St. Joseph Valley Register.W. 1,763
Tribune..................D. 1,764
" ....W. 1,765
Indiana Courier..........W. 1,766
Northern Indiana Teacher......................M. 1,767

SPENCER, c. h., Owen Co., 1,517 p., on west branch of White r. and Indianapolis & Vincennes Rd., 53 m. S. E. of Indianapolis. It is surrounded by a fine agricultural district. Stock-raising and lumber trade the principal branches of industry.
Owen Co. Journal........W. 1,768
Republican..............W. 1,769

SPICELAND, Henry Co.
Reporter.................W. 1,770

SULLIVAN, c. h., Sullivan Co., 2,700† p., on Evansville & Crawfordsville Rd., 26 m. from Terre Haute. County seat of a comparatively new and growing county, in which are newly discovered coal mines of considerable extent.
Democrat................W. 1,771
Sullivan Co. Union......W. 1,772

TELL CITY, Perry Co., 3,000† p., on Ohio r., about 3 m. below Cannelton, 125 from Louisville and 75 from Evansville. Extensively engaged in various manufactures.
Anzeiger................W. 1,773
Commercial.............W. 1,774

TERRE HAUTE, c. h., Vigo Co., 25,000† p., on Wabash r., 73 m. W. of Indianapolis. One of the most important shipping points on the Wabash & Erie Canal. A rich and highly cultivated agricultural district. Immense coal mines are worked in this vicinity. Engaged in manufactures of various kinds.
Evening Gazette..........D. 1,775
Gazette..................W. 1,776
Express..................D. 1,777
Dollar Express..........W. 1,778
Journal..................D. 1,779
" ....W. 1,780
Republican...............D. 1,781
Banner..............T. W. 1,782
Indiana Post............W. 1,783
Saturday Evening Mail..W. 1,784

INDIANA.

THORNTOWN, Boone Co., 2,000† p., on the Indianapolis, Cincinnati & Lafayette Rd., 38 m. from Indianapolis.
Messenger................W. 1,785

TIPTON, c. h., Tipton Co., 2,000† p., on Indianapolis, Peru & Chicago Rd., 38 m. from Indianapolis. Surrounded by a fine agricultural district. Extensively engaged in shipping timber and staves.
Advance..................W. 1,786
Times.....................W. 1,787

UNION CITY, Randolph Co., 4,000† p., at the northern terminus of Dayton & Union Rd., 45 m. from Dayton. The Cleveland, Columbus, Cincinnati & Indianapolis intersects the Pittsburgh, Cincinnati & St. Louis Rd. at this point, 84 m. from Indianapolis. Engaged in manufacturing and centre of trade.
Eagle.....................W. 1,788
Times.....................W. 1,789

VALPARAISO, c. h., Porter Co., 3,500† p., on Pittsburgh, Fort Wayne & Chicago Rd., 42 m. from Chicago, in an agricultural district. Paper and wool are manufactured here to some extent.
Messenger................W. 1,790
Porter Co. Vidette.......W. 1,791

VEEDERSBURG, Fountain Co.
Review....................W. 1,792

VERNON, c. h., Jennings Co., 1,000† p., on Jefferson, Madison & Indianapolis Rd., 71 m. from Indianapolis and 72 from Cincinnati. Extensively engaged in various manufactures. Quarries of lime and magnesia stone of fine quality, which is shipped from here in large quantities.
Banner....................W. 1,793

VERSAILLES, c. h., Ripley Co., 600 p., on Laughrey Creek, 5 m. from Ohio & Mississippi Rd., 70 m. S. E. of Indianapolis and 56 from Cincinnati. It is situated in a rich farming region and has considerable trade.
Ripley Index............W. 1,794

VEVAY, c. h., Switzerland Co., 2,000† p., on Ohio r., 75 m. below Cincinnati. A place of active trade and a large hay market.
Democrat................W. 1,795
Reveille..................W. 1,796

VINCENNES, c. h., Knox Co., 5,440 p., on Wabash r., at intersection of Ohio & Mississippi with Evansville & Crawfordsville Rd., and at terminus of Indianapolis & Vincennes Rd., 116 m. from Indianapolis, 58 from Terre Haute and 51 from Evansville. Engaged in manufacturing, and a shipping point for large quantities of grain. Located within 20 m. of Daviess county coal mines.
Western Sun..........S. W. 1,797
" " ....W. 1,798
Reporter.................W. 1,799
Times.....................W. 1,800
Wochenblatt.............W. 1,801

WABASH, c. h., Wabash Co., 4,923† p., on Wabash r. and Toledo, Wabash & Western Rd., at the southern terminus of Cincinnati, Wabash & Michigan Rd., 42 m. from Fort Wayne. Place of active trade, surrounded by a fertile agricultural district. Extensively engaged in various manufactures. Seat of Wabash Female Seminary.

INDIANA.

Free Trader..............W. **1,802**
Plain Dealer..............W. **1,803**

WAKARUSA, Elkhart Co.
Sun..........................W. **1,804**

WALKERTON, St. Joseph Co.
Visitor......................W. **1,805**

WARSAW, c. h., Kosciusko Co., 3,500† p., on Tippecanoe r. and Pittsburgh, Fort Wayne & Chicago Rd., at intersection of Cincinnati, Wabash & Michigan Rd., 40 m. from Fort Wayne. Engaged in agriculture and lumber trade. Several manufactures are located here.
National Union............W. **1,806**
Northern Indianian......W. **1,807**
Saturday Northern Indianian..................W. **1,808**

WASHINGTON, c. h., Daviess Co., 2,900 p., on the Ohio & Mississippi Rd., 20 m. E. of Vincennes and 173 from St. Louis and Cincinnati. Engaged in mining and manufacturing. A large number of coal mines in the vicinity.
Cook's Real Estate Gazette W.
Daviess Co. Democrat....W. **1,810**
Gazette......................W. **1,811**

WATERLOO, De Kalb Co., 2,000† p., on Cedar Creek, at the intersection of the Lake Shore & Michigan Southern with the Fort Wayne, Jackson & Saginaw Rd., 78 m. from Toledo. A trade centre for a large agricultural district. Largest town in and principal shipping point for the counties of De Kalb and Steuben.
Press........................W. **1,812**

WEST LEBANON, Warren Co., 700 p., on Toledo, Wabash & Western Rd., 30 m. from Lafayette. A large market for the shipment of grain and stock. Engaged in manufactures.
Enterprise..................W. **1,813**

WILLIAMSPORT, c. h., Warren Co., 1,200† p., on Wabash r. and Toledo, Wabash & Western Rd., 24 m. below Lafayette, 64 from Indianapolis and 120 from Chicago. Engaged in agriculture and stock raising.
Warren Republican......W. **1,814**

WINAMAC, c. h., Pulaski Co., 906 p., on Tippecanoe r. and Pittsburgh, Cincinnati & St. Louis Rd., 92 m. from Chicago and 25 from Logansport.
Democrat....................W. **1,815**
Republican..................W. **1,816**

WINCHESTER, c. h., Randolph Co., 2,000† p., on White r., at intersection of Cleveland, Columbus, Cincinnati & Indianapolis by the Cincinnati, Richmond & Fort Wayne Rd., 75 m. from Indianapolis and 68 from Fort Wayne. A rich farming district and place of active trade, principally in the raising and shipment of grain.
Herald........................W. **1,817**
Journal......................W. **1,818**

WOLCOTTVILLE, La Grange Co.
Register......................W. **1,819**

WORTHINGTON, Greene Co., 1,600† p., on the Indianapolis & Vincennes Rd., near the confluence of Eel r. with the W. fork of the White r. An important business point, engaged in manufacturing.
Journal......................W. **1,820**
Times........................W. **1,821**
Our Little Folks..........M. **1,822**

INDIANA.

XENIA, Miami Co., 1,000† p., near line of Pittsburgh, Cincinnati & St. Louis Rd., about 30 m. from Logansport.
Gazette......................W. **1,823**

ZIONSVILLE, Boone Co.
Times........................W. **1,824**

IOWA.

ACKLEY, Hardin Co., 2,000† p., on Iowa division of Illinois Central Rd., at intersection of Central Rd. of Iowa, 43 m. from Marshalltown. Centre of a thriving trade, and extensively engaged in shipping grain and live stock.
Der Deutscher Fortscritt..W. **1,825**
Enterprise..................W. **1,826**

ADEL, c. h., Dallas Co., 1,000† p., on Coon r., 25 m. W. of Des Moines. Surrounded by a wealthy farming district and centre of a large trade.
Dallas Co. Gazette.......W. **1,827**
Dallas Co. News.........W. **1,828**

AFTON, c. h., Union Co., 1,500 p., on Burlington & Missouri River Rd., 50 m. S. W. of Des Moines and 180 W. of Burlington. Manufactures of various kinds are successfully carried on. The centre of a good trade and the principal shipping point for two counties.
News..........................W. **1,829**
Tribune......................W. **1,830**

AGENCY CITY, Wapello Co., 630 p., on Burlington & Missouri River Rd., 6 m. from Ottumwa and 70 from Burlington. Centre of a large trade.
Agency Independent.....W. **1,831**

ALBIA, c. h., Monroe Co., 2,000† p., at intersection of Burlington & Missouri River Rd. with Central Rd. of Iowa, 100 m. from Burlington. Surrounded by immense coal mines.
Industrial Era............W. **1,832**
Union.........................W. **1,833**

ALDEN, Hardin Co.
News..........................W. **1,834**

ALGONA, c. h., Kossuth Co., 860 p., on Des Moines r., and Iowa and Dakota division of Milwaukee & St. Paul Rd., 126 m. from McGregor, 120 N. by W. of Des Moines. Engaged in milling, the river furnishing abundant power. Surrounded by an agricultural and stock-raising district.
Republican..................W. **1,835**
Upper Des Moines.......W. **1,836**

ALLERTON, Wayne Co.
Wayne Co. News..........W. **1,837**
Wayne Co. Republican..W. **1,838**

AMES, Story Co., 900† p., on Iowa division of Chicago & Northwestern Rd., about 5 m. W. of Nevada.
Intelligencer...............W. **1,839**

ANAMOSA, c. h., Jones Co., 2,083 p., on Wapsipinicon r., and on Dubuque & Southwestern Rd., at junction and western terminus of Iowa Midland Rd., 54 m. from Dubuque and 71 from Clinton. Centre of a large farming region, having an active trade.
Eureka.......................W. **1,840**
Journal......................W. **1,841**

ATLANTIC, Cass Co., 3,000† p., on Chicago, Rock Island & Pacific Rd., 52 m. E.

of Council Bluffs and 82 W. of Des Moines. Engaged in manufacturing.

Cass Co. Messenger......W. **1,842**
North Western Journal..W. **1,843**
Telegraph................W. **1,844**

AVOCA, Pottawattamie Co., 1,500† p., situated on Chicago, Rock Island & Pacific Rd., 40 m. from Council Bluffs. Surrounded by an agricultural country. Centre of a good trade.

Delta....................W.

BEDFORD, c. h., Taylor Co., 1,000 p., on Creston and Bedford branch of Burlington & Missouri River Rd., 65 m. from St. Joseph and about 100 from Des Moines. It is situated in a fine agricultural district.

Argus...................W. **1,846**
Iowa South West........W. **1,847**

BELLE PLAINE, Benton Co., 1,488 p., on Iowa division of Chicago & Northwestern Rd., 34 m. W. of Cedar Rapids and 25 S. W. of Vinton.

Review...................W. **1,848**
Union....................W. **1,849**

BELLEVUE, Jackson Co., 1,800† p., on Mississippi r., 25 m. below Dubuque, 12 S. E. of Galena, Ill. It has a fine steamer landing, and large amounts of produce are shipped from the surrounding agricultural districts.

Leader...................W. **1,850**

BELMOND, Wright Co.

Herald...................W. **1,851**

BELOIT, Lyon Co.

*Times and Canton Eclipse*W. **1,852**

BIRMINGHAM, Van Buren Co., 800† p., about 12 m. N. of Keosauqua, 9 from Fairfield Station, on Burlington & Missouri River, at intersection of Chicago & Northwestern Rds. The Des Moines r. runs through the county. Considerable manufactures carried on.

Enterprise...............W. **1,853**

BLAIRSTOWN, Benton Co.

Advocate.................W. **1,854**

BLOOMFIELD, c. h., Davis Co., 1,553 p., near Fox r., at the junction of the North Missouri and Burlington & Southwestern Rds., 70 m. W. N. W. of Keokuk and 85 from Burlington. The centre of a fertile and thriving agricultural region, and the trade centre for a large section.

Commonwealth..........W. **1,855**
Davis Co. Republican....W. **1,856**
Democrat.................W. **1,857**
Odd Fellow's Banner....W. **1,858**

BONAPARTE, Van Buren Co., 1,000† p., on Des Moines River and Des Moines Valley Rd., 35 m. N. W. of Keokuk. An extensive grain and stock market, and engaged in manufacturing.

Van Buren Democrat....W. **1,859**

BOONE, Boone Co., 3,500† p., on Iowa division of Chicago & Northwestern Rd., 340 m. from Chicago and 121 W. of Cedar Rapids. There are various kinds of mills here, and coal mining is extensively carried on, the beds being about 90 feet below the surface. It is surrounded by a fine farming country.

Boone Co. Democrat.....W. **1,860**
Boone Co. Republican....W. **1,861**
Standard.................W. **1,862**

BRIGHTON, Washington Co., 1,200† p., on southwestern division of Chicago, Rock Island & Pacific Rd., 13 m. S. W. of Washington.

Star......................W. **1,863**

BROOKLYN, Poweshiek Co., 1,300 p., on Chicago, Rock Island & Pacific Rd., 105 m. from Davenport and 75 E. of Des Moines. Situated in a rich prairie. Is the centre of a large grain trade.

Chronicle.................W. **1,864**

BRUSH CREEK, Fayette Co.

News.....................W. **1,865**

BURLINGTON, c. h., Des Moines Co., 26,000† p., on Mississippi r., and Chicago, Burlington & Quincy Rd., at junction of several important railroads, 180 m. from Chicago. Considerable manufacturing done here. The centre of a large and flourishing trade, and has considerable river commerce.

Evening Gazette..........D. **1,866**
Gazette...................W. **1,867**
Hawk Eye.................D. **1,868**
" " ....S. W. **1,869**
" " ....W. **1,870**
Freie Presse...........T. W. **1,871**
" " ....W. **1,872**
Iowa Tribune...........T. W. **1,873**
" " ....W. **1,874**

CARROLL CITY, Carroll Co., 1,000† p., on Iowa division of Chicago & Northwestern Rd., 92 m. from Council Bluffs.

Carroll Herald..........W. **1,875**
Democrat.................W. **1,876**
Der Carroll Democrat...W. **1,877**

CASEY, Guthrie Co., 800† p., a station on Chicago, Rock Island & Pacific Rd., 51 m. from Des Moines.

Clarion...................W. **1,878**

CEDAR FALLS, Black Hawk Co., 3,450† p., on Cedar r., and on Iowa division of the Illinois Central, at the intersection of the Burlington, Cedar Rapids & Minnesota Rds., 162 m. from Burlington and 99 from Dubuque. A first-class manufacturing town, possessing excellent water power

Gazette ....W. **1,879**
Iowa Advocate............W. **1,880**
Recorder..................W. **1,881**

CEDAR RAPIDS, Linn Co., 10,000† p., on Red Cedar r., and Burlington, Cedar Rapids & Minnesota Rd., at intersection of Iowa divison of Chicago & Northwestern Rd., and junction of Dubuque & Southwestern Rd., 79 m. from Dubuque and 100 from Burlington. It has good water power, which is employed in a number of mills.

Republican...............D. **1,882**
" ....W. **1,883**
Standard.................W. **1,884**
Times.....................W. **1,885**
Farmer's Stock Journal..M. **1,886**
Progressive Farmer......M. **1,887**

CENTERVILLE, c. h., Appanoose Co., 2,500† p., about 80 m. S. S. E. of Des Moines, on the southwestern division of the Chicago, Rock Island & Pacific Rd., 137 m. from Davenport. Engaged in manufacturing and milling. The country is well timbered and rich in mineral resources.

Appanoose Times........W. **1,888**
Citizen...................W. **1,889**
Journal...................W. **1,890**

CENTRE POINT, Linn Co.

Lotus......................W. **1,891**

CHARITON, c. h., Lucas Co., 2,500 p., on Chariton r. and Burlington & Missouri River Rd., 55 m. from Ottumwa, at junction of Chariton branch. It is the central trading point between the Mississippi and Missouri rs.

Leader..................W. **1,892**
Lucas Co. Republican....W. **1,893**
Patriot.................W. **1,894**

CHARLES CITY, c. h., Floyd Co., 2,270† p., on Cedar r., and Iowa division of Illinois Central Rd., at intersection of Iowa & Dakota division of Milwaukee & St. Paul Rd., 139 m. from Dubuque and 90 from McGregor. It possesses good water power.

Floyd Co. Advocate......W. **1,895**
Intelligencer.............W. **1,896**
Western Patriarch.......W. **1,897**

CHELSEA, Tama Co.

Bugle.....................W. **1,898**

CHEROKEE, c. h., Cherokee Co., 790 p., on Little Sioux r., and on the division of the Illinois Central Rd., 59 m. from Sioux City. Surrounded by fine farming lands.

Leader..................W. **1,899**
Times....................

CLARINDA, c. h., Page Co., 1,022 p., on Nodaway r., 75 m. S. E. of Council Bluffs. Engaged in agriculture, stock raising and manufacturing.

Herald..................W. **1,901**
Page Co. Democrat......W. **1,902**

CLARION, c. h., Wright Co., 200 p., in central part of State, and about 25 m. N. E. of Fort Dodge. In a fine farming district.

Wright Co. Monitor......W. **1,903**

CLARKSVILLE, Butler Co., 1,500 p., on Shell Rock r. and Burlington, Cedar Rapids & Minnesota Rd., 186 m. from Burlington. Engaged in manufacturing and a trade centre.

Star......................W. **1,904**

CLEAR LAKE, Cerro Gordo Co., 945 p., on lake of same name, and on the Iowa & Dakota division of the Milwaukee & St. Paul Rd., 10 m. from Mason City.

Observer.................W. **1,905**

CLERMONT, Fayette Co., 650† p., on Turkey r., 36 m. from Lansing, 80 N. W. of Dubuque and 30 W. of McGregor. It has water power, which is employed in manufacturing.

People's Paper...........W. **1,906**

CLINTON, Clinton Co., 9,026† p., on Mississippi r., 42 m. above Davenport, on the Chicago & Northwestern Rd., at the junction of several other railroads. Extensively engaged in lumber and various other manufactures. The railroad repair shops are located here. It has a large and rapidly growing trade.

Herald...................D. **1,907**
" ....W. **1,908**
Age......................W. **1,909**
Iowa Volks Zeitung......W. **1,910**

COLUMBUS CITY, Louisa Co., 900† p., on Iowa r., 20 m. from Muscatine. In the centre of a fine agricultural region.

Columbus Nonpareil.....W. **1,911**

COLUMBUS JUNCTION, Louisa Co.

Columbus Safeguard.....W. **1,912**
Herald...................W. **1,913**

CORNING, Adams Co., 1,000 p., on Burlington & Missouri R Rd., 90 m. from Council Bluffs. A place of active trade; rapidly increasing in wealth and population.

Adams Co. Gazette......W. **1,914**
Adams Co. Union........W. **1915**

CORYDON, c. h., Wayne Co., 750† p., 65 m. S. by E. of Des Moines and about 4 N. of southwestern division of Chicago, Rock Island & Pacific Rd. Engaged in agriculture and stock raising.

Times....................W. **1,916**

COUNCIL BLUFFS, c. h., Pottawattamie Co., 11,000† p., on Missouri r., opposite Omaha, Neb., at terminus of Chicago, Rock Island & Pacific, Chicago & Northwestern, and Kansas City, St. Joseph & Council Bluffs Rds., 120 m. W. of Des Moines. A place of great business activity.

Globe....................D. **1,917**
" ....W. **1,918**
Nonpareil................D. **1,919**
" ....W. **1,920**
Bugle....................W. **1,921**
Christian Expositor...S. M. **1,922**

CRESCO, Howard Co., 1,500† p., on Milwaukee & St. Paul Rd., 260 m. from Milwaukee and 62 from McGregor. Engaged in manufactures of various kinds. Has a large grain trade.

Howard Co. Times......W. **1,923**
Iowa Plain Dealer.......W. **1,924**

CRESTON, Union Co., 2,800† p., on Burlington & Missouri R. Rd., and junction of Creston branch. The largest stock yards on the road are located here. The railroad round house, machine shop and coal shoots are also located here.

Democrat................W. **1,925**
Gazette...................W. **1,926**
Union Co. Independent.

DAKOTA, City, Humboldt Co., 600 p., on Des Moines r., about 80 m. from Des Moines and 18 N. of Fort Dodge, in an agricultural district. The river furnishes excellent water power.

Humboldt Co. Independent....................W. **1,928**

DALLAS CENTER, Dallas Co.

Globe....................W. **1,929**

DAVENPORT, c. h., Scott Co., 25,612† p., on Mississippi r., at the foot of the Upper Rapids, 183 m. from Chicago and 220 from St. Louis; at the junction of six important railroads. It is engaged in various kinds of manufactures, principally agricultural implements, and has a large and increasing grain and lumber business. Opposite the island of Rock Island, the location of the central armory of the United States, and connected therewith by a vast iron railway and carriage bridge.

Democrat................D. **1,930**
" ....W. **1,931**
Der Demokrat............D. **1,932**
" " ....W. **1,933**
Gazette...................D. **1,934**
" ....W. **1,935**
Iowa Commercial........W. **1,936**
Times....................W. **1,937**
Church Missionary.
Common School..........M. **1,939**

DECORAH, c. h., Winneshiek Co., 3,000 p., on branch of Milwaukee & St. Paul

IOWA.

Rd., 56 m. W. of McGregor. The county seat and centre of a large trade. Considerable manufacturing and milling done here.

Bee..................D. **1,940**
Saturday Bee............W. **1,941**
Independent Register....W. **1,942**
Posten..................W. **1,943**
Republican..............W. **1,944**

DELHI, c. h., Delaware Co., 800† p., on Davenport & St. Paul Rd., 85 m. from Davenport and near Maquoketa r.

Monitor.................W. **1,945**

DELMAR, Clinton Co.

Journal.................W. **1,946**

DENISON, c. h., Crawford Co., 749 p., on Boyer r. and Chicago & Northwestern Rd., 64 m. from Council Bluffs. Agriculture is the principal branch of industry.

Crawford Co. Bulletin...W. **1,947**
Review..................W. **1,948**

DES MOINES, c. h., State capital, Polk Co., 17,600† p., on Des Moines r., at mouth of Raccoon r., and on Chicago, Rock Island & Pacific Rd., at intersection of Des Moines Valley Rd., 176 m. from Davenport and 161 from Keokuk. A place of active trade. Engaged in agriculture and manufacturing. Coal mining and shipping.

Iowa State Leader........D. **1,949**
" " " ....W. **1,950**
Iowa State Register.......D. **1,951**
" " " ......W. **1,952**
Herald of Liberty....... W. **1,953**
Homestead and Western Farm Journal..........W. **1,954**
Iowa Staats Anzeiger....W. **1,955**
Plain Talk...............W. **1,956**
State Journal............W. **1,957**
Western Farmer and Patron's Helper.....W. **1,958**
Industrial Motor.........M. **1,959**
Iowa Gazette.............M. **1,960**
Western Jurist...........M. **1,961**

DE WITT, Clinton Co., 2,000 p., on the Chicago & Northwestern Rd., at the intersection of the Maquoketa branch of the Davenport & St. Paul Rd., 19 m. from Clinton and 25 from Davenport.

Observer.................W. **1,962**

DEXTER, Dallas Co., 800† p., an Chicago, Rock Island & Pacific Rd., 35 m. from Des Moines. Rapidly growing in population and wealth.

Herald...................W. **1,963**

DUBUQUE, c. h., Dubuque Co., 24,000† p., on Mississippi r. and Illinois Central Rd., at junction of several important Rds. Immense quantities of lead are mined in this vicinity. Extensively engaged in river commerce, and surrounded by a rich and highly cultivated agricultural district.

Herald...................D. **1,964**
" ....W. **1,965**
News.....................D. **1,966**
Telegraph................D. **1,967**
" ....W. **1,968**
Times....................D. **1,969**
" ....W. **1,970**
Der Presbyterianer.......W. **1,971**
Iowa.....................W. **1,972**
Luxemburger Gazette.....W. **1,973**
National Demokrat.......W. **1,974**

DUNLAP, Harrison Co., 1,000 p., on Iowa division of Chicago & Northwestern Rd., 47 m. E. of Council Bluffs. Engaged in agricultural pursuits.

Reporter.................W. **1,975**

DYERSVILLE, Dubuque Co.

Commercial...............W. **1,976**

EARLVILLE, Delaware Co.

Gazette..................W. **1,977**

EDDYVILLE, Wapello Co., 1,550† p., on Des Moines r. and Des Moines Valley Rd., at crossing of Central Rd. of Iowa, 89 m. from Keokuk and 75 from Des Moines. Excellent manufacturing advantages. Fine water power. Located in the midst of a fine coal field.

Advance..................W. **1,978**
Advertiser...............W. **1,979**

ELDON, Wapello Co.

Times....................W. **1,980**

ELDORA, c. h., Hardin Co., 2,100† p., on Iowa r., and Iowa Central Rd., 27 m. from Marshalltown and 70 N. N. E. of Des Moines. Surrounded by a fine agricultural region. Coal found here in abundance. An excellent shipping point for coal, live stock and grain.

Herald...................W. **1,981**
Ledger...................W. **1,982**

ELGIN, Fayette Co.

Times....................W. **1,983**

ELKADER, c. h., Clayton Co., 1,150† p., on Turkey r., 60 m. N. W. of Dubuque. Centre of a large grain and pork-raising district. Terminus of the Iowa Eastern Rd.

Clayton Co. Journal......W. **1,984**
Nord Iowa Herold.........W. **1,985**

EMMETSBURG, c. h., Palo Alto Co., 400 p., about 140 m. N. W. of Des Moines. The centre of an excellent trade; also a fine stock-raising country.

Palo Alto Pilot......... W. **1,986**
Palo Alto Reporter......W. **1,987**

ESTHERVILLE, c. h., Emmett Co., 600 p., 175 m. from Sioux City, on W. fork of Des Moines r., 166 m. (mail route) N. W. of Des Moines. Engaged in agriculture and manufactures.

Northern Vindicator.....W. **1,988**

EXIRA, c. h., Audubon Co., 540 p., on Nishnabatona r., 70 m. W. of Des Moines. The centre of a fine agricultural region.

Audubon Co. Defender...W. **1,989**

FAIRFIELD, c. h., Jefferson Co., 3,000† p., at intersection of Burlington & Missouri River Rd. with S. W. division Chicago, Rock Island & Pacific Rd., 50 m. from Burlington. An important trade centre.

Iowa Democrat...........W. **1,990**
Ledger...................W. **1,991**

FARMINGTON, Van Buren Co.

Gazette..................W. **1,992**

FAYETTE, Fayette Co.

News.....................W. **1,993**

FONDA, Pocahontas Co.

North Western Hawk Eye.W. **1,994**

FOREST CITY, c. h., Winnebago Co., 800 p., in the northern part of the State, 130 m. W. of Mississippi r. at Lansing, and about 30 m. W. by N. of Mason City. Located on Lime r. Centre of a thriving trade.

Winnebago Summit......W. **1,995**

FORT DODGE, c. h., Webster Co., 3,700†

p., on Des Moines r., 90 m. N. from Des Moines, at junction of Des Moines Valley Rd. with Iowa division of Illinois Central Rd., 192 m. W. of Dubuque. The country abounds in coal, gypsum, sandstone, limestone and cement.

Times....................W. **1,996**
Messenger................W. **1,997**

FORT MADISON, c. h., Lee Co., 5,000† p., on Mississippi r., and Burlington & Keokuk branch of Chicago, Burlington & Quincy Rd., 24 m. above Keokuk and 19 below Burlington. Considerable manufacturing done here, and large quantities of produce shipped from the surrounding farming district.

Democrat................W. **1,998**
Plain Dealer.............W. **1,999**

GARDEN GROVE, Decatur Co., 1,200† p., on Chariton branch of Burlington & Missouri R. Rd., 24 m. from Chariton.

Iowa Express.............W. **2,000**

GARNER, Hancock Co., on Iowa & Dakota division of Milwaukee & St. Paul Rd., 31 m. from Algona and 138 from McGregor. Principal town in the county. In the centre of a good farming country and growing rapidly.

Hancock Signal..........W. **2,001**

GLENWOOD, c. h., Mills Co., 1,500 p., on Keg Creek, and the Burlington Missouri R. Rd., 20 m. S. by E. of Council Bluffs and 271 W. of Burlington.

Mills Co. Journal.......W. **2,002**
Opinion..................W. **2,003**

GRAND JUNCTION, Greene Co., 779 p., on Chicago & Northwestern Rd., at intersection of Des Moines Valley Rd., 50 m. from Des Moines, 39 from Fort Dodge and 125 from Council Bluffs. Does a heavy trade in grain.

Head Light..............W. **2,004**

GREENE, Butler Co.

Butler Co. Press.........W. **2,005**

GREENFIELD, Adair Co.

Reporter..................W. **2,006**
Transcript................W. **2,007**

GRINNELL, Poweshiek Co., 1,500 p., situated in rich prairie country, at intersection of Chicago, Rock Island & Pacific Rd. with Central Rd. of Iowa, 54 m. E. of Des Moines and about 16 N. W. of Montezuma. It is the seat of Iowa College.

Herald...................W. **2,008**

GRUNDY CENTER, c. h., Grundy Co., 500 p., on Black Hawk Creek, a branch of Cedar r., about 70 m., air line N. E. of Des Moines and about 25 S. W. of Waterloo. Centre of trade, principally agricultural.

Grundy Co. Atlas........W. **2,009**
New Century..............W. **2,010**

GUTHRIE CENTER, c. h., Guthrie Co.

Beacon Light............W. **2,011**

HAMBURG, Fremont Co., 2,554† p., near Missouri r., and on Kansas City, St. Joseph & Council Bluffs Rd., at junction of Nebraska City branch of Burlington & Missouri R. Rd., 51 m. S. of Council Bluffs and 79 from St. Joseph, Mo.

Democrat.................W. **2,012**
Fremont Times...........W. **2,013**

HAMPTON, c. h., Franklin Co., 1,100† p., on Central Rd. of Iowa, 59 m. from Marshalltown and 29 from Mason City.

Franklin Recorder.......W. **2,014**
Magnet...................W. **2,015**

HARLAN, c. h., Shelby Co., 540 p., on Nishnabotona r., 10 m. N. of Chicago, Rock Island & Pacific Rd., 40 m. from Council Bluffs. Surrounded by a good agricultural district.

Herald...................W. **2,016**
Record...................W. **2,017**

HUMBOLDT, Humboldt Co.

Kosmos...................W. **2,018**

IDA, Ida Co., 450† p., on Maple r., about 50 m. E. by S. of Sioux City and 25 N. of Chicago & Northwestern Rd., and 25 m. S. of Illinois Central Rd.

Ida Co. Pioneer..........W. **2,019**

INDEPENDENCE, c. h., Buchanan Co., 3,600† p., on Wapsipinicon r. and the Iowa division of the Illinois Central Rd., 69 m. from Dubuque and 24 from Waterloo.

Buchanan Co. Bulletin..W. **2,020**
Conservative..............W. **2,021**

INDIANOLA, Warren Co., 2,000† p., on Indianola branch of Chicago, Rock Island & Pacific Rd., 21 m. from Des Moines. Surrounded by a rich agricultural and stock raising country.

Herald...................W. **2,022**
Tribune...................W. **2,023**
Warren Record...........W. **2,024**
Simpsonian...............W. **2,025**

IOWA CITY, c. h., Johnson Co., 5,914 p., on Iowa r. and on Chicago, Rock Island & Pacific Rd., 54 m. from Davenport. Seat of State University and Historical Society. Engaged in manufacturing.

Press.......................D. **2,026**
Iowa State Press.........W. **2,027**
Republican................W. **2,028**
Slovan Americky.........W. **2,029**
Volksfreund...............W. **2,030**
University Reporter......M. **2,031**
Annals of Iowa..........

IOWA FALLS, Hardin Co., 1,600 p., on Iowa r. and Iowa division of Illinois Central Rd., 143 m. from Dubuque and 40 from Cedar Falls.

Sentinel...................W. **2,033**

JEFFERSON, c. h., Greene Co., 1,500† p.

Bee........................W. **2,034**

JESUP, Buchanan Co.

Vindicator................W. **2,035**

KELLOGG, Jasper Co.

Reporter..................W. **2,036**

KEOKUK, Lee Co., 12,766 p., on Mississippi r., near mouth of Des Moines r., at head of navigation for the large class of river steamboats. Terminus of several important railroads. The river commerce is very extensive. One of the principal grain and produce markets in Iowa.

Constitution..............D. **2,037**
" ....W. **2,038**
Gate City.................D. **2,039**
" " ....W. **2,040**
Post.......................W. **2,041**

KEOSAUQUA, c. h., Van Buren Co., 1,200† p., on Des Moines r., 48 m. from Keokuk. It has excellent water power. Surrounded by a rich farming district, and centre of a large trade.

Republican...............W. **2,042**

KEOTA, Keokuk Co.

Eagle.....................W. **2,043**

IOWA.

KNOXVILLE, c. h., Marion Co., 2,500† p., about 8 m. S. W. of Des Moines r. and 45 S. S. E. of Des Moines. Surrounded by a rich coal and agricultural district. Water power, timber and stone in abundance.
Journal..................W. 2,044
Marion Co. Democrat....W. 2,045

LAKE CITY, c. h., Calhoun Co., 420 p., 25 m. S. W. of Fort Dodge and 75 N. W. of Des Moines.
Journal..................W. 2,046

LAKE MILLS, Winnebago Co., 435 p., about 15 m. N. of Forest City and 18 W. of Northwood.
Independent Herald.....W. 2,047

LANSING, Allamakee Co., 2,000† p., on Mississippi r. and on Chicago, Dubuque & Minnesota Rd., 50 m. above Prairie du Chien and 100 from Dubuque. An extensive grain market and place of active trade. Strictly an agricultural county.
Die Nord Iowa Post.....W. 2,048
Mirror..................W. 2,049
North Iowa Journal.....W. 2,050

LA PORTE CITY, Black Hawk Co., 1,200† p., on Burlington, Cedar Rapids & Minnesota Rd., 16 m. from Waterloo and 140 from Burlington. Centre of a large and fertile district of country.
Progress..................W. 2,051

LAWLER, Chickasaw Co.
Chickasaw Co. Times.....W. 2,052

LE MARS, c. h., Plymouth Co., 1,000† p., on Iowa division of Illinois Central Rd., 24 m. from Sioux City. One of the principal grain, stock and lumber markets of northwestern Iowa.
Iowa Liberal.............W. 2,053
Sentinel..................W. 2,054

LENOX, Taylor Co.
Time Table...............W. 2,055

LEON, c. h., Decatur Co., 1,200 p., 65 m. S. of Des Moines, 40 from Chariton. Situated in the midst of an agricultural region.
Decatur Co. Journal....W. 2,056
Reporter..................W. 2,057

LINEVILLE, Wayne Co.
Tribune...................W. 2,058

LISBON, Linn Co.
Harvey's Courier........W. 2,059
Sun........................W. 2,060

LOGAN, Harrison Co., 500† p., on Boyer r., and Iowa division of Chicago & Northwestern Rd., 29 m. from Council Bluffs. It is the centre of a rich agricultural district, from which it derives an active trade. 2 stone quarries here.
Harrison Co. Courier....W. 2,061

LONE TREE, Johnson Co.
Sentinel..................W. 2,062

LYONS, Clinton Co., 4,500† p., on Mississippi r., and the Iowa Midland and Clinton, Dubuque and Minn. Rds., 3 m. above Clinton and opposite Fulton, Ill., and 136 m. from Chicago. Considerable lumber is cut here. It has a large and flourishing business.
Clinton Co. Advertiser....W. 2,063
Mirror...................W. 2,064

McGREGOR, Clayton Co., 4,000† p., on Mississippi r., opposite Prairie du Chien, and on Chicago, Milwaukee & St. Paul Rd., at the eastern terminus of the Iowa and Dakota division, 61 m. above Dubuque and 190 from Milwaukee. The railroad car and repair shops are located here. Centre of an active trade.
News......................W. 2,065
North Iowa Times.......W. 2,066

MALVERN, Mills Co., 700 p., on Burlington & Missouri R. Rd., 35 m. from Omaha and 30 from Council Bluffs. Centre of a thriving trade. Extensively engaged in stock raising.
Leader....................W. 2,067
Mills Co. Chronicle.......W. 2,068

MANCHESTER, Delaware Co., 2,500† p., on Maquoketa r. and Illinois Central Rd., 47 m. from Dubuque. Engaged in manufacturing.
Democrat.................W. 2,069
Press......................W. 2,070

MAQUOKETA, c. h., Jackson Co., 2,469† p., on Iowa Midland Rd., at intersection of Davenport & St. Paul Rd., 38 m. from Clinton and 45 from Davenport.
Excelsior.................W. 2,071
Jackson Sentinel.........W. 2,072

MARBLE ROCK, Floyd Co.
Weekly....................W. 2,073

MARENGO, c. h., Iowa Co., 1,693 p., on Iowa division of Chicago, Rock Island & Pacific Rd., 85 m. from Davenport. Engaged in agricultural pursuits.
Democrat.................W. 2,074
Republican...............W. 2,075

MARION, c. h., Linn Co., 2,700† p., on Dubuque & Southwestern Rd., 6 m. from Cedar Rapids and 70 from Dubuque.
Linn Co. Pilot...........W. 2,076
Register..................W. 2,077
Advent and Sabbath Advocate.............S. M. 2,078

MARSHALLTOWN, c. h., Marshall Co. 4,500† p., on Iowa division of Chicago & Northwestern Rd., at crossing of Central Rd. of Iowa, 70 m. W. of Cedar Rapids. Surrounded by a fine agricultural country. Centre of a thriving trade. Considerable manufacturing carried on.
Marshall Times. ....D. 2,079
Marshall Co. Times......W. 2,080
Republican.............S. W. 2,081
" ....W. 2,082
Marshall Statesman .....W. 2,083
Ladies' Bureau..........S. M. 2,084

MARYSVILLE, Marion Co.
Miner.....................W. 2,085

MASON CITY, c. h., Cerro Gordo Co., 3,000† p., on the Iowa & Dakota division of the Milwaukee & St. Paul Rd., at the junction of the Mason City & Austin branch, 74 m. from McGregor and 115 N. of Des Moines. In a fine agricultural district.
Cerro Gordo Republican.W. 2,086
Express..................W. 2,087

MECHANICSVILLE, Cedar Co., 800† p., on Iowa division of Chicago & Northwestern Rd., 12 m. W. of Clarence and 26 from Cedar Rapids. Surrounded by an agricultural country.
Press.....................W. 2,088

MEDIAPOLIS, Des Moines Co.
Enterprise...............W. 2,089

MISSOURI VALLEY, Harrison Co., 1,200 p., the southern terminus of Sioux

IOWA.

City & Pacific Rd., at its junction with Iowa division of Chicago & Northwestern Rd., 20 m. N. of Council Bluffs and 6 from Missouri r.
Times....................W. **2,090**

MONROE, Jasper Co., 1,600† p., on Des Moines Valley Rd., 32 m. from Des Moines and 29 from Oskaloosa. Noted for its excellent coal.
Mirror....................W. **2,091**

MONTEZUMA, c. h., Poweshiek Co., 1,555 p., about 20 m. N. of Oskaloosa and 10 S. of the line the Chicago, Rock Island & Pacific Rd. Coal fields in the vicinity.
Republican..............W. **2,092**

MONTICELLO, Jones Co., 2,587† p., on Dubuque & Southwestern Rd., at intersection of Davenport & St. Paul Rd., 43 m. from Dubuque and 70 from Davenport.
Express..................W. **2,093**
Jones Co. Liberal........W. **2,094**

MORNING SUN, Louisa Co., 1,000† p., on Burlington, Cedar Rapids & Minnesota Rd., 23 m. from Burlington and 7 from Wapello. Shipping point for grain and produce.
Reporter.................W. **2,095**

MOULTON, Appanoose Co., 1,100† p., on the St. Louis, Kansas City & Northern Rd., at the intersection of the Burlington & Southwestern Rd., 100 m. from Burlington and 35 from Ottumwa. Milling, woolen factories and general trade is carried on.
Record...................W. **2,096**

MOUNT AYR, c. h., Ringgold Co., 640 p., about 75 m. S. S. W. of Des Moines and about 20 from the line of the Burlington & Missouri R. Rd. at Afton.
Journal..................W. **2,097**
Ringgold Record..........W. **2,098**

MOUNT PLEASANT, c. h., Henry Co., 4,563† p., on Burlington & Missouri R. Rd., 28 m. from Burlington. Centre of trade for a fertile county. There are several educational institutions located here.
Free Press...............W. **2,099**
Journal..................W. **2,100**

MOUNT VERNON, Linn Co., 1,200 p., on Iowa division of Chicago & Northwestern Rd., 16 m. E. of Cedar Rapids. Cornell College is located here.
Hawk-Eye.................W. **2,101**
Collegian................W. **2,102**

MUSCATINE, c. h., Muscatine Co., 7,537† p., on Mississippi r. and southwestern division of Chicago, Rock Island & Pacific Rd., 300 m. above St. Louis. The centering point of a very large trade. Extensively engaged in manufacturing lumber and other articles and the lumber trade. Various manufactories and several large pork packing establishments located here.
Journal..................D. **2,103**
" ....T. W. **2,104**
" ....W. **2,105**
Tribune..................D. **2,106**
" ....W. **2,107**
Duetsche Zeitung.........W. **2,108**
Humming Bird.............W. **2,109**

NASHUA, Chickasaw Co., 3,000 p., on Red Cedar r. and the Cedar Falls & Minnesota Rd., 35 m. from Waterloo and 30 above Cedar Falls.
Post.....................W. **2,110**

NEVADA, c. h., Story Co., 1,200† p., on Chicago & Northwestern Rd., 99 m. W. of Cedar Rapids, 35 N. N. E. of Des Moines and 180 W. of Mississippi r. Surrounded by an agricultural district. The Iowa Agricultural College is located in this county.
Representative...........W. **2,111**
Watchman.................W. **2,112**

NEW ALBIN, Allamakee Co.
Spectator................W. **2,113**

NEWELL, Buena Vista Co., 400† p., on the Iowa division of the Illinois Central Rd., 43 m. W. of Fort Dodge.
Mirror...................W. **2,114**

NEW HAMPTON, Chickasaw Co., 1,000† p., on the Iowa & Dakota division of the Milwaukee & St. Paul Rd., 70 m. from McGregor and 15 N. E. of Nashua.
Courier..................W. **2,115**

NEW SHARON, Mahaska Co.
Star.....................W. **2,116**

NEWTON, c. h., Jasper Co., 1,983 p., on Chicago, Rock Island & Pacific Rd., 139 m. from Davenport and 25 from Des Moines. Surrounded by a fine agricultural district
Free Press & Republican.W. **2,117**
Jasper Co. Head Light...W. **2,118**
Jasper Co. Independent..W. **2,119**

NORA SPRINGS, Floyd Co., 900† p., on Shell Rock r. and Burlington, Cedar Rapids & Minnesota Rd., at intersection of Iowa & Dakota division of Milwaukee & St. Paul Rd., 119 m. from Cedar Rapids and 107 from McGregor. It is a fine market for grain and stock.
Floyd Co. Press..........W. **2,120**

NORTHWOOD, c. h., Worth Co., 650 p., on Shell Rock r. and northern terminus of Central Rd. of Iowa, about 20 m. from Mason City. Surrounded by a rich grazing and farming region. The county seat and centre of considerable trade.
Pioneer..................W. **2,121**

OGDEN, Boone Co.
Reporter.................W. **2,122**

ONAWA, c. h., Monona Co., 850† p., on Sioux City & Pacific Rd., 7 m. from Missouri r., 37 from Sioux City and 55 N. of Council Bluffs. Centre of a rich agricultural region.
Monona Co. Gazette.......W. **2,123**
People's Press...........W. **2,124**

ORANGE CITY, Sioux Co., 300 p., about 45 m. N. of Sioux City. In an agricultural district.
Sioux Co. Herald.........W.
Volksvriend..............W. **2,126**

OSAGE, Mitchell Co., 2,000† p., on Red Cedar r. and northern branch of Iowa division of Illinois Central Rd., 60 m. above Cedar Falls. It is the county seat and centre of trade for a large and growing section of agricultural country. Manufactures carried on to a considerable extent.
Mitchell Co. News........W. **2,127**
Mitchell Co. Press.......W. **2,128**

OSCEOLA, c. h., Clarke Co., 1,701† p., on the Burlington & Missouri R. Rd., 156 m. from Burlington. In an agricultural and stock-raising district, and the centre of considerable trade.
Beacon...................W. **2,129**
New Era..................W. **2,130**
Sentinel.................W. **2,131**

IOWA.

OSKALOOSA, c. h., Mahaska Co., 5,000 p., on Des Moines Valley Rd., at intersection of the Central Rd. of Iowa, 62 m. from Des Moines and 24 from Ottumwa. Pleasantly situated and centre of an active trade. Surrounded by a fine agricultural district. Extensively engaged in coal and iron mining and manufacturing.

Herald..................W. **2,132**
Record and Evangelist...W. **2,133**
Standard................W. **2,134**
Welch's Reform Leader..W. **2,135**
Christian Sunday School Teacher..............M. **2,136**
Gem.....................M. **2,137**

OSSIAN, Winneshiek Co.

Enterprise...............W. **2,138**

OTTUMWA, c. h., Wapello Co., 10,000† p., on Des Moines r. and Burlington & Missouri R. Rd., at intersection of Des Moines Valley Rd; also northern terminus of St. Louis, Kansas City & Northern Rd., 75 m. from Burlington and 86 from Des Moines. Largely engaged in manufactures, and the centre of an extensive trade.

Courier..................D. **2,139**
" ....W. **2,140**
Democrat................W. **2,141**
Journal..................W. **2,142**
Spirit of the Times.......W. **2,143**

PANORA, c. h., Guthrie Co., 1,000 p., 44 m. W. by N. of Des Moines and 14 from Chicago, Rock Island & Pacific Rd. In an agricultural section. Some manufacturing carried on.

Guthrie Vedette..........W. **2,144**

PARKERSBURG, Butler Co., 700 p., on the Iowa division of the Illinois Central Rd., 119 m. W. of Dubuque and 19 from Cedar Falls. In the midst of an agricultural country.

Eclipse...................W. **2,145**

PELLA, Marion Co., 3,000 p., on Des Moines Valley Rd., 47 m. from Des Moines, 115 from Keokuk. Surrounded by a fine agricultural region and largely engaged in manufacturing.

Baptist Beacon..........W. **2,146**
Blade.....................W. **2,147**
Weekblad................W. **2,148**

PERRY, Dallas Co.

Chief.....................W. **2,149**

POSTVILLE, Allamakee Co.

Review...................W. **2,150**

PRAIRIE CITY, Jasper Co., 1,000† p., on Des Moines Valley Rd., 24 m. from Des Moines and about 20 S. W. of Newton, in an agricultural district. It is a principal shipping point for live stock and produce.

News.....................W. **2,151**

PRESTON, Jackson Co.

Clipper...................W. **2,152**

PRIMGHAR, c. h., O'Brien Co.

O'Brien Pioneer.........W. **2,153**

RAYMOND, Black Hawk Co.

Burroughs' Journal......W. **2,154**

RED OAK, c. h., Montgomery Co., 3,000 p., on Nishnabatona r., and on the line of the Burlington & Missouri R. Rd., about 40 m. S. E. of Council Bluffs and 241 from Burlington. Is a rapidly-growing town. Considerable manufacturing carried on.

Express...................W. **2,155**

IOWA.

New Era.................W. **2,156**
Record...................W. **2,157**

RICHLAND, Keokuk Co.

Mail......................W. **2,158**

RIVERSIDE, Washington Co.

News.....................W. **2,159**

RIVERTON, Fremont Co., 600† p., on Nebraska City branch of Burlington & Missouri R. Rd., about 20 m. from Nebraska City. Its present importance is derived from immense shipments of grain and live stock.

Advocate................W. **2,160**

ROCKFORD, Floyd Co., 732 p., on Shell Rock r., and Burlington, Cedar Rapids & Minnesota Rd., 49 m. from Cedar Falls.

Reveille..................W. **2,161**

ROCK RAPIDS, Lyon Co., 290 p., on Rock r., in N. W. corner of the State, about 60 m. N. of Sioux City. Engaged in agriculture. Surrounded by a fertile country.

Review...................W. **2,162**

SABULA, Jackson Co., 1,200† p., on Mississippi r., 58 m. below Dubuque, and at eastern terminus of Sabula, Ackley & Dakota Rd., and connected with Savanna, on Western Union Rd., by a ferry transfer.

Gazette..................W. **2,163**

SAC CITY, c. h., Sac Co., 475 p., on Coon r., 45 m. W. of Fort Dodge. It has fine water power. County especially adapted to stock raising and dairy purposes.

Sac Sun..................W. **2,164**

SCRANTON, Greene Co.

Gazette...................W. **2,165**

SEYMOUR, Wayne Co.

Head Light..............W. **2,166**
Reporter.................W. **2,167**

SHELDON, O'Brien Co.

Mail......................W. **2,168**

SHELL ROCK, Butler Co., 1,142 p., on the Shell Rock r. and the Burlington, Cedar Rapids & Minnesota Rd., 22 m. from Waterloo.

News.....................W. **2,169**

SHELLSBURG, Benton Co., 700† p., on the Burlington, Cedar Rapids & Minnesota Rd., 15 m. from Cedar Rapids. Centre of a good trade.

Benton Co. Record.......W. **2,170**

SHENANDOAH, Page Co., 950† p., on the Nebraska City branch of Burlington & Missouri R. Rd., half way between Hamburg and Red Oak. Centre of a thriving trade. Engaged in agricultural pursuits.

Reporter.................W. **2,171**

SIBLEY, Osceola Co., 600† p., on Iowa division of Sioux City & St. Paul Rd.

Gazette..................W. **2,172**

SIDNEY, c. h., Fremont Co., 1,500 p., 40 m. S. of Council Bluffs and 10 N. of Hamburg.

Union....................W. **2,173**

SIGOURNEY, c. h., Keokuk Co., 2,000† p., on Skunk r., and Sigourney branch of Chicago, Rock Island & Pacific Rd., about 75 m. N. W. of Burlington.

News.....................W. **2,174**
Review...................W. **2,175**

SIOUX CITY, c. h., Woodbury Co., 5,100† p., on Missouri r., and on Sioux City &

IOWA.

Pacific Rd., at the terminus of Iowa division of Illinois Central Rd., 96 m. above Council Bluffs. Centre of an agricultural region, and outfitting point for upper Missouri.

Journal..................D. 2,176
" ....W. 2,177
Times..................W. 2,178

SIOUX RAPIDS, c. h., Buena Vista Co.
Echo..................W. 2,179

SOUTH ENGLISH, Keokuk Co.
Western Herald..........W. 2,180

SPENCER, Clay Co., 400† p., on the Little Sioux r., 40 m. N. E. of Cherokee and 80 N. W. of Fort Dodge. The centre of a fine agricultural region.
News..................W. 2,181

SPIRIT LAKE, c. h., Dickinson Co., 350 p., near lake of same name, surrounded by several other beautiful lakes, 90 m. from Fort Dodge. One of the richest portions of Northwestern Iowa for agricultural purposes. Fast becoming celebrated as a summer resort.
Beacon..................W. 2,182

STATE CENTRE, Marshall Co., 900† p., on the Chicago & Northwestern Rd. Geographical centre of State. Surrounded by one of the richest agricultural countries in the West.
Enterprise..............W. 2,183

STORM LAKE, Buena Vista Co., 800† p., on Storm Lake and the Iowa division of the Illinois Central Rd., 245 m. from Dubuque and 81 from Sioux City. A fine agricultural region surrounding it.
Pilot..................W. 2,184

STRAWBERRY POINT, Clayton Co.
Free Press..............W. 2,185

STUART, Adair Co., 2,000† p., on Chicago, Rock Island & Pacific Rd., 40 m. from Des Moines and 110 from Council Bluffs. Situated in the centre of a rich agricultural country. Several locomotive and machine shops in successful operation.
Locomotive..............W. 2,186
Register..................W. 2,187

TAMA CITY, Tama Co., 1,500† p., on Iowa division of Chicago & Northwestern Rd., 51 m. W. of Cedar Rapids.
Tama Herald...........W. 2,188
Tama Press.............W. 2,189

TIPTON, c. h., Cedar Co., 1,650† p., 5 m. from Cedar r. and 25 N. of Muscatine and the Mississippi r. The centre of a fine, rich agricultural region.
Advertiser...............W. 2,190
Conservative.............W. 2,191

TOLEDO, c. h., Tama Co., 1,100† p., near Iowa division of Chicago & Northwestern Rd., about 20 m. E. of Marshalltown and 50 W. of Cedar Rapids. The centre of a thriving local trade.
Chronicle................W. 2,192
Tama Co. Independent...W. 2,193

TRAER, Tama Co.
Clipper..................W. 2,194

UNION, Hardin Co.
Star.....................W. 2,195

VICTOR, Iowa Co., 800† p., on Chicago, Rock Island & Pacific Rd., 96 m. from Davenport and 78 from Des Moines.
Index...................W. 2,196

IOWA.

VILLISCA, Montgomery Co., 1,000 p., on Burlington & Missouri R. Rd., 65 m. E. from Council Bluffs. Noted principally for its extensive trade in grain and live stock.
Review..................W. 2,197

VINTON, c. h., Benton Co., 2,500† p., on Red Cedar r., and Burlington, Cedar Rapids & Minnesota Rd., 25 m. N. W. of Cedar Rapids, 244 W. of Chicago. Surrounded by a fine agricultural district and a trade centre. Has a small manufacturing interest.
Eagle....................W. 2,198
People's Journal.........W. 2,199
Iowa Fine Stock Gazette.M. 2,200
Reformed Missionary....M. 2,201

WAPELLO, c. h., Louisa Co., 1,200 p., on Iowa r. and Burlington, Cedar Rapids & Minnesota Rd., about 30 m. from Burlington. Engaged in milling, manufacturing and general trade.
Louisa Co. Record........W. 2,202
Republican..............W. 2,203

WASHINGTON, c. h., Washington Co., 4,000 p., on the Chicago, Rock Island & Pacific Rd., at junction of Southwestern division with the main line, 75 m. S. W. from Davenport. Engaged in manufactures and a place of active trade.
Gazette..................W. 2,204
Washington Co. Press.....W. 2,205

WATERLOO, c. h., Black Hawk Co., 5,600† p., on the Cedar r. and the Burlington, Cedar Rapids & Minnesota, and the Iowa division of the Illinois Central Rds., 93 m. from Dubuque and 156 from Burlington. Surrounded by a fine agricultural district. Engaged in manufactures of various kinds. The Illinois Central Rd. repair shops are here.
Courier..................W. 2,206
Deutsch-Amerikaner......W. 2,207
Iowa State Reporter......W. 2,208

WAUKON, c. h., Allamakee Co., 1,800 p., in a rich farming and fruit-growing district, 18 m. W. of Mississippi r. and 30 N. W. of McGregor. Surrounded by a fine farming country; a large live stock market.
Standard.................W. 2,209

WAVERLY, c. h., Bremer Co., 2,291 p., on Red Cedar r. and Iowa division of Illinois Central Rd., 18 m. from Waterloo. Considerable manufacturing carried on.
Bremer Co. Independent..W. 2,210
Deutsch Volks-Zeitung....W. 2,211
Republican...............W. 2,212

WEBSTER CITY, c. h., Hamilton Co., 2,200† p., on Boone r. and Iowa division of Illinois Central Rd., 20 m. from Fort Dodge, 80 N. of Des Moines and 172 W. of Dubuque. In a coal mining and agricultural section.
Argus....................W. 2,213
Hamilton Freeman.......W. 2,214

WEST BRANCH, Cedar Co.
Times....................W. 2,215.

WEST LIBERTY, Muscatine Co., 1,500† p., on Chicago, Rock Island and Pacific Rd., at intersection of Burlington, Cedar Rapids & Minnesota Rd., 62 m. from Burlington, 39 W. of Davenport and 26 N W. of Muscatine. An agricultural and stock-raising district.
Enterprise..............W. 2,216.

WEST UNION, c. h., Fayette Co., 1,489 p. 80 m. N. W. of Dubuque and 80 from

Cedar Rapids. Engaged in agriculture and stock raising.
Fayette Co. Union........W. **2,217**
Republican Gazette.......W. **2,218**

WHEATLAND, Clinton Co.
News.....................W. **2,219**

WILLIAMS, Hamilton Co.
Press....................W. **2,220**

WILTON, Muscatine Co., 1,317 p., at junction of Southwestern division of Chicago, Rock Island & Pacific Rd. with the main road, 25 m. W. of Davenport and 12 N. of Muscatine.
Exponent.................W. **2,221**
Herald...................W. **2,222**

WINTERSET, c. h., Madison Co., 3,000† p. Surrounded by a fine agricultural region; also one of the principal stone fields of Iowa; 42 m. S. W. of Des Moines, connected with it by Rd. branch of the C., R., I. & P. Rd., and is the present terminus.
Madisonian...............W. **2,223**
News.....................W. **2,224**

WYOMING, Jones Co., 1,733 p., on Davenport & St. Paul Rd., 54 m. from Davenport. Engaged in agriculture and stock raising.
Journal..................W. **2,225**

KANSAS.

ABILENE, c. h., Dickinson Co., 1,000† p., on Kansas Pacific Rd., 163 m. W. of Leavenworth. A place of active business.
Dickinson Co. Chronicle.W. **2,226**

ALMA, c. h., Wabaunsee Co., 450† p., on Mill creek, 14 m. from Wamego and 40 from Topeka. Engaged in agriculture and stock raising.
Wabaunsee Co. News....W. **2,227**

ARKANSAS CITY, Crowley Co., 500 p., on Arkansas r., 80 m. from Florence, on Atchison, Topeka & Santa Fe Rd. Stock raising and grain growing the principal branch of business.
Traveler.................W. **2,228**

ATCHISON, c. h., Atchison Co., 13,600† p., on Missouri r. It is the eastern terminus of central branch of Union Pacific, the Atchison, Topeka & Santa Fe, and Atchison & Nebraska Rds. The western terminus of Missouri Pacific Rd.
Champion.................D. **2,229**
" ....W. **2,230**
Patriot..................D. **2,231**
" ....W. **2,232**
Der Courier..............W. **2,233**

AUGUSTA, Butler Co., 798† p., 150 m. S. W. of Topeka. Lies in the celebrated Walnut Valley, the most fertile in the State; the average wheat crop in the valley in 1875 being 33 bushels to the acre.
Southern Kansas Gazette.W. **2,234**

BAXTER SPRINGS, Cherokee Co., 1,500† p., on Spring r. and Missouri R., Fort Scott & Gulf Rd., 60 m. from Fort Scott. Engaged in cattle trade, lead mining and manufacturing, and a place of active business.
Republican...............W. **2,235**

BELLEVILLE, c. h., Republic Co., 350† p., in the central part of the county, and about 75 m. N. W. of Junction City. A mining district.
Republic.................W. **2,236**
Telescope................W. **2,237**

BELOIT, Mitchell Co., 600† p., on Solomon r., 130 m. W. by N. of Topeka. Situated in one of the best agricultural counties in the State. A fine water power within the corporate limits of the city, with a flouring and saw mill.
Gazette..................W. **2,238**

BLUE RAPIDS, Marshall Co., 700 p., on Blue r., at junction of the Big and the Little Blues. Has improved water power of 1,600 horse power. Has largest flouring, woolen, paper, gypsum and oil mills in the State. Is reached by the Central branch Union Pacific Rd., is 95 m. due W. of Atchison. Surrounded by excellent farming lands, with abundance of water and building stone.
Times....................W. **2,239**

BURLINGTON, c. h., Coffey Co., 1,200† p., on Neosho r. and Missouri, Kansas & Texas Rd., 68 m. from Parsons and 89 from Junction City. Centre of trade. Has water power, which is employed in manufacturing. Principal business stock-raising.
Independent..............W. **2,240**
Patriot..................W. **2,241**

CAWKER CITY, Mitchell Co.
Echo.....................W. **2,242**

CHANUTE, Neosho Co., 1,200 p., junction of Missouri, Kansas & Texas and Leavenworth, Lawrence & Galveston Rds. It is a railroad centre and a place of considerable trade.
Times....................W. **2,243**

CHEROKEE, Crawford Co.
Index....................W. **2,244**

CHETOPA, Labette Co., 1,200† p., on Missouri, Kansas & Texas Rd., on the southern line of the State and on the west bank of the Neosho r.
Herald...................W. **2,245**
*Southern Kansas Advance*W. **2,246**

CLAY CENTER, c. h., Clay Co., 600† p., on Republican r., 40 m. from Junction City and 120 from Leavenworth. In an agricultural section.
Clay Co. Dispatch........W. **2,247**

COFFEYVILLE, Montgomery Co.
Journal..................W. **2,248**

COLUMBUS, c. h., Cherokee Co., 1,000 p., on Missouri R., Fort Scott & Gulf Rd., 11 m. from Baxter Springs and 150 from Kansas City. Surrounded by an agricultural district. Coal found in the vicinity.
Courier..................W. **2,249**
Democrat.................W. **2,250**

CONCORDIA, c. h., Cloud Co., 600† p., 54 m. from Waterville, 175 from Leavenworth and 154 from Atchison A normal school and U. S. land office located here. Produces coal and stone for building purposes.
Empire...................W. **2,251**
Expositor................W. **2,252**

COTTONWOOD FALLS, c. h., Chase Co., 459 p., on Cottonwood r., and Atchison, Topeka & Santa Fe Rd., 81 m. from Topeka. Has fine water power, and sur-

KANSAS.

rounded by an agricultural and stock-raising country.
Chase Co. Courant.......W. **2,253**
Chase Co. Leader........W. **2,254**

COUNCIL GROVE, c. h., Morris Co., 1,000† p., on the Neosho division of Missouri, Kansas & Texas Rd., 37 from Junction City. Surrounded by an agricultural and stock-raising district.
Democrat...............W. **2,255**
Morris Co. Republican...W. **2,256**

ELDORADO, c. h., Butler Co., 950† p., on Walnut r. Surrounded by an agricultural and stock-raising district, which is rapidly filling up with immigrants.
Walnut Valley Times.....W. **2,257**

ELK FALLS, Elk Co., 300† p., on Elk r., 35 m. N. W. of Independence. Surrounded by an agricultural and stock-raising region.
Elk Co. Ledger...........W. **2,258**

ELLSWORTH, c. h., Ellsworth Co., 800 p., on Kansas Pacific Rd., 156 m. W. of Topeka. Stock raising and wheat growing.
Reporter.................W. **2,259**

EMPORIA, c. h., Lyon Co., 2,400† p., near Atchison, Topeka & Santa Fe Rd., at crossing of Missouri, Kansas & Texas Rd., between Cottonwood and Neosho rs., 65 m. S. W. of Lawrence. Commercial trade centre. Manufacturing interests of importance and rapidly improving.
Ledger...................W. **2,260**
News.....................W. **2,261**

EUREKA, c. h., Greenwood Co., 1,040 p., on Fall r., 40 m. S. of Emporia. Centre of trade for a rapidly growing agricultural district.
Censorial................W. **2,262**
Herald...................W. **2,263**

FORT SCOTT, c. h., Bourbon Co., 6,000† p., on Marmaton r. and Mission R., Fort Scott & Gulf Rd., and at intersection of Missouri, Kansas & Texas Rd., 100 m. from Kansas City and about 120 S. of Leavenworth. Engaged in agriculture, manufacturing and coal mining. A place of active trade.
Monitor..................D. **2,264**
" ....W. **2,265**
Pioneer..................W. **2,266**

FREDONIA, c. h., Wilson Co.
Wilson Co. Citizen.......W. **2,267**

GARNETT, c. h., Anderson Co., 1,500† p., 51 m. S. of Lawrence, on Leavenworth, Lawrence & Galveston Rd. Surrounded by an agricultural district.
Journal..................W. **2,268**
Plain Dealer.............W. **2,269**

GIRARD, c. h., Crawford Co., 1,000 p., on Missouri R., Fort Scott & Gulf Rd., 26 m. from Fort Scott and 160 S. E. of Topeka. Located in an agricultural district with heavy deposits of coal.
Crawford Co. News......W. **2,270**
Press.....................W. **2,271**

GREAT BEND, c. h., Barton Co.
Register.................W. **2,272**

HANOVER, Washington Co., 350 p., on Little Blue r. and St. Joseph & Denver City Rd., 127 m. W. of St. Joseph.
Western Independent....W. **2,273**

KANSAS.

HAYS CITY, c. h., Ellis Co.
Hays Sentinel...........W. **2,274**

HIAWATHA, c. h., Brown Co., 1,000 p., on St. Joseph & Denver City Rd., 42 m. W. of St. Joseph. Engaged in agriculture and stock raising.
Dispatch.................W. **2,275**
Kansas Herald..........W. **2,276**

HOLTON, c. h., Jackson Co., 426 p., on Kansas Central Rd., 56 m. from Leavenworth and 30 N. of Topeka.
Recorder and Express....W. **2,277**

HOWARD CITY, c. h., Elk Co., 250 p., situated in a mineral, agricultural and stock growing region.
Courant..................W. **2,278**

HUMBOLDT, Allen Co., 1,500 p., on Neosho r., at junction of Leavenworth, Lawrence & Galveston Rd. with Missouri, Kansas & Texas Rd., 44 m. from Fort Scott and 86 from Lawrence. Surrounded by an agricultural district and centre of trade. The river furnishes water power for manufacturing.
Union....................W. **2,279**

HUTCHINSON, c. h., Reno Co.
News.....................W. **2,280**
Reno Co. Independent...W. **2,281**

INDEPENDENCE, Montgomery Co., 2,500† p., on Verdigris r., 65 m. from Fort Scott. Terminus of the L., L. & G. Rd. It is the centre of an agricultural district and a shipping point. A United States Land Office is located here.
Evening Courier.........D. **2,282**
Courier..................W. **2,283**
Kansan...................W. **2,284**
South Kansas Tribune...W. **2,285**

IOLA, c. h., Allen Co., 1,759 p., on Leavenworth, Lawrence & Galveston Rd., 70 m. from Lawrence, 104 from Kansas City. The Neosho r. supplies water power for manufactures, and surrounding country is agricultural. Several machine shops for manufacture of stoves, agricultural implements, etc., are located here. Has a mineral well.
Register.................W. **2,286**

IRVING, Marshall Co., 900† p., on Central branch of Union Pacific Rd., 91 m. from Atchison.
Blue Valley Gazette......W. **2,287**

JEWELL CENTER, Jewell Co.
Jewell Co. Monitor......W. **2,288**

JEWELL CITY, Jewell Co., 360 p., on Buffalo Creek, 30 m. N. W. of Concordia. Sitnate in the midst of a stock raising and farm growing country.
Jewell Co. Diamond.....W. **2,289**

JUNCTION CITY, c. h., Davis Co., 2,000 p., on Smoky Hill fork of Kansas r., at junction of Missouri, Kansas & Texas Rd. with Kansas Pacific Rd., 71 m. from Topeka. Engaged in manufacturing and centre of a large trade. Railroad repair shops located here.
Tribune..................W. **2,290**
Union....................W. **2,291**

KINSLEY, Edwards Co.
Reporter.................W. **2,292**

KIRWIN, Philips Co.
Chief....................W. **2,293**

LA CYGNE, Linn Co., 694 p., on Osage

KANSAS.

r. and Missouri R., Fort Scott & Gulf Rd., 37 m. N. of Fort Scott.
Journal..................W. **2,294**

LARNED, c. h., Pawnee Co.
Press.....................W. **2,295**

LAWRENCE, c. h., Douglas Co., 8,320 p., on Kansas r., 38 m. from State line of Mo. The Kansas Pacific, Atchison, Topeka & Santa Fe and several other Rds. intersect here.
Evening Standard........D. **2,296**
Standard of Reform.....W. **2,297**
Republican Journal......D. **2,298**
" " ...T. W. **2,299**
Western Home Journal..W. **2,300**
Tribune....................D. **2,301**
Kansas Tribune..........W. **2,302**
Spirit of Kansas.........W. **2,303**
State Sentinel............W. **2,304**

LEAVENWORTH, c. h., Leavenworth Co., 22,000 p., on Missouri r. The metropolis of Kansas. Its railroad connections and river trade make it a point of commercial importance. Engaged in various manufactures. Coal mines in the vicinity. Site of Fort Leavenworth.
Appeal....................D. **2,305**
Commercial...............D. **2,306**
Kansas Freie Presse......D. **2,307**
" " " .....W. **2,308**
Times.....................D **2,309**
" ....W. **2,310**
Herald....................W. **2,311**
Home Record.............M. **2,312**
Western World............M. **2,313**

LINCOLN CENTER, c. h., Lincoln Co.
Saline Valley Register....W. **2,314**

LOUISVILLE, c. h., Pottawatomie Co., 500† p., 40 m. W. of Topeka and 3 N. of Kansas Pacific Rd. at Wamego. Rock creek furnishes water power.
Kansas Reporter.........W. **2,315**

LYNDON, Osage Co.
Osage Co. Chronicle......W. **2,316**
Times......................W. **2,317**

McPHERSON, c. h., McPherson Co.
Independent..............W. **2,318**

MANHATTAN, c. h., Riley Co., 1,173 p., at junction of Big Blue with Kansas r., and on Kansas Pacific Rd., 80 m. from Lawrence. Surrounded by an agricultural and stock-raising district.
Nationalist..............W. **2,319**

MARION CENTRE, c. h., Marion Co., 500 p., on Cottonwood r., 10 m. from Atchison, Texas & Santa Fe Rd., and 50 from Junction City. Surrounded by an agricultural and stock-raising region.
Marion Co. Record......W. **2,320**

MARYSVILLE, c. h., Marshall Co.
Marshall Co. News.......W. **2,321**

MINNEAPOLIS, c. h., Ottawa Co., 700† p., on Solomon r. It has water power. An agricultural and sheep-raising country.
Independent.............W. **2,322**
Sentinel..................W. **2,323**

MOUND CITY, c. h., Linn Co., 635 p., 24 m. N. by W. of Fort Scott, 95 S. of Leavenworth and 6½ W. of the Missouri R., Fort Scott & Gulf Rd.
Linn Co. Clarion........W. **2,324**
Western Enterprise......W. **2,325**

NEODESHA, Wilson Co., 800† p., at junction of Verdigris and Fall rs., 65 m. from Fort Scott and 120 from Lawrence. A young town, rapidly rising, with large water power and coal mines.
Free Press................W. **2,326**

NEOSHO FALLS, c. h., Woodson Co., 1,500 p., on Neosho r. and the Missouri, Kansas & Texas Rd., 18 m. from Burlington and 100 from Kansas City.
Woodson Co. Post........W. **2,327**

NEWTON, c. h., Harvey Co., 1,200† p., on Atchison, Topeka & Santa Fe Rds., at the junction of Wichita branch, and 134 m. from Topeka.
Harvey Co. News.........W. **2,328**
Kansan....................W. **2,329**

OLATHE, c. h., Johnson Co., 2,300† p., on Missouri R., Fort Scott & Gulf Rd., at junction of Kansas City division of Leavenworth, Lawrence & Galveston Rd., 21 m. from Kansas City and 32 from Ottawa.
Condenser................W. **2,330**
Mirror and News Letter..W. **2,331**
Western Progress.........W. **2,332**

OSAGE CITY, Osage Co., 1,000 p., on Atchison, Topeka & Santa Fe Rd., 35 m. S. of Topeka. Coal fields and quarries of stone flagging located here.
Free Press................W. **2,333**

OSAGE MISSION, Neosho Co., 1,230† p., on Sedalia division of Missouri, Kansas & Texas Rd., 14 m. from Parsons and 35 from Fort Scott.
Neosho Co. Journal......W. **2,334**

OSBORNE CITY, c. h., Osborne Co.
Osborne Co. Farmer.....W. **2,335**

OSKALOOSA, c. h., Jefferson Co., 800 p., 22 m. N. by W. of Lawrence, 25 from Leavenworth, 25 from Topeka, 28 from Atchison. Engaged in agriculture, stock raising and fruit culture.
Independent..............W. **2,336**
Sickle and Sheaf.........W. **2,337**

OSWEGO, c. h., Labette Co., 1,200† p., on Neosho r., and Missouri, Kansas & Texas Rd., 16 m. from Parsons. The river furnishes good power, which is employed in manufacturing flour and breadstuffs.
Independent.............W. **2,338**

OTTAWA, c. h., Franklin Co., 2,941 p., on Osage r. and Leavenworth, Lawrence & Galveston Rd., at junction of Kansas City branch, 25 m. S. of Lawrence and 53 from Kansas City. Centre of a flourishing trade. Railroad machine shops located here.
Republican..............W. **2,339**
Triumph..................W. **2,340**

PAOLA, c. h., Miami Co., 1,811 p., on Missouri R., Fort Scott & Gulf Rd., at intersection of Osage division of Missouri, Kansas & Texas Rd., 45 m. S. by W. of Kansas City. It is the centre of a district of agricultural country.
Miami Republican......W. **2,341**
Western Spirit..........W. **2,342**

PARSONS, Labette Co., 2,500† p., at junction of Sedalia, Cherokee and Neosho divisions of Missouri, Kansas & Texas Rd., 49 m. from Fort Scott.
Sun.......................W. **2,343**

PEABODY, Marion Co.
Gazette.................. W. **2,344**

PEACE, Rice Co.
Rice Co. Gazette..........W. **2,345**

KANSAS.

PERU, c. h., Miami Co.
Chautauqua News.......W. 2,346

PLEASANTON, Linn Co., 1,200 p., on Missouri R., Fort Scott & Gulf Rd., 74 m. from Kansas City and 24 from Fort Scott. Centre of a thriving coal and stock trade.
Observer..................W. 2,347

RUSSELL, c. h., Russell Co.
Kansas Plainsman......W. 2,348
Russell Co. Record.......W. 2,349

SABETHA, Nemaha Co.
Advance..................W. 2,350

ST. MARY'S, Pottawatomie Co., 1,205 p., on Kansas Pacific Rd., 23 m. from Topeka and 48 from Junction City.
Times....................W. 2,351

SALINA, c. h., Saline Co., 2,500† p., on Smoky Hill, and on Kansas Pacific Rd., 185 m. W. by S. of Leavenworth, the same W. of Kansas City and 118 W. of the capital of the State.
Farmer's Advocate......W. 2,352
Herald...................W. 2,353
Saline Co. Journal......W. 2,354
Kansas Central Land Journal................M. 2,355

SEDAN, c. h., Chautauqua Co.
Chautauqua Journal....W. 2,356

SENECA, c. h., Nemaha Co., 1,000† p., on Nemaha r. and St. Joseph & Denver City Rd., 77 m. from St. Joseph. Surrounded by an agricultural and stock raising district.
Courier..................W. 2,357

SMITH CENTRE, c. h., Smith Co.
Smith Co. Pioneer.......W. 2,358

SOLOMON CITY, Saline Co., 581 p., on Solomon r., near its junction with Smoky Hill r., and on Kansas Pacific Rd., 104 m. W. of Topeka.
Solomon Reporter.......W. 2,359

STOCKTON, c. h., Rooks Co.
News......................W. 2,360

THAYER, Neosho Co., 500 p., on Leavenworth, Lawrence & Galveston Rd., 108 m. from Lawrence. Surrounded by coal fields.
Head Light..............W. 2,361

TOPEKA, Shawnee Co., State capital, 8,000† p., on Kansas r. and on Kansas Pacific Rd., and Atchison, Topeka & Santa Fe Rd., 29 m. from Lawrence and 60 W. of Kansas City. Engaged in milling and manufacturing and the centre of an active trade. Agricultural district surrounding. Coal mines and stone quarries in the vicinity. Several institutions of learning are located here.
Blade.....................D. 2,362
Commonwealth...........D. 2,363
"   ....W. 2,364
Times.....................D. 2,365
" ....W. 2,366
Kansas Democrat.......W. 2,367
Kansas Farmer.........W. 2,368
American Young Folks..W. 2,369

TROY, c. h., Doniphan Co., 1,100† p., on St. Joseph & Denver City Rd., at the intersection of the Atchison & Nebraska Rd., 14 m. W. of St. Joseph, Mo., and 16 from Atchison. Coal abounds in the vicinity.
Kansas Chief............W. 2,370

VALLEY FALLS, Jefferson Co., 1,000 p., on Delaware r., and Atchison, Topeka & Santa Fe Rd., at intersection of Kansas Central Rd., 25 m. from Topeka and 35 from Leavenworth. It has fine water power, which is employed in manufacturing. Surrounded by an agricultural region.
Kansas New Era........W. 2,371

WAMEGO, Pottawatomie Co., 1,000 p., on Kansas r. and Kansas Pacific Rd., 37 m. from Topeka. Engaged principally in agricultural pursuits.
Blade.....................W. 2,372

WASHINGTON, c. h., Washington Co., 400† p., on Mill Creek, 100 m. W. of Atchison and 100 S. W. of Hanover. An agricultural district.
Republican...............W. 2,373

WATERVILLE, Marshall Co., 1,584 p., on Central branch Union Pacific Rd., 100 m. W. of Atchison and 5 from Blue Rapids.
Telegraph................W. 2,374

WATHENA, Doniphan Co., 1,200† p., on Missouri r. and St. Joseph & Denver City Rd., 5 m. from St. Joseph.
Reporter..................W. 2,375

WELLINGTON, Sumner Co.
Sumner Co. Press........W. 2,376

WICHITA, c. h., Sedgwick Co., 3,700† p., at the mouth of Great Arkansas r., and on the Wichita branch of Atchison, Topeka & Santa Fe Rd., 160 m. S. W. of Topeka. Engaged in stock raising and wheat growing. An important shipping point for Texas cattle and grain.
Beacon....................W. 2,377
City Eagle ....W. 2,378

WINFIELD, c. h., Cowley Co., 960† p., on Walnut r., 43 m. S. E. of Wichita, 75 W. of Independence.
Courier...................W. 2,379
Cowley Co. Democrat....W. 2,380
Cowley Co. Telegram.....W. 2,381

WYANDOTTE, c. h., Wyandotte Co., 4,000 p., on Missouri r., near the mouth of Kansas r., and 3 m. above Kansas City, Mo. A place of active trade.
Gazette...................W. 2,382
Herald....................W. 2,383

KENTUCKY.

ASHLAND, Boyd Co., 3,500† p., on Ohio r., 150 m. from Cincinnati, 40 from Portsmouth. Terminus of Lexington & Big Sandy Rd. Engaged in the manufacture of pig iron, and coal and iron mining. Some forty furnaces are located within a radius of 10 miles.
Journal...................W. 2,384

AUGUSTA, Bracken Co., 2,000† p., on Ohio r., 45 m. above Cincinnati and 18 below Maysville. The centre of trade, and engaged in manufactures of various kinds. Engaged in tobacco growing.
Bracken Co. Chronicle...W. 2,385

BARDSTOWN, c. h., Nelson Co.
Nelson Co. Record.......W. 2,386

BLANDVILLE, c. h., Ballard Co.
Ballard News...........W. 2,387

BOWLING GREEN, c. h., Warren Co., 5,250 p., on Big Barren r., at the head of navigation, and on Louisville & Nashville Rd., 113 m. from Louisville.

KENTUCKY.

Democrat................W. **2,388**
Green River Pantagraph. W. **2,389**

BURKSVILLE, c. h., Cumberland Co.
Cumberland Courier.....W. **2,390**

BURLINGTON, c. h., Boone Co.
Boone Co. Recorder......W. **2,391**

CADIZ, c. h., Trigg Co., 1,200 p., on Little r., about 10 m. from its entrance into the Cumberland r., and about 75 S. of Henderson.
Trigg Co. Democrat......W. **2,392**

CALHOUN, c. h., McLean Co.
McLean Co. Progress....W. **2,393**

CARLISLE, c. h., Nicholas Co., 1,350† p., on Maysville & Lexington Rd., about 25 m. of Lexington. Considerable tobacco raised and bought and manufactured in the county.
Mercury..................W. **2,394**

CARROLLTON, c. h., Carroll Co., 1,800† p., on Ohio r., near the mouth of Kentucky r., 45 m. N. by W. of Frankfort, 82 from Cincinnati and 62 from Louisville. Shipping point for stock, tobacco and grain. Engaged in manufactures.
Democrat.................W. **2,395**

CARRSVILLE, Livingston Co.
Livingston Era...........W. **2,396**

CATLETTSBURG, c. h., Boyd Co., 1,250 p., on Ohio r., at the mouth of Big Sandy r., 150 m. E. by N. of Frankfort. This is the shipping point for the surplus timber, lumber and produce shipped annually from the Big Sandy Valley.
Central Methodist.......W. **2,397**
Sentinel..................W. **2,398**

COLUMBUS, Hickman Co., 1,574 p., on Mississippi r., about 15 m. below Cairo, Ill., at junction of Mobile & Ohio and St. Louis & Iron Mountain Rds., at an equal distance between Memphis and St. Louis. Engaged in lumber business and agriculture.
Messenger................W. **2,399**

COVINGTON, c. h., Kenton Co., 28,574† p., on Ohio r., opposite Cincinnati, with which it is connected by a bridge, and at terminus of Kentucky Central Rd. One of the largest manufacturing and commercial cities of the West.
Ticket.................T. W. **2,400**
" ....W. **2,401**
Commonwealth...........W. **2,402**
Journal..................W. **2,403**
Church News...........
Kentucky Presbyterian...M. **2,405**

CYNTHIANA, c. h., Harrison Co., 1,800 p., on South Licking r. and Kentucky Central Rd., 66 m. from Covington and 37 N. E. of Frankfort.
Democrat.................W. **2,406**
News.....................W. **2,407**

DANVILLE, c. h., Boyle Co., 3,000† p., 5 m. from Knoxville Branch Rd., and 42 S. of Frankfort. Is the educational centre of Kentucky; two large male and one female college. The Theological Seminary and Institution for the Deaf and Dumb are located here. It is surrounded by an agricultural district.
Kentucky Advocate......W. **2,408**

ELIZABETHTOWN, c. h., Hardin Co., 1,700† p., on Valley Creek and Louisville & Nashville Rd., at junction of Louisville, Paducah & Southwestern Rd., 42 m. from Louisville.
News.....................W. **2,409**

ELKTON, c. h., Todd Co.
Witness..................W. **2,410**

EMINENCE, Henry Co., 1,650† p., on Lexington branch of Louisville, Cincinnati & Lexington Rd., 40 m. from Louisville.
Constitutionalist. ....W. **2,411**

FALMOUTH, c. h., Pendleton Co., 1,000 p., on Licking r. and Kentucky Central Rd., 40 m. from Cincinnati.
Independent.............W. **2,412**

FLEMINGSBURGH, c. h., Fleming Co., 1,050 p., 17 m. S. of Ohio r. at Maysville.
Democrat................W. **2,413**
Rambler..................W. **2,414**

FRANKFORT, c. h., Franklin Co., State capital, 5,396 p., on Kentucky r., 60 m. from its mouth, on Louisville & Lexington Rd., 28 m. from Lexington and 65 from Louisville. Engaged in lumber, whisky and other manufactures. Has an extensive coal trade.
Kentucky Yeoman....T. W. **2,415**
" " ....W. **2,416**

FRANKLIN, c. h., Simpson Co., 1,808 p., on Louisville & Nashville Rd., 134 m. from Louisville and 85 from Nashville. Situated in an agricultural and stock raising region. Some manufacturing carried on.
Patriot...................W. **2,417**

FULTON, Fulton Co.
State Line News.........W. **2,418**

GEORGETOWN, c. h., Scott Co., 1,800 p., about 12 m. N. of Lexington and 18 E. of Frankfort. Engaged in agriculture and stock raising. College and seminary located here.
Times.....................W. **2,419**

GLASGOW, c. h., Barren Co., 2,050† p., near the line of Louisville & Nashville Rd., connected with it by a branch, 90 m. S. of Louisville. Large uantities of petroleum and tobacco shipped from this place. Extensive coal oil wells located two miles from Glasgow.
Times.....................W. **2,420**

GREENUP, c. h., Greenup Co., 1,100 p., on Ohio r., 10 m. from Ironton, 29 from Portsmouth and 235 from Cincinnati. In the centre of the mineral region of Kentucky. Extensively engaged in iron and coal mining
Independent.............W. **2,421**

HARRODSBURG, c. h., Mercer Co., 2,205 p., about 30 m. S. of Frankfort. Surrounded by an agricultural section.
Observer and Reporter...W. **2,422**

HARTFORD, c. h., Ohio Co.
Herald....................W. **2,423**

HAWESVILLE, c. h., Hancock Co.
Plaindealer..............W. **2,424**

HENDERSON, c. h., Henderson Co., 12,000† p., on Ohio r., and St. Louis, Evansville, Henderson & Nashville Rd., about 12 m. below Evansville, Ill., and 170 W. of Frankfort. Engaged in manufacturing tobacco, whisky and flour. A place of considerable river commerce.
Chronicle.
News.....................W. **2,426**
Reporter.................W. **2,427**

KENTUCKY.

HICKMAN, c. h., Fulton Co., 2,000† p., on Mississippi r., at terminus of Nashville & Northwestern Rd., 170 m. from Nashville and 35 below the mouth of Ohio r. A trade centre and shipping point.
Courier..................W. **2,428**

HOPKINSVILLE, c. h., Christian Co., 4,500† p., on St. Louis & S. E. Rd., 73 m. from Nashville, 204 S. W. of Frankfort. Engaged in the cultivation of tobacco and wheat.
Democrat..................W. **2,429**
Kentucky New Era......W. **2,430**

LA GRANGE, c. h., Oldham Co.
Oldham Era..................W. **2,431**

LANCASTER, c. h., Garrard Co., 1,340 p., on Richmond branch of Louisville, Nashville & Great Southern Rd., 113 m. from Louisville and about 30 S. of Lexington.
Letter..................W. **2,432**
Franklin Educator....B. M. **2,433**

LEBANON, Marion Co., 3,000 p., on Knoxville branch of Louisville & Nashville Rd., 67 m. from Louisville. Centre of a thriving trade and shipping point for several counties.
Standard..................W. **2,434**
Times and Kentuckian...W. **2,435**

LEXINGTON, c. h., Fayette Co., 22,700† p., on Kentucky Central Rd., at junction of three other railroads, 29 m. from Frankfort and 100 from Cincinnati. Located in the centre of the famous Blue Grass region of Kentucky, which is noted for the wealth and liberality of its people and the fertility of its soil. One of the finest stock-raising sections of the country. Considerable manufacturing done here.
Press..................D. **2,436**
" ....W. **2,437**
Dispatch..................T. W. **2,438**
" ....W. **2,439**
Kentucky Gazette........W. **2,440**
American Citizen........W. **2,441**
Apostolic Times..........W. **2,442**
Kentucky Live Stock Record..................W. **2,443**
Children's Friend.....S. M. **2,444**
Good Words for the Children..................S. M. **2,445**

LITCHFIELD, c. h., Grayson Co.
Grayson Journal........W. **2,446**

LONDON, c. h., Laurel Co.
Mountain Echo..........W. **2,447**

LOUISVILLE, c. h., Jefferson Co., 155,000† p., on Ohio r., 130 m. below Cincinnati. Extensively engaged in commerce and manufactures; nine railroads centre here.
Anzeiger..................D. **2,448**
" ....S. W. **2,449**
" ....W. **2,450**
Commercial..................D. **2,451**
" ....W. **2,452**
Courier-Journal..........D. **2,453**
" " ....W. **2,454**
Globe..................D. **2,455**
Ledger..................D. **2,456**
" ....W. **2,457**
Volksblatt..................D. **2,458**
" ....S. W. **2,459**
" ....W. **2,460**
American Medical Weekly W. **2,461**
Catholic Advocate........W. **2,462**
Christian Observer and Free Christ'n Commonwealth W. **2,463**
Farmer's Home Journal. W. **2,464**
Jeffersonian Democrat...W. **2,465**
Katholischer Glaubensbote W. **2,466**
National Granger.......W. **2,467**
Omnibus..................W. **2,468**
Price Current..................
Riverside Weekly.........W. **2,470**
Saturday Review.........W. **2,471**
Southern Agriculturist..W. **2,472**
Western Recorder........W. **2,473**
Manufacturers' and Merchants' Advertiser.....S. M. **2,474**
American Practitioner...M. **2,475**
Home and School..........M. **2,476**
Kentucky Freemason.....M. **2,477**
Richmond and Louisville Medical Journal........M. **2,478**

MADISONVILLE, c. h., Hopkins Co., 602 p., on Evansville, Henderson & Nashville Rd., 38 m. S. of Henderson.
South West..................W. **2,479**
Times..................W. **2,480**

MAYFIELD, c. h., Graves Co., 1,500† p., on Paducah & Memphis Rd., 30 m. from Paducah, 24 from Ohio, 26 from Mississippi and 25 from Tennessee rs. Surrounded by a region engaged in growing cotton, tobacco, wheat and oats.
Democrat..................W. **2,481**
Monitor..................W. **2,482**

MAYSVILLE, c. h., Mason Co., 5,000† p., on Ohio r., 61 m. above Cnicinnati, Maysville & Lexington Rd. A place of active trade. Heavy manufacturing interests and an important shipping point for the products of the surrounding country.
Bulletin..................W. **2,483**
Eagle..................W. **2,484**
Republican..................W. **2,485**
Methodist Times..........M. **2,486**

MIDWAY, Woodford Co.
Sun..................W. **2,487**

MOUNT OLIVET, c. h., Robertson Co.
Robertson Co. Tribune....W. **2,488**

MOUNT STERLING, c. h., Montgomery Co., 1,040 p., on Western division of Elizabethtown, Lexington & Big Sandy Rd., 33 m. E. of Lexington.
Kentucky Sentinel.......W. **2,489**

MURRAY, c. h., Calloway Co., 600† p., near Clarks r., 40 m. S. by E. of Paducah.
Gazette..................W. **2,490**

NEWPORT, Campbell Co., 2,000† p., on Ohio r., at the mouth of Licking r. and opposite Cincinnati. Engaged in manufacturing.
Leader..................W. **2,491**

NICHOLASVILLE, c. h., Jessamine Co.
Jessamine Journal.......W. **2,492**

OWENSBORO, c. h., Daviess Co., 8,500† p., on Ohio r. and Owensboro & Russellville Rd., 40 m. above Evansville, Ind., and 250 below Louisville. It has a steamboat landing and is the principal shipping point for the county.
Examiner..................W. **2,493**
Monitor..................W. **2,494**

OWENTON, c. h., Owen Co., 800† p., 77 m. from Louisville and 60 from Cincinnati, and about 10 from the Kentucky r.
Owen News..................W. **2,495**

OWINGSVILLE, c. h., Bath Co., 1,050

KENTUCKY.

p., about 5 m. from Licking r. and 30 S. of Maysville.
Bath Co. News...........W. **2,496**

PADUCAH, c. h., McCracken Co., 7,560 p., on Ohio r., 50 m. above Cairo, and just below the mouth of the Tennessee r., and at terminus of Paducah & Memphis and Elizabethtown & Paducah Rds. Engaged in manufacturing and has a large river trade.
News....................D. **2,497**
" ....W. **2,498**
Tribune.................D. **2,499**
Herald..................W. **2,500**
Sentinel................W. **2,501**
Baptist Herald..........M. **2,502**

PARIS, c. h., Bourbon Co., 5,000† p., on the Kentucky Central and Maysville & Lexington Rds., 80 m. from Covington. Fine stock market. Bourbon whisky largely manufactured.
Saturday Night..........W. **2,503**
True Kentuckian.........W. **2,504**
Western Citizen.........W. **2,505**

PRINCETON, c. h., Caldwell Co., 1,650 p., on Louisville, Paducah & Southwestern Rd., about 45 m. E. of Paducah. Surrounded by an extensive coal region and engaged in manufactures.
Banner..................W. **2,506**

RICHMOND, c. h., Madison Co., 3,000† p., on Richmond branch of Louisville & Nashville Rd., 125 m. E. of Louisville and 125 E. of Cincinnati, 50 S. by E. of Frankfort. In the centre of the celebrated Blue Grass region. An agricultural district. Large quantities of fine stock raised and shipped to the Southern and Eastern markets.
Kentucky Register.......W. **2,507**

RUSSELLVILLE, c. h., Logan Co., 4,000† p., on Louisville, Nashville & Great Southern Rd., 143 m. from Louisville.
Herald..................W. **2,508**

SCOTTSVILLE, c. h., Allen Co.
Argus...................W. **2,509**

SHELBYVILLE, c. h., Shelby Co., 3,000† p., on the Shelbyville division of Louisville, Cincinnati & Lexington Rd., 30 m. from Louisville. Seat of Shelby College.
Shelby Republican.......W. **2,510**
Shelby Sentinel..........W. **2,511**

SOMERSET, c. h., Pulaski Co.
Reporter................W. **2,512**
Children's Star..........S. M. **2,513**
Church Advocate..........S. M. **2,514**

STANFORD, c. h., Lincoln Co., 1,500† p., on Knoxville branch of Louisville, Nashville & Great Southern Rd., 104 m. from Louisville.
Interior Journal.........W. **2,515**

TAYLORSVILLE, c. h., Spencer Co., 500† p., on E. fork Salt r., about 32 m. S. E. of Louisville and on Cumberland & Ohio Rd. The river affords water power here.
Spencer Journal..........W. **2,516**

UNIONTOWN, Union Co.
Union Local..............W. **2,517**

VANCEBURG, c. h., Lewis Co., 1,545 p., on Ohio r., 40 m. above Maysville.
Kentuckian...............W. **2,518**

VERSAILLES, Woodford Co., 2,300† p., a few miles E. of Kentucky r., and about midway between Frankfort and Lexington. Engaged in manufacturing, and surrounded by an agricultural and stock-raising region.
Woodford Weekly..........W. **2,519**

WARSAW, c. h., Gallatin Co., 1,125 p., on Ohio r., 50 m. from Cincinnati and Louisville, 25 from Madison and 8 from Cincinnati & Louisville Rd. Corn, wheat, tobacco, &c., are shipped from here. The shipping point for Owen County.
Gallatin News.

WILLIAMSTOWN, c. h., Grant Co.
Sentinel.................W. **2,521**

WINCHESTER, c. h., Clark Co., 2,500† p., on the line of Lexington & Big Sandy Rd., about 20 m. E. of Lexington. There are two academies here. Principally engaged in stock-raising.
Clark Co. Democrat.......W. **2,522**

LOUISIANA.

ABBEVILLE, c. h., Vermillion Co., 545 p., on Bayou Vermillion, 55 m. W. by S. of Baton Rouge and 160 W. of New Orleans.
Meridional.

ALEXANDRIA, c. h., Rapides Co., 2,496† p., on Red r., about 130 m. N. W. of Baton Rouge. Engaged in the cultivation of sugar cane, corn and cotton.
Louisiana Democrat.......W. **2,524**
Rapides Gazette..........W. **2,525**

AMITE CITY, c. h., Tangipahoa Co., 900 p., on New Orleans, Jackson & Great Northern Rd., 68 m. from New Orleans.
Democrat.................W. **2,526**
Independent..............W. **2,527**

BASTROP, c. h., Morehouse Co., 500 p., about 60 m. N. by W. of Vicksburg, Miss. In a cotton-growing section.
Morehouse Clarion........W. **2,528**
Republican...............W. **2,529**

BATON ROUGE, East Baton Rouge Co., 6,498 p., on the Mississippi r., 129 m. above New Orleans. Extensive sugar and cotton plantations in the parish.
Advocate.................D. **2,530**
" ....W. **2,531**
Grand Era................W. **2,532**

BELLEVUE, c. h., Bossier Parish, 200 p., on Lake Bodeau, 20 m. N. E. of Shreveport. Cotton is the chief product.
Bossier Banner...........W. **2,533**
Bossier Sentinel.

CLINTON, c h., East Feliciana Co., 1,300† p., on Clinton and Port Hudson Rd., 32 m. from Baton Rouge. Centre of cotton trade.
Patriot Democrat.........W. **2,535**

COLUMBIA, c. h., Caldwell Co.
Herald...................W. **2,536**

CONVENT, c. h., St. James Co., 520† p., on Mississippi r., 65 m. above New Orleans. Sugar cane, corn and rice are the chief products.
St. James Sentinel.......W. **2,537**

COUSHATTA, Red River Parish, 650† p., on Red r., and about 60 m. S. E. of Shreveport.
Citizen..................W. **2,538**

COVINGTON, c. h., St. Tammany Co., 585 p., on Bayou Phalia, in the central part of the parish, and 60 m. E. of Baton Rouge.
St. Tammany Farmer...W. **2,539**

LOUISIANA.

DELTA, c. h., Madison Co., 400† p., on Vicksburg, Shreveport & Texas Rd., opposite Vicksburg. Engaged in the production of cotton.
Madison Journal........W. **2,540**

DONALDSONVILLE, c. h., Ascension Co., 2,218† p., on Mississippi r. and Louisiana division of the New Orleans, Mobile and Texas Rd., 63 m. above New Orleans. A shipping point.
Chief....................W. **2,541**

EDGAR, c. h., St. John Baptist Co., 1,000† p., on Mississippi r., about 40 m. above New Orleans. Engaged in the cultivation of sugar cane, rice and corn.
Meschacebe..............W. **2,542**

FARMERVILLE, c. h., Union Co., 416† p., near Bayou d' Arbonne, 30 m. N. W. of Monroe and 95 W. by N. of Vicksburg, Miss.
Union Record...........W. **2,543**

GRETNA, Jefferson Parish.
Jefferson Sentinel........W. **2,544**

HAHNVILLE, St. Charles Parish.
St. Charles Herald.......W. **2,545**

HARRISONBURG, c. h., Catahoula Parish, 350† p., on Ouchita r., about 100 m. N. by W. of Baton Rouge and about 30 N. W. of Natchez.
Catahoula News.........W. **2,546**

HOMER, c. h., Claiborne Co., 1,560 p., 200 m. N. W. of Baton Rouge and 50 from Shreveport. Engaged in the cultivation of cotton and corn.
Blackburn's Homer Iliad.

HOUMA, c. h., Terre Bonne Co., 593 p., 50 m. W. by S. of New Orleans. An agricultural district, which produces sugar, molasses, rice and corn.
Terrebonne Republican...W. **2,548**

JACKSON, East Feliciana Co., 934 p., about 30 m. N. of Baton Rouge and 10 W. of Clinton.
Feliciana Leader.

LAKE CHARLES, c. h., Calcasieu Co., 520† p., on Calcasieu r., in the S. W. part of the State.
Echo.....................W. **2,550**

LAKE PROVIDENCE, c. h., Carroll Parish.
True Republican........W. **2,551**

MANSFIELD, c. h., De Soto Co, 600† p., about 15 m. from Bayou Pierre and about 40 S. of Shreveport. Cotton and corn largely produced.
Reporter.................W. **2,552**

MARKSVILLE, c. h., Avoyelles Co., 600 p., about 3 m. from Red r. and about 30 W. of the Mississippi r. Cotton, corn, sugar cane and sweet potatoes are the chief productions.
Avoyelles Republican... W. **2,553**

MINDEN, Claiborne Co., 1,200 p., on Bayou Dorcheat, about 30 m. E. by N. of Shreveport.
Democrat................W. **2,554**

MONROE, c. h., Ouachita Co., 5,000† p., on Ouachita and Eldorado rs., at crossing of North Louisiana & Texas Rd., 75 m W. of Vicksburg, Miss. Steamboats make regular landings in passing up and down the river. An agricultural and cotton-growing country.

LOUISIANA.

Louisiana Intelligencer..W. **2,555**
Ouachita Telegraph......W. **2,556**

MORGAN CITY, Parish of St. Mary.
Attakapas Register.......W. **2,557**
Brashear News..........W. **2,558**

NATCHITOCHES, c. h., Natchitoches Co., 2,000 p., on Cane r., 80 m. S. E of Shreveport. It has a good steamboat landing, and is the centre of trade in corn and cotton.
People's Vindicator......W. **2,559**
Republican...............W. **2,560**

NEW IBERIA, c. h., Iberia Co., 2,000 p., near Bayou Teche and 150 m. W. of New Orleans. Engaged in sugar planting. Centre of cotton trade for surrounding country.
Iberia Progress..........W. **2,561**
Louisiana Sugar Bowl...W. **2,562**

NEW ORLEANS, c. h., Orleans Co., 191,000 p., on Mississippi r., 110 m. from its mouth. The centre of several railroads. The great commercial emporium of the South and largest cotton market in the world. The foreign and domestic commerce is immense. Steamboats make regular trips to all points on the Mississippi and its tributaries. The largest city in the South.
Bulletin..................D. **2,563**
Deutsche Zeitung.........D. **2,564**
" " ....W. **2,565**
Sonntags Blatt........Sund. **2,566**
L'Abeille.................D. **2,567**
" ....W. **2,568**
Picayune..................D. **2,569**
" ....W. **2,570**
Republican................D. **2,571**
" ....W. **2,572**
Times.....................D. **2,573**
" ....W. **2,574**
Price Current, Commercial Intelligencer and Shipping List.......S. W. **2,575**
Budget....................W. **2,576**
Christian Advocate.......W. **2,577**
Co-operative News.......W. **2,578**
Iron Preacher............W. **2,579**
Le Dimanche...........W. **2,580**
Louisiana State Register. W. **2,581**
Louisianian..............W. **2,582**
Morning Star and Catholic Messenger..........W. **2,583**
Orleanian................W. **2,584**
Our Home Journal and Rural Southland.......W. **2,585**
Over the Country.........W. **2,586**
Propagateur Catholique..W. **2,587**
Son of the Soil............W. **2,588**
South-Western Granger...W. **2,589**
South-Western Presbyterian.....................W. **2,590**
Familienfreund.......B. W. **2,591**
South-Western Advocate.................B. W. **2,592**
Kinderfreund.............M. **2,593**
Medical and Surgical Journal.................B. M. **2,594**

OPELOUSAS, c. h., St. Landry Parish, 2,000 p., 45 m. W. by S. of Baton Rouge and 175 W. by N. of New Orleans. Engaged in agriculture and stock raising; chief productions cotton, corn and sweet potatoes.
Courier..................W. **2,595**
Journal..................W. **2,596**

LOUISIANA.

PLAQUEMINE, c. h., Iberville Co., 1,460 p., on the Mississippi r., at the outlet of Plaquemine Bayou, 20 m. below Baton Rouge and 112 above New Orleans. Engaged in agriculture and lumber trade. Sugar and molasses very largely produced.
Iberville Republican......W. **2,597**

POINT COUPEE, c. h., Point Coupee Co.
Echo.

POINTE A LA HACHE, c. h., Plaquemine Co., 500 p., on Mississippi r., about 40 m. below New Orleans. Sugar, rice, oranges and garden products are raised here in abundance.
Observer..................W. **2,599**

PORT VINCENT, Livingston Co., 280 p., on Lake Ponchartrain, about 20 m. N. of New Orleans.
Triune..................W. **2,600**

RAYVILLE, c. h., Richland Co., 350 p., on Vicksburg, Shreveport & Texas Rd., 51 m. W. of Vicksburg, Miss.
Richland Beacon........W. **2,601**

ST. FRANCISVILLE, West Feliciana Co., 1,100 p., beautifully situated on an elevation one-half mile from Mississippi r., at Bayou Sara, 165 m. above New Orleans. The West Feliciana, Woodville & Bayou Sara Rd. runs past this place. A cotton shipping point.
Feliciana Ledger.........W. **2,602**

ST. JOSEPH, Tensas Parish, 500 p., on Mississippi r., 370 m. from New Orleans and 30 above Natchez, Miss. In a cotton district, and a shipping point for that staple.
North Louisiana Journal.W. **2,603**

ST. MARTINSVILLE, c. h., St. Martins Co., 750 p., on Bayou Teche, 125 m. W. of Baton Rouge.
Echo....................W. **2,604**
La Sentinelle des Attakapas..................W. **2,605**

ST. SOPHIE, Plaquemines Co.
Sentinel..................W. **2,606**

SHREVEPORT, c. h., Caddo Co., 7,500† p., on Red r. The initial point of the Southern Pacific Rd., 300 m. N. W. of Baton Rouge and 700 above New Orleans. Situated at the head of steamboat navigation, in the centre of cotton growing district. It has an extensive trade and river commerce.
Evening Telegram........D. **2,607**
South Western Telegram.W. **2,608**
Times....................D. **2,609**
" ....W. **2,610**

SPARTA, c. h., Bienville Co., 500† p., about 40 m. S. E. of Shreveport and 60 from Monroe. A trade centre for a very large section.
Rural Times.............W. **2,611**

THIBODAUX, c. h., La Fourche Co., 2,600† p., on Bayou La Fourche, 3 m. from Morgans, Louisiana & Texas Rd. and 55 from New Orleans. The largest town in the parish and the centre of a thriving trade. Surrounded by an agricultural and rice and sugar cane growing district.
Lafourche Republican...W. **2,612**
Sentinel.................W. **2,613**

VERMILIONVILLE, c. h., La Fayette Co., 2,000† p., on Vermilion Bayou, 180 m. W. by N. of New Orleans and 60 W. by S. of Baton Rouge.
La Fayette Advertiser....W. **2,614**
Louisiana Cotton Boll...W. **2,615**

VIDALIA, c. h., Concordia Co., 300 p., on Mississippi r., opposite Natchez, 147 m. above Baton Rouge. A large cotton growing district.
Concordia Eagle.........W. **2,616**

VIENNA, c. h., Lincoln Co.
Sentinel..................W. **2,617**

WASHINGTON, St. Landry Co.
Enterprise................W. **2,618**

WEST BATON ROUGE, West Baton Rouge Co., 300 p., on Mississippi r., opposite Baton Rouge. Engaged in the cultivation of sugar cane and cotton.
Sugar Planter............W. **2,619**

WINNSBOROUGH, c. h., Franklin Co., 540 p., on Turkey Creek, about 40 m. N. by W. of Natchez, Miss.
Franklin Sun............W. **2,620**

MAINE.

AUBURN, c. h., Androscoggin Co.
Maine Reformer.........W. **2,621**

AUGUSTA, c. h., Kennebec Co., State capital, 10,000 p., on Portland & Kennebec Rd. and on Kennebec r., at head of sloop navigation. Engaged in commerce and manufactures.
Kennebec Journal........D. **2,622**
" " ....W. **2,623**
Gospel Banner...........W. **2,624**
Maine Farmer..........W. **2,625**
Maine Standard.........W. **2,626**
Our Fireside Journal....W. **2,627**
" " " .....M. **2,628**
People's Literary Companion....................W. **2,629**
Vickery's Fireside Visitor.M. **2,630**

BANGOR, c. h., Penobscot Co., 19,380 p., on Penobscot r., at eastern terminus of Maine Central and western terminus of European & North American Rd. Engaged in the lumber trade, and the centre of supplies for a large portion of the central part of the State. Largest city in Maine excepting Portland.
Commercial..............D. **2,631**
Democrat................W. **2,632**
Whig and Courier........D. **2,633**
" " " ....W. **2,634**
Dirigo Rural............W. **2,635**
Northern Border..........W. **2,636**

BATH, c. h., Sagadahoc Co., 10,000† p., on Maine Central Rd. and Kennebec r., 12 m. from its mouth. Engaged in ship building and the lumber trade, and enjoys superior advantages for navigation. A line of steamers connect with Boston.
Times....................D. **2,637**
American Sentinel.......W. **2,638**

BELFAST, c. h., Waldo Co., 5,278 p., at head of Penobscot Bay, possessing a fine harbor, and is the terminus of the Belfast branch of Maine Central Rd., 132 m. from Portland. Engaged in ship building and foreign and domestic commerce.
Progressive Age..........W. **2,639**
Republican Journal......W. **2,640**

BIDDEFORD, York Co., 12,000† p., on

MAINE.

Saco r., opposite Saco, and on Portland, Saco & Portsmouth Rd., 15 m. from Portland. A thriving cotton-manufacturing and commercial city.
Maine Democrat........W. **2,641**
Union and Journal......W. **2,642**

BRIDGTON, Cumberland Co., 3,000† p., 40 m. from Portland, on Sebago Lake. A steamboat line, known as Sebago Lake Route, touches here. Engaged in woolen and other manufactures.
News....................W. **2,643**

BRUNSWICK, Cumberland Co., 3,000† p., on Androscoggin r. and Maine Central Rd., at the junction of branch railroads running to Bath, Lewiston and Farmington, 26 m. from Portland and Augusta. Engaged in lumber trade, ship building and manufacturing, and the centre of an increasing country trade. Seat of Bowdoin College and the Medical School of Maine.
Telegraph................W. **2,644**
Bowdoin Orient.......B. W. **2,645**

CALAIS, Washington Co., 6,500† p., at head of navigation on St. Croix r., and opposite St. Stephens, N. B. The market of all the up-river counties and of the Province of New Brunswick. Engaged in ship building and lumber trade.
Advertiser...............W. **2,646**
Times...................W. **2,647**

CAMDEN, Knox Co., 4,514 p., on Penobscot Bay, 8 m. N. of Rockland and 48 from Bangor. Ship building and the production of lime are carried on.
Herald.................W. **2,648**

CHASE'S MILLS, Androscoggin Co.
Chase's Chronicle........W. **2,649**

DEXTER, Penobscot Co., 3,100 p., the terminus of Dexter & Newport branch of Maine Central Rd., 30 m. N. W. of Bangor, is on a branch of Sebasticook r., which furnishes good water power for woolen mills and other manufactories located here.
Gazette..................W. **2,650**

DOVER, c. h., Piscataquis Co., 2,000 p., on Piscataquis r., 12 m. N. of Dexter.
Piscataquis Observer.....W. **2,651**

EASTPORT, Washington Co., 4,000 p., on Moose Island. Great fish depot. Engaged in foreign and domestic commerce.
Sentinel.................W. **2,652**

ELLSWORTH, c. h., Hancock Co., 6,000† p., on Union r., 26 m. from Bangor. Engaged in the lumber trade and ship building.
American................W. **2,653**

FAIRFIELD, Somerset Co., 850 p., on Kennebec r. and Maine Central Rd., at junction of Lewiston division, 83 m. from Portland. Engaged in manufacturing.
Chronicle................W. **2,654**

FARMINGTON, c. h., Franklin Co., 3,251 p., on Sandy r. The terminus of the Androscoggin Rd., 54 m. from Lewiston, 36 from Augusta and 93 from Portland. Surrounded by an agricultural district. Some manufactures carried on.
Chronicle...............W. **2,655**

FORT FAIRFIELD, Aroostook Co., 2,000† p., on south side of Aroostook r., 150 m. N. E. by N. of Bangor. Surrounded by an agricultural region. Terminus of N. B. Rd. Centre of a large lumber trade.
Aurora..................W. **2,656**

GARDINER, Kennebec Co., 5,000 p., on Maine Central Rd., and at the head of steamboat and ship navigation on the Kennebec r., 7 m. S. of Augusta. Has extensive water power and is largely engaged in manufactures, commerce and lumber trade.
Home Journal..........W. **2,657**
Kennebec Reporter.......W. **2,658**

HALLOWELL, Kennebec Co.
Eastern Examiner.......W. **2,659**

HOULTON, c. h., Aroostook Co., 2,850 p., on European & North American Rd., 190 m. N. E. of Augusta. Terminus of the New Brunswick & Canada Rd. Engaged in farming and manufactures.
Aroostook Pioneer.......W. **2,660**
Aroostook Times..........W. **2,661**

LEWISTON, Androscoggin Co., 20,000† p., on Androscoggin r., and Maine Central and Androscoggin Rds. **AUBURN,** c. h., on the opposite bank of the Androscoggin, is a city of over 10,000 p. The two cities are connected by 4 bridges, and are practically one city. The river furnishes water power, which is employed in manufacturing. Cotton, woolen, lumber, machinery and boots and shoes are the chief articles manufactured.
Evening Journal.........D. **2,662**
Journal.................W. **2,663**
Christian Mirror........W. **2,664**
Gazette..................W. **2,665**
Bates' Student...........M. **2,666**

MACHIAS, c. h., Washington Co., 2,525 p., on Machias r. Engaged in ship building and coast and lumber trade.
Republican..............W. **2,667**
Union...................W. **2,668**

MECHANIC FALLS, Androscoggin Co.
Androscoggin Herald....W. **2,669**

NORTH ANSON, Somerset Co., 1,745 p., on Kennebec r., 10 m. from Skowhegan. Engaged in agriculture, manufactures and the lumber trade.
Union Advocate..........W. **2,670**

NORWAY, Oxford Co., 1,958 p., 1 m. from Grand Trunk Rd. and 48 from Portland. Has an extensive water power and is engaged in manufactures.
Oxford Register..........W. **2,671**

PARIS, c. h., Oxford Co., 2,765 p., on the Grand Trunk Rd., 48 m. from Portland. The shire town of the county and centre of trade. Engaged in manufactures.
Oxford Democrat........W. **2,672**

PORTLAND, c. h., Cumberland Co., 31,418 p., on Casco Bay. Has one of the finest harbors on the coast. Connected by rail and steamer with all parts of Maine and the British Provinces. Two lines of railroad and a daily steamer connect with Boston, Mass. Has a new line of railroad reaching into New Hampshire, and is the winter port of the Allan line of steamers from Liverpool. Has a large trade from the West Indies.
Advertiser...............D. **2,673**
" ....W. **2,674**
Eastern Argus...........D. **2,675**
" " ....T. W. **2,676**
" " ....W. **2,677**

MAINE.

Press....................D. 2,678
Maine State Press.......W. 2,679
American Citizen........W. 2,680
Home and Fireside......W. 2,681
" " " .....M. 2,682
Sunday Times...........W. 2,683
Transcript..............W. 2,684
Zion's Advocate.........W. 2,685
Helping Hand...........M. 2,686
North East..............M. 2,687
Union Bible Teacher.....M. 2,688
Masonic Token..........Qr. 2,689

PRESQUE ISLE, Aroostook Co., 1,200† p., on Presque r., having a fine water power, 150 m. from Bangor, 42 from Houlton and 17 from steamboat navigation, on the St. Johns r. Terminus of New Brunswick Rd. Engaged in agriculture and the lumber trade.

North Star..............W. 2,690
Sunrise.................W. 2,691

ROCKLAND, c. h., Knox Co., 8,000 p., on Penobscot Bay, at eastern terminus of Knox & Lincoln Rd., 49 m. from Bath. Engaged in ship building and foreign and domestic commerce. Has extensive lime-stone quarries.

Courier..................W. 2,692
Free Press...............W. 2,693
Gazette..................W. 2,694
Opinion..................W. 2,695
Knox Co. Journal.......W. 2,696

SACO, York Co., 5,755 p., opposite Biddeford, on Saco r., 6 m. from its mouth. and on Portland, Saco & Portsmouth Rd., 13 m. S. W. of Portland. A large amount of capital is invested in lumber, cotton, iron and other manufactures.

York Co. Independent....W. 2,697

SKOWHEGAN, c. h., Somerset Co., 5,000† p., on Kennebec r., terminus of Skowhegan branch of Maine Central Rd., 30 m. from Augusta and 100 from Portland. Engaged in lumbering, farming and manufacturing.

Somerset Reporter.......W. 2,698

SPRINGVALE, York Co.

Reporter.................W. 2,699

WALDOBORRO, Lincoln Co.

Lincoln Co. News........W. 2,700

WATERVILLE, Kennebec Co., 4,852 p., on Kennebec r., 18 m. from Augusta, at junction of Maine Central and Portland & Kennebec Rds. Ticonic Falls furnish water power, which is partially developed.

Mail.....................W. 2,701

WISCASSET, c. h., Lincoln Co., 2,100† p., port of entry, with fine harbor, on Sheepscot r. and Knox & Lincoln Rd., 10 m. E. of Bath and 50 from Portland. Devoted to coast and fishing trade, ship building and manufacturing of lumber.

Eclectic Miscellany.
Seaside Oracle...........W. 2,703

MARYLAND.

ANNAPOLIS, c. h., Anne Arundel Co., State capital, 5,744 p., on Severn r., 2 m. from Chesapeake Bay and 30 from Baltimore. The Annapolis & Elk Ridge Rd. connects it with Baltimore & Washington Rd. The seat of St. John's College and of United States Naval Academy. The most important branch of business is its oyster trade.

Anne Arundel Advertiser.W. 2,704
Gazette..................W. 2,705
Maryland Republican and State Capital Advertiser W. 2,706
Maryland Ploughman & Chesapeake Granger....M. 2,707

BALTIMORE, Baltimore Co., 302,893† p., on Patapsco r., near Chesapeake Bay. The metropolis of Maryland, on Philadelphia, Wilmington & Baltimore Rd., and terminus of Baltimore & Ohio, Northern Central and Baltimore & Potomac Rds.. 98 m. from Philadelphia and 38 from Washington. Engaged in foreign and domestic commerce and manufactures. Great oyster and tobacco market; also celebrated for canned fruits and vegetables of all descriptions.

American and Commercial Advertiser..........D. 2,708
American................W. 2,709
Bee.......................D. 2,710
Deutsche Correspondent...D. 2,711
" " ..W. 2,712
Gazette...................D. 2,713
" ....W. 2,714
News......................D. 2,715
Sunday News.............W. 2,716
Sun........................D. 2,717
" ....W. 2,718
Wecker....................D. 2,719
" ....W. 2,720
Baltimorean..............W. 2,721
Bulletin...................W. 2,722
Catholic Mirror..........W. 2,723
Commercial...............W. 2,724
Die Biene von Baltimore.W. 2,725
Enquirer..................W. 2,726
Episcopal Methodist......W. 2,727
Jewish Chronicle.........W. 2,728
Journal of Commerce and Price Current..........W. 2,729
Katholische Volks-Zeitung W. 2,730
Methodist Protestant.....W. 2,731
Our Church Work.......W. 2,732
Presbyterian Weekly.....W. 2,733
Sunday Herald...........W. 2,734
Sunday Telegram.........W. 2,735
Underwriter..............W. 2,736
Conservative Churchman..................S. M. 2,737
Grocer and Provision Dealer................S. M. 2,738
American Engineer.......M. 2,739
American Farmer.......M. 2,740
American Journal of Dental Science.
Baptist Visitor.
Maryland Farmer.......M. 2,743
Missionary...............M. 2,744
North Baltimore..........M. 2,745
Phi Kappa Psi Monthly..M. 2,746
Physician and Surgeon...M. 2,747
Sunday School Companion M. 2,748

BEL AIR, c. h., Harford Co., 1,300† p., 22 m. from Baltimore and 9 from Philadelphia, Wilmington & Baltimore Rd. Centre of considerable trade and an agricultural region of country.

Aegis and Intelligencer...W. 2,749
Harford Democrat.......W. 2,750

BOONSBORO, Washington Co., 1,050 p., 10 m. from Hagerstown.

Odd Fellow..............W. 2,751

CAMBRIDGE, c. h., Dorchester Co., 1,983 p., on Choptank r., 20 m. from Chesa-

MARYLAND.

peake Bay. Terminus of Dorchester & Delaware Rd., and engaged in the oyster and lumber trade, also in agriculture and fruit growing.

Chronicle............W. **2,752**
Democrat and News.....W. **2,753**

CENTREVILLE, c. h., Queen Anne Co., 975 p., on Chester r., at terminus of Queen Anne & Kent Rd. Steamers connect with Baltimore.

Maryland Citizen.......W. **2,754**
Observer................W. **2,755**
Record..................W. **2,756**

CHESTERTOWN, c. h., Kent Co., 1,871 p., on Chester r., 30 m. from its entrance into Chesapeake Bay, terminus of steamboat navigation and about 45 m. N. E. of Annapolis. The Kent County Rd. terminates here. Washington College, founded in 1783, is located here. Engaged in agriculture. Has a large canning factory.

Conference Advocate....W. **2,757**
Kent News...............W. **2,758**
Transcript..............W. **2,759**

CRISFIELD, Somerset Co., 780 p., on Chesapeake Bay, at terminus of Eastern Shore Rd. Engaged in oyster fishery.

Leader..................W. **2,760**

CUMBERLAND, c. h., Alleghany Co., 13,000† p., on Potomac r. and Baltimore & Ohio Rd., at junction of Pittsburgh, Washington & Baltimore and Cumberland & Pennsylvania Rds., and on Chesapeake & Ohio Canal, 178 m. from Baltimore, 149 from Pittsburgh. Engaged in trade, coal mining.

Alleganian..............D. **2,761**
" ....W. **2,762**
News....................D. **2,763**
Times...................D. **2,764**
Mountain City Times....W. **2,765**
Civilian.................W. **2,766**

DENTON, c. h., Caroline Co., 675 p., on Choptank r., 65 m. from Annapolis and 25 S. W. of Dover, Del.

American Union........W. **2,767**
Journal.................W. **2,768**

EASTON, c. h., Talbot Co., 3,000† p., on Maryland & Delaware Rd., 109 m. from Philadelphia and 60 from Baltimore. Engaged in raising grain and fruit. Has a large mercantile trade. Some manufactures carried on. One of the most important business centres in the State.

Gazette..................W. **2,769**
Ledger...................W. **2,770**
Star.....................W. **2,771**

ELKTON, c. h., Cecil Co., 2,000† p., on Elk r., and Philadelphia, Wilmington & Baltimore Rd., 50 m. from Baltimore and 46 from Philadelphia. The Elk r. furnishes fine water power, which is employed in various manufactures.

Cecil Democrat..........W. **2,772**
Cecil Whig..............W. **2,773**

ELLICOTT CITY, c. h., Howard Co., 2,100† p., a narrow gorge on both sides of Patapsco r., which furnishes excellent water power. The Baltimore & Ohio Rd. connects it with Baltimore, 13 m. E.

American Progress......W. **2,774**
Times...................W. **2,775**

FEDERALSBURG, Dorchester Co., 800† p., on Nanticoke r., and Dorchester & Delaware Rd., 100 m. from Baltimore or Philadelphia.

Maryland Courier......W. **2,776**

FREDERICK, c. h., Frederick Co., 9,000 p., 44 m. from Washington and 61 from Baltimore. Connected with Baltimore & Ohio Rd. by a branch 3 m. long. Engaged in manufactures and a place of active trade.

Examiner................W. **2,777**
Maryland Union.........W. **2,778**
Republican Citizen.......W. **2,779**
Times....................W. **2,780**

FROSTBURGH, Alleghany Co.

Mining Journal..........W. **2,781**
National Relief Journal.W. **2,782**

HAGERSTOWN, c. h., Washington Co., 5,799 p., near Antietam r., at terminus of Cumberland Valley Rd., 86 m. from Baltimore. A place of active trade.

Free Press.
News......................D. **2,784**
" ....W. **2,785**
Twice a Week........S. W. **2,786**
Herald and Torch Light W. **2,787**
Mail......................W. **2,788**

HAVRE DE GRACE, Harford Co., 2,900† p., on Phila., Wilmington & Baltimore Rd., 36 m. N. E. of Baltimore and southern terminus of Tidewater Canal. It has a large coal and lumber trade. The Susquehanna r. empties into Chesapeake Bay at this point.

Havre Republican.......W. **2,789**

LEONARDTOWN, c. h., St. Mary's Co., 568 p., on Britton r., 55 m. S. of Annapolis.

St. Mary's Beacon.......W. **2,790**

LIBERTYTOWN, Frederick Co., 700† p., 12 m. from Frederick and 18 from Westminster. Surrounded by an agricultural district.

Banner of Liberty.......W. **2,791**

LONACONING, Alleghany Co.

George's Creek Press.....W. **2,792**

MECHANICSTOWN, Frederick Co., 850 p., on Western Maryland Rd., near Monocacy r., 20 m. from Frederick and 60 from Baltimore. Iron and copper mining carried on. Within a short distance of St. Mary's College and St. Joseph's Sisterhood.

Catoctin Clarion.........W. **2,793**

MIDDLETOWN, Frederick Co., 900† p., on the National Turnpike, 8 m. W. of Frederick, 53 from Baltimore and Washington. Surrounded by an agricultural district.

Valley Register..........W. **2,794**

NEWTOWN, Worcester Co., 1,700† p., on Pocomoke r., 150 m. from Philadelphia. Engaged in agriculture, fruit growing and the lumber trade.

Record and Gazette......W. **2,795**

OAKLAND, c. h., Garrett Co.

Garrett Co. Gazette......W. **2,796**
Garrett Co. Herald......W. **2,797**
Republican Ensign......W. **2,798**

PORT TOBACCO, c. h., Charles Co., 350 p., at the head of Port Tobacco Bay on Potomac r., 30 m. below Washington. Engaged in agriculture.

Maryland Independent..W. **2,799**
Times and Charles Co. Advertiser.............W. **2,800**

MARYLAND.

PRINCE FREDERICK, Calvert Co., 456 p., 35 m. S. of Annapolis, and about 5 W. of Chesapeake Bay and 6 E. of Patuxent r.
Calvert Journal..........W. **2,801**

PRINCESS ANNE, Somerset Co., 1,000† p., on Manokin r., 10 m. from its mouth, and the Eastern Shore Rd., 19 m. from Crisfield.
Somerset Herald.........W. **2,802**
True Marylander.........W. **2,803**

ROCKVILLE, c. h., Montgomery Co.
Montgomery Advocate....W. **2,804**

ST. MICHAELS, Talbot Co., 2,000† p., 12 m. from Easton, 60 from Baltimore and 6 from Maryland & Delaware Rd. Engaged in ship building, farming, fish and oyster trade.
Comet and Advertiser...W. **2,805**

SALISBURY, c. h., Wicomico Co., 2,500 p., on Wicomico r. and eastern Shore Rd., at junction of Wicomico and Pocomoke Rd., 95 m. S. E. of Annapolis. Engaged in wood and lumber trade and the production of grain.
Advertiser................W. **2,806**
Eastern Shoreman.......W. **2,807**

SMITHSBURG, Washington Co.
People's Guide...........W. **2,808**

SNOW HILL, c. h., Worcester Co., 1,195 p., on Pocomoke r., 20 m. from Pembroke Sound, at the head of steamboat navigation and terminus of Worcester Rd. Engaged in the lumber, oyster, fruit and trucking trade, supplying Philadelphia and New York markets.
Democratic Messenger...W. **2,809**
Worcester Co. Shield.....W. **2,810**

TOWNSONTOWN, c. h., Baltimore Co., 2,000 p., 7 m. N. of Baltimore and near the line of Northern Central Rd.
Baltimore Co. Herald...W. **2,811**
Baltimore Co. Union.....W. **2,812**
Maryland Journal.

UNION BRIDGE, Carroll Co.
People's Voice...........W. **2,814**

UPPER MARLBOROUGH, Prince George's Co., 492 p., 17 m. from Washington City, on the Baltimore & Potomac Rd. Patucent r. steamers within 2½ miles. Engaged principally in farming. Tobacco and grain the principal crops.
Marlborough Gazette.....W. **2,815**
Prince Georgian.........W. **2,816**

WESTMINSTER, c. h., Carroll Co., 3,000 p., on Western Maryland Rd., 58 m. from Annapolis and 29 from Baltimore. Engaged in manufactures.
American Sentinel.......W. **2,817**
Democratic Advocate.

WILLIAMSPORT, Washington Co., 1,500 p., on Potomac r., Chesapeake & Ohio Canal, 9 m. from Hagerstown. A place of considerable business importance.
Pilot.....................W. **2,819**

WOODBERRY, Baltimore Co.
News.....................W. **2,820**

MASSACHUSETTS.

ABINGTON, Plymouth Co.
Plymouth Co. Journal...W. **2,821**

MASSACHUSETTS.

AMESBURY, Essex Co., 5,581 p., on Amesbury branch of Eastern Rd., 27 m. N. of Salem, 42 from Boston and 5 from Newburyport. Devoted to woolen and carriage manufacturing.
Merrimac Journal.......W. **2,822**
Villager..................W. **2,823**

AMHERST, Hampshire Co., 4,035 p., on New London Northern Rd., 20 m. from Palmer, 23 from Springfield and 100 from Boston. Seat of Amherst College and State Agricultural College of Massachusetts.
Record...................W. **2,824**
Student...............B. W. **2,825**
Summerland Messenger..M. **2,826**

ANDOVER, Essex Co., 5,097† p., on Boston & Maine Rd., 26 m. from Boston and 3 from Lawrence.
Bibliotheca Sacra and Theological Eclectic.....Qr. **2,827**

ARLINGTON, Middlesex Co.
Advocate.................W. **2,828**

ASHLAND, Middlesex Co., 2,186 p., on Sudbury r. and Boston & Albany Rd., 25 m. from Boston, 20 from Worcester. Engaged in boot and shoe and cotton manufactures.
Advertiser................W. **2,829**

ATHOL, Worcester Co., 4,134† p., on Miller's r., and Vermont & Massachusetts Rd., at terminus of Athol & Enfield Rd., 33 m. W. of Fitchburg.
Transcript...............W. **2,830**
Worcester West Cronicle..W. **2,831**

ATTLEBORO, Bristol Co., 9,238† p., on Boston & Providence Rd., 12 m. from Providence and 31 from Boston. Manufacture of jewelry the principal business.
Advocate..................W. **2,832**
Chronicle.................W. **2,833**

AYER, Middlesex Co., 1,850† p., on the Boston & Fitchburg Rd., Worcester & Nashua Rd., Peterboro & Shirley and Lowell & Ayer Rds., 17 m. to Nashua, 28 to Worcester, 30 to Boston and 15 to Lowell, 12 to Fitchburg. Engaged in manufactures and a place of active trade.
Public Spirit..............W. **2,834**

BARNSTABLE, c. h., Barnstable Co., 5,000 p., on Barnstable Bay and Cape Cod Rd., 73 m. from Boston. Engaged in fishing and coast trade.
Patriot...................W. **2,835**

BARRE, Worcester Co., 2,500† p., on Ware r., about 23 m. N. E. of Palmer. Surrounded by an agricultural district. An active trade centre. Engaged in manufactures.
Gazette...................W. **2,836**

BEVERLY, Essex Co., 6,507 p., on Ann Harbor, 2 m. from Salem and 18 from Boston. Engaged in commerce, fishery and shoe manufacturing.
Citizen....................W. **2,837**

BOSTON, c. h., Suffolk Co., State capital, 341,919† p., on Massachusetts Bay. The commercial metropolis of New England, the "Athens of America." Second city in the United States in commercial importance. Engaged in trade with all parts of the world. Depot for New England manufactories of every nature.
Advertiser.................D. **2,838**

MASSACHUSETTS.

Advertiser.............S. W. 2,839
" ....W. 2,840
Evening Transcript.......D. 2,841
" " ......W. 2,842
Evening Traveller.........D. 2,843
" " .....S. W. 2,844
American Traveller......W. 2,845
Globe.....................D. 2,846
" ....W. 2,847
Herald....................D. 2,848
Sunday Herald...........W. 2,849
Hotel Reporter............D. 2,850
Journal..................D. 2,851
" ....S. W. 2,852
" ....W. 2,853
Post......................D. 2,854
Press and Post........S. W. 2,855
Statesman and Post......W. 2,856
Commercial and Shipping List................S. W. 2,857
American Architect and Building News.........W. 2,858
American Cabinet Maker.W. 2,859
American Canadian.....W. 2,860
American Justifier.
American Protestant.....W. 2,862
American Union.........W. 2,863
Apples of Gold...........W. 2,864
Banner of Light.........W. 2,865
Beacon and Dorchester News-Gatherer..........W. 2,866
Brighton Messenger......W. 2,867
Bunker Hill Times......W. 2,868
Charlestown Advertiser W. 2,869
Christian Register.......W. 2,870
Commercial Bulletin.....W. 2,871
Commonwealth..........W. 2,872
Congregationalist and Recorder..................W. 2,873
Courier...................W. 2,874
Cultivator................W. 2,875
Der Pionier..............W. 2,876
East Boston Advocate....W. 2,877
Golden Rule.............W. 2,878
Harry Hazel's Yankee Blade...................W. 2,879
Home Circle.............W. 2,880
Illustrated Police News...W. 2,881
Independent.............W. 2,882
Index.....................W. 2,883
Investigator..............W. 2,884
Journal of Commerce....W. 2,885
Littell's Living Age......W. 2,886
Massachusetts Ploughman...................W. 2,887
Medical and Surgical Journal..................W. 2,888
Messiah's Herald........W. 2,889
Myrtle....................W. 2,890
New England Journal...W. 2,891
New Age..................W. 2,892
New England Dial......W. 2,893
Dial Express List........Qr. 2,894
New England Farmer...W. 2,895
New England Journal of Education.............W. 2,896
New England Pythian Record..................W. 2,897
New England Rural Home...................W. 2,898
People's Ledger..........W. 2,899
Pilot......................W. 2,900
Railway and Steamship Chronicle..............W. 2,901
Roxbury Gazette.........W. 2,902
Saturday Evening Express ....W. 2,903
*Saturday Evening Gazette*W. 2,904

MASSACHUSETTS.

South Boston Enquirer..W. 2,905
Spiritual Scientist.......W. 2,906
Suffolk Co. Journal.....W. 2,907
Times.....................W. 2,908
Trade Record............W. 2,909
True Flag................W. 2,910
Universalist..............W. 2,911
Watchman................W. 2,912
Waverley Magazine..... W. 2,913
West Roxbury Gazette...W. 2,914
Woman's Journal.......W. 2,915
World's Crisis and Second Advent Messenger......W. 2,916
Youth's Companion......W. 2,917
Zion's Herald............W. 2,918
Dwight's Journal of Music...............B. W. 2,919
Temperance Album....S. M. 2,920
Young Pilgrim........S. M. 2,921
Advocate of Peace.........M. 2,922
American Naturalist.....M. 2,923
Angel of Peace...........M. 2,924
Atlantic Monthly........M. 2,925
Ballou's Monthly Magazine...................M. 2,926
Baptist Missionary Magazine....................M. 2,927
Child at Home...........M. 2,928
Christian..................M. 2,929
Christian Banner........M. 2,930
Contributor...............M. 2,931
Cottage Hearth...........M. 2,932
Day Spring...............M. 2,933
Dexter Smith's Paper.
Firemen's Monthly.......M. 2,935
Folio......................M. 2,936
Gleason's Monthly Companion.................M. 2,937
Gray's New England Real Estate Journal.........M. 2,938
Herald of the Age to Come.M. 2,939
Home Guardian..........M. 2,940
Howe's Musical Monthly.M.
Illustrated Home Guest...M. 2,942
Index.
Journal of Chemistry....M. 2,944
Laboratory...............M. 2,945
Literary World..........M.
Little Christian..........M. 2,947
Little Wanderer's Advocate....................M. 2,948
Macedonian and Helping Hand....................M. 2,949
Missionary Herald.......M. 2,950
Musician and Artist......M. 2,951
New England Insurance Gazette.................M. 2,952
New England Medical Gazette...................M. 2,953
Nursery...................M. 2,954
Old Curiosity Shop.
Our Dumb Animals......M. 2,956
Pastor and People........M. 2,957
Patent Star and Journal of Progressive Industry.M. 2,958
Pathfinder Railway Guide.M. 2,959
Scientific Farmer.........M. 2,960
Sunday School Helper....M. 2,961
Times of Refreshing......M. 2,962
Unitarian Review and Religious Magazine.
Wide Awake.............M. 2,964
Young Crusader.........M. 2,965
Ætna ....Qr. 2,966
American Journal of Numismatics..............Qr. 2,967
American Law Review.
Congregational Quarterly.Qr. 2,969

New England Historical and Genealogical Register....Qr. **2,970**
North American Review.
United States Official Postal Guide....Qr. **2,972**
Universalist Quarterly...Qr. **2,973**

BRIDGEWATER, Plymouth Co., 3,950 p., on Old Colony & Newport Rd., 27 m. from Boston. Engaged in manufacturing cotton gins, boots and shoes, and other articles. Location of a State Normal School and several educational institutions.
Banner....W. **2,974**

BROCKTON, Plymouth Co., 10,576† p., on Old Colony & Newport Rd., 20 m. from Boston. Engaged in manufacture of boots and shoes. Centre of a local trade.
Gazette....W. **2,975**

BROOKFIELD, Worcester Co.
News....W. **2,976**

BROOKLINE, Norfolk Co., 7,500† p., on N. Y. & N. E. branch of Boston & Albany Rd., 4 m. from Boston. A place of residence for persons doing business in Boston.
Chronicle....W. **2,977**

CAMBRIDGE, Middlesex Co., 50,000† p., on Charles r., connected with Boston by two bridges. Engaged in various manufactures. Seat of Harvard College.
Chronicle....W. **2,978**
Press....W. **2,979**
Harvard Advocate....W. **2,980**
Psyche....M. **2,981**

CAMBRIDGEPORT, Middlesex Co.
Vox Humana....W. **2,982**

CHATHAM, Barnstable Co., 2,411 p., at S. E. extremity of Cape Cod, 80 m. S. E. of Boston. Cod and mackerel fishing are carried on, but the people are more largely engaged in the coasting and foreign carrying trade. The harbor on the ocean side of the town is subject to constant changes, caused by the action of the waves, especially during easterly storms accompanied by high tides.
Monitor....W. **2,983**

CHELSEA, Suffolk Co., 22,000† p., on Eastern Rd., 3 m. from Boston. An important suburb of Boston, and residence of a large number doing business there. Connected with Boston by a ferry, and to Charlestown and East Boston by bridges.
Public....W. **2,984**
Record....W. **2,985**
Telegraph and Pioneer....W. **2,986**

CLINTON, Worcester Co., 6,780 p., on Nashua r., at intersection of Nashua & Worcester and Boston, Clinton & Fitchburg Rds., 45 m. from Boston and 16 from Worcester. Engaged in manufactures.
Courant....W. **2,987**

CONCORD, c. h., Middlesex Co.
Freeman....W. **2,988**

DANVERS, Essex Co., 6,500 p., on a branch of Boston & Maine Rd., about 5 m. from Salem and 16 from Boston. Engaged in shoe and leather manufacturing.
Advance....W. **2,989**
Mirror....W. **2,990**
Monitor....W. **2,991**

DEDHAM, c. h., Norfolk Co., 7,342 p., on Charles r., at terminus of Dedham Branch Rd., 10 m. from Boston. Boston & Providence and Boston, Hartford & Erie Rds. pass through the town. Centre of an agricultural district. Engaged in the manufacture of woolen goods, brushes, furniture, piano fortes and iron wares.
Transcript....W. **2,992**

EAST HAMPTON, Hampshire Co.
Leader....W. **2,993**

EDGARTOWN, c. h., Duke's Co., 1,516 p., 30 m. from New Bedford. Engaged in the whale fishery and domestic commerce. The famous Martha's Vineyard camp meeting held annually at this place in August.
Vineyard Gazette....W. **2,994**

ESSEX, Essex Co.
Enterprise....W. **2,995**

EVERETT, Middlesex Co., 3,653† p., on Eastern Rd., 3 m. from Boston.
Free Press....W. **2,996**

FALL RIVER, 45,360† p., on Old Colony & Newport Rd. and Taunton r., near its entrance to Mt. Hope Bay. Has a good harbor, and is one of the largest cotton manufacturing cities in New England. The commerce, both foreign and domestic, is quite extensive. A daily line of steamers run between this point and New York city. Contains a granite quarry.
Border City Herald....D. **2,997**
Evening News....D. **2,998**
News....W. **2,999**
Labor Journal....W. **3,000**
La Republique....W. **3,001**
Le Protecteur Canadien..W. **3,002**
Monitor....W. **3,003**
Saturday Morning Bulletin....W. **3,004**

FITCHBURG, Worcester Co., 12,300† p., at junction of five important Rds., 50 m. from Boston and 25 N. of Worcester. The manufactures of Fitchburg are extensive, the principal being chairs, engines, machinery, cotton and woolen goods, paper, mowing machines, edge tools, &c. Most important place in North Worcester Co.
Press....D. **3,005**
Reveille....W. **3,006**
Sentinel....D. **3,007**
"....W. **3,008**

FOXBORO, Norfolk Co.
Journal....W. **3,009**
Times....W. **3,010**

FRANKLIN, Norfolk Co., 2,986† p., on N. Y. & N. E. Rd., 27 m. from Boston.
Register and Norfolk Co. Journal....W. **3,011**

GARDNER, Worcester Co., 3,730† p., on Vt. & Mass. and Worcester & Gardner Rds., 15 m. from Fitchburg and 27 from Worcester. Engaged in the manufacture of chairs.
News....W. **3,012**

GEORGETOWN, Essex Co.
Advocate....W. **3,013**

GLOUCESTER, Essex Co., 17,000 p., on Cape Ann and branch of Eastern Rd., 32 m. from Boston. The largest fishing port in the United States. The foreign and domestic commerce is quite extensive.
Cape Ann Advertiser....W. **3,014**
Telegraph....W. **3,015**

GRAFTON, Worcester Co.
Herald....W. **3,016**

MASSACHUSETTS.

GREAT BARRINGTON, Berkshire Co., 4,320 p., on Housatonic Rd., near junction of State Line branch, 85 m. from Bridgeport, Ct. Engaged in various manufactures. It has quarries of variegated marble.
Berkshire Courier......W. **3,017**

GREENFIELD, c. h., Franklin Co., 3,589 p., on Connecticut r., Vermont and Massachusetts, Troy & Greenfield Rds., 36 m. from Springfield. Engaged in manufactures, and agriculture, the centre of trade for a large territory.
Franklin Co. Times......W. **3,018**
Gazette and Courier......W. **3,019**

HARWICH, Barnstable Co., 3,451† p., on Cape Cod Rd., 12 m. from Barnstable.
Independent............W. **3,020**

HAVERHILL, Essex Co., 14,628† p., on Merrimac r. and the Boston & Maine Rd., 32 m. from Boston. Engaged in various manufactures, of which boots and shoes are the principal.
Bulletin..................D. **3,021**
" ....W. **3,022**
Publisher.............T. W. **3,023**
Gazette................S. W. **3,024**
Essex Banner...........W. **3,025**

HINGHAM, Plymouth Co., 4,654† p., on S. E. side of Boston Harbor, and on South Shore Rd., 17 m. from Boston. A summer resort.
Journal and South Shore Advertiser.............W. **3,026**

HOLLISTON, Middlesex Co.
Transcript..............W. **3,027**

HOLYOKE, Hampden Co., 16,260† p., on Connecticut r., and Connecticut R. Rd., 8 m. from Springfield. Engaged in manufacturing, the falls in the river affording unlimited power.
Independent Journal....W. **3,028**
New England Staaten Zeitung..................W. **3,029**
Transcript...............W. **3,030**

HOPKINTON, Middlesex Co.
News.....................W. **3,031**

HUDSON, Middlesex Co., 2,500 p., on Marlboro branch of Fitchburg Rd., and about 27 m. W. of Boston. Engaged principally in the manufacture of shoes.
Pioneer.................W. **3,032**
Reformer..............S. M. **3,033**

HYDE PARK, Norfolk Co.
Norfolk Co. Gazette......W. **3,034**

IPSWICH, Essex Co., 3,800† p., on Eastern Rd. and Ipswich r., 27 m. from Boston. Engaged in the manufacturing of woolen and cotton hosiery.
Chronicle................W. **3,035**

LAWRENCE, Essex Co., 34,907† p., on Merrimac r., the Boston & Maine, Manchester & Lawrence and Lowell & Lawrence Rds., 26 m. from Boston, having immense water power, and one of the largest cotton and woolen manufacturing cities in the United States.
American................D. **3,036**
" ....W. **3,037**
Eagle....................D. **3,038**
Essex Eagle..............W. **3,039**
Journal and Citizen.....W. **3,040**
Sentinel.................W. **3,041**
New England Odd Fellow.M. **3,042**

MASSACHUSETTS.

LEE, Berkshire Co., 3,866 p., on Housatonic Rd., 50 m. from Albany and Springfield and 99 from Bridgeport. Engaged in various manufactures and quarrying marble.
Valley Gleaner and Berkshire Farmer's Advocate.................W. **3,043**

LEOMINSTER, Worcester Co.
Enterprise..............W. **3,044**

LEXINGTON, Middlesex Co., 2,277 p., Lexington & West Cambridge Branch Rd., 11 m. N. W. of Boston.
Minute Man..............W. **3,045**

LOWELL, Middlesex Co., 49,688† p., on Merrimac r., at the junction of six railroads. The river furnishes immense power, which is used in the mills and manufactories, which gives employment to thousands of operatives. The largest cotton manufacturing city of the United States.
Citizen and News.........D. **3,046**
American Citizen.........W. **3,047**
Courier..................D. **3,048**
Journal..................W. **3,049**
Times....................D. **3,050**
" ....W. **3,051**
Vox Populi..............W. **3,052**
Saturday Vox Populi....W. **3,053**

LYNN, Essex Co., 28,233 p., on Massachusetts Bay and Eastern Rd., 11 m. from Boston. The great centre of shoe manufacturing of the United States. Annual sales, $20,000,000. Rapidly increasing in wealth and population, the valuation having doubled during last seven years.
Reporter..............S. W. **3,054**
City Item...............W. **3,055**
Record..................W. **3,056**
Transcript...............W. **3,057**
Everett Monthly.........W. **3,058**

MALDEN, Middlesex Co., 10,000† p., 5 m. from Boston, on Boston & Maine Rd., and Eastern Saugus branch. Several large manufactories are located here.
Mirror..................W. **3,059**

MANCHESTER, Essex Co.
Beetle and Wedge.......M. **3,060**

MANSFIELD, Bristol Co.
News.....................W. **3,061**

MARBLEHEAD, Essex Co., 8,000 p., on Marblehead branch of Eastern Rd., about 4 m. S. E. of Salem. Shoe manufacturing and fishing. Centre of a large trade in shoes.
Messenger................W. **3,062**

MARLBORO, Middlesex Co., 8,446† p., on Boston, Clinton & Fitchburg Rd., 32 m. from Boston. Engaged in shoe manufacturing.
Mirror-Journal..........W. **3,063**

MAYNARD, Middlesex Co.
Journal..................W. **3,064**

MEDFORD, Middlesex Co., 6,627† p., on Mystic r. and Boston & Maine and Boston & Lowell Rds., 5 m. from Boston. Some manufacturing done here.
Chronicle................W. **3,065**

MEDWAY, Norfolk Co., 4,242† p., on Woonsocket division of Boston, Hartford & Erie Rd., 25 m. from Boston and 13 from Woonsocket.

MASSACHUSETTS.

Gazette..................W. **3,066**
Journal.................W. **3,067**

MELROSE, Middlesex Co., 4,000† p., on Boston & Maine Rd., 7 m. from Boston.
Journal.................W. **3,068**
Record..................W. **3,069**

MIDDLEBOROUGH, Plymouth Co., 5,500† p., on Old Colony & Newport Rd., at junction of Cape Cod Branch Rd., 34 m. from Boston. Engaged in manufactures.
Gazette..................W. **3,070**

MILFORD, Worcester Co., 9,890 p., on Charles r. and Milford branch Boston & Albany Rd., 35 m. from Boston and 14 from South Framingham. Engaged in boot and shoe manufacturing. Several tanneries here.
Journal.................W. **3,071**

NANTUCKET, c. h., Nantucket Co., 3,200† p., on Nantucket Island. Engaged in whale, cod and mackerel fishery and coast trade. A summer resort.
Island Review............W. **3,072**
Inquirer and Mirror.....W. **3,073**

NATICK, Middlesex Co., 7,500† p., on Boston & Albany Rd., 17 m. from Boston. Engaged in the manufacture of boots and shoes.
Bulletin..................W. **3,074**

NEEDHAM, Norfolk Co.
Chronicle and Wellesley Advertiser............ W. **3,075**

NEW BEDFORD, Bristol Co., 25,876† p., on Buzzard's Bay and New Bedford Rd., about 55 m. S. of Boston. It is more extensively engaged in whale fishery than all the rest of the world combined. Engaged in manufactures and commerce.
Evening Standard........D. **3,076**
Republican Standard....W. **3,077**
Mercury..................D. **3,078**
" ....W. **3,079**
Whalemen's Shipping List....................W. **3,080**

NEWBURYPORT, Essex Co., 12,976† p., on Merrimac r. and Eastern Rd., 36 m. from Boston. Engaged in commerce and fishery. The cotton and woolen manufacturing is also important.
Herald....................D. **3,081**
" ....S. W. **3,082**
Merrimac Valley Register W. **3,083**

NEWTON, Middlesex Co., 18,000† p., comprising ten villages, on the Boston & Albany Rd., 7 m. from Boston. Engaged in paper and other manufactures. It is the residence of a large number of persons doing business in Boston.
Journal...................W. **3,084**
Republican...............W. **3,085**

NORTH ADAMS, Berkshire Co., 15,000† p., on Troy & Boston and Pittsfield & North Adams Rds. Engaged in cotton, woolen, shoes and other manufactures. The west entrance of Hoosac tunnel is 1 m. from the town centre.
Adams Transcript.......W. **3,086**
Hoosac Valley News.....W. **3,087**

NORTHAMPTON, c. h., Hampshire Co., 11,000† p., on Connecticut r. and Connecticut R. Rd., at the junction of New Haven & Northampton Rd., 17 m. from Springfield. A farming district. There are several manufactories here.
Hampshire Gazette......W. **3,088**

MASSACHUSETTS.

Journal and Free Press..W. **3,089**
Le Jean Baptiste.........W. **3,090**

NORTHBORO, Worcester Co.
Farmer...................W. **3,091**

NORTH EASTON, Bristol Co., 2,500 p., on Old Colony & Newport Rd., 24 m. from Boston. Tributaries of the Taunton r. flow through the township, furnishing an abundant motive power, which is employed in various manufactures.
Easton Journal..........W. **3,092**

PALMER, Hampden Co., 4,553† p., at junction of Boston & Albany with New London, Northern, Ware R. Rds., 16 m. from Springfield. Engaged in manufacturing.
Journal..................W. **3,093**

PEABODY, Essex Co., 8,060† p., about 5 m. from Salem and near the line of Salem & Lowell Rd. Engaged in tanning and shoe manufacturing.
Press.....................W. **3,094**

PITTSFIELD, c. h., Berkshire Co., 12,278† p., on Boston & Albany Rd., and at junction of the Housatonic and Pittsfield & North Adams Rds., 53 m. from Springfield and 50 from Albany. Engaged in manufacturing and the centre of a large trade.
Berkshire Co. Eagle......W. **3,095**
Sun.......................W. **3,096**

PLYMOUTH, c. h., Plymouth Co., 6,328† p., on Plymouth Bay and E. branch of Old Colony Rd., 37 m. from Boston. Engaged in manufacturing, commerce and fishery.
Old Colony Memorial....W. **3,097**
Press.....................W. **3,098**

PRINCETON, Worcester Co.
Word......................M. **3,099**

PROVINCETOWN, Barnstable Co., 4,400† p., on northern extremity of Cape Cod, 120 m. from Boston. Terminus of Old Colony Rd. Has the most commodious and accessible harbor on the Atlantic coast. Engaged in mackerel, cod and whale fisheries and ship building. Is considerable of a summer resort. Celebrated as the first landing place of the pilgrims in America.
Advocate.................W. **3,100**

QUINCY, Norfolk Co., 7,442 p., on Quincy Bay and r. and Old Colony Rd., 8 m. from Boston. Celebrated for its granite quarries, from which large quantities are shipped to all parts of the United States.
Patriot...................W. **3,101**

RANDOLPH, Norfolk Co., 6,000 p., on Old Colony Rd., 12 m. S. of Boston. Engaged in the manufacture of boots and shoes.
Norfolk Co. Register.....W. **3,102**

READING, Middlesex Co.
Chronicle.................W. **3,103**
Reporter..................W. **3,104**

ROCKLAND, Plymouth Co., 4,278† p., on Old Colony Rd., 18 m. from Boston. Engaged in the manufacture of boots and shoes. One of the most prominent shoe manufacturing towns in the State.
Standard..................W. **3,105**

ROCKPORT, Essex Co.
Gleaner...................M. **3,106**

SALEM, c. h., 25,958† p., on Eastern Rd., 16 m. from Boston. One of the oldest cities in New England, having a fine and well-protected harbor.

MASSACHUSETTS.

Gazette...... ....S. W. **3,107**
Essex Co. Mercury.......W. **3,108**
Register..............S. W. **3,109**
Observer ....W. **3,110**
Post.......................W. **3,111**
Fireside Favorite.........M. **3,112**

SANDWICH, Barnstable Co., 3,417† p., on an arm of Cape Cod Bay and on Cape Cod Rd., 56 m. S. E. of Boston. Engaged in glass and other manufactures.
Seaside Press............W. **3,113**

SHREWSBURY, Worcester Co.
News.....................W. **3,114**

SOMERVILLE, Middlesex Co., 21,000† p., a suburb of Boston, on Mystic r., intersected by the Eastern, Boston & Maine, Boston & Lowell and Fitchburg Rds., 2 m. from Boston.
Journal..................W. **3,115**

SOUTH ABINGTON, Plymouth Co.
Times ....W. **3,116**

SOUTH ACTON, Middlesex Co.
Acton Patriot............W. **3,117**

SOUTH ADAMS, Berkshire Co.
Saturday Freeman......W. **3,118**

SOUTHBORO, Worcester Co.
Press.....................W. **3,119**

SOUTHBRIDGE, Worcester Co., 5,721† p., on Quinnebaug r. and a branch of Boston, Hartford & Erie Rd., 70 m. from Boston and 20 S. W. from Worcester. Engaged in manufacturing. Business centre for most of the towns in the S. part of Worcester County.
Journal.................W. **3,120**
Temple Star..............M. **3,121**

SOUTH FRAMINGHAM, Middlesex Co.
Framingham Gazette and Enterprise.............W. **3,122**

SPENCER, Worcester Co.
Sun........................W. **3,123**

SPRINGFIELD, c. h., Hampden Co., 26,703 p., on Connecticut r., at the junction of Boston & Albany, Hartford & New Haven and Connecticut R. Rds., and largest city in western Massachusetts. Manufactures various and extensive.
Republican...............D. **3,124**
" ....W. **3,125**
Union......................D. **3,126**
" ....W. **3,127**
Herald of Life...........W. **3,128**
New England Homestead.W. **3,129**
Sunday Telegram........W. **3,130**

STONEHAM, Middlesex Co., 4,984† p., on Stoneham branch of Boston & Lowell Rd., 12 m. N. of Boston. Extensive shoe and leather manufactories here.
Independent..............W. **3,131**
National Sovereign.......W. **3,132**
Sentinel...................W. **3,133**

STOUGHTON, Norfolk Co., 4,841† p., on Old Colony and a branch of Boston & Providence Rd., 19 m. from Boston. Engaged in boot and shoe making.
Sentinel...................W. **3,134**

SWAMPSCOTT, Essex Co.
Enterprise...............W. **3,135**

TAUNTON, c. h., Bristol Co., 18,629 p., on Taunton r. and Old Colony Rd., 34 m. from Boston and at junction of Taunton & New Bedford Rd. Engaged in manufacturing locomotives and other machinery.

MASSACHUSETTS.

Gazette...................D. **3,136**
" ....W. **3,137**
Bristol Co. Republican...W. **3,138**

TURNER'S FALLS, Franklin Co., 2,500 p., on Connecticut r. and a branch of the Vermont & Massachusetts Rd., 3 m. from Greenfield. The river affords power, which is employed in manufacturing.
Reporter..................W. **3,139**

UXBRIDGE, Worcester Co.
Worcester South Compendium...................W. **3,140**

WAKEFIELD, Middlesex Co., 5,649† p., on Boston & Maine Rd., 10 m. from Boston. Engaged in the manufacture of iron castings, rattan goods, paper collars and shoes.
Citizen and Banner......W. **3,141**
Local News...............W. **3,142**

WALPOLE, Norfolk Co., 2,137 p., on Boston, Hartford & Erie Rd., at intersection of Framingham & Mansfield division of Boston, Clinton & Fitchburg Rd., 19 m. from Boston.
Standard.................W. **3,143**

WALTHAM, Middlesex Co., 9,065 p., on Charles r. and Fitchburg Rd., 9 m. from Boston. Engaged in manufacturing. Waltham watches are made here.
Free Press ....W. **3,144**
Sentinel ....W. **3,145**

WARE, Hampshire Co., 4,300 p., on Ware R. Rd., 10 m. from Palmer and about 21 from Springfield. Engaged in woolen and other manufactures.
Gazette...................W. **3,146**
Standard..................W. **3,147**

WAREHAM, Plymouth Co., 3,000 p., on Buzzard's Bay and Cape Cod Rd., 48 m. from Boston.
News.....................W. **3,148**

WEBSTER, Worcester Co., 5,059† p., on Norwich & Worcester Rd., 15 m. from Worcester.
Times....................W. **3,149**
Evenings at Home.

WESTBOROUGH, Worcester Co., 5,141† p., on Boston & Albany Rd., 32 m. from Boston. Engaged in manufacturing boots and shoes and various other articles. State Reform School for boys located here.
Chronotype...............W. **3,151**

WESTFIELD, Hampden Co., 8,429† p., on Westfield r. and Boston & Albany, New Haven & Northampton, Holyoke & Westfield Rds., 10 m. from Springfield. Engaged in manufacturing steam heaters, whips and cigars.
Western Hampden Times and News Letter.......W. **3,152**

WEYMOUTH, Norfolk Co., 10,000† p., on South Shore Rd. Comprises several villages, engaged in various manufactures.
Gazette and Braintree Reporter..............W. **3,153**

WILLIAMSTOWN, Berkshire Co., 3,679† p., on Troy & Boston Rd., 20 m. N. of Pittsfield, 40 from Troy and in the N. W. extremity of the State. The manufactures comprise woolen goods, boots and shoes, carriages, hardware, etc. Seat of Williams College, founded in 1793, one of the most renowned institutions of learning in the country.
Williams Athenæum.B. W. **3,154**

MASSACHUSETTS.

WINCHENDON, Worcester Co., 3,776† p., on Cheshire Rd., at junction of Monadnock Rd. Miller's r. crosses the town and affords water power, which is partially developed for manufacturing purposes.
Journal................W. **3,155**

WOBURN, Middlesex Co., 10,000† p., on the Woburn branch of the Boston & Lowell Rd., 10 m. from Boston. Engaged in leather and other manufactures.
Advertiser..............W. **3,156**
Journal................W. **3,157**

WORCESTER, c. h., Worcester Co., 50,000† p., in the centre of the State, at junction of six important railroads and 40 m. from Boston. Manufactories of various kinds located here.
Evening Gazette..........D. **3,158**
Aegis and Gazette........W. **3,159**
Press....................D. **3,160**
" ....W. **3,161**
Spy......................D. **3,162**
Massachusetts Spy.......W. **3,163**
Le Travailleur...........W. **3,164**

WRENTHAM, Norfolk Co., 2,397† p., about 12 m. from Woonsocket and about 25 S. W. of Boston.
Recorder................W. **3,165**

YARMOUTH PORT, Barnstable Co., 2,425 p., on Old Colony Rd., 75 m. from Boston. Engaged in coast trade and mackerel fishing.
Port Yarmouth Register..W. **3,166**

MICHIGAN.

ADRIAN, c. h., Lenawee Co., 9,000† p., on Raisin r. and Lake Shore & Michigan Southern Rd., 37 m. from Monroe, 210 E. of Chicago, 70 from Detroit and 32 from Toledo. Rich and populous agricultural district and centre of active trade. Engaged in manufactures of various kinds.
Press....................D. **3,167**
" ....W. **3,168**
Times and Expositor......D. **3,169**
" " " ......W. **3,170**
Journal..................W. **3,771**
College Recorder..........M. **3,172**

ALBION, Calhoun Co., 3,500† p., on Kalamazoo r. and Michigan Central Rd., at junction of Lansing division of Lake Shore & Michigan Southern Rd., 20 m. from Jackson, 40 from Lansing. An active business place.
Mirror...................W. **3,173**
Recorder.................W. **3,174**

ALLEGAN, c. h., Allegan Co., 3,500† p., on Kalamazoo r. and junction of Kalamazoo division of Lake Shore & Michigan Southern and Michigan Lake Shore Rds., 20 m. from Lake Michigan and 23 from Kalamazoo, 23 from Paw Paw and 40 from Grand Rapids. Engaged in lumber trade and various manufactures. Exellent water power furnished by the Kalamazoo r.
Allegan Co. Democrat...W. **3,175**
Journal..................W. **3,176**

ALMONT, Lapeer Co., 2,056 p.
Herald...................W. **3,177**

ALPENA, c. h., Alpena Co., 4,500† p., on Thunder Bay, at the mouth of Thunder Bay r., 250 m. N. of Detroit 100 from Bay City. Has a fine harbor. Large lumber business done here. Nineteen large steam saw and shingle mills.
Alpena Co. Pioneer......W. **3,178**
Argus....................W. **3,179**

ANN ARBOR, Washtenaw Co., 7,363 p., on Huron r. and Michigan Central Rd., 38 m. from Detroit. In a farming district and contains several manufactories. The State University is located here.
Michigan Argus.........W. **3,180**
Peninsular Courier......W. **3,181**
Register.................W. **3,182**
Chronicle...............B. W. **3,183**

BALDWIN, Lake Co.
Lake Co. Star............W. **3,184**

BANGOR, Van Buren Co.
Reflector................W. **3,185**

BATTLE CREEK, Calhoun Co., 5,838 p., at junction of Battle Creek with Kalamazoo r., on Michigan Central, at intersection of Peninsular Rd., 23 m. from Kalamazoo. River furnishes water power, which is employed in various manufactures. It is surrounded by a fruit and farming country, and noted for its flourishing schools.
Journal..................D. **3,186**
" ....W. **3,187**
Advent Review and Sabbath Herald...........W. **3,188**
Michigan Tribune.......W. **3,189**
Advent Tidende..........M. **3,190**
Health Reformer.........M. **3,191**
Svensk Advent Harold....M. **3,192**
Youth's Instructor.......M. **3,193**

BAY CITY, c. h., Bay Co., 16,000† p., on Saginaw r., 6 m. from its mouth, and Flint & Pere Marquette and Jackson, Lansing & Saginaw Rds., and 15 m. below Saginaw. Engaged in the lumber trade and lake fishery, and also in extensive salt works.
Tribune..................D. **3,194**
Chronicle................W. **3,195**
Lumberman's Gazette....W. **3,196**
Michigan Odd Fellow....W. **3,197**

BELLEVUE, Eaton Co., 800† p., on Battle Creek and the Peninsular Rd., 32 m. from Lansing. Surrounded by a rich agricultural district. Produces a very fine quality of quick-lime. Engaged in shipping produce.
Gazette..................W. **3,198**

BENTON HARBOR, Perrien Co., 1,500† p., at the mouth of the St. Joseph and Paw Paw rs., and on Chicago & Michigan Lake Shore Rd., 60 m. from Chicago by lake, 103 by rail. The river furnishes good water power, which is employed in manufacturing. Surrounded by a fine fruit-growing district. A large lumber interest centres here. Shipping point for a fine wheat-growing country.
Palladium...............W. **3,199**
Times....................W. **3,200**

BENZONIA, c. h., Benzie Co., 235† p., on Betsie r., 7 m. from Lake Michigan, 130 m. N. of Grand Rapids.
Benzie Co. Journal......W. **3,201**

BERRIEN SPRINGS, c. h., Berrien Co., 1,381 p.
Berrien Co. Journal.....W. **3,202**
Era......................W. **3,203**

BIG RAPIDS, c. h., Mecosta Co., 3,500† p., on Muskegon r. and Grand Rapids &

MICHIGAN.

Indiana Rd., 56 m. from Grand Rapids. Engaged in lumbering and general manufacturing. Has excellent water power and surrounded by a rich farming country.
Magnet..................W. 3,204
Pioneer..................W. 3,205

BLISSFIELD, Lenawee Co., 2,048 p.
Advance..................W. 3,206

BLOOMINGDALE, Van Buren Co., 1,690 p.
Tidings..................W. 3,207

BRIGHTON, c. h., Livingston Co., 1,000† p., on Detroit, Lansing & Lake Michigan Rd., 9 m. from Howell and 43 from Detroit.
Citizen..................W. 3,208

BUCHANAN, Berrien Co., 3,200† p., on St. Joseph r. and the Michigan Central Rd., 53 m. from Kalamazoo, 90 from Chicago. Engaged in lumber manufactures. Surrounded by an agricultural and fruit-growing region.
Berrien Co. Record......W. 3,209

CARO, c. h., Tuscola Co., 500 p., on Cass r., near Vassar, 30 m. from East Saginaw. The centre of an agricultural district.
Tuscola Advertiser.......W. 3,210

CARSON CITY, Montcalm Co.
Commercial..............W. 3,211

CASSOPOLIS, c. h., Cass Co., 1,100 p., on Stone and Diamond Lakes, at crossing of Air Line and Chicago & Lake Huron Rds.
National Democrat......W. 3,212
Vigilant.................W. 3,213

CEDAR SPRINGS, Kent Co., 1,500† p., 20 m. from Grand Rapids.
Clipper...................W. 3,214

CENTREVILLE, St. Joseph Co., 793 p., on Prairie r. and Michigan Air Line Rd., 30 m. from Kalamazoo, in a productive section.
St. Joseph Co. Republican..................W. 3,215

CHARLEVOIX, c. h., Charlevoix Co., 600 p., on Greene r., 2 m. from Lake Michigan and 50 N. E. of Traverse City.
Sentinel..................W. 3,216

CHARLOTTE, c. h., Eaton Co., 3,200† p., on Grand R. Valley division of Michigan Central Rd., at crossing of Peninsular Rd., 20 m. from Lansing. Good agricultural region. Fine ash and walnut lumber region. A rapidly growing place.
Leader..................W. 3,217
Republican..............W. 3,218

CHEBOYGAN, c. h., Cheboygan Co.
Northern Tribune........W. 3,219

CHELSEA, Washtenaw Co., 1,500 p., on Michigan Central Rd., midway between Jackson and Ann Arbor.
Herald..................W. 3,220

CLAM LAKE, Wexford Co., 1,500† p., on Grand Rapids & Indiana Rd., 96 m. from Grand Rapids.
News..................W. 3,221

COLDWATER, c. h., Branch Co., 4,500† p., on Cold Water r. and the Lake Shore & Michigan Southern Rd., 115 m. from Detroit. The centre of a large and flourishing trade.
Republican...........S. W. 3,222
Reporter................W. 3,223

COLON, St. Joseph Co., 1,340 p., on Swan Creek and Air Line division of Michigan Central Rd., 16 m. from Three Rivers.
Enterprise..............W. 3,224

CONCORD, Jackson Co., 1,465 p., on Air Line division of Michigan Central Rd., 55 m. from Three Rivers.
News....................W. 3,225

CONSTANTINE, St. Joseph Co., 3,200† p., on St. Joseph r. and Michigan division of Lake Shore & Michigan Southern Rd. Engaged in various manufactures. Produce shipping point.
St. Joseph Co. Advertiser. W. 3,226

COOPERSVILLE, Ottawa Co.
Courier..................W. 3,227

CORUNNA, c. h., Shiawassee Co., 1,408 p., on Shiawassee r. and Detroit & Milwaukee Rd., 75 m. from Detroit. The river furnishes power, which is employed in manufactures. It has recently developed coal mines, which are being successfully worked. Fire clay is also found.
Shiawassee Co. American. W. 3,228

DECATUR, Van Buren Co., 2,200 p., on Michigan Central Rd., 24 m. from Kalamazoo and 23 from Niles. In an agricultural district.
Van Buren Co. Republican....................W. 3,229

DETROIT, c. h., Wayne Co., 105,000† p., and the great emporium of Michigan, on Detroit r., 18 m. from Lake Erie, having one of the finest harbors on the Lakes. A city of great commercial importance, being connected by railroads with the principal points west, and by means of the Lakes and railroads with the east. Immense quantities of grain, pork, wool and copper ore are shipped from here to eastern markets. The manufactures are extensive and various; fine cut tobacco and segars among the most important.
Abend Post..............D. 3,230
Famillien Blaetter........W. 3,231
Evening News.............D. 3,232
Detroit Free Press........D. 3,233
" " " ....T. W. 3,234
" " " ....W. 3,235
Michigan Journal.........D. 3,236
" " ....W. 3,237
Michigan Volksblatt......D. 3,238
" " ......W. 3,239
Post.....................D. 3,240
" ....T. W. 3,241
" ....W. 3,242
Sun......................D. 3,243
" ....W. 3,244
Tribune..................D. 3,245
" ....T. W. 3,246
" ....W. 3,247
Commercial Advertiser and Michigan Home Journal................W. 3,248
Die Stimme der Wahrheit. W. 3,249
Herald and Torchlight...W. 3,250
Journal of Commerce....W. 3,251
Michigan Christian Advocate..................W. 3,252
Michigan Farmer and State Journal of Agriculture...............W. 3,253
National Granger........W. 3,254
Price Current...........W. 3,255
Public Leader............W. 3,256
Truth for the People......W. 3,257

MICHIGAN.

Western Home Journal. W. 3,258
American Observer...... W. 3,259
Amphion................ W. 3,260
Military Gazette.......... M. 3,261
Our Dioceses.............. M. 3,262
Peninsular Journal of Medicine.................... M. 3,263
Review of Medicine and Pharmacy............ M. 3,264
Scientific Manufacturer.. M. 3,265
Song Journal............ M. 3,266
Sunday Guest............ M. 3,267
Mayhew College Journal. Qr. 3,268

DEXTER, Washtenaw Co., 2,000 p., at junction of Mill Creek with Huron r., on Michigan Central Rd., 9 m. W. of Ann Arbor. There is abundant water power for several mills located here.
Leader.................. W. 3,269

DOWAGIAC, Cass Co., 2,500† p., on the Michigan Central Rd., 35 m. from Kalamazoo, 107 E. of Chicago and 177 W. of Detroit. Large grain and produce market. Engaged in general manufactures.
Cass Co. Republican..... W. 3,270

DUNDEE, Monroe Co., 2,384 p., on Raisin r., about 12 m. W. of Monroe.
Enterprise............... W. 3,271

EAST SAGINAW, Saginaw Co., 17,500† p., on Saginaw r., at junction of Flint & Pere Marquette and Jackson, Lansing & Saginaw Rds. Business centre, having a large and flourishing trade. Saginaw Valley is noted for its manufactories of lumber and salt, annual shipments of which reach 700,000,000 feet of lumber and 800,000 barrels of salt. For 20 miles the bank of the Saginaw r. is occupied by over 100 saw mills and an equal number of salt works.
Republican............... D. 3,272
Saginaw Republican..... W. 3,273
Saginaw Courier......... D. 3,274
" " .... W. 3,275
Saginaw Zeitung........ W. 3,276

EATON RAPIDS, Eaton Co., 2,500† p., on Grand r. and Grand R. Valley division of the Central Michigan Rd., 25 m. N. W. from Jackson and 20 from Lansing. Noted for its magnetic springs, which are visited yearly by invalids.
Saturday Journal....... W. 3,277

EDWARDSBURGH, Cass Co.
Argus.................... W. 3,278

ELK RAPIDS, c. h., Antrim Co., 500† p., on E. arm of Grand Traverse Bay, 17 m. from Grand Traverse City. Principal business manufacturing iron, lumber and flour.
Traverse Bay Progress... W. 3,279

ESCANABA, c. h., Delta Co., 3,120 p., on Little Bay de Noquet, at the mouth of Escanaba r., and Peninsular division of Chicago & Northwestern Rd., 75 m. S. of Marquette, 486 N. W. of Lansing and 100 from Green Bay, Wis. Engaged in farming and lumber trade. Important shipping point for iron ore.
Tribune................. W. 3,280

EVART, Osceola Co., 713 p.
Review.................. W. 3,281

FARWELL, Clare Co., 700 p., on Flint & Pere Marquette Rd., 55 m. from East Saginaw.
Register................. W. 3,282

FENTON, Genesee Co., 3,806† p., on Shiawassee r., and the Detroit & Milwaukee Rd., 52 m. from Detroit. The river furnishes power, which is employed in various manufactures. Centre of a fine agricultural district.
Gazette.................. W. 3,283
Independent............. W. 3,284

FLINT, c. h., Genesee Co., 10,000† p., on the Flint & Pere Marquette Rd., at junction of Port Huron & Lake Michigan Rd., 64 m. from Detroit. The Flint river furnishes extensive water power, which is employed in mills and manufactories. A place of active trade and centre of a fertile agricultural district.
Genesee Democrat....... W. 3,285
Globe.................... W. 3,286
Wolverine Citizen........ W. 3,287

FOWLERVILLE, Livingston Co., 1,200† p., on Detroit, Lansing & Lake Michigan Rd., 9 m. from Howell and 24 from Lansing.
Review.................. W. 3,288

FRANKFORT, Benzie Co., 1,200† p., on Lake Michigan, 30 m. N. of Muskegon. Has a good harbor, and is engaged in iron and lumber manufacturing, and surrounded by an agricultural region.
Express.................. W. 3,289

FREMONT CENTRE, Shiawasse Co.
Fremont Times........... W. 3,290

GRAND HAVEN, c. h., Ottawa Co., 4,500† p., at mouth of Grand r., on Lake Michigan. Has a fine harbor. Chicago and Milwaukee steamers touch here daily. Terminus of Detroit & Milwaukee Rd., and junction with Michigan Lake Shore Rd., 189 m. from Detroit. Engaged in lumber manufacturing.
Herald.................. W. 3,291
News.................... W. 3,292

GRAND LEDGE, Eaton Co., 1,200 p., a few miles from Charlotte. Important for its deposits of stone and coal. Has an excellent water power.
Independent............. W. 3,293

GRAND RAPIDS, c. h., Kent Co., 33,000 p., on Grand r., 40 m. from its mouth, 30 from Lake Michigan, and on Detroit & Milwaukee Rd., at intersection of Grand Rapids & Indiana Rd. Grand Rapids division of Lake Shore & Michigan Southern Rd. and Grand River Valley division of Michigan Central Rd. terminate here. Steamboats run to Grand Haven, at mouth of river, where they connect with Lake steamers. River furnishes unlimited power, which is employed in a large number of factories. There are several gypsum beds located here. United States Courts for W. district of Michigan are held here.
Eagle.................... D. 3,294
" .... W. 3,295
Morning Democrat....... D. 3,296
" " .... W. 3,297
Morning Times........... D. 3,298
" " .... W. 3,299
De Standard............. W. 3,300
Michigan Staats Zeitung. W. 3,301
Saturday Evening Post.. W. 3,302
Vrijheids Banier........ W. 3,303

GREENVILLE, Montcalm Co., 3,500† p., on Flat r., a good lumbering stream, 28 m. N. E. of Grand Rapids, and on Detroit, Lansing & Lake Michigan Rd. Base of sup-

MICHIGAN.

plies for a lumbering region, and a fine agricultural district.

Democrat................W. **3,304**
Independent.............W. **3,305**

HANCOCK, Houghton Co., 2,068 p.

Northwestern Mining Journal..............W. **3,306**

HART, c. h., Oceana Co., 1,004 p., 8 m. from Pentwater.

Oceana Co. Journal......W. **3,307**

HARTFORD, Van Buren Co., 1,000† p., on Chicago & Michigan Lake Shore Rd., 78 m. from Grand Rapids. Surrounded by an agricultural region.

Day Spring..............W. **3,308**

HASTINGS, c. h., Barry Co., 2,519 p., on Thornapple r. and Grand R. Valley division of Michigan Central Rd., 42 m. from Lansing, 32 from Grand Rapids, 62 from Jackson and 138 from Detroit. Surrounded by a wheat-growing district. The river furnishes extensive water power, which is employed in manufacturing.

H[illegible]e Journal...........W. **3,309**
R[illegible]lican Banner......W. **3,310**

HERSEY, c. h., Osceola Co., 700† p., on Muskegon r. and Flint & Pere Marquette Rd., about 4 m. from junction with Grand Rapids & Indiana Rd. Lumbering carried on. An agricultural district.

Osceola Outline..........W. **3,311**

HESPERIA, Oceana Co.

Hesperian...............W. **3,312**

HILLSDALE, c. h., Hillsdale Co., 3,518 p., on Lake Shore & Michigan Southern Rd., at junction of Detroit, Hillsdale & South Western Rd. Hillsdale derives its name from the undulating country in centre of which it is located.

Business.................W. **3,313**
Democrat................W. **3,314**
Standard.................W. **3,315**

HOLLAND, Ottawa Co., 3,000 p., at mouth of Black r., on Michigan, Lake Shore and Chicago & Michigan Lake Shore Rds., 21 m. from Grand Haven. Agricultural, fruit and lumbering district. Tanning carried on.

City News...............W. **3,316**
De Hollander............W. **3,317**
De Hope.................W. **3,318**
Grondwet................W. **3,319**
De Wachter..........B. W. **3,320**

HOLLY, Oakland Co., 2,437 p., on Shiawassee r. and Detroit & Milwaukee Rd., at terminus of Flint & Holly Rd., 47 m. from Detroit. Agricultural market for surrounding country.

Register.................W. **3,321**
Times....................W. **3,322**

HOMER, Calhoun Co., 1,575 p., on Air Line division of Michigan Central Rd., at crossing of Lansing division of Lake Shore & Michigan Southern Rd.

Index....................W. **3,323**

HOUGHTON, c. h., Houghton Co., 3,000† p., on Portage Lake, about 90 m. N. W. of Marquette and about 300 N. of Fond du Lac, Wis. Copper mined in this vicinity.

Portage Lake Mining Gazette..................W. **3,324**

HOWARD CITY, Montcalm Co., 950† p., 33 m. N. of Grand Rapids, at intersection of Grand Rapids & Indiana with Detroit, Lansing & Lake Michigan Rds. Engaged in manufacturing lumber for the southern markets.

Howard Record..........W. **3,325**

HOWELL, c. h., Livingston Co., 3,000† p., on Detroit, Lansing & Lake Michigan Rd.; 50 m. from Detroit and 33 from Lansing. Surrounded by an agricultural region. Manufacturing carried on. One of the best markets in the State.

Livingston Democrat.
Livingston Republican...W. **3,327**

HUBBARDSTON, Ionia Co., 531 p., 6 m. from Detroit & Milwaukee Rd., at Pewamo. Base of supplies for large section of country. Engaged in lumbering and manufacturing.

Advertiser...............W. **3,328**

HUDSON, Lenawee Co., 2,650 p., on Lake Shore & Michigan Southern Rd., 17 m. from Adrian.

Gazette..................W. **3,329**
Post......................W. **3,330**

IMLAY CITY, Lapeer Co., 1,880 p.

Advance..................W. **3,331**

IONIA, Ionia Co., 4,000† p., on Grand r., and on Detroit & Milwaukee and Detroit, Lansing & Lake Michigan Rds., 124 m. from Detroit and 35 E. of Grand Rapids. Agricultural and lumber region.

Sentinel..................W. **3,332**
Standard.................W. **3,333**

ISHPEMING, Marquette Co., 4,692 p., on Peninsular division of Chicago & Northwestern Rd. Iron, silver, copper and lead mines located within limits, which furnish nearly one-half aggregate product of district.

Iron Home...............W. **3,334**

ITHACA, c. h., Gratiot Co., 600† p., 42 m. N. of Lansing and 100 N. W. of Detroit. Situated in the centre of an agricultural district.

Gratiot Co. Journal......W. **3,335**

JACKSON, c. h., Jackson Co., 15,000† p., on Michigan Central Rd.. 76 m. from Detroit. Besides the Michigan Central it possesses the following railroad facilities—viz: Lake Shore & Michigan Southern branch to Toledo; Jackson, Lansing & Saginaw Rd.; Michigan Air Line to Niles; Grand River Valley to Grand Rapids; Fort Wayne, Jackson & Saginaw Rd. The Michigan State Prison is located here.

Citizen....................D. **3,336**
"   ....W. **3,337**
Patriot....................D. **3,338**
"   ....W. **3,339**

JONESVILLE, Hillsdale Co., 2,000† p., on Lake Shore & Michigan Southern Rd., at crossing of Fort Wayne, Jackson & Saginaw Rd., 37 m. from Adrian, 73 from Toledo, Ohio, 110 from Detroit, Mich., 75 from Fort Wayne, Ind., 50 from Lansing, 171 from Chicago. Surrounded by an agricultural district. Manufacturing carried on.

Independent.............W. **3,340**

KALAMAZOO, c. h., Kalamazoo Co., 11,573† p., on Kalamazoo r. and Michigan Central, Lake Shore & Michigan Southern, Grand Rapids & Indiana, South Haven & Kalamazoo Rds., 144 m. from Detroit and 141 E. of Chicago. Engaged in various manufactures. Has a large and flourishing

MICHIGAN.

trade. Seat of Kalamazoo College and several other institutions of learning.
Telegraph..................D. 3,341
" ....W. 3,342
Gazette..................W. 3,343
Times..................W. 3,344
Michigan Freemason.....M. 3,345
Michigan Teacher........M. 3,346

KALKASKA, c. h., Kalkaska Co., 297 p.
Kalkaskaian..............W. 3,347

LAKEVIEW, Montcalm Co.
Citizen..................W. 3,348

L'ANSE, Houghton Co., 1,466 p.
News..................W. 3,349

LANSING, State capital, Ingham Co., 7,500† p., on Grand r., 87 m. N. W. of Detroit. Jackson, Lansing & Saginaw, Detroit, Lansing & Lake Michigan, Chicago & Lake Huron and Lansing division of the Lake Shore & Michigan Southern Rds. centre here. River furnishes water power, which is employed in mills and manufactories.
Republican............S. W. 3,350
" ....W. 3,351
Journal..................W. 3,352

LAPEER, c. h., Lapeer Co., 3,200† p., on Flint r., and Port Huron & Lake Michigan Rd., 46 m. from Port Huron and 60 from Detroit. Agricultural and lumber country.
Clarion..................W. 3,353
Democrat..................W. 3,354

LAWRENCE, Van Buren Co., 1,726 p
Advertiser..................W. 3,355

LESLIE, Ingham Co., 1,600 p., on Jackson, Lansing & Saginaw Rd., 22 m. S. of Lansing. Location of magnetic wells. Increasing in population and business.
Herald..................W. 3,356

LEXINGTON, c. h., Sanilac Co., 2,500 p., on Lake Huron, about 85 m. from Detroit.
Sanilac Jeffersonian.....W. 3,357

LITCHFIELD, Hillsdale Co., 1,836 p.
Gazette..................W. 3,358

LOWELL, Kent Co., 1,800† p., on Grand r., and on Detroit & Milwaukee Rd., about 18 m. E. of Grand Rapids.
Journal..................W. 3,359

LUDINGTON, Mason Co., 2,500† p., on Lake Michigan, about 70 m. N. of Grand Haven and 110 from Milwaukee. Engaged in the lumber business and raising fruit.
Appeal..................W. 3,360
Mason Co. Record.......W. 3,361

MANCHESTER, Washtenaw Co., 2,516 p., on Jackson division of Lake Shore & Michigan Southern Rd., at intersection of Detroit, Hillsdale & Indiana Rd., 25 m from Adrian. In an agricultural district Has several manufactories. Town growing rapidly.
Enterprise..................W. 3,362

MANISTEE, c. h., Manistee Co., 5,000 p., on Lake Michigan, at mouth of Manistee r., about 100 m. from Grand Haven. Milling and lumber manufacturing carried on.
Advocate..................W. 3,363
Times..................W. 3,364
Times and Standard.....W. 3,365

MAPLE RAPIDS, Clinton Co.
Messenger..................W. 3,366

MARCELLUS, Cass Co., 1,552 p.
Messenger..................W. 3,367

MICHIGAN.

MARINE CITY, St. Clair Co.
Gazette..................W. 3,368

MARQUETTE, c. h., Marquette Co., 5,242† p., on Lake Superior, at terminus of Peninsular Rd., which extends to Escanaba on Lake Michigan. E. terminus Marquette, Houghton & Ontonagon Rd., 200 m. N. of Green Bay and 400 N. of Chicago. Iron mines, blast furnaces, rolling mills and other manufacturing are chief industries.
Mining Journal.........W. 3,369

MARSHALL, c. h., Calhoun Co., 5,228† p., on Kalamazoo r. and Michigan Central and Cold Water, Marshall & Mackanac Rds., 108 m. from Detroit and 176 from Chicago. Place of active business. Several manufactories are located here. Surrounded by an agricultural region. Excellent water power.
Democratic Expounder..W. 3,370
Statesman..................W. 3,371

MASON, c. h., Ingham Co., 2,100† p., on Jackson, Lansing & Saginaw Rd., 12 m. S. of Lansing and 25 N. of Jackson. Surrounded by an agricultural district.
Ingham Co. News........W. 3,372

MENDON, St. Joseph Co., 1,000† p., on Grand Rapids & Indiana Rd., 21 m. from Kalamazoo. Surrounded by an agricultural country. Possessed of water power Centre of trade.
Times..................W. 3,373

MENOMINEE, c. h., Menominee Co., 1,500 p., on W. shore of Green Bay, at mouth of Menominee r. and on Chicago & Northwestern Rd., about 50 m. N. E. of Green Bay City. Extensive lumber mills here. Outlet of large iron-ore mines and marble quarries, which are in course of development.
Herald..................W. 3,374
Journal..................W. 3,375
Lumberman and Miner.

MIDDLEVILLE, Barry Co., 1,000† p., on Thornapple r. and Grand R. Valley division of Michigan Central Rd., 22 m. from Grand Rapids. Surrounded by an agricultural district, and possessing fine water power.
Barry Co. Republican...W. 3,377

MIDLAND, c. h., Midland Co., 2,500 p., on Tittawassee r., and the Flint & Pere Marquette Rd., 20 m. from Saginaw. Engaged in lumber and other manufactures.
Times..................W. 3,378

MILFORD, Oakland Co., 1,767 p., on Holly, Wayne & Monroe Rd., 40 m. from Detroit. In a farming country, possessing water power.
Times..................W. 3,379

MONROE, c. h., Monroe Co., 6,500† p., on Raisin r., a port of entry on Lake Erie, and at junction of Holly, Wayne & Monroe and Detroit & Toledo and Detroit & Chicago divisions of Lake Shore & Michigan Southern Rd., 40 m. from Detroit. Depot for the shipment of grain. Manufacturing done here.
Commercial..................W. 3,380
Monitor..................W. 3,381

MONTAGUE, Muskegon Co., 500 p., on N. bank of White Lake, navigable for steamers, and on Chicago, Michigan & Lake Shore Rd., 17 m. from Muskegon.
Lumberman..................W. 3,382

MICHIGAN.

MORENCI, Lenawee Co., 1,500† p., about 20 m. S. W. of Adrian, on the C. & C. Rd., 70 from Detroit.
State Line Observer......W. 3,383

MOUNT CLEMENS, c. h., Macomb Co., 3,500† p., on Grand Trunk Rd., 25 m. from Detroit, at head of navigation on Clinton r. Engaged in ship building and lumber trade.
Monitor..................W. 3,384
Press....................W. 3,385
Reporter.................W. 3,386

MT. PLEASANT, c. h., Isabella Co., 1,500† p., on Chippewa r., 12 m. S. of Clare. Centre of agricultural and lumber country.
Isabella Co. Enterprise..W. 3,387
Morgan's Watchtower....W. 3,388

MUIR, Ionia Co., 1,500† p., on Maple R., Detroit & Milwaukee Rd., 6 m. from Ionia. Engaged in manufacturing.
Grand River Herald.....W. 3,389

MUSKEGON, c. h., Muskegon Co., 9,000† p., on Chicago & Michigan Lake Shore Rd., near mouth of Muskegon r., 15 m. from Grand Haven, 6 from Lake Michigan, 100 from Chicago and 80 from Milwaukee. Manufacturing annually about 400,000,000 feet of lumber; capacity of mills, 600,000,000. Centre of great fruit belt of State.
News and Reporter....S. W. 3,390
Chronicle................W. 3,391
Lakeside Register........W. 3,392

NASHVILLE, Barry Co., 642 p., on Grand R. Valley division of Michigan Central Rd., 12 m. from Hastings.
News....................W. 3,393

NEGAUNEE, Marquette Co.
Iron Herald.............W. 3,394

NEWAYGO, c. h., Newaygo Co., 1,121† p., on Muskegon r., 36 m. from Grand Rapids. River furnishes water power, which is employed in lumbering and manufacturing.
Republican..............W. 3,395
Tribune.................W. 3,396

NEW BUFFALO, Berrien Co., 1,444 p.
Independent.............W. 3,397

NILES, Berrien Co., 4,630 p., on St. Joseph's r. and Michigan Central, Michigan Air Line and Niles & South Bend Rds., 90 m. from Chicago and 47 from Kalamazoo. River is navigable for small steamboats to this point, and affords water power, which is employed in several mills. Centre of a good agricultural district.
Democrat...............W. 3,398
Republican.............W. 3,399

NORRIS, Wayne Co.
Suburban................W. 3,400

NORTH BRANCH, Lapeer Co., 937 p.
Observer.................W. 3,401

NORTHPORT, c. h., Leelenaw Co.
Leelanau Tribune........W. 3,402

NORTHVILLE, Wayne Co., 800 p., on W. branch Rouge r., and Flint & Pere Marquette Rd., 27 m. N. W. of Detroit. Several mills and factories here are run by the water power of the river. School and church furniture manufactured here.
Record.................S. M. 3,403

ONTONAGON, c. h., Ontonagon Co., 800 p., on Lake Superior, at mouth of Ontonagon r., 45 m. from Houghton. Shipping point for copper mines which are worked in vicinity.
Miner...................W. 3,404

OTSEGO, Allegan Co., 2,118 p.
Union...................W. 3,405

OTSEGO LAKE, Otsego Co.
Otsego Co. Herald........W. 3,406

OVID, Clinton Co., 2,553 p., on Detroit & Milwaukee Rd., 88 m. from Detroit. Engaged in agriculture, with a large lumber trade.
Register.................W. 3,407

OWOSSO, Shiawassee Co., 1,500† p., on Shiawassee r., 79 m. from Detroit, at intersection of Jackson, Lansing & Saginaw with Detroit & Milwaukee Rd. Engaged in manufacturing and has a large trade in wool.
New Era..................W. 3,408
Press.....................W. 3,409

OXFORD, Oakland Co., 1,342 p.
Journal..................W. 3,410

PAW PAW, c. h., Van Buren Co., 2,000† p., on Paw Paw r. and Paw Paw branch of Michigan Central Rd., 9 m. from Decatur. Engaged in farming, lumber and general trade.
Courier..................W. 3,411
True Northerner..........W. 3,412
Van Buren Co. Press....W. 3,413
Pythian Journal and Record.

PENTWATER, Oceana Co., 1,370 p., on Lake Michigan, at mouth of Pentwater r., about 60 m. from Grand Haven, and terminus of Chicago & Michigan Lake Shore Rd. Engaged in manufacture of lumber and shingles. Centre of thriving trade.
News.....................W. 3,415

PETOSKEY, Emmett Co.
Emmett Co. Democrat...W. 3,416

PLAINWELL, Allegan Co., 1,600† p., on Kalamazoo r., at junction of Lake Shore & Michigan Southern and Grand Rapids & Indiana Rds. Surrounded by an agricultural district. Possesses water power, which is employed in manufacturing.
Allegan Co. Republic.....W. 3,417

PLYMOUTH, Wayne Co., 3,009 p.
Chronicle................W. 3,418

PONTIAC, c. h., Oakland Co., 4,864 p., on Clinton r. and Detroit & Milwaukee Rd., 26 m. from Detroit. One of the principal wool and produce markets in the State, and a place of active trade.
Bill Poster..............W. 3,419
Gazette..................W. 3,420

PORT AUSTIN, c. h., Huron Co., 778 p., on Lake Huron, at head of Saginaw Bay, 100 m. from Bay City. Principal industries are quarrying grind stones, building stone, and manufacturing salt and lumber.
Huron Co. News.........W. 3,421

PORT HURON, St. Clair Co., 5,973 p., on Lake Huron & Grand Trunk and Port Huron & Lake Michigan Rds., 62 m. from Detroit. Engaged in lumbering, ship building, repairing and lake commerce.
Times....................D. 3,422
" ....W. 3,423
Commercial...............D. 3,424
Sunday Commercial.....W. 3,425
Journal..................W. 3,426

MICHIGAN.

PORTLAND, Ionia Co., 1,800† p., on Detroit, Lansing & Lake Michigan Rd., at junction of Grand and Looking Glass rs., 12 m. S. E. of Ionia. Has water power, which is being improved by various manufacturing enterprises.
Observer..................W. **3,427**

QUINCY, Branch Co., 1,116† p., on Lake Shore & Michigan Southern Rd., 6 m. E. of Coldwater. Engaged in agriculture and stock raising.
Times..................W. **3,428**

READING, Hillsdale Co., 1,657 p., on Fort Wayne, Jackson & Saginaw Rd., 36 m. from Jackson.
Press..................W. **3,429**

REED CITY, Osceola Co.
Clarion..................W. **3,430**

ROCHESTER, Oakland Co.
Era..................W. **3,431**

ROCKFORD, Kent Co.
Register..................W. **3,432**

SAGINAW, c. h., Saginaw Co., 10,064† p., on Saginaw r., 22 m. from its mouth. River navigable to this point. Also on Jackson, Lansing & Saginaw and 2 m. from East Saginaw Rds. Engaged in lumber trade.
Saginawian..............W. **3,433**
Valley News..............W. **3,434**

ST. CLAIR, c. h., St. Clair Co., 2,000† p., on St. Clair r., at mouth of Pine r., 50 m. from Detroit. Surrounded by agricultural district. Engaged in manufactures.
Republican..............W. **3,435**

ST. JOHNS, c. h., Clinton Co., 2,200 p., on the Detroit & Milwaukee Rd., 98 m. from Detroit.
Clinton Independent.....W. **3,436**
Clinton Republican......W. **3,437**

ST. JOSEPH, Berrien Co., 2,994 p., at mouth of St. Joseph's r., and on Chicago & Michigan Lake Shore Rd., 60 m. from Chicago. Engaged in the lumber trade. Centre of the celebrated peach region of the Northwest.
Republican..............W. **3,438**
Traveler and Herald.....W. **3,439**

ST. LOUIS, Gratiot Co., 868 p., on Pine r., 8 m. N. of Ithaca, 30 W. of Saginaw and 60 N. of Lansing. Surrounded by an extensive lumber region. The celebrated magnetic springs of the State are located here.
Herald..................W. **3,440**

SALINE, Washtenaw Co., 1,802 p.
Oracle..................W. **3,441**

SARANAC, Ionia Co.
Reporter..................W. **3,442**

SAUGATUCK, Allegan Co., 1,575 p., on Lake Michigan, at mouth of Kalamazoo r., 25 m. N. W. of Allegan. Engaged in manufacturing lumber, and the wood and bark trade. Surrounded by a fruit-growing district.
Lake Shore Commercial..W. **3,443**

SCHOOLCRAFT, Kalamazoo Co., 1,000 p., at junction of Lake Shore & Michigan Southern, Chicago and Lake Huron Rds., about 15 m. S. of Kalamazoo. Agricultural region.
Dispatch and News......W. **3,444**

SHERMAN, Wexford Co., 300 p., on Manistee r., about 30 m. above Manistee. Lumber business and farming the chief industries.
Wexford Co. Pioneer.....W. **3,445**

SOUTH HAVEN, Van Buren Co., 1,500 p., on Lake Michigan and South Haven division of Michigan Central Rd., 39 m. from Kalamazoo, about 25 N. of St. Joseph.
Sentinel..................W. **3,446**

SPRING LAKE, Ottawa Co., 1,156 p., on Grand r., opposite Grand Haven, in heart of great fruit belt of Michigan. Centre of thriving trade. Engaged in manufacture of pine lumber.
Independent..............W. **3,447**

STANTON, c. h., Montcalm Co., 1,500† p., near centre of the county, and 15 m. N. E. of Greenville.
Montcalm Co. Journal...W. **3,448**
Montcalm Herald..........W. **3,449**

STURGIS, St. Joseph Co., 300† p., on Lake Shore & Michigan Southern, and Grand Rapids & Indiana Rds., 79 m. from Adrian. Engaged in agriculture and manufactures.
Journal and Times......W. **3,450**
St. Joseph Co. Democrat.W. **3,451**

TAWAS CITY, c. h., Iosco Co., 700† p., on Tawas Bay, about 30 m. N. by E. of Bay City. Has a fine harbor. Engaged in lumbering, and increasing in population and business.
Iosco Co. Gazette.........W **3,452**

TECUMSEH, Lenawee Co., 2,500† p., on Jackson division of Lake Shore & Michigan Southern Rd., 33 m. from Jackson and 13 from Adrian, 40 m. N. of Toledo. Agricultural district. Engaged in manufacturing.
Herald..................W. **3,453**
Raisin Valley Record....W. **3,454**

THREE OAKS, Berrien Co., 1,316 p.
Echo..................W. **3,455**

THREE RIVERS, St. Joseph's Co., 2,600 p., on St. Joseph's r. The Lake Shore & Michigan Southern and Michigan Central Air Line Rds. pass through here. Has water power, which is employed in various kinds of manufacture.
Herald..................W. **3,456**
Reporter..................W. **3,457**

TRAVERSE CITY, c. h., Grand Traverse Co., 1,500† p., on the west arm of Grand Traverse Bay, 125 m. N. of Grand Rapids.
Grand Traverse Herald..W. **3,458**
Traverse Bay Eagle......W. **3,459**

UNION CITY, Branch Co., 2,123 p., on St. Joseph's r. and Air Line division of the Michigan Central Rd., at head of navigation, 115 m. from Detroit. A manufacturing town. Business centre for a large tract of rich farming country.
Register..................W. **3,460**

VASSAR, Tuscola Co., 1,500† p., on Cass r., 18 m. from Saginaw and 22 from Bay City. Engaged in agriculture, manufacturing and lumbering.
Tuscola Co. Pioneer......W. **3,461**

VERMONTVILLE, Eaton Co., 1,718 p.
Enterprise..............W. **3,462**

VICKSBURG, Kalamazoo Co.
Monitor..................W. **3,463**

MICHIGAN.

WAYNE, Wayne Co.
Pilot....................W. 3,464

WENONA, Bay Co., 3,000† p., on the southern shore of Saginaw Bay immediately opposite Bay City, 79 m. N. E. of Lansing. The northern terminus of Jackson, Lansing & Saginaw Rd. One of the most important shipping points on Lake Huron. Engaged in lumber and salt business.
Herald..................W. 3,465

WHITEHALL, Muskegon Co., 1,323 p., on White Lake and Chicago & Michigan Lake Shore Rd., 16 m. from Muskegon. Engaged in lumbering and fruit growing. Has 16 mills, which cut 500,000 feet of lumber daily, and manufacture 200,000 shingles daily.
Forum..................W. 3,466

WHITE PIGEON, St. Joseph Co., 1,713 p.
Argus....................W. 3,467

WILLIAMSTON, Ingham Co.
Enterprise...............W. 3,468

WYANDOTTE, Wayne Co., 3,375† p., on Detroit r. and Lake Shore & Michigan Southern Rd., 17 m. from Detroit. The location of extensive furnaces, rolling mills and various manufactures.
Wayne Co. Courier......W. 3,469

YPSILANTI, Washtenaw Co., 6,300† p., on Huron r. and Michigan Central Rd., at junction of Detroit, Hillsdale & Indiana Rd., 30 m. from Detroit. In an agricultural district. The river furnishes water power, which is employed in various manufactures. Seat of State Normal School.
Commercial.............W. 3,470
Sentinel.................W. 3,471
School....................M. 3,472
Good Templar...........Qr. 3,473

MINNESOTA.

ALBERT LEA, c. h., Freeborn Co., 1,500† p., on two small lakes and Southern Minnesota Rd., 128 m. from La Crosse.
Enterprise...............W. 3,474
Freeborn Co. Standard...W. 3,475

ALEXANDRIA, c. h., Douglas Co., 800† p., in a region of lakes, 65 m. N. W. of St. Cloud, with which it is connected by stages. In a farming community, staple products, wheat, oats and raising of stock.
Post....................W. 3,476

ANOKA, c. h., Anoka Co., 2,500 p., on Mississippi r., at mouth of Rum r. and St. Paul & Pacific Rd., about 15 m. above Minneapolis. The river furnishes good water power, which is employed to considerable extent in manufactures. Lumbering is its principal branch of industry. Surrounded by an agricultural district.
Anoka Co. Republican...W. 3,477
Anoka Co. Union........W. 3,478
Journal.................W. 3,479

AUDUBON, Becker Co.
Journal.................W. 3,480

AUSTIN, c. h., Mower Co., 3,000† p., on Cedar r. and Milwaukee & St. Paul Rd., at junction of Austin & Mason City branch, and Burlington, Cedar Rapids & Minnesota Rds., 104 m. from St. Paul, 111 from McGregor, and about 40 S. W. of Rochester. Centre of trade for an agricultural community.
Mower and Fillmore Co.
Republican............W. 3,481
Mower Co. Transcript....W. 3,482
Register.................W. 3,483

MINNESOTA.

BEAVER FALLS, c. h., Renville Co., 150† p., 2 m. from Minnesota r. and 37 from New Ulm.
Renville Times...........W. 3,484

BENSON, c. h., Swift Co.
Times....................W. 3,485

BLUE EARTH CITY, c. h., Faribault Co., 1,956† p., on Blue Earth r., about 10 m. from Southern Minnesota Rd., 40 S. of Mankato. County seat and centre of trade of a prairie region.
Bee......................W. 3,486
Post.....................W. 3,487

BRAINERD, Crow Wing Co., 750 p., on Mississippi R. & Northern Pacific Rd., 115 m. from Duluth.
Tribune..................W. 3,488

CALEDONIA, c. h., Houston Co., 1,000† p., 14 m. from Brownsville and 18 S. W. of La Crosse, Wis.
Houston Co. Journal.....W. 3,489

CAMBRIDGE, c. h., Isanti Co.
Isanti Co. Press..........W. 3,490

CARVER, Carver Co.
Carver Co. Free Press....W. 3,491

CHASKA, c. h., Carver Co., 1,200 p., on Minnesota r. and Northern Pacific Rd., at junction of Hastings & Dakota Rd., 5 m. above Chakopee and about 28 from St. Paul.
Valley Herald...........W. 3,492

CHATFIELD, Fillmore Co., 1,600† p., about 60 m. from La Crosse, Wis.
Democrat................W. 3,493

CROOKSTON, c. h., Polk Co.
Independent.............W. 3,494

DELANO, Wright Co., 600† p., on Crow r. and St. Paul & Pacific Rd.
Wright Co. Eagle........W. 3,495

DETROIT, Becker Co., 280 p., on Detroit Lake and Northern Pacific Rd., 206 m. from Duluth.
Becker Co. Banner.......W. 3,496
Record..................W. 3,497

DODGE CENTRE, Dodge Co.
Press....................W. 3,498

DULUTH, c. h., St. Louis Co., 4,500 p., on extreme western shore of Lake Superior, and terminus of Lake Superior & Mississippi Rd., and lake terminus of Northern Pacific Rd., 170 m. N. E. of St. Paul. Engaged in commerce, manufacturing and general trade. Large grain market.
Minnesotian-Herald.....W. 3,499
Tribune..................W. 3,500

ELK RIVER, Sherburne Co., 900† p., on Mississippi r. and Mississippi R. branch of St. Paul & Pacific Rd., 40 m. N. W. of St. Paul. Several mills and manufactories here.
News....................W. 3,501
Sherburne Co. Star......W. 3,502

ELYSIAN, Le Sueur Co.
Messenger...............W. 3,503

EYOTA, Olmstead Co., 600† p., on Winona & St. Peter Rd., 13 m. E. of Rochester and

MINNESOTA.

37 W. of Winona. Centre of a wheat growing district.
Advertiser..............W. 3,504

FAIRMONT, c. h., Martin Co., 750† p., 20 m. from Winnebago City and 40 S. by W. of Mankato. The county seat of an agricultural county. Centre of a thriving trade.
Martin Co. Sentinel......W. 3,505

FARIBAULT, c. h., Rice Co., 5,534† p., on Iowa & Minnesota division of Milwaukee & St. Paul Rd., 65 m. from St. Paul and 15 from Owatonna. Seat of several institutions of learning, and the Asylum for the Deaf, Dumb and Blind. Surrounded by an agricultural region. Manufacturing carried on. Has seven flouring mills.
Democrat................W. 3,506
Republican..............W. 3,507

FARMINGTON, Dakota Co., 2,400 p., on Hastings & Dakota division at crossing of Iowa & Minnesota division of Milwaukee & St. Paul Rd. Surrounded by a farming country.
Press....................W. 3,508

FERGUS FALLS, Otter Tail Co., 700† p., on Otter Tail r., 200 m. N. W. of Minneapolis. It has a fine water power, and is surrounded by forests of pine and hardwood lumber. Engaged principally in lumber manufacturing.
Advocate................W. 3,509
Journal..................W. 3,510

GLENCOE, c. h., McLeod Co., 1,000† p., terminus of Hastings & Dakota division of Milwaukee & St. Paul Rd., 74 m. from Hastings and 59 W. of St. Paul, 50 W. of Minneapolis.
Register.................W. 3,511

GLENWOOD, c. h., Pope Co., 200† p., situated at the head of White Bear Lake, about 75 m. W. of St. Cloud. Fine water power for manufacturing purposes.
Pope Co. Press..........W. 3,512

GRANITE FALLS, c. h., Yellow Medicine Co.
Journal.................W. 3,513

HASTINGS, c. h., Dakota Co., 3,455 p., on Mississippi r., at eastern terminus of Hastings & Dakota division of Milwaukee & St. Paul Rd., also a station on Chicago division, 25 m. below St. Paul. Engaged in milling and manufacturing, and a shipping point for grain.
Gazette..................W. 3,514
Union....................W. 3,515

HENDERSON, c. h., Sibley Co., 800† p., on Minnesota r., and St. Paul & Sioux City Rd., 60 m. S. W. of St. Paul.
Sibley Co. Independent...W. 3,516

HOKAH, Houston Co.
Blade....................W. 3,517

HOMER, Winona Co.
Novelty Press............W. 3,518

HUTCHINSON, McLeod Co.
Enterprise...............W. 3,519

JACKSON, c. h., Jackson Co., 450† p., on Des Moines r., 164 m. S. W. of St. Paul and 75 from Mankato. The centre of a thriving trade and growing rapidly.
Republic.................W. 3,520

JAMESVILLE, Waseca Co.
Argus....................W. 3,521

KASSON, Dodge Co., 1,500† p., on Winona & St. Peter Rd., 65 m. W. of Winona. In an agricultural region.
Dodge Co. Republican...W. 3,522

LAC QUI PARLE, c. h., Lac Qui Parle Co.
Lac Qui Parle Co. Press.W. 3,523

LAKE CITY, Wabasha Co., 3,000† p., on Lake Pepin, an expansion of Mississippi r., and St. Paul and Chicago division of Milwaukee & St. Paul Rd., 72 m. below St. Paul. Centre of an agricultural region. Manufactures carried on. Summer resort.
Leader..................W. 3,524
Wabashaw Co. Sentinel...W. 3,525

LANESBORO, Fillmore Co., 1,175† p., on Southern Minnesota Rd., 51 m. W. of La Crosse, Wis.
Journal..................W. 3,526

LE ROY, Mower Co.
Independent.............W. 3,527

LE SUEUR, c. h., Le Sueur Co., 1,500 p., on Minnesota r., and St. Paul & Sioux City Rd., 63 m. from St. Paul.
Sentinel.................W. 3,528

LITCHFIELD, c. h., Meeker Co., 1,200† p., on Lake Ripley, and St. Paul & Pacific Rd., 78 m. W. of St. Paul.
News-Ledger..............W. 3,529

LITTLE FALLS, c. h., Morrison Co.
Courier..................W. 3,530

LONG PRAIRIE, c. h., Todd Co.
Todd Co. Argus..........W. 3,531

LUVERNE, c. h., Rock Co.
Rock Co. Herald.........W. 3,532

MADELIA, c. h., Watonwan Co., 675 p., on St. Paul & Sioux City Rd., 23 m. from Mankato and 110 from St. Paul. Surrounded by an agricultural district.
Times....................W. 3,533
Watonwan Co. Record...W. 3,534

MANKATO, c. h., Blue Earth Co., 5,750† p., at junction of Minnesota and Blue Earth rs. Centre of an agricultural district. Has considerable trade and manufacturing interests.
Minnesota Beobachter....W. 3,535
Record...................W. 3,536
Review...................W. 3,537
Union....................W. 3,538

MANTORVILLE, c. h., Dodge Co., 760 p., about 2½ m. from Kasson and 17 W. of Rochester.
Express..................W. 3,539

MARSHALL, c. h., Lyon Co.
Messenger...............W. 3,540

MINNEAPOLIS, c. h., Hennepin Co., 33,747† p., on Mississippi r., at junction of Milwaukee, St. Paul & Minneapolis, St. Paul & Pacific, Minneapolis & St. Louis and Minneapolis & Duluth Rds., 10 m. from St. Paul. The river furnishes power, which is employed in milling and manufacturing.
Evening Mail............D. 3,541
Dollar Mail..............W. 3,542
Tribune..................D. 3,543
" ....W. 3,544
Business Mirror......S. W. 3,545
Budstikken...............W. 3,546
Citizen..................W. 3,547
Farmers' Union..........W. 3,548
Freie Presse............W. 3,549

MINNESOTA.

Liberty 'Blade and Monday Morning News.....W. **3,550**
Rural Times..........S. M. **3,551**

MINNESOTA FALLS, Yellow Medicine Co.
Sentinel..................W. **3,552**

MONTICELLO, Wright Co., 1,200† p., on Mississippi r., 48 m. N. W. of St. Paul. Surrounded by a rich farming country.
Wright Co. Times........W. **3,553**

MOORHEAD, Clay Co., 420 p., on Red r. and Northern Pacific Rd., 252 m. from Duluth.
Red River Star.......... W. **3,554**

NEW ULM, c. h., Brown Co., 2,200† p., on Minnesota r. and Winona & St. Peter Rd., about 25 m. above Mankato. Centre of trade. Considerable manufacturing carried on.
Herald..................W. **3,555**
Post....................W. **3,556**

NORTHFIELD, Rice Co., 2,278 p., on Iowa & Minnesota division of Milwaukee & St. Paul Rd., 37 m. from St. Paul and 14 from Faribault. Centre of an agricultural region. Seat of Carleton College.
Rice Co. Journal........W. **3,557**

OWATONNA, c. h., Steele Co., 2,873 p., on Straight r., at intersection of Winona & St. Peter Rd. with Iowa and Minnesota division of Milwaukee & St. Paul Rd., 67 m. from St. Paul and 90 from Winona. Wheat and produce market for surrounding country. Shipping and manufacturing point. A vichy water spring located here.
Journal..................W. **3,558**
People's Press...........W. **3,559**

PERHAM, Otter Tail Co.
News.................... W. **3,560**

PRESTON, c. h., Fillmore Co., 1,500† p., 44 m. W. by S. of La Crosse, Wis. Surrounded by an agricultural district.
Republican..............W. **3,561**

PRINCETON, c. h., Mille Lacs Co.
Appeal..................W. **3,562**

RED WING, c. h., Goodhue Co., 5,630† p., on W. bank of Mississippi r. and St. Paul & Chicago Rd., about 41 m. from St. Paul.
Argus...................W. **3,563**
Goodhue Co. Republican.W. **3,564**
Grange Advance.........W. **3,565**

REDWOOD FALLS, c. h., Redwood Co., 700† p., on Redwood r., 40 m. from New Ulm and 45 from Willmar. Engaged in farming and manufactures. U. S. Local Land Office.
Redwood Gazette ....W. **3,566**

REED'S LANDING, Wabasha Co.
Press....................W. **3,567**

ROCHESTER, c. h., Olmstead Co., 5,000 p., on Winona & St. Peter Rd., 50 m. from Winona. The most important place on this railroad. Surrounded by an agricultural district and centre of an active trade.
Post.....................W. **3,568**
Record and Union.......W **3,569**

RUSH CITY, Chisago Co.
Chisago Co. Post.........W. **3,570**

RUSHFORD, Fillmore Co., 1,750 p., on Root R. & Southern Minnesota Rd., 30 m. from La Crosse. Water power furnished by the river and Rush Creek, which is used in manufactures of various kinds.
Star.....................W. **3,571**

MINNESOTA.

ST. CHARLES, Winona Co., 1,500† p., on Winona & St. Peter Rd., 28 m. W. of Winona. Centre of an agricultural district.
Times...................W. **3,572**

ST. CLOUD, c. h., Stearns Co., 3,300† p., on Mississippi r. and St. Paul & Pacific Rd., 80 m. from St. Paul. Largest place in N. part of State, and centre of manufacturing trade. Agricultural district surrounding.
Journal..................W. **3,573**
Press.................... W. **3,574**
Times....................W. **3,575**

ST. PAUL, c. h., Ramsey Co., State capital, 33,175† p., on Mississippi r., 9 m. below the falls of St. Anthony and at the head of navigation. Engaged in milling, manufacturing and trade. An important railroad centre.
Dispatch..................D. **3,576**
" .... T. W. **3,577**
" ....W. **3,578**
Pioneer Press.............D. **3,579**
" " ....T. W. **3,580**
" " ....W. **3,581**
Minnesota Staats Zeitung................ T. W. **3,582**
Minnesota Staats Zeitung.W. **3,583**
Anti-Monopolist..........W. **3,584**
Der Wanderer........... .W. **3,585**
L'Etoile du Nord.........W. **3,586**
Minnesota Volksblatt....W. **3,587**
North-Western Chronicle.W. **3,588**
Svenska Nybyggaren.....W. **3,589**

ST. PETER, c. h., Nicollet Co., 3,300† p., on Minnesota r., on St. Paul & Sioux City and Winona & St. Peter Rds., 70 m. from St. Paul. Engaged in manufacturing.
Commercial Advertiser...W. **3,590**
Tribune...................W. **3,591**

SAUK CENTRE, Stearns Co., 1,200† p., on Sauk r., on the St. Vincent branch of the N. P. Rd., about 45 m. W. N. W. of St. Cloud.
Herald...................W. **3,592**

SAUK RAPIDS, c. h., Benton Co.
Sentinel..................W. **3,593**

SHAKOPEE, c. h., Scott Co., 2,000 p., on Minnesota r., 28 m. from St. Paul, at junction of St. Paul & Sioux City, Hastings & Dakota and Minneapolis & St. Louis Rds. Surrounded by a farming district and centre of an active trade. Lime kilns and railroad machine shop located here.
Argus....................W. **3,594**

SPRING VALLEY, Fillmore Co., 1,400† p., on Southern Minnesota Rd., 75 m. W. of La Crosse. Engaged in manufacturing and agriculture.
Western Progress........W. **3,595**

STILLWATER, c. h., Washington Co., 5,000 p., head of Lake St. Croix and terminus of Stillwater branch of Lake Superior & Mississippi division of Northern Pacific Rd.; also of Stillwater branch of Northern Wisconsin Rd., 20 m. from Mississippi r. and 18 from St. Paul. Engaged in lumber trade. Surrounded by an agricultural region. Steamer runs daily to Taylor's Falls.
Gazette...................W. **3,596**
Lumberman..............W. **3,597**
Messenger................W. **3,598**

TAYLOR'S FALLS, Chisago Co., 1,003 p., on St. Croix r., about 47 m. N. E. of St. Paul. Engaged in lumber, manufactures

MINNESOTA.

and agriculture. Water power. Steamers make daily trips between this point and Stillwater.
Journal .... W. 3,599

WABASHA, c. h., Wabasha Co., 3,000† p., on Mississippi r., 3 m. below Lake Pepin, 30 above Winona. Grain market and centre of trade. Termination of the Midland Rd.
Herald .... W. 3,600

WASECA, Waseca Co., 1,875† p., on Winona & St. Peter Rd., 105 m. W. of Winona.
Minnesota Radical ...... W. 3,601

WATERVILLE, Le Sueur Co.
Echo .... W. 3,602

WELLS, Faribault Co., 1,000 p., on Southern Minnesota Rd., 40 m. S. E. of Mankato and 25 E. of Blue Earth City. The centre of an agricultural district. The railroad repair shops are located here.
Gazette .... W. 3,603

WILLMAR, c. h., Kandiyohi Co., 800† p., on Foot Lake and St. Paul & Pacific Rd., 104 m. from St. Paul and 95 from Minneapolis. An agricultural district. One of the best wheat markets on the road. The railroad machine shops are located here.
Gazette .... W. 3,604
Republican .... W. 3,605

WINDOM, Cottonwood Co., 500 p., on Sioux City & St. Paul Rd., 145 m. from St. Paul and 120 from Sioux City. Doing a considerable trade. An agricultural district.
Reporter .... W. 3,606

WINNEBAGO CITY, Faribault Co., 900 p., on Blue Earth r. and Southern Minnesota Rd., 33 m. S. of Mankato and market for an agricultural country.
Press .... W. 3,607

WINONA, c. h., Winona Co., 11,000† p., on Mississippi r. and Chicago & St. Paul Rd., about 25 m. above La Crosse. E. terminus of Winona & St. Peter Rd. Large quantities of grain are shipped from this point. Principal exporting point for wheat in the State.
Republican .... D. 3,608
" .... W. 3,609
Adler .... W. 3,610
Herald .... W. 3,611
Parish Messenger .... M. 3,612

WORTHINGTON, Nobles Co., 350 p., on Okabena Lake and St. Paul & Sioux City Rd., 178 m. from St. Paul. An agricultural and stock-raising section.
Advance .... W. 3,613

ZUMBROTA, Goodhue Co.
Independent .... W. 3,614

MISSISSIPPI.

ABERDEEN, c. h., Monroe Co., 5,000† p., on Tombigbee r. and branch of Mobile & Ohio Rd., 232 m. from Mobile and about the same distance from Columbus, Ky. The river is navigable to this point a large portion of the year, and large quantities of cotton are shipped down the river to Mobile.
Examiner .... T. W. 3,615
" .... W. 3,616
True Republican .... W. 3,617

MISSISSIPPI.

ASHLAND, c. h., Benton Co.
Benton Co. Argus .... W. 3,618

AUSTIN, c. h., Tunica Co., 500 p., on Mississippi r., 70 m. below Memphis and 35 N. W. of Sardis. Cotton-shipping point.
Cotton Plant .... W. 3,619

BAY ST. LOUIS, c. h., Hancock Co., 3,000 p., on Bay St. Louis and New Orleans, Mobile & Texas Rd., 50 m. from New Orleans and 212 S. by E. of Jackson. A watering place, and doing considerable trade in lumber, naval stores, cattle and cotton.
Herald .... W. 3,620
Sea Coast Republican .... W. 3,621

BILOXI, Harrison Co.
Mirror .... W. 3,622

BOLTON, Hinds Co.
Weekly .... W. 3,623

BOONEVILLE, c. h., Prentiss Co., 1,100 p., on Mobile & Ohio Rd., 21 m. from Corinth and 173 from Meridian. In a cotton-growing district.
Prentiss Pleader .... W. 3,624

BRANDON, c. h., Rankin Co., 756 p., on Vicksburg & Meridian Rd., 14 m. from Jackson, 60 from Vicksburg and 80 from Meridian. In a cotton district.
Republican .... W. 3,625

BROOKHAVEN, c. h., Lincoln Co., 2,030 p., on New Orleans, Jackson & Great Northern Rd., 95 m. from Jackson. Engaged in lumber business and a manufacturing town.
Citizen .... W. 3,626
Ledger .... W. 3,627

CANTON, c. h., Madison Co., 2,465 p., on New Orleans, St. Louis & Chicago Rd., 23 m. from Jackson. Cotton mart.
American Citizen .... W. 3,628
Mail .... W. 3,629

CARROLLTON, c. h., Carroll Co., 700† p., about 96 m. N. of Jackson and 20 W. by S. of Grenada.
Mississippi Conservative. W. 3,630

CARTHAGE, c. h., Leake Co., 600† p., about 40 m. N. E. of Jackson.
Carthaginian .... W. 3,631

CHARLESTON, c. h., Tallahatchee Co., 800 p., 10 m. W. of Mississippi & Tennessee Rd. at Oakland, 144 N. of Jackson.
Tallahatchee News .... W. 3,632

COLUMBUS, Lowndes Co., 6,000† p., on Tombigbee r., 140 m. from Jackson. A branch railroad connects with Mobile & Ohio Rd. at Artesia. The river is navigable for steamboats to this point, making it an important shipping point for cotton, which is cultivated in the vicinity.
Democrat .... W. 3,633
Index .... W. 3,634
Lowndes Independent ... W. 3,635
Press .... W. 3,636
Patron of Husbandry ..... M. 3,637

CORINTH, c. h., Alcorn Co., 1,512 p., on Mobile & Ohio Rd., at intersection of Memphis & Charleston Rd., 94 m. from Memphis. Engaged in cotton manufacturing.
News .... W. 3,638
Sub-Soiler and Democrat. W. 3,639

CRYSTAL SPRINGS, Copiah Co.
Monitor .... W. 3,640

MISSISSIPPI.

DRY GROVE, Hinds Co.
Diocesan Record of Mississippi....M. **3,641**

EDWARDS, Hinds Co.
Courier....W. **3,642**

ENTERPRISE, c. h., Clark Co., 2,000 p., at junction of Chunky and Oakabilla rs., forming the Chickasaha, on Mobile & Ohio Rd., 120 m. from Mobile and 95 E. by S. of Jackson. An agricultural and lumber district.
Courier.

FAYETTE, c. h., Jefferson Co., 780 p., 30 m. E. by N. of Natchez.
Chronicle....W. **3,644**
Vindicator.

FOREST, Scott Co., 560 p., on Vicksburg & Meridian Rd., 45 m. E. of Jackson.
Register....W. **3,646**

FRIARS POINT, c. h., Coahoma Co., 2,000† p., on Mississippi r., 270 m. above Vicksburg.
Delta....W. **3,647**

GREENWOOD, c. h., Le Flore Co.
Valley Sentinel....W. **3,648**

GRENADA, c. h., Grenada Co., 2,000 p., junction Mississippi Central and Mississippi & Tennessee Rds., head of navigation on Yalabusho r., 112 m. from Jackson, 100 from Memphis. A cotton-growing region.
Republican....W. **3,649**
Sentinel....W. **3,650**
Southern Rural Gentleman....W. **3,651**

HANDSBORO, Harrison Co., 650 p., near New Orleans, Mobile & Texas Rd., about 2 m. N. of Mississippi City, on Mississippi Sound, and 60 W. of Mobile. Engaged in lumber, milling and manufacturing.
Democrat....W. **3,652**

HAZELHURST, Copiah Co., 1,700 p., on New Orleans, St. Louis & Chicago Rd., 34 m. from Jackson and 149 from New Orleans.
Copiahan....W. **3,653**
Copiah Herald....W. **3,654**
Mississippi Democrat....W. **3,655**

HERNANDO, c. h., De Soto Co., 1,200 p., on Mississippi & Tennessee Rd., 22 m. from Memphis and 78 from Grenada.
Press and Times....W. **3,656**

HOLLY SPRINGS, c. h., Marshall Co., 3,000 p., on Mississippi Central division of New Orleans, Jackson & Great Northern Rd., 50 m. from Memphis and 180 from Jackson, engaged in cotton trade.
Mississippi Tribune.
Reporter....W. **3,658**
South....W. **3,659**

HOUSTON, Chickasaw Co., 720 p., on Vicksburg & Nashville Rd., about 40 m. N. W. of Columbus.
Chickasaw Messenger....W. **3,660**

JACKSON, c. h., Hinds Co., State capital, 5,850† p., on Pearl r., and New Orleans, St. Louis & Chicago Rd., at intersection of Vicksburg & Meridian Rd., 183 m. from New Orleans and 45 E. of Vicksburg. In a fertile and populous cotton-growing district, and place of active trade.
Times....D. **3,661**
Times and Republican....W. **3,662**
Clarion....W. **3,663**
Farmer's Vindicator....W. **3,664**

MISSISSIPPI.

Mississippi Pilot....W. **3,665**
People's Defense....W. **3,666**
Mississippi Teacher....M. **3,667**

KOSCIUSKO, c. h., Attala Co., 2,000† p., 15 m. E. of New Orleans, St. Louis & Chicago Rd., 18 from Mississippi Central Rd., and 70 N. by E. of Jackson. Engaged principally in agriculture.
Central Star....W. **3,668**

LEXINGTON, c. h., Holmes Co., 1,300 p., about 60 m. N. of Jackson and 12 from line of New Orleans, Jackson & Great Northern Rd.
Advertiser....W. **3,669**
Holmes Co. Aegis....W. **3,670**

LIBERTY, c. h., Amite Co., 300† p., about 25 m. from line of New Orleans, St. Louis & Chicago Rd. and 100 S. by W. of Jackson.
Advocate....W. **3,671**
Southern Herald....W. **3,672**

LOUISVILLE, c. h., Winston Co., 450† p., 26 m. W. of Mobile & Ohio Rd., at Macon, 113 N. E. of Jackson. Centre of trade and engaged in agriculture.
Banner.

McCOMB CITY, Pike Co.
Intelligencer....W. **3,674**

MACON, c. h., Noxubee Co., 975 p., on Mobile & Ohio Rd., 35 m. from Columbus, 198 from Mobile. Railroad repair shops are located here. Engaged in agriculture. A shipping point for cotton.
Beacon....W. **3,675**
Mississippi Sun....W. **3,676**

MAGNOLIA, Pike Co., 530 p., on New Orleans, St. Louis & Chicago Rd., 85 m. S. of Jackson and 98 from New Orleans.
Herald....W. **3,677**

MERIDIAN, Lauderdale Co., 6,000 p., on Mobile & Ohio Rd., 135 m. from Mobile, at junction of Vicksburg & Meridian and Alabama & Chattanooga Rds. Has an excellent trade and is growing rapidly.
Mercury....T. W. **3,678**
" ....W. **3,679**
Gazette....W. **3,680**
Southern Baptist....W. **3,681**
Southern Homestead....W. **3,682**

MONTICELLO, c. h., Lawrence Co.
Sunny South....W. **3,683**

MORTON, Scott Co.
Scott Co. Democrat....W. **3,684**

NATCHEZ, c. h., Adams Co., 9,057 p., on Mississippi r., 279 m. above New Orleans and 100 below Vicksburg. River trade is important, steamboats making regular trips between here and other points on the river. Noted for its healthful climate.
Democrat and Courier....D. **3,685**
" " " ....W. **3,686**
New South....W. **3,687**

NEW ALBANY, c. h., Union Co.
Union....W. **3,688**

NEWTON, Newton Co., 400 p., on Vicksburg & Meridian Rd., 60 m. E. of Jackson and 31 from Meridian. Centre of a corn and cotton growing section.
Bulletin....W. **3,689**

OKOLONA, Chickasaw Co., 1,620 p., on Mobile & Ohio Rd., 28 m. from Columbus.
Prairie News....W. **3,690**
Southern States....W. **3,691**

MISSISSIPPI.

OXFORD, c. h., La Fayette Co., 1,422 p., on New Orleans, Jackson & Great Northern Rd., 167 m. from Jackson.
Falcon....................W. 3,692
Ricochet....................W. 3,693

PASCAGOULA, Jackson Co.
Star of Pascagoula.......W. 3,694

PITTSBORO, c. h., Calhoun Co.
Calhoun Democrat.......W. 3,695
Calhoun Times..........W.

PORT GIBSON, c. h., Claiborne Co., 1,900† p., on Little Bayou Pierre, about 7 m. from Mississippi r., 35 from Vicksburg and 68 S. W. of Jackson. A cotton-growing district.
Southern Reveille........W. 3,697
Standard..................W. 3,698

RAYMOND, c. h., Hinds Co., 500 p., about 16 m. W. by S. of Jackson. Engaged in the cotton trade.
Hinds Co. Gazette........W. 3,699

RIPLEY, c. h., Tippah Co., 1,000† p., about 30 m. W. by S. of Corinth and 30 E. of Holly Springs.
Advertiser...............W. 3,700

SARDIS, c. h., Panola Co., 2,500 p., on Memphis and Tennessee Rd., 50 m. from Grenada and 50 from Memphis.
Panola Star.............W. 3,701

SATARTIA, Yazoo.
Sentinel..................W. 3,702

SENATOBIA, c. h., Tate Co.
Republican Signet.......W. 3,703
Tidal Wave................W. 3,704

STARKVILLE, c. h., Oktibbeha Co., 850 p., 25 m. W. of Columbus and 125 from Jackson.
East Mississippi Times...W. 3,705
News......................W. 3,706
Whig.

SUMMIT, Pike Co., 1,000 p., on New Orleans and Chicago Rd., 75 m. from Jackson.
Sentinel..................W. 3,708
Times.....................W. 3,709

TUPELO, Lee Co., 1,500† p., on Mobile & Ohio Rd., 45 m. from Corinth and 74 from Columbus.
Journal...................W. 3,710

VAIDEN, Carroll Co.
Record....................W. 3,711

VICKSBURG, c. h., Warren Co., 15,000† p., on Mississippi r., at W. terminus of Vicksburg & Meridian Rd., 45 m. from Jackson and 400 N. from New Orleans. Engaged in river trade. Large quantities of cotton are shipped from this point. Some manufacturing carried on.
Herald....................D. 3,712
" ....W. 3,713
Sentinel..................W. 3,714

WATER VALLEY, Yallabusha Co., 3,500† p., on New Orleans, St. Louis & Chicago Rd., 28 m. from Grenada.
Courier...................W. 3,715
Mississippi Central......W. 3,716

WEST POINT, Lowndes Co., 1,392 p., on Mobile & Ohio Rd., 97 m. from Meridian, 230 from Mobile and about 15 N. E. of Columbus. Engaged in agricultural pursuits. Cotton the principal production.
Southern Advertiser.....W. 3,717

WESTVILLE, c. h., Simpson Co., on New Orleans, St. Louis & Chicago Rd., about 40 m. S. E. of Jackson.
News......................W. 3,718

WINONA, Montgomery Co., 1,800† p., on Mississippi Central division of Great Jackson Rd., 89 m. from Jackson.
Advance...................W. 3,719

WOODVILLE, c. h., Wilkinson Co., 1,000 p., 35 m. S. of Natchez. Railroad connects it with Bayou Sara, La. Engaged in raising corn, cotton and fruits. Trade centre.
Republican...............W. 3,720

YAZOO CITY, c. h., Yazoo Co., 2,500 p., on Yazoo r., 50 m. N. by W. of Jackson, and about 25 W. of line of New Orleans, Jackson & Great Northern Rd. A shipping point for cotton, which is cultivated in large quantities in the vicinity.
Banner....................W. 3,721
Democrat..................W. 3,722
Herald....................W. 3,723

MISSOURI.

ALBANY, c. h., Gentry Co., 1,000 p., about 50 m. N. E. of St. Joseph. Centre of a farming and stock-raising country.
American Freeman.....W. 3,724
Democrat..................W. 3,725
Ledger.....................W. 3,726

ALEXANDRIA, Clark Co., 1,000† p., on Mississippi r., at mouth of Des Moines r. E. terminus of Missouri, Iowa & Nebraska Rd., opposite Warsaw, Ill., and 4 m. from Keokuk, Iowa.
Commercial...............W. 3,727

ALTON, c. h., Oregon Co.
South Missourian.........W. 3,728

APPLETON CITY, St. Clair Co., 1,000† p., on Sedalia division of Missouri, Kansas & Texas Rd., 60 m. S. W. of Sedalia. A farming district. Shipping point for St. Clair and Bates counties. Coal mines in operation in the vicinity.
Appleton Democrat......W. 3,729
Pilot.......................W. 3,730

BELTON, Cass Co.
Progress..................W. 3,731

BETHANY, c. h., Harrison Co., 1,200† p., on a branch of Big Creek, 60 m. N. E. of St. Joseph, 26 m. east of C. R. I. & P. Rd. Centre of trade.
Harrison Co. Herald....W. 3,732
Harrison Co. Republican.W. 3,733

BILLINGS, Christian Co.
Reformer..................W. 3,734

BLOOMFIELD, c. h., Stoddard Co., 750 p., 280 m. S. E. of Jefferson City, 30 W. of Charleston and 160 from St. Louis. Cotton, corn and tobacco are the chief products.
Stoddard Co. Messenger..W. 3,735

BOLIVAR, c. h., Polk Co., 1,000 p., 110 m. S. W. of Jefferson City, 240 S. W. from St. Louis, 30 N. of Springfield and 80 E. of Fort Scott. Farming and stock-raising country, with large mineral resources, but little developed.
Free Press...............W. 3,736
Herald....................W. 3,737

BOONEVILLE, c. h., Cooper Co., 6,500† p., on Missouri r., and Booneville branch of

MISSOURI.

Pacific Rd. of Missouri, 48 m. N. W. of Jefferson City. Engaged in trade and river commerce. The grape is cultivated in this vicinity. Mines of iron, lead, marble and stone coal are found here.

Advertiser..................D. **3,738**
" ....W. **3,739**
Central Missourier.......W. **3,740**
Eagle.......................W. **3,741**

BOWLING GREEN, c. h., Pike Co., 600 p., on Louisiana division of Chicago & Acton Rd., 10 m. from Louisiana and 92 from Jefferson City.

Post-Observer.............W. **3,742**

BRECKENBRIDGE, Caldwell Co.

Bulletin.....................W. **3,743**

BROOKFIELD, Linn Co., 2,500 p., on Hannibal & St. Joseph Rd., 102 m. from St. Joseph. Centre of agricultural district. Railroad machine shops located here.

Chronicle...................W. **3,744**
Gazette......................W. **3,745**

BROWNSVILLE, Saline Co., 2,200† p., on Black r., about 20 m W. of Sedalia.

Herald.......................W. **3,746**
Missouri Temperance Companion..............W. **3,747**
Saline Co. Messenger......W. **3,748**

BRUNSWICK, Chariton Co., 2,500† p., on Missouri r., at mouth of Grand r.. and on St. Louis, Kansas City & Northern Rd., at junction of Brunswick & Chillicothe branch, 185 m. from St. Louis and 90 from Kansas City. Engaged in manufacturing, river commerce.

Brunswicker...............W. **3,749**
News.........................W. **3,750**

BUFFALO, c. h., Dallas Co., 600 p., 32 m. N. of Springfield, 220 from St. Louis and 100 from Fort Scott. Lead and coal mines located here.

Dallas Co. Courier........W. **3,751**
Reflex........................W. **3,752**

BUTLER, c. h., Bates Co., 1,200 p., about 65 m. S. of Kansas City and 30 N. E. of Fort Scott, Kansas. Centre of an agricultural and grazing country.

Bates Co. Democrat......W. **3,753**
Bates Co. Record.........W. **3,754**

CALIFORNIA, c. h., Moniteau Co., 2,000† p., on Missouri & Pacific Rd., 25 m. from Jefferson City. County rich in mineral resources; lead and coal predominate.

Democrat...................W. **3,755**

CAMERON, Clinton Co., 2,000† p., at intersection of Hannibal & St. Joseph Rd. and Chicago, Rock Island & Pacific Rds., and junction of Kansas City division of former, 35 m. E. of St. Joseph and 53 from Kansas City. Engaged in manufacturing and surrounded by an agricultural district.

Observer....................W. **3,756**

CANTON, Lewis Co., 3,000 p., on Mississippi r. and St. Louis, Keokuk & Northwestern Rd., 22 m. below Keokuk and 200 above St. Louis. Shipping point for produce of surrounding country.

Press..........................W. **3,757**

CAPE GIRARDEAU, Cape Girardeau Co., 5,500† p., on Mississippi r., 50 m. above Cairo, Ill., 150 below St. Louis. Has a landing and river commerce. Surrounded by an agricultural country. Minerals found here. Seat of St. Vincent College and the Southeast Missouri State Normal School. Noted for its fine flour.

News.........................W. **3,758**
Western Press.............W. **3,759**
Westliche Presse..........W. **3,760**
College Message...........M. **3,761**

CARROLLTON, c. h., Carroll Co., 2,500 p., on St. Louis, Kansas City & Northern Rd., about 6 m. from Missouri r., 66 from Kansas City and 124 N. W. of Jefferson City.

Carroll Journal............W. **3,762**
Democrat...................W. **3,763**
Wakanda Record..........W. **3,764**

CARTHAGE, c. h., Jasper Co., 6,000† p., near Spring r., 220 m. S. W. of Jefferson City and 60 W. of Springfield. Engaged in manufactures. Centre of trade.

Advance.....................W. **3,765**
Banner.......................W. **3,766**
Patriot.......................W. **3,767**
People's Press.............W. **3,768**

CASSVILLE, c. h., Barry Co., 400 p., near S. W. corner of the State, 55 m. S. W. of Springfield.

Democrat...................W. **3,769**

CEDAR CITY, Callaway Co., 1,657 p., on Missouri r., opposite Jefferson City, and terminus of Louisiana division of Chicago & Alton Rd.

Gazette......................W.

CENTRALIA, Boone Co., 500† p., on St. Louis, Kansas City & Northern Rd., at junction of Columbia branch, 121 m. from St. Louis and 22 fom Columbia. Centre of a grazing and agricultural district. Principal stock shipping point for four counties. Place of active trade in produce and grain.

Our Fireside Guard......W. **3,771**

CHAMOIS, Osage Co.

Osage Co. Leader.........W. **3,772**

CHARLESTON, c. h., Mississippi Co., 1,100† p., on Iron Mountain Rd., 179 m. from St. Louis and 12 from Mississippi r. and Cairo, Ill. In a lumber region, with rich soil for general agricultural purposes.

Courier.......................W. **3,773**
Gazette.......................W. **3,774**

CHILLICOTHE, c. h., Livingston Co., 5,000 p., on Hannibal & St. Joseph Rd., at crossing of St. Louis, Council Bluffs & Omaha branch of St. Louis, Kansas City & Northern Rd., and Grand r., 130 m. from Hannibal. An agricultural and stock-raising region. Important trade centre. Manufactures of various kinds carried on.

Constitution................W. **3,775**
Tribune.......................W. **3,776**

CLARENCE, Shelby Co., 800† p., on Hannibal & St. Joseph Rd., 59 m. from Hannibal.

Tribune.......................W. **3,777**

CLARKSVILLE, Pike Co., 1,800 p., on Mississippi r., 100 m. above St. Louis. Engaged in agriculture and river commerce.

Sentinel......................W. **3,778**

CLINTON, c. h., Henry Co., 3,000 p., on Sedalia division of Missouri, Kansas & Texas Rd., 40 m. from Sedalia, 175 W. from St. Louis. Engaged in agriculture, manufacturing and stock raising.

Advocate....................W. **3,779**
Henry Co. Democrat......W. **3,780**

MISSOURI.

COLUMBIA, c. h., Boone Co., 3,200 p., 35 m. from Jefferson City and 10 from Missouri r., on Columbia branch of St. Louis, Kansas City & Northern Rd. Place of active trade and seat of State University. Also seat of "Christian Female College" and "Stephens' Female College."
Golden Age..............W. **3,781**
Missouri Herald..........W. **3,782**
Missouri Statesman......W. **3,783**
University Missourian ...M. **3,784**

COMMERCE, c. h., Scott Co., 1,267 p., on Mississippi r., about 170 m. below St. Louis and 35 above Cairo, Ill.
Dispatch..................W. **3,785**

CUBA CITY, Crawford Co.
Crawford Mirror........W. **3,786**

CURRYVILLE, Pike Co.
Pike Co. Express.........W. **3,787**

DE SOTO, Jefferson Co.
Phœnix..................W. **3,788**

DEXTER CITY, Stoddard Co.
Enterprise...............W. **3,789**

DONIPHAN, c. h., Ripley Co.
Prospect..................W. **3,790**

EASTON, Buchanan Co.
Banner, Times and Observer..................W. **3,791**

EDINA, c. h., Knox Co., 807 p., about 35 m. S. W. of Keokuk, Iowa, on Quincy, Missouri & Pacific Rd., 47 m. W. by N. of Quincy, Ill. Engaged in agriculture and stock raising. Centre of trade.
Knox Co. Democrat......W. **3,792**
Sentinel..................W. **3,793**

EMINENCE, c. h., Shannon Co.
Current Wave............W. **3,794**

FARMINGTON, c. h., St. Francois Co., 900† p., about 10 m. E. of the Iron Mountain Rd. and 60 S. of St. Louis.
New Era..................W. **3,795**
Times.....................W. **3,796**

FAYETTE, c. h., Howard Co., 1,200† p., about 12 m. from Missouri r., 60 N. W. of Jefferson City and 100 from St. Louis. In a farming district.
Howard Co. Advertiser..W. **3,797**

FORSYTH, c. h., Taney Co., 560 p., on White r., 45 m. S. of Springfield. Engaged in agriculture, fruit growing, stock raising and lumber manufacturing.
Pioneer Farmer..........W. **3,798**
Times.....................W. **3,799**

FREDERICKTOWN, c. h., Madison Co., 2,000† p., on St. Francis r. and Iron Mountain Rd., 155 m. from St. Louis. Lead and iron found in this vicinity.
Farmer and Miner......W. **3,800**
Plain Dealer.............W. **3,801**

FULTON, c. h., Callaway Co., 2,500† p., on Louisiana division of Chicago & Alton Rd., 20 m. from Jefferson City. State Lunatic and Deaf and Dumb Asylums and Westminster College located here. Earthenware manufactured. Centre of a stock-growing country.
Enterprise...............W. **3,802**
Telegraph................W. **3,803**

GALLATIN, c. h., Daviess Co., 1,600† p., near Grand r. and on Chillicothe & Omaha division of St. Louis, Kansas City and Northern Rd., about 50 m. E. of St. Joseph. Surrounded by a well watered agricultural district.

MISSOURI.

Democrat................W. **3,804**
North Missourian.......W. **3,805**

GAYOSO, c. h., Pemiscot Co., 700 p., near Mississippi r., at Walker's bend, 40 m. by water below New Madrid and 310 E. of Jefferson City.
South-East Missouri Statesman....................W. **3,806**

GLASGOW, Howard Co., 2,000† p., on Missouri r., 75 m. from Jefferson City and 12 from Fayette. Shipping point for produce of county. Large quantities of tobacco are raised. Engaged in manufacturing.
Journal...................W. **3,807**

GLENWOOD, Schuyler Co., 680 p., on northern division of St. Louis, Kansas City & Northern Rd., 227 m. from St. Louis and 50 from Ottumwa, Iowa. Centre of an agricultural district. Coal found here.
Criterion.................W. **3,808**

GRAHAM, Nodaway Co.
Headlight................W. **3,809**

GRANBY, Newton Co.
Miner....................W. **3,810**

GRANT CITY, c. h., Worth Co., 700 p., 291 m. (mail route) N. W. of Jefferson City, 60 N. of St. Joseph and 6 from Iowa line. A thriving place in the centre of an agricultural and stock raising district.
Star.......................W. **3,811**
Worth Co. Times.........W. **3,812**

GREENFIELD, c. h., Dade Co., 650 p., on Big Sac r., 35 m. N. W. of Springfield. In an agricultural and stock raising district.
Dade Co. Advocate.......W. **3,813**
Vedette...................W. **3,814**

HAMILTON, Caldwell Co., 1,250 p., on Hannibal & St. Joseph Rd., 50 m. from St. Joseph, Mo. A shipping point for counties N. and S. Engaged in agriculture and manufacturing.
News.....................W. **3,815**

HANNIBAL, Marion Co., 15,000† p., on Mississippi r., 153 m. above St. Louis and 20 below Quincy, Ill., and on Hannibal & St. Joseph and other Rds. Engaged in trade and river commerce. One of the most important shipping points in the State. Considerable manufacturing done here.
Clipper....................D. **3,816**
" ....W. **3,817**
Courier...................D. **3,818**
" ....W. **3,819**
Monitor...................W. **3,820**

HARRISONVILLE, c. h., Cass Co., 1,032 p., on Osage division of Missouri, Kansas & Texas Rd., 22 m. from Holden and 32 from Paola, Kansas. In an agricultural and coal district.
Cass Co. Courier.........W. **3,821**

HARTVILLE, c. h., Wright Co., on Gasconade r., 150 m. (mail route) S. of Jefferson City and 20 E. by S. of Springfield. Lead, copper and iron ore are found in the vicinity.
News.....................W. **3,822**

HERMANN, c. h., Gasconade Co., 1,500† p., on Missouri r. and Missouri Pacific Rd., 81 m. from St. Louis.
Advertiser................W. **3,823**
Gasconade Co. Courier...W. **3,824**
Hermanner Volksblatt...W. **3,825**

MISSOURI.

HERMITAGE, c. h., Hickory Co., 300† p., on Pomme de la Terre r., 90 m. from Jefferson City.
New Era....W. 3,826

HILLSBORO, c. h., Jefferson Co., 500 p., 4½ m. from St. Louis & Iron Mountain Rd. and 40 from St. Louis. Engaged in horticultural pursuits. Milling and manufacturing also carried on. Also a mining centre.
Jefferson Democrat....W. 3,827

HOLDEN, Johnson Co., 2,027 p., on Missouri Pacific Rd., at junction of Osage division of Missouri, Kansas & Texas Rd., 50 m. S. E. of Kansas City and 14 W. of Warrensburg. Agricultural district and centre of trade.
Enterprise....W. 3,828

HOPKINS, Nodaway Co.
Journal....W. 3,829

HOUSTON, c. h., Texas Co., 350 p., 100 m. S. of Jefferson City, 116 from St. Louis and 55 from Rolla, the county seat.
Democrat....W. 3,830
Texas Co. Pioneer....W. 3,831

HUNTSVILLE, c. h., Randolph Co., 2,500† p., on St. Louis & Northern Rd., 153 m. from St. Louis and 119 from Kansas City. Centre of trade. Engaged in manufactures. Surrounding country contains deposits of stone coal. Seat of Mount Pleasant College.
Herald....W. 3,832

INDEPENDENCE, c. h., Jackson Co., 3,500† p., on Missouri Pacific Rd., 10 m. from Kansas City.
Herald....W. 3,833
Sentinel....W. 3,834

IRONTON, c. h., Iron Co., 1,500 p., on St. Louis, Iron Mountain & Southern Rd., 90 m. from St. Louis. Agriculture and manufacturing are the chief industries.
Iron Co. Register....W. 3,835
South-East Missouri Enterprise.

JACKSON, Cape Girardeau Co., 750 p., 10 m. W. of Cape Girardeau and 10 from line of St. Louis & Iron Mountain Rd. Centre of an agricultural region.
Missouri Cash Book....W. 3,837

JAMESPORT, Daviess Co.
Independent....W. 3,838

JEFFERSON CITY, c. h., Cole Co., State capital, 6,000† p., on Missouri r. and Pacific Rd. of Missouri, and terminus of Louisiana division of Chicago & Alton Rd., 125 m. from St. Louis. Surrounded by an agricultural and mining district.
State Journal....D. 3,839
" "....W. 3,840
Missouri Volksfreund....W. 3,841
People's Tribune....W. 3,842

JOPLIN, Jasper Co.
Bulletin....W. 3,843
Mining News....W. 3,844

KAHOKA, Clark Co.
Gazette....W. 3,845

KANSAS CITY, Jackson Co., 42,000† p., on Missouri r., near mouth of Kansas r., and centering point of 11 railroads. Engaged in manufactures and commerce.
Evening Mail....D. 3,846
Journal of Commerce....D. 3,847
" " "....T. W. 3,848

MISSOURI.

Journal of Commerce....W 3,849
Kansas Courier....D. 3,850
News....D. 3,851
"....W. 3,852
Post and Tribune....D. 3,853
Westliche Volkszeitung....W. 3,854
Times....D. 3,855
"....T. W. 3,856
"....W. 3,857
Price Current....W. 3,858
Coin and Stamp Journal.M. 3,859

KENNETT, c. h., Dunklin Co.
South-East Advertiser....W. 3,860

KEYTESVILLE, Chariton Co., 529 p., on Chariton r. and St. Louis, Kansas City & Northern Rd., 174 m. from St. Louis.
Herald....W. 3,861

KINGSTON, c. h., Caldwell Co., 700 p., about 8 m. from Hannibal & St. Joseph Rd. and 50 E. of St. Joseph. Surrounded by an agricultural district. Engaged in milling and manufacturing.
Caldwell Citizen....W. 3,862
Caldwell Co. Sentinel....W. 3,863

KIRKSVILLE, c. h., Adair Co., 2,200 p., on Quincy, Missouri & Pacific Rd., at crossing of St. Louis, Kansas City & Northern Rd., 70 m. W. of Quincy, Ill. An agricultural district. A point of considerable trade. State Normal School located here.
Journal....W. 3,864
North Missouri Register..W. 3,865

KNOB-NOSTER, Johnson Co., 1,600 p., on Missouri Pacific Rd., 207 m. W. of St. Louis and 20 from Sedalia.
Taylor's Local....W.

LACLEDE, Linn Co., 1,000† p., on Hannibal & St. Joseph and Burlington & Southwestern Rds., 109 m. from Hannibal and 21 from Chillicothe. In the midst of an agricultural country.
Centennial....W. 3,867

LA GRANGE, Lewis Co., 1,825 p., on Mississippi r. and Mississippi Valley & Western Rd., 12 m. from Quincy, Ill., and 28 below Keokuk. Engaged in trade and river commerce.
Baptist Battle Flag and Church Historian....W. 3,868
Democrat....W. 3,869

LAMAR, c. h., Barton Co., 1,050 p., 150 m. S. W. of Jefferson City and 40 from Fort Scott, Kansas.
Barton Co. Advocate....W. 3,870
Independent....W. 3,871

LANCASTER, c. h., Schuyler Co., 800 p., on Missouri, Iowa & Nebraska Rd., 60 m. W. by N. of Keokuk, Iowa, and 140 N. by E. of Jefferson City. Engaged in agriculture, stock raising and manufacturing. Wood, coal and water in abundance.
Excelsior....W. 3,872

LA PLATA, Macon Co., 546 p., on Northern division of St. Louis, Kansas City & Northern Rd., 43 m. from Moberly and 88 from Ottumwa, Iowa.
Advocate....W. 3,873

LATHROP, Clinton Co., 780 p., on Kansas City division of Hannibal & St. Joseph Rd., at crossing of Lexington and St. Joseph branch of St. Louis, Kansas City & Northern Rd., 38 m. N. of Kansas City

and about 10 from Plattsburg. A trading point, in centre of an agricultural county.
Monitor..................W. **3,874**

LEBANON, c. h., Laclede Co., 1,500† p., on Atlantic & Pacific Rd., 185 m. from St. Louis and about 85 from Jefferson City. Engaged in agriculture and manufacturing. A trade centre.
Anti-Monopolist.........W. **3,875**
Journal...................W. **3,876**

LEXINGTON, c. h., La Fayette Co., 4,373 p., on Missouri r. and Lexington branch of Missouri Pacific Rd., 120 m. from Jefferson City. Engaged in agriculture, manufacturing and river commerce. Coal beds in vicinity.
Intelligencer..............W. **3,877**
Missouri Thalbote........W. **3,878**
Register...................W. **3,879**

LIBERTY, c. h., Clay Co., 1,710 p., on Kansas City division of Hannibal & St. Joseph Rd., 15 m. from Kansas City. Agriculture the chief industry. Manufacturing done here.
Advance..................W. **3,880**
Tribune...................W. **3,881**

LINN, c. h., Osage Co., 300† p., 21 m. E. of Jefferson City and 12 from Missouri Pacific Rd. Centre of an agricultural country
Osage Co. News..........W. **3,882**

LINNEUS, c. h., Linn Co., 2,000 p., about 10 m. N. W. of Brookfield. In an agricultural section.
Bulletin...................W. **3,883**

LOUISIANA, Pike Co., 4,509 p., on Mississippi r., 27 m. below Hannibal and 115 N. of St. Louis. On Louisiana division of Chicago & Alton Rd. Shipping point for the produce from surrounding agricultural district. Engaged in manufacturing.
Journal....................W. **3,884**
Riverside Press...........W. **3,885**

MACON, c. h., Macon Co., 4,000 p., on Hannibal & St. Joseph Rd., at crossing of St. Louis, Kansas City & Northern Rd., 70 m. from Hannibal, 136 from St. Joseph and 169 from St. Louis. Centre of an agricultural district. Engaged in manufacturing and trade.
Examiner...................W. **3,866**
Missouri Granger........W. **3,887**
Republican................W. **3,888**
Messenger of Peace....B. W. **3,889**

MARBLE HILL, c. h., Bollinger Co., 800 p., on St. Louis & Iron Mountain Rd., 134 m. S. of St. Louis. Agriculture, mining and lumber business are the chief industries.
Herald.....................W. **3,890**

MARSHALL, Saline Co., 1,800† p., about 15 m. from Missouri r., at two almost opposite points, and about 87 W. by N. of Jefferson City.
Saline Co. Democrat......W. **3,891**
Saline Co. Progress.......W. **3,892**

MARSHFIELD, c. h., Webster Co., 1,000 p., on Atlantic & Pacific Rd., 24 m. N. E. of Springfield and 217 S. W. of St. Louis. Surrounded by an agricultural and mineral country.
Democrat..................W. **3,893**
Farmer's Friend.........W. **3,894**

MARYVILLE, c. h., Nodaway Co., 3,000† p., on Maryville branch of Kansas City, St. Joseph & Council Bluffs Rd., 45 m. N. of St. Joseph. A farming region, suitable for grain, hogs and cattle.
Nodaway Co. Republican.W. **3,895**
Nodaway Democrat......W. **3,896**

MAYSVILLE, c. h., De Kalb Co., 600 p., 30 m. E. by N. of St. Joseph. Engaged in stock-raising and agriculture.
Register...................W. **3,897**

MEMPHIS, c. h., Scotland Co., 1,500† p., on Missouri, Iowa & Nebraska Rd., about 40 m. W. of Keokuk and 140 N. of Jefferson City. Ships large quantities of wool. and is surrounded by a farming and stock-raising district.
Conservative..............W. **3,898**
Reveille....................W. **3,899**
Scotland Co. News.......W. **3,900**

MEXICO, c. h., Audrain Co., 4,500† p., on Salt r. and St. Louis, Kansas City & Northern Rd., at crossing of Louisiana division of Chicago & Alton Rd., 108 m. from St. Louis and 52 from Jefferson City.
Intelligencer..............W. **3,901**
Missouri Messenger......W. **3,902**

MIAMI, Carroll Co.
Index.......................W. **3,903**

MILAN, c. h., Sullivan Co., 1,000 p., 31 m. N. of Hannibal & St. Joseph Rd., at La Clede, and 35 N. E. of Chillicothe.
Republican................W. **3,904**
Sullivan Standard........W. **3,905**

MOBERLY, Randolph Co.
Daily........................D. **3,906**
Enterprise-Monitor.......D. **3,907**
" "   ......W. **3,908**
Headlight..................W. **3,909**

MONROE CITY, Monroe Co., 400 p., on Hannibal & St. Joseph Rd., 30 m. W. of Hannibal and 20 N. E. of Paris.
News........................W. **3,910**

MONTGOMERY CITY, Montgomery Co., 1,800† p., on St. Louis, Kansas City & Northern Rd., 80 m. from St. Louis. Centre of trade. Best business point in county.
Montgomery Standard...W. **3,911**
Ray..........................W. **3,912**

MORLEY, Scott Co.
Transcript................W. **3,913**

MOUND CITY, Holt Co.
Globe.......................W. **3,914**

MOUNT VERNON, c. h., Lawrence Co., 1,200 p., about 8 m. from Atlantic & Pacific Rd. and 32 W. of Springfield. Its industries are agriculture, stock-raising and fruit-growing.
Fountain and Journal...W. **3,915**
Lawrence Chieftain.....W. **3,916**

NEOSHO, c. h., Newton Co., 1,100 p., on Atlantic & Pacific Rd., 73 m. S. W. of Springfield. In the newly-discovered lead regions of southwest Missouri. Surrounded by an agricultural district and engaged in manufacturing and trade.
Journal.....................W. **3,917**
Times.......................W. **3,918**

NEVADA, c. h., 2,000 p., on Sedalia division of Missouri, Kansas & Texas Rd., 90 m. from Sedalia, 90 S. of Kansas City and 20 E. of Fort Scott, Kan.
Ledger......................W. **3,919**
Living Democrat..........W. **3,920**

NEW CAMBRIA, Macon Co.
Enterprise.................W. **3,921**

MISSOURI.

NEW LONDON, c. h., Ralls Co., 410 p., on Salt r., 10 m. S. of Hannibal. Surrounded by a fertile agricultural district and rapidly increasing in population.
Ralls Co. Record.........W. **3,922**

NEW MADRID, c. h., New Madrid Co., 855 p., on Mississippi r., about 40 m. S. by W. of Cairo, Ill. Has considerable river commerce.
Record...................W. **3,923**

NORBORNE, Carroll Co.
Independent.............W. **3,924**

NORTH SPRINGFIELD, Greene Co.
South-West..............W. **3,925**

OAK RIDGE, Cape Girardeau Co.
School World.............M. **3,926**

OREGON, c. h., Holt Co., 1,200 p., 2½ m. from Missouri r., and about 25 in a direct line from St. Joseph, 2 from Kansas City, St. Joseph & Council Bluffs Rd., and 100 from Omaha. Agricultural region and trade centre. Some manufacturing done.
Holt Co. Sentinel........W. **3,927**
Missouri Valley Times...W. **3,928**

OSCEOLA, c. h., St. Clair Co., 800† p., on Osage r., 132 m. from Jefferson City and 60 S. by W. of Sedalia. The Osage r. is navigable for boats to this point.
Sentinel..................W. **3,929**

OZARK, Christian Co., 500 p., 15 m. S. E. of Springfield. Surrounded by a fruit and tobacco growing and farming country.
Monitor and Leader......W. **3,930**

PACIFIC, Franklin Co., 1,500 p., at junction of Atlantic & Pacific with Pacific Rd. of Missouri, 37 m. from St. Louis. A centre of business.
Franklin Co. Democrat..W. **3,931**

PALMYRA, c. h., Marion Co., 4,000 p., on Hannibal & St. Joseph Rd., at junction of Quincy branch, 12 m. from Quincy. Agriculture, manufacture and trade carried on.
Marion Co. Democrat....W. **3,932**
Spectator.................W. **3,933**

PARIS, c. h., Monroe Co., 1,450† p., on Hannibal & Central Missouri division of Toledo, Wabash & Western Rd., 40 m. W. S. W. of Hannibal. Surrounded by a farming district.
Mercury..................W. **3,934**
Monroe Co. Appeal......W. **3,935**

PEIRCE CITY, Lawrence Co., 1,500† p., on Atlantic & Pacific Rd., at junction of Memphis, Carthage & Northwestern Rd., 50 m. from Springfield and 27 from Carthage.
Record...................W. **3,936**

PERRYVILLE, c. h., Perry Co., 1,000 p., about 12 m. from Mississippi r. and 85 S. of St. Louis.
People's Forum..........W. **3,937**
Union.....................W. **3,938**

PIEDMONT, Wayne Co., 1,000† p., on the Iron Mountain Rd., 112 m. from St. Louis. A trade centre. Engaged in agriculture and lumber trade.
Times.....................W. **3,939**

PLATTE CITY, c. h., Platte Co., 650 p., on Platte r., 7 m. from Missouri r. and 20 N. by W. of Kansas City.
Landmark................W. **3,940**
Platte Co. Advocate......W. **3,941**

MISSOURI.

PLATTSBURG, c. h., Clinton Co., 1,700 p., on S. W. division of Chicago, Rock Island & Pacific Rd., at intersection of Lexington & St. Joseph branch of St. Louis, Kansas City & Northern Rd., 28 m. S. E. of St. Joseph, 33 from Kansas City and 37 from Leavenworth.
Clinton Co. Register......W. **3,942**
Lever......................W. **3,943**

PLEASANT HILL, Cass Co., 1,554 p., on Missouri Pacific Rd., 37 m. S. E. of Kansas City and 248 from St. Louis. Engaged in manufacturing.
Cass Co. Times..........W. **3,944**
Review....................W. **3,945**
Western Dispatch........W. **3,946**

POPLAR BLUFF, c. h., Butler Co.
Bluff Citizen.............W. **3,947**
New Era..................W. **3,948**

POTOSI, c. h., Washington Co., 1,000 p., on Potosi branch of Iron Mountain Rd., 65 m. from St. Louis. Extensively engaged in the lumber trade. Rich mines of iron and lead are worked in the vicinity.
Independent...............W. **3,949**
Washington Co. Journal.W.

PRINCETON, c. h., Mercer Co., 600 p., on Grand r. and on the line of the Southwestern branch of Chicago, Rock Island & Pacific Rd., about 45 m. N. of Chillicothe.
Advance..................W. **3,951**
Telegraph.................W. **3,952**

QUEEN CITY, Schuyler Co.
Globe......................W. **3,953**

RICHLAND, Pulaski Co.
Sentinel..................W. **3,954**

RICHMOND, c. h., Ray Co., 2,500 p., about 7 m. from Missouri r. and 40 E. by N. of Kansas City, on branch of St. Louis, Kansas City & Northern Rd., 68 m. from St. Joseph. Surrounded by an agricultural district. It has fine mercantile and manufacturing interests.
Conservator..............W. **3,955**
Ray Co. Chronicle.......W. **3,956**

ROCK PORT, c. h., Atchison Co., 1,000 p., about 8 m. E. of Missouri r., 60 N. W. of St. Joseph, and 4 from Kansas City, St. Joseph & Council Bluffs Rd. Centre of an agricultural region.
Atchison Co. Journal....W. **3,957**

ROLLA, c. h., Phelps Co., 2,500 p., on Atlantic & Pacific Rd., 113 m. W. S. W. of St. Louis. Situated in an iron mining district. Several smelting furnaces in the vicinity. State mining school located here.
Eagle......................W. **3,958**
Herald....................W. **3,959**
Phelps Co. New Era.....W. **3,960**

ST. CHARLES, c. h., St. Charles Co., 7,000 p., on Missouri r. at crossing of St. Louis, Kansas City & Northern Rd., 20 m. from St. Louis. Engaged in woolen and other manufactures and a place of active business. Mines of coal are worked in the vicinity.
Cosmos....................W. **3,961**
Demokrat.................W. **3,962**
News......................W. **3,963**
Zeitung...................W. **3,964**
Gossip.....................M. **3,965**

ST. GENEVIEVE, c. h., St. Genevieve Co., 1,521 p., on Mississippi r., 60 m. below St. Louis. Shipping point for the products

MISSOURI.

of the iron works at Iron Mountain. Large quantities of white sand are exported from here to be used in the manufacture of glass. Fruit culture and wine making carried on to a considerable extent.

Fair Play................W. **3,966**
Free Press.

ST. JOSEPH, c. h., Buchanan Co., 19,565 p., on Missouri r., at terminus of several important Rds., 206 m. from Hannibal and 275 from St. Louis.

Das Westliche Volksblatt..D. **3,968**
" " " .W. **3,969**
Gazette..................D. **3,970**
" ....W. **3,971**
Herald..................D. **3,972**
" ....W. **3,973**
Saturday Chronicle......W. **3,974**

ST. LOUIS, c. h., St. Louis Co., 310,864 p., on Mississippi r., about 20 m. below the mouth of Missouri r. The great metropolis of the West, and centre of trade and commerce of the two great rivers and their tributaries. Steamboats ply between St. Louis and almost all of the cities and towns in the West and Northwest that can be reached by water communication. Railroads connect, east and west, with all the principal cities in the United States.

Amerika.................D. **3,975**
" ....W. **3,976**
Amerika Sonntags-blatt................Sund. **3,977**
Anzeiger des Westens.....D. **3,978**
" " " ....W. **3,979**
Dispatch.................D. **3,980**
" ....W. **3,981**
Globe-Democrat...........D. **3,982**
" " ....S. W. **3,983**
" " ....W. **3,984**
Journal..................D. **3,985**
" ....W. **3,986**
Republican...............D. **3,987**
" ....T. W. **3,988**
Missouri Republican......W. **3,989**
Times....................D. **3,990**
" ....T. W. **3,991**
" ....W. **3,992**
Westliche Post...........D. **3,993**
" " ....W. **3,994**
South St. Louis News..S. W. **3,995**
Carondelet Review.......W. **3,996**
Central Baptist..........W. **3,997**
Central Christian Advocate....................W. **3,998**
Central Law Journal....W. **3,999**
Christian................W. **4,000**
Christian Advocate......W. **4,001**
Coleman's Rural World..W. **4,002**
Commercial..............W. **4,003**
Commercial Advocate....W. **4,004**
Commercial Gazette......W. **4,005**
Der Herold des Glaubens.W. **4,006**
Die Abendschule..........W. **4,007**
Bieblatt..................M. **4,008**
Dry Goods and Grocery Reporter................W. **4,009**
Journal of Agriculture and Farmer...........W. **4,010**
Journal of Commerce....W. **4,011**
" " ..S. M. **4,012**
" " .... M. **4,013**
Little Watchman.........W. **4,014**
" " ....M. **4,015**
Live Stock and Commercial Record........W. **4,016**
Mines, Metals and Arts..W. **4,017**
Presbyterian.............W. **4,018**
Price Current............W. **4,019**
Trade Journal............W. **4,020**
Western Watchman......W. **4,021**
Der Lutheraner ....S. M. **4 022**
Hardware, Stove and Tin Trade Journal.......S. M. **4,023**
American Journal of Education................M. **4,024**
American Medical Journal....................M. **4,025**
American Sunday School Worker................M. **4,026**
Central Magazine.........M. **4,027**
Christian News...........M. **4,028**
Church News.............M. **4,029**
Clinical Record..........M. **4,030**
Evangelist...............M. **4,031**
Fireside Visitor..........M. **4,032**
Ford's Christian Repository.....................M. **4,033**
Inland Magazine..........M. **4,034**
Irving Union.............M. **4,035**
Medical and Surgical Journal................M. **4,036**
Medical Brief.............M. **4,037**
Mercantile Circulator....M.
Midland Farmer..........M. **4,039**
Mississippi Valley Progress....................M. **4,040**
Missouri Dental Journal.M. **4,041**
Post Office Bulletin.......M. **4,042**
Truth....................M. **4 043**
Ware's Valley Monthly...M. **4,044**
Western..................M. **4,045**
Western Insurance Review..................M. **4,046**
Printers' Register.....B. M. **4,047**
Journal of Speculative Philosophy............Qr. **4,048**
Southern Law Review....Qr. **4,049**
Southern Review.........Qr. **4,050**

SALEM, c. h., Dent Co., 1,500† p., 25 m. S. E. of Atlantic & Pacific Rd., at Rolla, and 120 S. W. of St. Louis. Centre of an agricultural region.

Monitor..................W. **4,051**
Western Success.........W. **4,052**

SALISBURY, Chariton Co., 1,500† p., on St. Louis, Kansas City & Northern Rd., 18 m. E. of Brunswick. Tobacco raised here.

Press.....................W. **4,053**

SAVANNAH, c. h., Andrew Co., 1,600† p., on Hopkins branch of Kansas City, St. Joseph & Council Bluffs Rd., 15 m. from St. Joseph. Engaged in agriculture and stock raising.

Andrew Co. Republican..W. **4,054**
Mason's and Odd Fellow's Reporter................W. **4,055**
Patron of Husbandry....W. **4,056**

SEDALIA, c. h., Pettis Co., 5,800 p., on Missouri Pacific Rd., at junction of Lexington branch and terminus of Sedalia division of Missouri, Kansas & Texas Rd., 64 m. from Jefferson City. Surrounded by an agricultural region. Coal in abundance. Engaged in manufacturing.

Bazoo.....................D. **4,057**
" ....W. **4,058**
Sunday Morning Bazoo..W. **4,059**
Democrat.................D. **4,060**
" ....W. **1,061**
Opinion..................W. **4,062**
Times....................W. **4,063**
Great South-West...... M. **4,064**

MISSOURI.

SHELBINA, Shelby Co., 1,500 p., on Hannibal & St. Joseph Rd., 47 m. W. of Hannibal. Engaged in tobacco and stock raising.
Democrat................W. **4,065**

SHELBYVILLE, c. h., Shelby Co., 900 p., 8 m. from the Hannibal & St. Joseph Rd. and 90 N. N. E. of Jefferson City.
Shelby Co. Herald........W. **4,066**

SPRINGFIELD, c. h., Greene Co., 8,500† p., on Atlantic & Pacific Rd., 130 m. S. W. of Jefferson City, 241 S. W. of St. Louis. The most important place in this section of the State and centre of an agricultural district.
Advertiser...............W. **4,067**
Leader...................W. **4,068**
Missouri Patriot.........W. **4,069**
Times....................W. **4,070**

STEELVILLE, c. h., Crawford Co., 400 p., about 10 m. S. of line of Atlantic & Pacific Rd., 95 m. S. W. of St. Louis. Engaged in agriculture, coal and iron mining.
Register.................W. **4,071**

STOCKTON, c. h., Cedar Co., 500 p., 50 m. N. W. of Springfield. Engaged in agriculture and stock raising.
Journal..................W. **4,072**

STOUTLAND, Camden Co.
Country Standard .....W. **4,073**
Rustic. ....W. **4,074**

STURGEON, Boone Co., 1,000 p., on St. Louis, Kansas City & Northern Rd., 129 m. from St. Louis. Centre of a thriving trade. In the midst of an agricultural and stock-raising section.
Leader...................W. **4,075**

TRENTON, c. h., Grundy Co., 4,000† p., near Grand r., and on S. W. division of Chicago, Rock Island & Pacific Rd., 100 m. from St. Joseph and 26 N. W. of Chillicothe. Engaged in agriculture and manufacturing. Railroad machine shops located here.
Grundy Co. Times ....W. **4,076**
Republican...............W. **4,077**

TROY, c. h., Lincoln Co., 800 p., about 15 m. W. of Mississippi r., 15 N. E. of Warrenton and 55 N. W. of St. Louis. Principally engaged in agriculture. A coal mine within six miles of town.
Herald...................W. **4,078**

TUSCUMBIA, c. h., Miller Co., 540 p., on Osage r., 35 m. S. by W. of Jefferson City. Principal branch of industry is mining lead and iron. Possesses water power. Timber in great abundance in the vicinity.
Helmet...................W. **4,079**
Miller Co. Vidette........W. **4,080**

UNION, c. h., Franklin Co., 600† p., about 8 m. S. of Washington, 55 W. of St. Louis.
Franklin Co. Record.....W. **4,081**

UNIONVILLE, c. h., Putnam Co., 1,200† p., about 150 m. N. by W. of Jefferson City, on Burlington & Southwestern Rd., 130 m. from Burlington. An agricultural county.
Putnam Co. Ledger......W. **4,082**
Republican..............W. **4,083**

UTICA, Livingston Co.
Herald...................W. **4,084**

VANDALIA, Audrain Co.
Leader...................W. **4,085**

VERSAILLES, Morgan Co., 600 p., 46 m. S. W. of Jefferson City and 160 W. of St. Louis. Engaged in lead mining. Coal, iron and copper are found here.
Gazette..................W. **4,086**

VIENNA, c. h., Maries Co.
Courier..................W. **4,087**

WARRENSBURG, c. h., Johnson Co., 5,000† p., on Missouri Pacific Rd., 218 m. from St. Louis and 70 from Kansas City. Centre of a fertile and productive farming district. Engaged in manufactures.
News.....................D. **4,088**
Standard ....D. **4,089**
" ....W. **4,090**
Democrat................W. **4,091**
Journal..................W. **4,092**

WARRENTON, c. h., Warren Co., 800 p., on St. Louis, Kansas City & Northern Rd., 58 m. from St. Louis and about 15 from Missouri r. A place of active trade, surrounded by an agricultural district.
Missouri Banner........W. **4,093**
Warren Co. Citizen......W. **4,094**

WARSAW, c. h., Benton Co., 1,000 p., on Osage r., 80 m. S. W. of Jefferson City. Engaged in agriculture, mining and manufacturing lumber.
Democratic Press........W. **4,095**
Times....................W. **4,096**

WASHINGTON, Franklin Co., 5,614 p., on Missouri r. and on Pacific Rd. of Missouri, 54 m. from St. Louis. A shipping point for produce of surrounding country.
Die Washingtoner Post...W. **4,097**
Franklin Co. Observer....W. **4,098**

WAYNESVILLE, c. h., Pulaski Co., 850 p., 65 m S. of Jefferson City and 10 from the Atlantic & Pacific Rd.
Gasconade Valley Plain-Dealer...............W. **4,099**

WESTON, Platte Co., 2,200 p., on Missouri r. and Kansas City, St. Joseph & Council Bluffs Rd., 7 m. above Leavenworth, Kansas, and 30 direct from St. Joseph. An important commercial point. Engaged in milling, pork packing, distilling and manufacturing furniture.
Commercial............. W. **4,100**

WEST PLAINS, c. h., Howell Co., 1,000† p., about 130 m. S. of Jefferson City. Engaged in agriculture and lumber trade.
Journal..................W. **4,101**

NEBRASKA.

ALBION, c. h., Boone Co.
Review...................W. **4,102**

ASHLAND, c. h., Saunders Co., 653 p., on Saline r. and Burlington & Missouri R. Rd., 21 m. E. of Lincoln. Trade centre.
Saunders Co. Republican.W. **4,103**

AURORA, Hamilton Co.
Republican..............W. **4,104**

BEATRICE, c. h., Gage Co., 1,500† p., on Big Blue r. and Beatrice branch of Burlington & Missouri R. Rd., 51 m. from Lincoln and about 128 S. W. of Omaha. Has water power, which is employed in manufacture of flour and lumber.
Courier..................W. **4,105**
Express..................W. **4,106**
Nebraska Teacher........M. **4,107**

BEAVER CITY, c. h., Furnas Co.
Western Leader..........W. **4,108**

NEBRASKA.

BELL CREEK, Washington Co.
Sentinel..................W. **4,109**

BLAIR, c. h., Washington Co., 850† p., 3 m. from Missouri r., at crossing of Sioux City & Pacific & Omaha and Northwestern Rds., 26 m. N. of Omaha and 3 from Missouri r. A corn and wheat-producing section.
Pilot..................W. **4,110**
Times..................W. **4,111**

BLOOMINGTON, c. h., Franklin Co.
Guard..................W. **4,112**

BROWNVILLE, c. h., Nemaha Co., 2,386 p., on Missouri r., in an agricultural district, 125 m. below Omaha and an equal distance from St. Joseph.
Nebraska Advertiser.....W. **4,113**
Nemaha Co. Granger....W. **4,114**

CALAMUS, Valley Co.
Valley Co. Herald.......W. **4,_.5**

CENTRAL CITY, c. h., Merrick Co., 500† p., near Platte r. and on Union Pacific Rd., 132 m. W. of Omaha. A manufacturing place and trade centre.
Courier..................W. **4,116**

COLUMBUS, c. h., Platte Co., 600 p., on Platte r., at junction of Loup r. and Union Pacific Rd., 92 m. from Omaha. Business centre of a farming and grazing district.
Era..................W. **4,117**
Journal..................W.
Republican..................W. **4,119**

CRETE, Saline Co., 1,200† p., on Big Blue r., at crossing of Burlington & Missouri R. Rd., and junction of Beatrice branch, 20 m. from Lincoln.
Saline Co. Post..........W. **4,120**
Sentinel..................W. **4,121**

DAKOTA CITY, c. h., Dakota Co., 500 p., on Missouri r., 5 m. from Sioux City, Iowa, and 90 from Omaha. Engaged in agriculture, commerce, manufactures and mercantile pursuits.
Mail..................W. **4,122**

DAVID CITY, c. h., Butler Co.
Butler Co. Press.........W. **4,123**

DE WITT, Saline Co.
Opposition..................W. **4,124**

EDGAR, Clay Co.
Exponent..................W. **4,125**

FAIRBURY, c. h., Jefferson Co., 640 p., on St. Joseph & Denver City Rd., 65 m. S. W. of Lincoln.
Gazette..................W. **4,126**

FAIRMONT, Filmore Co., 500† p., on Burlington & Missouri R. Rd., 53 m. W. of Lincoln.
Bulletin..................W. **4,127**
Filmore Co. Review......W. **4,128**

FALLS CITY, c. h., Richardson Co., 607 p., on Atchison & Nebraska Rd., 55 m. from Atchison, 102 from Lincoln, 125 below Omaha and about 20 W. of Missouri r. at Rulo. Centre of an agricultural district. Fall wheat and corn the principal products. Engaged in stock-raising.
Globe Journal...........W. **4,129**
Press..................W. **4,130**

FREMONT, c. h., Dodge Co., 2,500† p., 3 m. from Platte r., on Union Pacific Rd., 47 N. W. of Omaha and at junction of Sioux City & Pacific Rd.
Herald..................D. **4,131**

NEBRASKA.

Herald..................W. **4,132**
Tribune..................W. **4,133**

GRAND ISLAND, c. h., Hall Co., 1,700† p., on Union Pacific Rd., 1½ m. from Platte r., and 154 from Omaha. Engaged in agriculture, fruit growing and lumber trade.
*Platte Valley Independent*W. **4,134**
Times..................W. **4,135**

HARVARD, Clay Co.
Advocate..................W. **4,136**

HASTINGS, Adams Co.
Journal..................W. **4,137**

HEBRON, c. h., Thayer Co., 400 p., on Little Blue r., 75 m. S. W. of Lincoln. Centre of an agricultural and stock-raising country.
Journal..................W. **4,138**
Thayer Co. Sentinel......W. **4,139**

JUNIATA, c. h., Adams Co., 275† p., 100 m. W. of Lincoln, on B. & M. Rd.
Adams Co. Gazette.......W. **4,140**

KEARNEY, Buffalo Co.
Press..................D. **4,141**
Central Nebraska Press..W. **4,142**
Times..................D. **4,143**
"..................W. **4,144**

LA PORTE, c. h., Wayne Co.
Wayne Co. Review.......W. **4,145**

LINCOLN, Lancaster Co., 7,000† p., State capital, on Salt Creek, 89 m. S. W. of Omaha, on Burlington & Missouri R. and Midland Pacific and Atchison & Nebraska Rds. State buildings located here, also several institutions of learning. Some manufacturing carried on.
Evening Star.
Farmers' Blade.
State Journal............D. **4,148**
Nebraska State Journal..W. **4,149**
Nebraska Staats-Zeitung..W. **4,150**
Spy.
Hesperian Student.......M. **4,152**

LOWELL, Kearney Co.
Register..................W. **4,153**

MADISON, Madison Co.
Review..................W. **4,154**

NEBRASKA CITY, c. h., Otoe Co., 8,000 p., on Missouri r., at junction of Kansas City, St. Joseph & Council Bluffs, Burlington & Missouri R., and eastern terminus of Nebraska Rds., 46 m. S. by E. of Omaha. Place of trade.
Nebraska Press............D. **4,155**
" "..........W. **4,156**
News..................W. **4,157**

NELIGH, Antelope Co.
Journal..................W. **4,158**

NELSON, c. h., Nuckolls Co.
Nuckolls Co. Inter-Ocean.W. **4,159**

NIOBRARA, c. h., Knox Co., on Missouri r., 40 m. above Yankton, Dakota, the terminus of the Dakota Southern Rd.
Pioneer..................W. **4,160**

NORTH PLATTE, c. h., Lincoln Co., 1,200† p., near junction of North and South Platte rs., and on Union Pacific Rd., 291 m. from Omaha. Devoted to agriculture and stock-raising.
Republican..............W. **4,161**
Western Nebraskian......W. **4,162**

OMAHA, c. h., Douglas Co., 16,083 p., on Missouri r., opposite Council Bluffs. Eastern terminus of Union Pacific Rd. Western terminus of Chicago & Northwestern Rd., Chicago, Rock Island & Pacific, Chicago, Burlington & Missouri R., Kansas City, Council Bluffs & St. Joseph Rds. Important place for trade and manufactures. Repair shops of Union Pacific Rd. located here. Largest city in the State.

Bee........................D. **4,163**
" ....W. **4,164**
Herald....................D. **4,165**
" ....W. **4,166**
Republican...............D. **4,167**
" ....W. **4,168**
Center Union Agriculturist........................W. **4,169**
Den Danske Pioneer.....W. **4,170**
Folkets Tidning..........W. **4,171**
Pokrok Zapadu...........W. **4,172**
Post and Beobachter......W. **4,173**
High School..............M. **4,174**
Nebraska Journal of Commerce...................M. **4,175**
Railroad Conductors' Brotherhood Magazine.....M. **4,176**

OSCEOLA, c. h., Polk Co.
Record....................W. **4,177**

PAPILLION, c. h., Sarpy Co., 600† p., on Union Pacific Rd., 15 m. from Omaha.
Times.....................W. **4,178**

PAWNEE CITY, c. h., Pawnee Co., 1,200 p., about 40 m. S. W. of Missouri r., at Brownsville, 70 m. from St. Joseph and 85 from Atchison, Kansas. In an agricultural and stock raising district.
Pawnee Republican......W. **4,179**

PLATTSMOUTH, Cass Co., 4,000 p., at the confluence of the Platte and Missouri rs. The initial point of Burlington & Missouri Rd., and on Kansas City and St. Joseph & Council Bluffs and the Nebraska Trunk Rds., about 20 m. direct S. of Omaha. It has a steamboat landing and does a large grain, cattle and lumber trade.
Nebraska Herald.........W. **4,180**
Nebraska Watchman.....W. **4,181**

PLEASANT HILL, c. h., Saline Co.
News......................W. **4,182**

PLUM CREEK, Dawson Co.
Dawson Co. Pioneer.....W. **4,183**

PONCA, c. h., Dixon Co.
Northern Nebraska Journal.....................W. **4,184**

RED CLOUD, c. h., Webster Co.
Chief......................W. **4,185**

REPUBLICAN CITY, Harlan Co.
News......................W. **4,186**

ST. HELENA, Cedar Co.
Cedar Co. Advocate......W. **4,187**

ST. PAUL, Howard Co.
Howard Co. Advocate...W. **4,188**

SARPY CENTRE, Sarpy Co.
Sarpy Co. Sentinel.......W. **4,189**

SCHUYLER, c. h., Colfax Co., 600 p., on Union Pacific Rd., 75 m. from Omaha. Centre of trade for four counties.
Sun.......................W. **4,190**

SEWARD, Seward Co., 1,600† p., about 25 m. W. by N. of Lincoln. Centre of an agricultural district. Has water power and a trade from surrounding counties.
Nebraska Reporter.......W. **4,191**

SIDNEY, c. h., Cheyenne Co.
Telegraph................W. **4,192**

STANTON, c. h., Stanton Co.
Bugle.....................W. **4,193**

STEELE CITY, Jefferson Co.
News......................W. **4,194**

SUTTON, c. h., Clay Co.
Globe......................W. **4,195**
Times.....................W. **4,196**

SYRACUSE, Otoe Co.
Reporter.................W. **4,197**

TECUMSEH, c. h., Johnson Co., 850 p., 28 m. W. of Missouri r., at Brownsville, on Atchison & Nebraska Rd., 57 m. E. of Lincoln. Big Nemaha r. affords water power for mills here.
Chieftain.................W. **4,198**
Herald....................W. **4,199**

TEKAMAH, c. h., Burt Co., 650† p., 45 m. N. of Omaha. Place of general trade.
Burtonian...............W. **4,200**

WAUHOO, c. h., Saunders Co.
Independent..............W. **4,201**
Nebraska Reveille........W. **4,202**

WEEPING WATER, Cass Co.
Nebraska Register........W. **4,203**

WEST POINT, c. h., Cuming Co., 1,200† p., on Elkhorn r. and Fremont & Elkhorn Valley Rd., 90 m. from Omaha. Has water power, which is employed in various manufactories. Centre of trade for a large district.
Republican...............W. **4,204**

WISNER, Cuming Co.
Times.....................W. **4,205**

YORK, York Co., 350 p., about 36 m. W. by N. of Lincoln.
Sentinel ....W. **4,206**

NEVADA.

AUSTIN, c. h., Lander Co., 4,000 p., near Reese r., 165 m. E. of Virginia City, 90 S. of Central Pacific Rd. at Battle Mountain. Several quartz mills are here and large quantities of silver produced annually. Silver mining the chief industrial pursuit.
Reese River Reveille......W. **4,207**

BELMONT, c. h., Nye Co.
Courier...................W. **4,208**

CARSON CITY, c. h., Ormsby Co., State capital, 3,042 p., on Virginia & Truckee Rd., 4 m. from Carson r. and 170 in a direct line from San Francisco. The city derives its support from State business and lumber trade from Sierra Nevada Mountains.
Appeal.
Nevada Tribune..........D. **4,210**

COLUMBUS, Esmeralda Co.
Borax Miner.

ELKO, c. h., Elko Co., 1,500† p., on Humboldt r. and Central Pacific Rd., 460 m. N. E. of Sacramento, Cal., and 275 W. of Ogden. Some manufacturing done here.
Independent..............D. **4,212**
" ....W. **4,213**
Post......................W. **4,214**

EUREKA, Lander Co., 6,000† p., 85 m. from Central Pacific Rd. and 80 E. of Aus-

NEVADA.

tin. Terminus of E. P. Rd. Engaged in mining and smelting silver ores and refining silver.

Sentinel..................W. **4,215**

GENOA, c. h., Douglas Co.

Carson Valley News.....W. **4,216**

GOLD HILL, Storey Co., 6,000 p., 14 m. N. by E. of Carson City, and connected to it by a railroad. In the mountains and surrounded by rich mines of gold and silver, which are extensively worked, producing large quantities of precious metal annually.

News......................D. **4,217**

HAMILTON, c. h., White Pine Co., 1,825 p., in a rich silver mining district, about 200 m. E. of Carson City. The Treasure Hill mining districts are among the richest in the State. Large and comprehensive reduction works are located here. Stage lines connect with all the town and mining districts in this section of the route, making it a trade centre.

White Pine News........W. **4,218**

PIOCHE, Lincoln Co., 3,000† p., about 100 m. S. E. of Hamilton, and near Utah line. Rich mines found here, which are being developed in a rapid and quite satisfactory manner. Machinery and appliances for reduction of ore are being put in operation on an extensive scale, making it a place of activity and rapid growth.

Journal....................D. **4,219**

Record....................D. **4,220**

RENO, Washoe Co., 2,500† p., on Truckee r. and Central Pacific Rd., 11 m. from E. base of Sierra Nevada mountains and 22 from Virginia City. Centre of trade. The river furnishes water power, which is partially developed.

Nevada State Journal.....D. **4,221**

" " " ....W. **4,222**

SILVER CITY, Lyon Co.

Lyon Co. Times..........W. **4,223**

SUTRO, Lyon Co.

Independent.............W. **4,224**

VIRGINIA CITY, c. h., Storey Co., 7,008 p., 15 m. N. E. of Carson City and 20 from Reno. Metropolis of the State. A city of active trade. Rich mines of gold and silver in the vicinity. Machinery for hoisting and reduction of ore is brought into use, giving employment to large amount of capital and labor.

Chronicle..................D. **4,225**

Territorial Enterprise....D. **4,226**

" " ...W. **4,227**

WINNEMUCCA, Humboldt Co., 1,500† p., on Humboldt r. and Central Pacific Rd., 324 m. N. E. of Sacramento, Cal., and 420 from Ogden. Centre of trade, and surrounded by a farming and mining country.

Humboldt Register........D. **4,228**

" " ....W. **4,229**

Silver State...............D. **4,230**

NEW HAMPSHIRE.

AMHERST, c. h., Hillsborough Co., 1,500 p., on Souhegan r., 18 m. S. of Concord and 10 S. W. of Manchester.

Farmers' Cabinet........W. **4,231**

CLAREMONT, Sullivan Co., 4,200 p., on Connecticut r. and Southern division of Vermont Central Rd., 7 m. from Windsor and 42 from Brattleboro. Considerable manufacturing done here.

Compendium.

Granite State Journal....W. **4,233**

National Eagle..........W. **4,234**

Northern Advocate.......W. **4,235**

COLEBROOK, Coos Co., 1,600† p., on Connecticut r., 140 m. from Concord. Surrounded by an agricultural district. Engaged in manufacturing.

Northern Sentinel........W. **4,236**

CONCORD, State capital, Merrimack Co., 13,000 p., on Merrimac r., and at junction of four railroads, near centre of State, 75 m. from Boston and 48 from Lowell. Centre of trade and engaged in manufacturing.

Monitor...................D. **4,237**

Independent Statesman..W. **4,238**

Patriot....................D. **4,239**

New Hampshire Patriot..W. **4,240**

People......................W. **4,241**

New England Monthly....M. **4,242**

DOVER, c. h., Strafford Co., 10,112† p., on Cocheco r., Boston & Maine and Portsmouth & Dover Rds., 12 m. from Portsmouth and 67 from Boston. Centre of business for this part of State. Engaged in manufacturing.

Foster's Democrat........D. **4,243**

" " ....W. **4,244**

Democratic Press..........D. **4,245**

Enquirer...................W. **4,246**

Morning Star..............W. **4,247**

EAST CANAAN, Grafton Co., 1,877 p., on Northern Rd., 51 m. N. of Concord and 120 from Boston. Railroad station for four adjoining towns. Engaged in lumbering

Canaan Reporter........W. **4,248**

EXETER, c. h., Rockingham Co., 4,000 p., on Exeter r. and Boston & Maine Rd., 50 m. from Boston. Engaged in cotton and other manufactures.

News Letter..............W. **4,249**

FISHERSVILLE, Merrimack Co.

Rays of Light...........W. **4,250**

FRANKLIN FALLS, Merrimack Co., 3,000† p., on Merrimac r. and Northern Rd., at junction of Bristol branch, 19 m. N. of Concord. Engaged in manufacturing.

Merrimack Journal......W. **4,251**

GREAT FALLS, Strafford Co., 4,504 p., on Salmon Falls r., Boston & Maine and Portland, Great Falls & Conway Rds., 74 m. from Boston. One of the largest cotton and woolen manufacturing places in the State.

Journal.................. W. **4,252**

HANOVER, Grafton Co., 2,085 p., 60 m. from Concord, on Connecticut r. Dartmouth College located here.

Dartmouth...............W. **4,253**

Granite State Journal....W. **4,254**

HILLSBORO' BRIDGE, Hillsborough Co., 1,595 p., at terminus of Contoocook R. Rd., 26 m. from Concord. Centre of trade, and engaged in manufacturing and lumber business.

Hillsboro' Messenger.....W. **4,255**

HINSDALE, Cheshire Co., 1,342 p., on Connecticut and Ashuelot rs. and Ashuelot Rd., 60 m. from Concord, 55 N. of Springfield, Mass., and 70 from Boston. Engaged in manufacturing.

NEW HAMPSHIRE.

Star Spangled Banner....M. **4,256**
Mirror....................Qr. **4,257**

KEENE, c. h., Cheshire Co., 6,500† p., at junction of Cheshire and Ashuelot Rds. Engaged in trade and manufactures.
Cheshire Republican......W. **4,258**
Granite State Journal....W. **4,259**
New Hampshire Sentinel. W. **4,260**
United States............M. **4,261**

LACONIA, c. h., Belknap Co., 2,309 p., on Boston, Concord & Montreal Rd., 27 m. from Concord. Engaged in manufacturing.
Democrat.................W. **4,262**

LAKE VILLAGE, Belknap Co., 3,361 p., at outlet of Winnipiseogee Lake, on Boston, Concord & Montreal Rd., 29 m. from Concord. Engaged in woolen and hosiery manufactures, and has several large machine shops.
Times....................W. **4,263**

LANCASTER, c. h., Coos Co., 2,548 p., on Israel's r., near junction with Connecticut, and on Boston, Concord & Montreal Rd., 135 m. N. of Concord, 25 from White Mountains. Centre of trade for Southern Coos.
Coos Republican..........W. **4,264**
Independent Gazette.....W. **4,265**

LEBANON, Grafton Co., 3,094 p., on Northern Rd., 65 m. from Concord. Centre of considerable trade. Engaged in manufactures.
Granite State Free Press. W. **4,266**
New Hampshire News....W. **4,267**

LITTLETON, Grafton Co., 2,446 p., on Boston, Concord & Montreal Rd., 113 m. N. of Concord. Engaged in manufactures and centre of trade. A summer resort. Connected by stages with all the principal points in the White and Franconia Mountains.
Argus.....................W. **4,268**
White Mountain Republic W. **4,269**

LOUDON RIDGE, Merrimack Co., 1,282 p., on Soucook r., 12 m. from Concord. Engaged in agriculture and manufactures.
Household Messenger.....M. **4,270**

MANCHESTER, Hillsborough Co., 23,536 p., on Merrimac r., at junction of several Rds. The river furnishes water power, which is very largely employed in cotton, woolen and other manufactures.
Mirror and American....D. **4,271**
Mirror and Farmer.....W. **4,272**
Union.....................D. **4,273**
Union Democrat..........W. **4,274**
New Hampshire Sunday Globe....................W. **4,275**
Saturday Night Dispatch. W. **4,276**
Whitney's New Hampshire Journal of Music......M. **4,277**

MILFORD, Hillsborough Co.
Enterprise................W. **4,278**

NASHUA, Hillsborough Co., 12,000† p., on Nashua r., near its junction with Merrimac r. A manufacturing place and terminus of six Rds.
Gazette...................D. **4,279**
" ....W. **4,280**
Telegraph.................D. **4,281**
" ....W. **4,282**

NEW MARKET, Rockingham Co.
Rockingham Co. Advertiser...................W. **4,283**

NEW HAMPSHIRE.

NEWPORT, c. h., Sullivan Co., 2,500 p., on Sugar r., 35 m. N. W. by W. of Concord. Engaged in manufactures.
New Hampshire Argus and Spectator...............W. **4,284**

PETERBORO, Hillsborough Co., 2,236 p., on Monadnock Rd., Contoocook r., 60 m. from Boston, 30 from Nashua and Manchester, and 50 from Concord. Cotton, woolen and general manufacturing done here.
Transcript.................W. **4,285**

PLYMOUTH, c. h., Grafton Co.
Grafton Co. Journal.....W. **4,286**

PORTSMOUTH, c. h., Rockingham Co., 10,000† p., and commercial metropolis of the State, on Piscataqua r., and only seaport in the State. Engaged in manufacturing and ship building. A United States Navy Yard is located on the opposite side of the river.
Chronicle..................D. **4,287**
New Hampshire Gazette. W. **4,288**
Evening Times............D. **4,289**
States and Union........W. **4,290**
Journal...................W. **4,291**

ROCHESTER, Strafford Co., 6,000† on Dover & Winnipiseogee Rd., 10 m. N. of Dover. A manufacturing place.
Courier and Farmington Advertiser..............W. **4,292**

SUNCOOK, Merrimack Co.
Journal...................W. **4,293**

WILTON, Hillsborough Co.
Journal...................W. **4,294**

WOLFBOROUGH, Carroll Co., 1,995 p., on Winnipiseogee Lake, 40 m. from Concord, 80 from Boston, and in direct communication with all of the thoroughfares in the State. A summer resort. Engaged in manufacturing.
Granite State News...... W. **4,295**

NEW JERSEY.

ARLINGTON, Hudson Co.
Journal and Saturday Gazette..................W. **4,296**

ASHBURY PARK, Monmouth Co.
Journal...................W. **4,297**

ATLANTIC CITY, Atlantic Co.
Atlantic Co. Review......W. **4,298**

BAYONNE CITY, Hudson Co., 3,834 p., on New Jersey Central Rd., about 4 m. S. W. of Jersey City. Place of residence for merchants and others doing business in the city.
Bayonne Herald and Greenville Register............W. **4,299**
Hudson Co. Times.......W. **4,300**

BELLEVILLE, Essex Co.
Record.....................W. **4,301**

BELVIDERE, c. h., Warren Co., 1,800 p., on Pequest r., near its junction with the Delaware, 50 m. above Philadelphia, and on Belvidere, Delaware & Flemington Rd. The falls in the river furnish water power, which is employed in manufactures.
Apollo....................W. **4,302**
Warren Journal.........W. **4,303**

BEVERLY, Burlington Co., 1,418 p., on Delaware r., above the outlet of Rancocas

NEW JERSEY.

Creek, and on Amboy division of Pennsylvania Rd., 15 m. N. E. of Philadelphia. Engaged in fruit and truck-raising and canning.
Visitor..................W. **4,304**

BLOOMFIELD, Essex Co., 6,000 p., on Bloomfield branch of Morris & Essex Rd. and Morris Canal. Engaged in manufacturing. Residence of persons doing business in Newark and New York.
Record..................W. **4,305**

BOONTON, Morris Co., 4,000† p., on Rockaway r., Morris Canal and Boonton branch of Delaware, Lackawanna & Western Rd., 32 m. from New York.
Bulletin..................W. **4,306**

BORDENTOWN, Burlington Co., 6,041 p., at mouth of Delaware and Raritan Canal, on Amboy division of Pennsylvania Rd., 57 m. from New York and 28 from Philadelphia. Connected by rail with Trenton. Engaged in manufactures.
Register..................W. **4,307**

BRICKSBURG, Ocean Co 3,000† p., on New Jersey Southern Rd., 22 m. from Long Branch.
Times and Journal......W. **4,308**

BRIDGETON, c. h., Cumberland Co., 7,000† p., on Cohansy r., at terminus of West Jersey Rd., at its junction with New Jersey Southern Rd., 38 m. from Philadelphia. Has manufactories of glass, iron and nails. Surrounded by a farming country.
Daily..................D **4,309**
Chronicle..................W. **4,310**
Advertiser and Review...W. **4,311**
New Jersey Patriot......W. **4,312**
West Jersey Pioneer.....W. **4.313**
American Favorite.......M. **4,314**

BURLINGTON, Burlington Co., 6,842 p., on Delaware r. and Amboy division of Pennsylvania Rd., 18 m. from Philadelphia. Engaged in commerce and manufactures. Seat of Burlington College. Connected by daily line of steamers with Philadelphia.
New Jersey Enterprise...W. **4,315**
New Jersey Gazette and Burlington Co. Advertiser..................W. **4,316**

CAMDEN, c. h., Camden Co., 20,045 p., on Delaware r., opposite Philadelphia, 87 m. from New York. Engaged in commerce and manufactures and an important suburb of Philadelphia, to which it is connected by ferries. Several railroads centre here.
Post..................D. **4,317**
Democrat..................W. **4,318**
New Republic..................W. **4,319**
Sunday Argus...........W. **4,320**
West Jersey Press........W. **4,321**

CAPE MAY CITY, Cape May Co., 1,300† p., on Atlantic Ocean, at southern point of New Jersey, terminus of Millville & Cape May Rd., 81 m. S. of Philadelphia. Fashionable summer resort.
Star of the Cape.........W. **4,322**
Wave..................W. **4,323**

CARLSTADT, Bergen Co., 2,500† p., on Hackensack branch of Erie Rd., 10 m. from New York.
Freie Presse.............W. **4,324**

CLINTON, Hunterdon Co., 1,000 p., on New Jersey Central Rd., 52 m. W. of Jersey City. Several mills here obtain water power from a branch of Raritan r.
Democrat..................W. **4,325**

CRANFORD, Union Co.
Courier..................W. **4,326**

DECKERTOWN, Sussex Co.
Sussex Co. Independent..W. **4,327**

DOVER, Morris Co., 3,044 p., on Morris & Essex division of Delaware, Lackawanna & Western Rd. Chester and Hibernia Rds. form a junction at this place with Delaware, Lackawanna & Western Rd. Surrounded by an agricultural district and engaged in manufactures.
Index..................W. **4,328**
Iron Era..................W. **4,329**

EAST ORANGE, Essex Co.
Gazette..................W. **4,330**

EGG HARBOR, Atlantic Co., 1,503† p., on Mullica r. at its entrance into Swan Bay, 42 m. from Philadelphia, on Camden & Atlantic Rd. Cigar and cloth and shoe factories located here.
Atlantic Democrat.......W. **4,331**
Atlantic Journal.........W. **4,332**
Der Pilot..................W. **4,333**
Der Zeitgeist.............W. **4,334**

ELIZABETH, c. h., Union Co., 25,800† p., on Staten Island Sound, at intersection of New Jersey and Central Rds., 11 m. from New York. Engaged in manufactures and domestic commerce.
Herald..................D. **4,335**
Central New Jersey Herald..................W. **4,336**
Journal..................D. **4,337**
New Jersey Journal.....W. **4,338**
Monitor..................D. **4,339**
Freie Presse...........S. W. **4,340**
Freie Zeitung.............W. **4,341**

ELIZABETHPORT, Union Co., 8,000 p.
Register..................W. **4,342**

ENGLEWOOD, Bergen Co., 5,000† p., on Northern Rd. of New Jersey, 15 m. from New York. Thriving village and home of a large number of New York business men.
Times..................W. **4,343**

FLEMINGTON, c. h., Hunterdon Co., 1,800 p., on Flemington and New Jersey Central Rds., 50 m. from Philadelphia. Centre of a large mercantile trade.
*Hunterdon Co. Democrat*W. **4,344**
Hunterdon Republican...W. **4,345**

FREEHOLD, c. h., Monmouth Co., 4,800† p., on Jamesburg branch of Pennsylvania Rd. Engaged in agriculture and centre of trade.
Monmouth Democrat W. **4,346**
Monmouth Inquirer.....W. **4,347**

FRENCHTOWN, Hunterdon Co., 912 p., on Delaware r. and on Belvidere & Delaware Rd., 32 m. N. W. of Trenton and 18 from Easton, Pa. Engaged in milling of various kinds.
Hunterdon Independent..W. **4,348**
Press..................W. **4,349**

GLOUCESTER CITY, Camden Co., 2,710 p., on West Jersey Rd. opposite Philadelphia and adjoining Camden. Engaged in manufactures.
Reporter..................W. **4,350**

HACKENSACK, c. h., Bergen Co., 7,000 p., on Hackensack r. and Rd., 13 m. from

NEW JERSEY.

New York. Residence of a large number of New York business men.
New Jersey Citizen....S. W. **4,351**
Bergen Co. Democrat and New Jersey State Register....................W. **4,352**
Bergen Index............W. **4,353**
New Jersey Republican and Bergen Co. Watchman....................W. **4,354**

HACKETTSTOWN, Warren Co., 2,202 p., on Morris & Essex division of Delaware, Lackawanna & Western Rd., 62 m. from New York. An agricultural district. Engaged in manufactures.
Gazette.................W. **4,355**
Herald..................W. **4,356**

HADDONFIELD, Camden Co.
Basket...................W. **4,357**

HAMMONTON, Atlantic Co., 2,000 p., on the Camden & Atlantic and New Jersey Southern Rds., 28 m. from Camden, 30 from Philadelphia and 90 from New York. Engaged in fruit growing and shoe and other manufactures.
Item....................W. **4,358**
South Jersey Republican.W. **4,359**

HARRISON, Gloucester Co.
Dispatch.................W. **4,360**
East Newark Record......W. **4,361**

HIGHTSTOWN, Mercer Co., 1,500 p., in East Windsor township, on Amboy division of Pennsylvania Rd., 49 m. from New York. Branch railroad radiates from this point, extending to Pemberton and Mt. Holly.
Gazette..................W. **4,362**

HOPEWELL, Mercer Co.
Herald...................W. **4,363**

JERSEY CITY, c. h., Hudson Co., 120,000† p., on Hudson r., opposite New York and 1 m. distant, connected by lines of ferry boats. Commerce and manufactures are extensive. Thousands reside here who do business in New York.
Argus....................D. **4,364**
Evening Journal.........D. **4,365**
Hudson Co. Volksblatt....D. **4,366**
Die Wacht am Hudson..W. **4,367**
Press....................D. **4,368**
Herald..................W. **4,369**
Hudson Co. Democrat...W. **4,370**
Hudson Co. Journal.....W. **4,371**
" " " (*Ger.*) W. **4,372**
Jersey Times and Bergen Index...................W. **4,373**
Society Courier..........W. **4,374**
Standard.................W. **4,375**

KEYPORT, Monmouth Co., 2,613† p., on Raritan Bay, 24 m. from New York. Does shipping trade. Oysters, clams, canned fruits, trucking and fruit growing in surrounding country.
Weekly...................W. **4,376**

LAMBERTVILLE, Hunterdon Co., 4,500† p., on Delaware r. and Belvidere & Delaware Rd., at junction of Flemington Rd., 46 m. from Philadelphia. Engaged in manufacturing.
Beacon...................W. **4,377**
Record...................W. **4,378**

LONG BRANCH, Monmouth Co., 3,800 p., on Long Branch & Seashore Rd., 33 m. from New York. A fashionable summer resort.
News.................. W. **4,379**

NEW JERSEY.

MATAWAN, Monmouth Co., 1,500† p., on Raritan Bay, near Keyport.
Journal..................W. **4,380**

MILLVILLE, Cumberland Co., 8,000† p., on Maurice r. and Millville & Cape May Rd., 40 m. from Philadelphia. Engaged in manufactures of cotton, iron and glass.
Herald...................W. **4,381**
Republican...............W. **4,382**

MORRISTOWN, c. h., Morris Co., 5,737† p., on Delaware, Lackawanna & Western Rd., 32 m. from New York. Centre of an agricultural district.
Jerseyman...............W. **4,383**
Morris Republican.......W. **4,384**
True Democratic Banner.W. **4,385**

MOUNT HOLLY, Burlington Co., 4,100† p., on Rancocas r., 7 m. from Burlington, 18 from Camden, and connected thereto by railroad. Railroad also connects with Medford. Engaged in agriculture and manufacturing.
Herald...................W. **4,386**
New Jersey Mirror.......W. **4,387**

NEWARK, c. h., Essex Co., 123,000† p., on Passaic r., 9 m. from New York, on New Jersey and Morris & Essex and Newark & New York Rds. Engaged in manufactures amounting to about $25,000,000 annually. Domestic commerce is quite extensive. Large number of persons living here have business in New York.
Advertiser...............D. **4,388**
Sentinel of Freedom......W. **4,389**
Evening Courier..........D. **4,390**
" " ....W. **4,391**
Journal..................D. **4,392**
" ....W. **4,393**
Morning Register.........D. **4,394**
New Jersey Freie Zeitung.D. **4,395**
Der Erzaehler............W. **4,396**
Catholic Citizen..........W. **4,397**
Essex Co. Press...........W. **4,398**
Helvetia..................W. **4,399**
New Jersey Hausfreund.W. **4,400**
Sunday Call..............W. **4,401**
Die Gegenwart.........S. M. **4,402**
Artisan...................M. **4,403**
New Jersey Pharmaceutical Record.............M. **4,404**
Young Men's Advocate...M. **4,405**
New Jersey Eclectic Medical and Surgical Journal.................B. M. **4,406**
American Church Review.Qr. **4,407**

NEW BRUNSWICK, c. h., Middlesex Co., 18,000† p., on Raritan r. and Pennsylvania Rd., 30 m. from New York. Engaged in manufactures.
Fredonian................D. **4,408**
" ....W. **4,409**
Times.....................D. **4,410**
" ....W. **4,411**
Home Advocate..........M. **4,412**
Targum...................M. **4,413**

NEWFIELD, Gloucester Co., 500 p., on West Jersey Rd., 30 m. S. of Philadelphia. Engaged in manufacturing and fruit-growing.
Rural Banner.

NEW MONMOUTH, Monmouth Co.
Spirit of the Age.

NEWTON, c. h., Sussex Co., 2,600† p., on Sussex Rd., 60 m. from New York. Trade centre. Engaged in agriculture and mining.

NEW JERSEY.

New Jersey Herald and Sussex Co. Democrat...W. **4,416**
Sussex Register..........W. **4,417**

OCEAN GROVE, Monmouth Co.
Record..................W. **4,418**

ORANGE, Essex Co., 10,919† p., on Morris & Essex Rd., 12 m. from New York. Engaged in manufacturing.
Chronicle..................W. **4,419**
Journal..................W. **4,420**
Volksbote..................W. **4,421**

PASSAIC, Passaic Co., 3,200 p., on Passaic r. and Erie & Boonton branch of Delaware, Lackawanna & Western Rds., 5 m. from Paterson, 13 from New York city. Engaged in manufacturing.
Herald..................W. **4,422**
Item..................W. **4,423**

PATERSON, c. h., Passaic Co., 39,000† p., on Passaic r. and Morris canal, and Erie, Boonton branch of Delaware, Lackawanna & Western, New Jersey Midland and Paterson & Newark Rds., 16 m. from New York and 13 from Newark. The falls in the river furnish water power, which is employed in manufactures.
Guardian..................D. **4,424**
" ....W. **4,425**
Press..................D. **4,426**
" ....W. **4,427**
Volksfreund..........S. W. **4,428**
New Jersey Staats Zeitung W. **4,429**

PERTH AMBOY, Middlesex Co., 3,755† p., at head of Raritan Bay, 25 m. from New York. Engaged in domestic commerce. At terminus of Perth Amboy & Woodbridge branch of Pennsylvania Rd., opposite Tottenville, at southern terminus of Staten Island Rd., and connected with it by steamer. Also on the line of the New York & Long Branch Rd.
Gazette..................W. **4,430**
Middlesex Co. Democrat..W. **4,431**

PHILLIPSBURG, Warren Co., 7,328† p., on Delaware r. and New Jersey Central Rd., opposite Easton, Penn., and 74 m. from New York. Engaged in manufactures.
Warren Democrat........W. **4,432**

PLAINFIELD, Union Co., 11,000† p., on New Jersey Central Rd., 24 m. from New York. An agricultural district.
Central New Jersey Times W. **4,433**
Constitutionalist.........W. **4,434**

PRINCETON, Mercer Co., 4,000 p., at the terminus of Princeton branch of Pennsylvania Rd., and on Delaware and Raritan Canal, 49 m. from New York. Seat of Princeton College.
Press..................W. **4,435**

RAHWAY, c. h., Union Co., 8,000† p., on Rahway r. and New Jersey Rd., 20 m. from New York, and at junction of Woodbridge & Perth Amboy Rd. Engaged in manufactures.
Advocate and Times.....W. **4,436**
National Democrat......W. **4,437**

RED BANK, Monmouth Co., 5,447 p., on Neversink r., and Port Monmouth branch of New Jersey Southern Rd., 26 m. from New York.
New Jersey Standard....W. **4,438**

RUTHERFORD, Bergen Co.
Bergen Co. Herald......W. **4,439**

NEW JERSEY.

SALEM, c. h., Salem Co., 4,555 p., on Salem r., 2½ m. from Delaware r., at terminus of Salem Rd., 34 m. from Philadelphia. Centre of an agricultural district and place of active trade. Glass manufactories located here.
National Standard.......W. **4,440**
Sunbeam..................W. **4,441**

SMITHVILLE, Burlington Co., on Rancocas r. and Camden & Burlington Co. Rd., 2 m. E. of Mt. Holly. Engaged in manufacturing all kinds of wood working machinery.
New Jersey Mechanic....W. **4,442**

SOMERVILLE, c. h., Somerset Co., 3,243† p., on Raritan r. and New Jersey Central Rd., 36 m. from New York. In the midst of a prosperous agricultural district.
Somerset Gazette.........W. **4,443**
Somerset Messenger......W. **4,444**
Somerset Unionist........W. **4,445**

SOUTH AMBOY, Middlesex Co.
Argus..................W. **4,446**

SOUTH ORANGE, Essex Co., 2,963 p., on Morris & Essex Rd., 8 m. from Newark and 16 from New York. Prosperous town, rapidly increasing in importance.
Bulletin..................W. **4,447**

SWEDESBORO, Gloucester Co., 1,200 p., on the Swedesboro & West Jersey Rd., 17 m. from Philadelphia. Manufacturing, farming and fruit-growing are the principal industrial pursuits.
Times..................W. **4,448**

TOM'S RIVER, Ocean Co., 3,062 p., at head of Tom's r. Bay and terminus of Tom's R. branch Rd. Engaged in coasting trade and cranberry culture.
New Jersey Courier......W. **4,449**
New Jersey Good Templar..................W. **4,450**

TRENTON, c. h., Mercer Co., State capital, 30,000† p., on Delaware r., at head of steamboat navigation, 30 m. from Philadelphia and 60 from New York, and on main branch of Camden & Amboy Rd. and Delaware & Raritan Canal. Possesses abundant water power. Several potteries located here.
Emporium..................D. **4,451**
Evening Star..................D. **4,452**
Free Press..................D. **4,453**
" " ....W. **4,454**
State Gazette..................D. **4,455**
" " ....W. **4,456**
True American..................D. **4,457**
" " ....W. **4,458**
Herald..................W. **4,459**
New Jersey Staats Journal..................W. **4,460**
Public Opinion..........W. **4,461**

TUCKERTON, Burlington Co.
New Jersey Coast News...W. **4,462**

VINELAND, Cumberland Co., 7,077 p., on West Jersey & Vineland Rd., 35 m. from Philadelphia. Rapidly increasing in population. Engaged in fruit-growing and general farming.
Journal..................D. **4,463**
Advertiser..................W. **4,464**
Independent..................W. **4,465**
Weekly..................W. **4,466**
Bible Banner............M. **4,467**

WASHINGTON, Warren Co., 2,280† p.,

NEW JERSEY.

on Morris & Essex and Delaware, Lackawanna & Western Rds., 65 m. W. of Jersey City. A branch railroad connects with the Central Rd. at Hampton Junction. Farming interests centre here. Cabinet organs and canal boats are made here.
Star....................W. **4,468**

WEST HOBOKEN, Hudson Co., 4,132 p., on Palisades, W. of and adjoining Hoboken City, ½ m. from Hudson r. Residence of many business men from New York. Engaged in manufactures.
Palisade News...........W. **4,469**

WHITE HOUSE, Hunterdon Co., 500† p., ¼ m. from New Jersey Central Rd., 45 m. W. of Jersey City.
Family Casket...........W. **4,470**

WOODBURY, c. h., Gloucester Co., 2,028† p., on West Jersey Rd., 8 m. from Philadelphia, 7 from Camden and 3 from Delaware r. Centre of agricultural region, supplying New York and Philadelphia markets.
Constitution and Farmers' and Mechanics' Advertiser....................W. **4,471**

WOODSTOWN, Salem Co., 1,914 p., 10 m. from the Delaware r. and 25 from Philadelphia. Stage lines connect daily with trains on Salem and West Jersey & Swedesport Rds.; also steamboat landing for Philadelphia. Marl deposits and limestone quarries are located here. Surrounded by an agricultural region.
Register ....W. **4,472**

NEW YORK.

ADAMS, Jefferson Co., 1,352 p., on Rome, Watertown & Ogdensburgh Rd., 14 m. from Watertown and 59 from Rome. Situated in an agricultural region, and containing several mills and manufactories. Central business point for the southern portion of the county.
Jefferson Co. Journal....W. **4,473**

ADDISON, Steuben Co., 2,218 p., on Canisteo r. and Erie Rd., 30 m. from Elmira, 300 from New York, 150 from Buffalo. Dairying and lumber manufacturing carried on. An iron foundry and woolen factory are located here. Centre of an agricultural district.
Advertiser.................W. **4,474**

ALBANY, c. h., Albany Co., State capital, 86,013† p., on Hudson r., 142 m. from New York. Centre of an immense trade; at junction of several railroads, and at the entrance of Erie Canal to the Hudson. Connected by river and canals to Lake Erie, Lake Ontario and Lake Champlain. Engaged in lumber trade.
Argus....................D. **4,475**
" ....S. W. **4,476**
" ....W. **4,477**
Evening Journal.........D. **4,478**
" " .....S. W. **4,479**
" " ....W. **4,480**
Evening Post.............D. **4,481**
Evening Times...........D. **4,482**
" " ....W. **4,483**
Freie Blaetter............D. **4,484**
Herold.....................D. **4,485**
Knickerbocker............D. **4,486**
Morning Express.........D. **4,487**
Cultivator and Country Gentleman............W. **4,488**
Law Journal.............W. **4,489**
Press and Legislative Journal.................W. **4,490**
Sunday Press............W. **4,491**

ALBION, c. h., Orleans Co., 3,322 p., on Erie Canal and New York Central Rd., 30 m. from Rochester. A trade centre, and contains several mills and manufactories.
Orleans American.......W. **4,492**
Orleans Republican......W. **4,493**

ALFRED CENTER, Allegany Co., 2,500 p., near line of Erie Rd., 340 m. from New York and 11 W. of Hornellsville.
Sabbath Recorder........W. **4,494**

ALLEGANY, Cattaraugus Co.
Journal...................W. **4,495**

AMENIA, Dutchess Co., 1,250 p., on New York & Harlem Rd., 88 m. from New York.
Times.....................W. **4,496**

AMSTERDAM, Montgomery Co., 5,426 p., on Mohawk r., 33 m. from Albany and on New York Central Rd. Engaged in the manufacture of knit goods and other articles, which creates an active business in all branches of trade.
Democrat................W. **4,497**
Recorder.................W. **4,498**

ANDES, Delaware Co., 2,840 p., 12 m. from Rondout & Oswego Rd. and 60 from Kingston, in a farming and lumbering district.
Recorder.................W. **4,499**

ANDOVER, Allegany Co., 2,000 p., on Erie Rd., 18 m. S. W. of Hornellsville. Centre of a farming region.
Citizen....................W. **4,500**

ANGELICA, c. h., Allegany Co., 1,708 p., on Genesee Valley Canal and r., and Erie Rd. In a lumbering district and possessing mills and manufactories.
Republican...............W. **4,501**

ANTWERP, Jefferson Co.
Gazette...................W. **4,502**

ARCADE, Wyoming Co., 900† p., in China township, and on Buffalo, New York & Philadelphia Rd., 35 m. from Buffalo. Centre of a dairy country, doing a thriving trade. The largest village within a radius of 15 miles.
Leader....................W. **4,503**

ATTICA, Wyoming Co., 2,200† p., on Tonawanda r. and Hornellsville branch of Erie Rd., 31 m. from Buffalo. A branch railroad connects with the New York Central at Batavia.
News.......................W. **4,504**

AUBURN, c. h., Cayuga Co., 20,000† p., at outlet of Owasco Lake, and on New York Central and Southern Central, Midland & Auburn and Homer Rds., 326 m. from New York. Possesses water power, and engaged in manufacturing and agriculture. One of the State Prisons is located here.
Advertiser................D. **4,505**
Journal...................W. **4,506**
Bulletin....................D. **4,507**
Morning News...........D. **4,508**
News and Democrat......W. **4,509**
Cayuga Co. Independent.W. **4,510**
True Press................W. **4,511**

AVON SPRINGS, Livingston Co.
Avonian..................W. **4,512**

BABYLON, Suffolk Co., 1,500† p., on Southern, also on the Flushing, North Side & Central Rd., and on Great South Side Bay, 35 m. E. of Brooklyn. Agricultural country surrounding.
South Side Signal........W. **4,513**

BAINBRIDGE, Chenango Co., 1,000 p., on Susquehanna r. and Albany & Susquehanna Rd., 31 m. from Binghamton.
Republican and Review..W. **4,514**

BALDWINSVILLE, Onondaga Co., 2,220† p., on Seneca r. and Oswego & Syracuse Rd., 12 m. from Syracuse and connected with it by canal. Engaged in manufactures.
Onondaga Gazette........W. **4,515**

BALLSTON SPA, c. h., Saratoga Co., 2,970 p., on Rensselaer & Saratoga Rd., 30 m. from Albany, 25 from Troy and 7 from Saratoga Springs. Engaged in manufactures and is a place of summer resort.
Ballston Democrat.......W. **4,516**
Ballston Journal........W. **4,517**

BATAVIA, c. h., Genesee Co., 5,000† p., on Tonawanda Creek and Erie, New York Central & Hudson R. Rds., at junction of Canandaigua, Tonawanda & Attica branches, 37 m. from Buffalo, 32 from Rochester. Surrounded by an agricultural district. Centre of trade. Several manufactories are located here.
Progressive Batavian....W. **4,518**
Republican Advocate.....W. **4,519**
Spirit of the Times.......W. **4,520**

BATH, c. h., Steuben Co., 6,236 p., on Rochester division of Erie Rd., 75 m. from Rochester. Surrounded by an agricultural district and centre of trade. Some manufacturing done here.
Steuben Courier.........W. **4,521**
Steuben Farmers' Advocate...................W. **4,522**

BELMONT, c. h., Allegany Co., 860† p., on Genesee r. and on Erie Rd. Has water power, which is employed in manufacturing. Centre of lumber and wool-growing district.
Alleganian..............W. **4,523**

BINGHAMTON, c. h., Broome Co., 16,000† p., at junction of Chenango and Susquehanna rs. and on Erie Rd., terminus of Albany & Susquehanna, Syracuse & Binghamton and Valley Rds. The water power is very good. Manufacturing and mercantile business done here.
Democrat.................D. **4,524**
" ....W. **4,525**
Republican...............D. **4,526**
Broome Republican......W. **4,527**
Times....................D. **4,528**
" ....W. **4,529**
Democratic Leader......W. **5,530**

BOONVILLE, Oneida Co., 1,700† p., on Black R. Canal and Utica & Black R. Rd., 31 m. from Utica.
Herald...................W. **4,531**

BREWSTER, Putnam Co., 1,110 p., on New York & Harlem Rd., 55 m. N. of New York. Centre of a milk producing country. Two iron mines are located here. Second village in size on Harlem Rd.
Putnam Co. Standard...W. **4,532**

BROCKPORT, Monroe Co., 2,847 p., on the Erie Canal and New York Central Rd., 17 m. W. of Rochester. Engaged in manufacturing agricultural implements and other articles.
Democrat...............W. **4,533**
Republic................W. **4,534**

BROOKLYN, c. h., Kings Co., 484,616† p., on W. end of Long Island. Separated from New York by East r. Engaged in commerce and manufactures, and the dwelling place of many business men of New York. The United States have a Navy Yard here.
Brooklyner Presse........D. **4,535**
Times...................D. **4,536**
Gazette..................W. **4,537**
Triangle...............S. M. **4,538**
Argus....................D. **4,539**
Brooklyner Freie Presse..D. **4,540**
Long Islander........Sund. **4,541**
Eagle.....................D. **4,542**
Programme..............D. **4,543**
Union....................D. **4,544**
Anzeiger..................W. **4,545**
Friden's Harold.........W. **4,546**
Leader and New Lots Journal.
Reform...................W. **4,548**
Review...................W. **4,549**
South Brooklyn News....W. **4,550**
Sunday Sun...............W. **4,551**
National Monitor.....B. W. **4,552**
Church Magazine.........M. **4,553**

BUFFALO, c. h., Erie Co., 152,000 p., at eastern extremity of Lake Erie, and connected with Albany by Erie Canal and New York Central Rd. Lake commerce is extensive, centering here from all points West. Manufactures are various and important, embracing iron, leather, agricultural implements, machinery, distilled spirits, &c.
Commercial Advertiser...D. **4.554**
" " T. W. **4,555**
Commercial Patriot and Journal................W. **4,556**
Courier...................D. **4,557**
Evening Republic.........D. **4,558**
Courier....................W. **4,559**
Demokrat.................D. **4,560**
Weltbuerger..............W. **4,561**
Express....................D. **4,562**
" ....W. **4,563**
Freie Presse..............D. **4,564**
" " ....W. **4,565**
Post.......................D. **4,566**
Taglicher Republikaner...D. **4,567**
Volk's-Freund............D. **4,568**
" " ....W. **4,569**
Aurora....................W. **4,570**
Catholic Union...........W. **4,571**
Christian Advocate.......W. **4,572**
Le Phare des Lacs.......W. **4,573**
Scientific Commercial....W. **4,574**
Sonntags-Herold..........W. **4,575**
Sunday Independent Leader.................W. **4,576**
Sunday News.............W. **4,577**
Tribune...................W. **4,578**
Globe.....................M. **4,579**
Medical and Surgical Journal...............M. **4,580**
Our Record...............M. **4,581**
Our Young Men's Paper.M. **4,582**
Homœopathic Quarterly.
Knowlton's Hand-Book of Business Education...Qr. **4,584**

NEW YORK.

CAMBRIDGE, Washington Co., 1,850. p., on White Creek and Rensselaer & Saratoga Rd., 33 m. from Albany.
Washington Co. Post.....W. **4,585**

CAMDEN, Oneida Co., 1,703 p., on Rome, Watertown & Ogdensburgh Rd., 18 m. from Rome.
Advance..................W. **4,586**
Journal..................W. **4,587**

CANAJOHARIE, Montgomery Co., 1,882 p., on Mohawk r. and Erie Canal, and New York Central Rd., 55 m. from Albany and 40 E. of Utica. Centre of a large farming and dairy section and engaged in manufactures.
Radii and Tax Payer's Journal...............W. **4,588**

CANANDAIGUA, c. h., Ontario Co., 4,862 p., at outlet of Canandaigua Lake, and on Auburn branch of New York Central Rd., 29 m. E. of Rochester and at intersection of Northern Central Rd. Centre of trade, surrounded by an agricultural district.
Ontario Co. Journal.....W. **4,589**
Ontario Co. Times.......W. **4,590**
Ontario Repository and Messenger..................W. **4,591**

CANASERAGA, Allegany Co., 800 p., on Buffalo division of Erie Rd., 79 m. S. E. of Buffalo and 12 from Hornellsville. Centre of trade.
Times....................W. **4,592**

CANASTOTA, Madison Co., 1,418† p., on New York Central Rd. and Erie Canal, and the terminus of the Canastota & Cazenovia Rd., 20 m. E. of Syracuse.
Herald..................W. **4,593**

CANTON, c. h., St. Lawrence Co., 2,540 p., on Grasse r., and a branch of Rome, Watertown & Ogdensburgh Rd., about 18 m. from Ogdensburgh. Several manufactories are located here.
*St. Lawrence Plaindealer*W. **4,594**

CAPE VINCENT, Jefferson Co., 1,200 p., on the St. Lawrence r., 25 m. from Watertown, and connected with it by railroad. A steam ferry connects with Kingston, Ont.
Eagle.....................W. **4,595**

CARMEL, c. h., Putnam Co., 500† p., 4 m. from New York & Harlem Rd., and 55 from New York. Devoted to farming and dairying.
Putnam Co. Courier.....W. **4,596**
Putnam Co. Monitor.....W. **4,597**

CARTHAGE, Jefferson Co., 2,860 p., on Black r., 16 m. from Watertown, on Utica & Black R. Rd., 17 from Watertown. Surrounded by an agricultural district and largely engaged in manufacturing.
Farmer's Journal.......W. **4,598**
Northern New Yorker....W. **4,599**
Republican..............W. **4,600**

CASTILE, Wyoming Co.
Castilian................W. **4,601**

CATSKILL, c. h., Greene Co., 6,000† p., on Hudson r., 111 m. from New York. The passage-way through which thousands of pleasure seekers proceed to the wonderful natural scenery of the Catskill Mountains. Engaged in manufactures.
Examiner................W. **4,602**
Recorder................W. **4,603**

CAZENOVIA, Madison Co., 1,821† p., on

NEW YORK.

Cazenovia, Canastota & De Ruyter Rd., also Syracuse & Chenango Rd. Agriculture and the manufacture of cheese comprise the principal industrial pursuits. Favorite summer resort.
Republican..............W. **4,604**

CENTRAL SQUARE, Oswego Co.
Union....................W. **4,605**

CHAMPLAIN, Clinton Co., 5,080 p., at head of Lake Champlain, on Chazy r. and western division of Vermont Central Rd., 114 m. from Ogdensburgh.
Journal..................W. **4,606**

CHATEAUGAY, Franklin Co., 3,000 p., on Chateaugay r. and Western division of Vermont Central Rd., 72 m. from Ogdensburgh and 12 from Malone.
Star.......................W. **4,607**

CHATHAM VILLAGE, Columbia Co., 2,000 p., on New York & Harlem Rd., at its intersection with Boston & Albany Rd., 128 m. from New York and 24 from Albany. Manufacture of paper is carried on.
Chatham Courier........W. **4,608**

CHERRY VALLEY, Otsego Co., 844† p., at terminus of Cherry Valley branch of Albany & Susquehanna Rd., 23 m. from Cobleskill.
Gazette..................W. **4,609**
Temperance Investigator.W. **4,610**

CHITTENANGO, Madison Co., 1,500 p., on Chittenango Creek and New York Central Rd., 14 m. E. of Syracuse.
Madison Co. Times......W. **4,611**

CLAYTON, Jefferson Co.
Independent..............W. **4,612**

CLEVELAND, Oswego Co., 900† p., on Oneida Lake, and New York & Oswego Midland Rd., 41 m. from Oswego. 30 from Fulton.
Lake-Side Press..........W. **4,613**

CLINTON, Oneida Co., 1,640 p., in Kirkland township, 9 m. from Utica, on Chenango Canal and Utica, Clinton & Binghamton Rd. Engaged in cotton, lumber, iron and other manufactures. Several institutions of learning are located here.
Courier...................W. **4,614**
Hamilton Literary Monthly.......................M. **4,615**

CLYDE, Wayne Co., 3,200 p., in Galen township, on Clyde r., Erie Canal and Central Rd., 8 m. from Lyons and 38 W. of Syracuse, 45 E. of Rochester. Engaged in manufacturing and a place of active trade.
Times....................W. **4,616**

COBLESKILL, Schoharie Co., 1,700† p., on Albany & Susquehanna Rd., 45 m. from Albany. A branch railroad connects with Cherry Valley. Agricultural works here.
Index....................W. **4,617**

COEYMANS, Albany Co., 850† p., on Hudson r., 12 m. from Albany, 1 from Athens & Schenectady Rd. and 1½ from Hudson R. Rd. Engaged in manufactures. Blue stone quarrying carried on.
Herald...................W. **4,618**

COHOCTON, Steuben Co.
Valley Times.............W. **4,619**

COHOES, Albany Co., 17,516† p., on Mohawk r., New York Central and Rensselaer & Saratoga Rds., and Erie and

NEW YORK.

Champlain Canals, 9 m. from Albany and 3 from Troy. Has water power, which is employed in manufacturing.
Eagle......................D. **4,620**
News......................D. **4,621**
Cataract.................W. **4,622**
Democrat...................W. **4,623**
L'Avenir National.......W. **4,624**
La Patrie Nouvelle......W. **4,625**

COLD SPRING, Putnam Co., 2,379† p., on Hudson r. and Rd., 52 m. from New York.
Recorder..................W. **4,626**

COLLEGE POINT, Queens Co.
Long Island Central Zeitung....................W. **4,627**

COOPERSTOWN, c. h., Otsego Co., 2,300 p., at outlet of Otsego Lake, on Cooperstown & Susquehanna Valley Rd., connected with Albany & Susquehanna Rd., 75 m. from Albany. Business place and centre of trade.
Freeman's Journal......W. **4,628**
*Republican and Democrat*W. **4,629**

CORNING, Steuben Co., 5,300† p., on Chemung r. and Erie Rd., at the junction of Rochester branch. Corning & Blossburg Rd. here forms a junction with Erie. Engaged in manufacture and lumber trade.
Democrat...................W. **4,630**
Independent..............W. **4,631**
Journal...................W. **4,632**

CORNWALL, Orange Co.
Times......................W. **4,633**

CORTLAND, c. h., Cortland Co., 4,100 p., on Tioughnioga r., and Syracuse, Binghamton & New York Rd., at its junction with Ithaca & Cortland Rd., 36 m. from Syracuse.
Cortland Co. Democrat..W. **4,634**
Standard and Journal...W. **4,635**

COXSACKIE, Greene Co., 4,000 p., on Hudson r. and Athens & Schenectady Rd., 22 m. from Albany. Engaged in brick making and back country trade.
News......................W. **4,636**

CUBA, Allegany Co., 2,500 p., on Erie Rd., 50 m. W. of Hornellsville. Surrounded by an agricultural district. Noted for its dairy products.
Herald....................W. **4,637**
Patriot...................W. **4,638**

DANSVILLE, Livingston Co., 3,387 p., on Canaseraga Creek, at the terminus of the Dansville & Mt. Morris branch of the Erie Rd., 49 m. from Rochester. Engaged in milling and various manufactures, and the centre of an agricultural district.
Advertiser................W. **4,639**
Express...................W. **4,640**
Laws of Life and Journal of Health..............M. **4,641**
National Record.........M. **4,642**

DELHI, c. h., Delaware Co., 1,530† p., on west branch of Delaware r. Terminus of a branch of Midland Rd., and the centre of a fine grazing and butter producing country.
Delaware Express.......W. **4,643**
Delaware Gazette.........W. **4,644**
Delaware Republican....W. **4,645**

DEPOSIT, Broome Co., 2,000 p., on Erie Rd., 175 m. from New York. Located partly in Delaware Co. Freight houses of company located here.
Courier...................W. **4,646**
Times and Democrat.....W. **4,647**

NEW YORK.

DE RUYTER, Madison Co., 625† p., on a branch of the New York & Oswego Midland Rd.
New Era................W. **4,648**

DOWNSVILLE, Delaware Co.
News......................W. **4,649**

DRYDEN, Tompkins Co., 1,250 p., on Southern Central Rd., 36 m. from Auburn and 34 from Owego. Centre of an agricultural district.
Herald...................W. **4,650**

DUNDEE, Yates Co., 1,500 p., in Starkey township, near Seneca Lake and Northern Central Rd. Centre of an agricultural district.
Record..................W. **4,651**

DUNKIRK, Chautauqua Co., 7,000† p., a port of entry on Lake Erie, at junction of Erie and Lake Shore & Michigan Southern Rds. The Dunkirk, Warren & Pittsburgh Rd. also forms a junction here, opening a direct route to the oil, coal and iron region of Pennsylvania. A commercial centre and place of active trade.
Advertiser and Union....W. **4,652**
Journal..................W. **4,653**

EAST ALBANY, Albany Co.
News......................W. **4,654**

EAST AURORA, Erie Co.
Erie Co. Advertiser......W. **4,655**

EAST NEW YORK, Kings Co. 12,300† p., just E. of Brooklyn, with which it is connected by horse cars. The Brooklyn Central & Jamaica Rd. runs E. from here.
Long Island Record......W. **4,656**
Sentinel..................W. **4,657**

EDGEWATER, Richmond Co., E. side of Staten Island. Connected to New York city by a ferry.
Staten Island Leader....W. **4,658**

ELIZABETHTOWN, c. h., Essex Co., 1,488 p., on Bouquet r., 9 m. from Lake Champlain and 126 from Albany. Surrounded by a district containing immense quantities of iron ore.
Post.......................W. **4,659**

ELLENVILLE, Ulster Co., 3,300† p., on Ellenville branch of Oswego & Midland Rd., and on Delaware & Hudson Canal, 75 m. from New York. Centre of trade. Considerable manufacturing done here.
Banner of Liberty.......W. **4,660**
Journal..................W. **4,661**
Press......................W. **4,662**

ELLICOTTVILLE, c. h., Cattaraugus Co., 1,000 p., in an agricultural district. 12 m. from Erie Rd. at Salamanca.
Cattaraugus Union......W. **4,663**

ELMIRA, c. h., Chemung Co., 20,500† p., on Chemung r. and Canal, and Erie, Lehigh Valley and Northern Central Rds. Engaged in manufacturing. Seat of the new State Reformatory.
Advertiser.................D. **4,664**
" ....W. **4,665**
Gazette....................D. **4,666**
" ....W. **4,667**
Chemung Co. Journal....W. **4,668**
Husbandman...........W. **4,669**
Leader...................W. **4,670**
Sunday Morning Herald.W. **4,671**
Weed.....................M. **4,672**
Bistoury................Qr. **4,673**

NEW YORK.

FAIRPORT, Monroe Co.
Herald..................W. **4,674**

FAYETTEVILLE, Onondaga Co., 1,800† p., near Erie Canal, 7½ m. from Syracuse. Engaged in milling, lime and plaster, with one of the best water powers in the county.
Recorder.................W. **4,675**

FISHKILL, Dutchess Co., 795† p., on Fishkill Creek and Dutchess & Columbia Rd. Centre of an agricultural district, 5 m. from Fishkill Landing.
Journal.................W. **4,676**

FISHKILL LANDING, Dutchess Co., 2,500 p., on Hudson r. and Hudson R. Rd., at junction of Dutchess & Columbia Rd., opposite Newburgh, 60 m. from New York. Centre of trade and engaged in various manufactures.
Fishkill Standard........W. **4,677**

FLATBUSH, Kings Co., 6,309 p., 3 m. S. of Brooklyn.
Kings Co. Rural Gazette.W. **4,678**

FLUSHING, Queens Co., 8,000† p., situated on Flushing Bay, Long Island, Flushing & North Side Rd., 8 m. from New York.
Times.....................D. **4,679**
Long Island Times......W. **4,680**
Journal..................W. **4,681**

FONDA, c. h., Montgomery Co., 1,750 p., on Mohawk r. and New York Central Rd., at junction of Johnstown & Gloversville branch, 42 m. from Albany.
*Mohawk Valley Democrat*W. **4,682**

FORESTVILLE, Chautauqua Co., 722 p., on Erie Rd., 8 m. E. of Dunkirk
Chautauqua Farmer.....W. **4,683**

FORT COVINGTON, Franklin Co.
St. Lawrence Valley Record..................W. **4,684**

FORT EDWARD, Washington Co., 5,126† p., on Hudson R. & Rensselaer & Saratoga Rd., at junction of Glens Falls branch, 49 m. from Troy. Engaged in paper and other manufactures.
Gazette...................W. **4,685**

FORT PLAIN, Montgomery Co., 1,797 p., in Minden township, on Mohawk r. and Erie Canal, 58 m. from Albany.
Mohawk Valley Register.W. **4,686**

FRANKLIN, Delaware Co., 1,150 p., on Ouleout Creek, 3 m. S. of Albany & Susquehanna Rd. at Otego. An agricultural community and seat of Delaware Literary Institute.
Register.................W. **4,687**

FRANKLINVILLE, Cattaraugus Co.
Argus...................W. **4,688**

FREDONIA, Chautauqua Co., 300† p., on Dunkirk, Warren & Pittsburgh Rd. State Normal School is located and manufacturing done here.
Censor..................W. **4,689**

FRIENDSHIP, Allegany Co., 1,500† p., on Erie Rd., 42 m. W. of Hornellsville, 84 E. of Dunkirk. Dairying and farming are the principal industries.
Register.................W. **4,690**

FULTON, Oswego Co., 5,000† p., on Oswego r. and Delaware, Lackawanna & Western Rd., and New York & Oswego Midland Rd., 25 m. from Syracuse and 12 from Oswego. Has water power, which is employed in manufactories.
Patriot and Gazette......W. **4,691**
Times....................W. **4,692**

NEW YORK.

FULTONVILLE, Montgomery Co., 1,500 p., in Glen township, on Mohawk r., and Erie Canal and Central Rd., 44 m. from Albany. Coal, grain, cheese and produce depot.
Montgomery Co. Republican..................W. **4,693**

GENESEO, c. h., Livingston Co., 2,500 p., on Genesee r. and Danville & Mt. Morris branch of Erie Rd., 28 m. from Rochester.
Livingston Republican...W. **4,694**

GENEVA, Ontario Co., 6,027† p., on Seneca Lake, and Cayuga & Seneca Canal and New York Central Rd. Interested in nursery business. Connected by steamer with Watkins, on Canandaigua & Elmira Rd.
Courier..................W. **4,695**
Gazette..................W. **4,696**

GLEN COVE, Queens Co., on Hempstead Harbor, on a branch of Long Island Rd., 28 m. N. E. of Brooklyn
Echo.....................W. **4,697**
Gazette..................W. **4,698**

GLEN'S FALLS, Warren Co., 6,500† p., on Hudson r. and connecting with Rensselaer & Saratoga Rd. by a branch to Fort Edward, 50 m. above Albany.
Messenger...............W. **4,699**
Republican..............W. **4,700**

GLOVERSVILLE, Fulton Co., 7,500† p., 8 m. from Fonda and Erie Canal, 50 from Albany, and on Fonda, Johnstown & Gloversville Rd. Engaged in manufacturing gloves and mittens. Does a thriving wholesale trade with the northern counties.
Advertiser...............
Century.................W. **4,702**
Intelligencer and Republican..................W. **4,703**
Standard.................W. **4,704**

GOSHEN, c. h., Orange Co., 3,000 p., on Erie Rd., 58 m. from New York. An agricultural district.
Democrat................W. **4,705**
Independent..............W. **4,706**

GOUVERNEUR, St. Lawrence Co., 1,627 p., on Oswegatchie r., and Rome, Watertown & Ogdensburgh Rd., 34 m. from Ogdensburgh. Manufacturing done here, the river furnishing abundant power. Centre of a thriving trade.
Herald..................W. **4,707**
Times...................W. **4,708**

GOWANDA, Cattaraugus Co., 1,290 p., on Buffalo & Jamestown Rd., 32 m. from Buffalo on the north and 24 from Jamestown on the south.
Gazette..................W. **4,709**

GRANVILLE, Washington Co., 850 p., on Albany & Rutland and Rensselaer & Saratoga Rds., and Methawee r., 68 m. from Albany. Engaged in manufactures of various kinds. Slate quarries are worked in this vicinity.
Sentinel..................W. **4,710**

GREENBUSH, Rensselaer Co., 7,000† p., on Hudson R. and Boston, Harlem & Albany Rds. Engaged in pork packing, flour mills and general manufacturing.
Evening Star............W. **4,711**
Rensselaer Co. Gazette...W. **4,712**

NEW YORK.

GREENE, Chenango Co., 1,025 p., on Chenango r., Chenango Canal and Utica division of Delaware, Lackawanna & Western Rd., 56 m. from Syracuse and 20 from Binghamton. A thriving place, in an agricultural district.
Chenango American.....W. **4,713**

GREENPORT, Suffolk Co., 2,000† p., at E. terminus of Long Island Rd., 95 m. from New York. Engaged in foreign and domestic commerce and agriculture.
Flood and Field..........W. **4,714**
Republican Watchman...W. **4,715**
Suffolk Times............W. **4,716**

GREENWICH, Washington Co., 2,000 p., in Greenwich township, on Battenkill r., 8 m. N. W. of Cambridge. Engaged in manufacturing.
People's Journal.........W. **4,717**

GROTON, Tompkins Co., 1,560 p., on Owasco Inlet, in N. E. part of county, on Southern Central Rd., 15 m. from Ithaca and 27 from Auburn, N. Y. Centre of a dairying country. Engaged in manufacturing carriages, agricultural implements and other articles.
Journal..................W. **4,718**

HAMBURG, Erie Co.
Erie Co. Independent... W. **4,719**

HAMILTON, Madison Co., 1,548† p., 28 m. from Utica, on the Utica, Clinton & Binghamton Rd. and Chenango Canal. Seat of Madison University, Theological Seminary and several other schools, also Colgate Academy.
Democratic Republican..W. **4,720**
Democratic Volunteer....W. **4,721**
Madisonensis..........S. M. **4,722**

HAMMONDSPORT, Steuben Co., 1,000 p., on Crooked Lake, 8 m. from Bath. Engaged in grape-growing and manufacturing wine.
Herald..................W. **4,723**

HANCOCK, Delaware Co., 3,069 p., on Erie Rd., 164 m. N. W. of New York. Engaged in tanning and lumber manufactures.
Herald..................W. **4,724**

HANNIBAL, Oswego Co., 840 p., about 12 m. S. of Oswego.
Reveille.................W. **4,725**

HAVANA, Schuyler Co., 1,500† p., on Northern Central Rd., 3 m. from Watkins and 18 from Elmira.
Enterprise..............W. **4,726**
Journal..................W. **4,727**

HAVERSTRAW, Rockland Co., 6,412 p., on Hudson r., 37 m. from New York. Engaged in manufacturing brick.
Rockland Co. Messenger..W. **4,728**

HEMPSTEAD, Queens Co., 2,316 p., on South Side Rd., 20 m. from New York. Rockaway Beach, noted as a summer resort, is in this township. Engaged in manufacturing, agriculture and the oyster trade.
Inquirer................W. **4,729**
Queens Co. Sentinel......W. **4,730**

HERKIMER, c. h., Herkimer Co., 2,250† p., on Mohawk r., New York Central Rd. and Erie Canal, 78 m. from Albany. In a great cheese and dairy district.
Democrat and Gazette....W. **4,731**

NEW YORK.

HIGHLAND, Ulster Co.
Journal..................W. **4,732**

HIGHLAND FALLS, Orange Co.
Journal..................W. **4,733**

HOLLEY, Orleans Co., 1,200 p., on Erie Canal and New York Central Rd., 22 m from Rochester. Engaged in general trade and manufacturing.
Standard................W. **4,734**

HOMER, Cortland Co., 2,008 p., on Syracuse & Binghamton Rd., 34 m. from Syracuse and 3 from Cortland. Some manufacturing done here.
Cortland Co. Republican.W. **4,735**

HONEOYE FALLS, Monroe Co., 921 p., on Honeoye Creek, and on Canandaigua branch of New York Central Rd., 19 m. from Canandaigua and 16 S. of Rochester. Engaged in a variety of manufactures.
Free Press.

HOOSICK FALLS, Rensselaer Co.
Rensselaer Co. Standard.W. **4,737**

HOPE, Hamilton Co.
Hamilton Co. Press......W. **4,738**

HORNELLSVILLE, Steuben Co., 8,000† p., on Canisteo r. and Erie Rd. Buffalo branch of Erie Rd. radiates from this point. A place of business and centre of trade.
Canisteo Valley Times....W. **4,739**
Herald..................W. **4,740**
Tribune..................W. **4,741**

HORSEHEADS, Chemung Co., 3,400† p., 6 m. from Elmira, on Chemung Canal and Northern Central Rd. Engaged in farming, milling and general manufacturing.
Free Press..............W. **4,742**
Journal..................W. **4,743**

HUDSON, c. h., Columbia Co., 8,615 p., on E. bank of Hudson r. and on Hudson R. Rd., at terminus of Hudson branch of Boston & Albany Rd., 116 m. from New York. Engaged in commerce and manufactures.
Register..................D. **4,744**
Gazette..................W. **4,745**
Star......................D. **4,746**
Columbia Republican and Star..................W. **4,747**
Columbia Co. Farmer....W. **4,748**
Helping Hand...........M. **4,749**

HUNTINGTON, Suffolk Co., 2,500† p., on Huntington Bay and Syosset branch of Long Island Rd., 35 m. from New York.
Long Islander...........W. **4,750**
Suffolk Bulletin..........W. **4,751**

ILION, Herkimer Co., 4,500† p., on Mohawk r., New York Central Rd. and Erie Canal, 11 m. from Utica. Engaged in manufacturing arms, sewing machines, agricultural implements and other articles.
Citizen..................W. **4,752**
Watchword..............W. **4,753**

IRVINGTON, Westchester Co.
Courier and Tarrytown News..................W. **4,754**

ITHACA, c. h., Tompkins Co., 9,658† p., at the head of Cayuga Lake, at junction of Cayuga division of Delaware, Lackawanna & Western with Ithaca & Cortland Rd. Cayuga Lake steamboat line touches here. Engaged in manufactures. Seat of Cornell University.
Journal..................D. **4,755**
" ....W. **4,756**

NEW YORK.

Cornell Era..............W. **4,757**
Democrat................W. **4,758**
Ithacan.................W. **4,759**
Poultry Organ of Central New York.............M. **4,760**

JAMAICA, c. h., Queens Co., 3,791 p., on Long Island & South Side and Brooklyn Central Rds., 12 m. from Brooklyn. Residence of merchants doing business in New York city. Engaged in market gardening.
Katholische Kirchen Zeitung...................W. **4,761**
Long Island Democrat...W. **4,762**
Long Island Farmer....W. **4,763**
Standard................W. **4,764**

JAMESTOWN, Chautauqua Co., 7,500† p., at outlet of Chautauqua Lake, on Atlantic & Great Western Rd., connected by steamers with various points on the lake. Engaged in manufacturing.
Democrat................D. **4,765**
Chatauqua Democrat....W. **4,766**
Journal..................D. **4,767**
" ....W. **4,768**
Folket's Rost.............W. **4,769**
Grange..................W. **4,770**

JEFFERSON, Schoharie Co., 1,712 p., in the southern part of the county, about 12 m. from the line of Albany & Susquehanna Rd.
Jeffersonian.............W. **4,771**

JEFFERSONVILLE, Sullivan Co., 700 p., on Callicoons Creek, about 10 m. from Erie and the same distance from Midland Rd., about 16 N. W. of Monticello.
Sullivan Co. Record.....W. **4,772**

JOHNSTOWN, c. h., Fulton Co., 4,600† p., in Johnstown township, on Cayadutta Creek and Fonda, Johnstown & Gloversville Rd., 4 m. from Fonda. Engaged in mercantile pursuits, manufacturing, &c. A large number of glove and mitten factories are located here.
Fulton Co. Democrat....W. **4,773**
Fulton Co. Republican...W. **4,774**
Journal..................W. **4,775**

JORDAN, Onondaga Co., 1,500† p., on Erie Canal and New York Central Rd., 17 m. from Syracuse. Engaged in manufactures.
Transcript..............W. **4,776**

KATONAH, Westchester Co.
Recorder................W. **4,777**

KEESEVILLE, Essex Co., 2,500 p., on Au Sable r., 4 m. from Lake Champlain and 14 from Burlington, Vt. Some manufacturing done here.
Essex Co. Republican....W. **4,778**

KINDERHOOK, Columbia Co., 4,060† p., on Boston & Albany Rd., 5 m. from Hudson r. at Stuyvesant Landing, 16 from Albany. Engaged in cotton warp and paper manufacture.
Rough Notes.............W. **4,779**

KINGSTON, c. h., Ulster Co., 20,000 p., on Hudson r. at the mouth of Rondout Creek, 91 m. from New York, at terminus of Hudson & Delaware Canal and Rondout & Oswego Rd. Engaged in manufactures. Has a large river commerce. The amount of business transacted here is as large as at any point on the Hudson between New York and Albany.
Freeman.................D. **4,780**

NEW YORK.

Freeman................W. **4,781**
Argus...................W. **4,782**
Courier.................W. **4,783**
Journal.................W. **4,784**
Press...................W. **4,785**

LANSINGBURGH, Rensselaer Co., 7,000 p., on Hudson R. & Bennington Rd. A suburb of the city of Troy and 10 m. above Albany. Engaged in manufacturing brushes and oil-cloth.
Courier.................W. **4,786**
Gazette.................W. **4,787**

LE ROY, Genesee Co., 2,634 p., on Oatka Creek and New York Central Rd., 46 m. from Buffalo and 28 S. W. of Rochester. Location of Ingham University; largest female university in western New York.
Gazette.................W. **4,788**
Genesee Courier..........W. **4,789**

LIBERTY, Sullivan Co., 700 p., on New York & Oswego Midland Rd., 100 m. from New York. In an agricultural district.
Local Echo..............W. **4,790**

LIMA, Livingston Co., 2,915† p., 7 m. E. of Erie Rd. at Avon and 4 S. of Honeoye Falls. The seat of Genesee College and the Wesleyan Seminary.
Recorder................W. **4,791**

LISLE, Broome Co., 3,443† p., on Tioughnioga r. and Syracuse & Binghamton Rd., 23 m. from Binghamton. Lumber district. Large quantities of butter shipped from here.
Gleaner.................W. **4,792**

LITTLE FALLS, Herkimer Co., 5,989† p., on Mohawk r. and New York Central Rd., 20 m. from Utica. The falls in the river furnish immense power. Considerable manufacturing done here. Engaged in dairying and the manufacture of cheese.
Herkimer Co. News......W. **4,793**
Journal and Courier.....W. **4,794**
Central New Yorker.....W. **4,795**

LIVERPOOL, Onondaga Co., 1,555 p., in central part of State, on Syracuse Northern Rd. and Oswego Canal, 5 m. from Syracuse. Large manufacturing interests and market gardening. Principal branch of industry is manufacture of salt.
Gazette.................W. **4,796**

LIVONIA, Livingston Co.
Gazette.................W. **4,797**

LOCKPORT, c. h., Niagara Co., 15,000† p., on Erie Canal and New York Central Rd., 19 m. from Niagara Falls. The locks in the canal furnish water power, which is used in manufacturing. Stone quarrying is done here and it is in the centre of an agricultural district.
Journal.................D. **4,798**
Niagara Journal.........W. **4,799**
Times...................D. **4,800**
" ....W. **4,801**
Union...................D. **4,802**
Niagara Democrat.......W. **4,803**
Catholic Visitor..........W. **4,804**
Niagara Pionier.........W. **4,805**

LONG ISLAND CITY, Queens Co., 10,000 p., on East r., N. of Brooklyn, and at W. terminus of Long Island & Flushing and North Side Rds. An important suburb of New York city. Engaged in manufactures.
Courier.................W. **4,806**
Star....................W. **4,807**

NEW YORK.

LOWVILLE, c. h., Lewis Co., 2,000 p., on Utica & Black R. Rd., 59 m. from Utica, 1 from Black r. and Canal, and 26 from Watertown. Centre of a dairy and agricultural district.
Journal and Republican. W. **4,808**
Lewis Co. Democrat...... W. **4,809**

LYONS, c. h., Wayne Co., 5,200† p., on Erie Canal and Central Rd., 36 m. from Rochester.
Republican.............. W. **4,810**
Wayne Democratic Press. W. **4,811**

MADRID, Franklin Co.
News..................... W. **4,812**

MALONE, c. h., Franklin Co., 7,186 p., on Salmon r. and Western division of Vermont Central Rd., 60 m. from Ogdensburgh. Equal distance from Rouse's Point. An agricultural district and centre of trade. Engaged in manufacturing.
Franklin Gazette......... W. **4,813**
Palladium................ W. **4,814**

MARATHON, Cortland Co., 896† p., on Syracuse & Binghamton Rd. and Tioughnioga r., 50 m. from Syracuse and 30 from Binghamton. A farming district, producing butter and other produce.
Independent.............. W. **4,815**

MARGARETVILLE, Delaware Co., 500† p., on E. branch of Delaware r., 23 m. S. E. of Delhi.
Utilitarian............... W. **4,816**

MATTEAWAN, Dutchess Co., 4,106† p., on Fishkill Creek, 1 m. above Fishkill Landing, and on Dutchess & Columbia Rd. Engaged in manufactures.
Gould's Household Companion.

MATTITUCK, Suffolk Co.
Fancier's Herald......... M. **4,818**

MAYVILLE, c. h., Chautauqua Co., 1,300† p., on Chautauqua Lake and Buffalo, Corry & Pittsburgh Rd., 20 m. from Jamestown, to which it is connected by steamer. An agricultural district.
Sentinel.................. W. **4,819**

MEDINA, Orleans Co., 3,732† p., on Orchard r., Erie Canal and New York Central Rd., 40 m. from Rochester and 50 from Buffalo. Centre of trade. Has water power, which is used in various manufactures.
Orleans Democrat....... W. **4,820**
Tribune.................... W. **4,821**

MEXICO, Oswego Co., 1,300 p., on Salmon Creek, near Lake Ontario and Rome & Oswego Rd. Agricultural implements and other articles manufactured here. A centre of trade.
Deaf-Mutes' Journal.... W. **4,822**
Independent............. W. **4,823**

MIDDLEBURGH, Schoharie Co., 1,000 p., on Middleburgh & Schoharie Valley Rd., 5 m. from Schoharie, 38 W. of Albany.
Gazette................... W. **4,824**

MIDDLEPORT, Niagara Co.
Mail....................... W. **4,825**

MIDDLETOWN, Orange Co., 6,049 p., on Erie Rd., at intersection of New York & Oswego Midland Rd., 67 m. from New York. A trade centre.
Argus..................... D. **4,826**
" .... W. **4,827**
Evening Press............ D. **4,828**

NEW YORK.

Orange Co. Press......... W. **4,829**
Mercury................... W. **4,830**
Signs of the Times..... S. M. **4,831**

MOHAWK, Herkimer Co.
Independent............. W. **4,832**
Prohibitionist............ W. **4,833**

MOIRA, Franklin Co.
Journal................... W. **4,834**

MONTGOMERY, Orange Co., 4,000 p., on Walkill r. and Montgomery & Walkill Valley branch of Erie Rd., 69 m. from New York city and 10 from Goshen. A farming region, having some manufactures.
Republican and Standard W. **4,835**

MONTICELLO, c. h., Sullivan Co., 1,200† p., on Monticello and Port Jervis branch of New York & Erie Rd., 90 m. from New York, near centre of Sullivan Co.
Republican Watchman... W. **4,836**
Sullivan Co. Republican.. W. **4,837**

MORAVIA, Cayuga Co., 2,350† p., on Owasco Lake and Southern Central Rd., 18 m. S. S. E. of Auburn. Surrounded by a farming district, making it a market for the sale of agricultural produce. Manufacturing done here.
Valley Register........... W. **4,838**

MORRIS, Otsego Co., 2,550 p., on Butternut's Creek, in a thickly settled farming country. Hops and wool, butter and cheese are the principal products.
Chronicle................. W. **4,839**

MORRISVILLE, c. h., Madison Co., 850 p., 3 m. from New York & Oswego Midland Rd., and 12 S. of Oneida.
Madison Observer........ W. **4,840**

MOUNT KISCO, Westchester Co.
Weekly.................... W. **4,841**

MOUNT MORRIS, Livingston Co., 2,500 p., on Genesee Valley Canal, at terminus of Dansville & Mt. Morris branch of Erie Rd. Engaged in manufacturing and agriculture.
Enterprise................ W. **4,842**
Union and Constitution.. W. **4,843**

MOUNT VERNON, Westchester Co., 4,200 p., on Harlem & New Haven Rd., 17 m. N. of New York.
Chronicle................. W. **4,844**
Eastchester Independent.. W. **4,845**
Westchester Co. Anzeiger. W. **4,846**

NAPLES, Ontario Co., 1,200† p., on Canandaigua inlet, 4 m. from Lake and about 20 S. of Canandaigua.
Record.................... W. **4,847**

NEWARK, Wayne Co., 2,500† p., in Arcadia township, on Erie Canal and on the direct branch of N. Y. C. & H. R. Rd. and the Ontario Southern Rd., 30 m. E. of Rochester and 50 W. of Syracuse.
Courier.................... W. **4,848**
Union...................... W. **4,849**

NEWARK VALLEY, Tioga Co.
Tioga Co. Herald......... W. **4,850**

NEW BALTIMORE, Greene Co.
Sun........................ W. **4,851**

NEW BERLIN, Chenango Co., 2,460 p., on Unadilla r. and Sidney Plains & New Berlin branch of New York & Oswego Midland Rd., 20 m. from Sidney Plains.
Gazette.................... W. **4,852**

NEWBURGH, c. h., Orange Co., 17,014 p., on W. bank of Hudson r., 61 m. from

NEW YORK.

New York. A branch railroad connects it with Erie Rd. at Goshen. Engaged in cotton, woolen and other manufactures and centre of trade. Surrounded by an agricultural district.

Journal..................D. **4,853**
" ....W. **4,854**
Telegraph..................D. **4,855**
" ....W. **4,856**
Home, Farm and Orchard..................W. **4,857**
Our Friend..............M. **4,858**

NEW LEBANON, Columbia Co., 2,086 p., on Harlem Extension Rd., 18 m. from Chatham Four Corners. Some manufacturing done here.

Druggist..................M. **4,859**
*Journal of Materia Medica*M. **4,860**

NEW PALTZ, Ulster Co., 950 p., on Walkill r. and Montgomery & Walkill Valley Rd., 37 m. from Goshen and 12 from Kingston. Country agricultural.

Independent..............W. **4,861**
Times..................W. **4,862**

NEW ROCHELLE, Westchester Co., 4,678† p., on New York & New Haven Rd., 20 m. from New York.

Pioneer..................W. **4,863**
Press..................W. **4,864**

NEWTOWN, Queens Co.

Long Island Journal and Volks-Blatt............W. **4,865**
Queens Co. Safeguard....W. **4,866**
Register..................W. **4,867**

NEW YORK, c. h., New York Co., 926,341 p., on Manhattan Island. Great commercial and business centre of the United States.

Bulletin and Auction Record..................D. **4,868**
City Record..............D. **4,869**
Commercial Advertiser...D. **4,870**
Spectator and Commercial Advertiser.............W. **4,871**
Courrier des Etats Unis..D. **4,872**
" " " " ..W. **4,873**
Evening Express........D. **4,874**
" " ......S. W. **4,875**
" " ....W. **4,876**
Evening Mail.............D. **4,877**
" " ....W. **4,878**
Evening Post.............D. **4,879**
" " ....S. W. **4,880**
" " ....W. **4,881**
Evening Telegram........D. **4,882**
Sunday Telegram........W. **4,883**
Financial Record and Investor's Manual........D. **4,884**
Graphic..................D. **4,885**
Herald..................D. **4,886**
" ....W. **4,887**
Journal of Commerce.... D. **4,888**
" " " ..S. W. **4,889**
" " " ....W. **4,890**
Le Messager Franco-Americain..................D. **4,891**
Le Messager Franco-Americain..................S. W. **4,892**
News..................D. **4,893**
" ....W. **4,894**
" ....Sund. **4,895**
New Yorker Demokrat....D. **4,896**
" " " ....W. **4,897**
Beobachter am Hudson.Sund.**4,898**
New Yorker Journal......D. **4,899**
" " " ......W. **4,900**

NEW YORK.

New Yorker Presse.......D. **4,901**
" " " ......W. **4,902**
New Yorker Tages-Nachrichten..................D. **4,903**
Sonntags Nachrichten....W. **4,904**
Register..................D. **4,905**
Skandinavisk Post........D. **4,906**
" " ....W. **4,907**
" " ....Sund. **4,908**
Staats-Zeitung............D. **4,909**
" " ....W. **4,910**
" " ....Sund. **4,911**
Stage..................D. **4,912**
Star..................D. **4,913**
Sunday Star.............W. **4,914**
Sun..................D. **4,915**
" ....W. **4,916**
" ....Sund. **4,917**
Times..................D. **4,918**
" ....S. W. **4,919**
" ....W. **4,920**
Tribune..................D. **4,921**
" ....S. W. **4,922**
" ....W. **4,923**
Witness..................D. **4,924**
" ....W. **4,925**
World..................D. **4,926**
" ....S. W. **4,927**
" ....W. **4,928**
El Cronista...........S. W. **4,929**
La Independencia ....S. W. **4,930**
Reporter and Harlem Local..................S. W. **4,931**
Shipping and Commercial List and Price-Current..................S. W. **4,932**
Advertisers' Gazette..... W. **4,933**
Albion..................W. **4,934**
American Art Journal...W. **4,935**
American Commercial Times..................W. **4,936**
American Grocer........W. **4,937**
American Newspaper Reporter and Printers' Gazette..................W. **4,938**
American Railroad Journal..................W. **4,939**
American Trade Journal.W. **4,940**
Appleton's Journal......W. **4,941**
Arcadian..................W. **4,942**
Army and Navy Journal.W. **4,943**
Atlantische Blaetter und New Yorker Kladderadatsch..................W. **4,944**
Baptist Union............W. **4,945**
Baptist Weekly............W. **4,946**
Belletristisches Journal...W. **4,947**
Boys of New York........W. **4,948**
Boys of the World.......W. **4,949**
Bulletin of the Hours of Closing the Foreign Mails..................W. **4,950**
Catholic Review...........W. **4,951**
Chimney Corner..........W. **4,952**
Christian Advocate......W. **4,953**
Christian at Work.......W. **4,954**
" " " ....M. **4,955**
Christian Intelligencer...W. **4,956**
Christian Union..........W. **4,957**
Chronicle..................W. **4,958**
Church Journal and Gospel Messenger..........W. **4,959**
Churchman..................W. **4,960**
Church Union............W. **4,961**
Clipper..................W. **4,962**
Coal Trade Journal......W. **4,963**
Commercial and Financial Chronicle..........W. **4,964**

NEW YORK.

Commercial Gazette and Shoe and Leather Chronicle.
Corner Stone............W. **4,966**
Counting-House Monitor.W. **4,967**
Courier..................W. **4,968**
Crockery and Glass Journal..........................**4,969**
Day-Book................W. **4,970**
Days' Doings............W. **4,971**
Der Freischutz...........W. **4,972**
Deutscher Volksfreund...W. **4,973**
Deutsches Volksblatt.....W. **4,974**
Digest....................W. **4,975**
Dispatch.................W. **4,976**
Dramatic News..........W. **4,977**
Druggists' Journal.......W. **4,978**
Dry Goods Journal......W. **4,979**
Echo.....................W. **4,980**
Engineering and Mining Journal................W. **4,981**
Era.......................W. **4,982**
Evangelist................W. **4,983**
Examiner and Chronicle.W. **4,984**
Family Story Paper......W. **4,985**
Fireside Companion......W. **4,986**
Forest and Stream.......W. **4,987**
Fortschritt...............W. **4,988**
Frank Leslie's Boys' and Girls' Weekly..........W. **4,989**
Frank Leslie's Illustrated Newspaper.............W. **4,990**
Erank Leslie's Illustrirte Zeitung................W. **4,991**
Frank Leslie's Lady's Journal................W. **4,992**
Free Lance...............W. **4,993**
Freeman's Journal and Catholic Register.......W. **4,994**
Germania................W. **4,995**
Girls and Boys of America....................W. **4,996**
Gospel Sower............W. **4,997**
Grocer...................W. **4,998**
Grocer and Country Merchant...................W. **4,999**
Grocer's Price-Current....W. **5,000**
Grocery and Provision Review...................W. **5,001**
Handels-Zeitung.........W. **5,002**
Hardware Price-Current.W. **5,003**
Harness and Carriage Journal................W. **5,004**
Harper's Bazar...........W. **5,005**
Harper's Weekly.........W. **5,006**
Hebrew Leader...........W. **5,007**
Home Journal...........W. **5,008**
Humphrey's Paint and Oil Trade and Wholesale Druggist..........W. **5,009**
Illustrated Christian Weekly..................W. **5,010**
Illustrated Weekly.......W. **5,011**
Independent.............W. **5,012**
Insurance and Real Estate Journal........W. **5,013**
Internal Revenue Record and Customs Journal..W. **5,014**
Irish American..........W. **5,015**
Irish Democrat..........W. **5,016**
Irish World..............W. **5,017**
Iron Age.................W. **5,018**
Jewish Gazette...........W. **5,019**
Jewish Messenger........W. **5,020**
Jewish Times............W. **5,021**
Law and Equity Reporter...................W. **5,022**
Le Bulletin de New York.W. **5,023**

NEW YORK.

Ledger...................W. **5,024**
Liberal Christian........W. **5,025**
Living Issue.............W. **5,026**
Mackey's A. B. C. Guide.W. **5,027**
Mackey's Office Directory.W. **5,028**
Maritime Register.......W. **5,029**
Medical Record..........W. **5,030**
Mercantile Journal......W. **5,031**
Metal Worker............W. **5,032**
Methodist................W. **5,033**
Mirror....................W. **5,034**
Moore's Rural New Yorker.................W. **5,035**
Morrisania Tagblatt.....W. **5,036**
Nachrichten aus Deutschland und der Schweiz..W. **5,037**
Nation...................W. **5,038**
National Police Gazette..W. **5,039**
Nautical Gazette.........W. **5,040**
Neue Heim..............W. **5,041**
*New Jerusalem Messenger*W. **5,042**
New Yorker.
New Yorker Musik Zeitung...................W. **5,044**
Norden...................W. **5,045**
Nordstjernan............W. **5,046**
North New Yorker and Westchester Clarion....W. **5,047**
Observer.................W. **5,048**
Oil, Paint and Drug Reporter...................W. **5,049**
Paper Trade Journal....W. **5,050**
Paper Trade Reporter....W. **5,051**
People's Pulpit..........W. **5,052**
Progressive American....W. **5,053**
Public....................W. **5,054**
Publishers' Weekly.......W. **5,055**
Railroad Gazette.........W. **5,056**
Real Estate Record and Builders' Guide.......W. **5,057**
Rod and Gun............W. **5,058**
Saturday Journal.......W. **5,059**
Schnedderedengg........W. **5,060**
School Journal..........W. **5,061**
Scientific American......W. **5,062**
Scotsman and Caledonian Advertiser.............W. **5,063**
Scottish American Journal....................W. **5,064**
Sheldon's Dry Goods Price List..............W. **5,065**
Shoe and Leather Reporter...................W. **5,066**
South....................W. **5,067**
Spirit of the Times.......W. **5,068**
Sporting New Yorker....W. **5,069**
Sportsman................W. **5,070**
Stockholder..............W. **5,071**
Story Teller..............W. **5,072**
Sunday Citizen..........W. **5,073**
Sunday Democrat........W. **5,074**
Sunday Mercury.........W. **5,075**
Sunday School Advocate.W. **5,076**
" " " S. M. **5,077**
Sunday Times and Noah's Messenger..............W. **5,078**
Tablet....................W. **5,079**
Telegrapher.............W. **5,080**
Thompson's Bank Note and Commercial Reporter...................W. **5,081**
Thompson's Bank Note and Commercial Reporter................S. M. **5,082**
Thompson's Bank Note and Commercial Reporter.................M. **5,083**
Tobacco Leaf............W. **5,084**

NEW YORK.

Touchstone .... W. **5,085**
Trade Bureau........... W. **5,086**
Trade Journal...... .... W. **5,087**
Trade Reporter.......... W. **5,088**
Truth Seeker............. W. **5,089**
Turf, Field and Farm... W. **5,090**
United States Economist and Dry Goods Reporter W. **5,091**
Vindicator .... W. **5,092**
Wall Street Journal..... W. **5,093**
Weekly .... W. **5,094**
Westchester Times........ W. **5,095**
Westchester Union....... W. **5,096**
Wild Oats................ W. **5,097**
Wine and Fruit Reporter W. **5,098**
Woodhull and Claflin's Weekly................. W. **5,099**
Young American........ W. **5,100**
Young Christian Soldier. W. **5,101**
Catholic Total Abstinence Union.............. B. W. **5,102**
Heart and Hand...... B. W. **5,103**
Heirath's Anzeiger.... B. W. **5,104**
Lutherische Herold.... B. W. **5,105**
Notions and Fancy Goods Record....... B. W. **5,106**
Advocate and Family Guardian............ S. M. **5,107**
American Bookseller... S. M. **5,108**
American Gas Light Journal and Chemical Repertory............ S. M. **5,109**
American Stationer.... S. M. **5,110**
Appleton's Railway and Steam Navigation Guide .... S. M. **5,111**
Bonfort's Wine and Liquor Circular........ S. M. **5,112**
Deutsch-Amerikanische Gewerbe und Industrie Zeitung......... S. M. **5,113**
El Educador Popular.. S. M. **5,114**
El Mundo Nuevo America Illustrada.. S. M. **5,115**
Fraternity Record...... S. M. **5,116**
Journal of the Telegraph S. M. **5,117**
Munson's Phonographic News................ S. M. **5,118**
Music Trade Review... S. M. **5,119**
National Bankruptcy Register Reports..... S. M. **5,120**
Operator............... S. M. **5,121**
Road .... S. M. **5,122**
Shipper's Gazette and Traveler's Guide.......... S. M. **5,123**
United States Counterfeit Detector.
Aldine.................... M. **5,125**
American Age............ M. **5,126**
American Agriculturist... M. **5,127**
American Brewers' Gazette and Malt and Hops Trades Review.......... M. **5,128**
American Builder....... M. **5,129**
American Checker Player M. **5,130**
American Chemist....... M. **5,131**
American Industries..... M. **5,132**
American Journal of Microscopy................ M. **5,133**
American Law Times and Reports................ M. **5,134**
American Mechanic...... M. **5,135**
American Messenger...... M. **5,136**
American Missionary.... M. **5,137**
American Progress....... M. **5,138**
American Register and Hotel Guide............. M. **5,139**
Amerikanische Bierbrauer M. **5,140**

NEW YORK.

Amerikanischer Botschafter.................. M. **5,141**
Animal Kingdom........ M. **5,142**
Anthony's Photographic Bulletin................ M. **5,143**
Aquatic Monthly and Nautical Review............ M. **5,144**
Bankers' Magazine...... M. **5,145**
Bee Keepers' Magazine... M. **5,146**
Bible Society Record...... M. **5,147**
Book Buyer............... M. **5,148**
Browne's Phonographic Monthly................ M. **5,149**
Cæcilia.................. M. **5,150**
Carpet Trade............ M. **5,151**
Carpet Trade Review.
Carrier Dove............. M. **5,153**
Catholic World.
Child's Paper........... M. **5,155**
Christian Patriot......... M. **5,156**
Christian World......... M. **5,157**
Chronotype.
Church Gazette........... M. **5,159**
Clothier and Hatter...... M. **5,160**
Comic Monthly.......... M. **5,161**
Commercial Bulletin..... M. **5,162**
Confectioner............ M. **5,163**
Cricket on the Hearth.... M. **5,164**
Cutters' Monthly Journal of American Fashions.. M. **5,165**
Das Archiv.............. M. **5,166**
Delineator............... M. **5,167**
Demorest's Illustrated Monthly............... M. **5,168**
Deutsche Kirchenblatt.... M. **5,169**
Domestic Monthly....... M. **5,170**
Druggists' Advertiser..... M. **5,171**
Druggists' Circular and Chemical Gazette....... M. **5,172**
Eclectic Magazine.... ... M. **5,173**
El Ateneo................ M. **5,174**
El Comercio............. M. **5,175**
El Espejo................ M. **5,176**
Family Journal.......... M. **5,177**
Fire Record.............. M. **5,178**
Foreign Missionary...... M. **5,179**
Frank Leslie's Boys of America............... M. **5,180**
Frank Leslie's Budget of Fun.................. M. **5,181**
Frank Leslie's Lady's Magazine.............. M. **5,182**
Frank Leslie's Popular Monthly............... M. **5,183**
Galaxy.................. M. **5,184**
Good Cheer.............. M. **5,185**
Good Words............. M. **5,186**
Grand Army Gazette..... M. **5,187**
Guide to Holiness......... M. **5,188**
Hall's Journal of Health. M. **5,189**
Harper's New Monthly Magazine.............. M. **5,190**
Hat, Cap and Fur Trade Review................ M. **5,191**
Herald of Health......... M. **5,192**
Historical Magazine..... M. **5,193**
Home Journal of Health. M. **5,194**
Home Missionary........ M. **5,195**
Housekeeper............. M. **5,196**
Hub..................... M. **5,197**
Importer and United States Customs Record. M. **5,198**
Insurance Age........... M. **5,199**
Insurance Law Journal.. M. **5,200**
Insurance Monitor....... M. **5,201**
Insurance Times......... M. **5,202**
Jeweler's Circular and Horological Review..... M. **5,203**

NEW YORK

Johnstons' Dental Miscellany.................M. 5,204
Journal of Education....M. 5,205
Journal of Homœopathy.
Kind Words.............M. 5,207
La Creme de la Creme....M. 5,208
Ladies' Floral Cabinet and Pictorial Home Companion............M. 5,209
Le Beau Monde..........M. 5,210
Life Boat ....M. 5,211
Linthicum's Journal of New York Fashions....M. 5,212
Little Gem and Young Folks' Favorite.........M. 5,213
Manufacturer & Builder..M. 5,214
Manufacturers' Review & Industrial Record......M. 5,215
Matrimonial Advertiser..M. 5,216
Medical Journal.........M. 5,217
Merry Masker...........M. 5,218
Methodist Episcopal Church Missionary Advocate..................M. 5,219
Millers' Journal and Hydraulic Engineer.......M. 5,220
*Milliner and Dressmaker*M. 5,221
Millinery Trade Review..M. 5,222
Mirror.
Mirror of Fashion.......M. 5,224
Missionary Echo & Standard Bearer.
Monthly Record of Scientific Literature.........M. 5,226
Monthly Record of the Five Points House of Industry...............M. 5,227
Morning.................M. 5,228
Morning Light...........M. 5,229
Mother's Magazine.......M. 5,230
Musical Globe............M. 5,231
My Paper................M. 5,232
National Agriculturist and Working Farmer.......M. 5,233
National Bank Note Reporter and Financial Gazette................M. 5,234
National Car Builder....M. 5,235
National Protestant......M. 5,236
National Teacher's Monthly................M. 5,237
National Temperance Advocate...................M. 5,238
New Century.............M. 5,239
New Era.................M. 5,240
New Remedies............M. 5,241
Normal Class.............M. 5,242
Novo Mundo..............M. 5,243
Old and Young...........M. 5,244
Orpheus..................M. 5,245
Our Own Fireside........M. 5,246
Painters' Magazine......M. 5,247
Parish Visitor.
Patent Right Gazette.....M. 5,249
Patron's Gazette.........M. 5,250
Pen and Plow.
Peters' Household Melodies....................M. 5,252
Peters' Parlor Music.....M. 5,253
Pet Stock, Pigeon and Poultry Bulletin.
Philomathean.
Phrenological Journal and Life Illustrated.........M. 5,256
Phunny Fellow...........M. 5,257
Pictorial World..........M. 5,258
Pleasant Hours..........M. 5,259
Plumbers' and Gasfitters' Journal.

NEW YORK.

Popular Science Monthly.M. 5,261
Record of the Year.......M. 5,262
Register of the American Church Missionary Society.
Safeguard.................M. 5,264
Sailors' Magazine and Seamen's Friend........M. 5,265
*St. Chrysostom's Magazine*M. 5,266
St. Nicholas..............M. 5,267
Sanitarian................M. 5,268
Schermerhorn's Monthly..M. 5,269
Science of Health.........M. 5,270
Scribner's Monthly........M. 5,271
Sewing Machine Journal..M. 5,272
Sewing Machine World...M. 5,273
Sheltering Arms.........M. 5,274
Spectator.................M. 5,275
Spirit of Missions.
Student's Journal........M. 5,277
Sunbeam.
Sunday School Class Classmate.
Sunday School Journal..M. 5,280
Tailors' Monthly Review..M. 5,281
Technologist or Industrial Monthly...............M. 5,282
Temperance Magazine and Home Gem............M. 5,283
Texas New Yorker........M. 5,284
Treasure Trove...........M. 5,285
Underwriter and General Joint Stock Register....M. 5,286
Union in Christ..........M. 5,287
United States Insurance Gazette..................M. 5,288
United States Mail and Post Office Assistant....M. 5,289
Van Nostrand's Eclectic Engineering Magazine.M. 5,290
Voice from the Old Brewery....................M. 5,291
Watchmaker and Jeweler.M. 5,292
Work and Play..........M. 5,293
Working Church.........M. 5,294
Workshop .... M. 5,295
Young Catholic.
Your Paper..............M. 5,297
Youth's Temperance Banner......................M. 5,298
American Bibliopolist.B. M. 5,299
Catholic Book News...B. M. 5,300
International Review..B. M. 5,301
Medical Eclectic.......B. M. 5,302
American Garden.......Qr. 5,303
American Journal of Obstetrics...................Qr. 5,304
American Life Assurance Magazine and Journal of Actuaries............Qr. 5,305
Circular del Joyero.......Qr. 5,306
Fur, Fin and Feather....Qr. 5,307
Happy Hours............Qr. 5,308
Little Wanderer's Friend.
Methodist Quarterly Review .... Qr. 5,310
Musical Monitor..........Qr. 5,311
National Quarterly Review .... Qr. 5,312
Physician and Pharmacist.......................Qr. 5,313
Presbyterian Quarterly and Princeton Review..Qr. 5,314
Typographic Messenger...Qr. 5,315

NIAGARA FALLS, Niagara Co., 3,600† p., on Niagara r., near the Falls, 22 m. from Buffalo. A place of summer resort. Noted for its scenery.

Gazette..................W. 5,316

NEW YORK.

NICHOLVILLE, St. Lawrence Co.
Herald..................W. **5,317**

NORTHPORT, Suffolk Co.
Advertiser..............W. **5,318**
Suffolk Co. Journal......W. **5,319**

NORWICH, c. h., Chenango Co., 5,000 p., on Chenango r. and New York & Oswego Midland and the Delaware, Lackawanna & Western Rds., 40 m. from Binghamton, 50 from Utica. Engaged in manufactures.
Chenango Telegraph......W. **5,320**
Chenango Union.........W. **5,321**

NORWOOD, St. Lawrence Co.
Commercial Advertiser...W. **5,322**

NUNDA, Livingston Co., 1,875 p., 2½ m. from line of Buffalo division of Erie Rd. and 67 from Buffalo. Engaged in manufactures.
Livingston Democrat.....W. **5,323**
News....................W. **5,324**

NYACK, Rockland Co., 3,438 p., on Hudson r. and terminus of Northern New Jersey Rd., 29 m. from New York. Largest village in Rockland County.
City and Country........W. **5,325**
Rockland Co. Journal....W. **5,326**

OGDENSBURGH, St. Lawrence Co., 12,000† p., on St. Lawrence r., at mouth of Oswegatchie, and at terminus of Ogdensburgh & Lake Champlain and Rome, Watertown & Ogdensburgh Rds. Engaged in commerce and manufacturing.
Journal..................D. **5,327**
St. Lawrence Republican..W **5,328**
Advance..................W. **5,429**

OLEAN, Cattaraugus Co., 1,327 p., on Alleghany r. and Genesee Valley Canal, at junction of Buffalo, New York & Philadelphia Rd. with Erie Rd., 69 m. from Buffalo. Lumbering business of Olean important. Situated in an agricultural region.
Times....................W. **5,330**
American Socialist......W. **5,331**

ONEIDA, Madison Co., 3,289† p., in Lenox township, at intersection of New York Central Rd. with New York & Oswego Midland Rd., 26 m. from Syracuse, 27 from Utica and 12 from Rome. Centre of an agricultural and hop-growing district.
Democratic Union......W. **5,332**
Dispatch................W. **5,333**

ONEONTA, Otsego Co., 3,000† p., on Susquehanna r. and Albany & Susquehanna Rd., 82 m. from Albany, 60 from Binghamton. Engaged in manufactures. Albany & Susquehanna Rd. machine shops located here.
Commercial..............W. **5,334**
Herald and Democrat....W. **5,335**

ONTARIO, Wayne Co.
Sun......................W. **5,336**

OSWEGO, c. h., Oswego Co., 20,910 p., on Oswego Canal and Oswego r., at its entrance to Lake Ontario, and terminus of four important railroads. Has extensive commerce, flour being one of the principal articles of trade. Manufactures are carried on here, river furnishing power. Leading lake port for grain and lumber.
Palladium................D. **5,337**
" ....W. **5,338**
Times....................D. **5,339**
" ....W. **5,340**

OVID, c. h., Seneca Co., 800 p., between Seneca and Cayuga Lakes, about 20 m. S. of Waterloo.
Independent.............W. **5,341**

OWEGO, c. h., Tioga Co., 5,246† p., 250 m. W. of New York city, on Erie Rd., Chenango Canal and Southern Central Rd., and Owego r., at its junction with the Susquehanna. Engaged in manufactures and lumber trade.
Gazette..................W. **5,342**
Times....................W. **5,343**
Tioga Co. Record........W. **5,344**

OXFORD, Chenango Co., 3,500 p., on Chenango r. and Canal, New York & Oswego Midland Rd., and Delaware, Lackawanna & Western Rd. (Utica branch), 33 m. from Binghamton, 60 from Utica. Centre of a rich agricultural district and somewhat engaged in manufacturing.
Times....................W. **5,345**

PAINTED POST, Steuben Co., 1,415 p., at junction of Conhocton and Tioga rs., and on Erie Rd., at junction of Susquehanna and Rochester divisions, 20 m. W. of Elmira. Engaged in general manufacturing.
Gazette..................W. **5,346**
Times....................W. **5,347**

PALMYRA, Wayne Co., 3,000† p., on Erie Canal and line of New York Central Rd., 22 m. from Rochester.
Courier..................W. **5,348**
Wayne Co. Journal......W. **5,349**

PARISH, Oswego Co.
Mirror....................W. **5,350**

PATCHOGUE, Suffolk Co., a small town near south shore of Long Island, about 60 m. E. of New York.
Advance..................W. **5,351**

PAWLING, Dutchess Co., 1,743 p., on Harlem Rd., 67 m. N. of New York.
Rural Home..............W. **5,352**

PEEKSKILL, Westchester Co., 7,000† p., on Hudson r. and Hudson R. Rd., 48 m. from New York. Several iron foundries are located here, and give employment to a large number of men.
Highland Democrat......W. **5,353**
Messenger................W. **5,354**

PENN YAN, c. h., Yates Co., 4,200† p., in Milo township, at outlet of Crooked Lake, on Northern Central Rd., 43 m. from Elmira. Crooked Lake furnishes water power, which is employed in manufactures. Surrounded by a farming and fruit-growing district.
Democrat................W. **5,355**
Express..................W. **5,356**
Yates Co. Chronicle.....W. **5,357**

PERRY, Wyoming Co., 1,200 p., at outlet of Silver Lake and on Rochester & Pine Creek Rd., 45 m. from Rochester. Possesses water power from the lake.
Star......................W. **5,358**

PHELPS, Ontario Co., 1,850 p., on Flint Creek and New York Central Rd., 5 m. from Geneva and 15 E. of Canandaigua. Centre of a wealthy agricultural district. Engaged in raising fruit and stock for the New York market. An important gypsum and plaster depot.
*Ontario Citizen and News*W. **5,359**
Neighbors' Home Mail... W. **5,360**

PHŒNIX, Oswego Co., 1,418 p., on Oswe-

NEW YORK.

go r. and Canal, and near line of New York & Oswego Midland and Oswego & Syracuse Rds., 16 m. from Syracuse and 20 from Oswego. A farming district. Fine water power, which is employed in manufacturing.
Register..................W. 5,361

PINE PLAINS, Dutchess Co., 750 p., on Dutchess & Columbia and Poughkeepsie & Eastern Rds., 26 m. from Poughkeepsie.
Herald..................W. 5,362

PITCHER, Chenango Co.
Otselic Valley Register...W. 5,363

PLATTSBURGH, c. h., Clinton Co., 8,396 p., with harbor on Lake Champlain, and at junction of Plattsburgh & Montreal and Whitehall & Plattsburgh Rds. Sarenac r. furnishes water power. Engaged in manufactures and lake commerce.
News..................W. 5,364
Republican..................W. 5,365
Sentinel..................W. 5,366

PORT BYRON, Cayuga Co., 1,200† p., on New York Central Rd. and Erie Canal, 7 m. from Auburn and 26 from Syracuse. Engaged in manufacturing.
Chronicle..................W. 5,367

PORT CHESTER, Westchester Co., 3,797 p., on New Haven Rd., 29 m. N. E. of New York. Situated near Long Island Sound. Engaged in iron and other manufactures.
Journal..................W. 5,368

PORT HENRY, Essex Co., 3,000† p., on Lake Champlain. Engaged in manufactures and iron mining.
Herald..................W. 5,369
Record..................W. 5,370

PORT JEFFERSON, Suffolk Co., 2,000† p., a village on Port Jefferson Bay and Long Island Sound, about 63 m. E. of Brooklyn.
Long Island Leader.....W. 5,371

PORT JERVIS, Orange Co., 9,000† p., on Delaware r. and Erie Rd. and Delaware & Hudson Canal, 88 m. from New York. Engaged in manufactures. Erie Rd. machine shops located here.
Union..................D. 5,372
Tri-States Union..........W. 5,373
Evening Gazette......T. W. 5,374
Gazette..................W. 5,375

POTSDAM, St. Lawrence Co., 2,891 p., on Racket r. and Rome, Watertown & Ogdensburgh Rd. A place of active trade. Engaged in lumber and other manufactures. One of the State Normal and Training Schools located here.
Courier and Freeman....W. 5,376

POUGHKEEPSIE, c. h., Dutchess Co., 20,080 p., on E. bank of Hudson r., terminus of Poughkeepsie, Hartford & Boston and on Hudson R. Rds., 75 m. from New York. Engaged in manufacturing and river commerce and centre of trade. Several institutions of learning are located here. Styled the "City of Schools."
Eagle..................D. 5,377
" ....W. 5,378
News..................D. 5,379
" ....W. 5,380
Press..................D. 5,381
Telegraph..................W. 5,382
Dutchess Farmer..........W. 5,383
Stern am Hudson........W. 5,384

NEW YORK.

Sunday Courier..........W. 5,385
Real Estate Register and Commercial Advertiser.M. 5,386

PRATTSBURGH, Steuben Co., 700 p., in the Northern part of Steuben County, 50 m. from Rochester.
News..................W. 5,387

PRATTSVILLE, Greene Co.
News..................W. 5,388

PULASKI, c. h., Oswego Co., 1,800 p., on Salmon r., 4 m. from Lake Ontario, and on Oswego branch of Rome, Watertown & Ogdensburgh Rd., 24 m. from Oswego. Engaged in manufacturing.
Democrat..................W. 5,389

RANDOLPH, Cattaraugus Co., 2,500† p., on Atlantic & Great Western Rd., 16 m. E. of Jamestown. Engaged in agriculture and manufacturing butter and cheese. Has a good lumber trade.
Register..................W. 5,390

RED HOOK, Dutchess Co., 1,000 p., about 3 m. from Barrytown, on Hudson r. and Hudson R. Rd., 20 m. N. of Poughkeepsie. In an agricultural district.
Journal..................W. 5,391
Aurora Borealis..........Qr. 5,392

REMSEN, Oneida Co.
Y Cenhadwr Americanaido..................M. 5,393

RENSSELAERVILLE, Albany Co., 2,492 p., on Catskill Creek, 20 m. S. W. of Albany.
Press..................W. 5,394

RHINEBECK, Dutchess Co., 1,800† p., on E. bank of Hudson r., opposite Kingston, and on Hudson R. Rd. Some manufacturing done here and market for a farming district.
Gazette..................W. 5,395

RICHFIELD SPRINGS, Otsego Co., 1,000† p., on Utica, Chenango and Susquehanna Valley Rd., 35 m. from Utica and 10 N. of Cooperstown.
Mercury..................W. 5,396

RICHMONDVILLE, Schoharie Co., 630 p., on Albany & Susquehanna Rd., 50 m. from Albany. Engaged in manufacturing. Centre of trade for the surrounding country.
Schoharie Co. Democrat..W. 5,397

RIVERHEAD, c. h., Suffolk Co., 1,800† p., on Peconic r. at its entrance into Great Peconic Bay, and on Long Island Rd., 73 m. E. of Brooklyn.
News..................W. 5,398

ROCHESTER, c. h., Monroe Co., 90,039† p., on Genesee r., 7 m. from Lake Ontario. The river has several falls within the city limits that furnish abundant power, which is very largely employed for manufacturing purposes. A number of flouring mills are located here. This is the centre of the nursery interest of New York State and is an agricultural market. The commerce is important, having communication with Lake Ontario through Genesee r., and with Buffalo and Albany by means of the Erie and Genesee Valley Canals, and the Central Rd. and its branches, several of which converge at this point. A branch of the Erie Road also connects with the main line at Corning.
Beobachter..................D. 5,399
" ....W. 5,400

NEW YORK.

Democrat and Chronicle..D. **5,401**
" " " S. W. **5,402**
" " " W. **5,403**
Evening Express..........D. **5,404**
" " ......T. W. **5,405**
" " ....W. **5,406**
Union and Advertiser....D. **5,407**
" " " S. W. **5,408**
Republican............... W. **5,409**
Volksblatt..................D. **5,410**
" ....W. **5,411**
American Rural Home..W. **5,412**
Times......................W. **5,413**
Von Nah und Fern......W. **5,414**
Earnest Christian and Golden Rule............M. **5,415**
Fruit Recorder.............M. **5,416**
Hospital Review...........M. **5,417**
Industrial School Advocate......................M. **5,418**
University Record.........M. **5,419**
West End Journal and Orphan's Advocate.....M. **5,420**
Vick's Floral Guide.......Qr. **5,421**

ROCKVILLE CENTER, Queens Co., 650 p., about 17 m. from New York.
South Side Observer.......W. **5,422**

ROME, c. h., Oneida Co., 11,000 p., on Mohawk r., at junction of Black r. & Erie Canal, New York Central and terminus of Rome, Watertown & Ogdensburgh, Oswego & Rome and Rome & Clinton Rds., 14 m. from Utica. An active business place, engaged in railroad iron and other manufactures. In the heart of a farming and dairy region.
Roman Citizen...........W. **5,423**
Sentinel...................W. **5,424**

ROSENDALE, Ulster Co.
Blade.......................W. **5,425**

SAG HARBOR, Suffolk Co., 1,723 p., on branch of Long Island Rd., 100 m. from New York. Engaged in commerce and whale fishery. Centre of trade for surrounding towns.
Corrector..................W. **5,426**
Express....................W. **5,427**

ST. JOHNSVILLE, Montgomery Co.
Interior New Yorker.....W. **5,428**

SALAMANCA, Cattaraugus Co.
Cattaraugus Republican. W. **5,429**

SALEM, c. h., Washington Co., 1,500 p., on Albany & Rutland Rd., 48 m. from Albany.
Press......................W. **5,430**

SANDY CREEK, Oswego Co., 1,100† p., on Sandy Creek and Rome, Watertown & Ogdensburgh Rd., 47 m. from Rome.
News......................W. **5,431**

SANDY HILL, c. h., Washington Co., 2,500† p., on Hudson r., and Glen's Falls branch of Rensselaer & Saratoga Rd., 52 m. N. of Albany. Has water power and engaged in manufacturing.
Herald....................W. **5,432**
Saw Mill.

SARATOGA SPRINGS, Saratoga Co., 7,516 p. in winter and about 25,000 in summer, 38 m. from Albany, on Rensselaer & Saratoga Rd. A fashionable watering place.
Saratogian................D. **5,434**
" ....W. **5,435**
Saratoga Democratic Banner.......................W. **5,436**

NEW YORK.

Saratoga Sentinel... ....W. **5,437**
Saratoga Sun.............W. **5,438**

SAUGERTIES, Ulster Co., 3,731 p., on Hudson r. at mouth of Esopus Creek, 12 m. above Kingston. Country almost exclusively agricultural.
Telegraph..................W. **5,439**

SCHENECTADY, c. h., Schenectady Co., 13,000† p., on Mohawk r. and Erie Canal and New York Central Rd., at junction of Schenectady division of Rensselaer & Saratoga Rd., 16 m. from Albany. Engaged in manufacturing, and surrounded by an agricultural district. Seat of Union College.
Evening Star..............D. **5,440**
Reflector...................W. **5,441**
Union.......................D. **5,442**
" ....W. **5,443**
Deutscher Anzeiger......W. **5,444**
Gazette.......... ....W. **5,445**
Poultry Graphic.........S. M. **5,446**
College Spectator..........M. **5,447**

SCHENEVUS, Otsego Co., 800† p., on Albany & Susquehanna Rd., 67 m. from Albany. Thriving town. Centre of trade.
Monitor....................W. **5,448**

SCHOHARIE, c. h., Schoharie Co., 1,650 p., on Schoharie r. & Schoharie Valley branch of Albany & Susquehanna Rd., 40 m. from Albany.
Republican.................W. **5,449**
Union.......................W. **5,450**

SCHUYLERVILLE, Saratoga Co., 1,367 p., on Hudson r. & Champlain Canal, about 28 m. N. of Troy.
Saratoga Co. Standard..W. **5,451**

SENECA FALLS, Seneca Co., 6,000 p., on Seneca r. and New York Central Rd., 43 m. from Syracuse. The river has a fall at this point which affords a fine water power, which is employed in manufacturing agricultural implements, fine engines and other articles.
Reveille....................W. **5,452**
Seneca Co. Courier.......W. **5,453**
Cowing's Illustrated Journal.

SHAKERS, Albany Co., 3,000 p., about 8 m. N. W. of Albany. Engaged in raising seeds and manufacture of brooms.
Shaker.....................M. **5,455**

SHARON SPRINGS, Schoharie Co.
Gazette............... ...W. **5,456**

SHERBURNE, Chenango Co., 2,915† p., on Chenango r. and Utica, Chenango & Susquehanna Valley Rd., 9 m. from Norwich and 43 from Utica.
News.......................W. **5,457**

SING SING, Westchester Co., 6,000 p., in Ossining township, on Hudson r. and Hudson R. Rd., 33 m. from New York. Quarries of lime-stone are located here. Also file and other manufactories.
Democratic Register.....W. **5,458**
Republican................W. **5,459**

SKANEATELES, Onondaga Co., 2,200† p., on Skaneateles Lake, and 7 m. from Auburn and 18 from Syracuse. Engaged in manufacturing and an active business place. A summer resort.
Democrat.................W. **5,460**
Free Press.................W. **5,461**

SMYRNA, Chenango Co.
Citizen....................W. **5,462**

SODUS, Wayne Co.
Wayne Co. Alliance......W. **5,463**

SOUTHOLD, Suffolk Co., 1,500† p., on Long Island Rd., 4 m. from Greenport.
Long Island Traveler....W. **5,464**

SPRING VALLEY, Rockland Co.
Rockland Advocate.......W. **5,465**

SPRINGVILLE, Erie Co., 850† p., on Spring Creek, 30 m. from Buffalo, in a farming district.
Journal and Herald.....W. **5,466**

STAMFORD, Delaware Co., 1,571† p., 60 m. from Albany and 75 from Rondout. Engaged in agriculture and manufacturing.
Mirror..................W. **5,467**

STAPLETON, Richmond Co., 9,000 p., on Staten Island, 6 m. from New York, and to which it is connected by a steamboat.
Richmond Co. Gazette....W. **5,468**

SUSPENSION BRIDGE, Niagara Co., 2,500 p., on Niagara r. and New York Central Rd., 18 m. from Lockport, 12 from St. Catharines, Ont.
Journal.................W. **5,469**

SYRACUSE, c. h., Onondaga Co., 54,099† p., on Onondaga Lake and Erie Canal, at intersection with Oswego Canal. Several railroads centre here. Engaged in the manufacture of salt and other articles.
Courier..................D. **5,470**
Onondaga Courier......W. **5,471**
Journal...................D. **5,472**
" ....W. **5,473**
Standard.................D. **5,474**
" ....W. **5,475**
Freie Presse...........S. W. **5,476**
American Wesleyan......W. **5,477**
Central Demokrat........W. **5,478**
Northern Christian Advocate....................W. **5,479**
Sunday News............W. **5,480**
Union.....................W. **5,481**
Children's Banner.....S. M. **5,482**
Aurora Brazileira........M. **5,483**
School Bulletin and New York State Educational Journal................M. **5,484**
Typo.......................M. **5,485**

TARRYTOWN, Westchester Co., 5,000 p., on Hudson R. Rd., 27 m. from New York.
Argus.....................W. **5,486**

TICONDEROGA, Essex Co.
Sentinel..................W. **5,487**

TONAWANDA, Niagara Co., 6,000† p., on Niagara r., at outlet of Tonawanda Creek, opposite Grand Island and on Erie Canal, where it is crossed by Buffalo & Niagara Falls Rd., also Erie Rd., 10 m. N. of Buffalo. Engaged in manufacturing lumber and other articles.
Herald....................W. **5,488**
Lake Shore Enterprise....W. **5,489**

TROY, c. h., Rensselaer Co., 48,253† p., at head of steamboat navigation, on E. bank of Hudson r., 6 m. from Albany. Hudson R., New York Central, Rensselaer & Saratoga and Troy & Boston Rds. centre here. Engaged in manufactures, stoves, iron, steel, being the principal, and having a large river commerce.
Press......................D. **5,490**
" ....W. **5,491**
Times......................D. **5,492**
" ....W. **5,493**
Whig.......................D. **5,494**
" ....W. **5,495**
Northern Budget.........W. **5,496**
Sunday Trojan............W. **5,497**
Volksfreund..............W. **5,498**

TRUMANSBURG, Tompkins Co., 1,400 p., 2 m. from Cayuga Lake and 9 from Ithaca.
Tompkins Co. Sentinel...W. **5,499**

UNADILLA, Otsego Co., 1,000 p., on Susquehanna r. and Albany & Susquehanna Rd., 95 m. from Albany. Some manufacturing done here.
Times......................W. **5,500**

UNION, Broome Co., 2,538 p., on Erie Rd., 9 m. from Binghamton and 13 from Owego. Engaged in lumber business, farming and dairying.
News......................W. **5,501**

UNION SPRINGS, Cayuga Co., 1,500 p., on Lake Cayuga, 9 m. S. W. of Auburn. Engaged in manufacturing agricultural implements, carriage hubs, etc. Centre of trade.
Advertiser................W. **5,502**

UTICA, c. h., Oneida Co., 33,800† p., on Mohawk r., Erie Canal and New York Central Rd., 95 m. from Albany, at terminus of Chenango Canal and centering point for several railroads extending north and south. Engaged in various manufactures. Centre of an agricultural district.
Morning Herald and Gazette.....................D. **5,503**
Herald and Gazette......W. **5,504**
Observer..................D. **5,505**
" ....W. **5,506**
Deutsche Zeitung.....T. W. **5,507**
Christian Leader.........W. **5,508**
Y Drych...................W. **5,509**
Steam Engine.............M. **5,510**
Y Cyfaill o'r Hen Wlad..M. **5,511**
American Journal of Insanity.....................M.

WALDEN, Orange Co., 1,448† p., on Walkill r. and Montgomery & Walkill Valley branch of Erie Rd., 4 m. from Montgomery and 10 N. W. of Newburgh.
Herald and Recorder....W. **5,513**

WALTON, Delaware Co., 1,380† p., on W. branch of Delaware r. and New York & Oswego Midland, at junction of Delhi Branch Rd., 17 m. S. W. of Delhi and 23 from Sidney Plains.
Chronicle.................W. **5,514**

WAPPINGERS FALLS, Dutchess Co., 3,000† p., on Wappingers Creek, 1¼ m. from Hudson R. Rd. Manufacturing done here.
Wappingers Chronicle...W. **5,515**

WARSAW, c. h., Wyoming Co., 3,206 p., on Allen's Creek and Hornellsville Branch Rd., 48 m. from Buffalo. A business place.
Arcade Times............W. **5,516**
Western New Yorker.....W. **5,517**
Wyoming Co. Democrat.W. **5,518**

WARWICK, Orange Co., 1,096† p., on branch of Erie Rd., 9 m. from Greycourt.
Advertiser...............W. **5,519**
Orange Co. Crusader....W. **5,520**

WATERFORD, Saratoga Co., 4,700† p., on Rensselaer & Saratoga Rd. and Hudson r., near the mouth of Mohawk r., 4 m.

NEW YORK

from Troy and 10 above Albany. Engaged in various manufactures.
Advertiser................W. 5,521

WATERLOO, c. h., Seneca Co., 4,086 p., on New York Central Rd. and Cayuga and Seneca Canal, 18 m. from Auburn. Engaged in manufacturing shawls and woolen goods, agricultural implements, carriages and other articles.
Observer..................W. 5,522

WATERTOWN, c. h., Jefferson Co., 9,336 p., on Black r. and on Rome, Watertown & Ogdensburgh Rd., 71 m. from Rome and on Utica & Black R. Rd., 91 m. from Utica. A railroad extends from here to Cape Vincent, on the St. Lawrence r. The falls here furnish power, which is developed to some extent. The manufactures are various and extensive.
Despatch..................D. 5,523
Re-Union................W. 5,524
Times......................D. 5,525
Reformer.................W. 5,526
Post.......................W. 5,527

WATERVILLE, Oneida Co., 1,600† p., in Saugerfield township, on Utica, Chenango & Susquehanna Valley Rd., 21 m. from Utica.
Times.....................W. 5,528

WATKINS, c. h., Schuyler Co., 3,000† p., on Seneca Lake, on Northern Central Rd., connected with Geneva at the other end of the lake, about 35 m. distant, by steamers, and 20 from Elmira. In an agricultural and grape-growing district. The famous Watkins Glen is located here. it is annually visited by from 50,000 to 75,000 people.
Express..................W. 5,529
Schuyler Co. Democrat...W. 5,530

WAVERLY, Tioga Co., 4,150† p., on Chemung r. and Erie Rd., at junction of Lehigh Valley and Geneva, Ithaca & Athens Rds., 17 m. from Elmira. Surrounded by farming lands, and shipping point for grain and butter.
Advocate.................W. 5,531
Enterprise................W. 5,532
Review...................W. 5,533
For Everybody.

WAYLAND, Steuben Co.
Press......................W. 5,535

WEEDSPORT, Cayuga Co., 1,800† p., on Erie Canal and New York Central & Southern Central Rd., 10 m. from Auburn. Engaged in manufacturing, etc.
Sentinel..................W. 5,536

WELLS, Hamilton Co., 817 p., on Sacondaga r., 80 m. N. W. of Albany.
Journal and Republican..W. 5,537

WELLSVILLE, Allegany Co., 4,000† p., on Genesee r. and Erie Rd., 27 m. W. of Hornellsville. Engaged in tanning, and has considerable trade with Northern Pennsylvania.
Allegany Co. Reporter...W. 5,538
Allegany Democrat......W. 5,539

WESTCHESTER, Westchester Co., 6,015 p., on Westchester Creek, 5 m. from Harlem. Country residences for New York merchants.
Manhattan Monthly.....W. 5,540

WESTFIELD, Chautauqua Co., 3,000 p., on Lake Shore & Michigan Southern Rd., 57 m. from Buffalo and 31 from Erie, Pa. Engaged in manufacturing agricultural implements and other articles.
Republican...............W. 5,541

WEST NEW BRIGHTON, Richmond Co., 6 m. from New York city, with which it is connected by ferry. Manufacturing done here.
North Shore Advocate... W. 5,542

WEST TROY, Albany Co., 12,000 p., on W. bank of Hudson r., opposite Troy, and to which it is connected by bridge and a steam ferry. Engaged in manufacturing and lumber trade. Watervliet Arsenal—an important United States post—is located at this place.
Albany Co. Democrat....W. 5,543
Herald....................W. 5,544

WEST WINFIELD, Herkimer Co., 1,561 p., on Richfield Springs branch of Utica; Chenango & Susquehanna Valley Rd., 21 m from Utica and 13 from Richfield Springs.
Winfield Standard.......W. 5,545

WHITEHALL, Washington Co., 5,000 p., on Lake Champlain, at mouth of Poultney r. Connected to various ports on the Lake by steamers, and by railroad to Troy and Albany. Some manufacturing done here.
Chronicle.................W. 5,546
Times.....................W. 5,547

WHITE PLAINS, c. h., Westchester Co., 2,630 p., on New York & Harlem Rd., 26 m. from New York.
Eastern State Journal...W. 5,548
Westchester News........W. 5,549

WHITESTONE, Queens Co., 2,500† p. Terminus of Flushing & North Side Rd. Engaged in commerce and manufacturing.
Herald....................W. 5,550

WHITNEY'S POINT, Broome Co.
Nioga Reporter.......... W. 5,551

WINDHAM, Greene Co., 1,488† p., on Batavia Creek, 25 m. W. of Catskill.
Journal..................W. 5,552

WINDSOR, Broome Co.
Advance..................W. 5,553

WOLCOTT, Wayne Co.
Lake Shore News.........W. 5,554

WORCESTER, Otsego Co.
Times.................... W. 5,555

YONKERS, Westchester Co., 18,000† p., on Hudson r. and Hudson R. Rd., 17 m. from New York. Engaged in various manufactures and the residence of many persons doing business in New York. Several institutions of learning are located here.
Gazette...................W. 5,556
Herald....................W. 5,557
New York Republikaner..W. 5,558
Statesman................W. 5,559
Westchester Deutsche Zeitung....................W. 5,560

NORTH CAROLINA.

ASHEBORO, c. h., Randolph Co.
Randolph Regulator......W. 5,561

ASHEVILLE, c. h., Buncombe Co., 2,500† p., near French Broad r., 255 m. W. of Raleigh.

North Carolina Citizen..W. **5,562**
Pioneer.................W. **5,563**
Western Expositor.......W. **5,564**

BAKERSVILLE, c. h., Mitchell Co.
Independent.............W. **5,565**

CHARLOTTE, c. h., Mecklenburg Co., 6,000 p., on Sugar Creek and Wilmington, Charlotte & Rutherford Rd., at terminus of North Carolina division of Richmond & Danville and Charlotte, Columbia & Augusta Rds.
Bulletin..................D. **5,566**
" ....T. W. **5,567**
Courier...................W. **5,568**
Observer..................D. **5,569**
" ....W. **5,570**
Democrat..................W. **5,571**
Southern Home.............W. **5,572**
Southern Mechanic.........M. **5,573**

CONCORD, c. h., Cabarrus Co.
Register..................W. **5,574**
Sun.......................W. **5,575**

DANBURY, c. h., Stokes Co., 500 p., 112 m. N. N. W. of Raleigh and 10 from Virginia State line.
Reporter..................W. **5,576**

DURHAM, Orange Co., 3,000† p., on North Carolina Rd., 25 m. from Raleigh. Tobacco manufacturing the principal branch of industry.
Tobacco Plant.............W. **5,577**

ELIZABETH CITY, c. h., Pasquotank Co., 2,000 p., on Pasquotank r., 20 m. from Albemarle Sound. Connected by a daily line of steamers with Norfolk, Va. Engaged in lumber and grain trade.
Economist.................W. **5,578**
North Carolinian...........W. **5,579**

FAYETTEVILLE, c. h., Cumberland Co., 5,000† p., on Cape Fear r., at the head of navigation, and terminus of Western Rd. Centre of trade, and a shipping point for lumber, tar, turpentine, &c. Engaged in the manufacture of cotton goods.
Educator.
North Carolina Gazette...W. **5,581**
Public Spirit.............W. **5,582**

GOLDSBORO, c. h., Wayne Co., 3,000† p., on Neuse r. and Wilmington & Weldon Rd., 84 m. from Wilmington. The Atlantic & North Carolina Rd. terminates here; also E. terminus of North Carolina division of Richmond & Danville Rd. One of the most important trade centres in State. In centre of cotton region and agricultural section.
Carolina Messenger...S. W. **5,583**
Transcript and Messenger W. **5,584**
Carolina Household Magazine.

GRAHAM, c. h., Alamance Co.
Alamance Gleaner.........W. **5,586**

GREENSBORO, c. h., Guilford Co., 4,000† p., on the North Carolina division of Richmond & Danville Rd., at the junction of Richmond, Danville & Piedmont Rd., 81 m. from Raleigh. A place of trade. Engaged in manufacturing.
Central Protestant........W. **5,587**
Masonic Journal...........W. **5,588**
New North State...........W. **5,589**
Patriot...................W. **5,590**

GREENVILLE, c. h., Pitt Co., 1,500 p., on Tar r., about 30 m. above Washington and 103 E. of Raleigh. Tar and turpentine are products of vicinity.
Register..................W. **5,591**
Tar River Beacon..........W. **5,592**

HENDERSON, Granville Co.
Tribune...................W. **5,593**

HENDERSONVILLE, c. h., Henderson Co.
Henderson Co. Advertiser.W. **5,594**

HICKORY, Catawba Co., 2,000† p., on Western North Carolina Rd., about 30 m. W. of Statesville and 30 from Blue Ridge. Corn, wheat and tobacco raised. A watering place.
Piedmont Press............W. **5,595**

HILLSBOROUGH, c. h., Orange Co., 1,500 p., on Eno r., an affluent of the Neuse, and on the North Carolina Rd., 39 m. from Raleigh.
Recorder..................W. **5,596**

LA GRANGE, Lenoir Co.
Baptist Review............W. **5,597**

LENOIR, c. h., Caldwell Co.
Caldwell Messenger........W. **5,598**

LEXINGTON, c. h., Davidson Co.
Central...................W. **5,599**

LINCOLNTON, c. h., Lincoln Co.
Lincoln Progress..........W. **5,600**

LOUISBURG, c. h., Franklin Co., 1,000 p., on Tar r., 10 m. from the Raleigh & Gaston Rd., and 30 N. by E. of Raleigh. A market for the agricultural productions of the county.
Franklin Courier..........W. **5,601**

LUMBERTON, c. h., Robeson Co., 850 p., on Wilmington, Charlotte & Rutherford Rd., 68 m. N. W. of Wilmington and 33 S. W. of Fayetteville. Engaged in cotton, corn and lumber trade, and in turpentine.
Robesonian................W. **5,602**

MAGNOLIA, Duplin Co., on Wilmington & Weldon Rd., 48 m. from Wilmington and 37½ from Goldsboro.
Record....................W. **5,603**

MILTON, Caswell Co.
Chronicle.................W. **5,604**
Mercury...................W. **5,605**

MONROE, c. h., Union Co.
Enquirer..................W. **5,606**
Monthly Messenger.........W. **5,607**

MORGANTON, c. h., Burke Co.
Blue Ridge Blade..........W. **5,608**

MOUNT AIRY, Surry Co., 1,250 p., on Ararat r., near Virginia State line, 170 m. N. W. of Raleigh.
Surry Visitor.............W. **5,609**
Watchman..................W. **5,610**

MURFREESBORO, Hertford Co.
Enquirer..................W. **5,611**

MURPHY, c. h., Cherokee Co.
Cherokee Herald...........W. **5,612**

NEW-BERNE, c. h., Craven Co., 5,849 p., at the confluence of the Neuse and Trent rs., 40 m. from Pamlico Sound, on the Atlantic & North Carolina Rd., 59 m. from Goldsboro. Engaged in turpentine distilleries. Has a cotton and lumber trade, and is engaged in various manufactures. Surrounded by an agricultural section.
Nut Shell.................D. **5,613**
Newbernian..............S. W. **5,614**

NORTH CAROLINA.

Journal of Commerce....W. 5,615
Times and Republic-Courier....................W. 5,616

OXFORD, c. h., Granville Co.
Torch Light..............W. 5,617

PLYMOUTH, c. h., Washington Co., 1,500 p., connected with Albemarle Sound by Roanoke r. Has an extensive trade.
Roanoke Cressett.
Spirit of the Press.

POLKTON, Anson Co.
Ansonian................W. 5,620

RALEIGH, c. h., State capital, Wake Co., 7,790 p., on North Carolina, Raleigh & Gaston Rd., 148 m. N. by W. of Wilmington. Railroads connect with Wilmington, Newbern, Gaston and Charlotte, which render it a point of trade. Cotton, corn and tobacco produced.
News......................D. 5,621
" ....W. 5,622
Sentinel...................D. 5,623
" ....S. W. 5,624
" ....W. 5,625
Biblical Recorder.........W. 5,626
Christian Advocate.......W. 5,627
Era........................W. 5,628
Friend of Temperance....W. 5,629
Spirit of the Age.........W. 5,630
North Carolina Journal of Education.
Our Living & Our Dead..M. 5,632

REIDSVILLE, Rockingham Co., 500 p., on Richmond & Danville Rd., 24 m. from Greensboro.
News.....................W. 5,633
Times.....................W. 5,634

ROCKINGHAM, c. h., Richmond Co., 850† p., on Wilmington, Charlotte & Rutherford Rd., 117 m. from Wilmington.
Pee Dee Courier.........W. 5,635
Spirit of the South........W. 5,636

ROCKY MOUNT, Edgecomb Co., 550† p., on Wilmington & Weldon Rd., 37 m. from Weldon.
Mail......................W. 5,637

RUTHERFORDTON, c. h., Rutherford Co., 790 p., 260 m. W. of Raleigh and 65 W. of Charlotte. Centre of an agricultural and mining district.
New Regime.............W. 5,638

SALEM, Forsythe Co., 1,594 p., 25 m. W. of Greensboro. Engaged in manufacturing. Seat of Salem Female Academy.
People's Press...........W. 5,639

SALISBURY, c. h., Rowan Co., 4,000† p., on North Carolina Rd., at junction of Western North Carolina Rd., 131 m. from Raleigh.
Carolina Watchman.....W. 5,640

SHELBY, c. h., Cleveland Co., 1,100† p., 55 m. W. of Charlotte. Head of Carolina Central Rd.
Banner...................W. 5,641

SMITHFIELD, c. h., Johnston Co.
Johnston Courier........W. 5,642

STATESVILLE, c. h., Iredell Co., 1,800† p., on Western North Carolina Rd., 25 m. from Salisbury. Chief town in county and centre of trade.
American..............W. 5,643
Landmark..............W. 5,644

TARBORO, c. h., Edgecomb Co., 1,340 p., on Tar r., 50 m. above Washington, and connected with Rocky Mount, on Wilmington & Weldon Rd., by a branch. Engaged in raising cotton and corn.
Southerner...............W. 5,645

TIOSNOT, Wilson Co.
Transcript...............W. 5,646

WADESBORO, c. h., Anson Co., 1,250† p., 10 m. W. of Pee Dee r. and 120 S. W. of Raleigh.
North Carolina Argus...W. 5,647
Pee Dee Herald..........W. 5,648

WARRENTON, Warren Co., 500 p., on Raleigh & Gaston Rd., 62 m. from Raleigh.
Centennial...............W. 5,649
Gazette...................W. 5,650

WASHINGTON, c. h., Beaufort Co., 2,094 p., on Tar r., 40 m. from Pamlico Sound and 128 E. of Raleigh.
Echo......................W. 5,651

WELDON, Halifax Co., 1,500 p., on Roanoke r., 60 m. from Petersburg. The Wilmington & Weldon, Seaboard & Roanoke, Petersburg & Weldon, and Raleigh & Gaston Rds. centre here, making it a place of active trade.
Roanoke News.........S. W. 5,652

WILMINGTON, c. h., New Hanover Co., 19,000† p., on Cape Fear r., 34 m. from sea. Engaged in commerce and manufactures. Railroads connect with Raleigh and Weldon and Manchester, S. C. Foreign commerce increasing and now constitutes two-thirds of export trade. Manufactures of cotton goods, cane fibre for paper stock, machinery, &c. Railway connections with Charlotte and the West, Columbia, Augusta and Charleston, S. C., Raleigh, Newberne, Weldon, &c.
Evening Review..........D. 5,653
Journal...................D. 5,654
" ....W. 5,655
Star.......................D. 5,656
" ....W. 5,657
North Carolina Presbyterian....................W. 5,658
Post.......................W. 5,659
Pythian Echo............W. 5,660

WILSON, c. h., Wilson Co., 2,000† p., on Wilmington & Weldon Rd., 24 m. from Goldsboro, 100 from Wilmington, 134 from Portsmouth and Norfolk, Va. In centre of an agricultural section. Sheep raised.
Advance.................W. 5,661
Plain Dealer.............W. 5,662
Watch-Tower...........S. M. 5,663
Zion's Landmark......S. M. 5,664

WINDSOR, c. h., Bertie Co.
Albemarle Times..........W. 5,665

WINSTON, Forsythe Co., 1,600 p., 120 m. W. by N. of Raleigh, and adjoining Salem. Tobacco raising, manufacturing and fruit culture the principal branches of industry.
Union Republican.......W. 5,666
Western Sentinel.........W. 5,667

OHIO.

ADA, Hardin Co., 1,700† p., on Pittsburgh, Fort Wayne & Chicago Rd., 15 m. E. of Lima.
Record..................W. 5,668

AKRON, Summit Co., 14,500 p., on Atlantic & Great Western Rd., at intersection of Cleveland, Mount Vernon & Delaware Rd.,

40 m. from Cleveland. The Ohio and Erie Canal here forms a junction with the Pennsylvania & Ohio Canal. Actively engaged in manufacturing agricultural implements.
Argus..................D. **5,669**
"..................S. W. **5,670**
Beacon..................D. **5,671**
Summit Co. Beacon.....W. **5,672**
City Times..............W. **5,673**
Germania................W. **5,674**
Commercial..............M. **5,675**

ALLIANCE, Stark Co., 4,520† p., on Mahoning r. and Pittsburgh, Fort Wayne & Chicago Rd., at intersection of Cleveland & Pittsburgh Rd., and Lake Erie, Alliance and Wheeling Rds., 56 m. from Cleveland. Engaged in manufactures and surrounded by a farming community.
Leader..................W. **5,676**
Monitor.................W. **5,677**
Review..................W. **5,678**
Sunday Telegraph.

ANTWERP, Paulding Co., 1,600† p., on Maumee r. and Toledo, Wabash & Western Rd., 71 m. from Toledo.
Gazette..................W. **5,680**

ASHLAND, Ashland Co., 3,300† p., on Atlantic & Great Western Rd., 85 m. from Columbus and 60 from Cleveland. An agricultural district.
Press....................W. **5,681**
Times....................W. **5,682**

ASHLEY, Delaware Co.
Enterprise............S. M. **5,683**

ASHTABULA, Ashtabula Co., 3,700† p., on Ashtabula r., 3 m. from Lake Erie and on Lake Shore & Michigan Southern Rd., at junction of Ashtabula, Youngstown & Pittsburgh Rd., 55 m. from Cleveland. Lake steamers have a harbor at the mouth of the river. Engaged in agriculture and dairying.
News....................W. **5,684**
Telegraph................W. **5,685**

ATHENS, c. h., Athens Co., 2,500 p., on Hocking r. and Marietta & Cincinnati Rd., at terminus of Columbus & Hocking Valley Rd., 76 m. from Columbus and 159 from Cincinnati. Seat of Ohio University. Engaged in agriculture, coal mining and manufacturing.
Journal..................W. **5,586**
Messenger................W. **5,687**

BAINBRIDGE, Ross Co.
Paint Valley Times......W.

BARNESVILLE, Belmont Co., 2,100 p., on Baltimore & Ohio Rd., 32 m. from Wheeling, W. Va. An agricultural district and trade centre.
Enterprise................W. **5,689**

BASIL, Fairfield Co.
Fairfield Co. News.......W. **5,690**

BATAVIA, c. h., Clermont Co., 1,000† p., on E. branch of Little Miami r., 18 m. from Cincinnati and 11 from Milford. In an agricultural county.
Clermont Courier........W. **5,691**
Clermont Sun............W. **5,692**
Patrons' Advance.......W. **5,693**

BELLAIRE, Belmont Co., 7,081† p., on Ohio r. and Baltimore & Ohio Rd., at junction of Central Ohio division; also terminus of river division of Pittsburgh, Fort Wayne & Chicago Rd., 5 m. from Wheeling, W. Va. Engaged in coal mining and manufactures.
Independent.............W. **5,694**
Leader....................W. **5,695**

BELLE CENTRE, Logan Co.
Press.

BELLEFONTAINE, c. h., Logan Co., 3,753 p., on Cincinnati, Sandusky & Cleveland Rd., at crossing of C., C., C. & I. Rd., 57 m. from Dayton and 98 from Sandusky. In a farming district and centre of trade.
Examiner................W. **5,697**
Press....................W. **5,698**
Republican...............W. **5,699**

BELLEVUE, Huron Co., 3,219† p., on Lake Shore & Michigan Southern Rd., 12 m. W. of Norwalk, 65 from Cleveland and 25 from Toledo. Engaged in manufacturing, and a trade centre and shipping point for grain.
Gazette..................W. **5,700**
Local News...............W. **5,701**

BELLVILLE, Richland Co., 1,200† p., on Lake Erie division of Baltimore & Ohio Rd., 50 m. from Columbus and 14 from Mansfield. Engaged in various manufactures.
Weekly...................W. **5,702**

BELPRE, Washington Co.
Courant.
News.....................W. **5,704**

BEREA, Cuyahoga Co., 3,000 p., on C., C., C. & I. and Lake Shore & Michigan Southern Rds., 13 m. S. W. of Cleveland. Engaged in manufacturing. Quarries of grindstones, building stone, &c. Seat of Baldwin University and Wallace College.
Grindstone City Advertiser....................W. **5,705**

BIRMINGHAM, Erie Co.
Poultry Nation...........M. **5,706**

BLANCHESTER, Clinton Co., 1,000 p., on Marietta & Cincinnati Rd., at junction of Hillsboro branch, 15 m. from Wilmington and 42 from Cincinnati. Surrounded by a grain region. An important shipping point.
Press.....................W. **5,707**

BLOOMVILLE, Seneca Co.
Banner...................W. **5,708**

BLUFFTON, Allen Co.
News.....................W. **5,709**

BOWLING GREEN, c. h., Wood Co., 906 p., 7 m. from Dayton & Michigan Rd. and 21 S. of Toledo. Agriculture the principal branch of industry.
Wood Co. Sentinel.......W. **5,710**

BRYAN, Williams Co., 3,300† p., on Air Line division of Lake Shore & Michigan Southern Rd., 54 m. from Toledo. Surrounded by an agricultural region. Centre of trade. Has factories of various kinds.
Democrat................W. **5,711**
Press.....................W. **5,712**

BUCYRUS, c. h., Crawford Co., 3,550† p., on Sandusky r., Pittsburgh, Fort Wayne & Chicago Rd., 62 m. from Columbus. Centre of trade. A thickly populated district, noted for its schools and manufactories.
Forum................S. W. **5,713**
"..................W. **5,714**
Deutscher Courier.......W. **5,715**
Journal..................W. **5,716**

OHIO.

BURTON, Geauga Co.
Geauga Leader..........W. **5,717**

CADIZ, c. h., Harrison Co., 1,436 p., 17 m. from Wheeling, W. Va. A branch railroad, 8 m. long, connects it with Pittsburgh, Cincinnati & St. Louis Rd. Centre of an extensive wool-growing district.
Republican..............W. **5,718**
Sentinel..................W. **5,719**

CALDWELL, c. h., Noble Co., 600 p., in Olive township, on W. fork of Duck Creek and Marietta & Pittsburgh Rd., about 30 m. from Zanesville and 35 from Marietta. In Duck Creek oil regions.
Citizen's Press...........W. **5,720**
Noble Co. Republican....W. **5,721**

CALEDONIA, Marion Co.
Argus....................W. **5,722**

CAMBRIDGE, c. h., Guernsey Co., 2,193 p., on Wills Creek and Baltimore & Ohio Rd., 24 m. from Zanesville, 50 W. of Wheeling and 85 E. of Columbus. Engaged in coal mining, salt making and stock raising.
Boy in Blue.............W. **5,723**
Guernsey Times.........W. **5,724**
Jeffersonian.............W. **5,725**
News....................W. **5,726**

CANAL DOVER, Tuscarawas Co., 1,593 p., on Ohio Canal and Tuscarawas branch of Cleveland & Pittsburgh Rd.
Iron Valley Reporter.....W. **5,727**

CANAL FULTON, Stark Co., 1,048 p., on Ohio Canal and Cleveland, Mount Vernon & Delaware Rd., 31 m. from Cleveland.
Fulton Signal...........W. **5,728**

CANAL WINCHESTER, Franklin Co., 633 p., on Hocking Canal and Columbus & Hocking Valley Rd., 16 m. from Columbus.
Times....................W. **5,729**

CANFIELD, c. h., Mahoning Co., 800 p., 10 m. from Youngstown, on Niles & New Lisbon Rd., 21 m. from New Lisbon. An agricultural district.
Mahoning Valley News..W. **5,730**
Golden Mean............M. **5,731**

CANTON, c. h., Stark Co., 12,000† p., on Pittsburgh, Fort Wayne & Chicago Rd., 102 m. from Pittsburgh. Nimishillen Creek furnishes water power, which is employed in the manufacture of farming tools and other articles.
Ohio Staats Zeitung.....W. **5,732**
Repository...............W. **5,733**
Stark Co. Democrat......W. **5,734**

CARDINGTON, Morrow Co., 918 p., on C., C., C. & I. Rd., 38 m. from Columbus and 93 from Cleveland. Trade centre for an agricultural district.
Independent.............W. **5,735**

CAREY, Wyandot Co.
Times....................W. **5,736**

CARROLLTON, c. h., Carroll Co., 1,000† p., about 75 m. S. by E. of Cleveland. Carrollton & Oneida Rd. connects with Pittsburgh & Cleveland Rd. at Bayard.
Carroll Co. Chronicle....W. **5,737**
Carroll Free Press.......W. **5,738**

CELINA, c. h., Mercer Co., 859 p., near source of Wabash r., about 20 m. W. of Wapakoneta and 65 N. by W. of Dayton.
Mercer Co. Standard.....W. **5,739**
Western Democrat.......W. **5,740**

OHIO.

CHAGRIN FALLS, Cuyahoga Co.
Exponent.................W. **5,741**

CHARDON, c. h., Geauga Co., 1,200† p., on Youngstown & Painsville Rd., 38 m. from Cleveland and 14 from Lake Erie. An agricultural district. A shipping point for large quantities of cheese, wool and fruits.
Geauga Republican......W. **5,742**

CHICAGO, Huron Co.
Herald..................W. **5,743**

CHILLICOTHE, c. h., Ross Co., 11,000† p., on Scioto r. and Ohio & Erie Canal, 45 m. from Columbus, also on Cincinnati & Marietta Rd., 99 m. from Cincinnati. Engaged in various manufactures and centre of a fine agricultural district.
Advertiser...............W. **5,744**
Ross Co. Register........W. **4,745**
Scioto Gazette............W. **5,746**
Scioto Valley Post.......W. **5,747**

CINCINNATI, c. h., Hamilton Co., 216,239 p., on Ohio r. The metropolis of Ohio and the great centre of the pork trade. Connected with all points by railroads and steamboats. Has an extensive trade with all parts of the South and West. The manufacturing interests are large and form an important branch of industry. Largest city in the State.
Commercial...............D. **5,748**
" ....W. **5,749**
Enquirer.................D. **5,750**
" ....W. **5,751**
Freie Presse..............D. **5,752**
Sonntagsblatt Freie Presse..............Sund. **5,753**
Gazette...................D. **5,754**
" ....S. W. **5,755**
" ....W. **5,756**
Star......................D. **5,757**
" ....W. **5,758**
Times....................D. **5,759**
" ....W. **5,760**
Volksblatt.................D. **5,761**
" ....W. **5,762**
Westliche Blaetter......Sund. **5,763**
Volksfreund..............D. **5,764**
" ....W. **5,765**
Sonntagmorgen..........W. **5,766**
American Christian Review..................W. **5,767**
American Israelite.......W. **5,768**
Catholic Telegraph.......W. **5,769**
Christian Standard......W. **5,770**
Christian World.........W. **5,771**
Clinic.....................W. **5,772**
Der Christliche Apologete.W. **5,773**
Grange Bulletin.........W. **5,774**
Hebrew Sabbath School Visitor.................W. **5,775**
Herald and Presbyter....W. **5,776**
Journal and Messenger..W. **5,777**
Kikeriki...................W. **5,778**
Laborers' National Union.
Law Bulletin.............W. **5,780**
Live Stock Review.......W. **5,781**
Merchants' and Manufacturers' Bulletin........W. **5,782**
National A. O. U. W. Bulletin.................W. **5,783**
New Temperance Era....W. **5,784**
Post.......................W. **5,785**
Price Current and Commercial Review........W. **5,786**
Protestantische Zeitblaetter....................W. **5,787**
Record....................W. **5,788**

OHIO.

Saturday Night..........W. 5,789
Star in the West..........W. 5,790
Suburban News..........W. 5,791
Trade List..........W. 5,792
Wahrheitsfreund..........W. 5,793
Western Christian Advocate..........W. 5,794
Western Tobacco Journal.W. 5,795
Leaves of Light.......B. W. 5,796
Guiding Star..........S. M. 5,797
Sonntag Schul Glocke..S. M. 5,798
Christian Press..........M. 5,799
Church's Musical Visitor.M. 5,800
Dental Register..........M. 5,801
Deutsche Pionier..........M. 5,802
Eclectic Medical Journal..M. 5,803
Golden Hours..........M. 5,804
Haus und Herd..........M. 5,805
Hydraulic Engineer......M. 5,806
Ladies' Repository........M. 5,807
Lancet and Observer......M. 5,808
Literary Journal and People's Golden Visitor....M. 5,809
Masonic Review..........M. 5,810
Medical Advance..........M. 5,811
Medical News..........M. 5,812
Miller and Millwright....M. 5,813
Missionary..........M. 5,814
Pansy..........M. 5,815
Physio-Medical Recorder..M. 5,816
Post Office Bulletin........M. 5,817
Sabbath School Monthly...M. 5,818
Christian Quarterly.......Qr. 5,819
Heidelburg Teacher.......Qr. 5,820
Ryman's Western Reporter..........Qr. 5,821

CIRCLEVILLE, c. h., Pickaway Co., 5,600† p., on Scioto r. and Ohio Canal, 25 m. from Columbus and on Cincinnati & Muskingum Valley Rd., 64 from Zanesville. River furnishes water power, which is employed in manufacturing. A rich and populous agricultural district and centre of trade.

Advertiser..........W. 5,822
Democrat and Watchman.W. 5,823
Herald..........W. 5,824
Herald and Union........W. 5,825

CLEVELAND, c. h., Cuyahoga Co., 160,000† p., on Lake Erie and Cuyahoga r.. 125 m. from Columbus and 195 from Buffalo, N. Y. Engaged in commerce, manufactures and ship building, and a centre for the exchange of produce of Ohio and the West for the manufactures of the East. Railroads connect with all principal cities East and West.

Anzeiger..........D. 5,826
" ....W. 5,827
Herald..........D. 5,828
" ....T. W. 5,829
" ....W. 5,830
Leader..........D. 5,831
News..........D. 5,832
Leader..........T. W. 5,833
" ....W. 5,834
Plain Dealer..........D. 5,835
" " ....T. W. 5,836
" " ....W. 5,837
Wæchter am Erie..........D. 5,838
" " " ....W. 5,839
Columbia..........T. W. 5,840
" ....W. 5,841
Die Biene..........T. W. 5,842
Sonntagsblatt..........W. 5,843
Pokrok..........T. W. 5,844
" ....W. 5,845
Catholic Universe........W. 5,846

OHIO.

Christliche Botschafter...W. 5,847
Delnicke Listy..........W. 5,848
Der Sendbote..........W. 5,849
Evangelical Messenger...W. 5,850
Manufacturing and Trade Review..........W. 5,851
Ohio Farmer..........W. 5,852
Reformirte Kirchenzeitung und Evangelist...W. 5,853
*South Cleveland Advocate*W. 5,584
Standard of the Cross ...W. 5,855
Sunday Morning Voice..W. 5,856
Sunday Post..........W. 5,857
Sunday Times..........W. 5,858
Christliche Kinderfreund..........S. M. 5,859
Sunday School Messenger..........S. M. 5,860
*Brainard's Musical World*M. 5,861
Christian Harvester.......M. 5,862
Der Muntere Saemann...M. 5,863
Evangelical Sunday School Teacher..........M. 5,864
Evangelische Magazin....M. 5,865
Living Epistle..........M. 5,866
Machinist's and Blacksmith's Journal........M. 5,867
Miners' National Record.M. 5,868
Morgenstern..........M. 5,869
Printing Gazette..........M. 5,870
Ohio Medical and Surgical Reporter..........B. M. 5,871
Composing Stick..........Qr. 5,872

CLYDE, Sandusky Co., 2,000 p., on Cincinnati, Sandusky & Cleveland Rd., at intersection of Lake Shore & Michigan Southern Rd., 17 m. from Sandusky, 75 from Cleveland and 38 from Toledo. Centre of trade. Manufactures of various kinds carried on.

Review..........W. 5,873
Sentinel..........W. 5,874

COLUMBIANA, Columbiana Co., 1,200† p., on Pittsburgh, Fort Wayne & Chicago Rd., 60 m. from Pittsburgh. Engaged in manufacturing and a trade centre.

Independent Register....W. 5,875
True Press..........W. 5,876

COLUMBUS, c. h., Franklin Co., State capital, 45,000† p., on Scioto r. and branch of Ohio Canal, near centre of State. Connected by railroads and canal with all the principal towns and cities in all directions; 120 m. from Cincinnati, 135 from Cleveland and 140 from Wheeling. Has an extensive grain, wool and stock trade. Engaged in iron and other manufactures.

Dispatch..........D. 5,877
Dollar Dispatch..........W. 5,878
Ohio State Journal.......D. 5,879
" " " ......W. 5,880
Der Wesbote..........S. W. 5,881
" " ....W. 5,882
Catholic Columbian.......W. 5,883
Gazette..........W. 5,884
Lutheran Standard.......W. 5,885
Mute's Chronicle..........W. 5,886
Ohio Statesman..........W. 5,887
Sunday Herald..........W. 5,888
Sunday Morning News...W. 5,889
Lutherische Kirchen-Zeitung..........S. M. 5,890
Companion and American Odd-Fellow..........M. 5,891
Der Odd-Fellow..........M. 5,892
Knight..........M. 5,893

OHIO.

COLUMBUS GROVE, Putnam Co.
Putnam Co. Vidette.....W. **5,894**

CONNEAUT, Ashtabula Co., 1,600† p., on a creek 2 m. from Lake Erie and on Lake Shore & Michigan Southern Rd., 69 m. from Cleveland and 28 from Erie, Pa. Has a good harbor and trade, being a point of supply for an agricultural district. Manufacturing carried on.
Reporter.................W. **5,895**

COSHOCTON, c. h., Coshocton Co., 2,756† p., on Muskingum r., Ohio Canal and Pittsburgh, Cincinnati & St. Louis Rd., 69 m. from Columbus. Principal industries are coal mining and manufacturing.
Age ....W. **5,896**
Democrat................W. **5,897**

COVINGTON, Miami Co., 1,010 p., on Stillwater Creek and Chicago division of Pittsburgh, Cincinnati & St. Louis Rd., 6 m. from Piqua, 79 from Columbus, 88 N. of Cincinnati and 236 E. of Chicago. In an agricultural region. Manufacturing carried on.
Gazette...................W. **5,898**

CRESTLINE, Crawford Co., 2,279 p., on Pittsburgh, Fort Wayne & Chicago Rd., at crossing of C., C., C. & I. Rd., 12 m. E. of Bucyrus. Railroad shops here.
Advocate................W. **5,899**
Crawford Co. Democrat.W. **5,900**

CUYAHOGA FALLS, Summit Co., 1,861 p., on Cuyahoga r. and Cleveland, Mount Vernon & Delaware Rd., 6 m. from Akron. Engaged in milling and manufacturing paper and other articles.
Reporter..................W. **5,901**

DALTON, Wayne Co.
Gazette................B. W. **5,902**

DAYTON, c. h., Montgomery Co., 38,000† p., on Great Miami r. and Miami Canal, 60 m. from Cincinnati and 67 from Columbus. Engaged in manufacturing and centre of several important railroads. Railroad repair shops are located here.
Democrat................D. **5,903**
" ....W. **5,904**
Herald and Empire......D. **5,905**
Empire...................W. **5,906**
Journal...................D. **5,907**
" ....W. **5,908**
Volkszeitung..........T. W. **5,909**
" ....W. **5,910**
Froehliche Botschafter...W. **5,911**
*Herald of Gospel Liberty*W. **5,912**
Religious Telescope.......W. **5,913**
Children's Friend......S. M. **5,914**
Jugend Pilger.........S. M. **5,915**
Missionary Visitor....S. M. **5,916**
Sunday School Herald.S. M. **5,917**
Our Bible Teacher........M. **5,918**

DEFIANCE, c. h., Defiance Co., 5,000† p., at confluence of Maumee and Auglaize rs., and on Wabash & Erie Canal and Toledo, Wabash & Western and Chicago division of Baltimore & Ohio Rds., 51 m. from Toledo. Centre of a thriving trade. Engaged in manufactures.
Democrat ....W. **5,919**
Express..................W. **5,920**

DE GRAFF, Logan Co.
Banner...................W. **5,921**

DELAWARE, c. h., Delaware Co., 7,000† p., on Olentangy r., and C., C., C. & I. Rd., at junction of Cleveland and Columbus branches, 25 m. from Columbus. A place of active trade. Seat of Ohio Wesleyan University and Wesleyan Female College. Engaged in manufacturing hemp, jute, woolen goods and agricultural implements.
News ....S. W. **5,922**
Gazette..................W. **5,923**
Herald...................W. **5,924**
Signal...................W. **5,925**
College Transcript.....B. W. **5,926**

DELPHOS, Allen Co., 4,000† p., on Pittsburgh, Fort Wayne & Chicago Rd., and Miami & Erie Canal, 14 m. N. W. of Lima and 90 from Toledo. Has water power. Centre of an agricultural district. Principal business manufacturing.
Herald...................W. **5,927**

DELTA, Fulton Co.
Avalanche................W. **5,928**

DOYLESTOWN, Wayne Co.
Journal..................W. **5,929**

DRESDEN, Muskingum Co., 1,500† p., on Pittsburgh, Cincinnati & St. Louis Rd., at junction of Cincinnati & Muskingum Valley Rd., and at head of navigation on Muskingum r., 15 m. above Zanesville. Water power is abundant. Coal and iron ore in the vicinity. The Ohio Canal empties into the Muskingum r. at this point.
Doings...................W. **5,930**

DUNKIRK, Hardin Co.
Standard................W. **5,931**

EAST LIVERPOOL, Columbiana Co., 3,000† p., on Ohio r., and river division of Cleveland & Pittsburgh Rd., 48 m. W. of Pittsburgh, Pa. A number of potteries here. Situated in an agricultural country and has some mechanical works.
Gazette..................W. **5,932**
Tribune ....W. **5,933**

EAST TOLEDO, Lucas Co.
East Side................W. **5,934**

EATON, c. h., Preble Co., 2,500† p., on Cincinnati, Richmond & Chicago Rd., 53 m. from Cincinnati. An agricultural district. Engaged in manufacturing.
Democrat ....W. **5,935**
Register..................W. **5,936**

ELMORE, Ottawa Co., 1,131 p., on Lake Shore & Michigan Southern Rd., 17 m. S. E. of Toledo. Centre of a large farming district. Engaged in manufacturing.
Tribune ....W. **5,937**

ELYRIA, c. h., Lorain Co., 3,038 p., on Black r., and Cleveland & Toledo branch of Lake Shore & Michigan Southern Rd., 26 m. from Cleveland. Engaged in manufactures, the falls in the river furnishing water power. Surrounded by an agricultural and dairy country.
Constitution.............W. **5,938**
Independent Democrat...W. **5,939**
Republican..............W. **5,940**
Volksfreund.............W. **5,941**

FAIRVIEW, Guernsey Co.
Enterprise...............W. **5,942**

FAYETTE, Fulton Co.
Record ....W. **5,943**

FINDLAY, c. h., Hancock Co., 3,316 p., on Blanchard's fork of Auglaize r., and terminus of Lake Erie & Louisville and Cary & Findlay branch of Cleveland, Sandusky & Cincinnati Rd., 90 m. N. W. of

OHIO.

Columbus. An agricultural district and trade centre.
American Patron........W. **5,944**
Hancock Courier........W. **5,945**
Jeffersonian..............W. **5,946**

FOREST, Hardin Co.
News.....................W. **5,947**

FOSTORIA, Seneca Co., 3,500† p., on Lake Erie & Louisville Rd., 22 m. from Fremont and 15 from Findlay. Several saw and grist mills here.
Democrat................W. **5,948**
Review....................W. **5,949**
Common School Visitor..W. **5,950**

FRANKLIN, Warren Co.
Advertiser................W. **5,951**

FREDERICKTOWN, Knox Co., 850 p., on Owl Creek and Erie division of Baltimore & Ohio Rd., 7 m. from Mount Vernon.
Free Press...............W. **5,952**

FREMONT, c. h., Sandusky Co., 5,455 p., on Sandusky r., at head of navigation, 24 m. from Sandusky, on Lake Shore & Michigan Southern Rd., at junction of Lake Erie & Louisville Rd., 30 m. from Toledo and 83 from Cleveland. Steamers run from here to various ports on Lake Erie. Has a large and flourishing business.
Courier...................W. **5,953**
Democratic Messenger....W. **5,954**
Journal...................W. **5,955**

GALION, Crawford Co., 5,075† p., on C., C., C. & I. Rd., at crossing of Atlantic & Great Western Rd., 89 m. from Cleveland and 59 from Columbus. Manufacturing carried on.
Review...................W. **5,956**
Sun.......................W. **5,957**

GALLIPOLIS, Gallia Co., 3,711 p., on Ohio r., 91 m. above Portsmouth and 103 below Marietta.
Bulletin..................W. **5,958**
Journal...................W. **5,959**
Ledger....................W. **5,960**

GAMBIER, Knox Co.
Argus.....................W. **5,961**

GARRETTSVILLE, Portage Co., 658 p., on Mahoning r. and Mahoning division of Atlantic & Great Western Rd., 37 m. from Cleveland.
Journal...................W. **5,962**

GENEVA, Ashtabula Co., 3,500† p., on Lake Shore & Michigan Southern Rd., 45 m. from Cleveland. Engaged in manufacturing and a trade centre.
Times.....................W. **5,963**

GEORGETOWN, c. h., Brown Co., 1,000 p., on White Oak Creek, 7 m. from Ohio r. and 40 from Cincinnati. A farming district, having an active trade.
Brown Co. News..........W. **5,964**
Sentinel..................W. **5,965**

GERMANTOWN, Montgomery Co., 1,440 p., on Twin r., 44 m. from Cincinnati and 12 from Dayton. Whisky distilling, tobacco culture and manufacture of cigars are the principal branches of industry.
Independent Press........W. **5,966**

GREENFIELD, Highland Co., 1,800† p., on Paint Creek and Marietta & Cincinnati Rd., 75 m. from Cincinnati. Situated in an agricultural community and has a large mercantile trade.
Highland Chief...........W. **5,967**

GREENVILLE, c. h., Drake Co., 3,500† p., on Pittsburgh, Cincinnati & St. Louis Rd., at crossing of Dayton & Union Rd., 35 m. from Dayton and 94 from Columbus.
Darke Co. Courier........W. **5,968**
Democrat..................W. **5,969**
Journal....................W. **5,970**

HAMDEN, Geauga Co.
Leader....................W. **5,971**

HAMILTON, c. h., Butler Co., 14,000† p., on Miami r. and Cincinnati, Hamilton & Dayton Rd., at junction of Cincinnati, Richmond & Chicago and Cincinnati & Indianapolis Junction Rds., 20 m. from Cincinnati. Mills and manufactories are located here.
Allgemeiner Beobachter.
Butler Co. Democrat.....W. **5,973**
National Zeitung..........W. **5,974**
Telegraph.................W. **5,975**

HARRISON, Hamilton Co.
News......................W. **5,976**

HAYESVILLE, Ashland Co.
Journal...................W. **5,977**

HICKSVILLE, Defiance Co.
Independent..............W. **5,978**

HILLSBOROUGH, c. h., Highland Co., 6,000 p., at terminus of a branch railroad 21 m. long, which connects with Marietta & Cincinnati Rd. at Blanchester.
Gazette...................W. **5,979**
Highland News...........W. **5,980**

HUBBARD, Trumbull Co., 1,800† p., 18 m. S. E. of Warren, on Mahoning branch of Atlantic & Great Western Rd., 6 m. from Youngstown. Centre of a mineral district, mining being its principal branch of industry.
Laborer's Vindicator.....W. **5,981**

HUDSON, Summit Co.
Enterprise................W. **5,982**

HURON, Erie Co.
Times......................W. **5,983**

IRONTON, c. h., Lawrence Co., 5,686 p., on Ohio r., 145 m. above Cincinnati. Engaged in iron and coal mining. Several iron manufactories located here. The river commerce is quite important. Iron Rd., 13 m. in length, extends back from the river to Center. In the Hanging Rock iron region.
Journal..................T. W. **5,984**
" ....W. **5,985**
Commercial...............W. **5,986**
Democrat.................W. **5,987**
Register...................W. **5,988**
Wæchter am Ohio........W. **5,989**

JACKSON, c. h., Jackson Co., 3,000† p., on Portsmouth branch of Marietta & Cincinnati Rd., 145 m. from Cincinnati and 44 from Portsmouth. In centre of pig iron and stove coal region of Southern Ohio.
Herald....................W. **5,990**
Standard..................W. **5,991**

JEFFERSON, Ashtabula Co., 1,000 p., on Jamestown branch of Lake Shore & Michigan Southern Rd., 60 m. from Cleveland and 50 from Erie, in the centre of an agricultural and dairy district.
Ashtabula Sentinel.......W. **5,992**

KENT, Portage Co., 3,000 p., on Cuyahoga

OHIO.

r., 10 m. N. E. of Akron and on Atlantic & Great Western Rd. Railroad machine shops are located here. Has a fine water power and engaged in various manufactures.

Saturday Bulletin.......W. **5,993**

KENTON, c. h., Hardin Co., 2,610 p., on Scioto r. and Cincinnati, Sandusky & Cleveland Rd., 74 m. from Sandusky and 24 from Bellefontaine. An agricultural and lumber district.

Hardin Co. Democrat....W. **5,994**
Republican ....W. **5,995**

LANCASTER, c. h., Fairfield Co., 7,000† p., at intersection of Cincinnati & Muskingum Valley Rd. with Columbus & Hocking Valley Rd., and connected by Hocking Canal to Ohio Canal at Carroll. An agricultural district and centre of trade.

Gazette..................W. **5,996**
Ohio Eagle...............W. **5,997**

LEAVITT, Carroll Co.

Good Will...............W. **5,998**

LEBANON, c. h., Warren Co.

Patriot..................W. **5,999**
Western Star.............W. **6,000**

LEETONIA, Columbiana Co., 1,200 p., on Pittsburgh, Fort Wayne & Chicago Rd., at crossing of Niles & New Lisbon Rd., 63 m. from Pittsburgh, Pa., and 21 from Alliance.

Reporter.................W. **6,001**

LIMA, c. h., Allen Co., 7,000† p., on Ottawa r., at intersection of the Pittsburgh, Fort Wayne & Chicago with Dayton & Michigan Rd., 130 m. from Cincinnati and 60 from Fort Wayne. Engaged in manufacturing and trade.

Allen Co. Democrat......W. **6,002**
Gazette..................W. **6,003**
Sun......................W. **6,004**

LOGAN, c. h., Hocking Co., 1,847 p., on Hocking r., Hocking Canal and Hocking Valley Rd., at junction of Straitsville branch, 49 m. from Columbus. Coal and iron ore mines are located here.

Hocking Sentinel.........W. **6,005**
Republican...............W. **6,006**

LONDON, c. h., Madison Co., 2,937† p., on Pittsburgh, Cincinnati & St. Louis Rd., at junction of London branch of Cincinnati, Sandusky & Cleveland Rd., 24 m. from Columbus, 20 from Springfield and 30 from Xenia.

Enterprise ....W. **6,007**
Madison Co. Democrat..W. **6,008**
Times....................W. **6,009**

LOUDONVILLE, Ashland Co., 1,700† p., on Black fork of Michigan r. and Pittsburgh, Fort Wayne & Chicago Rd., 19 m. from Mansfield and 70 N. by E. of Columbus. Centre of a grain and stock-raising country.

Advocate.................W. **6,010**

McARTHUR, c. h., Vinton Co., 1,000† p., 3 m. from line of Marietta & Cincinnati Rd., 34 from Chillicothe and 133 from Cincinnati. Situate in Southern Ohio coal and iron region. Engaged in iron and general manufacturing, coal mining and stock-raising.

Christian Union Witness or the Olive Branch of Peace ....W. **6,011**
Enquirer ....W. **6,012**
Vinton Record...........W. **6,013**

OHIO.

McCONNELLSVILLE, c. h., Morgan Co., 1,646 p., on Muskingum r., 38 m. from its junction with the Ohio, 27 below Zanesville. Salt and other manufactures carried on.

Democrat................W. **6,014**
Herald..................W. **6,015**

MADISON, Lake Co.

Gazette..................W. **6,016**

MANCHESTER, Adams Co., 1,200 p., on Ohio r., 72 m. from Cincinnati and 40 from Portsmouth. Centre of trade, with considerable river commerce.

Gazette..................W. **6,017**

MANSFIELD, c. h., Richland Co., 8,029 p., 176 m. from Pittsburgh and 180 from Cincinnati, on Atlantic & Great Western Rd., at intersection of Pittsburgh, Fort Wayne & Chicago Rd. and Lake Erie division of Baltimore & Ohio Rd. It has large manufacturing interests and surrounded by an agricultural district.

Courier..................W. **6,018**
Herald...................W. **6,019**
Ohio Liberal.............W. **6,020**
Richland Shield and Banner ....W. **6,021**

MARIETTA, c. h., Washington Co., 8,500† p., on Muskingum r., at its entrance into Ohio r., and at terminus of Marietta & Cincinnati and Marietta, Pittsburgh & Cleveland Rds. The Muskingum r. is navigable from this point to Zanesville, a distance of 80 m. In the coal oil regions of Ohio. Engaged in various manufactures and river commerce, and centre of a large and flourishing trade.

Register.................W. **6,022**
Times....................W. **6,023**
Zeitung..................W. **6,024**

MARION, c. h., Marion Co., 2,531 p., on Atlantic & Great Western, and C., C., C. & I. Rds., 44 m. from Columbus. Engaged in agriculture.

Democratic Mirror......W. **6,025**
Independent..............W. **6,026**

MARTIN'S FERRY, Belmont Co., 1,835 p., on river division of Cleveland & Pittsburgh Rd., 20 m. from Steubenville.

Ohio Valley News........W. **6,027**

MARYSVILLE, c. h., Union Co.

Journal..................W. **6,028**
Tribune..................W. **6,029**

MASSILLON, Stark Co., 9,000† p., at junction of Pittsburgh, Fort Wayne & Chicago, Massillon & Cleveland and Lake Shore & Tuscarawas Valley Rds. On the Ohio Canal, which furnishes cheap water transportation to the Ohio r. and Lake Erie. 110 m. from Pittsburgh and 55 from Cleveland. It is in the midst of the rich Tuscarawas coal fields, and ships anually about 500,000 tons of coal. Large manufacturing centre for iron works and agricultural machinery. Large and celebrated sandstone quarries are within the corporate limits. Is surrounded by a rich agricultural region.

American.................W. **6,030**
Democrat................W. **6,031**
Independent.............W. **6,032**
Stark Co. Times..........W. **6,033**

MECHANICSBURG, Champaign Co., 1,500† p., on Springfield branch of C., C., C. & I. Rd. Centre of a stock-raising dis-

OHIO.

trict. Shipping point for stock and grain to Eastern markets.

Central Ohio News.......W. **6,034**

MEDINA, c. h., Medina Co., 1,159 p., 28 m. S. by W. of Cleveland. Cheese, wool, stock-raising and general agriculture are the branches of industry carried on here.

Democrat................W. **6,035**
Medina Co. Gazette......W. **6,036**

MIAMISBURG, Montgomery Co., 1,800† p., on Great Miami r., Miami & Erie Canal and Cincinnati, Hamilton & Dayton Rd., 11 m. S. of Dayton and 50 N. of Cincinnati. Several mills here, run by water power from Miami r. In the tobacco-growing region of Miami Valley.

Bulletin.................W. **6,037**

MIDDLEPORT, Meigs Co., 3,000† p., on Ohio r., 2 m. from Pomeroy. Engaged in coal mining and river trade.

Meigs Co. Republican....W. **6,038**

MIDDLETOWN, Butler Co., 3,046 p., on Miami r., 37 m. from Cincinnati. Cincinnati & Dayton Rd. passes up the opposite side of the river. Engaged in manufacturing.

Journal..................W. **6,039**

MILAN, Erie Co., 2,000 p., on Huron r., 8 m. from Lake Erie.

Advertiser..............W. **6,040**

MILLERSBURG, c. h., Holmes Co., 2,500† p., on Cleveland, Mount Vernon & Columbus Rd., 87 m. from Cleveland and 80 from Columbus. Rich coal fields and iron ore mines located here. Country principally agricultural.

Holmes Co. Farmer......W. **6,041**
Holmes Co. Republican..W. **6,042**

MINERVA, Stark Co., 2,567 p., on Tuscarawas branch of Cleveland & Pittsburgh Rd., 14 m. S. of Alliance.

Commercial..............W. **6,043**

MINSTER, Auglaize Co.

Stern des Westlichen Ohio.W. **6,044**

MONROEVILLE, Huron Co., 1,344 p., on Huron r., at crossing of Lake Shore & Michigan Southern and Lake Erie division of Baltimore & Ohio Rds., 60 m. W. of Cleveland. A grain market and manufacturing town.

Spectator................W. **6,045**

MOUNT GILEAD, c. h., Morrow Co., 1,200† p., 1½ m. E. of C., C., C. & I. Rd., 42 from Columbus, on E. branch of Olentongy r. Some manufacturing done here.

Morrow Co. Sentinel......W. **6,046**
Union Register...........W. **6,047**

MOUNT VERNON, c. h., Knox Co., 5,500† p., on Kokosing r. and Lake Erie division of Baltimore & Ohio and Cleveland, Mount Vernon & Columbus Rds., 55 m. from Columbus. In a populous district and centre of trade.

Democratic Banner......W. **6,048**
Republican..............W. **6,049**
Orphan's Friend.........M. **6,050**
Park's Floral Gazette....M. **6,051**

NAPOLEON, c. h., Henry Co., 3,000† p., on Maumee r. and Toledo, Wabash & Western Rd., 36 m. from Toledo. Wabash and Erie Canal passes through here. Surrounded by an agricultural district; has water power and several manufacturing establishments.

OHIO.

Democratic North-West..W. **6,052**
Henry Co. Signal........W. **6,053**

NELSONVILLE, Athens Co., 3,000† p., on Columbus & Hocking Valley Rd., 14 m. from Athens.

Ohio Mining Gazette.....W. **6,054**

NEVADA, Wyandot Co., 1,050† p., on Pittsburgh, Fort Wayne & Chicago Rd., 34 m. from Mansfield.

Enterprise..............W. **6,055**

NEWARK, c. h., Licking Co., 6,698 p., on Licking r. and Ohio Canal, 37 m. from Columbus, and at junction of Baltimore & Ohio and Pittsburgh, Cincinnati & St. Louis Rds., also junction of Erie division with main line. A railroad centre, having trade in coal, grain and live stock. Engaged in manufactures.

Advocate.................W. **6,056**
American................W. **6,057**
Banner...................W. **6,058**

NEW BALTIMORE, Stark Co.

Enterprise...............W. **6,059**

NEWCOMERSTOWN, Tuscarawas Co.

Argus....................W. **6,060**

NEW LEXINGTON, c. h., Perry Co., 953 p., on Cincinnati & Muskingum Valley Rd., 21 m. from Zanesville. Engaged in manufactures and mining.

Democratic Herald.
Tribune...................W. **6,062**

NEW LISBON, c. h., Columbiana Co., 2,000 p., on Beaver r., 56 m. from Pittsburgh, Pa., on Niles & New Lisbon Rd. Centre of an agricultural and wool-growing district. Woolen and other manufactories are located on the river, which furnishes power.

Buckeye State............W. **6,063**
Journal...................W. **6,064**
Ohio Patriot..............W. **6,065**

NEW LONDON, Huron Co., 678 p., on C., C., C. & I. Rd., 48 m. S. W. of Cleveland. Centre of a large and prosperous agricultural region. Engaged in various kinds of manufactures.

Record....................W. **6,066**

NEW PHILADELPHIA, c. h., Tuscarawas Co., 3,143 p., on Tuscarawas r. and Ohio Canal, and at terminus of Tuscarawas branch of Cleveland & Pittsburgh Rd. Engaged in the manufacture of agricultural implements and woolen goods. Salt, coal and iron mining.

Der Deutsche Beobachter.W. **6,067**
Ohio Democrat...........W. **6,068**
Tuscarawas Advocate....W. **6,069**

NEW RICHMOND, Clermont Co., 3,000† p., on Ohio r., 20 m. from Cincinnati. Largest town in the county. Engaged in manufacturing.

Independent.............W. **6,070**

NEW VIENNA, Clinton Co.

Christian Worker......S. M. **6,071**
Messenger of Peace......M. **6,072**
Olive Leaf................M. **6,073**

NILES, Trumbull Co., on Mahoning r., Pennsylvania & Ohio Canal and Mahoning division of Atlantic & Great Western Rd., at junction of Niles & New Lisbon Rd., 5 m. S. E. of Warren. A place of active business.

Trumbull Co. Independent....................W. **6,074**

OHIO.

NORTH AMHERST, Lorain Co.
Amherst Free Press......W. **6,075**

NORTH LEWISBURG, Champaign Co.
Gazette..................W. **6,076**
Star......................W. **6,077**

NORWALK, c. h., Huron Co., 6,500† p., on Lake Shore & Michigan Southern Rd., 55 m. from Cleveland and 58 from Toledo. Engaged in manufacturing.
Experiment..............W. **6,078**
Huron Co. Chronicle.....W. **6,079**
Reflector..................W. **6,080**

OAK HARBOR, Ottawa Co.
Press......................W. **6,081**

OBERLIN, Lorain Co., 3,250† p., on Lake Shore & Michigan Southern Rd., 32 m. from Cleveland and 8 from Elyria. Seat of Oberlin College and other literary institutions.
News......................W. **6,082**

ORRVILLE, Wayne Co., 745 p., on Pittsburgh, Fort Wayne & Chicago Rd., at intersection of Cleveland, Mount Vernon & Delaware Rd., 64 m. from Cleveland. An agricultural and stock-raising region.
Crescent..................W. **6,083**
Evenings at Home......M. **6,084**

OTTAWA, Putnam Co., 1,500† p., on Dayton & Michigan Rd., 51 m. from Toledo and 91 from Dayton. Engaged in agriculture, stock raising and lumber.
Putnam Co. Sentinel....W. **6,085**

OXFORD, Butler Co., 1,738 p., on Cincinnati & Indianapolis Junction Rd., 32 m. from Cincinnati. Seat of Miami University, Oxford Female College and Western Female Seminary.
Citizen....................W. **6,086**

PAINESVILLE, c. h., Lake Co., 5,000† p., on Grand r., and Lake Shore & Michigan Southern Rd., at junction of Painesville & Youngtown Rd., 3 m. from Lake Erie and 29 from Cleveland. Engaged in manufacturing and a place of trade. Has a harbor and shipping. Surrounded by an agricultural district.
Advertiser................W. **6,087**
Northern Ohio Journal...W. **6,088**
Telegraph.................W. **6,089**

PAULDING, c. h., Paulding Co., 448 p., on Crooked Creek, 7 m. from Toledo, Wabash & Western Rd., and about the same distance from Indiana State line.
Democrat.................W. **6,090**

PERRYSBURG, Wood Co., 2,500† p., on Maumee r., at head of navigation, 9 m. from Toledo and on Dayton & Michigan Rd. Surrounded by agricultural land.
Buckeye Granger........W. **6,091**
Journal...................W. **6,092**

PIQUA, Miami Co., 7,000† p., on Great Miami r. and Pittsburgh, Cincinnati & St. Louis Rd., at intersection of Dayton & Michigan Rd., 73 m. from Columbus and 28 from Dayton. The Miami & Erie Canal passes through here. Engaged in manufacturing; a place of trade.
Journal...................W. **6,093**
Miami Democrat.........W. **6,094**
Miami Helmet............W. **6,095**

PLAIN CITY, Madison Co.
Press......................W. **6,096**

PLYMOUTH, Richland Co., 1,200 p., on Lake Erie division of Baltimore & Ohio Rd., 36 m. from Sandusky and 20 from Mansfield.
Advertiser................W. **6,097**

POMEROY, c. h., Meigs Co., 8,000† p., on Ohio r., 86 m. below Marietta and 106 from Portsmouth. Engaged in coal mining and manufacture of salt.
Meigs Co. Telegraph......W. **6,098**
Ohio Waisenfreund......W. **6,099**

PORT CLINTON, c. h., Ottawa Co., 1,000 p., at the mouth of Portage r., on Lake Erie, 30 m. from Toledo and on Lake Shore & Michigan Southern Rd. Engaged in grape culture and fishing.
Ottawa Co. News........W. **6,100**
Ottawa Co. Reporter.....W. **6,101**

PORTSMOUTH, c. h., Scioto Co., 15,500† p., on Ohio r. and Portsmouth branch of Marietta & Cincinnati Rd., near the mouth of Scioto r., at terminus of Ohio & Erie Canal, 115 m. above Cincinnati. Steamboats ply regularly between here and Cincinnati and other river ports. Has a large and increasing business, and is extensively engaged in wood and iron manufactures.
Globe......................D. **6,102**
Correspondent............W. **6,103**
Republican................W. **6,104**
Times......................W. **6,105**
Tribune....................W. **6,106**

PROSPECT, Marion Co.
Union......................W. **6,107**

QUAKER CITY, Guernsey Co.
Independent..............W. **6,108**

RAVENNA, c. h., Portage Co., 3,500 p., one of the most healthy towns in the State, 38 m. from Cleveland, on the Cleveland & Pittsburgh Rd., and is also one of the most important stations of the Atlantic & Great Western Rd.
Portage Co. Republican-Democrat..............W. **6,109**

RICHWOOD, Union Co., 1,300† p., on Atlantic & Great Western Rd., 15 m. from Marion and 49 from Springfield.
Gazette....................W. **6,110**

RIPLEY, Brown Co., 2,327 p., on Ohio r., 56 m. above Cincinnati. Engaged in trade, river commerce and manufacturing.
Bee.........................W. **6,111**

SABINA, Clinton Co.
Telegram..................W. **6,112**

ST. CLAIRSVILLE, c. h., Belmont Co., 1,200† p., on National Road, 12 m. from Wheeling, W. Va., near Baltimore & Ohio Rd. Surrounded by an agricultural district.
Belmont Chronicle........W. **6,113**
Gazette....................W. **6,114**

ST. MARYS, Auglaize Co., 1,800† p., on Miami & Erie Canal, about 10 m. W. of Wapakoneta.
Commercial...............W. **6,115**

ST. PARIS, Champaign Co., 650 p., on Indianapolis & Chicago division of Pittsburgh, Cincinnati & St. Louis Rd., 11 m. from Urbana and 15 from Piqua.
New Era...................W. **6,116**

SALEM, Columbiana Co., 3,700 p., on Pittsburgh, Fort Wayne & Chicago Rd., 70 m. from Pittsburgh, Pa., and 60 from Cleveland. Surrounded by a farming dis-

OHIO.

trict and a trade centre. Engaged in manufacturing.

Era......................W. 6,117
Republican..............W. 6,118
Ohio Educational Monthly and National Teacher..M. 6,119
Sheet Metal Builder.....W. 6,120

SALINEVILLE, Columbiana Co., 2,500† p., on Cleveland & Pittsburgh Rd., 86 m. from Cleveland. Coal mining and shipping the principal features of industry.

Index......................W. 6,121

SANDUSKY, c. h., Erie Co., 18,000 p., on Sandusky Bay, near its entrance to Lake Erie, and at terminus of Cincinnati, Sandusky & Cleveland, Lake Erie division of Baltimore & Ohio, and Sandusky line of Lake Shore & Michigan Southern Rds. Engaged in lake commerce, having one of the finest harbors on Lake Erie.

Register..................D. 6,122
"..................T. W. 6,123
"......................W. 6,124
Demokrat..............S. W. 6,125
"......................W. 6,126
Journal & Erie Co. News..W. 6,127
Fireside Visitor..........M. 6,128

SEVILLE, Medina Co., 1,000† p., on C., T., V. & Wheeling Rd., 20 m. W. of Akron and 9 S. of Medina.

Times......................W. 6,129

SHELBY, Richland Co., 1,807 p., on C., C., C. & I. Rd., at intersection of Erie division of Baltimore & Ohio Rd., 67 m. from Cleveland. A grain market and has a general manufacturing trade.

Independent News........W. 6,130

SHILOH, Richland Co., 600 p., on C., C., C. & I. Rd., 61 m. from Cleveland.

Review......................W. 6,131

SHREVE, Wayne Co., 600 p., on Pittsburgh, Fort Wayne & Chicago Rd., about 10 m. N. E. of Wooster.

Journal......................W. 6,132

SIDNEY, c. h., Shelby Co., 2,808 p., on Great Miami r., Miami & Erie Canal and Dayton & Michigan Rd., at intersection of C., C., C. & I. Rd., 40 m. from Dayton and 100 from Cincinnati. Engaged in manufacturing. Surrounded by a rich agricultural country.

Journal......................W. 6,133
Shelby Co. Democrat.....W. 6,134

SMITHFIELD, Jefferson Co.

Independent..............W. 6,135

SOMERSET, Perry Co., 1,153 p., on Straitsville division of Baltimore & Ohio Rd., 24 m. from Newark.

Press......................W. 6,136

SOUTH CHARLESTON, Clark Co.

Banner....................W. 6,137

SPRINGFIELD, c. h., Clark Co., 19,000† p., near confluence of Mad r. and Lagonda Creek, 43 m. W. of Columbus. Six railroads centre here, connecting it with the principal cities in all directions. Flouring mills located here and in vicinity. Centre of an agricultural district and a place of active trade.

Republic..................D. 6,138
"..................T. W. 6,139
"......................W. 6,140
Advertiser................W. 6,141
Gazette....................W. 6,142
Springfielder Journal....W. 6,143

OHIO.

Transcript................W. 6144
Grange Visitor and Farmer's Monthly Magazine......................M. 6,145
Leffel's Illustrated Milling & Mechanical News.M. 6,146

STEUBENVILLE, c. h., Jefferson Co., 12,000 p., on Ohio r., 70 m. from Pittsburgh by water, 43 by rail. Pittsburgh, Cincinnati & St. Louis, and river division Cleveland & Pittsburgh Rds. pass through the city. Extensively engaged in manufacture of iron, nails, glass and woolen goods.

Gazette......................D. 6,147
"......................W. 6,148
Herald......................D. 6,149
"......................W. 6,150

SUNBURY, Delaware Co.

Spectator..................W. 6,151

TIFFIN, c. h., Seneca Co., 10,000† p., in Clinton township, on Sandusky r. and Cincinnati, Sandusky & Cleveland Rd., 34 m. from Sandusky and 42 from Toledo. Engaged in manufactures.

Star......................D. 6,152
"......................W. 6,153
Presse......................W. 6,154
Seneca Advertiser........W. 6,155
Tribune......................W. 6,156
College Times..............M. 6,157

TIPPECANOE CITY, Miami Co., 1,500† p., on Great Miami r. and Canal, and on Dayton & Michigan Rd., 14 m. from Piqua. Several mills here.

Herald......................W. 6,158

TOLEDO, c. h., Lucas Co., 55,000† p., on Maumee r., 4 m. from Lake Erie, and on Wabash & Erie Canal and Lake Shore & Michigan Southern, Toledo, Wabash & Western and Dayton & Michigan Rds. The river furnishes a harbor for lake commerce. Manufacturing forms an important branch of industry. An important point for shipping productions of the West to Eastern markets. One of the leading ports on the lake in point of business activity.

Blade......................D. 6,159
"..................T. W. 6,160
"......................W. 6,161
Commercial................D. 6,162
"..................T. W. 6,163
"......................W. 6,164
Express....................D. 6,165
"......................W. 6,166
Review..................S. W. 6,167
Argus......................W. 6,168
Sunday Journal............W. 6,169
*American Farm Journal*M. 6,170
Fellowship..................M. 6,171
*Locke's National Monthly*M. 6,172
Lyceum.
Whitney's Musical Guest and Literary Journal..M. 6,174

TROY, c. h., Miami Co., 4,500† p., on Miami r. and Dayton & Michigan Rd., 80 m. from Cincinnati. Engaged in manufactures. Surrounded by a fertile valley.

Free Press..................W. 6,175
Globe......................W. 6,176
Miami Union................W. 6,177

UHRICHSVILLE, Tuscarawas Co., 1,541 p., on Stillwater Creek and Pittsburgh, Cincinnati & St. Louis Rd., 10 m. S. E. of New Philadelphia, 93 from Pittsburgh and 100 from Columbus. Location

OHIO.

of railroad repair shops. Engaged in wool growing and agriculture.
Tuscarawas Chronicle....W. **6,178**

UPPER SANDUSKY, c. h., Wyandot Co., 3,000 p., on Sandusky r. and Pittsburgh, Fort Wayne & Chicago Rd., 43 m. E. of Lima.
*Wyandot Co. Republican*W. **6,179**
Wyandot Democratic Union..................W. **6,180**

URBANA, c. h., Champaign Co., 7,000† p. on Sandusky, Dayton & Cincinnati Rd., at crossing of Atlantic & Great Western Rd., 42 m. from Columbus. Columbus & Indianapolis Rd. also passes through the place. Centre of trade.
News....................W. **6,181**
Citizen and Gazette.......W. **6,182**
Union Democrat.........W. **6,183**

VAN WERT, c. h., Van Wert Co., 2,625 p., on Pittsburgh, Fort Wayne & Chicago Rd., 32 m. from Fort Wayne and 27 from Lima. Engaged in lumber works.
Bulletin................W. **6,184**
Press....................W. **6,185**
Times....................W. **6,186**

VERSAILLES, Darke Co.
Independent.............W. **6,187**

WADSWORTH, Medina Co., 1,224† p., on Atlantic & Great Western Rd., 14 m. from Akron and 35 from Cleveland. Engaged in coal mining. In an agricultural region.
Enterprise...............W. **6,188**
Home Scientist...........M. **6,189**
Young Folks' Gem.......M. **6,190**

WAKEMAN, Huron Co.
Independent Press.......W. **6,191**

WAPAKONETA, c. h., Auglaize Co., 2,800† p., on Auglaize r. and Dayton & Michigan Rd., 95 m. from Columbus, 60 N. of Dayton and 80 S. of Toledo. Centre of a mercantile trade and extensive manufactures.
Auglaize Co. Democrat..W. **6,192**

WARREN, c. h., Trumbull Co., 6,000 p., on Mahoning r. and Mahoning branch of Atlantic & Great Western Rd., 52 m. from Cleveland, 23 from Ravenna. Centre of dairy and wood district.
Constitution.............W. **6,193**
Record..................W. **6,194**
*Western Reserve Chronicle*W. **6,195**

WASHINGTON, c. h., Fayette Co., 2,115 p., at Point Creek, on Cincinnati & Muskingum Valley Rd., 77 m. from Cincinnati. Manufacturing carried on.
Fayette Co. Herald......W. **6,196**
News....................W. **6,197**
Ohio State Register.......W. **6,198**

WAUSEON, c. h., Fulton Co., 2,000† p., on Air Line division of Lake Shore & Michigan Southern Rd., 32 m. from Toledo.
Democratic Expositor....W. **6,199**
*North-Western Republican*W. **6,200**

WAVERLY, Pike Co., 1,500† p., on Ohio Canal and Scioto r., 61 m. from Columbus, 29 from Portsmouth, 16 from Chillicothe and 115 from Cincinnati. Does a thriving trade. Engaged in manufactures, agriculture and stock-raising.
Pike Co. Republican......W. **6,201**
Watchman...............W. **6,202**

WAYNESVILLE, Warren Co., 800† p., on Little Miami r., 51 m. from Cincinnati. The Little Miami division of Pittsburgh, Cincinnati & St. Louis Rd. passes down the opposite side of the river.
Miami Gazette...........W. **6,203**

WELLINGTON, Lorain Co., 2,000† p., on C., C., C. & I. Rd., 36 m. S. W. of Cleveland.
Enterprise................W. **6,204**

WELLSVILLE, Columbiana Co.
Union....................W. **6,205**

WESTERVILLE, Franklin Co., 1,200 p., on C., C., C. & I. Rd., 14 m. N. E. of Columbus. Surrounded by a rich agricultural district. Engaged in manufacturing.
Banner..................W. **6,206**

WEST LIBERTY, Logan Co.
Independent.............W. **6,207**

WESTON, Wood Co.
Free Press................W. **6,208**

WEST SALEM, Wayne Co., 713 p., on Atlantic & Great Western Rd., 36 m. from Akron and 31 from Mansfield.
Monitor..................W. **6,209**

WEST UNION, c. h., Adams Co., 540† p., 7 m. from Ohio r. and 84 from Columbus.
People's Defender........W. **6,210**
Scion.....................W. **6,211**

WILMINGTON, c. h., Clinton Co., 2,500† p., on Cincinnati & Muskingum Valley Rd., 56 m. from Cincinnati. Engaged in manufacturing. Quaker College located here.
Clinton Republican......W. **6,212**
Journal..................W. **6,213**

WOODSFIELD, c. h., Monroe Co., 753 p., 120 m. E. of Columbus, 35 S. W. of Wheeling, W. Va., and 12 from Ohio r.
Monroe Democrat.......W. **6,214**
Spirit of Democracy.....W. **6,215**

WOOSTER, c. h., Wayne Co., 7,300† p., on Killbuck Creek, and Pittsburgh, Fort Wayne & Chicago Rd., 52 m. from Cleveland and 41 from Mansfield. Manufacturing done here. Location of University of Wooster.
Republican..............W. **6,216**
Wayne Co. Democrat....W. **6,217**
University Review........M. **6,218**

XENIA, c. h., Greene Co., 6,377 p., on Pittsburgh, Cincinnati & St. Louis Rd., at junction of several other railroads, 61 m. from Columbus and 65 from Cincinnati. A place of active trade.
Gazette..................W. **6,219**
News....................W. **6,220**
Torchlight................W. **6,221**

YOUNGSTOWN, Mahoning Co., 15,000† p., on Mahoning r. and Lawrence branch of Pittsburgh, Fort Wayne & Chicago Rd., also a station on Mahoning division of Atlantic & Great Western Rd., 65 m. from Cleveland and 65 from Pittsburgh, Pa. Centre of block coal basin. Engaged in iron manufacture and agriculture.
Register and Tribune.....D. **6,222**
" " " ....W. **6,223**
Commercial..............W. **6,224**
Morning Star.............W. **6,225**
Rundschau...............W. **6,226**
Vindicator...............W. **6,227**

ZANEFIELD, Logan Co.
Mad-River Blade......S. M. **6,228**

OHIO.

ZANESVILLE, c. h., Muskingum Co., 18,000† p., on Muskingum r., at intersection of Baltimore & Ohio and Cincinnati & Muskingum Valley Rds. Engaged in manufactures. Steamboats run to Pittsburgh, Cincinnati and other points on the Ohio r., connected by the Ohio Canal to Cleveland. Centre of trade and a fertile agricultural region.
Courier..................D. **6,229**
" ....W. **6,230**
Farmers' and Mechanics' Advocate..............W. **6,231**
Post......................W. **6,232**
Signal......................W. **6,233**
Sunday Morning Times..W. **6,234**
Blandy's Monthly Journal......................M. **6,235**

OREGON.

ALBANY, Linn Co., 2,980† p., on Willamette r., at mouth of the Callapooia, 81 m. from Portland and 28 S. of Salem, and on Oregon & California Rd. Engaged in milling and manufacture of agricultural implements and various other articles. Surrounded by an agricultural district.
Evening Democrat........D. **6,236**
State Rights Democrat...W. **6,237**
Oregon Cultivator........W. **6,238**
Register..... ....W. **6,239**

ASTORIA, c. h., Clatsop Co.
Astorian..................W. **6,240**

BAKER CITY, c. h., Baker Co., 312 p., on S. fork of Powder r., in an agricultural, stock-raising and silver mining region.
Bedrock Democrat.......W. **6,241**

CORVALLIS, c. h., Benton Co., 1,200 p., on Willamette r., at head of navigation, 80 m. S. of Portland. Engaged in river commerce and a place of trade. Surrounded by an agricultural district.
Benton Democrat........W. **6,242**
Gazette....................W. **6,243**

DALLAS, c. h., Polk Co., 1,000† p., on Rickreal r., 15 m. W. of Salem. Surrounded by an agricultural district and a place of commercial activity.
Itemizer..................W. **6,244**

EMPIRE CITY, c. h., Coos Co.
Coos Co. Record.........W. **6,245**

EUGENE CITY, c. h., Lane Co., 1,600† p., on Willamette r., at head of Willamette Valley, on Oregon & California Rd., 125 m. S. of Portland and 72 S. of Salem. Grain producing the principal branch of industry.
Guard......................W. **6,246**
Oregon State Journal....W. **6,247**

HILLSBORO, c. h., Washington Co.
Washington Independent.W. **6,248**

JACKSONVILLE, c. h., Jackson Co., 1,000 p., on Rogue r., 240 m. S. of Salem and 60 N. of Yreka, Cal. Engaged in mining, agriculture and stock raising.
Democratic Times........W. **6,249**
Oregon Sentinel..........W. **6,250**

LAFAYETTE, c. h., Yam Hill Co.
Courier..................W. **6,251**

OREGON.

McMINNVILLE, Yam Hill Co., 500† p., on Yam Hill r., 60 m. from Portland and about 20 N. W. of Salem. A fertile region, exporting wheat and wool. River navigable to this point.
Yamhill Co. Reporter....W. **6,252**

MONMOUTH, Polk Co., 750 p., 9 m. from Dallas, 3 W. of Salem and 3¼ W. of Willamette r. Site of Christian College.
Christian Messenger.....W. **6,253**

OREGON CITY, c. h., Clackamas Co., 1,382 p., on Willamette r., and Oregon & California Rd., 16 m. from Portland and 37 from Salem. A manufacturing place and shipping point for freight from Upper Willamette r. The river has a fall of 40 feet at this point, rendering it necessary to trans-ship all freight for the upper river. The immense water power afforded by this fall is but partially developed.
Enterprise...............W. **6,254**

PENDLETON, c. h., Umatilla Co.
East Oregonian......... W. **6,255**

PORTLAND, c. h., Multnomah Co., 12,000† p., on Willamette r., 15 m. from its mouth, 10 from its junction with the Columbia and 53 N. E. of Salem. Head of ship navigation, and terminus of Oregon & California and Oregon Central Rds. Largest commercial city in Oregon and centre of trade. Steamers run regularly between Portland and San Francisco.
Bee.......................D. **6,256**
Dollar Bee............... W. **6,257**
Morning Oregonian...... D. **6,258**
" " ......W. **6,259**
Catholic Sentinel.........W. **6,260**
Commercial Reporter.... W. **6,261**
New North-West..........W. **6,262**
Oregon Churchman......W. **6,263**
Oregon Deutsche Zeitung.W. **6,264**
Pacific Christian Advocate....................W. **6,265**
Standard.................W. **6,266**
Star of the West..........W. **6,267**
Sunday Welcome.........W. **6,268**
West Shore...............M. **6,269**

ROSEBURG, c. h., Douglas Co., 1,000† p., on Umpqua r. and Oregon & California Rd., 19 m. S. of Oakland. Engaged in agriculture, and stock raising and mining.
Plaindealer..............W. **6,270**

SALEM, c. h., Marion Co., 6,000† p., State capital, on Willamette r. and Oregon & California Rd., 53 m. S. by W. of Portland. The river is navigable for a large part of the year. Manufacturing carried on. Centre of an agricultural country.
Evening Mercury.........D. **6,271**
" " ....W. **6,272**
Oregon Statesman........D. **6,273**
" " ....W. **6,274**
Willamette Farmer......W. **6,275**
Oregon Educational Monthly...............M. **6,276**

THE DALLES, c. h., Wasco Co., 1,500 p., on Columbia r., about 90 m. E. of Portland. The only place of any importance in the county and centre of trade A steamer connects with Portland.
Mountaineer.
Oregon Tribune..........W. **6,278**

UNION, Union Co.
Mountain Sentinel.......W. **6,279**

PENNSYLVANIA.

ADAMSTOWN, Lancaster Co.
Press .... W. 6,280

AKRON, Lancaster Co.
Globe .... W. 6,281

ALLEGHENY, Allegheny Co., 73,000† p., at junction of Allegheny with Ohio r., and on Pittsburgh, Fort Wayne & Chicago, Western Pennsylvania and Cleveland & Pittsburgh Rds. Connected by several bridges with Pittsburgh.
Mail.......................D. 6,282
Journal..................W. 6,283

ALLENTOWN, c. h., Lehigh Co., 19,000† p., on Lehigh r. and Canal, 51 m. from Harrisburg, at junction of Lehigh Valley, Lehigh & Susquehanna and East Pennsylvania Rds., 60 m. from Philadelphia and 90 from New York. Engaged in iron manufacturing. Surrounded by a populous agricultural district.
Chronicle and News......D. 6,284
Lehigh Register..........W. 6,285
Herald ....D. 6,286
Lecha Bote................D. 6,287
Friedens-Bote............W. 6,288
Democrat.................W. 6,289
Lutherische Zeitschrift...W. 6,290
Unabhaengiger Republikaner...................W. 6,291
Vaterland.
Welt-Bote .... W. 6,293
Der Jugend-Freund......M. 6,294

ALTOONA, Blair Co., 16,000† p., on Pennsylvania Central Rd., 238 m. from Philadelphia and 117 E. of Pittsburgh. Railroad repair shops and several manufactories located here. A trade centre for this section.
Mirror.......................D. 6,295
Blair Co. Radical........W. 6,296
Sun.........................W. 6,297
Tribune .... W. 6,298

APOLLO, Armstrong Co.
Lacon and Kiskiminetas Valley Review..........W. 6,299

ASHLAND, Schuylkill Co., 5,714 p., on Mine Hill & E. Mahanoy branch of Philadelphia & Reading Rd., 12 m. from Pottsville. Engaged in coal trade. A mining and manufacturing town.
Advocate ....W. 6,300
Record ....W. 6,301

ATHENS, Bradford Co., 1,500 p., at the junction of Susquehanna and Chemung rs., Pa. and N. Y. Rd., 18 m. from Towanda and 4 from Waverly Junction on Erie Rd. Engaged in manufacturing.
Bradford Democrat......W. 6,302
Gazette....................W. 6,303
Advertiser......... ..... M. 6,304

BADEN, Beaver Co., 1,000† p., on Ohio r., near mouth of Beaver r., and P., Ft. W. & C. Rd., 20 m. from Pittsburgh. Surrounded by an agricultural and stock-raising district. Coal and stone are found in this vicinity.
Beaver Co. Citizen.......M. 6,305

BALDWIN, Butler Co.
Token of Progress........W. 6,306

BARNHART'S MILLS, Butler Co.
Millerstown Review......W. 6,307

BEAVER, Beaver Co., 2,000† p., on Ohio r., near mouth of Beaver r., and river division of Cleveland & Pittsburgh Rd., 28 m. from Pittsburgh. Beaver r. furnishes water power for several factories.
Argus and Radical......W. 6,308
Democrat.................W. 6,309
Times.....................W. 6,310

BEDFORD, c. h., Bedford Co., 2,500† p., on Rayston branch of Juniata r. and Bedford division of Pennsylvania Central Rd., 52 m. from Huntingdon. Situated near Bedford Mineral Springs. Developing an iron manufacturing interest. Deposits of hematite and fossil ores and lime-stone found.
Gazette...................W. 6,311
Inquirer ....W. 6,312

BELLEFONTE, c. h., Center Co., 3,000† p., in Spring township, at terminus of Bellefonte branch of Bald Eagle division of Pennsylvania Central Rd., 33 m. from Tyrone. Engaged in iron manufactures, mining and general trade.
Democratic Watchman...W. 6,313
Republican...............W. 6,314
Christian Giver...........M. 6,315
Christian Temperance Alliance .... M. 6,316

BENTON, Columbia Co.
Independent Weekly......W. 6,317

BERWICK, Columbia Co., 923 p., in Briar Creek township, on Susquehanna r. and Canal, and Lackawanna & Bloomsburg Rd., 43 m. from Scranton and 26 from Wilkes-Barre. Engaged in manufacturing.
Independent .... W. 6,318

BETHLEHEM, Northampton Co., 4,512 p., on Lehigh r. and North Pennsylvania, Lehigh Valley and Lehigh & Susquehanna Rds., 54 m. from Philadelphia, 87 from New York. Engaged in manufactures. Centre of an iron and coal-producing region.
Times.................... W. 6,319
Der Brueder Botschafter. W. 6,320
Moravian .... W. 6,321
Little Missionary.........M. 6,322

BLOOMSBURG, c. h., Columbia Co., 3,400 p., on N. branch of Susquehanna r., and Lackawanna & Bloomsburg and Cattawissa Rds. and North Branch Canal, 147 m. from Philadelphia. Engaged in agriculture and iron manufacturing.
Columbian ....W. 6,323
Democratic Sentinel......W. 6,324
Republican...............W. 6,325

BLOSSBURG, Tioga Co., 1,500 p., on Tioga r. and Blossburg & Corning Rd., 130 m. from Harrisburg and 41 from Corning, N. Y. Engaged in mining and agriculture.
Register..................W. 6,326

BOYERTOWN, Berks Co., 1,200† p., on Colebrookdale branch of Philadelphia & Reading Rd., 9 m. from Pottstown and about 18 E. of Reading.
Demokrat................ W. 6,327

BRADFORD, McKean Co.
New Era..................W. 6,328

BRISTOL, Bucks Co., 4,000† p., on Delaware r. and New York division of Philadelphia Rd., 21 m. from Philadelphia. Terminus of Delaware division of Pennsylvania Canal. Engaged in manufacturing.
Bucks Co. Gazette........W. 6,329
Observer..................W. 6,330

PENNSYLVANIA.

BOCKWAYVILLE, Jefferson Co.
Free Press..............W. **6,331**

BROOKVILLE, c. h., Jefferson Co., 1,942 p., on Red Bank Creek and Bennett's branch extension of Allegheny Valley Rd., 65 m. N. E. of Pittsburgh. Engaged principally in the lumber business. Coal and iron abundant.
Jeffersonian.............W. **6,332**
Republican..............W. **6,333**

BROWNSVILLE, Fayette Co., 1,749 p., on Monongahela r., 35 m. from Pittsburgh. Coal abounds here. Manufacturing carried on. Steamboats from Pittsburgh run to this place.
Clipper..................W. **6,334**
Methodist Missionary....M. **6,335**

BUTLER, c. h., Butler Co., 4,000† p., on Conequenessing Creek and Butler extension of Western Pennsylvania division of Pennsylvania Central Rd., 40 m. from Pittsburgh. Surrounded by an agricultural district.
Butler Co. Citizen.......W. **6,336**
Eagle...................W. **6,337**
Ziegler's Democratic Herald..................W. **6,338**

CALIFORNIA, Washington Co.
Times...................W. **6,339**

CAMBRIDGEBORO, Crawford Co., 1,000† p., on Atlantic & Great Western Rd., 14 m. from Meadville. In an agricultural section.
Cambridge Index........W. **6,340**

CANONSBURG, Washington Co.
Herald..................W. **6,341**

CANTON, Bradford Co., 1,840 p., on Northern Central Rd., 40 m. N. of Williamsport.
Sentinel.................W. **6,342**

CARBONDALE, Luzerne Co., 6,393 p., on Lackawanna r. and Jefferson branch of Erie Rd., at its junction with Delaware & Hudson Rd. Coal is found in this vicinity.
Advance.................W. **6,343**
Leader..................W. **6,344**

CARLISLE, c. h., Cumberland Co., 7,000 p., on Cumberland Valley Rd., at junction of Pine Grove Branch, 18 m. from Harrisburg. In an agricultural district. Seat of Dickinson College.
Mirror..............S. W. **6,345**
American Volunteer.....W. **6,346**
Herald..................W. **6,347**
Valley Sentinel..........W. **6,348**
Dickinsonian............M. **6,349**

CATASAUQUA, Lehigh Co., 4,500† p., on Lehigh Valley Rd., Lehigh & Susquehanna Canal, and Catasauqua & Fogelsville Rd., 97 m. from New York and 22 from Philadelphia. Engaged in iron manufacturing.
Dispatch.................W. **6,350**
Valley Record...........W. **6,351**

CENTER HALL, Center Co., 800 p., on turnpike road from Bellefonte to Lewistown, 75 m. N. W. of Harrisburg.
Centre Reporter..........W. **6,352**

CHAMBERSBURG, c. h., Franklin Co., 6,500† p., on Cumberland Valley Rd., 52 m. from Harrisburg, 150 from Philadelphia and 140 from Baltimore. Centre of trade, being surrounded by a populous agricultural district.
Franklin Repository.....W. **6,353**

PENNSYLVANIA.

Public Opinion..........W. **6,354**
Valley Spirit............W. **6,355**

CHESTER, Delaware Co., 15,000† p., on Delaware r. and Philadelphia & Wilmington and Baltimore Rd., 15 m. from Philadelphia. Engaged in ship-building and manufacturing of various kinds. It has a good harbor, and is engaged in commerce and trade.
Evening News............D. **6,356**
Delaware Co. Advocate...W. **6,357**
Delaware Co. Democrat..W. **6,358**
Delaware Co. Mail.......W. **6,359**
*Delaware Co. Republican*W. **6,360**
Democratic Pilot.........W. **6,361**

CLARION, c. h., Clarion Co., 1,250 p., on Clarion r., 75 m. N. by E. of Pittsburgh. Situated in an agricultural and mining district.
Democrat................W. **6,362**
Jacksonian...............W. **6,363**
Republican...............W. **6,364**

CLEARFIELD, c. h., Clearfield Co., 2,000† p., on W. branch of Susquehanna r., and terminus of Tyrone & Clearfield division of Pennsylvania Central Rd., 41 m. from Tyrone and 172 from Pittsburgh. Industries, manufacturing lumber, agriculture and mining coal.
Raftsman's Journal.....W. **6,365**
Republican...............W. **6,366**

COATESVILLE, Chester Co., 3,500† p., on Pennsylvania Central Rd., at intersection of Wilmington & Reading Rd., 39 m. from Philadelphia. A centre for paper and woolen mills.
Chester Valley Union....W. **6,367**

COLUMBIA, Lancaster Co., 10,000† p., in West Hempfield township, on Susquehanna r., 28 m. from Harrisburg, on Columbia branch of Pennsylvania Central Rd., at junction of Reading & Columbia Rd. A lumber depot and engaged in manufacturing iron.
Courant.................W. **6,368**
Herald..................W. **6,369**
Spy.....................W. **6,370**
Mutual Underwriter.....M. **6,371**

CONNEAUTVILLE, Crawford Co., 1,100 p., in Spring township, on Erie Extension Canal and Erie & Pittsburgh Rd., 113 m. from Pittsburgh and 35 from Erie. Agriculture and manufacturing are the chief industries.
Courier..................W. **6,372**

CONNELLSVILLE, Fayette Co., 3,500† p., on Pittsburgh, Baltimore & Washington Rd., 57 m. E. of Pittsburgh. Coal, lime-stone, iron and lumber are the principal features of industry.
Fayette Monitor..........W. **6,373**
Tribune..................W. **6,374**

CONSHOHOCKEN, Montgomery Co., 4,000† p., on Schuylkill r. and Philadelphia & Reading Rd., 14 m. N. W. of Philadelphia. Engaged in the manufacture of gas and water pipes, and iron manufactures generally.
News and Recorder......W. **6,375**

CORRY, Erie Co., 6,809 p., on Philadelphia & Erie Rd., at crossing of Atlantic & Great Western Rd., and terminus of the Buffalo, Corry & Pittsburgh and Oil Creek & Allegheny Valley Rds., 37 m. from Erie. A centre of trade and rapidly increasing

in population. Engaged in oil lumber and iron manufactures
Local News............W. **6,376**
Telegraph...............W. **6,377**

COUDERSPORT, c. h., Potter Co., 950† p., on Allegheny r., 174 m. N. of Harrisburg.
Potter Enterprise........W. **6,378**
Potter Journal..........W. **6,379**

CURWENSVILLE, Clearfield Co., 700† p., on W. branch of Susquehanna r., 6 m. above Clearfield.
Clearfield Co. Times.....W. **6,380**

DANVILLE, c. h., Montour Co., 8,336 p., on N. branch of Susquehanna r., 67 m. from Harrisburg, on Lackawanna & Bloomsburg, Catawissa & Danville, Hazelton & Wilkes-Barre Rds., 150 m. from Philadelphia and 175 from New York. Iron works and other manufactures located here.
Intelligencer.............W. **6,381**
Montour American......W. **6,382**
Record..................W. **6,383**

DELTA, York Co.
Times...................W. **6,384**

DILLSBURG, York Co.
New Era..............S. M. **6,385**

DOWNINGTON, Chester Co., 1,077 p., on Pennsylvania Central Rd., at junction of Waynesburg branch, and at terminus of Chester Valley division of Philadelphia & Reading Rd., 33 m. from Philadelphia.
Chester Co. Archive......W. **6,386**

DOYLESTOWN, c. h., Bucks Co., 2,550 p., on Doylestown branch of North Pennsylvania Rd., 28 m. from Philadelphia. In an agricultural district and centre of trade.
*Bucks Co. Intelligencer*S. W. **6,387**
Bucks Co. Express and Reform...... ....W. **6,388**
Bucks Co. Mirror........W. **6,389**
Democrat...............W. **6,390**
Demokratische Wacht....W. **6,391**
Morgenstern.............W. **6,392**

DUNCANNON, Perry Co.
Record..................W. **6,393**

EAST BRADY, Clarion Co., 728 p., 18 m. S. W. of Clarion.
Independent.............W. **6,394**

EASTON, c. h., Northampton Co., 17,000† p., on Delaware r., 57 m. from Philadelphia. Centre of six railroads. Engaged in manufactures and a centre of trade.
Express..................D. **6,395**
Free Press................D. **6,396**
" " ....W. **6,397**
Argus....................W. **6,398**
Northampton Correspondent.....................W. **6,399**
Sentinel...... ....W. **6,400**
American Mechanic's Advocate..................M. **6,401**

EBENSBURG, c. h., Cambria Co., 1,500† p., at terminus of Ebensburg & Cresson branch of Pennsylvania Central Rd., 11 m. from Cresson. Manufacturing, lumber and coal mining are the principal means of employment. Shipping point for northern part of county.
Cambria Freeman...... W **6,402**
Cambria Herald........W. **6,403**

ELIZABETH, Allegheny Co.
Herald ....W. **6,404**

ELIZABETHTOWN, Lancaster Co., 1,000 p., on Pennsylvania Central Rd., 18 m. from Lancaster City and an equal distance from Harrisburg. Situated in a densely populated agricultural district.
Chronicle................W. **6,405**

EMLENTON, Venango Co., 1,200† p., on Allegheny r. and Allegheny Valley Rd. In the oil regions. Engaged in iron manufacturing, mercantile pursuits and the production of oil.
Times....................W. **6,406**

EMPORIUM, c. h., Cameron Co., 1,600† p., on Philadelphia & Erie Rd., 99 m. W. from Williamsport.
Cameron Co. Press...... W. **6,407**
Independent.............W. **6,408**

EPHRATA, Lancaster Co.
Mountain Echo..........W. **6,409**

ERIE, c. h., Erie Co., 26,000† p., on Lake Erie, Erie & Beaver Canal, Erie & Pittsburgh, Philadelphia & Erie and Lake Shore & Michigan Southern Rds., 90 m. from Buffalo. Engaged in lake commerce, lumber trade and manufactures. Gas wells are located here.
Dispatch.................D. **6,410**
" ....W. **6,411**
Gazette..................W. **6,412**
Sunday Morning Gazette.W. **6,413**
Lake Shore Visitor......W. **6,414**
Leuchtthurm............W. **6,415**
Observer.................W. **6,416**
Zuschauer am Erie......W. **6,417**
Florist's Friend and Gardener's Manual..........M. **6,418**

EVERETT, Bedford Co.
Bedford Co. Press.......W. **6,419**

FARMERSVILLE, Lancaster Co.
West Earl Banner ....M. **6,420**

FRANKLIN, c. h., Venango Co., 3,908 p., on French Creek, near Allegheny r., and on Atlantic & Great Western, Franklin division of Lake Shore & Michigan Southern and Allegheny Valley Rds., 28 m. from Meadville. Engaged in oil trade. In the oil regions of Pennsylvania.
Independent Press.......W. **6,421**
Venango Citizen..........W. **6,422**
Venango Spectator.......W. **6,423**

FREEBURG, Snyder Co., 700† p., 5 m. from Susquehanna r. and 50 from Harrisburg.
Courier ....W. **6,424**

FREEPORT, Armstrong Co., 1,640 p., on Allegheny r., and Western Pennsylvania division of Pennsylvania Central Rd., 29 m. from Pittsburgh.
Valley Times............W. **6,425**

GETTYSBURG, c. h., Adams Co., 3,074 p., near Rock Creek and on Hanover, Hanover Junction & Gettysburg Rd., 36 m. from Harrisburg, 52 from Baltimore and 112 from Philadelphia.
Century..................W. **6,426**
Compiler.................W. **6,427**
Star and Sentinel........W. **6,428**

GIRARD, Erie Co., 1,800 p., on Lake Shore & Michigan Southern Rd., at junction of Erie & Pittsburgh Rd., 16 m. from Erie. Surrounded by an agricultural district.
Cosmopolite ....W. **6,429**

GLEN ROCK, York Co., 850 p., on Northern Central Rd., 42 m. from Baltimore and

Harrisburg, and 16 from York. A growing town, in centre of an agricultural and iron mining region. Iron, woolen and rope manufactories located here.
Item....................W. **6,430**

GREAT BEND, Susquehanna Co.
Reporter....................W. **6,431**

GREENCASTLE, Franklin Co., 1,750 p., on Cumberland Valley Rd., 63 m. from Harrisburg. Situated in an agricultural district, and engaged in manufacturing agricultural implements and other articles.
Valley Echo....................W. **6,432**

GREENSBURG, c. h., Westmoreland Co., 1,642 p., on Pennsylvania Central Rd., 32 m. from Pittsburgh. In an agricultural district and centre of trade. The Westmoreland & Pennsylvania Gas Coal Company ship coal from this point.
Democratic Times.......W. **6,433**
Pennsylvania Argus.....W. **6,434**
Tribune and Herald......W. **6,435**
Westmoreland Democrat.W. **6,436**

GREENVILLE, Mercer Co., 1,848 p., on Shenango r. and Pittsburgh & Erie and Atlantic & Great Western Rds., at terminus of Allegheny & Chenango Rd., 63 m. from Erie, 80 from Pittsburgh and 60 from Cleveland. Several mills, manufactories and coal mines here. Centre of a farming region.
Advance.
Shenango Valley Argus..W. **6,438**

HAMBURGH, Berks Co., 2,200† p., in Windsor township, on Schuylkill R. Canal, and Philadelphia & Reading Rd., 17 m. from Reading and 70 N. of Philadelphia. Has trade in grain, leather and iron. Second town in county in population and business importance.
Hamburger Schnellpost..W. **6,439**

HANOVER, York Co., 2,000† p., on Penn. Rd., Frederick division, at junction of railroad to Gettysburg, 35 m. from Harrisburg, 42 from Frederick, Md. Centre of a highly cultivated district.
Citizen....................W. **6,440**
Citizen (German)........W. **6,441**
Herald....................W. **6,442**
Spectator....................W. **6,443**

HARRISBURG, c. h., Dauphin Co., State capital, 30,000† p., on Susquehanna r. and Pennsylvania Central Rd., at junction of several railroads, 106 m. W. of Philadelphia. Engaged in the manufacture of iron and other articles.
Patriot....................D. **6,444**
" ....W. **6,445**
Telegraph....................D. **6,446**
" ....W. **6,447**
Church Advocate.........W. **6,448**
Pennsylvanische Staats-Zeitung....................W. **6,449**
Saturday Chronicle.......W. **6,450**
Temperance Vindicator and Keystone Good Templar....................W. **6,451**
Vaterland's Waechter....W. **6,452**
Sunday School Gem.......M. **6,453**

HATBORO, Montgomery Co.
Public Spirit............W. **6,454**

HAWLEY, Wayne Co.
Times....................W. **6,455**

HAZLETON, Luzerne Co., 7,000 p., on Lehigh Valley Rd., 15 m. from Mauch Chunk, 120 from New York and 105 from Philadelphia. A coal mining town.
Sentinel....................D. **6,456**
Anthracite Sentinel.......W. **6,457**
Volksblatt....................W. **6,458**

HOLLIDAYSBURG, c. h., Blair Co., 2,952 p., on Juniata r. and Pennsylvania Canal, connected with Pennsylvania Central Rd. at Altoona by a branch 8 m. long. Iron and coal mines are found here. Centre of trade. Iron manufacturing and coal mining the chief industries.
Democratic Standard....W. **6,459**
Register....................W. **6,460**

HONESDALE, c. h., Wayne Co., 9,000† p., on Lackawaxen Creek, at terminus of Delaware & Hudson Canal, and on Honesdale division of Erie Rd., 135 m. from New York city, 32 from Scranton. Engaged in manufacturing and the coal trade. Delaware & Hudson Canal transports coal from this point to the Hudson r.
Citizen....................W. **6,461**
Das Journal..............W. **6,462**
Wayne Co. Herald.......W. **6,463**

HUGHESVILLE, Loudon Co.
Enterprise....................W. **6,464**

HULMEVILLE, Bucks Co., 400 p., on Nishuming Creek, 20 m. from Philadelphia, 8 from Trenton, N. J., and 5 from Bristol. Centre of trade. Engaged in cotton and lace manufacturing.
Beacon....................W. **6,465**

HUMMELSTOWN, Dauphin Co., 1,200† p., on E. Pennsylvania & Lebanon Valley branch of Philadelphia & Reading Rd., 9 m. from Harrisburg.
Sun....................W. **6,466**

HUNTINGDON, c. h., Huntingdon Co., 3,034 p., on Juniata r., Pennsylvania Canal and Pennsylvania Central Rd., at junction of Huntingdon & Broad Top Rd., 96 m. from Harrisburg. Engaged in manufacturing and mining.
Local News.............S. W. **6,467**
Globe....................W. **6,468**
Journal....................W. **6,469**
Monitor....................W. **6,470**
Pilgrim....................W. **6,471**

INDIANA, c. h., Indiana Co., 3,000† p., at terminus of Indiana branch of Pennsylvania Central Rd., 16 m. from Blairsville. Engaged in manufacturing and a shipping point for produce, lumber, etc.
Democrat....................W. **6,472**
Messenger....................W. **6,473**
Progress....................W. **6,474**

IRWIN, Westmoreland Co.
Spray.

JAMESTOWN, Mercer Co.
Sun....................W. **6,476**

JERSEY SHORE, Lycoming Co., 1,440† p., on W. branch of Susquehanna R. and Philadelphia & Erie Rd., 12 m. from Williamsport and 13 from Lock Haven.
Herald....................W. **6,477**

JOHNSTOWN, Cambria Co., 6,028 p., on Pennsylvania Central Rd., 78 m. from Pittsburgh. Engaged in iron, steel and woolen manufacturing.
Tribune....................D. **6,478**
" ....W. **6,479**
Democrat....................W. **6,480**
Freie Presse....................W. **6,481**
Voice and Echo..........W. **6,482**

PENNSYLVANIA.

KITTANNING, c. h., Armstrong Co., 1,889 p., on Allegheny r. and Allegheny Valley Rd., 45 m. from Pittsburgh. Coal and iron mines and manufactories and iron works located here.
Armstrong Republican...W. **6,483**
Democratic Sentinel......W. **6,484**
Union Free Press....... W. **6,485**

KUTZTOWN, Berks Co., 1,290† p., on Allentown Rd., 4½ m. from Topton and about 17 N. E. of Reading.
American Patriot........W. **6,486**
Journal..................W. **6,487**
National Educator.......W. **6,488**

LANCASTER, c. h., Lancaster Co., 23,-000† p., on Pennsylvania Central Rd., at junction of Columbia branch, 68 m. from Philadelphia. Centre of trade for a populous agricultural district. Engaged in agriculture and manufactures.
Evening Express..........D. **6,489**
" " ....W. **6,490**
Examiner.................D. **6,491**
Examiner and Herald....W. **6,492**
Intelligencer.............D. **6,493**
" ....W. **6,494**
Bar...................... W. **6,495**
Die Laterne.............. W. **6,496**
Inquirer.................W. **6,497**
Review...................W. **6,498**
Volksfreund und Beobachter...................W. **6,499**
Christliche Kundschafter..M. **6,500**
College Days.............M. **6,501**
Farmer...................M. **6,502**
Pennsglvania School Journal.....................M. **6,503**
Reformed Church Monthly........................M. **6,504**
Waffenlose Waechter.....M. **6,505**

LANSDALE, Montgomery Co., 993 p., on N. Pennsylvania Rd., 22 m. from Philadelphia, at junction of Doylestown Branch Rd. Engaged in manufacturing. A trade centre.
Montgomery Co. Presse...W. **6,506**
Reporter..................W. **6,507**

LAPORTE, c. h., Sullivan Co., 750 p., 107 m. from Harrisburg. Mining, lumbering and farming the chief industries.
Press and Standard.
Sullivan Co. Democrat....W. **6,509**

LATROBE, Westmoreland Co.
Advance ....W. **6,510**

LEBANON, c. h., Lebanon Co., 6,727 p., on Lebanon Valley branch of Philadelphia & Reading Rd., 25 m. from Harrisburg. Connected with the Schuylkill Company coal mines by Lebanon & Fremont Rd., and with the Cornwall oil mines by Cornwall Rd.
News......................D. **6,511**
Times.....................D. **6,512**
Valley Standard.........W. **6,513**
Advertiser .... W. **6,514**
Courier.................. W. **6,515**
Laborer...................W. **6,516**
Pennsylvanier............W. **6,517**
Review....................W. **6,518**
United Brethren Tribune.W. **6,519**
Wahrer Demokrat ....W. **6,520**
Musical Visitor and Lesson Manual...............M. **6,521**

LEECHBURG, Armstrong Co.
Enterprise................M. **6,522**

PENNSYLVANIA.

LEHIGHTON, Carbon Co., 1,485 p., on Lehigh r. and Lehigh & Susquehanna division of Central Rd. of New Jersey, 3 m. from Mauch Chunk and 42 W. N. W. of Easton. Iron works in the vicinity.
Carbon Advocate..........W. **6,523**

LEWISBURG, c. h., Union Co., 3,121 p., in Buffalo township, on W. branch of Susquehanna r., 69 m. from Harrisburg. In a populous agricultural district.
Chronicle.................W. **6,524**
Journal...................W. **6,525**
College Herald...........M. **6,526**

LEWISTOWN, c. h., Mifflin Co., 2,731 p., on Juniata r. and Pennsylvania Canal, 1 m. from Pennsylvania Central Rd., on Mifflin & Center County branch, 61 m. W. of Harrisburg. Engaged in agriculture and manufactures and centre of trade.
Democratic Sentinel.....W. **6,527**
Gazette....................W. **6,528**
True Democrat...........W. **6,529**

LINESVILLE, Venango Co.
Leader....................W. **6,530**

LITIZ, Lancaster Co.
Gazette...................W. **6,531**

LITTLESTOWN, Adams Co., 1,100 p., on Littlestown Rd., 10 m. S. E. of Gettysburg and 42 from Baltimore. In an agricultural neighborhood. Centre of a coal, lumber and grain trade, and engaged in manufacturing.
News.....................W. **6,532**

LOCK HAVEN, c. h., Clinton Co., 8,500† p., on W. branch of Susquehanna r. and Pennsylvania Canal, and on Philadelphia & Erie Rd., at junction of Bald Eagle division of Pennsylvania Central Rd. Engaged in lumber trade and manufacturing.
Clinton Democrat.......W. **6,533**
Clinton Republican......W. **6,534**
Enterprise...............W. **6,535**

LYKENS, Dauphin Co., 1,800† p., on Lykens Valley Rd., 43 m. from Harrisburg. Several coal mines here. The base of supplies of Lykens Valley coal region.
Record...................W. **6,536**
Register.................W. **6,537**

McCONNELSBURG, c. h., Fulton Co., 600† p., 70 m. W. by S. of Harrisburg. Engaged in manufactures, agriculture and salt making.
Fulton Democrat.........W. **6,538**
Fulton Republican.......W. **6,539**

McKEESPORT, Allegheny Co., 2,523 p., on Monongahela r., and Pittsburgh, Washington & Baltimore Rd., 15 m. from Pittsburgh. Centre of coal and lumber trade. Engaged in manufacturing.
Paragon.................W. **6,540**
Times....................W. **6,541**

McVEYTOWN, Mifflin Co.
Journal..................W. **6,542**

MAHANOY CITY, Schuylkill Co., 6,500† p., on the Mahanoy Creek, 13 m. N. E. of Pottsville. Railroad connections by the East Mahanoy branch of Philadelphia & Reading Rd. and the Mahanoy branch of the Lehigh Valley Rd.
Mahanoy Gazette.... ...W. **6,543**
Mahanoy Valley Record..W. **6,544**

MANHEIM, Lancaster Co., 1,500† p., on Reading & Columbia Rd., at junction of Pine Grove Rd., 10 m. N. of Lancaster.

PENNSYLVANIA.

Engaged in agriculture, iron mining and cigar manufacturing.
Sentinel and Advertiser..W. **6,545**

MANSFIELD, Tioga Co., 1,200† p., on Blossburg & Corning Rd., 10 m. from Blossburg and 31 from Corning.
Advertiser..................W. **6,546**

MANSFIELD VALLEY, Allegheny Co.
Mansfield Item..........W. **6,547**

MARIETTA, Lancaster Co., 6,000† p., in East Donegal township, on Susquehanna r. and Columbia branch of Pennsylvania Central Rd., 16 m. from Lancaster. Has several iron furnaces and rolling mills. Engaged in coal and lumber trade.
Register..................W. **6,548**

MARTINSBURG, Blair Co.
Cove Echo.

MAUCH CHUNK, c. h., Carbon Co., 5,000† p., on Lehigh r. and Canal, Lehigh Valley Rd., and Lehigh & Susquehanna division of Central Rd. of New Jersey, at junction of Nesquehoning branch, 46 m. from Easton, 88 from Philadelphia and 121 from New York. A centre of coal trade.
Coal Gazette..............W. **6,550**
Democrat..................W. **6,551**

MEADVILLE, c. h., Crawford Co., 10,000† p., on Atlantic & Great Western Rd., at junction of Franklin branch. Centre of a wealthy and populous district. Engaged in manufacturing.
Republican................D. **6,552**
" ....W. **6,553**
Crawford Democrat.....W. **6,554**
Crawford Journal.......W. **6,555**

MECHANICSBURG, Cumberland Co., 3,500† p., on Cumberland Valley Rd., 8 m. from Harrisburg. In a fertile agricultural district abounding in deposits of iron ores. Engaged in various manufactures.
Farmer's Friend.........W. **6,556**
Independent Journal....W. **6,557**

MEDIA, c. h., Delaware Co., 1,300† p., on Westchester & Philadelphia Rd., 13 m. from Philadelphia.
Dalaware Co. American.W. **6,558**

MERCER, c. h., Mercer Co., 1,235 p., on Neshannock Creek and Shenango & Allegheny Rd., 60 m. from Pittsburgh and 17 from Greenville. Agriculture, mining and stock raising carried on. The county is rich in mineral resources and rapidly filling with iron works.
Dispatch..................W. **6,559**
Western Press............W. **6,560**

MERCERSBURG, Franklin Co., 971 p., in Montgomery township, 15 m. S. W. of Chambersburg. Seat of Marshall College.
Journal..................W. **6,561**

MEYERSDALE, Somerset Co.
Independent..............W. **6,562**
Primitive Christian......W. **6,563**

MIDDLEBURG, c. h., Snyder Co., 600 p., on Middle Creek and Lewiston division of Pennsylvania Central Rd., 33 m. from Lewiston and 69 from Harrisburg.
Post..................W. **6,564**

MIDDLETOWN, Dauphin Co., 4,100† p., in Lower Swatara township, on Susquehanna r., Pennsylvania Central Rd., 9 m. from Harrisburg.
Journal..................W. **6,565**

PENNSYLVANIA.

MIFFLINBURG, Union Co., 1,200† p., on Buffalo Creek, 9 m. from Lewisburg. In an agricultural district.
Telegraph................W. **6,566**

MIFFLINTOWN, c. h., Juniata Co., 1,200 p., on Juniata r., 49 m. from Harrisburg. The Pennsylvania Central Rd. passes along the opposite side of the river.
Democrat and Register...W. **6,567**
Independent..............W. **6,568**
Juniata Sentinel and Republican................W. **6,569**
Juniata Tribune..........W. **6,570**

MILFORD, c. h., Pike Co., 870† p., on Delaware r. and Delaware & Hudson Canal, 110 m. from Philadelphia.
Herald..................W. **6,571**

MILFORD SQUARE, Bucks Co., 1,000 p., 38 m. by railroad N. of Philadelphia. Centre of trade for an agricultural district.
Der Reformer und Agriculturist..................W. **6,572**
Mennonitische Friedensbote..................S. M. **6,573**
Himmel's Manna.........M. **6,574**
Our Home Friend.........M. **6,575**

MILLERSBURG, Dauphin Co.
Herald..................W. **6,576**

MILLERSTOWN, Perry Co.
Ledger..................W. **6,577**

MILLERSVILLE, Lancaster Co.
Era......................W. **6,578**

MILLHEIM, Centre Co.
Der Centre Berichter.....W. **6,579**

MILL VILLAGE, Erie Co.
Herald..................W. **6,580**
Home Weekly.............W. **6,581**

MILTON, Northumberland Co., 1,900 p., on W. branch of Susquehanna r. and Pennsylvania Canal, at junction of Catawissa with Philadelphia & Erie Rd., 13 m. N. of Sunbury. Iron manufacturing carried on.
Miltonian..............W. **6,582**

MILTON GROVE, Lancaster Co.
News....................W. **6,583**

MINERSVILLE, Schuylkill Co.
Schuylkill Republican....W. **7,584**

MONONGAHELA CITY, Washington Co., 4,316 p., on Monongahela r., 20 m. S. of Pittsburgh. Engaged in manufactures, mining and a place of active trade.
Monongahela Valley Republican..............W. **6,585**
Valley Record............W. **6,586**
Pennsylvania Reserve News Letter..............M. **6,587**

MONTROSE, c. h., Susquehanna Co., 1,500 p., 10 m. from Delaware, Lackawanna & Western Rd., 165 from Philadelphia. In an agricultural district.
Democrat.................W. **6,588**
Independent Republican..W. **6,589**

MT. HOLLY SPRINGS, Cumberland Co., 1,000† p., 6 m. S. of Carlisle and 20 S. W. of Harrisburg.
Mountain Echo..........W. **6,590**

MOUNT JOY, Lancaster Co., 1,896 p., on Pennsylvania Central Rd., 12 m. from Lancaster and 24 E. of Harrisburg. Engaged in various manufactures.
Herald..................W. **6,591**
Star......................W. **6,592**

PENNSYLVANIA.

MOUNT PLEASANT, Westmoreland Co
Dawn....................W. **6,593**

MOUNT UNION, Huntingdon Co.
Herald....................W. **6,594**
Times......................W. **6,595**

MUNCY, Lycoming Co., 1,040 p., on W. branch of Susquehanna r., and Philadelphia & Erie and Catawissa Rds., 14 m. from Williamsport. Muncy Creek affords water power, which is employed in various manufactures. Agriculture and lumber business are the chief industries.
Luminary................W. **6,596**

MYERSTOWN, Lebanon Co.
Chronicle.................W. **6,597**

NEW BETHLEHEM, Clarion Co.
Press.......................W. **6,598**

NEW BLOOMFIELD, c. h., Perry Co., 655 p., 27 m. from Harrisburg and 5 from Pennsylvania Central Rd. Centre of an agricultural district.
People's Advocate and Press..................W. **6,599**
Perry Co. Democrat......W. **6,600**
Perry Co. Freeman.......W. **6,601**
Times.....................W. **6,602**

NEW BRIGHTON, Beaver Co., 5,000† p., on Beaver R. Rd., 3 m. N. of Beaver. Mills and factories are furnished with water power from the river. Connected with Lake Erie by Beaver and Erie Canal. In a coal region. Engaged in manufacturing.
Beaver Valley News......W. **6,603**

NEW CASTLE, c. h., Lawrence Co., 8,000† p., on Shenango r. and Erie Canal, at junction of New Castle branch of Pittsburgh, Fort Wayne & Chicago with Erie & Pittsburgh Rd., 52 m. from Pittsburgh. Engaged in manufacturing iron and mining bituminous coal.
Courant..................W. **6,604**
Lawrence Guardian......W. **6,605**
Lawrence Paragraph....W. **6,606**
United Workman.........W. **6,607**

NEW HOLLAND, Lancaster Co.
Clarion....................W. **6,608**

NEWPORT, Perry Co., 946 p., on Juniata r. and Pennsylvania Central Rd., 28 m. N. W. of Harrisburg. Grain shipped from here and some manufacturing. Principal shipping point for Perry county.
News.......................W. **6,609**

NEWTOWN, Bucks Co., 859 p., 14 m. S. E. of Doylestown and 10 from Trenton, N. J. In a farming district.
Enterprise.................W. **6,610**

NEWVILLE, Cumberland Co., 907 p., on Cumberland Valley Rd., 30 m. from Harrisburg and 22 from Chambersburg.
Enterprise................W. **6,611**
Star of the Valley.........W. **6,612**

NICHOLSON, Wyoming Co., 1,546 p., on Delaware, Lackawanna & Western Rd., 21 m. from Scranton.
Examiner................W. **6,613**

NORRISTOWN, c. h., Montgomery Co., 10,753 p., on Schuylkill r and Canal and Philadelphia & Reading Rd., 16 m. from Philadelphia, at terminus of Philadelphia & Norristown and Chester Valley Rd. Engaged in iron, cotton and wool manufacturing.
Herald....................D. **6,614**
Herald and Free Press...W. **6,615**

PENNSYLVANIA.

Independent..............D. **6,616**
" ....W. **6,617**
Register..................D. **6,618**
" ....W. **6,619**
Montgomery Co. Post....W. **6,620**
National Defender.......W. **6,621**
*Schuylkill Valley Sentinel*W. **6,622**

NORTH EAST, Erie Co.
Sun........................W. **6,623**

NORTHUMBERLAND, Northumberland Co.
Public Press..............W. **6,624**

NORTH WALES, Montgomery Co.
Record....................W. **6,625**

OIL CITY, Venango Co., 7,000† p., 8 m. from Franklin, on Allegheny r. and Oil Creek. Several railroads centre here. 132 m. from Pittsburgh. Engaged in oil business, quantities being shipped to Pittsburgh by means of steamers.
Derrick....................D. **6,626**
Times......................W. **6,627**

ORBISONIA, Huntingdon Co.
Leader....................W. **6,628**

ORWIGSBURG, Schuylkill Co.
Times......................W. **6,629**

OSCEOLA, Tioga Co.
Industrial World.........W. **6,630**

OXFORD, Chester Co., 1,800† p., on Philadelphia & Baltimore Central Rd., 52 m. from Philadelphia. Centre of an agricultural district.
Press......................W. **6,631**

PARKER CITY, Armstrong Co., 3,000† p., on Allegheny Valley Rd., 83 m. from Pittsburgh.
Daily.......................D. **6,632**
Oilman's Journal.........W. **6,633**

PARKESBURG, Chester Co., 2,000 p., on Pennsylvania Central Rd., 44 m. W. of Philadelphia. Engaged in manufacturing.
Chester Co. Times.......W. **6,634**
American Stock Journal.M. **6,635**

PENNSBURGH, Montgomery Co., 500 p., about 20 m. N. by W. of Norristown
Bauern Freund und Demokrat...................W. **6,636**
Perkiomen Valley Press..W. **6,637**

PHILADELPHIA, c. h., Philadelphia Co., 765,000† p., on Delaware and Schuylkill rs. Great metropolis of Pennsylvania. Engaged in almost all of the various kinds of manufactures. The commerce of Philadelphia is extensive, especially the domestic coast trade.
Abend Post................D. **6,638**
Day........................D. **6,639**
Demokrat.................D. **6,640**
*Vereinigte Staaten Zeitung*W. **6,641**
Evening Bulletin.........D. **6,642**
Evening Chronicle........D. **6,643**
Evening Express..........D. **6,644**
Evening Star..............D. **6,645**
Freie Presse...............D. **6,646**
Die Republikanische Flagge..................W. **6,647**
Herald.....................D. **6,648**
Inquirer...................D. **6,649**
Item........................D. **6,650**
Journal and American Hotel Reporter.........D. **6,651**
North American and United States Gazette...D. **6,652**

PENNSYLVANIA.

*North American and United States Gazette*T. W. **6,653**
Press........D. **6,654**
" ....T. W. **6,655**
" ....W. **6,656**
Programme........D. **6,657**
Public Ledger........D. **6,658**
Public Record........D. **6,659**
Telegraph........D. **6,660**
Times........D. **6,661**
Volksblatt........D. **6,662**
Nord Amerika........W. **6,663**
*Bulletin of the American Iron & Steel Association*W. **6,664**
Business Advocate and Price Current........W. **6,665**
Catholic Standard........W. **6,666**
Centennial Gazette and Journal of the Exhibition........W. **6,667**
Christian Instructor and Western United Presbyterian........W. **6,668**
Christian Recorder........W. **6,669**
Christian Standard and Home Journal........W. **6,670**
Christian Statesman........W. **6,671**
*Chronicle and Advertiser*W. **6,672**
Commercial Manufacturers' Gazette........W. **6,673**
Commercial List and Price Current........W. **6,674**
Commonwealth........W. **6,675**
Episcopal Recorder........W. **6,676**
Episcopal Register........W. **6,677**
Fanciers' Journal and Poultry Exchange........W. **6,678**
*Frankford & Holmesburg*W. **6,679**
Frankford Herald........W. **6,680**
Friend.
Friends' Intelligencer........W. **6,682**
Friends' Review........W. **6,683**
Germantown Telegraph..W. **6,684**
Insurance Reporter........W. **6,685**
Iron and Metal Review..W. **6,686**
Jewish Record........W. **6,687**
Journal........W. **6,688**
Keystone........W.
Keystone Independent...W. **6,690**
Legal Gazette........W. **6,691**
Legal Intelligencer........W. **6,692**
Literary Society........W. **6,693**
Lutheran and Missionary........W. **6,694**
Lutheran Observer........W. **6,695**
Mail........W. **6,696**
Manayunk Sentinel........W. **6,697**
Market Journal........W. **6,698**
Medical and Surgical Reporter........W. **6,699**
Messenger........W. **6,700**
National Baptist........W. **6,701**
Neue Welt........W. **6,702**
Observer........W. **6,703**
Our Little Ones........W. **6,704**
People's Advocate and Western Journal of Commerce........W. **6,705**
Practical Farmer and Journal of the Farm...W. **6,706**
Presbyterian........W. **6,707**
Presbyterian Journal....W. **6,708**
Railway World........W. **6,709**
Roxborough Intelligencer.W. **6,710**
*Saturday Evening Mirror*W. **6,711**
Saturday Evening Post..W. **6,712**
Saturday Night........W. **6,713**
School, Church and Home.W. **6,714**

PENNSYLVANIA.

Steck's Philadelphia Guide and Strangers' Paper..W. **6,715**
Sunday Dispatch........W. **6,716**
Sunday Mercury........W. **6,717**
Sunday Press and Mirror of the Times........W. **6,718**
Sunday Republic........W. **6,719**
Sunday School Times.....W. **6,720**
Sunday Times........W. **6,721**
Sunday Transcript........W. **6,722**
Sunday World........W. **6,723**
Trade Journal........W. **6,724**
United States Journal....W. **6,725**
Vindicator.
Young Folks' News........W. **6,727**
Medical Times........B. W. **6,728**
Brethren's Messenger..S. M. **6,729**
Child's Treasury........S. M. **6,730**
Child's World........S. M. **6,731**
" " ....M. **6,732**
Intelligencer........S. M. **6,733**
Peterson's Counterfeit Detector and National Bank Note List....S. M. **6,734**
Peterson's Counterfeit Detector and National Bank Note List........M. **6,735**
Real Estate Reporter...S. M. **6,736**
Sabbath School Visitor.S. M. **6,737**
" " " ....M. **6,738**
Soldiers' and Sailors' Journal........S. M. **6,739**
United States Review...S. M. **6,740**
Young Reaper........S. M. **6,741**
" " ....M. **6,742**
Youth's Evangelist.....S. M. **6,743**
Advocate of Christian Holiness........M. **6,744**
American Exchange and Review........M. **6,745**
American Journalist.....M. **6,746**
American Journal af Homœopathic Materia Medica and Record of Medical Science........M. **6,747**
American Journal of Pharmacy........M. **6,748**
American Law Register..M. **6,749**
Arthur's Illustrated Home Magazine........M. **6,750**
Augsburg Sunday School Teacher........M. **6,751**
Baptist Teacher........M. **6,752**
Building Association Journal........M. **6,753**
Busy Bee........M. **6,754**
Camp News........M. **6,755**
Carpet Journal........M. **6,756**
Carriage Monthly........M. **6,757**
Catholic Record........M. **6,758**
Christian Child........M. **6,759**
Christian Woman........M. **6,760**
Confectioners' Journal...M. **6,761**
Crotzer's Centennial and Journal of the Exposition........M. **6,762**
Dental Cosmos........M. **6,763**
Evangelical Repository & United Presbyterian Worker........M. **6,764**
Expositor.
*Forest and Quarry and Builders' Price Current*M. **6,766**
Freedmen's Monitor and Workingman's Looking-Glass........M. **6,767**
Gardener's Monthly and Horticulturist........M. **6,768**

PENNSYLVANIA

Godey's Lady Book......M. **6,769**
Great Western Monthly.
Guardian..............M. **6,771**
Guardian Angel.........M. **6,772**
Hahnemannian Monthly M. **6,773**
I. O. B. U. Journal......M. **6,774**
Journal of the Franklin Institute..............M. **6,775**
Lammerhirte............M. **6,776**
Le Moniteur de la Mode.
Lippincott's Magazine....M. **6,778**
Lutheran Sunday School Herald...............M. **6,779**
*Medical News and Library*M. **6,780**
Monthly Abstract of Medical Science............M. **6,781**
North Philadelphia Gazette.
Observer................M. **6,783**
Penn Monthly............M. **6,784**
People's Journal.........M. **6,785**
Peterson's Journal.
Peterson's Ladies' National Magazine..............M. **6,787**
Photographer.
Polytechnic Review.......M. **6,789**
Potter's American Monthly......................M. **6,790**
Presbyterian at Work.....M. **6,791**
Presbyterian Monthly Record....................M. **6,792**
Printers' Circular........M. **6,793**
Sunday School World....M. **6,794**
Travelers' Official Railway Guide.................M. **6,795**
Underwriter..............M. **6,796**
Voice of Peace...........M. **6,797**
Woman's Temperance Union................M. **6,798**
Proof Sheet...........B. M. **6,799**
American Catholic Quarterly Review...........Qr. **6,800**
American Journal of the Medical Sciences......Qr. **6,801**
Baptist Quarterly........Qr. **6,802**
Druggists' Printer.
Mercersburg Review....Qr. **6,804**
Typographic Advertiser..Qr. **6,805**

PHILIPSBURG, Center Co., 1,086 p., on Clearfield & Tyrone branch of Pennsylvania Central Rd., 24 m. from Tyrone and 28 W. of Bellefonte.
Journal..................W. **6,806**

PHŒNIXVILLE, Chester Co., 6,000† p., on Schuylkill r., at mouth of French Creek, and Philadelphia & Reading Rd., at junction of Pickering Valley Rd., 27 m. from Philadelphia. Engaged in manufacturing iron, cotton, machinery and other articles.
Independent Phœnix.....W. **6,807**
Messenger................W. **6,808**

PITTSBURGH, c. h., Allegheny Co., 120,000† p., at junction of Allegheny and Monongahela rs., which here form the Ohio. Surrounded by mines of coal and iron. Manufactures are extensive, employing millions of capital and thousands of operatives. Iron founderies are more numerous and extensive than in any other city in the United States. Commerce is also extensive, the Ohio r. being navigable to this point for light draught steamboats, which run to all points on Ohio and Mississippi rs. Connected by railroads with all the principal cities. Pennsylvania Central, Pittsburgh, Fort Wayne & Chicago, St. Louis & Cincinnati, Pittsburgh, Washington & Baltimore and Allegheny Valley Rds. centre here.

PENNSYLVANIA.

Commercial..............D. **6,809**
" ....W. **6,810**
Das Volksblatt...........D. **6,811**
Pittsburgher Volksblatt..W. **6,812**
Allegheny Blaetter.....Sund. **6,813**
Dispatch.................D. **6,814**
" ....W. **6,815**
Evening Chronicle........D. **6,816**
" " ....W. **6,817**
Evening Leader...........D. **6,818**
Dollar Leader............W. **6,819**
Sunday Leader...........W. **6,820**
Evening Telegraph........D. **6,821**
" " ......W. **6,822**
Freiheits freund.........D. **6,823**
Freiheits Freund und Courier.....................W. **6,824**
Gazette..................D. **6,825**
" ....W. **6,826**
Post.....................D. **6,827**
" ....W. **6,828**
Republikaner.............D. **6,829**
" ....W. **6,830**
Advance.................W. **6,831**
American Manufacturer and Iron World........W. **6,832**
Business Guide..........W. **6,833**
Catholic.................W. **6,834**
Catholic Journal.........W. **6,835**
Christian Advocate......W. **6,836**
Commercial Bulletin and Review...............W. **6,837**
Critic...................W. **6,838**
Legal Journal...........W. **6,839**
Methodist Recorder......W. **6,840**
National Labor Tribune..W. **6,841**
Presbyterian Banner....W. **6,842**
Saturday Guide..........W. **6,843**
South Side Herald.......W. **6,844**
Temperance Agitator.....W. **6,845**
United Presbyterian.....W. **6,846**
Y Wasg..................W. **6,847**
Our Morning Guide...S. M. **9,848**
College Journal..........M. **6,849**
Home Companion.........M. **6,850**
Insurance World.........M. **6,851**
Quadrat..................M. **6,852**
Sewing Machine Gazette..M. **6,853**
Trumpet..................M. **6,854**
WoolenManufacturer.....M. **6,855**

PITTSTON, Luzerne Co., 6,760 p., on N. branch of Susquehanna r., 10 m. from Wilkes-Barre, on Lehigh Valley, Lehigh & Susquehanna, and Lackawanna & Bloomsburg Rds., 9 m. from Scranton. Coal mines are located in this vicinity.
Comet and Wyoming Valley Journal.............W. **6,856**
Gazette..................W. **6,857**

PLYMOUTH, Luzerne Co., 2,684 p., on Susquehanna r. and Lackawanna & Bloomsburg Rd., 4 m. S. W. of Wilkes-Barre. Several coal mines here.
Index...................W. **6,858**
Star.....................W. **6,859**

PORT ALLEGHENY, McKean Co.
Northern Tier Reporter.. W. **6,860**

PORTLAND, Northampton Co.
Enterprise..............W. **6,861**

POTTSTOWN, Montgomery Co., 4,125 p., on Schuylkill Canal and r., and Philadelphia & Reading Rd., at junction of Reading & Colebrookdale Rd., 35 m. from Philadelphia. Engaged in manufactures.
Ledger...................D. **6,862**
Montgomery Ledger......W. **6,863**
Advertiser..............W. **6,864**

PENNSYLVANIA.

POTTSVILLE, Schuylkill Co., 14,500† p., on Schuylkill r. and Canal, at terminus of Philadelphia & Reading Rd., 93 m. from Philadelphia. Several other railroads centre here. Mining and shipping coal the chief business.
- *Evening Chronicle*........D. **6,865**
- *Miner's Journal*..........D. **6,866**
- " " ....W. **6,867**
- *Amerikanischer Republikaner*..................W. **6,868**
- *Jefferson Demokrat*......W. **6,869**
- *Standard*.................W. **6,870**
- *Workingman* ....W. **6,871**
- *Emerald Vindicator*......M. **6,872**

PUNXSUTAWNEY, Jefferson Co., 600† p., on Big Mahoning Creek, 20 m. S. E. of Brookville and 75 N. E. of Pittsburgh. Engaged in agriculture and lumber trade.
- *Mahoning Argus*........W. **6,873**
- *Mahoning Valley Spirit*..W. **6,874**

READING, Berks Co., 45,000† p., on Schuylkill r. and Canal, and Philadelphia, Reading & Pottsville and other Rds., 52 m. from Philadelphia. Engaged in various manufactures. Centre of an agricultural district.
- *Die Post*..................D. **6,875**
- *Banner von Berks*.......W. **6,876**
- *Die Biene*.............Sund. **6,877**
- *Eagle* ....D. **6,878**
- *Gazette and Democrat*....W. **6,879**
- *Times and Dispatch*......D. **6,880**
- *Berks and Schuylkill Journal*.................W. **6,881**
- *Adler*.....................W. **6,882**
- *Der Pilger*...............W. **6,883**
- *Deutsche Eiche*...........W. **6,884**
- *Industrial Pioneer*.......W. **6,885**
- *Republikaner von Berks*..W. **6,886**
- *Saturday Evening Review*W. **6,887**
- *Sunday News*............W. **6,888**
- *Tribune and Commercial Advertiser* ....W. **6,889**
- *Reformirte Hausfreund*S. M. **6,890**

RENOVO, Clinton Co., 3,000† p., on W. branch of Susquehanna r. and Philadelphia & Erie Rd., 27 m. from Lock Haven. Centre of a lumbering region. Engaged in coal mining. Railroad machine shops located here.
- *Record*...................W. **6,891**

REYNOLDSVILLE, Jefferson Co.
- *Reynolds Herald*........W. **6,892**

RIDGWAY, Elk Co., 800 p., on Clarion r. and Philadelphia & Erie Rd., 118 m. from Erie. Engaged in coal mining, tanning and the lumber trade.
- *Elk Co. Advocate*........W. **6,893**
- *Elk Democrat*............W. **6,894**

ST. CLAIR, Schuylkill Co.
- *Review and Chronicle*....W. **6,895**

ST. MARY'S, Elk Co., 1,287 p., on Philadelphia & Erie Rd., 10 m. E. of Ridgway. In a coal and lumbering district.
- *Elk Co. Railroad and Mining Gazette*........W. **6,896**

ST. PETERSBURG, Clarion Co.
- *Record*...................W. **6,897**

SALTSBURG, Indiana Co.
- *Press*................... W. **6,898**

SANDY LAKE, Mercer Co.
- *News*.....................W. **6,899**

SCRANTON, Luzerne Co., 50,000† p., on Lackawanna r. and Delaware, Lackawanna & Western, Delaware & Hudson, Lehigh & Susquehanna, Lackawanna & Bloomsburg and Pennsylvania Coal Company Rds., 142 m. from New York. Extensive iron and steel works. A trade centre and the depot of anthracite coal trade.
- *Republican* ....D. **6,900**
- " ....W. **6,901**
- *Times*....................D. **6,902**
- " ....W. **6,903**
- *Baner America* ....W. **6,904**
- *City Journal*............W. **6,905**
- *Der Herold*..............W. **6,906**
- *Free Press*..............W. **6,907**
- *Sunday Morning Free Press* ....W. **6,908**
- *Law Times*...............W. **6,909**
- *Wochenblatt*.............W. **6,910**
- *Knights' Monthly Record*.M. **6,911**

SELINSGROVE, Snyder Co., 2,000 p., on Susquehanna r. and Northern Central Rd., at junction of Lewistown division of Pennsylvania Central Rd., 50 m. from Harrisburg. Surrounded by an agricultural district.
- *Snyder Co. Tribune*......W. **6,912**
- *Times* ....W. **6,913**
- *Our Flag.*

SHAMOKIN, Northumberland Co., 7,000† p., on Shamokin Valley Rd., 18 m. from Sunbury.
- *Herald*..................W. **6,915**
- *Times*...................W. **6,916**

SHARON, Mercer Co., 4,221 p., on Pittsburgh & Erie Rd., 75 m. from Pittsburgh. Terminus of Cleveland & Sharon and Sharon & Greenfield Rds. Engaged in iron manufacturing and coal mining.
- *Herald*..................W. **6,917**
- *Mercer Co. Eagle*........W. **6,918**
- *Times*...................W. **6,919**

SHARPSVILLE, Mercer Co., 550 p., on Erie & Pittsburgh Rd., 24 m. from New Castle.
- *Advertiser*...............W. **6,920**

SHENANDOAH, Schuylkill Co., 8,000† p., on Lehigh Valley and Philadelphia & Reading and Lehigh Valley Rds., 13 m. from Pottsville. In a coal mining section.
- *Herald*...................D. **6,921**
- " ....W. **6,922**

SHICKSHINNY, Luzerne Co.,
- *Mountain Echo*..........W. **6,923**

SHIPPENSBURG, Cumberland Co., 2,065 p., on Cumberland Valley Rd., 41 m. from Harrisburg. Surrounded by a populous agricultural district and a centre of trade. State Normal School located here.
- *Democratic Chronicle*....W. **6,924**
- *News*....................W. **6,925**

SHIPPACK, Montgomery Co.
- *Der Naturalist und Allgemeine Neuigkeits-Bote*.W. **6,926**

SLATINGTON, Lehigh Co., 2,000† p., on Lehigh r. and Lehigh Valley Rd., 16 m. N. W. of Allentown. Slate quarries here.
- *News*.....................W. **6,927**

SMETHPORT, McKean Co., 1,500† p., in Keating township, 196 m. N. W. of Harrisburg. Engaged in general business.
- *McKean Co. Miner*......W. **6,928**

SOMERSET, Somerset Co., 1,050† p., on Somerset branch of Pittsburgh, Washington & Baltimore Rd., 70 m. from Pitts-

PENNSYLVANIA.

burgh. Lumber and iron trade carried on. Coal found in this vicinity. Fine agricultural district.
Democrat..................W. **6,929**
Herald..................W. **6,930**

SOUTH BETHLEHEM, Northampton Co., 3,556 p., on Lehigh r., near Bethlehem, and on Lehigh Valley, North Pennsylvania and Lehigh & Susquehanna Rds. Engaged in iron mining and manufacturing.
Saturday Star...........W. **6,931**

SPRING CITY, Chester Co., 900† p., on Schuylkill r. and Canal, near the line of Philadelphia & Reading Rd., 32 m. from Philadelphia.
Sun......................W. **6,932**

STRASBURG, Lancaster Co., 1,008 p., 46 m. from Harrisburg and 10 S. E. of Lancaster.
Free Press............W. **6,933**

STROUDSBURG, Monroe Co., 2,500† p., on Broadhead's Creek and Delaware, Lackawanna & Western Rd., 89 m. from New York. Surrounded by an agricultural country; possesses water power and is engaged in manufactures.
Jeffersonian..............W. **6,934**
Monroe Democrat........W. **6,935**

SUGAR GROVE, Warren Co.
Home Journal..........W. **6,936**

SUMMIT HILL, Carbon Co.
Intelligencer.............W. **6,937**

SUNBURY, c. h., Northumberland Co., 4,500† p., on Susquehanna r., at junction of Philadelphia & Erie with Northern Central Rd., 56 m. from Harrisburg and 36 from Williamsport. The Shamokin Valley & Pottsville Rd. terminates here. Shipping point for Shamokin coal fields. Engaged in lumber trade.
American................W. **6,938**
Gazette..................W **6,939**
Northumberland Co. Democrat....................W. **6,940**

SUSQUEHANNA DEPOT, Susquehanna Co., 2,729 p., on Erie Rd., 8 m. E. of Great Bend and 23 E. of Binghamton, and 191 W. from New York city. Repair shops located here.
Susquehanna Gazette....W. **6,941**
Susquehanna Journal....W **6,942**

TAMAQUA, Schuylkill Co., on Tamaqua r. and Little Schuylkill Rd., 15 m. from Pottsville. Coal is found here. Some manufacturing carried on.
Item.........................D. **6,943**
Courier....................W. **6,944**

TERRE HILL, Lancaster Co.
Standard.................W. **6,945**

TIDIOUTE, Warren Co.,'1,638 p., on Allegheny r. and Oil City & Allegheny R. Rd., 15 m. from Titusville. In the oil region. Some manufacturing carried on.
Warren Co. News........W. **6,946**

TIOGA, Tioga Co., 1,000† p., on Blossburg & Corning, Tioga and Wellsboro & Lawrenceville Rds. In a farming district and centre of trade.
Tioga Co. Express....... W. **6,947**

TIONESTA, c. h., Forest Co., 500† p., on Allegheny r. and Oil Creek & Allegheny R. Rd., 13 m. from Oil City. Engaged in lumber trade.

PENNSYLVANIA.

Forest Press.............W. **6,948**
Forest Republican........W. **6,949**

TITUSVILLE, Crawford Co., 8,639 p., on Pittsburgh, Titusville & Buffalo Rd., at junction of Union & Titusville Rd., 28 m. from Meadville. Engaged in oil trade and location of a number of refineries.
Courier...................D. **6,950**
" ....W. **6,951**
Herald....................D. **6,952**
" ....W. **6,953**

TOWANDA, Bradford Co., 4,000† p., on Susquehanna r., and Lehigh Valley Rd., at junction of Barclay, State Line & Sullivan Rds., 77 m. from Pittston. Contains a flourishing Collegiate Institute and several manufactories.
Bradford Argus.........W. **6,954**
Bradford Reporter.......W. **6,955**
Bradford Republican....W. **6,956**
Journal....................W. **6,957**

TRAPPE, Montgomery Co.
Providence Independent..W. **6,958**

TREMONT, Schuylkill Co., 2,250† p., 13 m. from Pottsville, on Philadelphia & Reading Rd. Engaged in coal mining and iron manufactures.
News......................W. **6,959**

TROY, Bradford Co., 1,081 p., on Northern Central Rd., 25 m. from Elmira, N. Y. In an agricultural and butter-producing section, and centre of trade.
Northern Tier Gazette....W. **6,960**

TUNKHANNOCK, Wyoming Co., 13,000† p., on N. branch of Susquehanna r. and Lehigh Valley Rd., 23 m. from Pittston, 145 from Harrisburg and 24 from Scranton. The centre of a grain trade and engaged in various industrial pursuits.
Republican...............W. **6,961**
Wyoming Democrat.....W. **6,962**

TYRONE, Blair Co., 2,200† p., on Pennsylvania Central Rd., at junction of Tyrone & Clearfield & Bald Eagle divisions, and terminus of Lewisburg Center & Spruce Creek Rd., 14 m. from Altoona. Engaged in iron, lime, lumber and stone coal trade.
Democrat.................W. **6,963**
Herald....................W. **6,964**
Phonetic Magazine.......M. **6,965**

UNION CITY, Erie Co., 3,000† p., on Atlantic & Great Western, Philadelphia & Erie and Union & Titusville Rds., 26 m. from Erie. The centre of an agricultural district and engaged in manufactures.
Enterprise................W. **6,966**
Times......................W. **6,967**

UNIONTOWN, Fayette Co., 3,600† p., at terminus of Fayette Co. branch of Pittsburgh, Baltimore & Washington Rd., 72 m. from Pittsburgh. Surrounded by a thickly settled agricultural district. Centre of the coke and iron region of Pennsylvania.
American Standard.....W. **6,968**
Genius of Liberty........W. **6,969**

WARREN, Warren Co., 3,000† p., on Allegheny r. and Philadelphia & Erie Rd., at junction of Dunkirk, Warren & Pittsburgh Rd., 66 m. from Erie.
Ledger....................W. **6,970**
Mail.......................W. **6,971**
Monthly Nation..........M. **6,972**

WASHINGTON, Washington Co., 4,560† p., on Chartiers Creek and Chartiers & Hempfield Rds., 31 m. from Pittsburgh.

PENNSYLVANIA.

Engaged in manufacturing. Seat of the Washington and Jefferson Colleges.
Observer..................W. **6,973**
Reporter..................W. **6,974**
Review and Examiner...W. **6,975**
Monthly Elevator........M. **6,976**

WATSONTOWN, Northumberland Co., 2,000† p., on W. branch Susquehanna r., on Philadelphia & Erie Rd., 17 m. N. of Sunbury and 20 E. of Williamsport. Considerable manufacturing carried on. Surrounded by a good agricultural district.
Record..................W. **6,977**

WAYNESBORO, Franklin Co.
Village Record...........W. **6,978**

WAYNESBURG, Greene Co., 2,000† p., 45 m. S. of Pittsburgh. Engaged in agriculture and stock raising.
Independent.............W. **6,979**
Messenger.................W. **6,980**
Republican.................W. **6,981**

WELLSBORO, Tioga Co., 2,800† p., on Wellsboro & Lawrenceville Rd., 24 m. from Lawrenceville, 40 from Corning, N. Y. In an agricultural section.
Agitator..................W. **6,982**
Gazette....................W. **6,983**

WEST CHESTER, Chester Co., 6,500† p., 92 m. from Philadelphia and 16 from Wilmington, Del., on Philadelphia & West Chester and Philadelphia & Baltimore Central Rds. Situated in an agricultural district and a centre of trade.
Local News...............D. **6,984**
American Republican...W. **6,985**
Chester Co. Village Record W. **6,986**
Jeffersonian...............W. **6,987**

WESTFIELD, Tioga Co.
Idea.......................W. **6,988**

WILKES-BARRE, c. h., Luzerne Co., 23,000† p., on N. branch of Susquehanna r., Pennsylvania Canal, Lehigh Valley and Lehigh & Susquehanna Rds., at junction of Nauticoke branch, 19 m. from Scranton. Centre of an agricultural district. Coal mining and lumber manufacturing are among the chief branches of industry.
Record of the Times.......D. **6,989**
" " " ".......W. **6,990**
Demokratischer Waechter W. **6,991**
Luzerne Co. Volksfreund.W. **6,992**
Luzerne Legal Register..W. **6,993**
Luzerne Union...........W. **6,994**

WILLIAMSPORT, c. h., Lycoming Co., 18,000† p., on W. branch Susquehanna r. and Canal, and at junction of Catawissa, Philadelphia & Erie, and Northern Central Rds., 96 m. from Harrisburg. Engaged in various manufactures and centre of the lumber trade. About forty steam saw mills located here.
Banner....................D. **6,995**
"..........................W. **6,996**
Gazette and Bulletin......D. **6,997**
" " "......Sund. **6,998**
" " "......W. **6,999**
Susquehanna Zeitung.S. W. **7,000**
Sun and Lycoming Democrat....................W. **7,001**
Sunday Times............W. **7,002**
West Branch Beobachter.W. **7,003**
Parish Dial................M. **7,004**

WRIGHTSVILLE, York Co., 1,500† p., in Héllam township, on Susquehanna r., Susquehanna and Tidewater Canals, and York branch of Pennsylvania Central Rd., 31 m. from Harrisburg. Engaged in the lumber, coal, lime and iron trade.
Star.......................W. **7,005**

YORK, York Co., 4,500† p., on Codoms Creek and Northern Central Rd., at junction of York branch of Pennsylvania Central Rd., 82 m. from Philadelphia and 50 from Baltimore. In a thickly populated agricultural district. Engaged in manufacturing iron and steel. Centre of trade.
Daily......................D. **7,006**
Telegram.
American Lutheran.....W. **7,008**
Democratic Press.........W. **7,009**
Gazette (German)........W. **7,010**
Gazette....................W. **7,011**
Pennsylvanian............W. **7,012**
Republican................W. **7,013**
True Democrat...........W. **7,014**
Rural Journal............M. **7,015**
Teachers' Journal........M. **7,016**

YOUNGSVILLE, Warren Co.
Warren Co. Press.......W. **7,017**

RHODE ISLAND.

BRISTOL, Bristol Co., 6,000† p., on Narragansett Bay and Providence, Warren & Bristol Rd., 15 m. from Providence. Has a good harbor. Engaged in manufacturing, gardening and commerce.
Phœnix...................W. **7,018**

CENTRAL FALLS, Providence Co., 6,281† p., in Lincoln township of 7,889 p., on Blackstone r. and Providence & Worcester Rd., 1 m. from Pawtucket and 5 from Providence. Engaged in manufacturing. Several cotton mills here.
Visitor....................W. **7,019**

GREENWICH, Kent Co., 3,250† p., on Narragansett Bay and Stonington & Providence Rd., 15 m. from Providence. Engaged in commerce, manufactures and fishery.
Rhode Island Pendulum.W. **7,020**

NEWPORT, Newport Co., semi-State capital, 14,300† p., on Rhode Island, having a fine harbor. The Fall River line of steamers touch here. Connected to Boston by Old Colony & Newport Rd. A city of considerable commercial importance and a fashionable summer resort.
News.......................D. **7,021**
Journal....................W. **7,022**
Mercury...................W. **7,023**

PAWTUCKET, Providence Co., 18,460† p., on Blackstone r., 4 m. from Providence. Engaged in various manufactures. The commerce of Pawtucket is quite large. The first cotton manufactory in the U. S. was established here.
Gazette and Chronicle....W. **7,024**

PHENIX, Kent Co.
Pawtuxet Valley Gleaner W. **7,025**

PROVIDENCE, Providence Co., semi-State capital, 68,904 p., at head of Narragansett Bay. Connected to Boston, New York and other principal cities by railroads. The commerce and manufactures are extensive and important. The largest city in the State. Seat of Brown University.
Bulletin.................. D. **7,026**

RHODE ISLAND.

Evening Press............D. **7,027**
Rhode Island Press......W. **7,028**
Journal....................D. **7,029**
Manufacturers' and Farmers' Journal.......S. W. **7,030**
Rhode Island Country Journal................W. **7,031**
Star.......................D. **7,032**
General Advertiser and Gazette..................W. **7,033**
Sun.......................W. **7,034**
Sunday Dispatch........W. **7,035**
Town and Country.......W. **7,036**
Freemason's Repository..M. **7,037**
Temple of Honor........M. **7,038**

WAKEFIELD, Washington Co., 850 p., in South Kingston township, at head of Point Judith inlet. Engaged in manufactures.
Narragansett Times.....W. **7,039**

WARREN, Bristol Co., 4,000† p., on Narragansett Bay and Providence, Warren & Bristol Rd., 10 m. from Providence.
Gazette..................W. **7,040**

WESTERLY, Washington Co., 5,708† p., partly in R. I. and partly in Conn., on Pawtucket r. and the Providence & Stonington Rd., 44 m. from Providence. Engaged in cotton and other manufactures.
Narragansett Weekly....W. **7,041**

TOWN OF WOONSOCKET, Providence Co., 13,576† p., on Blackstone r. and Providence & Worcester Rd., 16 m. from Providence. Largely engaged in cotton, woolen and other manufactures.
Reporter..................D. **7,042**
Le Courrier Canadien...W. **7,043**
Patriot...................W. **7,044**

SOUTH CAROLINA.

ABBEVILLE, c. h., Abbeville Co., 3,034 p., on a branch of Greenville & Columbia Rd., 106 m. from Columbia and 60 from Augusta, Ga. Principally occupied in cultivation of cotton.
Medium....................W. **7,045**
Press and Banner........W. **7,046**

AIKEN, Barnwell Co., 2,259 p., on South Carolina Rd., 17 m. from Augusta, Ga., and 120 N. W. of Charleston. Engaged in agriculture and the shipping of cotton.
Courier-Journal..........W. **7,047**
Tribune....................W. **7,048**

ANDERSON, c. h., Anderson Co., 2,765† p., on Anderson branch of Greenville & Columbia Rd., and Southern terminus of Blue Ridge Rd., 127 m. from Columbia. A cotton market for the N. W. portion of the State.
Intelligencer..............W. **7,049**
Journal....................W. **7,050**

BARNWELL, Barnwell Co., 965† p., 10 m. from South Carolina Rd. at Blackville and 90 from Charleston.
Sentinel...................W. **7,051**

BEAUFORT, Beaufort Co., 1,739 p., on Port Royal r., about 15 m. from Atlantic Ocean and 80 S. W. of Charleston. Has a good harbor. Rice and sweet potatoes are cultivated in this section. Yellow pine and cypress lumber are exported.
Port Royal Standard and Commercial.............W. **7,052**
Tribune....................W. **7,053**

SOUTH CAROLINA.

BENNETTSVILLE, c. h., Marlborough Co., 1,736 p., on Crop Creek, 8 m. from the Great Pedee r.
Marlboro' Times..........W. **7,054**

BLACKVILLE, c. h., Barnwell Co., 600† p., on South Carolina Rd., 90 m. N. W. of Charleston and 30 from Aiken.
News......................W. **7,055**
Sun........................W. **7,056**

CAMDEN, c. h., Kershaw Co., 1,007 p., on Camden branch of South Carolina Rd., 5 m. E. of Wateree r.
Journal...................W. **7,057**
Kershaw Gazette.........W. **7,058**

CHARLESTON, c. h., Charleston Co., 54,000 p., at junction of Ashley and Cooper rs., 7 m. from Atlantic Ocean. It has a fine harbor and a large foreign and domestic trade. Railroads from the interior centre here, making it a shipping point for cotton and other produce.
News and Courier........D. **7,059**
" " " ....T. W. **7,060**
News......................W. **7,061**
Deutsche Zeitung......S. W. **7,062**
" " ....W. **7,063**
Independent..............W. **7,064**
Lutheran Visitor.........W. **7,065**
Sunday Times............W. **7,066**
*South-Eastern Advocate*B. W. **7,067**
Monthly Record..........M. **7,068**
Medical Journal and Review......................Qr. **7,069**

CHERAW, Chesterfield Co., 1,600† p., on Great Pedee r., at head of navigation, and at terminus of Cheraw & Darlington Rd., 142 m. from Charleston. Cotton is shipped from this point.
Chesterfield Democrat....W. **7,070**

CHESTER, c. h., Chester Co., 944 p., on Charlotte, Columbia & Augusta Rd., at junction of Kings Mountain Rd., 65 m. from Columbia, in a cotton-raising district.
Reporter..................W. **7,071**

CLINTON, Laurens Co.
Our Monthly.............M. **7,072**

COKESBURY, Abbeville Co.
Rural Carolinian........M. **7,073**

COLUMBIA, c. h., Richland Co., State capital, 9,298 p., on Columbia Canal and Congaree r., 130 m. from Charleston. Here converge the lines of South Carolina, Greenville & Columbia and Charlotte, Columbia & Augusta Rds., making it a business and manufacturing centre. Seat of South Carolina College.
Rigister...................D. **7,074**
Union-Herald.............D. **7,075**
Christian Neighbor......W. **7,076**
Southern Presbyterian...W. **7,077**
Temperance Advocate.
Working Christian.......W. **7,079**
Carolina Teacher.........M. **7,080**
Southern Presbyterian Review.....................Qr. **7,081**

CONWAYBORO, c. h., Horry Co., 1,400 p., on Waccamaw r., 40 m. above Georgetown, 100 m. N. E. of Charleston and 15 from Atlantic Ocean. The sandy soil produces pine, from which turpentine is manufactured. Naval stores are produced.
Horry News.............W. **7,082**

DARLINGTON, c. h., Darlington Co., 1,000 p., on Cheraw & Darlington Rd., 10

SOUTH CAROLINA.

m. from Florence and 112 from Charleston.
Southerner ....W. **7,083**

DUE WEST, Abbeville Co., 700† p., about 12 m. N. of Abbeville.
Associate Reformed Presbyterian...............W. **7,084**

EDGEFIELD, c. h., Edgefield Co., 846 p., 10 m. W. of Charlotte, Columbia & Augusta Rd., about 25 m. N. of Augusta, Ga., and 56 S. by W. of Columbia. Cotton-growing district.
Advertiser...............W. **7,085**

FLORENCE, Darlington Co.
Pioneer..................W. **7,086**

GEORGETOWN, c. h., Georgetown Co., 2,080 p., on Winyaw Bay, 15 m. from the sea. Has some domestic commerce and surrounded by a rice-growing district.
Comet...................W. **7,087**
Times...................W. **7,088**

GREENVILLE, Greenville Co., 2,758 p., at terminus of Greenville & Columbia Rd., 144 m. from Columbia. Seat of the Southern Baptist and Theological Seminary, Furman University, Female College and high school. The Atlanta & Richmond Air Line Rd. has an extensive depot in the city.
News.....................D. **7,089**
" ....W. **7,090**
Enterprise and Mountaineer................W. **7,091**

KINGSTREE, c. h., Williamsburg Co., 700 p., on Black r. and on Northeastern Rd., 64 m. N. of Charleston.
Star.....................W. **7,092**
Williamsburg Republican W. **7,093**

LANCASTER, c. h., Lancaster Co., 591 p., 72 m. N. of Columbia and 30 E. of Chesterville.
Ledger...................W. **7,094**

LAURENSVILLE, c. h., Laurens Co., 900 p., on a branch of Greenville & Columbia Rd., about 73 m. from Columbia.
Herald...................W. **7,095**

LEXINGTON, c. h., Lexington Co.
Dispatch.................W. **7,096**

MANNING, c. h., Clarendon Co., 1,000 p., 70 m. N. by W. of Charleston and 50 E. by S. of Columbia.
Clarendon Press.........W. **7,097**

MARION, c. h., Marion Co., 1,240 p., on Wilmington, Columbia & Augusta Rd., 110 m. from Columbia. In a cotton-growing district and centre of trade.
Merchant and Farmer ...W. **7,098**
Star.....................W. **7,099**

NEWBERRY, c. h., Newberry Co., 3,000† p., on Greenville & Columbia Rd., 47 m. from Columbia.
Herald...................W. **7,100**
Progressive Age..........W. **7,101**

NINETY SIX, Abbeville Co.
Herald...................W. **7,102**

ORANGEBURG, c. h., Orangeburg Co., 1,700† p., on South Carolina Rd., 51 m. from Columbia and 86 from Charleston. A trade centre.
Free Citizen.............W. **7,103**
News and Times.........W. **7,104**

PICKENS, c. h., Pickens Co., 400† p., between Wolf and Town Creeks, 7 m. from R. & A. Air Line Rd. and 20 from Greenville. Possesses water power. Centre of trade. Minerals are found here.
Sentinel.................W. **7,105**

ROCK HILL, York Co.
Granger..................W. **7106**

SPARTANBURG, c. h., Spartanburg Co., 1,080 p., on Spartanburg & Union Rd., 93 m. N. W. of Columbia. Gold and iron mines in this district.
Carolina Spartan.
Herald...................W. **7,108**
Southern Methodist......W. **7,109**
Way of Holiness.........M. **7,110**

SUMMIT, Lexington Co.
Courier..................W. **7,111**

SUMTER, c. h., Sumter Co., 1,807 p., on Wilmington & Weldon Rd., 50 m. from Columbia.
True Southron...........W. **7,112**
Watchman.............. W. **7,113**

TIMMONSVILLE, Darlington Co.
News......................W. **7,114**

UNION, c. h., Union Co., 1,250 p., on Spartanburg & Union Rd., 65 m. N. W. of Columbia. Gold and iron ore are found in this district.
Times.

WALHALLA, c. h., Oconee Co., 716 p., on Blue Ridge Rd., about 30 m. W. of Anderson. Surrounded by an agricultural district.
Keowee Courier..........W. **7,116**

WALTERBORO, c. h., Colleton Co., about 30 m. W. of Charleston and 10 N. of Charleston & Savannah Rd.
News.....................W. **7,117**

WINNSBORO, c. h., Fairfield Co., 1,124 p., on Charlotte, Columbia & Augusta Rd., 34 m. from Columbia.
News..................T. W. **7,118**
Fairfield Herald.........W. **7,119**

YORKVILLE, c. h., York Co., 1,000 p., on Kings Mountain Rd., 22 m. from Chesterville and 83 from Columbia. A place of active trade.
Enquirer.................W **7,120**
Family Visitor........S. M. **7,121**

TENNESSEE.

ALAMO, Crockett Co.
Crockett Co. Sentinel.....W. **7,122**

ARLINGTON, Houston Co.
Houston Co. Times.

ATHENS, c. h., McMinn Co., 1,000† p., on East Tennessee, Virginia & Georgia Rd., 55 m. from Knoxville.
News.......................W. **7,124**
Post.......................W. **7,125**

BELLVILLE, Crockett Co., 900† p., on Louisville and Memphis Rd., 69 m. from Memphis.
Enterprise...............W. **7,126**

BOLIVAR, c. h., Hardeman Co., 1,200† p., on Mississippi Central Rd., about 65 m. E. of Memphis.
Bulletin..................W. **7,127**

BRISTOL, Sullivan Co., 3,500† p., on East Tennessee, Virginia and Georgia Rd., at junction of Atlantic, Mississippi & Ohio Rd. The Virginia State line passes

TENNESSEE.

through the village, 130 m. from Knoxville.
Courier....................W. 7,128
Souvenir....................M. 7,129

BROWNSVILLE, c. h., Haywood Co., 3,000† p., on Memphis and Louisville division of Louisville, Nashville & Great Southern Rd., 117 m. W. S. W. of Nashville, 5 from Hatchie r. and 57 from Memphis. In a cotton-growing district and centre of trade.
Democrat....................W. 7,130
States....................W. 7,131

CALHOUN, McMinn Co.
Hiwassee Reporter.......W. 7,132

CAMDEN, c. h., Benton Co.
Benton Banner..........W. 7,133

CHATTANOOGA, Hamilton Co., 6,093 p., on Tennessee r., at terminus of Nashville & Chattanooga, Western & Atlantic, East Tennessee, Virginia & Georgia Rds., 151 m. from Nashville. The Tennessee r. is navigable to this point a great part of the year. A large amount of trade centres here, making it one of the most important points in east Tennessee. Engaged in manufacturing iron and various other articles.
Commercial..............D. 7,134
Times....................D. 7,135
" ....W. 7,136
Tennessee Journal.......W. 7,137

CLARKSVILLE, c. h., Montgomery Co., 3,200 p., on Cumberland r. and Memphis & Louisville Rd., 199 m. from Memphis and 45 N. W. of Nashville. Surrounded by a tobacco raising district and centre of trade. A shipping point for tobacco and other farm produce. Some manufacturing done here.
Chronicle................W. 7,138
Tobacco Leaf............W. 7,139

CLEVELAND, c. h., Bradley Co., 2,253 p., on East Tennessee, Virginia & Georgia Rd., at junction of Dalton branch, 30 m. from Chattanooga, 140 from Atlanta.
Banner..................W. 7,140
Herald..................W. 7,141

CLIFTON, Wayne Co.
Wayne Co. Citizen.......W. 7,142

CLINTON, c. h., Anderson Co.
Tribune..................W. 7,143

COLUMBIA, c. h., Maury Co., 2,550 p., on Duck r. and on Nashville & Decatur Rd., at junction of Mount Pleasant branch, 46 m. from Nashville. Has two large female colleges.
Herald and Mail.........W. 7,144
Journal..................W. 7,145
Guardian.

COOKEVILLE, c. h., Putnam Co., 420 p., 80 m. E. of Nashville. An agricultural county.
Middle Tennesseean......W. 7,147

COVINGTON, c. h., Tipton Co., 1,500 p., about 15 m. from Mississippi r. and 30 N. E. of Memphis. In an agricultural district and a trade centre.
Tipton Record...........W. 7,148

DOVER, c. h., Stewart Co., 850 p., on Cumberland r., 75 m. from Nashville and near Louisville & Memphis Rd.
Record..................W. 7,149

TENNESSEE.

DRESDEN, c. h., Weakley Co.
*West Tennessee Democrat*W. 7,150

DYERSBURG, c. h., Dyer Co., 1,300† p., on Forked Deer r., and 160 m. W. of Nashville and 70 m. N. of Memphis.
Dyer Co. Progress.......W. 7,151
Neal's State Gazette.......W. 7,152

ELIZABETHTON, c. h., Carter Co.
Republican..............W. 7,153

FAYETTEVILLE, c. h., Lincoln Co., 1,500† p., on Elk r. and Winchester & Alabama Rd., 73 m. S. by E. of Nashville. Centre of trade. Some manufacturing carried on.
Express..................W. 7,154
Observer..................W. 7,155

FRANKLIN, Williamson Co., 2,000† p., on Nashville & Decatur Rd., 19 m. from Nashville. In an agricultural and manufacturing section and seat of Tennessee Female College.
Review and Journal.....W. 7,156

GALLATIN, c. h., Sumner Co., 2,123 p., on Louisville & Nashville Rd., 26 m. from Nashville. Engaged in cotton and woolen manufacturing. Surrounded by an agricultural and stock-raising district.
Examiner................W. 7,157
Tenneseean..............W. 7,158

GRAND JUNCTION, Hardeman Co.
Bell Co. Times...........W. 7159

GREENVILLE, c. h., Greene Co., 1,039 p., on the East Tennessee & Virginia Rd., 74 m. from Knoxville.
Intelligencer.............W. 7,160
New Era..................W. 7,161
Union and American....W. 7,162

HARTSVILLE, Sumner Co., 1,000 p., near Cumberland r., about 45 m. E. by N. of Nashville.
Sentinel..................W. 7,163

HOME, Greene Co.
Christian Republic.......M. 7,164

HUMBOLDT, Gibson Co., 2,296 p., on Mobile & Ohio Rd., at intersection of Louisville & Memphis Rd., 82 m. from Memphis.
Grange Journal..........W. 7,165
Herald...................W. 7,166

HUNTINGDON, c. h., Carroll Co., 890 p., on Nashville & Northwestern Rd., 107 m. from Nashville. An agricultural, produce and cotton raising region.
Tennessee Republican....W. 7,167

JACKSON, Madison Co., 1,500 p., on Forked Deer r., 150 m. W. S. W. of Nashville. At junction of Mississippi Central and Mobile & Ohio Rds. A cotton market for several adjoining counties. Railroad repair shops located here.
Dispatch..................W. 7,168
Sun......................W. 7,169
Whig and Tribune.......W. 7,170
Whig Banner.............W. 7,171

JASPER, c. h., Marion Co., 720 p., on Sequatchy r., 6 m. from its entrance into the Tennessee and 20 W. of Chattanooga.
Valley Herald...........W. 7,172

JONESBOROUGH, c. h., Washington Co., 1,445 p., on East Tennessee, Virginia & Georgia Rd., 98 m. from Knoxville. An agricultural district. Principal productions corn, wheat, oats, grass, &c.
Herald and Tribune.....W. 7,173
Journal..................W. 7,174

KINGSTON, c. h., Roane Co., 1,000 p., at junction of Clinch and Tennessee rs., 145 m. E. by S. of Nashville and 20 W. by S. of Knoxville. A shipping point for the products of the surrounding country.
East Tennesseean........W. **7,175**

KNOXVILLE, c. h., Knox Co., 8,682 p., on Holston r., 185 m. E. of Nashville, the centering point for four railroads, 110 m. from Chattanooga and 310 from Lynchburg, Va. Steamboats ascend the river to this point, making it a place of business importance and centre of trade. Agriculture and commerce the principal branches.
Age........................D. **7,176**
Living Age and Grange Outlook..................W. **7,177**
Press and Herald.........D. **7,178**
Press and Messenger.....W. **7,179**
Tribune...................D. **7,180**
Whig and Chronicle......D. **7,181**
" " " .....W. **7,182**
Holston Methodist.......W. **7,183**
University Monthly......M. **7,184**

LAWRENCEBURG, c. h., Lawrence Co., 540 p., on Shoal r., about 80 m. S. by W. of Nashville.
Free Press................W. **7,185**

LEBANON, c. h., Wilson Co., 2,073 p., on Tennessee & Pacific Rd., 31 m. E. of Nashville. Surrounded by a tobacco-raising country. Engaged in manufacturing. Seat of Cumberland University.
Herald...................W. **7,186**

LEWISBURG, c. h., Marshall Co., 950 p., 60 m. S. of Nashville and 15 S. E. of Columbus. In an agricultural section.
Marshall Gazette.........W. **7,187**

LEXINGTON, c. h., Henderson Co.
Reporter...................W. **7,188**

LOUDON, Roane Co., 1,500† p., on Tennessee r. and East Tennessee, Virginia & Georgia Rd., 27 m. from Knoxville.
Times......................W. **7,189**

LYNCHBURG, Lincoln Co., 1,750 p., 10 m. W. by S. of Tullahama and 68 S. by E. of Nashville.
Sentinel...................W. **7,190**

McMINNVILLE, c. h., Warren Co., 1,700 p., 75 m. S. E. of Nashville, at terminus of McMinnville & Manchester Rd., and 34 from Tullahama. Centre of a fine trade. Engaged in manufacturing, and surrounded by an agricultural and fruit-growing district.
New Era.................W. **7,191**

MANCHESTER, c. h., Coffee Co., 600 p., on McMinnville & Manchester Rd., 70 m. from Nashville. Engaged in manufactures. Excellent water power.
Guardian................W. **7,192**

MARYVILLE, c. h., Blount Co., 811 p., on Knoxville and Charleston Rd., 16 m. S. of Knoxville. Seat of Maryville College.
Republican...........S. W. **7,193**
Independent...............W. **7,194**

MEMPHIS, c. h., Shelby Co., 60,000† p., on Miss. r., at head of perpetual navigation for largest sized steamboats. Fourth largest cotton receiving point in America—second largest in sales. Annual commerce $75,000,000, of which half cotton; terminus Memphis & Charleston, M. & Louisville, Miss. & Tenn., M. & Paducah and Memphis & Little Rock Rds., making it a great trade centre. Largest city in the State and chief business centre between St. Louis and New Orleans.
Appeal...................D. **7,195**
" ....W. **7,196**
Avalanche...............D. **7,197**
" ....W. **7,198**
Public Ledger............D. **7,199**
" " ....W. **7,200**
Baptist..................W. **7,201**
Christian Witness.
Planet...................W. **7,203**
Southern Catholic.........W. **7,204**
Southern Farmer.........W. **7,205**
Western Methodist........W. **7,206**
Southern Granger.....S. M. **7,207**
Masonic Jewel............M. **7,208**
Mayfield's Happy Home..M. **7,209**

MILAN, Gibson Co.
Exchange................W. **7,210**

MORRISTOWN, Hamblen Co., 1,200† p., on East Tennessee, Virginia & Georgia Rd., and at crossing of Cincinnati, Cumberland Gap & Charleston Rd., in an agricultural district near Holston r., 42 m. N. E. of Knoxville.
Baptist Reflector.........W. **7,211**
Gazette...................W. **7,212**
Spy.

MURFREESBORO, c. h., Rutherford Co., 4,000 p., on Nashville & Chattanooga Rd., 32 m. from Nashville. Surrounded by an agricultural and fruit-growing region. Cotton cultivated to a considerable extent.
News.....................W. **7,214**

NASHVILLE, c. h., State capital, Davidson Co., 25,865 p., on Cumberland r., 200 m. from its mouth. Engaged in river commerce and centre of trade. Several cotton mills located here. Iron and coal districts near. Railroads centre here from New Orleans, Memphis, Louisville, Chattanooga and other points.
American................D. **7,215**
" ....S. W. **7,216**
" ....W. **7,217**
Baptist Watchman......W. **7,218**
Bulletin...................W. **7,219**
Christian Advocate......W. **7,220**
Commercial and Legal Reporter..................W. **7,221**
*Cumberland Presbyterian*W. **7,222**
Good Templar.
Gospel Advocate..........W. **7,224**
Rural Sun................W. **7,225**
Southern Household.....W. **7,226**
Sunday-School Visitor....W. **7,227**
" " " ..S. M. **7,228**
" " " ....M. **7,229**
Tennessee Post.
Journal of Medicine and Surgery.................M. **7,231**
Ladies' Pearl..............M. **7,232**
Sunday Morning.
Sunday-School Magazine.M. **7,234**
Theological Medium.

PARIS, c. h., Henry Co., 1,797 p., on Memphis & Louisville Rd., 130 m. from Memphis and 110 W. of Nashville.
Intelligencer.............W. **7,236**

PULASKI, c. h., Giles Co., 3,041 p., on Nashville & Decatur division of Louisville, Nashville & Great Southern Rd., 75 m. S. of Nashville. Surrounded by an agricultural and stock raising district.
Citizen...................W. **7,237**

TENNESSEE.

RIPLEY, c. h., Lauderdale Co., 1,000 p., 60 m. from Memphis, in an agricultural district heavily timbered.
News......................W. **7,238**
Amethyst.

SAVANNAH, c. h., Hardin Co.
Tennessee Transcript.....W. **7,240**
District Directory.

SEWANEE, Franklin Co.
University Record........M. **7,242**

SHELBYVILLE, c. h., Bedford Co., 3,500† p., on a branch of Nashville & Chattanooga Rd., 60 m. S. E. of Nashville.
Commercial..............W. **7,243**
Gazette....................W. **7,244**

SOMERVILLE, c. h., Fayette Co., 1,600† p., 50 m. E. of Memphis, on a branch of Memphis & Charleston Rd. Centre of an agricultural district.
Falcon....................W. **7,245**

SPARTA, c. h., White Co., 500† p., on Calf-kill Creek, 75 m. E. by S. of Nashville.
Index.....................W. **7,246**

SPRINGFIELD, c. h., Robertson Co., 2,140 p., on Evansville, Henderson & Nashville Rd., 25 m. N. by W. of Nashville. Engaged in agriculture and stock-raising.
Record....................W. **7,247**

SWEETWATER, Monroe Co., 1,069 p., on East Tennessee, Virginia & Georgia Rd., about 130 m. E. S. E. from Nashville, 43 W. of Knoxville. Engaged in agriculture, stock-raising and minerals.
Enterprise................W. **7,248**

TRACY CITY, c. h., Grundy Co.
Miners' and Manufacturers' Reporter........W. **7,249**

TRENTON, c. h., Gibson Co., 3,000 p., on Mobile & Ohio Rd., 130 m. W. of Nashville, 56 from Columbus, Ky. Centre of an agricultural country. Engaged in manufacturing. Two colleges located here.
News......................W. **7,250**

TROY, c. h., Obion Co., 500 p., on Mobile & Ohio Rd., at junction of Paducah & Gulf Rd., 56 m. from Jackson.
Obion Co. News.

UNION CITY, Obion Co., 2,479 p., in N. W. part of State, near Obion r., and at intersection of Mobile & Ohio and Nashville & Northwestern Rds., 150 m. W. of Nashville. Centre of an agricultural district.
Reveille..................W. **7,252**

UNION DEPOT, Sullivan Co.
Sullivan Landmark......W. **7,253**

WAVERLY, Humphreys Co., 350† p., on Nashville & Northwestern Rd., 67 m. from Nashville.
Journal...................W. **7,254**

WINCHESTER, Franklin Co., 1,700† p., on Elk r. and Winchester & Alabama Rd., 84 m. from Nashville. Several institutions of learning located here.
Home Journal...... ...W. **7,255**

WOODBURY, Cannon Co., 420 p.
Press......................W. **7,256**
Baptist Messenger........M. **7,257**

TEXAS.

ATHENS, c. h., Henderson Co.
Courier...................W. **7,258**

AUSTIN, c. h., Travis Co., State capital, 15,000† p., on Colorado r., 230 m. N W. of Galveston. Engaged in manufacturing.
Democratic Statesman....D. **7,259**
" " ...W. **7,260**
Evening News............D. **7,261**
State Gazette.............D. **7,262**
" " ....W. **7,263**
Intelligencer Echo.
Texas Staats-Bulletin....W. **7,265**
Stylus.....................M. **7,266**

BASTROP, c. h., Bastrop Co., 2,500† p., on Colorado r., 35 m. below Austin.
Advertiser................W **7,267**

BELLVILLE, c. h., Austin Co.
Beacon...................W. **7,268**

BELTON, c. h., Bell Co., 2,000† p., on Leon r., 59 m. N. of Austin and 40 W. of Houston & Texas Central Rd.
Journal....................W. **7,269**
Review....................W. **7,270**

BLANCO CITY, c. h., Blanco Co.
Busy Bee.................W. **7,271**

BONHAM, c. h., Fannin Co., 1,250 p., 12 m. S. of Red r., 60 N. by E. of Dallas and 270 N. by E. of Austin. Situated in a corn and cotton growing region. Farming and stock raising the chief industries.
Christian Messenger.....W. **7,272**
News.......................W. **7,273**
North Texas Enterprise..W. **7,274**

BREMOND, Robertson Co.
Sentinel...................W. **7,275**

BRENHAM, c. h., Washington Co., 2,500 p., on western branch of Houston & Texas Central Rd., 60 m. N. W. of Houston and 10 W. of Brazos r. Agriculture the principal branch of industry. A number of manufactories located here.
Banner....................W. **7,276**
Der Texas Volksbote.....W. **7,277**

BROWNSVILLE, c. h., Cameron Co., 5,000 p., on Rio Grande r., 40 m. from its mouth, and opposite Matamoras, Mexico. Engaged in commerce and has a large Mexican trade. Stock raising is carried on in the surrounding district.
Evening Ranchero........D. **7,278**
Ranchero.................W. **7,279**
*Rio Grande Democrat*S. W. **7,280**
Sentinel................S. W. **7,281**
" ....W. **7,282**

BRYAN, c. h., Brazos Co., 3,500 p., near Brazos r., 100 m. N. W. of Houston, on Houston & Texas Central Rd. Seat of several institutions of learning.
Appeal....................W. **7,283**
Post.......................W. **7,284**

BURKEVILLE, Newton Co.
Baptist Messenger.......W. **7,285**

BURNET, c. h., Burnet Co.
Bulletin..................W. **7,286**
Western Texas Advertiser.

CALDWELL, c. h., Burleson Co.
Eagle.....................W. **7,288**

CALVERT, Robertson Co., 2,800 p., on Houston & Texas Central Rd., 130 m. N. W. of Houston. Situated in the geographical centre of the State and in the cotton belt.
Central Texan...........W. **7,289**

TEXAS.

CAMBRIDGE, Clay Co.
Texas North-West .... W. **7,290**

CENTREVILLE, c. h., Leon Co.
Texas Gladiator .... W. **7,291**

CLARKSVILLE, c. h., Red River Co., 617 p., 15 m. from Red r. and 330 N. E. of Austin. Surrounded by a farming region. Considerable lumber manufacturing carried on.
Standard.
Times .... W. **7,293**

CLEBURNE, Johnson Co., 686 p., 162 m. N. of Austin.
Chronicle .... W. **7,294**

COLUMBUS, c. h., Colorado Co., 2,000 p., on Colorado r., terminus of Galveston, Harrisburg & San Antonio Rd., 95 m. S. E. of Austin and 60 W. of Houston.
Colorado Citizen .... W. **7,295**

COMANCHE, c. h., Comanche Co.
Chief .... W. **7,296**

COOPER, c. h., Delta Co.
Delta Co. Record .... W. **7,297**

CORPUS CHRISTI, c. h., Neuces Co., 600 p., on Corpus Christi Bay, at mouth of Neuces r., 230 m. S. of Galveston. It has a good harbor and considerable commerce.
Times .... D. **7,298**
" .... W. **7,299**
Gazette .... W. **7,300**

CORSICANA, c. h., Navarro Co., 1,200 p., on Houston & Texas Central Rd., 20 m. W. of Trinity r. and 180 N. by E. of Austin.
Index .... W. **7,301**
Observer .... W. **7,302**
Odd-Fellow .... M. **7,303**

COTTON GIN, Freestone Co.
Freestone Herald .... W. **7,304**

CROCKET, c. h., Houston Co., 2,000† p., on Houston & Great Northern Rd., 100 m. N. of Houston. A centre of trade.
Texas Patron .... W. **7,305**

CUERO, De Witt Co.
Star .... W. **7,306**

DALLAS, c. h., Dallas Co., 3,000 p., on Trinity r. and Houston & Texas Central Rd., 261 m. from Houston and 215 N. by E. of Austin. Centre of a wheat-growing region. Engaged in manufacturing.
Commercial .... D. **7,307**
Commercial Sunday Press .... W. **7,308**
Herald .... D. **7,309**
" .... W. **7,310**
Norton's Union Intelligencer ... . W. **7,311**
Sunday Dispatch .... W. **7,312**
Texas Baptist .... W. **7,313**

DECATUR, Wise Co., 500 p., 75 m. N. W. of Dallas and 40 N. of Weatherford.
Advance Guard .... W. **7,314**

DENISON, Grayson Co.
Cresset .... D. **7,315**
" .... W. **7,316**
News .... D. **7,317**
" .... W. **7,318**

DENTON, c. h., Denton Co., 1,600† p., on Pecan Creek, 40 m. N. W. of Dallas and 241 N. of Austin.
Monitor .... W. **7,319**
Review .... W. **7,320**

ENNIS, Ellis Co.
Ellis Co. News .... W. **7,321**
Saturday Review .... W. **7,322**

FORT WORTH, Tarrant Co., 850 p., on Trinity r., 210 m. N. of Austin and 25 W. of Dallas.
Democrat .... W. **7,323**
Standard .... W. **7,324**

FREDERICKSBURG, c. h., Gillespie Co.
Sentinel .... W. **7,325**

GAINESVILLE, c. h., Cooke Co., 1,000 p., a few m. from Red r. and 270 N. of Austin. Centre of trade for country surrounding and a depot for supplies for drovers. Large droves of cattle pass northward every spring and fall.
Gazette .... W. **7,326**

GALVESTON, c. h., Galveston Co., 13,818 p., on an island at mouth of Galveston Bay. Engaged in commerce and trade, and having the finest harbor in the State. Largest city in the State.
Civilian .... D. **7,327**
" .... W. **7,328**
News .... D. **7,329**
" .... W. **7,330**
Texas Post .... D. **7,331**
" " .... W. **7,332**
Argus .... Sund. **7,333**
Christian Advocate ...... W. **7,334**
Spectator .... Sund. **7,335**
Texas Catholic .... Sund. **7,336**
Visitor .... M. **7,337**

GATESVILLE, c. h., Coryell Co., 1,455 p., on Leon r., 40 m. from Waco and Belton, and 80 N. of Austin. Engaged in agriculture and stock-raising.
Sun .... W. **7,338**

GEORGETOWN, c. h., Williamson Co., 1,200† p., about 25 m. N. of Austin. In an agricultural district.
County Record .... S. W. **7,339**

GIDDINGS, c. h., Lee Co.
Tribune .... W. **7,340**

GOLIAD, c. h., Goliad Co., 700 p., on San Antonio r., 120 m. S. by E. of Austin. Agriculture and stock-raising are the principal branches of industry. Fine water power.
Guard.

GONZALES, c. h., Gonzales Co., 1,500 p., on Guadaloupe r., at mouth of San Marcos r., 70 m. S. by E. of Austin. Engaged in farming and grazing.
Inquirer.

GRANBERY, c. h., Hood Co.
Vidette .... W. **7,343**

GREENVILLE, c. h., Hunt Co., 850 p., 50 m. N. E. of Dallas.
Independent .... S. M. **7,344**
Herald.

GROESBECK, c. h., Limestone Co.
Democrat .. .. W. **7,346**

HALLETTSVILLE, c. h., Lavacca Co., 500 p., on Lavacca r., 35 m. W. of Columbus. Engaged in growing cotton and corn, etc.
Herald and Planter ...... W. **7,347**

HEARNE, Robertson Co.
Enterprise .... W. **7,348**

HEMPSTEAD, Hempstead Co., 3,000 p., on Brazos r. and Houston & Texas Central Rd., at junction of Austin branch, 50 m.

TEXAS.

from Houston. Engaged in manufacturing.
Messenger................W. **7,349**
Waller Co. Courier.......W. **7,350**

HENDERSON, c. h., Rusk Co., 1,250 p., 160 m. N. by E. of Houston and 75 E. of Shreveport, La. In a cotton-growing region.
Times.

HENRIETTA, c. h., Clay Co.
Texas Star................W. **7,352**

HILLSBORO, c. h., Hill Co., 500† p., on Brazos r., 35 m. above Waco and 150 N. of Austin.
Hill Co. Expositor.......W. **7,353**

HONEY GROVE, Fannin Co.
Independent..............W. **7,354**

HOUSTON, c. h., Harris Co., 12,500 p., on Buffalo Bayou, 50 m. from Galveston. Steamboats run regularly between here and Galveston. Second city in the State in population and commercial importance. Centering point for several railroads. Surrounded by an agricultural district, producing cotton, sugar cane and corn.
Age.......................D. **7,355**
" ....W. **7,356**
Telegraph.................D. **7,357**
" ....W. **7,358**
Texas Baptist Herald.....W. **7,359**
Texas Deutsche-Zeitung..W. **7,360**

HUNTSVILLE, Walker Co., 1,500 p., on Houston & Great Northern Rd., 60 m. N. of Houston and 12 from Trinity r. Cotton market and shipping point. State penitentiary and two colleges located here.
Item......................W. **7,361**

JACKBORO, c. h., Jack Co.
Frontier Echo...........W. **7,362**

JASPER, c. h., Jasper Co., 600 p., near Nechese r., 150 m. N. E. of Galveston and 35 W. of Louisiana State line.
Newsboy..................W. **7,363**

JEFFERSON, c. h., Marion Co., 4,190 p., at the mouth of Big Cypress Bayou, 40 m. N. W. of Shreveport, La. Steamboats run to this point, making it a centre of trade, and shipping point for produce and live stock.
East Texas Leader........D. **7,364**
Trans-Continental Iron Age....................W. **7,365**
Jimplecute.................D. **7,366**
" ....W. **7,367**

KAUFMAN, c. h., Kaufman Co., 700† p., 35 m. S. E. of Dallas and 40 N. of Corsicana.
Telegraph.................W. **7,368**

KERRVILLE, c. h., Kerr Co.
Frontiersman.............W. **7,369**

LADONIA, Fannin Co.
Courier.

LA GRANGE, c. h., Fayette Co., 1,500† p., on Colorado r., 65 m. below Austin and 35 above Columbus.
Fayette Co. New Era....W. **7,371**
Fayette Co. Record.......W. **7,372**

LAMPASAS, c. h., Lampasas Co., 1,200 p., on Sulphur fork of Lampasas r., 60 m. N. by W. of Austin. Surrounded by an agricultural and stock-raising district.
Dispatch.................W. **7,373**

LAWRENCE, Kaufman Co.
Times....................W. **7,374**

TEXAS.

LINDEN, c. h., Cass Co.
Cass Co. Sun............W. **7,375**

LOCKHART, c. h., Caldwell Co.
News Echo................W. **7,376**

LONGVIEW, c. h., Gregg Co.
Texas New Era.

McKINNEY, c. h., Collin Co., 2,300† p., 135 m. N. by E. of Austin. Situate in a wheat-growing district.
Enquirer.................W. **7,378**
Texas Christian Monthly.M. **7,379**

MADISONVILLE, c. h., Madison Co.
Plaindealer...............W. **7,380**

MARLIN, c. h., Falls Co., 1,000† p., on Waco & Northwestern Rd., 18 m. from Bremond, 3 from Brazos r. and 97 N. E. of Austin.
Moving Ball..............W. **7,381**

MARSHALL, c. h., Harrison Co., 7,000† p., on Texas & Pacific Rd., 250 m. N. by E. of Galveston and 40 W. of Shreveport, La. In an agricultural district.
Herald................T. W. **7,382**
News.
Texas Presbyterian ......W. **7,384**

MERIDIAN, c. h., Bosque Co.
Bosque Co. Herald.

MEXIA, Limestone Co., 900† p., on Houston & Texas Central Rd., 181 m. from Houston.
Ledger...................W. **7,386**

MINEOLA, Wood Co.
Citizen.
Reporter..................W. **7,388**

MONTAGUE, c. h., Montague Co.
News.....................W. **7,389**

MOSCOW, Polk Co.
East Texas Democrat....W. **7,390**

MOUNT PLEASANT, Titus Co., 800 p., 80 m. N. W. of Shreveport, La.
Southern Patron.........W. **7,391**

NACOGDOCHES, c. h., Nacogdoches Co.
News.....................W. **7,392**

NAVASOTA, Grimes Co., 1,500 p., on Brazos r., at mouth of Navasota r., and on Houston & Texas Central Rd., 70 m. from Houston. Agricultural and cotton-growing district surrounding.
Tablet...................W. **7,393**

NEW BRAUNFELS, c. h., Comal Co.
Zeitung..................W. **7,394**

OAKVILLE, c. h., Live Oak Co.
Tribune..................W. **7,395**

PALESTINE, c. h., Anderson Co., 1,500 p., on International Rd., 10 m. from Trinity r., and 201 from Galveston, in an agricultural region. Considerable manufacturing carried on.
Advocate.................D. **7,396**
" ....W. **7,397**
New Era.................W. **7,398**

PARIS, c. h., Lamar Co., 4,000† p., 10 m. S. of Red r., 300 N. by E. of Austin, and 100 N. W. of Jefferson. Strictly an agricultural county. Cotton raised here to some extent.
Press....................D. **7,399**
" ....W. **7,400**
North Texan.............W. **7,401**

PEORIA, Hill Co.
Hill Co. Record..........W. **7,402**

TEXAS.

PITTSBURG, c. h., Camp Co.
Magnet..... ....W. **7,403**

PLEASANTON, c. h., Atascosa Co.
Western Stock Journal...W. **7,404**

QUITMAN, c. h., Wood Co., 1,000 p., 75 m. from Jefferson and 275 from Austin. Centre of trade.
News.....................W. **7,405**

RICHMOND, c. h., Fort Bend Co.
Four Counties...........W. **7,406**

ROCKDALE, Milam Co.
Messenger.............S. W. **7,407**
Tribune....................W. **7,408**

ROCKPORT, Aranzas Co., 900† p., on Aranzas Bay. Has a good harbor, and a steamship line which connects with New Orleans. Live stock, beef, hides and wool are shipped from this point.
Transcript................W. **7,409**

ROCKWALL, c. h., Rockwall Co.
Banner......................W. **7,410**

RUSK, c. h., Cherokee Co., 800 p., 120 m. N. of Houston, 150 from Galveston and 125 from Shreveport, La.
Texas Observer...........W. **7,411**

SAN ANTONIO, c. h., Bexar Co., 12,256 p., on San Antonio r., 80 m. S. by W. of Austin and 140 from Port Indianola. Centre of trade for the interior. Principal branch of industry, stock-raising.
Express......... ....D. **7,412**
" ....W. **7,413**
Freie Presse fur Texas....D. **7,414**
" " " " ....W. **7,415**
Herald......................D. **7,416**
" ....W. **7,417**

SAN MARCOS, c. h., Hays Co.
West Texas Free Press....W. **7,418**

SAN SABA, c. h., San Saba Co.
News.......................W. **7,419**

SEGUIN, Guadalupe Co., 1,320† p., 45 m. S. by W. of Austin.
Guadalupe Times........W. **7,420**

SHERMAN, c. h., Grayson Co., 1,430 p., 10 m. from Red r. and 270 N. by E. of Austin. Surrounded by a wheat and cotton region.
Courier....................W. **7,421**
Patriot.....................W. **7,422**
Register...................W. **7,423**

STEPHENVILLE, c. h., Erath Co.
Eclectic....................W. **7,424**
Empire.....................W. **7,425**

SULPHUR SPRINGS, Hopkins Co., 2,500† p., 80 m. E. by N. of Dallas and 80 N. W. of Jefferson. In an agricultural district. Has several flouring and other mills.
Gazette....................W. **7,426**
Temperance Vidette.

TERRELL, Kaufman Co.
Kaufman Star..........W. **7,428**

TEXARKANA, Bowie Co.
Gate City News..........W. **7,429**

TYLER, c. h., Smith Co., 2,500† p., 250 m. N. of Galveston and 100 W. by S. of Shreveport. In an agricultural district.
Democrat.................W. **7,430**
Grange Reporter.........W. **7,431**
National Index..........W. **7,432**

VICTORIA, c. h., Victoria Co., 4,800† p., on Guadaloupe r., 40 m. from Indianola. Situated on the Gulf, West Texas & Pacific Rd. Surrounded by an agricultural region, and engaged in raising cotton, corn, potatoes and sugar cane.
Advocate.................W. **7,433**

WACO, c. h., McLennan Co., 8,000† p., on Brazos r. and Waco & Great Northern Rd., 95 m. N. by E. of Austin and 250 from Galveston. Engaged in agricultural pursuits, stock raising and manufacturing. Has a wire suspension bridge 500 ft. span.
Examiner.................D. **7,434**
Examiner and Patron...W. **7,435**
Reporter...................D. **7,436**
*Business & Stock Reporter*W. **7,437**
Register.. ....W. **7,438**
Prairie Bird.............M. **7,439**

WAXAHACHIE, c. h., Ellis Co., 2,000† p., 180 m. N. E. of Austin. Surrounded by a cotton, wheat and corn-growing country
Enterprise................W. **7,440**

WEATHERFORD, c. h., Parker Co., 3,500 p., 11 m. from Brazos r. and 200 N. of Austin. Engaged in farming and stock raising. Centre of trade.
Times.....................W. **7,441**

WILLIS, Montgomery Co.
Observer..................W. **7,442**

WILL'S POINT, Van Zandt Co.
Observer..................W. **7,443**

VERMONT.

BARTON, Orleans Co., 2,000† p., on Passumpsic Rd., 28 m. from St. Johnsbury and 15 from Newport. In an agricultural district.
Orleans Co. Monitor.....W. **7,444**

BELLOWS FALLS, Windham Co., 2,000† p., on Connecticut r., and Vermont Central Rd., at terminus of Cheshire Rd., 114 m. from Boston. It has good water power, which is partially developed. The largest and best paper mills in New England are located here.
Times .... W. **7,445**

BENNINGTON, c. h., Bennington Co., 5,900† p., on Harlem Extension Rd., 36 m. from Troy and 200 from New York. Engaged in manufacturing.
News......................D. **7,446**
Banner ....W. **7,447**
Vermont Gazette.........W. **7,448**

BETHEL, Windsor Co., 1,817 p., on Vermont Central Rd., 38 m. S. of Montpelier. A soapstone quarry at this point.
White River Standard... W. **7,449**

BRADFORD, Orange Co., 1,492 p., on Connecticut r. and Passumpsic R. Rd. Centre of trade for eastern portion of Orange county. Engaged in manufacturing.
Opinion..................W. **7,450**
Vermont Journal........W. **7,451**

BRANDON, Rutland Co.
Union.......................W. **7,452**

BRATTLEBORO, Windham Co., 5,000 p., on Connecticut r., and Vermont Valley and Vermont & Massachusetts Rd. Engaged in manufacturing and a trade centre.
Vermont Journal........W. **7,453**
Vermont Phœnix.........W. **7,454**
Vermont Record and Farmer .... W. **7,455**

VERMONT.

Household .... M. **7,456**
Leisure Hour .... M. **7,457**

BURLINGTON, c. h., Crittenden Co., 18,000† p., on Lake Champlain and Vermont Central Rd. Engaged in lake commerce, extensive lumber manufacturing. Seat of the University of Vermont and largest city in the State.
Free Press and Times .... D. **7,458**
" " " " .... W. **7,459**
Sentinel .... D. **7,460**
Clipper .... W. **7,461**
Democrat and Sentinel ... W. **7,462**
Vermont Witness .... M. **7,463**

CHELSEA, c. h., Orange Co.
Post .... W. **7,464**

DANVILLE, Caledonia Co., 2,500 p., on Portland & Ogdensburg Rd., 12 m. from St. Johnsbury. Engaged in agriculture and manufacturing.
North Star .... W. **7,465**

GRAND ISLE, Grand Isle Co.
Recorder .... W. **7,466**

GUILDHALL, c. h., Essex Co.
Essex Co. Herald .... W. **7,467**

HYDE PARK, c. h., Lamoille Co., 1,624 p., near Lamoille r., 28 m. N. of Montpelier, on the Portland & Ogdensburg Rd. A business centre. Farming and manufacturing carried on.
Lamoille Newsdealer .... W. **7,468**

LUDLOW, Windsor Co., 1,827 p., on Black r. and Vermont Central Rd., 26 m. S. E. of Rutland. Cloths and various other articles manufactured here.
Black River Gazette ..... W. **7,469**

LYNDON, Caledonia Co., 2,350 p., on Passumpsic r. and Rd., 8 m. N. of St. Johnsbury. In an agricultural district. Some manufacturing done here. Passumpsic Rd. shops are located here.
Vermont Union .... W. **7,470**

MANCHESTER, Bennington Co., 2,000 p., on Battenkill r. and Harlem Extension Rd., 30 m. from Rutland. One of the first settled towns in the State.
Journal .... W. **7,471**

MIDDLEBURY, c. h., Addison Co., 3,086 p., on Otter Creek & Rutland division of Vermont Central Rd., half way between Rutland and Burlington. Engaged in manufactures. Seat of Middlebury College. Has one of the finest water powers in New England.
Register .... W. **7,472**

MONTPELIER, c. h., Washington Co., State capital, 4,000 p., on Onion r., in central part of State. Centre of trade.
Argus and Patriot .... W. **7,473**
Green Mountain Freeman W. **7,474**
Vermont Christian Messenger .... W. **7,475**
Vermont Chronicle .... W. **7,476**
Vermont Watchman and State Journal .... W. **7,477**

MORRISVILLE, Lamoille Co.
Vermont Citizen .... W. **7,478**

NEWPORT, Orleans Co., 2,050 p., at the head of Lake Memphremagog, at terminus of Passumpsic Rd. A summer resort. Surrounded by an agricultural region. Centre of trade and considerable manufacturing.
Express and Standard ... W. **7,479**

VERMONT.

NORTH TROY, Orleans Co.
Palladium.

POULTNEY, Rutland Co., 2,836 p., on Poultney r. and Rutland & Washington Rd., 18 m. from Rutland and 60 from Troy. Engaged in manufacturing and shipping slate roofing. Seat of several educational institutions.
Journal .... W. **7,481**

RICHFORD, Franklin Co., 1,348 p., on Missisquoi r., at junction with Clyde r., and on a branch of Vermont Central Rd., 28 m. from St. Albans and 70 from Montreal. The river furnishes water power, which is employed in manufacturing.
Frontier Sentinel .... W. **7,482**

RUTLAND, c. h., Rutland Co., 10,000 p., on Otter Creek, at junction of four railroads and centre of trade. Largest city in the State except Burlington. It is headquarters for the famous Vermont marble.
Globe .... D. **7,483**
" .... W. **7,484**
Herald .... D. **7,485**
" .... W. **7,486**

ST. ALBANS, Franklin Co., 7,014 p., on Central Vt. Rd., and at junction of Missisquoi Branch Rd., 63 m. from Montreal and 3 from Lake Champlain. The great butter market of New England and a trade centre.
Messenger .... D. **7,487**
" .... W. **7,488**
Advertiser .... S. W. **7,489**
Merchant's Home Visitor W. **7,490**

ST. JOHNSBURY, Caledonia Co., 4,600 p., on Passumpsic r. and Rd., at intersection of Portland & Ogdensburg Rd. On shortest line from great Lakes to tide-water and from Boston to Montreal and Quebec. Engaged in manufacturing. The manufactory of Fairbanks' patent weighing scales is located here, giving employment to 600 men, and manufacturing 1,000 scales per week.
Caledonian .... W. **7,491**
Vermont Farmer .... W. **7,492**
Vermont Journal .... W. **7,493**

SOUTH ROYALTON, Windsor Co., 1,000 p., on Vermont Central Rd., 18 m. from White River Junction.
Vermont Journal .... W. **7,494**

SPRINGFIELD, Windsor Co., 3,000 p., on Connecticut and Black rs. One of the largest manufacturing towns in the State.
Black River Standard .... W. **7,495**
Bulletin .... W. **7,496**
Vermont Journal .... W. **7,497**

VERGENNES, Addison Co., 1,570 p., on Otter Creek & Rutland division of Vermont Central Rd., 21 m. from Burlington, 7 from Lake Champlain. Engaged in manufactures.
Vermonter .... W. **7,498**

WATERBURY, Washington Co.
Biblical Messenger .... M. **7,499**

WEST RANDOLPH, Orange Co., 2,829 p., on Vermont Central Rd., 30 m. from Montpelier. Engaged in trade and manufacturing. Centre of an agricultural region. State Normal School for teachers is located here.
Green Mountain Herald .. W. **7,500**
Orange Co. Democrat .... W. **7,501**
Vermont Journal .... W. **7,502**

VERMONT.

WINDSOR, Windsor Co., 1,700 p., on Connecticut r., 25 m. N. of Bellows Falls. United States Court House and State Prison located here. In a superior agricultural section.
Valley Farmer...........W. **7,503**
Vermont Journal........W. **7,504**

WOODSTOCK, c. h., Windsor Co., 3,000 p., on Otta Quechee r., 14 m. from White River Junction, communication to which is Woodstock Rd.
Spirit of the Age..........W. **7,505**
Vermont Standard.......W. **7,506**

VIRGINIA.

ABINGDON, c. h., Washington Co., 1,200 p., on Atlantic, Mississippi & Ohio Rd., 189 m. from Lynchburg and 14 from Bristol. The most important point in this part of the State.
Virginian...............W. **7,507**

ALEXANDRIA, c. h., Alexandria Co., 13,570 p., on Potomac r. and Chesapeake and Ohio Canal, 7 m. below Washington. The Alexandria & Washington, Orange, Alexandria & Manassas, and Washington & Ohio Rds. centre here. Engaged in coal trade, and foreign and domestic commerce and manufactures.
Gazette...................D. **7,508**
" ....T. W. **7,509**
Virginia Sentinel.........D. **7,510**
" " ....W. **7,511**
Granger.................W. **7,512**
Southern Churchman....W. **7,513**

AMHERST, c. h., Amherst Co., 400† p., on Orange, Alexandria & Manassas Rd., 164 m. from Washington, D. C., and 14 from Lynchburg.
Enterprise...............W. **7,514**

BERRYVILLE, c. h., Clarke Co., 800 p., about 10 m. from Winchester and 50 W. by N. of Washington. An agricultural district.
Clarke Courier...........W. **7,515**

BOYDTON, c. h., Mecklenburgh Co., 763 p., near Roanoke r., 86 m. from Richmond, and an equal distance from Petersburg, 10 m. N. E. of Clarksville. Cultivation of tobacco the principal feature of industry.
Roanoke Valley..........W. **7,516**

BRISTOL, Washington Co., 1,200 p., at junction of Atlantic, Mississippi & Ohio with E. Tennessee, Virginia & Georgia Rd., and on State line between Virginia and Tennessee.
News.....................W. **7,5_7**

BURKEVILLE, Nattoway Co., 500† p., on Atlantic, Mississippi & Ohio Rd., at intersection of Richmond & Danville Rd., 54 from Richmond and 52 from Petersburg.
South Side Sentinel......W. **7,518**

CHARLOTTE, c. h., Charlotte Co.
Charlotte Gazette.........W. **7,519**

CHARLOTTESVILLE, c. h., Albemarle Co., 5,000† p., on Chesapeake & Ohio, at junction of C. & Ohio and Va. Midland Rds., 117 m. from Washington, D. C. Engaged in manufacturing and surrounded by an agricultural district. Seat of the University of Virginia.
Chronicle................W. **7,520**
Jeffersonian Republican.W. **7,521**

VIRGINIA.

CHASE CITY, Mecklenburgh Co.
Enterprise..............W. **7,522**
Young America's Advocate.....................M. **7,523**

CHRISTIANSBURG, c. h., Montgomery Co., 1,200† p., on Atlantic, Mississippi & Ohio Rd., 86 m. from Lynchburg.
Montgomery Messenger...W. **7,524**

CULPEPER, Culpeper Co., 2,200† p., on Va. Midland Rd., 69 m. from Washington. In an agricultural district and centre of trade.
Observer.................W. **7,525**
Times...................W. **7,526**

DANVILLE, Pittsylvania Co., 6,500† p., on Dan r. and Richmond & Danville Rd., 141 m. from Richmond. In an agricultural district. Engaged in tobacco raising. Has water power, which is employed in manufacturing.
Border Express..........D. **7,527**
News......................D. **7,528**
" ....W. **7,529**
Register..................W. **7,530**
Times.................... W. **7,531**

EMORY, Washington Co.
Banner................S. M. **7,532**

ESTILVILLE, c. h., Scott Co.
Scott Banner............W. **7,533**

FARMVILLE, Prince Edward Co., 2,500† p., on Appomattox r. and Atlantic, Mississippi & Ohio Rd., 55 m. from Lynchburg and 68 from Petersburg.
Mercury..................W. **7,534**

FINCASTLE, Botetourt Co., 800 p., about 40 m. W. of Lynchburg and 9 from James r. Centre of county trade.
Herald...................W. **7,535**

FREDERICKSBURG, Spottsylvania Co., 4,100 p., on Rappahannock r. and Richmond, Fredericksburg & Potomac Rd., 57 m. from Washington. Engaged in manufacturing and a trade centre.
News..................S. W. **7,536**
Virginia Herald......S. W. **7,537**
Virginia Star.........S. W. **7,538**
Independent.............W. **7,539**

FRONT ROYAL, c. h., Warren Co., 705 p., on Manassas division of Orange, Alexandria & Manassas Rd., 1 m. E. of Shenandoah r. and 140 N. N. W. of Richmond. Has fine water power, which is employed in various manufactures.
Warren Sentinel.........W. **7,540**
Zion's Advocate.......S. M. **7,541**

GLOUCESTER, c. h., Gloucester Co., 570 p., on York r., near Chesapeake Bay, 82 m. from Richmond.
Chesapeake Current......W. **7,542**

GORDONSVILLE, Orange Co.
Gazette...................W. **7,543**

HALIFAX, c. h., Halifax Co., 1,582 p., on Bannister r. and near Richmond, Danville & Piedmont Rds., 115 m. from Richmond, 60 from Lynchburg and 41 from Danville. Situated in an agricultural section. Several grist mills and iron founderies and two plumbago mines located in the county.
Record..................W. **7,544**

HAMILTON, Loudoun Co.
Loudoun Enterprise.....W. **7,545**

HAMPTON, c. h., Elizabeth City Co.
Southern Workman.......M. **7,546**

VIRGINIA.

HARRISONBURG, c. h., Rockingham Co., 3,500† p., at terminus of Manassas division of Orange, Alexandria & Manassas Rd., 25 m. N. of Staunton, 146 S. of Washington City and 125 N. W. of Richmond. Surrounded by an agricultural section and centre of trade.
Old Commonwealth......W. **7,547**
Rockingham Register....W. **7,548**
Ray of Hope..........S. M. **7,549**

HILLSVILLE, Carroll Co., 300† p., about 100 m. S. W. of Lynchburg and 20 S. of Atlantic, Mississippi & Ohio Rd. A place of considerable trade. Country rich in minerals.
Virginian................W. **7,550**

INDEPENDENCE, c. h., Grayson Co.
Grayson Clipper.........W. **7,551**

JACKSONVILLE, Floyd Co.
Floyd Reporter...........W. **7,552**

JONESVILLE, c. h., Lee Co.
Lee Co. Sentinel..........W. **7,553**

LAWRENCEVILLE, c. h., Brunswick Co.
Brunswick Advocate.....W. **7,554**

LEBANON, c. h., Russell Co.
Russell Progress..........W. **7,555**

LEESBURG, c. h., Loudoun Co., 1,650 p., on Washington & Ohio Rd., about 38 m. from Washington and 3 from Potomac r. An agricultural district, rapidly growing in wealth and population.
Mirror....................W. **7,556**
Washingtonian...........W. **7,557**
Independent..........S. M. **7,558**

LEXINGTON, c. h., Rockbridge Co., 2,873 p., on a fork of James r., 35 m. W. of Lynchburg.
Gazette....................W. **7,559**
Southern Collegian....S. M. **7,560**

LIBERTY, Bedford Co., 2,200† p., on Atlantic, Mississippi & Ohio Rd., 25 m. from Lynchburg. Engaged in tobacco and wheat raising and coal and lead mining. Centre of trade.
Bedford Sentinel.........W. **7,561**
Bedford Star.............W. **7,562**

LOUISA, c. h., Louisa Co.
Louisa Record...........W. **7,563**

LOVINGSTON, c. h., Nelson Co.
Nelson Co. Examiner....W. **7,564**

LURAY, c. h., Page Co., 900 p., 136 m. N. W. of Richmond and near S. fork of Shenandoah r.
Page Courier.............W. **7,565**

LYNCHBURG, Campbell Co., 15,000 p., on James r. and Canawha Canal, and Atlantic, Mississippi & Ohio Rd., at junction of Orange, Alexandria & Manassas Rd. The railroad and canal communication render it a shipping point for the produce of a productive district. Surrounded by a tobacco producing district.
Evening Star.............D. **7,566**
News.................... D. **7,567**
" ....T. W. **7,568**
" ....W. **7,569**
Virginian.................D. **7,570**
" ....T. W. **7,571**
" ....W. **7,572**
Press.................S. W. **7,573**
Press and Recorder......W. **7,574**

MANASSAS, Prince William Co.
Gazette...................W. **7,575**

VIRGINIA.

MANCHESTER, Chesterfield Co.
Courier...................W. **7,576**

MARION, c. h., Smythe Co., 1,100† p., on Holston r. and Atlantic, Mississippi & Ohio Rd., 160 m. from Lynchburg. Chiefly engaged in mining and agriculture.
Patriot and Herald......W. **7,577**

NEWBERN, c. h., Pulaski Co.
Virginia People.........W. **7,578**

NEW MARKET, Shenandoah Co., 700 p., on Valley branch of Baltimore & Ohio Rd., 43 m. N. by E. of Staunton and 150 N. W. of Richmond. Trade centre for an agricultural section.
Our Church Paper.......W. **7,579**
Shenandoah Valley......W. **7,580**
Sunday School............M. **7,581**

NORFOLK, c. h., Norfolk Co., 24,000† p., on Elizabeth r., 8 m. from Hampton Roads and 32 from Atlantic Ocean. Terminus of Atlantic, Mississippi & Ohio Rd., and connected with Albemarle Sound by Dismal Swamp Canal. Its harbor is large and safe, admitting vessels of the largest class. Engaged in foreign and domestic commerce. Second city in population and first in commercial importance in the State. Regular lines of steamships ply between Norfolk, Philadelphia and New York.
Day Book.................D. **7,582**
" " ....T. W. **7,583**
" " ....W. **7,584**
Evening Times............D. **7,585**
Landmark................D. **7,586**
" ....W. **7,587**
Virginian.................D. **7,588**
" ....W. **7,589**

ONANCOCK, Accomack Co.
Eastern Virginian......W. **7,590**

ORANGE, c. h., Orange Co., 800† p., on W. C., V. M. & G. S. Rd., 87 m. from Washington, D. C., and 91 from Lynchburg.
Piedmont Virginian.....W. **7,591**

PEARISBURG, c. h., Giles Co., 680 p., on New r., 90 m. W. of Lynchburg and 20 W. by N. of Christiansburg.
Gazette...................W. **7,592**

PETERSBURG, Dinwiddie Co., 23,000 p., on Appomattox r., 22 m. from Richmond and 10 from City Point, and on Atlantic, Mississippi & Ohio Rd., at junction of Richmond & Petersburg, Norfolk & Petersburg and Petersburg & Weldon Rds. A harbor for light draught vessels, and a shipping point for tobacco and other produce, and a centre of trade.
Evening Star..............D. **7,593**
Index and Appeal........D. **7,594**
" " " ....W. **7,595**
News.....................D. **7,596**
" ....W. **7,597**
Rural Messenger.........W. **7,598**

PITTSYLVANIA C. H., Pittsylvania Co., 1,200† p., in a planting district, 16 m. N. of Danville and 40 S. by W. of Lynchburg.
Chatham Tribune........W. **7,599**
Pittsylvania Courier....W. **7,600**

PORTSMOUTH, Norfolk Co.
Enterprise............... D. **7,601**

RICHMOND, Henrico Co., State capital, 60,000† p., on James r., at head of tidewater, and junction of five railroads and

VIRGINIA.

Kanawha Canal, 100 m. from Washington, D. C. Engaged in commerce and manufactures.
Anzeiger..................D. **7,602**
Dispatch..................D. **7,603**
" ....S. W. **7,604**
" ....W. **7,605**
Enquirer..................D. **7,606**
" ....S. W. **7,607**
" ....W. **7,608**
Guide and News..........D. **7,609**
State......................D. **7,610**
" ....W. **7,611**
Virginia Staats Gazette..D. **7,612**
Sonntags-Blatt........Sund. **7,613**
Whig......................D. **7,614**
" ....S. W. **7,615**
" ....W. **7,616**
Central Presbyterian.....W. **7,617**
Christian Advocate......W. **7,618**
Christian Examiner.....W. **7,619**
Commercial and Tobacco Leaf...................W. **7,620**
Religious Herald........W. **7,621**
Sunday School Record.
Virginia Patron.........W. **7,623**
Children's Friend.
Educational Journal of Virginia...............M. **7,625**
Foreign Mission Journal.
Insurance Advocate......M. **7,627**
Southern Historical Society Papers...........M. **7,628**
Southern Planter and Farmer...................M. **7,629**
*Virginia Medical Monthly*M. **7,630**

ROCKY MOUNT, c. h., Franklin Co.
Virginia Monitor........W. **7,631**

SALEM, c. h., Roanoke Co., 2,000† p., on Roanoke r. and Atlantic, Mississippi & Ohio Rd., 60 m. from Lynchburg. Surrounded by a tobacco raising and manufacturing district. Seat of Roanoke College and Hollins' Institute.
Register..................W. **7,632**
Roanoke Times..........W. **7,633**

SCOTTSVILLE, Albemarle Co., 600 p., on James r. and James R. Canal, about 18 m. S. of Charlottesville. A shipping point and centre of trade.
Courier..................W. **7,634**

SINGER'S GLEN, Rockingham Co.
Musical Casket...........M. **7,635**
Musical Million...........M. **7,636**

STAUNTON, c. h., Augusta Co., 7,000† p., on Chesapeake & Ohio & Valley Rds., 136 m. from Richmond, 93 from Harper's Ferry. Engaged in manufacturing and centre of an agricultural district. The State Insane and Deaf and Dumb Asylums are located here. Seat of several institutions of learning.
Spectator.................W. **7,637**
Valley Virginian.........W. **7,638**
Vindicator.................W. **7,639**

SUFFOLK, c. h., Nansemond Co., 2,000 p., at intersection of Atlantic, Mississippi & Ohio with Seaboard & Roanoke Rd., 17 m. from Norfolk, 58 from Petersburg and 17 from Portsmouth. Surrounded by a truck-growing district.
Christian Sun...........W. **7,640**
Herald.....................W. **7,641**
Little Christian........S. M. **7,642**
Unity.......................M. **7,643**

TAPPAHANNOCK, c. h., Essex Co., 576 p., on Rappahannock r., 50 m. N. E. of Richmond. Engaged in coast trade. Fish, grain and fruit are shipped from here. It has a United States Custom House.
Tidewater Index.........W. **7,644**

TAZEWELL C. H., Tazewell Co.
Southwest Virginian.....W. **7,645**

WARRENTON, c. h., Fauquier Co., 1,500† p., 9 m. from Orange, Alexandria & Manassas Rd., to which it is connected by a branch. Situated in an agricultural district and a centre of trade.
True Index...............W. **7,646**

WEST POINT, King William Co., 2,193 p., at confluence of Pamunkey and Mattapony rs., and at terminus of Richmond and York R. Rd., 38 m. from Richmond.
Star.......................W. **7,647**

WINCHESTER, c. h., Frederick Co., 6,000 p.
News.......................W. **7,648**
Times.......................W. **7,649**

WOODSTOCK, c. h., Shenandoah Co., 1,000† p., on fork of Shenandoah r., and on Baltimore & Ohio Rd., 100 m. W. of Washington City and 160 from Richmond.
Shenandoah Democrat...W. **7,650**
Shenandoah Herald......W. **7,651**

WYTHEVILLE, Wythe Co., 1,800† p., on Atlantic, Mississippi & Ohio Rd., 133 m. from Lynchburg and 260 from Richmond. Engaged in manufacturing and a trade centre.
South-West Virginia Enterprise..............S. W. **7,652**
Dispatch..................W. **7,653**

WEST VIRGINIA.

BERKELEY SPRINGS, c. h., Morgan Co., 700† p., 3 m. S. of Potomac r. and Baltimore & Ohio Rd., at Sir John's Run, and 50 N. W. of Harper's Ferry. An agricultural county.
Morgan Mercury........W. **7,654**

BUCKHANNON, Upshur Co., 780 p., on Buckhannon r., about 12 m. E. by S. of Weston.
Delta.....................W. **7,655**

CAMERON, Marshall Co.
Free Press...............W. **7,656**

CHARLESTON, Kanawha Co., 4,000 p., on Kanawha r. and Chesapeake & Ohio Rd., 52 m. from Huntington. The river is navigable to this point. Centre of trade. Surrounded by coal and iron regions. Salt works located within 7 m. Post office, Kanawha C. H.
Courier...............T. W. **7,657**
West Virginia Courier...W. **7,658**
Kanawha Chronicle.....W. **7,659**
West Virginia Journal..W. **7,660**

CHARLESTOWN, Jefferson Co., 1,605 p., on Winchester, Potomac & Strasburg division of Baltimore & Ohio Rd., 10 m. S. W. of Harper's Ferry. Engaged in agriculture and manufacturing.
Spirit of Jefferson........W. **7,661**
Virginia Free Press.....W. **7,662**

CLARKSBURG, c. h., Harrison Co., 3,000 p., on Parkersburg division of Baltimore & Ohio Rd., 120 m. from Cumberland. Coal is found in the vicinity.

WEST VIRGINIA.

News....................W. 7,663
Telegram..................W. 7,664

ELIZABETH, Wirt Co.
Wirt Co. Mentor.........W. 7,665

FAIRMONT, c. h., Marion Co., 1,300† p., on Monongahela r. and Baltimore & Ohio Rd., 77 m. from Wheeling. The river is navigable to this point. Mining and shipping of coal carried on. A branch of the State Normal School located here.
Index....................W. 7,666
West Virginian..........W. 7,667

FAIRVIEW, c. h., Hancock Co., 3 m. from Ohio r. at Wellsville, O., and 36 N. of Wheeling.
Hancock Co. Courier....W. 7,668

FAYETTEVILLE, c. h., Fayette Co.
Enterprise................W. 7,669

FORT GAY, Wayne Co.
Wayne Advocate.........W. 7,670

FRANKLIN, c. h., Pendleton Co.
Pendleton News..........W. 7,671

GERARDSTOWN, Berkeley Co.
Times....................W. 7,672

GRAFTON, Taylor Co., 4,000† p., on Tygert Valley r., 100 m. from Wheeling, on Baltimore & Ohio Rd. Lumber trade, coal mining and manufacturing the chief industries.
Sentinel..................W. 7,673

HARRISVILLE, c. h., Ritchie Co., 300 p., terminus of Pennsboro & Harrisville Rd., a branch of the Baltimore & Ohio Rd., 37 m. from Parkersburg. Post office, Ritchie C. H.
Ritchie Gazette ....W. 7,674

HINTON, c. h., Summers Co.
Mountain Herald.......W. 7,675

HUNTINGTON, Cabell Co., 3,000† p., on Ohio r., terminus of Chesapeake & Ohio Rd., 52 m. from Charleston. Shipping point for coal, lumber, iron and salt from the Kanawha regions.
Advertiser................W. 7,676
Commercial..............W. 7,677

KEYSER, c. h., Mineral Co., 1,200† p., on Baltimore & Ohio Rd., 23 m. from Cumberland, Md. A shipping point for grain and live stock.
West Virginia Tribune...W. 7,678

KINGWOOD, Preston Co., 1,500† p., on Cheat r., and 10 m. from Baltimore & Ohio Rd.
Preston Co. Herald......W. 7,679
Preston Co. Journal.....W. 7,680

LEWISBURG, c. h., Greenbrier Co., 1,200† p., 4 m. from Greenbrier r., 9 from Greenbrier White Sulphur Springs and 200 S. of Wheeling. Situated among the mountains and a centre of business. Engaged in agriculture and manufactures.
Greenbrier Independent..W. 7,681

MANNINGTON, Marion Co.
Ventilator and Golden Rule....................W. 7,682

MARTINSBURG, c. h., Berkeley Co., 4,863 p., on Baltimore & Ohio Rd., 19 m. from Harper's Ferry. Contains railroad repair shops and is a centre of trade.
Independent..............D. 7,683
" ....W. 7,684
Statesman................W. 7,685

WEST VIRGINIA.

MASON CITY, Mason Co.
Mason Co. Journal......W. 7,686

MOOREFIELD, c. h., Hardy Co., 900† p., on S. branch of Potomac r., 27 m. above Romney, 150 S. E. of Wheeling and 50 from Cumberland, Md. Principally engaged in stock raising.
Courier and Advertiser...W. 7,687
Examiner.................W. 7,688

MORGANTOWN, c. h., Monongalia Co., 1,500 p., on Monongahela r., 65 m. S. of Pittsburgh, Pa., with which it is connected by steamboats. Engaged in various manufactures.
Post.......................W. 7,689

MOUNDSVILLE, c. h., Marshall Co., 2,000 p., on Ohio r. and Baltimore & Ohio Rd., 11 m. below Wheeling. Surrounded by a farming country. Engaged in manufacturing and coal mining.
New State Gazette........W. 7,690
Reporter..................W. 7,691

NEW MARTINSVILLE, Wetzel Co., 520 p., on Ohio r., 40 m. below Wheeling.
Labor Vindicator........W. 7,692

PARKERSBURG, c. h., Wood Co., 7,000† p., on Ohio and Little Kanawha rs., 204 m. by rail and 96 by river below Wheeling, on Baltimore & Ohio Rd. Engaged in oil refining, manufacturing, and centre of trade. Second city in West Virginia in point of population and business importance.
Times......................D. 7,693
Times and Gazette.......W. 7,694
Inquirer...................W. 7,695
Sentinel...................W. 7,696
State Journal............W. 7,697
West Virginia Educational Monthly.............M. 7,698

PHILLIPPI, c. h., Barbour Co.
Barbour Jeffersonian....W. 7,699
Plaindealer...............W. 7,700

PIEDMONT, Mineral Co., 2,000 p., on Potomac r. and Baltimore & Ohio Rd., 5 m. from New Creek. Centre of trade. A great coal shipping point.
Independent.............W. 7,701

POINT PLEASANT, Mason Co., 773 p., just above the junction of Kanawha with Ohio r., 200 m. above Cincinnati. Agriculture, mining, coal and salt among the chief industries.
Register..................W. 7,702

RAVENSWOOD, Jackson Co., 950† p., on Ohio r., 35 m. below Parkersburg, 30 from Pomeroy and an equal distance from the oil region on Little Kanawha r. Surrounded by an agricultural district. Shipping point for several back counties.
Jackson Co. News ....W. 7,703

ROMNEY, c. h., Hampshire Co., 600† p., on S. branch of Potomac r., 24 m. in a direct line S. of Cumberland, Md.
South Branch Intelligencer..................W. 7,704

SHEPHERDSTOWN, Jefferson Co., 1,560 p., on Potomac r, on Baltimore & Ohio Rd., 12 m above Harper's Ferry.
Register..................W. 7,705

SUTTON, Braxton Co.
Mountaineer.............W. 7,706

UNION, c. h., Monroe Co., 650 p., about 15 m. from Lewisburg. Wheat, corn and to-

bacco are the chief products. Mineral springs are located here.
Border Watchman.......W. **7,707**
Monroe Co. Register.....W. **7,708**

WELLSBURG, c. h., Brooke Co., 1,500 p., on Ohio r., 16 m. from Wheeling. A wool-growing and agricultural district. Coal mines located in the vicinity.
Herald..................W. **7,709**
Pan-Handle News.......W. **7,710**

WEST COLUMBIA, Mason Co.
Monitor..................W. **7,711**

WESTON, c. h., Lewis Co., 1,200 p., on W. Fork r., 20 m. from Baltimore & Ohio Rd. at Clarksburg. In an agricultural district and location of State Insane Hospital. Engaged in agriculture and stock-raising.
Democrat................W. **7,712**

WEST UNION, c. h., Doddridge Co.
Baptist Messenger.......W. **7,713**
Observer................W. **7,714**

WHEELING, c. h., Ohio Co., 27,000† p., on Ohio r. at terminus of Hempfield Rd. and Wheeling division of Baltimore & Ohio Rd., 92 m. from Pittsburgh. Engaged in commerce, agriculture and manufacturing. Coal found in the vicinity. Largest and most important city in West Virginia.
Evening Standard........D. **7,715**
" " ....W. **7,716**
Intelligencer.............D. **7,717**
" ....S. W. **7,718**
" ....W. **7,719**
Register..................D. **7,720**
" ....T. W. **7,721**
" ....W. **7,722**
Arbeiter-Freund.........W. **7,723**
Sunday Leader..........W. **7,724**
United States Post-Office Bulletin..............M. **7,725**
United States Post-Office Bulletin...............Qr. **7,726**

WINFIELD, c. h., Putnam Co.
Independent.............W. **7,727**
West Virginia Agriculturist...................S. M. **7,728**

WISCONSIN.

AHNAPEE, Kewaunee Co.
Record..................W. **7,729**

ALMA, c. h., Buffalo Co., 600 p., on Mississippi r., about 14 m. above Wenona, Minn. Engaged in lumber trade.
Express..................W. **7,730**

APPLETON, c. h., Outagamie Co., 6,730† p., on Fox r., and on Chicago & Northwestern Rd., 36 m. from Fond du Lac. Steamers connect with the lakes on one hand and with the Mississippi r. on the other. It has water power and is engaged in various manufactures, principally woodenware. Seat of Lawrence University.
Crescent................W. **7,731**
Post.
Volksfreund.............W. **7,733**
Lawrence Collegian......M. **7,734**
Neoterian................M. **7,735**

ARCADIA, Trempealeau Co.
Leader..................W. **7,736**

ARENA, Iowa Co.
Star....................W. **7,737**

ASHLAND, c. h., Ashland Co.
Press....................W. **7,738**

AUGUSTA, Eau Claire Co., 1,100† p., on West Wisconsin Rd., 34 m. from Black r. Falls and 112 from St. Paul, Minn. Possesses water power and is surrounded by an agricultural district.
Eagle....................W. **7,739**

BALDWIN, St. Croix Co.
Bulletin.................W. **7,740**

BARABOO, c. h., Sauk Co., 4,000† p., on Baraboo r., and Wisconsin division of Chicago & Northwestern Rd., about 40 m. N. W. of Madison. Centre of an agricultural district. The river affords water power.
Republic.................W. **7,741**

BEAVER DAM, Dodge Co., 3,700† p., on Milwaukee & St. Paul Rd., 61 m. from Milwaukee. Surrounded by an agricultural district, possessing water power, which is employed in various manufactures. Seat of Wayland University.
Argus....................W. **7,742**
Dodge Co. Citizen........W. **7,743**

BELOIT, Rock Co., 5,000 p., on Western Union Rd., at intersection of Madison division of Chicago & Northwestern Rd., 69 m. from Racine, 93 from Chicago and 68 from Milwaukee. Engaged in manufacturing and centre of populous farming district. Several institutions of learning located here, among them Beloit College.
Free Press...............W. **7,744**
Round Table..........B. W. **7,745**

BERLIN, Green Lake Co., 3,500† p., on Fox r. and terminus of Berlin branch of Northern division of Milwaukee & St. Paul Rd., 98 m. from Milwaukee and 42 from Horicon junction, on Eastern division. Centre of trade for surrounding district. In a cranberry-growing country.
Courant..................W. **7,746**
Journal..................W. **7,747**

BLACK CREEK, Outagamie Co.
Journal..................W. **7,748**

BLACK EARTH, Dane Co., 900 p., on Black Earth Creek and Chicago, Milwaukee & St. Paul Rd., 20 m. W. of Madison. In an agricultural district. Shipping point for grain and stock.
Advertiser...............W. **7,749**

BLACK RIVER FALLS, c. h., Jackson Co., 1,800† p., on Black r. and West Wisconsin Rd., 45 m. from La Crosse. Engaged in the lumber trade and various manufactures.
Badger State Banner....W. **7,750**
Wisconsin Independent..W. **7,751**

BOSCOBEL, Grant Co.
Dial.....................W. **7,752**

BRANDON, Fond du Lac Co., 600 p., in Metomen township, on Milwaukee & St. Paul Rd., 74 m. from Milwaukee and 20 from Berlin.
Times....................W. **7,753**

BRODHEAD, Green Co., 1,548 p., on Sugar r. and Prairie du Chien division of Milwaukee & St. Paul Rd., 89 m. from Milwaukee and 20 from Janesville. Surrounded by an agricultural district.
Independent.............W. **7,754**

BURLINGTON, Racine Co., 1,589 p., on Fox r. and Western Union Rd., 27 m. from

WISCONSIN.

Racine. The river furnishes power, which is employed in several manufactories.
Standard .... W. **7,755**

CHILTON, c. h., Calumet Co., 2,000† p., on Manitowoc r., about 10 m. E. of Lake Winnebago and on Wisconsin Central Rd. 76 m. from Milwaukee. In a farming district.
Times .... W. **7,756**

CHIPPEWA FALLS, c. h., Chippewa Co., 2,507 p., on Chippewa r., at Chippewa Falls, about 80 m. from La Crosse. Has water power, and is engaged in the lumber trade and agriculture.
Chippewa Herald .... W. **7,757**
Chippewa Times .... W. **7,758**

CLINTON, Rock Co.
Independent .... W. **7,759**

COLUMBUS, Columbia Co., 1,888 p., on Milwaukee & St. Paul Rd., 63 m. from Milwaukee. Engaged principally in agriculture and a business centre.
Democrat .... W. **7,760**
Republican .... W. **7,761**

DARLINGTON, c. h., La Fayette Co., 2,773 p., on Pecatonica r. and Mineral Point Rd., 15 m. from Mineral Point and 150 from Chicago. Engaged in mining and manufacturing, and a depot for the shipment of grain and pork.
La Fayette Co. Democrat. W. **7,762**
Republican .... W. **7,763**

DELAVAN, Walworth Co., 2,000 p., on Turtle Creek and Western Union Rd., 46 m. from Racine, 13 from Clinton and 65 from Milwaukee.
Republican .... W. **7,764**

DE PERE, Brown Co., 4,000† p., on Fox r. and Chicago & Northwestern and Wis. Central Rds. Engaged in manufactures of various kinds, principally pig iron, agricultural implements, freight cars and wooden ware. Terminus of a line of propellers.
News .... W. **7,765**

DE SOTO, Vernon Co., 640 p., on Mississippi r., midway between La Crosse and Prairie du Chien.
Leader .... W. **7,766**

DODGEVILLE, c. h., Iowa Co., 2,000 p., 45 m. from Madison. Lead and copper mines are worked in this vicinity. Large amount of zinc ore raised here.
Chronicle .... W. **7,767**

DURAND, c. h., Pepin Co., 917 p., on Chippewa r., about 20 m. from its entrance into Mississippi r. Largest town in a radius of 25 m. and a business centre. Surrounded by a wheat-growing district.
Times .... W. **7,768**

EAU CLAIRE, c. h., Eau Claire Co., 8,543† p., on West Wisconsin Rd. and Chippewa r. at mouth of Eau Claire r., 70 m. N. of La Crosse. Several mills here engaged in the lumber business and centre of trade for a radius of 40 m.
Free Press .... D. **7,769**
" " .... W. **7,770**
Chippewa Anzeiger ...... W. **7,771**
News .... W. **7,772**

EDGERTON, Rock Co.
Independent .... W. **7,773**

ELKHORN, c. h., Walworth Co., 1,500† p., on Western Union Rd., at junction of Racine branch, 40 m. from Racine. In a fertile agricultural district.
Walworth Co. Independent .... W. **7,774**

ELLSWORTH, c. h., Pierce Co., 1,300† p., 18 m. E. of Prescott, 12 from River Falls. Engaged in miscellaneous manufactures.
Pierce Co. Herald .... W. **7,775**

ELROY, Juneau Co.
Head Light .... W. **7,776**

EVANSVILLE, Rock Co., 1,000 p., on Madison division of Chicago & Northwestern Rd., 25 m. from Beloit. Surrounded by a farming country.
Review .... W. **7,777**

FOND DU LAC, c. h., Fond du Lac Co., 16,068† p., at S. end of Lake Winnebago and on Chicago & Northwestern and Sheboygan & Fond du Lac Rds., 60 m. from Milwaukee and 177 from Chicago. A heavy grain, lumber and pork market. Considerable manufacturing carried on.
Commonwealth .... D. **7,778**
" .... W. **7,779**
Journal .... W. **7,780**
Nordwestlicher Courier .. W. **7,781**
Saturday Reporter .... W. **7,782**

FORT ATKINSON, Jefferson Co., 2,311† p., on Rock r. and Chicago & Northwestern Rd., 20 m. from Janesville and 111 from Chicago. In an agricultural district, and carrying on manufactures and mills. Centre of a grain and produce trade.
Jefferson Co. Union ...... W. **7,783**

FORT HOWARD, Brown Co., 3,860† p., on Fox r., opposite Green Bay. Northern terminus of Wisconsin division and southern terminus of Peninsula division of C. & N. W. Rd. and eastern terminus of G. B. & Minn. Rd.
Herald .... W. **7,784**
Monitor .... W. **7,785**

FOUNTAIN CITY, Buffalo Co., 900 p., on Mississippi r., 8 m. above Wenona and 40 above La Crosse. Has a steamer landing, and is a grain and wheat market for an agricultural district.
Buffalo Co. Republikaner W. **7,786**

FOX LAKE, Dodge Co., 1,570 p., on Milwaukee & St. Paul Rd., 65 m. from Milwaukee. In a wheat-growing section.
Representative .... W. **7,787**

FRIENDSHIP, c. h., Adams Co., 650 p., on Little Roche-a-Cris r. Engaged in raising hops, stock and grain.
Adams Co. Press .... W. **7,788**

GALESVILLE, c. h., Trempealeau Co., 1,068 p., 8 m. N. E. of Trempealeau.
Independent .... W. **7,789**

GENEVA, Walworth Co., 1,700† p., on Geneva Lake, and Fox R. branch of Chicago & Northwestern Rd., 8 m. S. E. of Elkhorn.
Geneva Lake Herald .... W. **7,790**

GRAND RAPIDS, c. h., Wood Co., 3,000 p., on Wisconsin r., 100 m. N. of Portage City. Engaged in the lumbering business.
Tribune .... W. **7,791**
Wood Co. Reporter ...... W. **7,792**

GRANTSBURG, c. h., Burnett Co.
Sentinel .... W. **7,793**

GREEN BAY, c. h., Brown Co., 7,000† p., on Green r., at head of Green Bay, and

WISCONSIN.

on Chicago & Northwestern Rd. and Lake Pequin & Green Bay Rd., 65 m. from Fond du Lac. Has harbor and large lake commerce. Engaged in lumber trade. Fish business carried on.

State Gazette......D. **7,794**
" " ......W. **7,795**
Advocate......W. **7,796**
Concordia......W. **7,797**
Volks Zeitung......W. **7,798**

HAMMOND, St. Croix Co.

Independent......W. **7,799**

HUDSON, c. h., St. Croix Co., 2,000 p., on St. Croix r. and West Wisconsin Rd., 20 m. E. of St. Paul, Minn. The river is navigable for large steamboats to this point. Engaged in manufacturing and a shipping point for wheat.

Star and Times......W. **7,800**
True Republican......W. **7,801**

JANESVILLE, c. h., Rock Co., 11,000† p., on Rock r. and on Chicago & Northwestern Rd., 91 m. from Chicago and 70 from Milwaukee. A branch of the Milwaukee & St. Paul Rd. passes through here, connecting with Milwaukee. Rock r. furnishes power, which is employed in manufacturing. Surrounded by an agricultural district.

Gazette......D. **7,802**
" ......S. W. **7,803**
" ......W. **7,804**
City Times......W. **7,805**
Rock Co. Recorder......W. **7,806**

JEFFERSON, c. h., Jefferson Co., 2,213† p., on Wisconsin division of Chicago & Northwestern Rd., 13 m. S. of Watertown, 117 from Chicago, 45 from Milwaukee and 30 from Madison. Rock r. furnishes water power for several mills and factories here.

Banner......W. **7,807**

JENNY, c. h., Lincoln Co.

Lincoln Co. Advocate...W. **7,808**

JUNEAU, c. h., Dodge Co., 600 p., on Chicogo & Northwestern Rd., 58 m. N. W. of Milwaukee and 145 from Chicago. Shipping point for produce.

Dodge Co. Democrat......W. **7,809**

KENOSHA, c. h., Kenosha Co., 4,500 p., on Lake Michigan, 35 m. S. of Milwaukee, on Milwaukee division of Chicago & Northwestern Rd; also eastern terminus of Kenosha, Rockford & Rock Island Rd. It has a good harbor and considerable lake commerce. Engaged in manufacturing wagons and thumble-skeins, and surrounded by a butter and cheese district.

Telegraph......W. **7,810**
Union......W. **7,811**

KEWAUNEE, c. h., Kewaunee Co., 1,200 p., on Lake Michigan, at mouth of Kewaunee r., 27 m. E. of Green Bay.

Enterprise......W. **7,812**

KILBOURN CITY, Columbia Co., 1,114 p., on La Crosse division of Milwaukee & St. Paul Rd., 17 m. N. W. of Portage. Wisconsin r. affords water power for several mills here.

Wisconsin Mirror......W. **7,813**

LA CROSSE, c. h., La Crosse Co., 12,000† p., on Mississippi r., and terminus of La Crosse division of Milwaukee & St. Paul Rd. Engaged in lumber and other manufacturing and river commerce. Centre of trade.

Liberal Democrat......D. **7,814**
" " ......W. **7,815**
Republican and Leader...D. **7,816**
" " " ..W. **7,817**
Faedrelandet og Emigranten......W. **7,818**
Nord Stern......W. **7,819**
North-Western Miller....W. **7,820**
Sun......W. **7,821**

LANCASTER, c, h., Grant Co., 3,000 p., on Grant r., about 14 m. from Mississippi r. and about 25 S. E. of Prairie du Chien. Lead mines are found in this vicinity. Centre of a mineral and agricultural county. Engaged in the manufacture of woolen goods.

Grant Co. Advocate......W. **7,822**
Grant Co. Herald......W. **7,823**

LODI, Columbia Co., 1,565 p., 20 m. from Madison, on Chicago & Northwestern Rd. Has fine water power. Surrounded by an agricultural district.

Valley News......W. **7,824**

LONE ROCK, Richland Co

Pilot......W. **7,825**

MADISON, State capital, Dane Co., 10,145 p., between Lakes Mendota and Monona, 96 m. from Milwaukee, at junction of four railroads. Increasing in population and business. Surrounded by an agricultural region.

Democrat......D. **7,826**
" ......W. **7,827**
Wisconsin State Journal..D. **7,828**
" " " T. W. **7,829**
" " " W. **7,830**
Nordvesten......W. **7,831**
Wisconsin Botschafter...W. **7,832**
Wisconsin Statesman....W. **7,833**
Soldiers' Record.
Wisconsin Journal of Education......M. **7,835**

MANITOWOC, c. h., Manitowoc Co., 6,000 p., on Lake Michigan, at mouth of Manitowoc r. and on Wisconsin Central Rd., 90 m. from Milwaukee. It has a harbor, and is engaged in ship building and lumber trade.

Journal......D, **7,836**
Sonntagsblatt......Sund. **7,837**
Nord-Westen......W. **7,838**
Pilot......W. **7,839**
Tribune......W. **7,840**

MARINETTE, Oconto Co., 2,800† p., on Chicago & Northwestern Rd. and on Green Bay, at mouth of Menominee r., 57 m. from Green Bay. Engaged in the lumber trade.

Marinette and Peshtigo Eagle......W. **7,841**

MAUSTON, Juneau Co., 1,200 p., on Lemonweir r. and Milwaukee & La Crosse Rd., 127 m. from Milwaukee.

Star......W. **7,842**

MAZOMANIE, Dane Co.

Sickle......W. **7,843**

MEDFORD, Taylor Co.

Taylor Co. News......W. **7,844**
Taylor Co. Star......W. **7,845**

MENASHA, Winnebago Co., 4,000† p., on Fox r., at outlet of Lake Winnebago, nearly opposite Neenah, 1 m. distant. Contains grist mills, saw mills, potteries, an iron foundry, and pail, chair, and sash and blind factories.

Press....................W. **7,846**

MENOMONIE, c. h., Dunn Co., 3,433 p., on Red Cedar r. and West Wisconsin Rd., 23 m. from Eau Claire and 40 from Wabasha, on Mississippi r. The river furnishes power, which is employed in saw mills. Engaged in the lumber trade and agriculture.

Dunn Co. News........W. **7,847**
Times....................W. **7,848**

MILWAUKEE, c. h., Milwaukee Co., 100,781† p., on Lake Michigan, at mouth of Milwaukee r. It has one of the finest harbors on the lakes and is engaged in commerce. One of the largest grain markets in the West. Railroads connect with Chicago and all of the principal cities east and west. The manufactures are various and important. Largest city in the State.

Banner und Volksfreund..D. **7,849**
Wisconsin Banner und Volksfreund..........W. **7,850**
Sonntags-Blatt........Sund. **7,851**
Commercial Times........D. **7,852**
Journal of Commerce....W. **7,853**
Der Socialist..............D. **7,854**
Evening Wisconsin.......D. **7,855**
" " ....S. M. **7,856**
" " ......W. **7,857**
Germania..................D. **7,858**
" ....W. **7,859**
Herold....................D. **7,860**
" ....W. **7,861**
Volks Magazin........Sund. **7,862**
News......................D. **7,863**
" ....S. W. **7,864**
" ....W. **7,865**
See-Bote...................D. **7,866**
" ....W. **7,867**
Sentinel...................D. **7,868**
" ....T. W. **7,869**
" ....W. **7,870**
Catholic Vindicator......W. **7,871**
Christian Statesman.....W. **7,872**
Columbia..................W. **7,873**
Cream City Courier.....W. **7,874**
Freidenker................W. **7,875**
Spectroscope..............W. **7,876**
Acker und Gartenbau Zeitung..................M. **7,877**
Catholic School Record...M. **7,878**
Citadel....................M. **7,879**
Erziehungs-Blætter........M. **7,880**
Fortschritt der Zeit.......M. **7,881**
Grand Army Sentinel....M. **7,882**
Monthly Magazine........M. **7,883**
Musical Echo.............M. **7,884**
Northwestern Illustrated Mechanical Journal...M. **7,885**
School Bulletin and North-western Journal of Education.................M. **7,886**
Young Churchman........M. **7,887**
Magazin..................Qr. **7,888**
North-Western............Qr. **7,889**

MINERAL POINT, Iowa Co., 3,600† p., at terminus of Mineral Point Rd., a branch of Illinois Central Rd., 33 m. from Warren, 180 from Chicago and 190 from Milwaukee. Surrounded by a mineral region, from which large quantities of copper and lead are exported annually. It is the grain and general produce market for a tract of country of 15 miles square.

National Democrat......W. **7,890**
Tribune...................W. **7,891**
Our Messenger...........M. **7,892**

MONDOVI, Buffalo Co.

Buffalo Co. Herald......W. **7,893**

MONROE, c. h., Green Co., 3,408 p., at terminus of Southern Wisconsin division of Milwaukee & St. Paul Rd., 34 m. from Janesville. Engaged in agriculture, stock raising and dairying, and the centre of an active trade.

Greene Co. Reformer....W. **7,894**
Sentinel..................W. **7,895**

MONTELLO, c. h., Marquette Co., 1,000 p., on Fox r., about 20 m. from Portage City and 12 from Princeton.

Express...................W. **7,896**

MUSCODA, Grant Co.

News......................W. **7,897**

NEENAH, Winnebago Co., 5,000† p., on Fox r., and Chicago & Northwestern and Wisconsin Central Rds., 14 m. from Oshkosh. Engaged in the manufacture of flour and paper. There are several first-class flour mills in the place. Lumber and other manufactures carried on.

City Times...............W. **7,898**
Gazette...................W. **7,899**
Teetotaler................W. **7,900**

NEILLSVILLE, c. h., Clark Co.

Clark Co. Press..........W. **7,901**
Clark Co. Republican....W. **7,902**

NEW LISBON, Juneau Co.

Juneau Co. Argus.......W. **7,903**

NEW LONDON, Waupaca Co., 3,000† p., on Wolf r., and Green Bay & Lake Pepin Rd., 40 m. from Green Bay, 60 from Oshkosh and 22 from Menasha. Trade centre for an agricultural district. Engaged in manufactures of various kinds.

News......................W. **7,904**
Times.....................W. **7,905**

NEW RICHMOND, St. Croix Co., 847 p., on North Wisconsin Rd., 18 m. from Hudson. A trade centre and shipping point for an agricultural district.

St. Croix Republican.....W. **7,906**

NORTH LA CROSSE, La Crosse Co.

Star........................W. **7,907**

OCONOMOWOC, Waukesha Co., 2,500† p., on La Crosse division of Milwaukee & St. Paul Rd., 31 m. from Milwaukee. Located in an agricultural district. Produce shipping point and summer resort.

Local......................W. **7,908**
Times.....................W. **7,909**
Wisconsin Free Press....W. **7,910**

OCONTO, c. h., Oconto Co., 4,463† p., on Green Bay, at mouth of Oconto r., and on Chicago & Northwestern Rd., 30 m. from Green Bay. Engaged in the lumber trade.

Lumberman..............W. **7,911**
Oconto Co. Reporter.....W. **7,912**

OMRO, Winnebago Co.

Journal....................W. **7,913**

OREGON, Dane Co.

Village Record..........W. **7,914**

OSCEOLA, Polk Co.

Polk Co. Press...........W. **7,915**

OSHKOSH, c. h., Winnebago Co., 17,011† p., on Lake Winnebago, at mouth of Fox r., and on Chicago & Northwestern Rd. Engaged in the lumber business. Some steamboat building done here. Three

WISCONSIN.

lines of steamers run from here during the summer season.

Northwestern............D. **7,916**
" ....W. **7,917**
Times....................W. **7,918**
Wisconsin Telegraph. ...W. **7,919**
Northwestern Prohibitionist...................W. **7,920**

PALMYRA, Jefferson Co.
Enterprise...............W. **7,921**

PLATTEVILLE, Grant Co.
Grant Co. Witness.......W. **7,922**

PLOVER, Portage Co., 1,200† p., on Wisconsin r., about 5 m. below Stevens' Point. Engaged in lumber business and centre of trade. Manufacture of flour carried on.
Times.....................W. **7,923**

PLYMOUTH, Sheboygan Co.
Reporter.................W. **7,924**

PORTAGE, c. h., Columbia Co., 3,945 p., on Milwaukee & St. Paul Rd., and Ship Canal, connecting Wisconsin and Fox rs. Terminus of the Madison & Portage Rd., northern division of Milwaukee, St. Paul, and the Portage & Stevens' Point Rd. Engaged in commerce and lumber trade.
Columbia Co. Wecker....W. **7,925**
Western Advance........W. **7,926**
Wisconsin State Register.W. **7,927**

PORT WASHINGTON, Ozaukee Co., 3,500† p., on Lake Michigan, 90 m. N. N. E. of Madison. Engaged in manufactures and is a trade centre.
Ozaukee Co. Advertiser..W. **7,928**
Zeitung.................W. **7,929**

POYNETTE, Columbia Co.
Reporter................W. **7,930**

PRAIRIE DU CHIEN, c. h., Crawford Co.
Courier.................W. **7,931**
Union...................W. **7,932**

PRESCOTT, Pierce Co.
Pierce Co. Plaindealer...W. **7,933**

PRINCETON, Green Lake Co., 1,250† p., on Fox r. and Sheboygan & Fond du Lac Rd., 35 m. from Fond du Lac and 13 S. W. of Berlin. A shipping point and trade centre.
Republic................W. **7,934**

RACINE, c. h., Racine Co.
Advocate................W. **7,935**
Journal..................W. **7,936**
Racine Co. Argus........W. **7,937**
Slavie...................W. **7,938**
College Mercury.......S. M. **7,939**

RANDOLPH, Dodge Co.
Enterprise..............W. **7,940**

REEDSBURG, Sauk Co., 1,200† p., on Madison division of Chicago & Northwestern Rd., 16 m. from Baraboo.
Free Press...............W. **7,941**

RICE LAKE, Barron Co.
Barron Co. Chronotype..W. **7,942**

RICHLAND CENTER, c. h., Richland Co., 1,200† p., on Pine r., about 12 m. from Wisconsin r. and near Milwaukee & St. Paul Rd. Engaged in agriculture, stock-raising, lumbering and manufacturing.
Richland Co. Republican.W. **7,943**

RIPON, Fond du Lac Co., 3,605† p., on Milwaukee & St. Paul Rd., at its junction with Oshkosh branch, 86 m. from Milwaukee, also on Sheboygan & Fond du Lac Rd. Surrounded by an agricultural district and seat of Ripon College.
Commonwealth..........W. **7,944**
Free Press...............W. **7,945**

RIVER FALLS, Pierce Co., 1,500 p., on Kinnickinnie r., 30 m. from St. Paul. Engaged in lumber trade and manufacturing.
Advance.................W. **7,946**
Journal..................W. **7,947**
Press....................W. **7,948**

SAUK CITY, Sauk Co., 1,200 p., on Wisconsin r., 15 m. S. of Baraboo. Engaged in hop culture.
Pionier am Wisconsin...W. **7,949**

SHARON, Walworth Co., 2,000† p., on Wisconsin division of Chicago & Northwestern Rd., 15 m. S. W. of Elkhorn. Engaged in agriculture and dairying.
Inquirer..................W. **7,950**

SHAWANO, c. h., Shawano Co., 920† p., on Wolf r., head of navigation, 58 m. N. of Oshkosh. Centre of farming district. Principal branch of industry, lumbering.
Shawano Co. Journal....W. **7,951**

SHEBOYGAN, c. h., Sheboygan Co., 6,000 p., on Lake Michigan and Sheboygan r., and at terminus of Sheboygan & Fond du Lac Rd., 62 m. N. of Milwaukee. Engaged in lake commerce, lumber trade and manufactures.
Herald...................W. **7,952**
National Demokrat......W. **7,953**
Times....................W. **7,954**
Tribun...................W. **7,955**

SPARTA, c. h., Monroe Co., 3,500 p., on La Crosse r. and Milwaukee & St. Paul Rd., 25 m. from La Crosse. In an agricultural district. Artesian wells here furnish water, which is used for medicinal purposes.
Herald...................W. **7,956**
Monroe Co. Republican..W. **7,957**

STEVENS' POINT, Portage Co., 4,000† p., on Wisconsin r. and Wisconsin Central Rd. There are several mills here, and large quantities of lumber are manufactured and exported.
Journal..................W. **7,958**
Wisconsin Pinery........W. **7,959**

STOUGHTON, Dane Co., 1,207† p., on Prairie du Chien division of Milwaukee & St. Paul Rd., 16 m. from Madison.
Courier..................W. **7,960**

STURGEON BAY, c. h., Door Co., 1,400 p., on Sturgeon Bay, an inlet from Green Bay, and about 8 m. from Lake Michigan. Engaged in lumbering, farming and shipping.
Door Co. Advocate......W. **7,961**
Expositor.................W. **7,962**
Evergreen................M. **7,963**

SUPERIOR, c. h., Douglas Co., 759† p., at W. extremity of Lake Superior, has a good harbor and regular lines of steamboats ply between here and Detroit, Chicago and other points on the Lakes. Surrounded by an agricultural country. Engaged in manufactures and exportation of lumber, fish and furs.
Times....................W. **7,964**

TOMAH, Monroe Co., 2,000 p., at junction of Milwaukee & St. Paul and Wisconsin Valley Rds., 42 m. from La Crosse. Engaged in agriculture and lumbering.
Journal..................W. **7,965**

WISCONSIN.

TREMPEALEAU, Trempealeau Co., 1,116† p., on Mississippi r. and Chicago & Northwestern Rd., 20 m. above La Crosse.
Trempealeau Co. Republican..................W. **7,966**

TWO RIVERS, Manitowoc Co., 1,951† p., on Lake Michigan, about 6 m. N. E. of Manitowoc. Engaged in lake commerce, ship building and the lumber business.
Manitowoc Co. Chronicle.W. **7,967**

VIROQUA, c. h., Vernon Co., 1,352 p., on Kiskoper r., 35 m. S. E. of La Crosse. An agricultural district surrounding. Some lumbering carried on.
Vernon Co. Censor......W. **7,968**
Vidette..................W. **7,969**

WATERLOO, Jefferson Co., 1,000† p., on Milwaukee & St. Paul Rd., 60 m. W. of Milwaukee and 24 E. of Madison. It commands a good trade. Engaged in manufactures.
Journal..................W. **7,970**

WATERTOWN, Jefferson Co., 9,524† p., on Rock r. and Chicago & Northwestern Rd., at intersection of Milwaukee & St. Paul Rd., 43 m. from Milwaukee and 39 from Janesville. The river furnishes water power, which is employed in manufacturing. Centre of trade.
Democrat................W. **7,971**
Republican...............W. **7,972**
Weltburger...............W. **7,973**

WAUKESHA, c. h., Waukesha Co., 4,000† p., on Fox r. and Milwaukee & St. Paul Rd., 18 m. from Milwaukee. Engaged in manufacturing and a place of trade. Stone quarries, mineral spring and State Industrial School located here
Freeman.................W. **7,974**
Plaindealer..............W. **7,975**
Waukesha Co. Democrat.W. **7,976**

WAUPACA, c. h., Waupaca Co., 2,100† p., on Waupaca r. and Wisconsin Central Rd., 50 m. N. by W. of Fond du Lac. Engaged in agriculture and manufactures.
Waupaca Co. Republican W. **7,977**

WAUPUN, Fond du Lac Co., 2,069† p., on Milwaukee & St. Paul and Chicago & Northwestern Rds., 18 m. from Fond du Lac and 64 from Milwaukee. Centre of an agricultural region. State Prison located here.
Leader...................W. **7,978**
Times....................W. **7,979**

WAUSAU, c. h., Marathon Co., 2,880† p., on Wisconsin r., 35 m. from Stevens' Point and 175 N. of Madison. Engaged in the lumber trade and manufacturing.
Central Wisconsin.......W. **7,980**
Wisconsin River Pilot....W. **7,981**
Wochenblatt..............W. **7,982**

WAUTOMA, c. h., Waushara Co., 800 p., 25 m. W. by N. of Berlin and 30 N. of Portage City.
Waushara Argus........W. **7,983**

WEST BEND, c. h., Washington Co., 2,300† p., on Milwaukee r., on the line of Chicago & W. W. Rd., 33 m. from Milwaukee. The river affords water power, which is employed in various manufactures.
Democrat ....W. **7,984**
Republican..............W. **7,985**

WEYAUWEGA, Waupaca Co., 2,000 p., on Waupaca r., 8 m. S. E. of Waupaca. The river affords power for the flour and saw mills here.
Times....................W. **7,986**

WHITEHALL, Trempealeau Co.
Trempeleau Co. Messenger....................W. **7,987**

WHITEWATER, Walworth Co., 4,395† p., on Milwaukee & St. Paul Rd., 51 m. from Milwaukee. An agricultural district and centre of trade.
Register.................W. **7,988**

WILSON, St. Croix Co.
Pioneer..................W. **7,989**

TERRITORIES.

ARIZONA.

PRESCOTT, c. h., Yavapai Co., 2,500† p., among the Pine Mountains, 140 m. E. of Colorado r. and 500 S. of Salt Lake City. In a mining and agricultural district and surrounded by vast forests of pine. A supply point for a large section of country.
Arizona Miner..........W. **7,990**

TUCSON, Pima Co., Territorial capital. 3,224 p., on Santa Cruz r., 485 m. from San Diego and 275 from Yuma. An agricultural and stock-raising country. On the overland route from the Southern States to California, and the centre of considerable trade. Mining is carried on to some extent in this section. Largest town in the territory.
Arizona Citizen.

YUMA, Yuma Co., 1,800† p., on Colorado r., at mouth of Gila r., 764 m. from San Francisco, 240 from San Diego and 175 from the Gulf of California. Steamers ascend the river to the mining districts, carrying on an extensive trade. Engaged in commerce and mining.
Arizona Sentinel........W. **7,992**

COLORADO.

ALMA, Park Co.
Mount Lincoln News....W. **7,993**

BOULDER, c. h., Boulder Co., 1,950† p., on Boulder Creek and Boulder Valley Rd., 28 m. N. W. of Denver. Engaged in gold, silver and coal mining, agriculture and stock raising.
Boulder Co. News........W. **7,994**
Colorado Banner.........W. **7,995**

CANON CITY, c. h., Fremont Co., 900† p., on Arkansas r., 45 m. from Pueblo and 90 from Denver.
Avalanche...............W. **7,996**
Times....................W. **7,997**

CASTLE ROCK, c. h., Douglas Co.
Douglas Co. News.......W. **7,998**

CENTRAL CITY, c. h., Gilpin Co., 5,000 p., in the Rocky Mountains, 40 m. W. by N. of Denver. Supply point for the surrounding mining district. Engaged in gold mining, milling and smelting.
Register..................D. **7,999**
" ....W. **8,000**

COLORADO.

COLORADO SPRINGS, c. h., El Paso Co.
Colorado Free Press......W. **8,001**
Colorado Mountaineer...W. **8,002**
Gazette and El Paso Co. News..................W. **8,003**

DEL NORTE, c. h., Rio Grande Co.
San Juan Prospector....W. **8,004**

DENVER, Arapahoe Co., Territorial capital, 21,000† p., at confluence of Cheery Creek and S. Platte r., terminus of Kansas Pacific, Denver Pacific, Colorado Central, and Denver & Rio Grande Rds., 620 m. from Omaha, Neb. Leading city in the Territory, and commercial centre for the mining and agricultural interests of Colorado and New Mexico.
Colorado Democrat.
Rocky Mountain News....D. **8,006**
" " "..W. **8,007**
Times....................D. **8,008**
"....................W. **8,009**
Tribune..................D. **8,010**
"..................W. **8,011**
Colorado Farmer and Live Stock Journal....W. **8,012**
Colorado Journal........W. **8,013**
Mirror..................W. **8,014**
Rocky Mountain Herald.W. **8,015**
Mining Review......B. W. **8,016**
Rocky Mountain Presbyterian..................M. **8,017**
Woman's Journal.......M. **8,018**

EVANS, Weld Co., on South Platte r. and Denver Pacific Rd., 48 m. from Denver.
Journal..................W. **8,019**

FAIRPLAY, c. h., Park Co.
Sentinel..................W. **8,020**

FORT COLLINS, c. h., Larimer Co.
Larimer Co. Express....W. **8,021**
Standard..................W. **8,022**

GEORGETOWN, c. h., Clear Creek Co., 5,000† p., in the Rocky Mountains, 50 m. W. of Denver. Mining extensively carried on.
Colorado Miner..........W. **8,023**

GOLDEN, c. h., Jefferson Co., 2,500† p., 16 m. W. of Denver, on a fork of South Platte r., which affords water power. Is the present terminus of the Colorado Central Rd., connecting with the Union Pacific and Kansas Pacific Rds. Rich gold mines near here. U. S. Land Office at this point. Manufactures carried on in the neighborhood. Altitude, 5,600 feet above the sea.
Colorado Transcript.....W. **8,024**
Globe....................W. **8,025**

GREELEY, Weld Co., 1,200 p., on Denver Pacific Rd., and on Cachia La Poudre r. at its junction with Platte r., 55 m. from Denver. Engaged in agriculture.
Colorado Sun............W. **8,026**
Tribune..................W. **8,027**
Colorado Horticulturist.

LONGMONT, Boulder Co., 550 p., 7 m. from railroad terminus and 30 from Denver. Centre of an agricultural region.
Press....................W. **8,029**

PUEBLO, c. h., Pueblo Co., 3,500† p., on Denver & Rio Grande Narrow Gauge Rd. and Arkansas r., 118 m. S. of Denver. The metropolis of southern Colorado, and surrounded by an agricultural and stock raising district.

COLORADO.

Colorado Chieftain.......D. **8,030**
" "......W. **8,031**
Republican............S. W. **8,032**

ROSITA, Fremont Co.
Index....................W. **8,033**

SAGUACHE, c. h., Saguache Co.
Chronicle................W. **8,034**

SILVERTON, c. h., La Plata Co.
La Plata Miner.........W. **8,035**

SUNSHINE, Boulder Co.
Courier..................W. **8,036**

TRINIDAD, c. h., Las Animas Co., 2,000† p., on Las Animas r., 220 m. from Denver City, 130 from Kit Carson, on Kansas Pacific Rd. Centre of a grazing country. Surrounded by fields of coal.
Colorado Pioneer........W. **8,037**
El Explorador..........W. **8,038**
*Enterprise and Chronicle*W. **8,039**

WALSENBURG, c. h., Huerfano Co.
Huerfano Independent...W. **8,040**

WEST LAS ANIMAS, Bent Co.
Las Animas Colorado Leader..................W. **8,041**

DAKOTA.

BISMARCK, Saguache Co.
Tribune...............T. W. **8,042**
"..................W. **8,043**

CANTON, c. h., Lincoln Co., 400 p., on Sioux City & Pembina Rd., 60 m. N. W. of Sioux City, Iowa. Has water power and is a place of active trade.
Sioux Valley News......W. **8,044**

ELK POINT, c. h., Union Co., 500 p., on Dakota Southern Rd., between Missouri and Sioux rs., 22 m. from Sioux City, Iowa, and 39 E. of Yankton. Grazing and farming country in vicinity. Some milling carried on.
Union Co. Courier.......W. **8,045**

FARGO, c. h., Cass Co.
Times....................W. **8,046**

GRAND FORKS, c. h., Grand Forks Co.
Plaindealer..............W. **8,047**

SIOUX FALLS, c. h., Minnehaha Co., 800† p., on Sioux r., 90 m. N. of Sioux City, Iowa. Rapidly growing business, having water power, which is only partially developed for manufacturing purposes.
Independent.............W. **8,048**
Pantagraph.............W. **8,049**

SPRINGFIELD, Bon Homme Co., 300 p., on Missouri r., 90 m. above Sioux City, Iowa, and 30 above Yankton. Base of supplies for an agricultural district and Black Hills out-fitting parties, and engaged in trade with the whole upper Missouri counties.
Times....................W. **8,050**

SWAN LAKE, c. h., Turner Co.
Era......................W. **8,051**

VERMILLION, c. h., Clay Co., 1,200† p., on Missouri r., at mouth of Vermillion r., 30 m. from Yankton and 35 from Sioux City, Iowa. Surrounded by a growing agricultural country.
Register.............. S. W. **8,052**
Dakota Republican......W. **8,053**

YANKTON, c. h., Yankton Co., Territor

DAKOTA.

ial capital, 3,200† p., on Missouri r., about 7 m. from mouth of Dakota r., on the line of Dakota Southern Rd. Largest city in the Territory and has an extensive trade with settlers. Surrounded by an agricultural district.

Press and Dakotian......D. **8,054**
" " " .....W. **8,055**
Dakota Freie Presse.....W. **8,056**
Dakota Herald..........W. **8,057**

IDAHO.

BOISE CITY, c. h., Boise Co., Territorial capital, 1,000 p., on N. bank of Boise r., about 30 m. W. S. W. of Idaho City. Trade centre, surrounded by an agricultural country. Mining regions are located within a short distance.

Statesman............T. W. **8,058**
" ....W. **8,059**

IDAHO CITY, c. h., Boise Co., 600† p., at confluence of Elk and Moor's Creeks, about 35 m. E. N. E. of Boise City. Gold and silver found near this place. Engaged in mining and farming.

Idaho World ....S. W. **8,060**
" " ....W. **8,061**

SILVER CITY, c. h., Owyhee Co., 1,347 p., on Jordan Creek, about 1 m. above Ruby City. Silver is found here in quartz rocks. It has several quartz mills. Connected to Winnemucca by stage.

Idaho Avalanche.........D. **8,062**
" " ....W. **8,063**

INDIAN.

ATOKA, Choctaw Nation, 380 p., on Missouri, Kansas & Texas Rd., 271 m. from Fort Scott, Kansas.

Vindicator..............W. **8,064**

CADDO, Choctaw Nation.

Oklahoma Star..........W. **8,065**

OSAGE AGENCY.

Indian Herald..........W. **8,066**

TAHLEQUAH, c. h., Cherokee Nation, about 200 m. S. of Fort Scott, Kansas, and 40 from the Arkansas State line.

Cherokee Advocate.......W. **8,067**

MONTANA.

BOZEMAN, c. h., Gallatin Co., 500† p., on E. Gallatin r., 400 m. from Salt Lake. Situate in an agricultural and stock-raising region. Mines of coal found in this vicinity.

Avant Courier...........W. **8,068**
Times...................W. **8,069**

DEER LODGE CITY C. H., Deer Lodge Co., 788 p., on Deer Lodge r., near W. base of Rocky Mountains, 43 m. from Helena, on the line of the Northern Pacific Rd. The richest, most numerous and most productive placer and quartz mines in the West are in this county.

New North West....... W. **8,070**

DIAMOND CITY, c. h., Meagher Co.

Rocky Mountain Husbandman..............W. **8,071**

MONTANA.

FORT BENTON, c. h., Choteau Co.

Record..................W. **8,072**

HELENA, c. h., Lewis and Clark Co., 4,000† p., near Prickley Pear Creek, 16 m. from Missouri r. Largest town in Montana and centre of trade. Surrounded by an agricultural district, and mines of gold and silver and iron.

Herald...................D. **8,073**
" ....W. **8,074**
Independent..............D. **8,075**
" ....W. **8,076**
Montana News..........D. **8,077**

MISSOULA, c. h., Missoula Co., 500 p., on Hell Gate r., 145 m. W. of Helena.

Missoulian..............W. **8,078**

VIRGINIA CITY, Madison Co., Territorial capital, 2,000 p., on Alder Creek, 125 m. S. of Helena. Surrounded by mining districts. Stages connect with Deer Lodge and other important points.

Montanian...............W. **8,079**

NEW MEXICO.

ALBUQUERQUE, c. h., Bernalillo Co., 2,000 p., on Rio Grande r., 75 m. from Santa Fe. Centre of trade in wool, hides, corn and wine. Silver, gold, copper, coal, lead and iron mines abound in the vicinity.

Republican Review.......W. **8,080**

CIMARRON, c. h., Colfax Co.

News and Press..........W. **8,081**

LAS CREUCES, Doña Ana Co.

Borderer.
El Fronterizo.

LAS VEGAS, San Miguel Co., on a branch of Rio Pecos r., about 40 m. E. of Santa Fe.

Gazette..................W. **8,084**
New Mexico Advertiser...W. **8,085**

MESILLA, c. h., Doña Ana Co.

News....................W. **8,086**

SANTA FE, c. h., Santa Fe Co., Territorial capital, 5,000 p., about 20 m. E. of Rio Grande r. The emporium of the overland trade.

New Mexican.
Regimental Flag.

SILVER CITY, Grant Co.

Herald.

UTAH.

BEAVER CITY, c. h., Beaver Co.

Enterprise............T. W. **8,090**

OGDEN, c. h., Weber Co., 5,000 p., on Weber r., at junction of Union Pacific, Central Pacific and Utah Central Rds., 36 m. from Salt Lake City. Centre of an agricultural district and has a thriving trade. Various kinds of manufacturing done here.

Junction................. D. **8,091**
" ....S. W. **8,092**

OGDEN CITY, c. h., Weber Co.

Ogden Freeman.......S. W. **8,093**

ST. GEORGE, c. h., Washington Co., 2,000† p., on Rio Virgin r., 330 m. S. of Salt Lake. Agricultural soil. Cotton, grapes, figs, pomegranates, and all the usual crops of fruits and vegetables in

UTAH.

warm climates grow freely. Silver and copper mines scattered all over the country.

Utah Promologist and Gardener..............M. **8,094**

SALT LAKE CITY, c. h., Salt Lake Co., Territorial capital, 21,000† p., on Utah Central Rd., 36 m. from Ogden, near the E. bank of Jordan r. and 22 S. E. of Great Salt Lake. An agricultural district. Surrounded by silver and base metal mines. The largest and most important city in the Territories and centre of trade.

Deseret News..............D. **8,095**
" " ....S. W. **8,096**
" " ....W. **8,097**
Salt Lake Herald..........D. **8,098**
" " " ......S. W. **8,099**
Salt Lake Tribune........D. **8,100**
" " " ....W. **8,101**
Utah Evening Mail......D. **8,102**
Utah Miner..............W. **8,103**
Utah Skandinav........W. **8,104**
Juvenile Instructor...B. W. **8,105**
Utah Educational Journal....................M. **8,106**

WASHINGTON.

KALAMA, Cowlitz Co., on Columbia r., about 40 m. N. by W. of Portland, Oregon.

Beacon.

OLYMPIA, c. h., Thurston Co., Territorial capital, 2,000 p., at S. extremity of Puget Sound, 150 m. from the sea. The town is rapidly growing in population and importance. Engaged in manufacturing and commerce.

Morning Echo...........D. **8,108**
" " ....W. **8,109**
Puget Sound Courier....W. **8,110**
Transcript..............W. **8,111**
Washington Standard...W. **8,112**

PORT TOWNSEND, c. h., Jefferson Co., 593 p., on Port Townsend Bay, 100 m. N. of Olympia. Engaged in commerce and the lumber trade.

Argus...................W. **8,113**

SEATTLE, c. h., Kings Co., 3,100† p., at mouth of Duwamish r., on Puget Sound, 60 m. N. N. E. of Olympia. Lumbering, agriculture and coal mining are the principal resources.

Dispatch..................D. **8,114**
Puget Sound Dispatch...W. **8,115**
Pacific Tribune.
Intelligencer.............W. **8,117**

STEILACOOM, c. h., Pierce Co.

Puget Sound Express...W. **8,118**

VANCOUVER, c. h., Clark Co., 750 p., on Columbia r., 10 m. from Portland, Oregon, to which it is connected by a daily line of steamers.

Independent.............W. **8,119**

WALLA WALLA, c. h., Walla Walla Co., 2,500† p., on Mill Creek, 30 m. from Columbia r. and about 410 E. by S. of Olympia. Surrounded by a farming and stock-raising district, and the trade centre for this portion of the Territory and northeastern Oregon.

Spirit................S. W. **8,120**
Statesman.
Union...................W. **8,122**

WHATCOM, c. h., Whatcom Co.

Bellingham Bay Mail...W. **8,123**

WYOMING.

CHEYENNE, c. h., Laramie Co., 3,000† p., on Union Pacific Rd., at junction of Denver Pacific Rd., 500 m. from Omaha, Neb., and 100 N. of Denver, Col. Central supply point, surrounded by agricultural, stock-raising and mining districts. Shipping point for all the forts and Indian agencies. Railroad repair shops located here.

Leader...................D. **8,124**
Wyoming Leader........W. **8,125**
Sun.......................D. **8,126**

EVANSTON, c. h., Uintah Co.

Age.......................D. **8,127**

LARAMIE CITY, c. h., Albany Co., on Laramie r. and Union Pacific Rd., 57 m. W. of Cheyenne. It derives its supplies from the stock-raising and timber interests in the vicinity.

Sentinel..................D. **8,128**
" ....W. **8,129**

HISTORICAL AND STATISTICAL DATA.

A SKETCH FOR THE BOOK OF THE CENTENNIAL NEWSPAPER EXHIBITION.

NEWSPAPERS IN 1776.

The first American newspaper was printed in Boston, Sept. 25, 1690. It was issued by Richard Pierce and published by Benjamin Harris, and was intended to be published once a month, but was immediately suppressed by the authorities. The only copy known to be in existence is in the State Paper Office in London. The *Boston News Letter*, published by John Campbell, appeared April 24, 1704, being issued weekly until 1776. It was followed by the *Boston Gazette*, Dec. 21, 1719, and by the *American Mercurie*, issued by William Bradford, at Philadelphia, Dec. 22, 1719. On Aug. 17, 1701, James Franklin, elder brother of Benjamin Franklin, established at Boston the *New England Courant*. Oct. 16, 1725, William Bradford, the founder of the *Mercurie* at Philadelphia, began the publication of the *New York Gazette*, the first paper issued in that city. In 1728 Benjamin Franklin established in Philadelphia the *Pennsylvania Gazette*. In 1754 four newspapers were published in Boston, two in New York, and two in Philadelphia. The *Virginia Gazette* was then printed at Williamsburg, having been first issued in 1736 by William Parks, who had previously given to the public for nine years the *Maryland Gazette*, at Annapolis. In 1776 seven journals were published in Massachusetts, one in New Hampshire, two in Rhode Island, four in Connecticut, four in New York, nine in Pennsylvania, two each in Maryland, Virginia, and North Carolina, three in South Carolina, and one in Georgia; in all thirty-seven. All were weeklies, with the exception of the *Advertiser*, of Philadelphia, which was semi-weekly.

NEWSPAPER STATISTICS IN 1876.

By the "American Newspaper Directory" for the current year, 1876, there appear to be now published in the United States and Territories, 738 daily, 70 tri-weekly, 121 semi-weekly, 6,235 weekly, 33 bi-weekly, 105 semi-monthly, 747 monthly, 13 bi-monthly, and 67 quarterly publications, making a total of 8,129 of all kinds.

Of the journals published in the country, the State of New York furnishes the largest number. Of all kinds, New York State prints 1,818; Pennsylvania follows with 738; Illinois is third; and then come in regular order Ohio, Iowa, Missouri and Indiana, all of which outstrip old Massachusetts, although she issues nearly 350. Only ten States print as many papers of all kinds as California, which ranks fourth in the number of its dailies. It seems to be peculiar to the new States at the West that they sustain daily papers. In many places the first newspaper established will be a daily, while in the old towns at the East such a thing was never heard of. Until within one or two years Florida has never had a daily paper.

At the present day it would seem that the United States print more newspapers than all the other nations of the world. Their growth has been rapid even in proportion to the increase of population. In 1776 we find we had thirty-seven papers and three millions of people. Now we have eight thousand papers and forty millions of people. These figures show that whilst one hundred years ago we printed one newspaper for every 30,000 souls, we now print one for every 5,000. This can be accounted for only on the hypothesis that the people are now more in the habit of reading than formerly. At the time Independence was declared probably no family took more than one paper, while now many take several.

NEWSPAPERS DEFINED.

A newspaper is defined by Webster to be "a sheet of paper printed and dis tributed at short intervals for conveying intelligence of passing events." In compiling a "Newspaper Directory" it is necessary to exercise a good deal of care to be able to say what should be called a newspaper. The definition given by Webster cannot be taken as an accurate description of the present-day newspaper, for numbers do not contain any news, while many sheets which do, are not considered newspapers. All the amateur publications, for example, are excluded, though the number is quite large of those printing considerable news; and many sheets devoted especially to advertising the business of some man or firm are also omitted. On the other hand, books and magazines—everything published at regular periods not exceeding three months—are classed as newspapers.

There has been of late a large increase of what are called "class papers." It is being recognized that every interest must be supported by a paper. There are religious papers, agricultural papers, commercial papers; those of a financial, insurance, masonic, and temperance complexion, and so on through the whole list of interests and isms. The class papers in many cases are very successful. They seem to be in receipt of an excellent advertising patronage, and for the obvious reason that they are taken by people to whose interests or theories they are specially devoted, so that when one wishes to communicate with this particular class they are *par excellence* the channels. An advertisement in the *Scientific American* will reach many thousands of mechanics, while the same advertisement in an ordinary paper would be read by possibly the same number of or more people, but by fewer mechanics. So an advertisement in the *American Builder* might reach more carpenters than one in the New York *Times*, although the circulation of the latter would surpass that of the former many times.

ADVERTISEMENTS THE LIFE-BLOOD OF NEWSPAPERS.

Among the newspapers which have been most successful in obtaining widespread circulations are certain story papers and Sabbath school journals, which do not contain news, and some of which are without advertisements. That some such journals can rely for profits upon their circulation for remuneration, does not render it less a fact that the advertisement is the life of newspapers. Daily papers are, in many instances, sold to newsboys at a price so low that it hardly pays the cost of the white paper on which they are printed. The editorial expenses, the setting of the types, the expensive presses, the magnificent incomes of the proprietors, are all the result of the advertising. Without the fast presses of to-day the editions of 50,000 copies could not be printed in two or three hours of a night as now, and but for the advertising patronage the papers could not be afforded at the low prices which make possible the immediate sale of such enormous numbers.

NEWSPAPER INCREASE.

The number of new papers started during the past five years has averaged not fewer than six per day, but the actual increase has been only two thousand one hundred and seventy-nine. Suspensions and consolidations account for the balance.

Since May 1, 1875, thirteen hundred and sixty-six papers have commenced pub. lication (an average of over four for each laboring day), and one thousand and ninety-seven have suspended. That the circulations are below what they were one year ago is also more than probable.

The States in which there has been an increase in number are: Arkansas, nine; California, twenty-eight; District of Columbia, eight; Georgia, five; Illinois, sixty-five; Indiana, eighteen; Iowa, twenty-two; Kansas, six; Kentucky, nine; Maine, one; Maryland, two; Massachusetts, ten; Michigan, eleven; Minnesota, two; Mississippi, five; Nebraska, seven; Nevada, two; New York, two; North Carolina, one; Ohio, thirty-one; Oregon, one; Pennsylvania, thirty-one; Texas, eighteen; Virginia, five; Wisconsin, eight; Territories, six; Dominion of Canada, twelve.

There has been a decrease in the following States: Alabama, six; Connecticut, two; Delaware, one; Florida, one; Louisiana, one; Missouri, twenty-three; New Hampshire, three; South Carolina, seven; Tennessee, five; Vermont, five; and in Newfoundland, two.

Exactly the same number as last year is issued in New Jersey—one hundred and seventy-seven—Rhode Island, twenty-seven, and West Virginia, seventy-five Divided geographically, the gain in number is: New England States, one; Middle States, thirty-four; Western States, one hundred and forty-seven; Southern States, forty; Pacific States, thirty-one; Territories, six; Canada and Newfoundland, ten.

INFLUENCES WHICH EFFECT NEWSPAPER CIRCULATIONS.

It is interesting to consider what influences chiefly contribute to extend or limit the circulation of papers. One reason why those of New York State should have a larger circulation than their contemporaries in the West is that the Occi dental States are largely peopled by emigrants from the Eastern, among whom there is a tendency to take a home paper. This swells the sale of Massachusetts and other New England papers. Another reason: New York is the metropolis of the country, the headquarters for all sorts of information; and the knowledge of this contributes to make people in every part of the country seek after the New York journals. It was notorious in the time of the war that the armies in the battle-field, officers and men, waited for the New York papers in order to get accounts of the battles they fought, as no others gave them so fully and accurately.

The leading morning papers of New York nearly all sell for four cents, but in the Western States five cents is the general price. Since, however, the hard times penny papers have come into fashion again, and it is quite a remarkable fact that most of the leading papers of the country were first brought into favor and notice as such.

The number of daily newspapers which stereotype their forms and use duplicate machinery is very limited, New York having as many as all the rest of the country combined.

The newspaper seems to be an institution specially calculated to advance in this country. Everybody reads it. Many men and women of more than ordinary intelligence read nothing else; and it would be wrong to assume that such do not educate themselves respectably, for he who studies thoroughly a well-conducted New York daily will not be badly informed on matters of importance. The necessities for newspapers seem to be endless. Politicians want them to advance their political interests; rings want them to influence the public mind; the public demands them to keep itself informed; religious denominations require their aid to propagate their distinctive tenets, and so on.

MODERN PRINTING PRESSES.

In the matter of printing presses there has been a great change in ideas in the past ten years. The Walter press, which has many points in its favor, is the only one used in the office of the New York *Times*. The St. Louis *Republican* also employs one of these machines. The Bullock press has superseded the Hoe in the New York *Herald*, *Sun*, and several other offices. Both these presses print from a continuous roll of paper. This feature alone implies a considerable saving in the working expenses of the press room. Another advantage they possess is their great compactness—a quality of much importance in large cities where room is scarce and expensive. The Bullock press is specially remarkable for this, and, other things being equal, bids fair, by virtue of its excellence in this regard, to advance to the very first rank. The Hoe press retains its position in most of the important offices outside the metropolitan cities, and is still used by the New York *Tribune*. Several manufacturers compete for the patronage in lower-priced machines. In the smaller weekly offices the old hand-press holds its own, and their sale is greater now than ever before, amounting to several hundred yearly.

WHAT KIND OF NEWSPAPERS THE PEOPLE WANT.

An impression prevails, particularly in country places, that the public want a large sheet of paper. The country newspaper publisher will almost always increase the size of his sheet if he can get advertising enough to pay the actual cost of the enlargement, and yet have no thought whatever of making a better paper. The notion that he is publisher of a large paper seems to gratify his pride. This idea that a big sheet is desirable would seem to be delusive, because we find, in going over the successful papers of the country, that those which really pay the best are, as a rule, the small ones.

NAMES OF NEWSPAPERS.

The publications of all kinds described in the "American Newspaper Directory" for 1876 are represented by 7,626 titles. In many cases several editions are issued from the same establishment, under substantially the same name, and in the figures just stated such several editions are counted as but one. The *Journals* are the most numerous, there being 487. Next in favor stand the *Times*. These num ber 310. There are 302 *Heralds*. The *News* number 298. The total of the *Gazettes* is 276. The *Democrats* come next in point of numbers, 268. To offset the Democratic phalanx there are 211 *Republicans*. The *Advertisers* number 92, and are naturally most frequent in localities where the populace is the most enlightened and progressive. There are 122 *Advocates*. This name appears to be a favorite of the religious publications, and at least three-fifths of the total are borne by religious papers. There are 60 papers known as the *Argus*, and with this quantity of professed eye-power, it is amazing that the frauds heretofore existing for years were not sooner discovered. There are 58 *Bulletins*, which are undoubtedly perused with care by the 51 *Citizens* described in the "Directory." Of *Chronicles* there are 89, while 143 *Couriers* stand in expectancy, ready to depart with 34 *Dispatches*. There are 89 *Enterprises*, most of them being located in the West. There are 45 *Expresses*, 34 *Farmers*, and 20 *Globes*. One of the latter is the Flint *Globe* of Michigan, and another the Golden *Globe* of Colorado Territory. Just 133 papers keep on the safe side by being *Independents*, though 49 *Leaders* are ready to direct them. There are 34 *Ledgers*, 47 *Observers*, and 16 *Pilots*. One of the latter is the Storm Lake *Pilot* of Iowa, and another the Lone Rock *Pilot* of Wisconsin. Each of these is remarkably co-incident in respect to the name of the place and the name of the paper. There are 59 *Posts*, 122 *Registers*, and 95 *Reviews*. The country enjoys the guardianship of 144 *Sentinels*, one of which is the Lone Tree *Sentinel* of Iowa. There are 76 *Standards*, 84 *Stars*, 50 *Suns*, and 93 *Tribunes*. Among the unusual or striking titles are the *Bistoury* (Elmira, N. Y.), *Jimplecute* (Jefferson, Tex.), *Luxapililan* (Fayette C. H., Ala.), the *Card Basket*—a society paper—of Washington, the Hope *Star of Hope* (Ark.), *Thistleton's Illustrated Jolly Giant* (San Francisco), *China Mail and Flying Dragon*, the *Elm Leaf* (East Hartford, Conn.), the *Eulenspiegel* (Owl's Mirror) of Chicago, *Jefferson Republican*, the *Southern Cross*—a Catholic paper—of Savannah, the *Egyptian Press* (Marion, Ill.), *Hoosier Patron and Lady Granger* (Indianapolis), *Hoosier State*, *Union Spy*—there is only one—*Condenser*, *Meschacebe*, *Wide Awake*—a literary paper—*Iron Home* (Ishpeming, Mich.), *Morgan's Watch-tower* (Mt. Pleasant, Mich.), the *Ricochet* (Oxford, Miss.), *Blætter und Kladderadatsch*, the *Schnedderdengg*, *Freedman's Monitor and Workingman's Looking Glass* (Phila.), the *I. C. B. U. Journal* (also in Phila.), the *Four Counties* of Richmond, Texas, the *Ventilator and Golden Rule* (Mannington, W. Va.), *Eurhetorian Argosy* (Sackville, Ont.), *Stylus*; *Lady Elgin* (Elgin, Ill.), *Over the Country*, *Pajaronian*, *Aurora Brazileira*, *Neighbor's Home Mail*, *Psyche*, *Madisonensis*, and the *Alpine Chronicle* of Silver Mountain, California. To these may be added the *Toledo Blade*, *Burlington Hawk Eye*, *Cape May Ocean Wave*, *Broad Axe of Freedom*, *Sentinel on the Border*, *Unterrified Democrat*, *Spirit Lake Beacon*, *Homer's Iliad*, *Horsehead's Journal*, *Painted Post Times*, *Roman Citizen*, and many others. Names popularly supposed to be frequent are in fact rare. It occasionally happens that the prominence attained by a single paper with a certain name brings the name so much before the people that it grows familiar to the public mind, though there may really be but few papers with the same designation. What the journalistic fancy of the Centennial year will devise in the way of newspaper titles is uncertain.

THE CO-OPERATIVE NEWSPAPERS—WHAT THEY ARE.

Within the past seven or eight years there has come up a class of newspapers known as co-operatives, or patent insides and outsides, by which it is understood that the publisher purchases at a central point a sufficient number of sheets for his issue with one side already printed. The persons with whom he contracts, having extensive offices, and wide arrangements with publishers through a great extent of country, are able to supply fifty or one hundred with the same matter, the geographical distribution of those papers being so distinct that the fact of the sides of two papers being alike becomes of no consequence. They do not go to the same readers. The system has been scoffed at; but it has grown nevertheless. It is found that the man who has a "patent inside" can in many cases make a better paper and a cheaper than he who plumes himself upon doing the thing "all at home." There are about 2,000 sheets printed on this plan—more than a fourth of all the weeklies published.

THE VALUE OF ADVERTISING SPACE.

The value of advertising space in a newspaper is generally supposed to be fixed by its circulation, but although the principal, this is not the only element to be considered. Advertisements in papers having large circulations are said to be worth half a cent a line in dailies, and one cent a line in weeklies, for each thousand issued. In papers of smaller circulation publishers have to obtain a higher price for advertisements which go in but a few times. Advertisements are attracted to those journals which contain other announcements of the same class. A man who wants to let a house advertises it in the paper in which he sees most announcements of houses to let; and in time in every city there will be some one paper monopolizing that class of advertisements, and it is almost impossible for any rival ever to displace it or deprive it of this peculiar patronage. It will hold it even after having lost its circulation.

The impression prevails that English papers are much more favored with advertisements than the American ones. This is not the case. Our journals have more and get much higher prices for them. No other paper in the world has so many as the New York *Herald*, whose advertising rates are fifty per cent. higher than those of the London *Times*, and *Harper's Weekly* charges four times as much as the *Illustrated London News* for the same space. The truth is, the advertising rates of American papers are higher throughout than those of the English, and the patronage extended to them is more munificent.

The one-price system for advertising is the one which pays. Publishers are apt to devote too much attention to advertising. They think that this is all they have need to strive after, and they often depend upon it to pay every expense. Some have even gone so far as to publish a paper to be given away, trusting to the advertising to even cover the cost of the white paper; but as the paper would be a great item of outlay, the temptation to defraud is so great that it is not in human nature to withstand it. Knowing this, advertisers have come to regard papers of free circulation as dishonest enterprises, and there are now none of them in existence which are of any account. Advertising space is generally charged for by the "square"—a term which may have had meaning once, but has not any now. A "square" means a space—a large or a small space, according to the arbitrary rules of offices. Thus, a man who orders two "squares" may find he has negotiated for eight or for sixty-four lines. A "square" is about as definite as "a piece of chalk."

Agate is the type used in all the great daily papers for advertisements. Smaller type would not do, and larger is never employed. In some of the higher priced weeklies they are set in nonpareil; in a few of the lower priced still larger type appears, and in some of the Southern papers we find the paid announcements displayed in long primer. Whenever a paper uses a larger type than nonpareil for its advertisements, the experienced advertiser knows that space can be bought at a low price.

It is, doubtless, true that the best managers of newspapers treat their advertising space as merchandise. They know what it costs and what it ought to be worth, and unless they obtain the price they value it at, do not sell. Experience teaches that the man who gets a reduction to-day will not advertise to-morrow unless a similar or greater concession be made; whilst he who is refused to-day comes in to-morrow with increased respect for the man who had the backbone to see him leave the office the day before. Yet, after all, advertising space is not like merchandise. Merchandise, if not sold, remains in store and possesses value, whilst advertising space, if not disposed of, must be filled up with reading matter, and the compositor, too, must be paid for setting it. This fact acts as a lever in the hands of the shrewd advertiser, and is by him used with great effect. In most of the country weeklies an advertisement for three months will cost no more than twice the sum which would be demanded for one month; and if double the price for three months be offered for a year's insertion, the chances are it will not be refused. Patent medicine men become very conversant with this condition of affairs.

Advertisements possess another value in addition to the money which they bring The "wanted" advertisements, those of school-books, etc., etc., are much sought after, they being supposed to give character to the columns of a paper. Patent medicine advertisements, although considered less desirable, are, as a general thing, taken at lower rates than those of banks and insurance companies, because it is understood that a man who advertises patent medicines must make the advertising pay, and that he will watch and know the result. The other classes extend their advertising more as favors, and have less faith in its efficacy.

NEWSPAPER CIRCULATIONS.

Of the circulation of newspapers in this country as compared with that in others we know very little. This is the only country in the world wherein any statistics of newspaper circulation are published regularly. People's ideas about circulation are very crude. Newspapers have by no means such large constituencies as they are supposed to have. A town of 50,000 inhabitants rarely will buy as many as 2,000 copies of a daily paper published in its midst; and many a daily paper is published which prints less than 300 copies per diem. Sometimes papers rarely heard of in the town of their publication, and thought but of little consequence there, are those printing the largest number of copies. In New York city the *News* undoubtedly prints more than 100,000 copies a day, yet many residents of the city do not see a copy from one end of the year to another. The largest regular circulation ever obtained by any daily newspaper in the United States is now possessed by the New York *Sun*, Its daily issue is about 140,000 copies. The London *Daily Telegraph* is the only paper in Europe whose circulation exceeds that of the New York *Sun*. That is said to issue about 180,000 copies daily, while the London *Times*, believed by the public in general to be the leading paper of the world (and justly so), prints barely one-third that number. It is almost superfluous to add that the most influential dailies are not always those of largest circulation.

The New York *Ledger* and the New York *Weekly* undoubtedly print more than 100,000 copies every issue—possibly twice that number; a child's paper in Boston issues 127,000, and *Harper's Weekly* can claim nearly 100,000. With these exceptions there is every reason for believing that there are no weekly papers which exceed an issue of 90,000.

A premium system of getting subscribers has been very much in fashion for some years past, which has at times been very successful. Many papers have run up an enormous circulation by this means, people often buying them for the premium, and not caring for the paper. But circulations so obtained do not hold good, and after the expansion has once receded, it is exceedingly difficult to restore it.

The religious paper having the largest circulation in the United States is the *Christian Advocate*, published in New York; next to it, probably, the New York *Observer*.

It is a remarkable fact that some of the most profitable papers have very small circulations. They obtain a good name and valuable advertising patronage; their small issue enables them to get along with low-priced presses. Having plenty of time to run off an edition, they do not employ many men. With them there is no rush or confusion. Everything goes slowly, comfortably, is done cheaply, and managed with economy, and a large portion of the money which comes in remains as profit.

AMOUNT OF CAPITAL REQUIRED TO START A NEWSPAPER.

The amount of capital required to start a newspaper is an interesting subject. It varies from three hundred dollars up to a million. Many an one has been commenced on as little money as the smallest sum named, while probably a million would hardly suffice to bring out in New York at the present time a daily which should successfully compete with the great dailies already in existence.

The largest profits ever made from newspaper enterprise have come from daily papers. They also sink money the most rapidly when they fail to pay. Weekly papers stand next in the order of lucrativeness; but semi-weekly and tri-weekly papers are rarely profitable. There is no instance in all the Northern States of a semi or tri-weekly paper having come up to the value of $15,000.

The sums of money sunk in establishing papers are often very heavy. On *Harper's Weekly* $100,000 was expended before it commenced to pay; the New York *Times'* outlay reached several hundred thousand dollars before the investors began to see a return; *Hearth and Home* entailed on its various proprietors losses not far short of $200,000 before it was finally suspended; and many a paper of which the public knows nothing has cost its owners sums ranging from $30,000 to $100,000. On the other hand, the profits, when success is met, are proportionately large. *Harper's Weekly* has undoubtedly paid as much as $100,000 a year in profits; the New York *Ledger* much more. The Philadelphia *Ledger*, New York *Herald*, New York *Times*, and New York *Sun* have often paid much larger profits than those even. It is reported that the Chicago *Tribune* earned from its advertising columns the money required for its new building as it was needed to pay the contractors. Monthlies rarely make much money. They are generally published for the pleasure of the thing. No temperance newspaper was ever known to pay. The same may be said of masonic publications and of those devoted to the interest of any of the various secret societies.

To establish a new daily paper in any of the large cities is considered a positively certain way of sinking all the money that is put in. In ten years there has been no new daily in New York that has made money; and one that is losing is a perfect maelstrom for the wrecking of capital. Such investments we have heard compared (and aptly) to "pouring water down a rat hole." There is hardly ever any end to it. The paper, however, that is making money will go on doing so, notwithstanding great mismanagement. That which does not quite pay, and loses a little more this year than last, will never pay; but the one which has struggled for twenty years, and for the last five has come a little nearer to a paying basis each twelvemonth, will in a few years make a fortune for its owners.

The causes of failure in newspaper enterprises may almost invariably be traced to poor business management. The paper that fails, fails in a way and from causes which would be foreseen by any intelligent observer who from day to day had an opportunity of overseeing such matters.

The value of newspaper property in this country is very great. It is very intangible, however. Probably the New York *Herald*, if offered for sale, would realize about two million dollars. There are two or three establishments worth a million of dollars each; a couple of dozen worth half a million; a larger number equal to a hundred thousand dollars apiece; and there exist plenty of offices throughout the country publishing little papers, which a journeyman printer, going in with $250, and giving his note for $250 more, could induce the proprietor to resign in his favor. There are many newspapers conducted in the country the proprietors of which do not realize more than $400 profit per annum as a recompense for their labor.

In the country, in small places, the job office is an important auxiliary. Many papers would be unable to exist without it, and in some the paper simply serves as a sort of a tender to the other department. It advertises and brings business to the printer. Next to the job office, the legal advertising is depended upon to furnish the sustenance of the newspaper. It is oftentimes the case that a man having a newspaper established in a frontier county (and consequently a sparsely-settled region) takes advantage of the absence of similar publications to publish a sheet at his own office, printing on it the name of the shiretown in a contiguous county. He then sends over one or two hundred copies and obtains subscribers there, and thus manages to get the legal advertising of the county. In this way the enterprise pays—perhaps not very handsomely, but it does pay.

The most successful newspapers are those conducted in two separate departments, having an editor and a publisher. The editor controls the columns of the paper. It is for him to say what course the paper shall take—what it shall say and what it shall not say; it is for the publisher to see that the bills are paid, to fix the prices for advertising, and to decide what shall be paid for of that which is published. These two positions need two very different descriptions of talent, and it is very rarely indeed that one man possesses both. It was well known that Mr. Greeley, the founder of the New York *Tribune*, was never a suitable man to have anything to do with the affairs of the counting-room. He, perhaps, knew this as well as anybody.

NEWSPAPER CHARACTER AND INFLUENCE.

The business of publishing a newspaper, in the hands of a good man, is a very respectable one, but in the hands of a man of another sort it becomes quite the reverse.

The editor who always tells the truth—who says in his columns only what he believes—exercises a great influence, and sometimes he is himself surprised to find to what an extent his statements are received. The newspapers which never take any stand upon political questions—the so-called independent papers, that are Republican to-day and Democratic to-morrow—do not wield much power over the minds of their readers. Senator Wilson, of Massachusetts, our late Vice-President, very accurately described their position when, in conversation one day with a Western editor who prided himself upon the influence of his "independent" paper, he said: "Your independent papers have not any influence. Your readers have been so educated by you that they are just as independent as you are, and when you take any stand different from that which you have been taking, your readers cut loose from you."

To make a good newspaper, to publish it, or to edit it, is said to require a peculiar training. Yet many successful newspaper men have never had any, and have gone into the business in middle life. They have, however, all been men who have shown themselves possessed of a peculiar tact which is not common by any means.

Editors are slow to learn that what interests them will not always interest their readers. If an editor has a personal grievance, he is greatly tempted to ventilate it in his paper, and in that way he reveals to his readers all about a rival or an enemy of whom they might otherwise never have heard. Thus he makes an antagonist of importance, who, if let alone, would have been of no consequence whatever.

NEWSPAPER SALARIES.

Where there are no official announcements, to report upon people's salaries is necessarily somewhat hazardous. It is an interesting point, however, and one that cannot be overlooked in a sketch of this kind. The largest salaries paid to editors probably do not exceed $15,000 a year, and this can only be secured on one or two of the leading New York journals. In cities outside of New York $100 a week is good pay, and it is only in cities like Chicago that so much is to be obtained. Probably no editor in Boston, Philadelphia, or any Eastern city, except New York, receives as much as $5,000 a year. Reporters and city editors, and all the minor positions on a paper are, as a rule, poorly paid—from $12 to $40 a week, according to the importance of the place. The business manager of a paper is frequently the best paid employe, and upon him the profits largely depend.

TOO MUCH ORIGINAL MATTER NOT DESIRABLE IN NEWSPAPERS.

Papers which are made up entirely of original matter are not, as a rule, very popular. It is a very common remark of shrewd newspaper men that they can steal better articles than they can buy. When an article is bought and paid for, there is a feeling that the whole of it must be used, even though in some parts it lack interest. On the other hand, there is no feeling of compunction in slicing down, to meet the exigencies of space or the needs of readers, a good article seen in a neighboring paper. The good points are saved and verbiage rejected. It is also a fact that the public seem to have an objection to too much reading matter. Among the most prosperous papers are those which have very little of it in their columns. In proof of this take, for instance, the Philadelphia *Ledger* and the New York *News*. The public also have an antipathy to supplements. Hardly any man finds an extra sheet in his morning paper without a feeling of annoyance, or without wishing it were not there. Yet these supplements cost a great deal of money.

It may not be out of place here to correct an erroneous idea which quite extensively prevails. It is thought that the conductors of newspapers, especially of those appearing diurnally, are very glad to have sensational reports—great trials, murders, scandals, and so forth. These cause the papers to be largely sold, and the public infer that the proprietors reap heavy profits from the increased circulation, whereas the fact is that the extra expense for telegraphic news, for reportorial labor, type setting, etc., vastly exceeds all the profit accruing from this source.

THE CIRCULATION AND DISTRIBUTION OF NEWSPAPERS.

In the list of dailies, in point of circulation the average of Maryland (11,336) stands at the head of the list, with Massachusetts (9,942) second, and New York (8,402) third. The large average of Maryland is due to the fact that six out of the eight dailies, whose circulations are given, are published in Baltimore and print from 8,278 to 20,094 copies each. Although the average circulation of the New York city dailies is 24,965, the large number of country dailies whose subscription lists fall below 1,000 each (23 per cent.), reduces the average for the whole State to a third place in the list. In Massachusetts 26 per cent. of the list exceeds 10,000 circulation, while in New York only 11 per cent. reaches that figure. The smallest daily average (734) is found in Mississippi, and the next (782) in Nebraska.

Among the weeklies the largest average (4,120) is found in New York, the next (3,777) in Massachusetts, and the next (3,375) in the District of Columbia. A comparison between the cities of New York and Boston shows an average weekly circulation of 12,124 in the former and of 10,702 in the latter. Nevada furnishes the smallest weekly average (400), and Florida (478) next. Among the total averages of all publications that of New York (4,991) ranks first, that of Massachusetts (4,582) second, and that of the District of Columbia (3,697) third, while Florida (470) is found at the foot of the list. Between the different classes of publications the monthlies take the lead, with an average circulation of 5,144, and the dailies next with 3,877. A further analysis shows that, while the daily average of a State is influenced to a marked degree by the large cities within its borders, that of the weeklies serve as an unfailing index of the prosperity and intelligence of the rural districts. In the Northern States the average is large, while in the Southern States and Territories it is small.

In a comparison of aggregates, New York heads the list with a daily circulation of 764,500 copies, or 244,640,000 copies per annum, of which number 599,161 copies are issued daily in New York city alone. The aggregate weekly circulation in the State is 2,459,503 copies, of which 1,782,163 copies are issued from the city offices, and the total aggregate amounts to 4,271,527 copies each issue, or 390,529,912 copies per annum. Of the total for each issue, New York city prints 3,340,300 copies, or over 78 per cent. of the aggregate circulation of the State. The next largest total aggregate for each issue is that of Pennsylvania (1,701,250), and the next Massachusetts (1,214,124). The total circulation of all the dailies in the United States amounts to 2,291,041 copies, of the weeklies 8,938,166 copies, and of all publications 13,940,304 copies each issue, or 1,250,024,590 copies per annum.

A comparison between the aggregate circulation of all publications in each State with its population (1870), shows that California issues 90 copies per annum for every individual on her census rolls, while New York and Massachusetts fall but little short of that number with an annual issue of 89 and 79 copies respectively. When the distance of California from the great newspaper centres of the East is considered, it will be seen that the local support which her publications receive is far better than a comparison with the averages of those States in near proximity to New York, Boston, or Philadelphia would indicate. At the other extreme we find Florida and Arkansas, the former issuing 3 and the latter 4 copies per annum to each person. Of the 42 separate States and Territores, 9 issue less then 10 copies, 23 less than 25 copies, and 34 less than 50 copies per annum to each person, while in the whole of them combined the average number issued is 32. It will be interesting to note that a high average is always found in those States where a high standard of education and good order exists—a fact of no slight significance in estimating the influence of newspapers upon the government and education of the people. The table shows that one periodical of some kind is printed for every three persons. With five persons to each family this will prove one of two things, either that there is more than one paper regularly printed and sold for every family, or that the circulations as given are too high.

In the Territories the average area for each publication is 7,443 square miles, in Nevada 4,339 square miles, while in the District of Columbia the minimum is reached with barely 2 square miles. In the New England States the average area ranges from 23 square miles in Massachusetts to 442 in Maine, in the Middle States from 43 in New York to 88 in Delaware, in the Western States from 70 in Ohio to 4,339 in Nevada, in the Southern States from 95 in Maryland to 1,976 in Florida.

THE CONNECTICUT COURANT.

A SKETCH FOR THE BOOK OF THE CENTENNIAL NEWSPAPER EXHIBITION.

The COURANT, of Hartford, is the oldest, most successful, most widely-known journal that is published in Connecticut; nor has any in New England a more thoroughly national reputation. The first regular number of its weekly edition—the CONNECTICUT COURANT—was issued November 19, 1764, by Thomas Green, who set up the first printing press in Hartford, in order to print this paper. Since then it has been continuously published in the same city and under the same title, and no other newspaper in the United States has for so long a time had a similarly uninterupted existence. It is, therefore, speaking strictly, *the oldest newspaper in America!*

It appeared in time to give early utterance to the complaints that, first by suggestion, then by plain statement, and later by most emphatic expression, gave unheeded warning of the coming revolution of a century ago. All through that trying period, save one brief interval when, delayed by lack of paper—the proprietors stopped publication long enough to build themselves a paper mill—the COURANT regularly appeared every week. And on through the settlement of the war, and the discordant times that followed, and on through three more wars through all our periods of national prosperity and adversity, the COURANT has unfailingly gone out to its thousands of readers prepared under the promise of its projector, to take "great care from Time to Time to collect all domestic Occurrences that are worthy the Notice of the Publick."

The whole history of the United States, written contemporaneously with the events, is spread out on record on its pages, while its advertising columns, and its home news are, from year to year, illustrative of the domestic and social life of the people and of its various changes.

The first COURANT was of four pages, with two columns to each page. The COURANT of to-day, still a four-paged journal, has nine columns to the page, and is more than eight times as large as was the first issue; while now all the issues of the COURANT, daily and weekly, give their readers nearly sixty times as much to look over in one week as was given in a week by the COURANT a century ago.

The HARTFORD DAILY COURANT was first printed in 1836, and is now the only morning newspaper in the city. The paper, owing, perhaps, in part to its long service and its being so firmly established in the households of all those older families of the State, with whom it has come to be an indispensable institution, has a wide popularity. From early days it has received frequent contributions from prominent citizens; Hartford people regarding it as the Englishmen are said to regard their London *Times*—as the place to appear in in print whenever they have anything to say. It would be hard to name any of the public characters of the city for a hundred years back who have not, participating in some discussion, or through some particular independent essay of their own, put their contributions in the "People's Column" of the COURANT. It has become a part and fixture of the city of Hartford and of the State of Connecticut. Its circulation is large through Connecticut, and its influence under judicious management has become very great. Outside of the State, the weekly, more especially than the daily, is taken by subscribers all over the country and by many New England people abroad.

The paper has changed proprietors ten times since 1764, either by total sale or by change of partnership, and since January 1, 1867, has been published by Hawley, Goodrich & Co. Gen. Joseph R. Hawley, the President of the Centennial Commission, is at the head of the firm, and when at home is the editor-in-chief. Mr. Charles Dudley Warner is associated with him, both in the partnership and as editor, and "My Summer in a Garden," Mr. Warner's first thoroughly successful literary production, was first printed in a series of contributions to this paper. Mr. Stephen A. Hubbard, formerly of the Winsted (Ct.) *Herald*, is the third associate partner and editor, and the manager. The business department is in charge of Mr. W. H. Goodrich, whose name appears in the firm, and who has been connected with the paper for many years.

All the regular facilities of the modern newspaper for collecting news "worthy the Notice of the Publick" are employed by the COURANT, and it has also its special correspondents in various parts, both of this country and Europe. Every effort is made to have it truly a newspaper. Conscious of its influence and jealously careful of its reputation for honesty and accuracy, the managers of the COURANT maintain for it a high moral tone and avoid that which is sensational and untrustworthy. By this wise conservatism they increase the respect for the paper and the weight attached to its expressions of opinions, which are positively and fearlessly outspoken in favor of what it believes to be right.

Relatively to its size Hartford is to-day the richest city in the United States. It has developed thus through a series of wisely-planned public measures and through the energy and private enterprise of its citizens. The COURANT has been found always ready to advocate that public policy which looked to the city's ultimate welfare, and it has always had a word of encouragement for those citizens who have made themselves active in opening new and promising paths of industry. It has seen the insurance business of Hartford grow from its very beginnings to the accumulation of the hundreds of millions of dollars of assets that the Hartford companies now have; it has watched the banks of Hartford from the founding of the first grow to be the richest in the State; and it has welcomed and assisted one after another the great manufactories that have so contributed to make Hartford famous. In a word, it has, from the first, identified itself with the best interests of the place, and as Hartford has prospered and grown, the COURANT has prospered and grown with it, and may to-day be taken as the exponent of New England intelligence, New England enterprise, New England honesty, and New England success, which is the product of these.

THE "PUBLIC LEDGER," PHILADELPHIA.

A SKETCH FOR THE BOOK OF THE CENTENNIAL NEWSPAPER EXHIBITION.

The Philadelphia PUBLIC LEDGER is among the journals which have chiefly contributed to establish the reputation of the American press. In point of enterprise as well as of originality of business procedure, the manager and proprietor of the LEDGER is not surpassed by those holding similar relations to any of our other great papers, and in no instance has the exercise of those qualities secured for their owners such widespread celebrity as is apparent in the case of GEO. W. CHILDS. It is not alone in the Western Hemisphere that this distinguished journalist's fame is a topic discussed far and wide; it is almost equally established and canvassed in European countries—France, Germany, England—where his achievements are held up as exemplars of American enterprise, power of surmounting colossal obstacles, and justice in rewarding merit. Biographies of him have been published in leading organs of those countries, the interest of the narratives being such that thousands of readers have perused them with avidity, and so widely discussed the matter of them that most Europeans who study our public men are acquainted intimately with the history of the popular proprietor of the PUBLIC LEDGER, of Philadelphia.

GEORGE W. CHILDS commenced life in a humble way, and has risen to wealth and eminence, and the same may be said of the PUBLIC LEDGER itself, which first appeared as a small four-page, one-cent sheet on the 25th of March, 1836. The talent employed on it was, however, of a high order, and quickly secured it favorable notice and hearty support. The first year of the LEDGER'S existence proved so propitious that larger accommodation was needed, and the paper was increased in size. Success continued to be proportionate to the enterprise displayed, and (as usual where profits are quickly realized) rivalry was induced. Other penny daily papers were started in opposition, but failed to loosen the firm hold on the people's regard which had been conceded the LEDGER as a reward of ability, consistency, and a progressive spirit. During and subsequent to the Abolition Riots of 1838 the LEDGER became famous as an uncompromising advocate of "free speech" as to slave labor, and notwithstanding that many of its readers were for a time alienated, and that the dangers of extreme measures at the hands of an excited mob were ominous, the LEDGER bravely held on its philanthropic course, and lived to see and now survives the abolition of what was so long our rebuke in the eyes of other nations. The first rotary press ever built was used to print the LEDGER, April 9, 1847. This was a four-cylinder press, invented by Richard M. Hoe. The proposition to place type on a cylinder and whirl it around was scouted as an absurdity by nearly all printers; but Mr. Swain, one of the then proprietors, had intelligent faith in Colonel Hoe's theory, and the machine proved, as is well known, a satisfactory success.

The great increase in the price of white paper and labor during the war rendered the publication of a one-cent journal impossible at a profit, and after having lost considerable money in their endeavors to supply it at the old rates, Messrs. Swain & Abell determined to sell out the entire establishment. This they did December 3, 1864, and the following Monday Mr. GEORGE W. CHILDS began his brilliant career as the publisher of the PUBLIC LEDGER, and received a warm welcome from the leading journals of the country, to which he was already known as the publisher of many valuable books. Not being disposed to follow up the course of his predecessors, by publishing the paper at a loss, Mr. Childs, on the 10th of December, 1864, increased the subscription price to twelve cents per week, but this was reduced a month later to ten cents—now twelve cents. The rates of advertising were also advanced. These mutations caused many to predict a disastrous decrease of support; but though there was an immediate declension, it proved only temporary, the excellency of the paper being such that few who had once been in the habit of regularly perusing it could long abstain from according it patronage, and the circulation speedily recovered and steadily increased, until in the first three months of 1876 it reached 7,221,500 copies—a daily average of 92,584.

"LEDGER" BUILDING.

The building in which the LEDGER is produced is among the grandest structural embellishments of the Quaker City, and as a newspaper office is complete in every particular. It is freely open at all times to citizens and strangers; and it is estimated that not less than one hundred thousand persons have availed themselves of the privilege of scrutinizing the establishment. Nothing that judicious liberality could secure has been left undone to provide for the comfort of all engaged in the production and issue of the paper.

The great influence exerted by the PUBLIC LEDGER is largely attributable to the care that has for many years been exercised to prevent the appearance of extravagant statements in its columns. The imperative rule is to understate rather than to overstate. Throughout its long career the LEDGER has advocated every improvement which has tended to increase the prosperity of Philadelphia and the welfare of its citizens, often in the face of strong hostility; and the wisdom of its pleadings has been demonstrated by the benefits which have accrued when its advice has been followed. The LEDGER may be said, among other things, to have created a class of advertisements which contributes largely to a newspaper's revenue. "Wants," "Boarding," "For Sale," "To Let," &c., had no existence as they now appear when the LEDGER started, but have grown with it.

Mr. GEORGE W. CHILDS has enlarged the usefulness and widely extended the influence of the PUBLIC LEDGER. His sagacity and tact enabled him to pilot his paper through a perilous passage in its course, and to make changes in its management which, in less skillful hands, might have proved disastrous. He has proved his capacity and fitness to control a great journal, which is at once an exponent and moulder of public opinion, and a power in the land. Colleagued with his rare intellectual qualities is a goodness of heart which constantly manifests itself in acts of considerate benevolence, and added to these is a magnetism of manner that draws and attaches to him multitudes of friends. "As a true journalist," said the Hon. John T. Hoffman, ex-Governor of New York, "he appreciates and understands the difference between the liberty of the press and the license of the press. He deals boldly with public matters and with public men in connection with them—but he is always careful to recollect that private character is private property, owned by that most sacred of all circles, the family circle, and that the man who needlessly assails it is as much a criminal as if he robbed the household of its dearest treasures, or plucked from it, for his own base uses, its fairest flower. He understands, what I wish all editors in America understood, not only the power of the press, but its proper uses and its great mission; and by his daily conduct and life declares his opinion that the man who owns a printing press and can use a pen has no more right to indite libels and stamp private reputation than the owner of a uniform and a sword has to cut and kill to please his fancies or to gratify his malice."

THE BOSTON JOURNAL.

A SKETCH FOR THE BOOK OF THE CENTENNIAL NEWSPAPER EXHIBITION.

The Boston JOURNAL is one of the best known newspapers published in New England, having been established in 1833. It occupies its own building at 264 Washington street, and is printed on an eight-cylinder and a six-cylinder Hoe press. It publishes two papers daily, Boston MORNING JOURNAL and Boston EVENING JOURNAL. The sworn statement of its publisher, subject to verification at any time by advertisers, shows an average daily circulation of 31,500 for the months of January, February, March, April, and May, 1876. The circulation for the last week prior to this writing is as follows:

1876.	
May 8	31,514
May 9	30,889
May 10	31 816
May 11	31,225
May 12	30,980
May 13	33,854
Average	31,713

The JOURNAL publishes weekly and semi-weekly editions. The weekly has a larger circulation in New England than any paper of like character emanating from a daily newspaper office in Boston. The official postage returns show that the Boston JOURNAL ranks the *sixth* paper in the United States in the amount of matter sent through the mails. The JOURNAL is published by the Journal Newspaper Co., Boston, Mass., and its managers are Messrs. S. N. Stockwell and Wm. W. Clapp. It is a political, commercial and literary newspaper. Its enterprise is best indicated by a few items of its expenses for the year ending April 1, 1876. Telegraphic expenses, $33,302.70; Editorial and News Department, $39,447.24; correspondence, $13,404.68; postage paid, $4,285.

THE SPIRIT OF THE TIMES, NEW YORK.

THE LEADING SPORTING JOURNAL OF AMERICA.

A SKETCH FOR THE BOOK OF THE CENTENNIAL NEWSPAPER EXHIBITION.

This great weekly newspaper is as well known throughout this country as the New York *Herald* or *Harper's Magazine*. It was founded in 1831, in compliance with a general demand for a journal which should reflect the tastes of the vast number who find pleasure in the sports of the turf, the field, the water, and other pastimes, sprang at once into popular favor, and has never since its foundation failed to hold its position as the recognized authority and acknowledged organ in the matters to which its broad columns are specially devoted. Its original editor was William T. Porter, *clarum et venerabile nomen*, who continued in its sole charge until 1856, in which year George Wilkes became associated with him. Mr. Porter died in 1859, and since then Mr. Wilkes has most ably edited the paper, being also its proprietor, until November 1, 1875, when E. A. Buck became equally interested in its ownership, and assumed editorial control. Great as had been its previous popularity, its rapidly-increasing circulation under the new management shows that it still holds first place in the esteem of the public. Labor and expense are lavished upon it as they have never been before, and the reading community is always quick to appreciate generosity in its behalf.

The SPIRIT OF THE TIMES has always been noted for its manly and independent manner of dealing with all sporting questions and events. Being thoroughly informed, it knows the right and dares to pursue it. Fraudulent practices find in it not an apologizer, but an armed and relentless foe. The true sportsman is the last to compromise or palter with rascality; and this paper has well earned the right to be considered the palladium of the interests of the true sportsman.

The sphere of the SPIRIT OF THE TIMES is very extensive. It has sympathetically expanded with the expanding wants and tastes of those to whom it is the special organ, until it now issues a weekly edition of twenty-eight closely-printed pages, which number it frequently increases to thirty-two, and on occasions to thirty-six. Each number contains more printed matter than any magazine or other periodical published in the United States. Its patrons may depend upon it that everything of value relating to outdoor or indoor sports will find its way into the broad columns of the SPIRIT.

Its several departments receive the especial attention of gentlemen fully competent to maintain them at the highest standard. As the organ of the turf, it gives most complete and accurate summaries of all events, besides graphic reports of the more important meetings. In this department it has no rival. Its dramatic and musical columns, to which matters several pages are devoted weekly, are made up of brilliant and incisive *critiques*, correspondence from every large town in this country and from many foreign cities, and the latest intelligence of the movements of stars. In this department it is admittted to be *facile princeps*, both at home and abroad. The rising interest in aquatic sports and rifle-practice has caused a full page to be set apart for each of these specialties, edited by experts in their respective lines, who will keep fully abreast of the times. One of the most remarkable features of this journal is its "Answers to Correspondents." Questions upon every imaginable subject from all parts of the country are showered in upon it for decision, and receive the most careful attention and prompt and correct answers. It is the authority for the decision of wagers throughout the United States. The veterinary department is conducted by a fully-educated surgeon, who deals conscientiously with every case submitted. Letters are continually received announcing the beneficial results of these prescriptions, which are afforded *gratis* to all who take the paper regularly. Besides these departments, billiards, athelctics, chess, etc., are given due attention. Editorially, the SPIRIT OF THE TIMES is the organ of no person, clique or party, but deals fearlessly with all questions of the day. Its contributed articles have a world-wide fame.

What has been said in a simple statement of facts, and combined with the circumstances that the circulation of the paper is enormous, that it is read by the wealthy and money-spending classes as well as by the vast army of "middle men" who are the strength of the country, that it goes to every club in the land, and that the majority of its subscribers preserve its issues in permanent form for future reference, it will be seen, without argument, how invaluable it is as an advertising medium. The publishers are constantly in receipt of letters saying, "My advertisement in the SPIRIT has brought me more applications than those in all the other papers."

The subscription price is $5 per annum, in advance, for which the paper will be sent, postage paid, to any address. All communcations should be sent to E. A. Buck, No. 3 Park Row, New York City.

THE AVALANCHE, MEMPHIS, TENN.

A SKETCH FOR THE BOOK OF THE CENTENNIAL NEWSPAPER EXHIBITION.

In the front rank of the most influential and valuable newspapers of the West and South, is the AVALANCHE, of Memphis, Tenn. This powerful and widely-known journal, since its establishment in 1857, has gradually acquired a position of which no competitor can easily deprive it. Under the long-continued judicious and enterprising management of its present publishers, Messrs. A. J. Kellar and R. A. Thompson—the latter of whom associated with Mr. Kellar at a comparatively recent date—the influence of the AVALANCHE has signally augmented in those wide sections where the paper was already so favorably known, and its reputation has experienced a merited extension in still broader regions. Its publishers have proved that they understand fully what the public expects of a first-class newspaper, and they have also attested their ability to produce and maintain a paper amply commensurate with those expectations of the public. The AVALANCHE is manifestly the leading independent and conservative newspaper of the Southern States. It is issued daily and weekly, and is thickly circulated throughout Tennessee, Arkansas, Mississippi, Alabama, Kentucky, Missouri, Western Texas, etc. The yearly subscription price of the daily is ten dollars, that of the weekly two dollars, and special rates for both or either are allowed to clubs. It is devoted to news, politics, commerce, agriculture, industries, literature, science, and the development of Southern interests, both material and social. To use its own words, it believes in the Constitution as it is, in the perpetuity of the Union of the States, and that the virtue and intelligence of the American people are equal to all the duties of self-government. It does not propose to ally itself with any political party except in so far as that alliance may accomplish good results. It does not look to nor care for the personal or political advancement of individuals, unless they represent vital principles whose enforcement is desirable; and its relations to all existing parties are such that it can afford to be fair in its dealings with them—to commend that in them which is good, and to condemn that which is hurtful.

1842. AMERICAN AGRICULTURIST. 1876.

AND DER

1858. AMERIKANISCHER AGRICULTURIST. 1876.

A SKETCH FOR THE BOOK OF THE CENTENNIAL NEWSPAPER EXHIBITION.

These important ournals well deserve a prominent place in a "description of the great newspapers of the day," and of the age, on account of their high character, great influence, and their immense circulation. The first named has run as high as *one hundred and fifty thousand* (150,000), regular edition, and has averaged fully one Hundred Thousand since 1862. For many years its circulation has far exceeded the combined editions of at least half a dozen of the largest of its cotemporaries of similar character and until the recent large multiplication of "agricultural papers," the AMERICAN AGRICULTURIST probably equaled or exceeded the combined circulation of *all* the other agricultural and horticultural papers in America. Its circulation and influence extend not only all over the United States and British America, but it is very largely taken in Australia, in the various English settlements on the African coast, and indeed almost everywhere in the world where the English language is spoken; while the German edition finds many readers all through Central Europe, Russia, etc.

The above facts do not favor the general opinion that farmers, as a class, "are more given to hard work than to reading about it." It is to be noted that among economical cultivators a wide system of "lending" and "exchanging" papers prevails. Statistics gathered by the publishers show, for example, that in a single neighborhood there were 107 families, comprising 506 persons, young and old, who regularly read the twenty-three copies of the AMERICAN AGRICULTURIST taken at that post-office—an average of TWENTY-TWO READERS TO EACH COPY. From the facts gathered, and the above ratio, it is probable that nearly, or quite, Two Million (2,000,000) persons read this journal.

The AMERICAN AGRICULTURIST is one of the highest authorities on Horticulture and kindred subjects. The managing editor, Dr. George Thurber, ranks with Prof. Asa Gray and men of like character and pursuits at home and abroad. While well versed in all matters connected with this journal, he is everywhere recognized as one of the foremost in a knowledge of botany, horticulture, etc. It would be a novelty to find in the AMERICAN AGRICULTURIST an erroneous recommendation, or item, in botany, horticulture, or, indeed, on any other subject.

It is to be noted, however, that the AMERICAN AGRICULTURIST, though taking this name at first and adhering to it, is not exclusively, by any means, an agricultural or horticultural journal. Its motto is: "For the Farm, Garden and Household." Its FORTY-FOUR large pages, contain much "plain, practical and reliable" information on all subjects that pertain to the labor and physical well-being of the people, whether they live in City, Village or Country. It is largely taken by professional men, by merchants by mechanics, by operatives in manufactories, who cultivate their little garden plots—indeed, by all classes. (For example, its circulation in Massachusetts alone sometimes runs as high as 17,000 copies.)

A special feature of the AMERICAN AGRICULTURIST for a quarter of a century has been its unsparing and persistent exposure of quackery and the swindlers that prey upon the pockets, the health and the lives of honest people, who, without dishonest purposes themselves, are least likely to be suspicious of the statements and assurances of others. By this course this journal has saved to its readers and to the country many millions of dollars that would otherwise have gone into the pockets of harpies. In connection with the above may be mentioned: The Advertising rules of the AMERICAN AGRICULTURIST, which are perhaps more strict and more closely lived up to "at all times and in all seasons," than in any other periodical. Those in charge of this Department are under positive directions to rigidly scan every advertisement and every advertiser; to admit nothing deceptive in substance or form; to exclude all quack and other medical advertisements, all secret things, all persons suspected of dishonesty—in short, "every person offering an advertisement, who is not known personally or by good and well-established repute, is required to furnish satisfactory references or other evidence that he has both the ABILITY and the INTENTION to do for his patrons just what his advertisements promise."

The above rules, adopted at first from conscientious motives, have, unexpectedly to the publishers, proved a financial success, and furnished an example well-worthy of imitation by other publishers. The readers of this journal, knowing the strict rules of the publishers, read the advertisements and respond to them with confidence. The good advertisers receive such large custom through this particular journal, that they find it to their interest to give it special attention in sending out their business notices—no matter what rules or requirements the paper may be compelled to adopt to keep its advertisements within desirable limits. Thus it has come to pass that, while the subscription rates of the AMERICAN AGRICULTURIST have been, and are, kept down to or below the cost of making and supplying the paper, its business columns have made this periodical a notable financial success, unequaled and even unapproached by any other similar journal in the world.

It begins the New Century in the highest vigor and influence, and 1976 will doubtless find it among the flourishing institutions of that day. To avoid any interruption of its business or its arrangements by the age or the decease of any of the business partners, or other causes, the Management was in 1873 changed to that of a Chartered Company, taking the name of the leading editor and publisher for many years, and it is now, therefore, published by the ORANGE JUDD COMPANY, at 245 Broadway, New York.

History.—The AMERICAN AGRICULTURIST was originated in April, 1842, by the venerable A. B. Allen, who still lives in retirement at Toms River, N. J. He employed others to assist in publishing and editing, having a different business growing on his hands. In May, 1853, he called to the editorial chair Mr. Orange Judd, who, brought up as a farmer at the West, had at mature age sought the advantage of a collegiate education, and after some years of subsequent investigation, had devoted three years (1850—1853) to the careful study of agricultural chemistry, and agricultural science generally, with Profs. Silliman, Norton, etc., in Yale College. After a short service as editor, Mr. Judd became sole proprietor, and continued thus until the magnitude of the business required him to call in business associates, including among others, Samuel Burnham, Esq., who has now been a "right hand man" for about ten years; C. C. North, Esq., the present treasurer, who came in in 1873. In 1859 Mr. Judd called to his editorial aid Dr. George Thurber, above alluded to, who has since given untiring attention to this journal, and also is now chiefly entrusted with the editorial management. Among its editorial and contributing corps may be named Henry Stewart, Col. Geo. E. Waring, Jr., Timothy Bunker, Esq., Col. Mason C. Weld, A. B. Allen, Peter Henderson, Prof. Asa Gray, Prof. W. O. Atwater, L. C. Root, Hon. Frederic Munch, "Aunt Sue," Faith Rochester, and others.

The German edition (*der Amerikanischer Agriculturist*) was started in 1858, and has been the only German agricultural and horticultural paper in this country that has had a continuous existence for a period of eighteen years.

THE CHURCHMAN, NEW YORK.

A SKETCH FOR THE BOOK OF THE CENTENNIAL NEWSPAPER EXHIBITION.

THE CHURCHMAN was established about one-third of a century ago, and its existence was continued under different names until the end of the year 1866, with indifferent pecuniary success, notwithstanding its editorial management was at various points of its history in the hands of very able men. In 1866 it was called the *Connecticut Churchman*, and its actual circulation was hardly 1,500.

In December of that year it was purchased by the present proprietors, and from that time on it has enjoyed uniform prosperity, its circulation rising rapidly from 1,500 up to 17,500, and this notwithstanding its subscription price is larger than that of any other religious journal in the United States.

This growth is due to the determined perseverance of the managers in their endeavor to make THE CHURCHMAN a religious paper which should exhibit, in all the matters pertaining to its specialty, the enterprise and the literary excellence of the best secular journals.

It occupies confessedly the first rank among religious and literary weeklies.

At the beginning of the year 1875 it made a great advance in meeting the need of the time. In effect a weekly journal of high character is a magazine, made up of matter which merits to be preserved as much as any of the best monthlies or quarterlies. Therefore its form should be adapted to this. Recognizing the principle, the managers of THE CHURCHMAN adopted its present shape and size. It contains thirty-two pages, nine by thirteen inches in size, and is sent to subscribers most conveniently pasted and folded. The folding, the pasting and the cutting are done by one process, on a machine built expressly for THE CHURCHMAN.

THE CHURCHMAN is the most reliable exponent of the attitude and the principles of the Protestant Episcopal Church.

It represents adequately the entire Church, and is not an organ for the dissemination of merely party principles, or the opinions of one man or one clique. It gives week by week with remarkable promptness all Church news, and treats ably the civil topics of the day, as viewed from a churchman's standpoint.

In brief, THE CHURCHMAN is a weekly magazine of ecclesiastical intelligence and devotional and general reading, and is the largest and most widely-circulated weekly in the Protestant Episcopal Church. It contains each year one-half more reading matter than "Harper's Magazine," more than twice as much as the "Galaxy" or "Scribner's," and three and a half times as much as the "Atlantic."

THE BOSTON DAILY ADVERTISER.

A SKETCH FOR THE BOOK OF THE CENTENNIAL NEWSPAPER EXHIBITION.

THE DAILY ADVERTISER BUILDING.

The Boston DAILY ADVERTISER was founded in 1813. In the following year it became the property of the late Nathan Hale, whose connection with it only ceased with his death. Mr. Hale was the first publisher and editor of a newspaper in the United States to print editorials daily and continuously, and his articles very soon acquired a national reputation. His writings were distinguished by breadth, intelligence and great candor. From the first, he rigidly excluded from the news and advertising columns of his paper everything which had an immoral intent or tendency, and this commendable rule is still adhered to. Mr. Hale likewise kept the editorial columns exclusively under his control *and for his own use;* and the frequent writings of Edward Everett, Jared Sparks, William Ellery Channing, and of numberless celebrated men of the day were inserted only as communications. The editorials were and are still the free and untrammelled expression of the editorial staff. No paper in the United States is edited with greater care and fidelity or with a more strict regard to the interests of our great nation. The expenses of its editorial and news departments are six times as great as they were only ten years ago. Its editor-in-chief and also its financial editor are proprietors, and constant writers, thus inducing the strongest sense of responsibility that self-interest can create. It has select and able special correspondents in the prominent cities of Europe and this country. It makes of literary, dramatic and fine art criticism a speciality, with the ablest writers to be had on its staff. The result is a large and increasing circle of readers, both in the business and the literary world, and among the very best people of the country. Indeed, the paper is the recognized organ of the banks and other monied institutions of Massachusetts, and of the different colleges and other literary institutions of New England.

The paper is located in a handsome building, of which a cut is herewith given, on Court street, and on the site of the very structure in which Benjamin Franklin made his advent as a journalist. Its composing room is lofty and commodious. Its editorial rooms are convenient and inviting; they occupy the entire fourth floor. The counting room, mailing room, and press room engross the first floor and basement. To accomplish the labor of printing and folding in season for mails, one of Hoe & Co's fastest presses, and four folding machines are run.

THE BALTIMORE AMERICAN.

A SKETCH FOR THE BOOK OF THE CENTENNIAL NEWSPAPER EXHIBITION.

THE BALTIMORE AMERICAN.

The BALTIMORE AMERICAN was established August 20, 1773, by Wm. Goddard, a native of New England, and is now one hundred and three years old, being not only the oldest paper in Baltimore, but also one of the oldest and most influential in the United States. It was first issued as the *Maryland Journal and Baltimore Advertiser*, a name it bore until 1799, when it was changed to that under which it appears at the present day, THE BALTIMORE AMERICAN AND COMMERCIAL ADVERTISER. Mr. Goddard conducted the journal until 1793, and from that time to 1853 it passed through several different ownerships. In 1853 the firm became Robert A. Dobbin and Charles C. Fulton (the present senior proprietor), and was conducted under that firm until 1862, when Mr. Dobbin died and Mr. Fulton purchased his interest, thus becoming sole proprietor, associating his son Albert K. Fulton, in the future conduct of the paper, and at this period commenced its most successful career, which has remained unbroken to the present day. It was in the columns of this journal that our national anthem, "The Star Spangled Banner," first saw the light, having been set up by Mr. Samuel Sands, a gentleman still living, a few hours after it was originally written by Mr. Keys, and it was several times during the war of 1812 that the issue of the paper was omitted on account of the editors and journeymen being engaged in repulsing the British attacking North Point. There are other very interesting circumstances connected with the history of the AMERICAN, but space forbids their mention. In 1875, its old quarters having been found too contracted for its steadily-increasing business, a handsome and commodious edifice was erected for its accommodation on the corner of South and Baltimore streets, and the AMERICAN is now the possessor of one of the finest and most imposing newspaper offices in the country, and well worth a visit from the many travelers in transit through Baltimore this summer. Its counting-room is universally conceded to be the handsomest in the country. Visitors to the Centennial will find a painting of the building, and also a fac-simile of the first issue of the AMERICAN, on exhibition in the newspaper building.

THE COURRIER DES ETATS-UNIS, NEW YORK.

A SKETCH FOR THE BOOK OF THE CENTENNIAL NEWSPAPER EXHIBITION.

1828—1876.

The "COURRIER" has arrived to-day at that period of complete development to which a half century of hard work, independence and progress has conducted it.

Started on the 1st March, 1828—the date of its first number—it passed through many trials and difficulties before it achieved success, and was assured of a permanent existence. The idea of its founder was an ambitious one, viz.: to publish in the States an organ in the French language—the language of the highest European society—and to excite attention to French literature, which at that time was entirely ignored in this country. At that time there was no question of politics or of commerce, manufactures, international interests or of any private interests; but simply to introduce and inculcate the taste for French literature, which, in consequence of the very spirit of the country, has not, even since that time, made the progress here which could naturally have been expected. However, the idea succeeded. With its 8 pages in quarto, of 3 columns each, appearing every Saturday—at the annual subscription price of $8—the "COURRIER," from its very commencement, was astonished at its success. Very soon, to keep pace with the demand for it, from new subscribers, it was obliged to reprint its earlier numbers. In less than two years from its start it became a semi-weekly; to its Saturday edition was added one on Wednesday; to be sure it consisted of 4 pages only, but it was one step in advance, and was justified by the patronage which it obtained.

However, the paper changed hands several times. In 1829 it passed into the possession of Mr. Felix Lacoste, who died consul-general of France at New York in 1859. In 1836 Mr. Lacoste transferred the "COURRIER" to Mr. Ch. de Behr, who was succeeded by Mr. Frederic Gaillardet.

It was in November, 1839, that Mr. Gaillardet took the editorship of the "COURRIER DES ETATS-UNIS," and from his very first number he inaugurated a programme which was a striking success. Mr. Gaillardet had seen clearly the brilliant opening that there was for a French newspaper in the United States. He said in substance—"There is a great field to be occupied by a newspaper which can become both the representative and the defender of the French nation in America, which will uphold the traditions of our manners, of our customs and of our language amongst the population of French origin; which can offer itself as a friend and ally to this population in upholding its native idioms and ideas, and in carrying the French diction to all parts of the new world—it will sustain and rally round it all those who speak this language and of these different scattered members it shall make, if it be possible to do it, one body and one spirit."

What Mr. Gaillardet said in 1839 we think to-day, and we repeat that a French newspaper in America has no higher duty and no position more useful than to act as an intermediary between all the groups of French nationality, not only in the United States, but throughout the whole of the new world; to make them known to each other; to bring them together as much as possible and to mutually assist them. It is this idea, constantly and energetically carried out, which is the secret of the greatest and most durable successes of the "COURRIER DES ETATS-UNIS."

It is this idea constantly kept in view by all those connected with its administration, since the time of Mr. Gaillardet up to the present date, which, repeated from the St. Lawrence to Cape Horn, has caused to spread in all the cities, towns and villages where Frenchmen are to be found, the name of one paper especially devoted to their interests and sufficiently established to defend them. Thus it is that, little by little, the

"COURRIER" is now to be found in the most distant points of the American continent, and that it is welcomed as a friend in all the French homes in the Canadas, Louisiana, the Pacific coast, Mexico, West Indies, and in Central and South America.

In saying this we do not fear any contradiction.

There may be great differences of opinion on political points, or on any other matter which is open to controversy; for we do not expect everybody to hold the same opinions as ourselves; but, at all events, we fear no denial when we proclaim positively that the "COURRIER," whilst continually reminding Frenchmen of the rights which have been conferred on them and the duties which are imposed upon them as members of the American family, has always been a newspaper thoroughly French; working ardently to rally—in the name of the mother country—the French people scattered throughout the vast extent of the American continent; studying their wants, sustaining their rights, and, above all, encouraging them with all the energy in its power to lay aside all useless differences and animosities, and to remember only that they are children of the same country, and that their highest interest, as well as their most imperative duty, is to hold together, to sustain and to help each other.

Few words are necessary to recall the progressive steps of THE COURRIER from its commencement up to the new epoch which opens to-day.

As we have previously stated, THE COURRIER DES ETATS-UNIS dates from the 1st March, 1828. Eighteen months after, a new edition, published on Wednesday, was added to the original Saturday one. This semi-weekly edition was sufficient at that time, when the news from Europe only reached us by sailing vessels, and when, besides, the postal communications with the interior of the country were so uncertain that, in the year 1833, our subscribers in Philadelphia complained that they only received their papers three days after publication.

Mr. Gaillardet's connection with the paper was coincident with the inauguration of trans-Atlantic steam navigation. Then commenced, also, the publication of this paper three times a week. The exciting period of 1848, in its turn created new demands, calling for frequent extras, making an average of four or five numbers per week. However, it was not until three years later—namely, in May, 1851—that the regular daily edition was commenced. A short time previously—namely, in the preceding month of April—was commenced a weekly edition of sixteen quarto pages specially intended for subscribers scattered throughout the interior of the country and for the benefit of our American readers. Towards the end of the same year—in November—THE COURRIER increased the size of its paper, thus enabling it to give more complete details of the subjects treated about. At last, on the 1st November, 1864, the paper was still further enlarged and appeared in its present form. Thus nothing further was needed (at least for the present) but the Sunday edition to meet the demands of a large and varied circulation.

To-day THE COURRIER DES ETATS-UNIS publishes a daily edition (seven numbers per week) at the price of $12 per year. A weekly edition especially for Europe, same size as the daily edition, at $6 per year. A weekly edition, containing twenty pages, at $5 per year.

This last edition, of which the circulation is very large, goes more especially into the Western States, Louisiana, Cuba, the West Indies, Mexico, California, and all the countries on the Pacific Coast as far as Chili.

Such is the present position of THE COURRIER DES ETATS-UNIS, and it is a source of much pleasure to us to acknowledge that its progress has been constantly sustained, encouraged and accelerated by the sympathy of the large majority of the French residents in America. We thank them most cordially, and assure them that we shall endeavor in the future, as we have done in the past, to merit their good-will by sustaining their special interests in America, whenever the occasion therefor arises, and also to inspire Americans with respect and love for France, in return for the affection and respect which she has always shown to their country.

CH. LASALLE & CO., Proprietors,

NO. 92 WALKER STREET, NEW YORK.

"THE SUN," NEW YORK.

A SKETCH FOR THE BOOK OF THE CENTENNIAL NEWSPAPER EXHIBITION.

The prosperity of THE NEW YORK SUN is without a parallel in the history of the daily newspaper press. In proof of this, let the following figures testify. They show the number of copies of THE SUN printed every week during the year ending March 11, 1876:

Week ending		*Copies printed.*	*Week ending*		*Copies printed.*
March	20	849,382	September	18	860,358
	27	845,802		25	858,778
April	3	857,956	October	2	863,935
	10	863,556		9	870,820
	17	855,076		16	878,082
	24	858,270		23	874,625
May	1	869,542		30	876,160
	8	867,550	November	6	908,580
	15	877,450		13	852,372
	22	874,946		20	847,815
	29	866,276		27	836,248
June	5	873,782	December	4	845,378
	12	869,769		11	1,042,716
	19	880,348		18	956,294
	26	883,846		25	933,864
July	3	898,862	January	1	933,987
	10	867,574		8	952,201
	17	877,400		15	953,019
	24	876,282		22	969,910
	31	874,216		29	967,850
August	7	865,558	February	5	993,030
	14	875,982		12	1,024,647
	21	880,488		19	1,027,209
	28	870,502		26	1,014,766
September	4	872,211	March	4	1,014,993
	11	860,755		11	1,028,951

Total.......................................46,799,769

In printing these papers no less than three million, four hundred and twenty-six thousand, six hundred and ten (3,426,610) pounds of paper were consumed.

This exhibit almost passes belief. Had we not examined the books of the establishment, and copied the figures ourselves, we should have feared that a mistake had been made somewhere. But no mistake has been made. The circulation of THE SUN for the fifty-two weeks given, reached the enormous aggregate of *forty-six million, seven hundred and ninety-nine thousand, seven hundred and sixty-nine!* And its average daily circulation, on week days, is now continuously over *one hundred and thirty-eight thousand copies!*

Such unparalleled success, such unexampled popularity, such vast prosperity, can only come from a wide-spread and deep-seated recognition of the trustworthiness of THE SUN as a purveyor of news, and of its fearlessness and faithfulness as an expositor of public affairs, an exposer of public wrongs, an advocate of morality and religion, and an upholder of the rights of the people; and, in truth, as to these grand features of journalism THE SUN has an exalted and commanding position. It is independent of party. It aims always to bring out the truth, no matter who may be helped or hurt by its publication; to support honest and capable men for office, no matter to what party they belong; to secure the enactment of good laws, no matter by whom they are proposed; never in any case to admit into the columns of the paper anything that is contrary to public or private morality, or which cannot be read in the family circle; and always to maintain an independent attitude in the decision of religious questions, treating all sides with fairness, and giving all sides a hearing, and endeavoring to measure and judge them all by the standard of the divine laws.

It is a common remark in New York that "everybody buys THE SUN." Everybody knows that THE SUN tells the truth about public measures, and public men, and public plunderers, without fear or favor. Everybody loves to read the truth about his conspicuous neighbors, no matter how cutting it may be; yea, though it be "sharper than any two-edged sword, piercing even to the dividing asunder of soul and spirit, and of the joints and marrow." This universal love of truth THE SUN, with marked success, perpetually aims to gratify, and therefore, in every number it has toothsome provender for the hungry multitude.

When one enters the first-floor corner door of the spacious and elegant edifice on the corner of Nassau and Frankfort streets, opposite the City Hall, which is known as THE NEW YORK SUN Building, he finds himself in

THE PUBLICATION OFFICE

of the establishment. This is a spacious room with lofty ceiling, running the whole depth of the building. It is divided into a front and rear office. In the front office are desks at which advertisers can write or modify their advertisements. One can hardly enter this office at any hour between 8 o'clock in the morning and 10 at night without finding it alive with employés and customers. There is a constant rush of persons bringing advertisements, coming for answers to advertisements, calling to purchase THE SUN, or to subscribe for it, and seeking information or bringing information; altogether presenting an animated spectacle.

The rear office in the Publication Room is fitted up with desks for the cashier, advertisement clerks, mail clerks, and other employés, and with the ponderous safes of the establishment. It also contains the inner and private office of the publisher, Isaac W. England, Esq., who, though not old in years, is a veteran in newspaper affairs. Mr. England is widely known among newspaper and business men. His integrity, though so unbending as to make things uncomfortable for those who have "crooked" interests to serve, is tempered with such genuine good nature and consideration for the rights and feelings of others, that honest, industrious people like to work under his authority. He is a large stockholder in THE SUN, and cherishes an enthusiastic affection for the paper which vitalizes and reinforces all his faculties, and enables him to thrive bodily on his labors, as well as pecuniarily on his profits.

Having surveyed the Publication Office, let us now ascend to the

EDITORIAL DEPARTMENT,

or "Brain Box," as printers call it, of the establishment. This is situated on the third floor, and consists of a suite of four spacious rooms, forming an L, fronting on Printing House Square, and running along Frankfort street the whole depth of the building from front to rear. We enter the rear room, which is occupied by the reporters and editorial attachés of THE SUN office—all young men, full of vitality and enthusiasm, who love their work, and are proud of their paper. They shirk nothing, but are always ready to start for Coney Island or California, for Alaska or Australia ; to take part in a railroad collision or a steamboat explosion ; to go down in a diving bell or up in a balloon. These young men contribute much to the vivacity and variety of THE SUN, and are to be estimated among the elements of its success.

From the reporters' room, we pass into the apartment of the MANAGING EDITOR.

The position of the Managing Editor of THE SUN is a most important and onerous one. He has to keep a wide-awake eye not only on the entire city, but also on the Union at large, and has the whole reportorial force of THE SUN under his command. With the exception of such persons as the Editor-in-Chief admits to an audience, the Managing Editor has to meet all inquirers, and pacify or discipline all grumblers, and dispose of all comers who, having axes to grind, visit the editorial rooms of THE SUN for the purpose of having them brought to an edge.

Another important member of the editorial force of THE SUN is the NIGHT EDITOR. The Night Editor comes on duty at 4 o'clock P.M., and stays till the last page is made up, ready for the stereotypers. He finds out what has been done by his associates before he came in ; looks over the proofs, makes needful corrections, and decides what must go in the paper and what can be omitted ; examines and condenses correspondence which comes by the night mail, and also the late telegrams ; writes notices of important matters and gives directions as to the nature and length of late reports, and fixes up news matters outside of the local departments. The Night Editor holds a position of great responsibility ; inasmuch as, with the exception of such articles as the Editor-in-chief or the Managing Editor has marked "Must"—which means that articles thus marked *must go in*—he has absolute control of the contents of the paper; consequently, on his judgment in selecting articles to go in, the character of the paper of the next morning in a great measure depends.

In addition to the foregoing, there are the City Editor, the Day Editor, the Financial Editor, the Political Editor, the Market Editor, the Literary Editor, the Musical Editor, the Agricultural Editor, and the Mail and Weekly Editor, whose several functions are indicated by their titles. Then there is the Ship News, and the Telegraphic News, furnished by associations, by correspondents, and by agents. Then there are the Special Correspondents stationed in the important cities of America and Europe. Then there is the army of Voluntary Correspondents which the enterprise and liberality of THE SUN have called forth, "and which covers the land for multitude." Nothing of importance can occur anywhere, that some agent or friend of THE SUN will not at once telegraph to it, or describe by letter in case there be no telegraph station in reach. Liberal pay inevitably awaits all such voluntary news-senders or news-bringers at THE SUN office.

And still further: Besides all the aforementioned persons, there are gentlemen of high culture and special gifts on the editorial pay-roll of THE SUN, who constitute a powerful force, and are able to furnish, on call, articles of the highest merit on any subject which it may be desired to discuss in the columns of the paper.

We have still to mention the most important member of the editorial force of THE SUN, to wit: Charles A. Dana, Esq., the EDITOR-IN-CHIEF, whose function is one of supreme importance. He must hold the entire force in a firm but elastic grasp, marshal all its diverse elements into harmony without impairing their individualities, and give consistency and unity to the general sweep and purpose of the journal. He must scan, day by day, the events of the world, and single out for publication and comment those which are either of the most general or special importance, and indicate to his subordinates what they are severally to write about, what the scope and tone of their articles shall be, and what shall be the policy of THE SUN on every subject.

Mr. Dana is the largest stockholder of the Company, and the editorial monarch of the establishment. His sway is imperial and despotic. No one does or can call *him* to account. He has had large experience in newspaper affairs, in subordinate as well as controlling positions. He has been reporter, city editor, managing editor, New York correspondent, Washington correspondent, Paris correspondent, and foreign correspondent generally. Like Napoleon, therefore, he knows his profession through all its grades, and can judge and do justice to all his subordinates, and pity all their woes because he has felt the same. He has a wide knowledge of public affairs, and also of business, commercial and scholastic matters; has traveled much, both in Europe and America; speaks the modern languages with fluency; has an intimate acquaintance with many of the leading scholars and statesmen of both hemispheres; is familiar with literature, philosophy, and metaphysics; sympathizes with the progressive and ameliorating movements of the times; has always been an audacious and plucky newspaper belligerent, but fights without malice, and is a generous conqueror. Several years ago it was said of Mr. Dana:

"He receives the hardest blows with serenity of countenance and of spirit, as though he heard gentle angels whispering: 'Peace, Charles, prithee peace! Possess thy soul in patience and bide thy time, for that vain man weareth a scalp wherewith, in the Providence of God, thou shalt ere long adorn thy wigwam!' and he doth possess his soul in patience, and he also bideth his time, and finally, like a true journalist, he conspicuously takes the scalp of the offender at the very time it would be most awkward for the victim to appear in society bereft of that ornamental hereditament."

This declaration seems to have been instigated by the spirit of prophecy. One after another the foes of THE SUN have gone down before the prowess of its "Chief," until there is no other wigwam in the country so rich in scalps as Mr. Dana's.

Mr. Dana is a hard worker. THE SUN is his pet. He loves it and is proud of it. He keeps a vigilant eye upon everything; and, like his subordinates, is ready to do any piece of work whatever that may come to his hand. His literary and editorial executiveness is surpassingly prompt and decisive. This helps him to go through his work with a celerity which relieves it of much of its burdensomeness. He is genial and companionable with his assistants, but no one can more effectively assume the imperial *role* when distinctions of position should be made apparent, and the lines of order should be sharply drawn.

Mr. Dana is in all respects a prosperous gentleman. His copyright as editor of Appleton's New *American Cyclopedia* is large, his receipts for salary and dividends from THE SUN are much greater, and altogether he has a most princely income.

The members of the editorial force of THE SUN, one hundred and five in number, are loyal to the paper, and to one another, from the Chief to the lowest member of the staff. The reporters stand by THE SUN; the Managing Editor stands by the reporters; and the Editor-in-Chief stands by the entire force. This is an important point, and gives a unity, and enthusiasm, and self-reliance to the men which nothing else could inspire.

And now let us see how all the work done by this array of accomplished and industrious men is finally brought to a focus in the pages of THE SUN.

It is 10 o'clock at night as we mount to the editorial rooms. The apartment of the Editor-in-Chief, in the northeast corner of the edifice, looking out upon City Hall Park, is all aglow. Ordinarily he only comes down at night to take a general survey of affairs and look over his proofs, but to-night matters of uncommon importance have come to hand, and he is at his post, with a full staff, at a later hour than usual.

Everybody seems to work as though under whip and spur. Reporters from the public meetings, fires, fights, and scenes of accident and crime, rush in with their notes and set to work as if for life. Messengers hurry to and fro from telegraph offices. Other messengers likewise hurry to and fro from divers other points. Visitors come hurrying in, all out of breath, wanting to see the Managing Editor or the Chief, on matters of pressing importance. and all are disposed of with promptness, celerity and courtesy. Mangled and tumbled papers from the city, the country, and the uttermost parts of the civilized world, lie in heaps upon the floors. The pens scratch, the scissors click, the Chief's bell rings sharply out for the boy, and the "condensers"—three men whose only business is to take the core out of correspondence, reports and extracts, and articles from other papers—are "refining as with a refiner's fire" the matter which is to appear in the morning's paper.

The space in THE SUN is too valuable to admit anything except the very cream and marrow of the news and information to its columns; wherefore, telegraphic dispatches are reduced to "Sparks," long communications to paragraphs, paragraphs to "Personals," and articles to "Jottings."

THE SUN Condensers are men who can see at a glance what is interesting in an article, and what is useful, and what is needful, and what is of no account; and they "kill" without mitigation or remorse.

And now midnight approaches; the turmoil has died away; the Chief and his immediate staff have disappeared; the reporters have gone, except a few who have but recently come in; and the Managing and Night Editors, with a few trusty assistants, are all that remain on duty. And now let us "follow copy" up-stairs to the

COMPOSING ROOM,

where the type-setters ply their nimble fingers.

The composing room of THE SUN office is a fine, light, airy apartment, and is fitted up with the utmost elegance and convenience. The exact cost of the outfit—including type, furniture, and materials for stereotyping—was $12,290.72. The regular force of compositors, or type-setters, is sixty-five; and a fine-looking, intelligent company of men they are.

The compositors have been at work for many hours. They take it easily at first, from 3 P.M. to 5; then there is a recess of two hours, and at 7 o'clock they come back for the real work of the day, and stay till 2 o'clock, A.M., or as much longer as may be necessary. As a usual thing, when 2 o'clock comes, all but four of the compositors are allowed to go, and the four retained are kept till the paper is sent to press. The compositors work by the piece, and their average earnings are $25 a week; but some of them make $45 a week, when they do their best.

After the type-setters have been at work for an hour, or less, the proof-taker begins his work. The type which has been set is put in an orderly way and fastened in its place on long brass beds called galleys, which are then run under the proof-press, whereby impressions, or proofs, are taken on long slips of paper. These are sent to the proof-readers, who read them over for errors, and mark all mistakes on the margins of the proofs, which are then taken back to the compositors, who correct the errors in the type, after which new proofs, called revises, are taken, to see if everything is right. If any errors are found in the revises they are also marked and corrected; and when everything has been at last set right in a galley of type, it is transferred to the make-up table; that is, to the table where the type is finally put in the forms or pages of the newspaper.

About 11 o'clock the foreman of the composition room sends word to the Night Editor that he is ready to "make up;" that is, that he is ready to put the type into the pages, and send them to the stereotypers. On receiving this notice the Night Editor appears with a separate set of proofs, taken expressly for him, and over which he has been studying and working for several hours.

There is already matter enough in type to fill the columns of the paper twice over, and more is coming all the time. The telegraphic lightnings are pouring it in; the reporters are writing it out by the column; and messengers are coming with all manner of communications—"Very important, sir, and *must* appear in the morning's paper, sir."

And so the Night Editor works away, studying over his proofs, gradually singling out what must go in, whether or no, and no mistake; also what *may* be left out; also what *shall* be left out. When, therefore, he receives notice from the foreman of the composition room, that he is ready to "make up," the Night Editor goes up to the fifth story with a clearly defined purpose. Under his direction the foreman rapidy lifts column after column of the news and editorials into the form which is to constitute the second or editorial page of the next morning's SUN. The last page and the third page, composed largely of advertisements, have already been made up and sent to the stereotypers. The first page, which is the last one made up, is yet to come. Meanwhile, let us step into

THE STEREOTYPING ROOM

and see what the Vulcans are about.

The stereotyping room is one of the most interesting departments of THE SUN establishment. It is occupied, and the stereotyping process performed by eight splendid fellows, whose brain and muscle, as well as their skill and fidelity, are of a high grade.

The stereotyping process is peculiar, and differs widely from that in ordinary use. The Bullock presses used in printing THE SUN require stereotype plates which can be affixed to their cylinders, and hence the plates must be cast in half-circles; and they must be cast, too, with the utmost expedition and in unusual numbers. There are seven presses used by THE SUN, each of which prints two complete copies of the paper at an impression. Therefore, *no less than fourteen complete sets of plates have to be cast for* THE SUN, *so that it can have fourteen papers printed consentaneously, in order to get off its immense edition within the brief period between the hour when the paper goes to press and the time of its delivery to buyers, and at the post-office for the early mails.* The process of stereotyping is performed in this wise:

The flat page of type is first warmed on a hollow iron table heated by steam, then a sheet of thick paper, such as steel engravings are printed on, which is chemically prepared by soaking in a mixture until it becomes nearly of the consistency of paste, is laid upon the face of the type, and beaten down with a heavy and stiff brush, until every letter, rule, and point is perfectly moulded in the soft mass of paper. All hollow places are then filled up with a preparation of plaster of Paris; after which another sheet of the prepared paper is laid upon the first, and beaten down in the same manner. By this means a substantial matrix of the entire page is formed. The type and matrix are then swathed in blankets, placed on the hollow, steam-heated table, run under a press on one end of the table, and subjected to a heavy pressure, while at the same time it is baked by the heat. It is then taken out and the paper matrix is removed from the type. It is firm, but pliable, and capable of resisting a high degree of heat. It is the flexibleness of the matrix, even more than the celerity with which it can be produced, which gives it its peculiar value; for it is its flexibleness which enables a cylindrical plate to be cast from it.

After the matrix has been perfected as above described, it is placed in a reversed position in an iron mould of the exact curvature of the press cylinder; the melted type metal is then poured in, and in two minutes a stereotype plate of the page of type in the form of a half-circle is taken out and handed over to the trimmers to be fitted to the press cylinder; the mould is again filled with metal, and another plate is cast; and so the process goes on, until fourteen casts of each page have been taken, trimmed, and sent down to the press-room.

We will now step on the elevator along with a set of the stereotype plates and descend with them to

THE PRESS-ROOM.

The Press-Room is situated in the basement of the edifice, and is a most capacious apartment. When we arrive at the press-room, at half past one o'clock in the morning, matters are in no very lively trim. Everything is quiet. There is not yet even a hiss of steam. Stalwart men are stretched out on huge piles of paper, fast asleep. Some of them lie face downward, with their arms stretched out at full length, and sleeping as though they would never again wake. Others are lying all in a heap, others flat on their backs, showing grimy but honest faces; and all are sleeping soundly. Other men are bringing in huge rolls of paper from the dampening room and arranging them conveniently at hand for the pressman.

The Bullock press, on which THE SUN is printed, prints from a continuous sheet, which is wound up in the form of a huge cylinder. The machine for wetting down or dampening the paper is so constructed that it unwinds it from one roll and at the same time winds it up into another roll; and as the paper thus passes from one roll to another it is subjected to a uniform shower of the finest spray, which dampens it in every fibre to just exactly the degree which is requisite for it to print to the best advantage—the construction of the press, the rapidity of the motion, and the force of the pressure, all considered. Attached to the dampening machine is an invention of Mr. England's, which ingeniously measures the roll of paper and tells just how many SUNS it will make. This is done for the purpose of checking the tendency of paper manufacturers to put so much body in their stock that a roll of paper of given weight sometimes falls short in length to the extent of many copies of THE SUN.

And now, as the pressmen have begun to wake up, and are beginning to put the stereotype plates on the cylinders, and the steam begins to give tokens of its coming, let us go up to the composition room again, where over the first page of THE SUN the final struggle of matter against space is to begin. "This," says the Night Editor, pointing at it as he speaks, "is the costliest page on this planet." It is now half-past one o'clock A.M. The form must be in the stereotyper's room in fifteen minutes. There is matter enough on the make-up table to fill four pages, and every line of it is important. What's to be done? especially as a fresh batch of copy has just come up marked "MUST," from the Managing Editor, who is still hard at work below. Now is seen the value of understanding *every part of one's business*, especially the mechanical part. The Night Editor is a practical printer, copy-cutter, proof-reader, anything and everything that may be needed. He looks over the type—does not have to resort to the proofs—and orders out this and cuts down that, and reads the proof of new articles from the type—and finally "Good Night" comes from the telegraph offices—and the page is completed, and the form is locked up (that is, fastened so the type cannot fall out) and trundled into the stereotyper's room exactly at 15 minutes to 2 o'clock A.M.

And now look at the stereotypers. They are also on the home-stretch, and how magnificently they work. Every man knows just exactly what to do, and does it to perfection just in the nick of time; and the total result is that four casts of the first page of THE SUN are on their way to the lower regions in just twenty minutes from the time the stereotypers received the form. That is only five minutes to a cast. The other ten casts follow at a more rapid rate.

From the stereotype room we now go down to the publication office, to see the newsmen and newsboys buy their checks. When the delivery of the paper begins, which will be in a few minutes, the rush will be so great that there will be no time to make change; and so newsmen and newsboys provide themselves with metal checks, about the size of a two-cent piece, on which is stamped the number of papers for which they have paid. If a newsboy wants 12 papers, he pays 16 cents—THE SUN is sold to him at 1⅓ cents a copy—and receives a check which entitles him to 12 papers. This check he presents to the man below of whom he gets his papers, who delivers his 12 SUNS to him, and drops the check through a hole in the delivery counter, into a box kept for the purpose. The smallest check calls for three papers, and the largest for eight thousand.

On entering the publication office, we find a number of men and boys buying their checks, and several tired little fellows lying asleep on the floor; and on the grating outside, through which the warm steam and hot air come up, are other children also lying asleep. It is a raw and chilly morning, and the "iron bedstead," as the little fellows call the grating, affords them a luxurious couch, through which the warmth comes upon their pinched and withered and ill-clad bodies like airs from Heaven.

And now back to the press-room again. At 7 minutes to 2 the first press starts and delivers 200 papers a minute. In a few minutes the counters begin to count off, and get the papers ready for delivery to the newsboys and newsmen. At 2 minutes after 2 the second press begins to throw of its 200 SUNS a minute. At 9 minutes after 2 the third press starts; and so they keep on until all the presses are running and throwing off fourteen hundred SUNS a minute, two of the presses printing 300 papers a minute each. Although the SUN now has seven presses in operation, the popular demand is so constantly increasing that it has ordered another of double size, and the capacity of 50,000 per hour, which, after being shown at the Centennial Exhibition, will be set up in the press-room.

The counting of the papers is one of the most interesting and astounding performances in the whole business. There is one man who counts 300 a minute, and another who can count 400 a minute. Let the readers of this article try to count 400 a minute on their fingers, or try to count 400 pins or 400 peas in a minute, and they will get some notion what it is to count that number in that time.

The fact is, the counting of newspapers in the SUN office has been refined into an art as delicate as that of piano playing, and it is performed very much in the same way. The counter throws a pile of damp papers on the table, strikes the heap in the stomach with his left hand, twitches up the edges with his right so that they stand slightly apart, and then, with the fingers of his left hand runs them off in groups of five, almost exactly as a pianist runs off arpeggios on his instrument, and with an equal precision and delicacy of touch.

The papers are usually counted off in bundles of fifty, but sometimes in larger quantities. The delivery of the papers to the buyers begins at half-past three. The number taken by the different buyers the morning we were present varied from 3 to 27,000. The three were taken by a little boy about seven years old, the 27,000 by a newsdealer, and we are informed that the whole number delivered by a quarter past 5 o'clock was 126,600. The additional sales, and the papers sent to mail subscribers, brought the whole number up to 138,993.

Having thus followed the NEW YORK SUN through its entire daily and nightly growth, from the first article written to the point where the presses are dropping fourteen hundred complete copies a minute at our feet, we now take our leave, and take a Third Avenue car for up-town. By the time the car arrives opposite THE SUN office it is comfortably filled, and a newsboy rushes in it, crying "Here's your NEW YORK SUN," and sells four papers on the spot. We look at the City Hall clock; it is just 48 minutes past 3 o'clock. Thus early does the sale of THE SUN in the streets commence.

The number of persons employed in THE SUN office is two hundred and forty-nine. The expenses of the establishment for the week ending March 11, 1876, were *fifteen thousand eight hundred and seventeen dollars and seventeen cents* ($15,817.17), and it was not an expensive week either, the items of which are as follows:

Editorial expenses, including salaries, telegrams, etc.,	$3,826.83	Ink,	$138.72
Publication salaries,	429.51	Paper,	7,074.55
Mail room,	197.00	Coal and Gas,	176.50
Composition,	1,486.91	Steam-power,	70.00
Stereotyping,	296.00	Postage,	330.68
Press room salaries,	940.47	General expenses,	750.00
" expenses and supplies,	100.00	Total for the week,	$15,817.17

Dividing this amount by seven, it gives a daily average of $2,259.59, the outlay incurred that every buyer of THE SUN may get his copy for two cents. If a buyer of THE SUN were to set to work to make the copy which he gets for two cents, he couldn't begin to do it for $2,259.59, without first incurring an outlay of a fortune to start with, and then spending a quarter of a century or so in learning how to do it.

The expenses of THE SUN are so enormous that one naturally wonders where the profits come in. They come from the sale of the papers and from subscriptions and advertisements.

In addition to their enormous daily issue, THE SUN PRINTING COMPANY publish THE SUNDAY SUN (8 pages), at $1.20 a year, and THE WEEKLY SUN (8 pages), at $1.20 a year. THE WEEKLY SUN is intended more particularly for country circulation, and is filled only with the choicest news of most interest and value to those who do not care to take the New York daily papers. Great care is bestowed upon its agricultural and market reports; the farmer and the country merchant are provided with such items of intelligence as most closely enter into the warp and woof of their prosperity, and the matron and children are not forgotten, but are supplied with such genial and instructive reading matter as one loves to peruse in the family circle and enjoy with those who sit around the same hearthstone.

It was supposed to be a dangerous experiment for THE SUN COMPANY to attempt to publish a two-cent paper at a cost surpassing that of any four-cent paper. But the experiment has succeeded so well that THE SUN could now live without an advertisement, and Mr. Dana's policy is always to make advertisements give way to the news. The people appreciate such enterprise and liberality, and THE NEW YORK SUN is having greater success than ever before. It is emphatically *the people's* paper. It always stands by the workingmen and all movements for the improvement of the condition of the masses, when they *need* support; and it also stands by them in an effective manner. It does them downright, substantial service. It also always takes the lead in exposing corruption in high places, and in bringing the people's unfaithful servants to the bar of public opinion. For these and many similar reasons, THE SUN has a strong, enduring hold on the affections of the masses and the confidence of the nation at large.

And then the fact that it gives all the news of the Associated Press at one-half the price which the other papers of the Association charge for it, in addition to what its own exclusive enterprise furnishes, and the fact that it gives the combined results of the labor and brains of two hundred and forty-nine men, winnowed of all chaff, skimmed of all scum, and purged of all sediment—the fact, in short, that it every morning gives every one of its buyers $2,259.59 for two cents, places the ever growing prosperity of THE NEW YORK SUN beyond all question. Its compactness is also a strong point in its favor. One can attack its contents with a fair hope of being able to master them within a reasonable period.

In the antediluvian days, when human beings lived away up towards the thousands, such a feature would not have been of so much importance. In those long-drawn times a sprightly girl of sixty, or a robust youth of ninety, or even a middle-aged man or woman two or three hundred years old, could take things moderately; but it is ordered otherwise in this day, and especially in this metropolis. Here, life is cut short at both ends, and crammed to choking in the middle; the day's hurly burly's never done, and there's only time to read THE SUN.

THE EVENING JOURNAL, OF JERSEY CITY, N. J.

A SKETCH FOR THE BOOK OF THE CENTENNIAL NEWSPAPER EXHIBITION.

The EVENING JOURNAL of Jersey City was established in May, 1867, its publication and editorial office being combined in one small room, and its total available capital at end of first week was $119.00. Its success has been remarkable, even in this land of rapid growths. It is strictly a "local paper," which, while giving all the telegraphic news of the day, yet concentrates its attention chiefly on the local news of the thriving community in which it is published, and it is therefore a favorite visitor at every tea-table and the leading advertising medium in Jersey City. The population of Jersey City, which in 1850 was about 16,000 is now 120,000, and rapidly increasing. The success of the JOURNAL is attested by the four-story handsome granite and brick building, size 25x90 feet, 37 Montgomery street, Jersey City, erected for it in 1874. It is printed from the most remarkable Web printing machine yet invented. Its proprietors, Messrs. Pangborn, Dunning & Dear, who are experienced newspaper men, and thoroughly appreciate the wants and requirements of the community amongst whom they labor, have brought the JOURNAL to a high pitch of excellence, and have received, as a reward of conscientious work, cordial support and approbation.

THE NEW YORKER STAATS ZEITUNG.

A SKETCH FOR THE BOOK OF THE CENTENNIAL NEWSPAPER EXHIBITION.

The progress, development, and present position of this paper form one of the most remarkable existing proofs of the success with which industry, energy, perseverance, and faithful and righteous management, when applied to the Press, are crowned in the United States. The New York STAATS ZEITUNG was first published in 1834, as a weekly paper. As such it was well received and supported, but the patronage accorded had so far augmented, and the demands of the Teutonic population so increased in 1842, that in that year it was issued as a tri-weekly publication. The mutation proved the calculations of the projector to be soundly based. The sale of the journal grew, and its reputation advanced correspondingly, and three years later, when it was converted into a daily paper, it entered on its more useful career with a propitious future before it. At this time, notwithstanding its reputation, the circulation of the paper was, however, comparatively insignificant, amounting to about only 3,000 copies, and it was not till 1849 that the grand development leading to its present commanding position can be said to have taken place. Even then, for some years, its progress was not over-rapid, and Mr. Oswald Ottendorfer, the present proprietor and chief editor, avers that if, in 1852, when he became first connected with the STAATS ZEITUNG, any one should have suggested the possibility of the paper reaching its present large circulation, he would have considered the idea visionary and absurd. But what was deemed a quarter of a century ago an impossibility is to-day an accomplished fact.

In order to present a trustworthy opinion of its circulation, we have carefully prepared from the office books the following statement of the average daily circulation of the N. Y. STAATS ZEITUNG for every week during the first quarter of the current year:

Week ending		*Average daily.*	*Week ending*		*Average daily.*
January	6	47,200	February	24	49,400
	13	47,300	March	2	49,600
	20	47,300		9	49,700
	27	47,400		16	49,800
February	3	48,500		23	49,900
	10	49,600		30	49,700
	17	49,800	April	6	49,600

In addition to this daily circulation, a weekly and a Sunday edition are printed, the circulation of the former being principally outside the city, in the Middle, Western, and Southern States. The Sunday edition is a prominent literary paper of acknowledged merits, and is very widely read.

The above statistics show that the New York STAATS ZEITUNG has the largest circulation of any daily paper printed in the German language. None in the United States will compare with it at all, and we are reliably informed that the principal journals issued in Germany—in Vienna, Berlin, Cologne or Frankfort—are not its peers. It is not necessary, however, to confine the comparison among German journals. The New York STAATS ZEITUNG will well bear to be contrasted with its English contemporaries of the city. There is that in its circulation which is remarkable, and indicates a superior class of readers. It is this: nearly all the copies of every issue are taken by regularly appointed carriers to the houses of subscribers. Compared with its English contemporaries, it is vended but little on the streets. Evidently, then, its subscription list is very heavy, it being very doubtful if even the *Herald* or *Sun* can claim a heavier.

When it first appeared, the ZEITUNG was published in Nassau street; next it was removed to Frankfort, and afterwards to William street. In 1857 it was located in an establishment specially erected for its accommodation, at 17 Chatham street, opposite the City Hall, whence it continued to issue for many years. But the constant increase of business, together with the prospect that the East River Bridge will, when complete, have its landing on the spot where that office is situate, constrained Mr. Ottendorfer to seek another place of publication. The choice of site was a matter of no little importance. Printing House Square is the most desirable location for the business place of a newspaper in the city. Therefore, to retain a holding there must be accomplished if possible. But no suitable building presented itself. Now it was that Mr. Ottendorfer determined to carry out his long cherished desire to erect an edifice for his paper which should be an ornament to the city and a monument of newspaper enterprise. In pursuance of his resolve, he bought several houses on Tryon Row, extending from Chatham to Centre streets, facing Broadway, and thereon has placed a structure whose dignity and gracefulness impress all beholders. It was completed in 1872, and first occupied in the early part of 1873, and no one who examines it can fail to admit that its projector, Mr. Ottendorfer, has succeeded remarkably in his efforts to secure a building exteriorly handsome and complete in its internal arrangements.

NEW YORKER STAATS ZEITUNG BUILDING.

The edifice forms the north side of Printing House Square, on which nearly all the principal daily morning papers published in the City—the *Sun*, the *Tribune*, the *Times*, and the *Herald*—have their palaces. It closes the circle formed by the City Hall, and the new Post Office, and gives an appropriate finish to one of the most interesting parts of the City. The style of architecture employed is the modern renaissance, the first story being built of the dark bluish Quincy Granite and those above it of the lighter Concord Granite. The effect of this combination is to relieve the building of the heavy appearance usually characterizing granite structures. The ornamentation, which is rich without being redundant, further aids the accomplishment of this end, whilst the portico, extending through two floors, and surmounted by bronze statues of Guttenberg and Franklin (the one the inventor and the other the American representative of printing) is a central feature which is never beheld without admiration. There is a pleasant harmony in the whole arrangement, and the remark is often made by gentlemen of cultivated taste and great experience that among all the majestic public buildings erected in the city in recent years, that of the STAATS ZEITUNG bears the palm for combining beauty and utility.

A model exterior was not, however, what Mr. Ottendorfer alone aimed at. His intention was that this should be an accompaniment only to a complete, thoroughly practical newspaper establishment. He therefore, in preparing the plans, made a careful study of all the improvements in newspaper economy, and introduced all such as commended themselves to his approbation. All other considerations were made subservient to this end, and how fully this was accomplished a visit to the STAATS ZEITUNG office will convince every observer.

Entering the publication office, situate on the ground floor at the south-east corner, one is immediately struck with the loftiness of the apartment, next with the elegance of its fittings, and then with the evidence of business-like arrangement everywhere present. For height and good ventilation the STAATS ZEITUNG publication office has not its equal in the city. The consequence of this grand provision being that the *employees* are healthy and vigorous, and that the evil effects of a vitiated atmosphere are never experienced even when the congregation of people at the office is greatest. The woodwork in this department is of rich polished walnut, exquisitely carved, and set off with artistic bronze adornments, affording a charming contrast to a splendid specimen of German marble (expressly imported for Mr. Ottendorfer) which forms the slab at the aperture through which advertisers and others confer with the clerks. Writing desks *en suite*, and of the most approved pattern, are placed on the elegant tiled floor for the accommodation of visitors ; all *minutiæ* are carefully disposed ; and pervading everything is a conformity with the architectural design.

Going up a noble stairway, the walls at the side of which are tastefully frescoed, the editorial rooms, situated on the fourth story, are reached. Whilst ascending, the sustained elegance of the building cannot fail to impress any visitor. The landing-place at each story is tiled just as the publication office is ; the same sort of adornments observable in the hall are presented at the top of the edifice ; everything bespeaks thoroughness.

The editors' rooms are arranged methodically and comfortably, being so placed as to expose the busy workers to the least danger of distraction. What hundreds of their literary brethren sigh for in vain—fresh air and plenty of it—they enjoy without let or hindrance. The several offices connect with each other, so that no difficulty stands in the way of ready communication between the editor-in-chief and his subordinates ; speaking tubes render the transmission of messages to printers or clerks easy ; and copy-lifts expedite the transmission of copy or correspondence to and from the *sanctum*.

Above the editorial department, on the top floor of the building, are the composing room and stereotyping foundry—the most excellent in the city—devised for the comfort of work-people and the facilitation of the operations conducted in them. Everything is clean, orderly, systematic, and the looks of the workmen betoken that the sanitary arrangements have not been carried out in vain.

The STAATS ZEITUNG forms are stereotyped every morning, and as the whole operation has to be completed in about 18 minutes, the most perfect machinery is necessarily employed. The pages of type having been trundled into the foundry, an accurate mould of them is taken on wet papier-maché, which, when dried by heat, is placed in a massive iron casting box of curved shape, into which the seething metal is poured. A good cast having been secured, the plate is transferred to the planing machine, where all irregularities are removed, and in a few minutes (the finishers having removed any crudities) it is fit to be affixed to the cylinder of either of the two splendid six-cylinder Hoe presses on which the issue is daily worked in the basement. In the foundry a small engine is used to drive the machinery, the steam being supplied from the basement. The means of heating the building are also furnished from this subficial department, and are very complete.

Descending by an elegantly fitted elevator to the press-room we enter a series of underground apartments. The elaborate machinery at once attracts notice, but the next subject to arrest the attention is the excellence of the light, which, though conveyed artificially, is so good as to render the use of gas unnecessary during the day, save in retired places. The two presses employed to print the STAATS ZEITUNG will turn off together 20,000 an hour, the motive power being given by a 36 horse-power engine constructed by Wright & Co. Two of these splendid machines stand side by side, though but one is used at a time, the object being to obviate delay in printing the paper in case accident should befall either. Near at hand are the folding machines, all of the most approved pattern and capable of folding neatly the papers as fast as they are printed. The mailing apparatus is likewise close at hand, this also being of the most approved construction. The immense boilers which furnish the steam for the machinery and the whole building are located in vaults under the sidewalk on the Chatham street side of the building. On a level with these, but on the opposite side of the floor, there is another vault for the storage of paper, in which several thousand reams are constantly kept, and an aperture for the purpose admits of fresh supplies being slid down a shute. In close contiguity is the distributing room, where the papers are handed every morning to the numerous carriers, who are invariably promptly on hand when an issue is coming from press. To this a half story is devoted. The government of this department is singularly excellent. Each carrier is a man of proved reliability. Promptness and precision are points which the indefatigable carriers vie with each other to excel in, and it is next to impossible for any subscriber to the NEW YORK STAATS ZEITUNG to be disappointed of his paper at the breakfast table. Each of the corps has a district assigned him, and is protected from the encroachments of rivals by provisions designed by Mr. Ottendorfer to benefit both the distributors and his patrons. There is not one of the other daily papers that has anything approaching to the completeness of this system.

Indeed, everything possible appears to have been done to obviate delay in the delivery of the paper. Even the building itself was from the first designed to subserve this end, and for that reason chiefly it was that each and every room in the whole of the colossal edifice was made independently fire-proof. It seems impossible that the building could be destroyed by fire, or that flames could even extend beyond the apartment in which they might have their origin. The success of the New York STAATS ZEITUNG, in a business point of view, is in no small degree due to the active interest which Mrs. Ottendorfer, the wife of the editor and proprietor, takes in it. This lady is every morning in the publication office, and superintends and directs the business affairs with an ability and circumspection only to be acquired by long experience, and that faculty of comprehensive tact which are commonly believed to be the exclusive characteristics of men ; her example demonstrates that, without claiming a larger sphere of rights for the so-called weaker sex, ladies can become eminently useful in the daily exertions of life, if they understand how to properly exercise their influence.

The New York STAATS ZEITUNG as it at present stands before the public is the result of the activity, industry and intelligence of our citizens of German descent. But it has in no small degree itself contributed to bring that class of our citizens to the respected position which they occupy. Its influence in the formation of their views, modeling their opinions, and its usefulness in correctly apprising them of important national and local issues, can hardly be over-estimated. If the secret of its great influence be sought it will alone be found in the sincerity and disinterestedness with which the STAATS ZEITUNG urges its arguments. These are the only qualities which could possibly have gained it the consideration it enjoys among such thoughtful and well-instructed people as compose the Teutonic element of our population. The tendency of the paper is conservative. Being inspired with a conviction of the necessity of the preservation of the Union, it supported before the war the democratic party, believing it to be the one giving the best guarantee for the undisturbed preservation of the Union, and after the outbreak of the Rebellion its editor and proprietor, in words and facts, enthusiastically supported the Union cause.

Of late years, however, the NEW YORK STAATS ZEITUNG has been independent in politics, its principal efforts being directed against corruption and the abuses in our public life and to endeavor to impress upon its readers the necessity of making honesty, faithfulness and capability the only standard by which candidates for all offices should be judged, regardless of party dictates or promptings. To this course it consistently adheres, and its increasing popularity is the best possible voucher that this stand is one which commends itself to public approbation.

THE NEW YORK TIMES.

A SKETCH FOR THE BOOK OF THE CENTENNIAL NEWSPAPER EXHIBITION.

The projectors of the N. Y. TIMES promised in their prospectus to make "at once the best and the cheapest daily family newspaper in the United States." Twelve months later, they were able to declare that it had been "immeasurably more successful, in all respects, than any new paper of a similar character ever before published in the United States." With justifiable exultation, and with strict adherence to truth, they asserted that "in circulation, in income, in influence, in everything which goes to make up the aggregate of a successful journal, it challenges a comparison with any other paper ever published." Such, in brief, is the story of "The Year One," as told by Mr. Raymond, on the 17th September, 1852.

The TIMES, then, was a success from the beginning. And it was a success because it met an urgent want of the community, because to enterprise in the acquisition and publication of news it added courage, moderation, dignity, ability and genuine consistency in the discussion of public affairs. The field was already largely occupied by journals which looked with no friendly eye upon the new comer. There was coarseness in the controversies of those days, and the contrast maintained was between indifference to principle on one hand, and a dangerous tendency to extreme principles on the other. The orthodox Whig newspaper vied with the organ of Democratic opinion in obedience to the slave power; the radical Whig became the champion of Socialism, and the cause of human liberty suffered from an advocacy which identified it with opinions that were repugnant to the American people. A need of journalism different from either was felt, and the TIMES met it boldly and well. "We shall be conservative in all cases where we think conservatism essential to the public good," was one of its opening assurances; "and we shall be radical in everything which may seem to us to require radical treatment and radical reform." This discriminating judgment was one of the secrets of the remarkable influence and prosperity which attended the establishment of the TIMES. Its excellence as a newspaper was a potent factor in the sum of its success. The care with which it was adapted to the tastes and wants of the family, the high standard of purity which it maintained, and the literary culture which shone in its columns, were marked and important sources of power. But its weight in political discussion—the authority it exercised alike in the affairs of the State and of the nation—was to a large extent traceable to the skill and effect with which it imposed restraint upon the conflicting ultraisms of the time. It infused the vitality of progress and the courage of conviction into the dominating conservatism; it held in check an aggressive radicalism, and subjected it to the discipline of the Constitution and the law. Never leaving its readers in doubt as to its position on any important question—never evading a question because it was beset with prejudice or linked with powerful vested interests, it adhered steadfastly to the course in the first instance marked out. It was vigorous, without being offensive; courteous, without being cowardly; and it appealed always to the intelligence and moral principle of its readers.

Identified with the Free Soil Whigs as long as the Whig party lasted, the TIMES largely contributed to the influences and purposes which culminated in the organization of the Republican party. The Pittsburg Convention and the nomination of Fremont were events with which the historian will associate the services of the TIMES. The previous four years witnessed a struggle bitter and unrelenting, in which the TIMES took a conspicuous and honorable part. As a newspaper, it had kept pace with the march of the age. Its size had expanded, and with the enlargement of its resources had come increased efficiency in all the general departments of a metropolitan journal. The principles which had governed it remained unchanged; the policy it did much towards moulding and crystallizing found final expression in the election of Lincoln. The position he assumed corresponded very closely with that which the TIMES had uniformly held. And when the madness of Southern faction forced upon the nation a struggle for its life, the TIMES accorded his administration an ungrudging, unqualified support. It had no doubts as to its duty, and never paused to count the cost of the difficulties it encountered. No better record of the war exists than that which might be compiled from its columns.

The views attributed to American statesmen by Victor Hugo and Louis Blanc in their appeal for the Philadelphia Exhibition reflect the policy upheld by the TIMES throughout the era of reconstruction. It exerted itself to "prevent hatred succeeding defeat." It contended that to permanently re-establish peace, and to win from peace the fruits it should yield, friendly feeling must be restored between the victors and the vanquished. The pursuit of these ideas for a brief period estranged from the TIMES the more extreme leaders of the Republican party. Experience has vindicated the motives of the TIMES, and moderated the rancor of those who at the moment quarreled with it. Its desire to promote sectional reconciliation continued unabated; its good will towards the South remained unaffected by the fate that attended the overtures which it encouraged. But it has insisted that magnanimity shall be tempered with justice—that while removing disabilities and fostering paternal feeling, the essential results of the war shall be preserved unimpaired. At every stage of the controversy the TIMES has made partisanship subordinate to patriotism, and has interpreted in their broadest aspects the principles which underlie the Republican organization, and are the key to all that is greatest and best in its career.

The demand for party purification and administrative reform harmonizes with the declarations embodied in the first number of the TIMES: "What is good we desire to preserve and improve; what is evil, to exterminate or reform." The paper stands where it has always stood when our institutions were menaced by corruption and intrigue. It never talked about terms with rascals or "Rings." It never concealed or apologized for wrong-doing in high places. It never hesitated to condemn what is evil because the perpetrators were members of the Republican party. It never recognized partisan obligations when the integrity of the government, local or national, was endangered. It never allowed party affiliations to fetter its judgment or to obstruct the discharge of its duty to the country. These are characteristics of which the TIMES may fairly boast, and they indicate more emphatically than mere promises the direction of its course in the present condition of affairs.

The TIMES was never blind to that rapidly growing demoralization of our municipal politics which culminated in the accession to power of the Tweed Ring. It followed with unsparing denunciation the outrages upon public honor which marked the administration of Mayor Wood, and it attacked persistently and vigorously the earlier evidence of a league between Judges of the Supreme Court and the spoilers of the city. In the great Erie warfare of 1868 the TIMES bore a prominent part. The shameful series of injunctions and receiverships by which corrupt judges enabled Fisk, Gould and Lane to take forcible possession of other people's property were followed by the outspoken condemnation of the TIMES. Its course at this juncture secured for it the bitter hostility of the confederate Tammany and Erie Rings. The indictment of its conductors was openly recommended to the Grand Jury by one of the Ring Judges, and it risked both property and personal safety in its warfare on the side of honesty and judicial purity. The stupendous naturalization frauds which paved the way for a period of corruption and wholesale plunder in the State and city were exposed and denounced in the TIMES. The political despotism which obtained possession of all the avenues of justice, of legislation and of administration, and to which even the best class of New York citizens had begun to submit with a feeling of hopeless despair, found its only formidable adversary in the TIMES. During 1870 and 1871, the TIMES waged, almost single-handed, a struggle which is probably without any example in journalism. The odds against it seemed overwhelming, and the vast majority of onlookers undoubtedly believed that the paper would come out of the unequal contest with its property sacrificed and its business ruined. The brilliant success which attended that onslaught upon the most colossal system of swindling known to modern times, tended to breed forgetfulness of the discouraging prospects which attended the early stages of the struggle, and the very substantial risks which had to be faced during the period when success appeared doubtful. The TIMES was never more true to the principles on which it was founded than when it deliberately staked its very existence upon the certainty that even in the dark days of Ring domination, against all obstacles, the cause of right and justice must ultimately triumph.

In the great movement for a higher standard of official fidelity and political purity which gained so decided an impetus from the overthrow of the Tammany Ring, the TIMES has taken a leading and effective part. It occupies to-day the position of perhaps the most powerful Republican journal in the country, devoted to all that is noblest and most progressive in the policy of its party, while ready to meet with the severest condemnation all abuse of the party name for base ends or ignoble personal ambition. In American journalism there is no more consistent and honorable record than that of the New York TIMES.

THE TIMES BUILDING.

The first number of the TIMES was issued from No. 113 Nassau street. Although, compared with subsequent accommodations, these premises were humble, they were in favorable contrast with other newspaper offices of that day, and were in themselves sufficient to prove that pluck, enterprise and capital were at the back of the new venture. On the 1st of May, 1854, it removed to ample quarters at the corner of Nassau and Beekman streets. But its sojourn here was to be of brief duration, for the business sagacity of the owners speedily saw and took advantage of an opportunity to place the paper in one of the best locations held by any newspaper in the United States. Early in the year 1857, the property of the "Old Brick Church," consisting of the triangular plot of ground bounded by Spruce, Nassau and Beekman streets and Park Row, was put upon the market, and the TIMES was fortunate enough to secure the northern half of it. The plot it obtained was somewhat irregular in shape, being 65 feet front on what has now come to be known as Printing House Square by 105 feet on Nassau street and 100 feet on Park Row. For this site $185,000 was paid, and on it ground was broken on the 1st of May, 1857, for the building which is still, and will be for indefinite years to come, occupied by the paper. This building, at the time it was constructed, was far superior to any then in existence, and with all the suggestions and improvements of the last twenty years which have been embodied in recent architecture, is not now surpassed by any in the world. It is constructed of Nova Scotia stone, is five stories high and has three fronts, as it extends over the area which has just been named. It is thoroughly fire-proof throughout, which was a feat never achieved or hardly attempted at the time it was constructed. It occupies an area of 13,750 square feet and contains 38 large rooms, many of which are sub-divided by partitions for business purposes and for the uses of the newspaper. This latter occupies in the publishing, editorial and composing departments altogether 23 rooms, some of which, however, are sub-divisions, and in addition there is the press room underneath the building, which by excavation under the sidewalks has been given an area of 206 feet by 104. The entire building is fully supplied with gas, water, speaking tubes and all other appliances for the convenience of tenants, or for that of the business for which it was specially intended. As a great newspaper can only be done justice by giving particulars, it is now intended to go through this building in detail, and give a view not only of each department, but of the manner in which it is conducted.

THE PUBLICATION DEPARTMENT.

The rooms of this department occupy 65 feet front on Printing House Square by about the same space in depth on both Nassau street and Park Row, thus giving them, in common with all the remainder of the building used for the newspaper, three fronts. First of all is the counting room, with entrances from three streets. Oblong in shape, it gives ample space for the vast business which must every day be transacted. The counter of black walnut extends across the entire length of the room, and is surmounted at short intervals with high plate glass screens, to insure the privacy of the clerks. It is here that the general business with advertisers and subscribers is transacted, and there is no hour in the twenty-four when it does not present a busy scène, but hardly at any time does it present an appearance so animated as during those hours when the army of newspaper readers are in bed and asleep.

In the rear of the counting room is another apartment of equal size, and connected with it by three arched passages, which is divided by partitions into five compartments. First on the Park Row side is the office of the cashier, and next to him is the private room of the publisher and chief proprietor, Mr. George Jones, and next beyond is the office of Mr. Gilbert Jones. The other small rooms are used for miscellaneous purposes; one of them being devoted to the mailing bureau, which is in itself no small portion of this department, for it is here that the huge mails of the paper are so arranged and systematized that the largest possible amount of work is done downstairs in the shortest possible space of time. The labors of this bureau, and indeed of the whole force of the paper, have been greatly increased since the introduction of the fast mail. This mail leaving the post office in New York at 4 A. M., it is easy to see that a morning newspaper having any pretensions to enterprise has hard work to make time, but the TIMES has done it with more success than any of its contemporaries.

THE EDITORIAL DEPARTMENT.

Leaving the Publishing Department and going up three flights of stairs we reach the editorial rooms of the paper. Here are thirteen rooms, all but two of which are devoted to the use of the editorial staff proper, and those two to the city department. One of these two latter is used exclusively by the City Editor and his assistants, and the other and larger rooms by the reporters, who number altogether about thirty. It is their business to scour the city far and near for whatever items of interest may appear from day to day, and the fullness and excellence of the TIMES' local news for many years past bear witness to the intelligence and faithfulness with which these gentlemen have discharged and still are discharging their duties. On the same floor are the rooms of the editorial writers: the Exchange Editor, the Telegraphic News Editors, the Night Editor, the Dramatic Editor, the Commercial and Financial Editor, the Literary Editor, the Index Editor. The habits of business in this department are methodical, but varied according to the necessities of the numerous departments of the work of a great daily newspaper.

It is the business of a newspaper like the TIMES to furnish its readers every morning with every item of interest which has transpired anywhere in the world during the previous day and night. To accomplish this end it not only needs and has a complete corps of capable editors and intelligent reporters, but a large retinue of foreign correspondents who have the tact and experience necessary to observe and correctly report all events of public interest in the localities in which they are stationed. Sometimes the news comes by mail, but if need be the telegraph is freely used. In addition to all these the TIMES' corps of domestic correspondents is among the largest and most efficient in the country. It has regular correspondents in Boston, Philadelphia, Chicago, Baltimore, Washington, Albany, Richmond, Wilmington, Hartford, Raleigh, Atlanta, New Orleans, Jackson, Memphis, Nashville, Knoxville, Louisville, Trenton, Harrisburg, Pittsburg, Columbus, Cincinnati, Detroit, Cleveland, St. Louis, Omaha, Denver, Salt Lake City and San Francisco, and many cities of lesser note. But this is not all, for no sooner does anything of any great public interest happen, than the TIMES immediately dispatches a special correspondent from the office in New York to the scene. Added to all these, the TIMES has an experienced corps of political correspondents, who, during times of political excitement, traverse the Union and furnish information in regard to passing events.

THE COMPOSING ROOM.

All the matter prepared by the staff of editors, correspondents and reporters, after undergoing requisite revision, is sent to the composing room, on the floor above, where it is put in type. Here it is only necessary to briefly mention facts in order to show the great resources and business of the establishment. There are 92 employés, which includes the night foreman, 7 assistants, a day assistant foreman, 83 compositors, and in addition there is the general foreman, making 93. To all these must be added 8 proof-readers, making a total of 101 employés on this floor. There are 68 cases at which printers work setting type, and that they are all necessary is shown by the fact that nearly 400,000 ems are set every day, and sometimes—when supplements are issued—a great deal more. The only deduction to be made from this large aggregate is that of the advertisements which stand over from day to day, and the number is comparatively small. The most of this work is done after 6 P. M. So admirably is the composing room organized that there is rarely any delay, never any disturbance, in the performance of the work. The books show that the average time at which the last "form" goes to the stereotype room is 2.37 A. M., and from this statement any one can see that there can be no idleness during these eight hours in the large, airy and well lighted apartment which constitutes the TIMES composing room.

THE STEREOTYPING ROOM.

After matter has been "set up," or put in type, the next process is to take impressions of these types on paper, and as a final result produce from stereotype plates the printed sheet with which the public is familiar. The first step is to cast stereotype plates of the several forms, for the TIMES does not and has not for many years printed from the types themselves. When a form is made up it is sent down in a box moved by steam power from the top floor to the basement, some 25 feet below the surface of the street, to the stereotyping room, where some layers of damp paper are laid upon it, and it is then driven twice through a machine having powerful rollers, which squeeze the paper down on the face of the type. Taken out of that, it is next placed—with its damp paper still on it—below a heavy screw-press, the sole or lower plate of which is a steam heated metal chamber. This hot chamber dries the paper rapidly, and at the same time the pressure put upon it prevents any cockling or inequality. In a short space of time the frame or page of type is drawn out from below this press and the dried paper peeled off its surface, when it forms a perfect matrix, or counterpart of the type, sufficiently deep to enable a casting to be taken from it which shall yield a page of clear-cut lettering ready for printing from. Before the casting is taken, however, this paper matrix is made absolutely dry by being placed on another hot plate. That only occupies a very brief space of time, and when it is satisfactorily finished the paper is trimmed carefully, and then placed face upward inside a semicircular mold, when its edges are fastened down by bands of iron of the thickness that the cast is meant to be. On these bands a counterpart of the mold is then let down from a small crane, and fastened so that a semicircular chamber is formed the size of the page of the newspaper, and about three-eighths of an inch deep all round. Into this a pot of molten stereotyping metal is poured by two men, the mold having first been turned on end so as to compel the metal to fill the cavity completely, and, after resting for a moment or two till the metal has set, the inner part of the mold is removed by the crane, the paper matrix is peeled off, scarcely browned, and capable of being used again and again, and the solid cast is swung round and deposited, still adhering to the mold, in another cavity exactly the shape of that from which it was taken. Here its edges are trimmed, and the lump of metal which formed the excess at the top of the casting sawed off by a small revolving saw driven by steam. That done, the cast may be said to be complete, having merely to be dressed a little along the edges of the outer columns of letters, and along the top and between the headings of articles, and to be pared on the back to make it lie perfectly true on the cylinder in the machine, all of which is accomplished in a very few moments. The page of lettering presents the appearance of a strong, solid half-cylinder of white metal, ribbed on the inside so as to facilitate the paring off of possible inequalities, and covered on its outer face with crisp, clean, shining letters, ready at once for the press. Only four men are employed in this room, and they do their work with marvelous rapidity. Only seventeen minutes are required in any case for making a matrix, and it has been done in twelve minutes.

THE PRESS ROOM.

But the chief marvel of the mechanical department of the New York TIMES is in its press room, which is the most perfect in the world, containing as it does not only all the latest improvements in machinery found elsewhere, but many which are peculiar to itself. Among these is the "wetting machine," for wetting the white paper. The TIMES is printed on rolls of continuous paper without joint or break, each of which is about five miles in length and 36 inches in width, and weighs about 900 pounds net. Five of these rolls can pass through the machine and be "wet down" in an hour, being unrolled from one side and rolled up on the other with the utmost exactness. The paper being ready for the press, the presses themselves are next in order. The TIMES is printed on three Walter presses, which are capable, without being pushed, of producing 13,500 impressions each per hour, or 40,500 per hour altogether. The stereotype plates having been placed on the presses, a roll of paper containing 6,000 copies of the TIMES is put in its place at the end of each press in a moment by one man, by means of a movable section of the floor raised by a hydraulic jack. The end of the roll is put in place and the press put in motion. The paper goes upward to where the stereotype plates forming the four pages of one side of a sheet of the paper are fastened on a cylinder just large enough to take a sheet to go round it. Against that cylinder there is another, identical in size, possessing a soft surface, which presses lightly against the edge of the type, and between these the sheet passes, taking up an impression as it goes. It is then carried downward round another large cylinder covered with cloth, the "set off" on which is taken off by another cylinder in contact with it, and that again by a rubber, in a fashion that is both simple and effective. The web of paper, still running on, passes between the second type-covered roller and its counterpart, taking the impression on its other side of the remaining four pages; and that done, it runs out between two more rollers of the same circumference. The machinery is so adjusted that the knife catches the paper exactly between each sheet, and, the paper being held hard on each side, cuts it in two, all but a couple of tags near each end, which are left for the purpose of pulling the sheet on between two sets of running tapes, until it is caught by a pair of small rollers, which are driven at a greater speed than the rest of the machine. These immediately tear the sheets apart where they have been all but cut, and the tapes hurry on what is now a completely printed newspaper up an inclined plane, at the top of which they carry it down an oscillating frame which moves pendulumwise so exactly that it delivers a paper precisely at each end of its short swing on to the face of another set of running tapes, which carry it downward on their outer face by the mere force of contact as they run. Between these tapes a frame like a huge comb swings backward and forward, catching up one delivered paper at every motion and flinging it down on a board. The current of air raised by the motion of this frame suffices to hold each succeeding sheet against the tapes along which it moves. Thus, two boys and the man who attends the machine are all the manual labor required, and the manner of delivering the papers alternately on to two inclined boards ready to receive them.

Formerly these presses required several boys each to attend them, but such improvements have been made in them by Mr. Gilbert Jones since they have been in the use of the TIMES that they have become as nearly automatic as any machines possibly can be. One man can put the roll in place, and the same man can take the printed sheets from the other side. Some boys and men are needed to carry away the printed sheets to the mailing and delivery rooms, but so little is human help required by these presses that only nineteen persons in all are employed in the press room, while formerly more than double that number were necessary. The machinery by

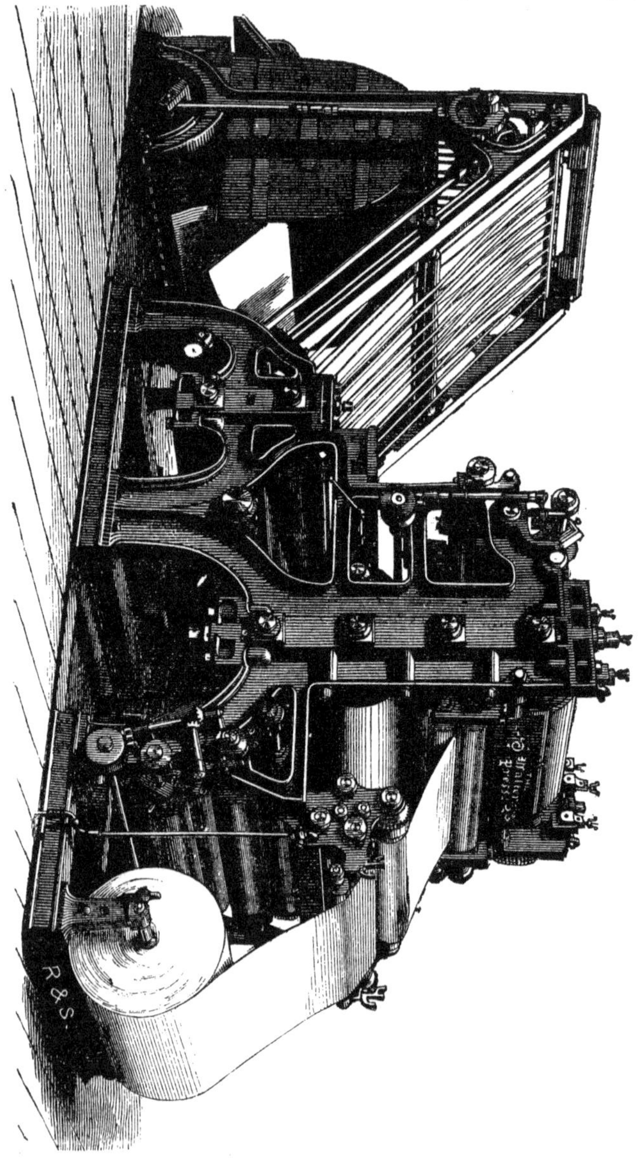

which all this is done is put in motion by two engines of 40 horse power each; but only one of them is generally used at a time, as it is the system of the TIMES to have duplicates of everything in the mechanical department, so that if any one piece should break down the other is on the spot ready for immediate use. It has another precaution against any interruption, for it has a complete machine shop in its press room, and skilled mechanics constantly in attendance to make any repairs which may be wanted. But with all this machinery in a space 106 feet by 104 feet, the TIMES press room does not appear crowded, so compact and well placed is everything. Great as are the powers of the Walter presses, they only occupy a few feet of space each, and the wetting machine could be placed on the top of a dining table of ordinary size. Nor is there the griminess usually found in such places, for the TIMES has made use of every possible appliance to avoid it. The feeding of presses with ink under the old method caused a vast deal both of foulness and waste, but under the TIMES' system, by which the ink is pumped from a reservoir into each press as it is needed, not a drop is spilled. All these facts are mentioned only to show that in its mechanical department, as in all others, the paper is second to none. It is universally admitted to be the most handsome in appearance of any paper printed, and it could not have reached nor have maintained this distinction without the most perfect mechanism.

In addition to the daily issue of the TIMES, there is the semi-weekly edition, issued on Tuesdays and Fridays, and the weekly edition on Wednesday of each week, all of which have large circulations. Complete in its mechanical appliances, strong in its resources, solid in its basis, independent and honest in its editorial management, sincere and decisive in its political convictions, but not devoted to the interests of any person or clique, presenting every morning all the news of the world for the previous day in the most perfect shape, the TIMES is the embodiment of the highest standards yet attained by American journalism.

"THE EVENING POST," NEW YORK.

ITS SEVENTY-FIFTH BIRTHDAY.

A SKETCH FOR THE BOOK OF THE CENTENNIAL NEWSPAPER EXHIBITION.

The New York EVENING POST is one of the oldest of the *great* American newspapers, and is the best evening Journal published in New York. It was established in 1801, and for more than fifty years has been under the wise editorial management of William Cullen Bryant, the honored poet and author. Under his guidance the EVENING POST has gained a reputation and an amount of influence equaled by very few American journals. Believing thoroughly in the principles of Republican government, it addresses and represents peculiarly the cultured class of our citizens, and its tone is very high. Even its advertising columns are jealously guarded against questionable or objectionable advertisements. This fastidiousness has made it a great family newspaper, and it is generally acknowledged to be the door by which access is to be gained to New York homes.

An introduction by the EVENING POST ensures an hospitable reception to any topic, charity or business. As a contemporary published in a neighboring city says: "The EVENING POST is most decidedly the one daily paper in New York that can fully claim, like the *Pall Mall Gazette*, to be conducted by gentlemen and for gentlemen."

Its Semi-Weekly and Weekly editions bear the same general character, both in the quality of their matter and their audience, although, of course, special attention is given to the Agricultural and other departments which are of peculiar interest to the country readers.

The fact that there are a larger number of really great newspapers published in the morning than in the evening gives the EVENING POST even more prominence than it could otherwise have attained.

Having gained its position, however, the publishers have wisely spared no expense to keep and advance it. The special dispatches, it is safe to assert, are more complete and are made a much greater feature in this than in any other afternoon journal published in New York, and as the most important events happen, as a rule, in the day time, and as the difference in time gives an evening journal the daily news of Europe, a reader of the EVENING POST, for instance, has spread before him in a concise form the daily events of the whole world.

He reads this record of the day at his home when he has both the time and the inclination for its careful perusal and consideration. Thus, an evening journal has the best possible opportunity for real influence.

The same thing is true, further, in respect to all announcements made in an evening newspaper; for, being read at home and left at home, it is naturally the medium consulted by the family in regard to most of the domestic needs and the family plans. The EVENING POST is very decided in its opinions, and as it has said of itself, it "is often called upon by a sense of duty to oppose itself to the general feeling of those from whom a commercial paper always must receive its support; it never hesitates to do so. It sometimes finds a powerful member of that community occupied with projects which it deems mischievous; it puts itself in his way and frustrates his designs if possible. In this way it makes bitter enemies, who would break it down if they could; it makes also warm friends by whom it is cordially supported. Its proprietors are satisfied with its success and its expectations." It may interest foreigners to know that the EVENING POST is the American Champion of Free Trade and the rights of Foreign Authors.

Its stately building (a picture of which is reproduced on the opposite page) is thoroughly appointed for the Newspaper business, and is on the corner of the two great commercial thoroughfares of New York, Broadway and Fulton street.

On Broadway the building has a front of sixty-two feet and ten inches, and extends one hundred and three feet, six inches on Fulton street. Its height above the side-

"THE EVENING POST" BUILDING.

walk is one hundred and twenty-five feet, though the cupola is fifteen feet higher. It is divided into nine stories, but the monotony of row upon row of windows is broken by a series of pilasters, arches, and ornamental pillars on both Broadway and Fulton street. The entire outside walls are of the best quality Philadelphia pressed front bricks and the trimmings of Dorchester stone.

THE NEW YORK EVENING EXPRESS.

A SKETCH FOR THE BOOK OF THE CENTENNIAL NEWSPAPER EXHIBITION.

THE NEW YORK EXPRESS was established as a daily morning journal in 1836, when the city commenced at the battery and ended at Niblo's Garden, on the corner of Prince street and Broadway. The up-town omnibuses then went no further, and Union Square was in the fields, and the head-quarters of the Manhattan Works, which supplied the city through wooden pipes with water, was in Chambers street. Of the morning papers then in existence only two survive, and of the evening only two, except the EXPRESS. All other daily journals have since disappeared, to the number of over one hundred.

The EXPRESS was started by the late JAMES BROOKS, with ROBERT E. HUDSON as Commercial Editor, and ERASTUS BROOKS as part owner and its Washington Editor, a post which he occupied during the sessions of Congress for nearly twenty consecutive years. Mr. James Brooks had occupied the same field years before, as editor of the *Portland Advertiser*, writing letters from thence, and both earlier and later from the South and Europe. He was among the earliest of the Washington correspondents, though not before Messrs. Coleman, Kingman and Mathew L. Davis, and perhaps some others. Mr. Brooks, senior, entered upon his editorial career in this city in June, 1836. Some years later the old *New York Advertiser* (Theo. Dwight and Wm. B. Townsend, proprietors), was merged in the NEW YORK EXPRESS, and the two papers were for over fifty years the corporation journal of the city, with pay at not over $250 a year for the honor of doing the work.

The EXPRESS was the first daily double sheet printed in the city, and as an experiment it failed to attract public interest, for the reason that the advertisements could not be found, and the MORNING EXPRESS, then nearly as large as the London Times, was pronounced too cumbersome. In most parts of the country the old folio form of the present EXPRESS is still the favorite with the public. In March, 1876, the NEW YORK EXPRESS was formed into a joint stock company, Erastus Brooks and James Wilton Brooks, only son of James Brooks, consenting to part with one-fifth of their interest, and to expend the new capital in the improvement of their paper. Since then its editorial and reportorial corps have been greatly increased, with large additions to its expenses and a corresponding increase in its business income.

Since 1836, the EXPRESS has occupied the old Tontine Buildings, at the corner of Wall and Water streets, the offices at the present, 112 and 114 Broadway, the corner of Wall and Nassau streets, opposite the Custom House, the narrow front and wider rear on Tryon Row, where the EVENING EXPRESS was started, 13 and 15 Park Row, where it was burned out in December, 1872, and for three years in its present premises, No. 23 Park Row, bought and built by J. & E. Brooks, and entirely adapted to its present large business, with its press-room far down in terra firma, and its editorial and composing rooms among the best ventilated and lightest rooms in the city. The premises extend from Park Row, opposite the Post Office, to Theatre Alley, with ample light and room to assure the health and comfort of all occupants in its seven stories.

THE SITE OF THE EXPRESS BUILDING.

Perhaps there is no plot of ground in the city that has a more memorable history than that on which the EXPRESS Building stands. Its early associations, like the principles disseminated from the structure, embraced the whole country. One hundred years ago it intersected the old "Commons" that stretched from St. Paul's to a cemetery that skirted the northwest line of Chambers Street. Beyond this point were the Collect or Great Pond, on which the Tombs was built; the "Tea Water Pump," in Chatham Street; "Gallows Hill," whose scaffold drank the blood of a member of Washington's Body Guard, who had sold his plans to the enemy, and the barracks and jails that stretched from the eastern section of the City Hall Park to Tryon Row and Centre Street. Farm houses, miles apart; wheat fields and orchards, relieved by small villages, such as Richmond Hill, in the neighborhood of Varick and Charlton Streets, and Greenwich (now Christopher Street) completed the scene. The "Commons," as all the ancient records inform us, was the scene of many an encounter between the "Liberty Boys" and the British loyalists, in 1775. The former fought for the principles of constitutional liberty, and for a government of and by the people; and the EXPRESS, on the self-same ground, is fighting the self-same battles over again, though happily with no effusion of blood.

Other associations connected with the site of the new EXPRESS Building also make it an object of public interest. Here was the old Park Theatre, with the row of ancient and uneven buildings which formed the block forty years ago, and it must necessarily share in all the histrionic glories of that ancient Thespian temple. Forrest, Placide, Charles Kean, Ellen Tree, Barrett (Gentleman George), Mme. Vestris, Charlotte Cushman, Vache, Fisher, Macready, Cooke, Blake, Peter Richings, and a host of other stars performed within its walls, "drawing crowded houses nightly." Opera, comedy, tragedy, burlesque, extravaganza, farce—succeeded each other. In those days, as now, play-going gallants espoused the cause of each attractive actress whom unsympathetic critics would place among less favored sisters in a stock company. On one occasion this theatre was the scene of a terrible row between the defenders and assailants of Mrs. John Wood, who was then playing a brief engagement within its walls. The gallant James Watson Webb attacked the lady's personations of several characters in his paper, the old *Courier and Enquirer*, and when she appeared on the stage the same evening, she was received by a storm of alternate applause and hisses, which was succeeded by a general melee, in which the house was practically converted into a prize-ring. The police finally separated the combatants.

On either side of the Park Theatre stood two memorable saloons. The first was kept by Jas. Sweeny, the father of Peter B. Sweeny, now in Paris, and James M. Sweeny, his brother, who recently died there. Both Peter B. and James M. were born in that house. The second saloon was owned by one Conroy, a brother-in-law of a "host" well known and respected in those days, named Malachi Fallon, who subsequently founded a cosy restaurant and social meeting-house in Elm street, which was known by the familiar name of "The Ivy Green."

We might multiply these by-gone scenes and incidents which give the site of the EXPRESS and those immediately connected with it a bright and varied page in our local history. In the cause of American liberty the place where the United States played an active part against the Georges of England, and for George Washington, of the American Colonies, the same good work is ours now, and with as brilliant prospects of success before the country, we trust, as when the old liberty boys met to defend the right at the mouth of the cannon. The weapon now used is the pen, which ought to be mightier than the sword, but which now is too often, we fear, used to pull down rather than build up the Republic.

THE BROOKLYN "EAGLE."

A SKETCH FOR THE BOOK OF THE CENTENNIAL NEWSPAPER EXHIBITION.

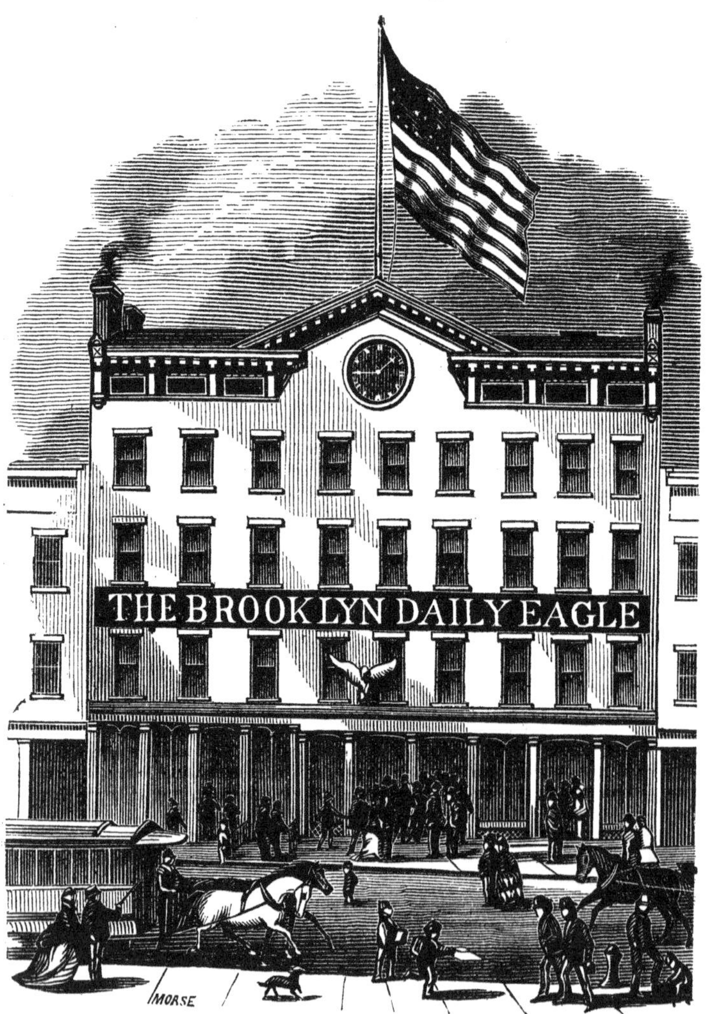

THE "EAGLE" BUILDINGS.

THE ESTABLISHMENT OF THE BROOKLYN EAGLE.

The BROOKLYN EAGLE is in an especial sense the journalistic representative of the city in which it is published, and it is published in the third city in the Union, in point of population, and the second in extent of area. The growth of Brooklyn has been marvelous among even American cities. The BROOKLYN DAILY EAGLE was founded in 1842 by Isaac Van Anden, who took an active interest in its business management up to the period of his death in 1875. Brooklyn, at the time the EAGLE was started, had been incorporated as a city but about seven years, and it then contained a population of only 30,000. Its population is now over 500,000. The EAGLE has steadily grown with the city, until it is now the most widely circulated evening journal published in this country. Its early contemporaries and rivals have all passed away, and, while there are three other daily papers published in Brooklyn at the present time, the newspaper business of the city may be said to be concentrated in the office of the EAGLE. Designed mainly to meet the wants of a concentrated population of half a million, it is exceptional among newspapers in the compactness and universality of its circulation within the sphere of its direct influence, so that it has long ago come to be accepted as a truism in Brooklyn that, "Everybody who can read at all, reads the EAGLE." As a medium of advertising, in order to reach the people of Brooklyn, it has no rival. The extent of its advertising patronage is exceeded by only one morning newspaper in New York, and by no evening paper in the world. Its circulation is believed to be larger than that of all the evening journals, of its class, published in New York, and is exceeded but by two or three of the Metropolitan morning newspapers, which, while they may have sharper competition, have a more extensive constituency. The circulation of the EAGLE has more than kept pace with the growth of Brooklyn. It is also sold at the principal centres of resort in New York; has a considerable and growing mail circulation, and is recognized throughout the country as one of its most influential and prosperous journals. In proportion to its circulation, the EAGLE is believed to be the cheapest advertising medium in either city. The income of the paper has grown to be very large, but in presenting not only the news of the world, but the most minute reflex of the daily life of Brooklyn, its expenditure has come to be so vast that rivalry with it has been found to be impossible.

HOW THE EAGLE BUILDINGS ARE OCCUPIED.

The EAGLE is issued from the extensive printing establishment known as Nos. 34, 36 and 38 Fulton street. These buildings extend to the adjoining street, and have been fitted up with the especial view of accommodating its business, and that of the very extensive Book and Job Printing office embraced in the establishment. These buildings are four stories in height, and are occupied as follows:

On the basement floor are the newspaper folding rooms, and the rooms for the clerks engaged in selling tickets, which are in turn passed to the folders, who count off the EAGLE with a rapidity perfectly incomprehensible to those who have not seen the quickness of the eye tested as an enumerator. At certain hours of the day the front room is given over to bustle and excitement—and to the newsdealers and "newsboys" who impatiently await their turn to get their papers—each one eager to be first on the street with a newspaper which everybody in Brooklyn reads.

On the first floor are the counting rooms, telegraph office, newspaper-file room, and private rooms of the business heads of the concern. In the counting rooms there is a "Gold and Stock Indicator," which records during business hours of the day all the operations of Wall street, ship arrivals and departures, and the principal news items of the day. The counting room is one of the most frequented centres of Brooklyn, and is usually crowded with people having business with the office. Nearly level with the first floor is a building especially constructed for the accommodation of the two eight-cylinder Hoe Lightning Presses, which can be seen from the counting rooms, from morning until late into the afternoon, and often into the night, throwing off the various editions of the EAGLE, at the rate of thirty-six thousand per hour. The EAGLE is now stereotyped, and hence its "forms" can be printed at the same time on both presses. The EAGLE is the only evening newspaper in the country printed on the Hoe Lightning Presses, which is under the necessity of duplicating its forms by stereotyping. The rear building, fronting on Doughty street, is occupied by the numerous presses required by the Job Office Department.

The second floor is devoted exclusively to the business of the Book and Job offices. Several weekly newspapers are printed here, and every description of work is turned out in large quantities.

The third floor—Very nearly one-half of this floor is devoted to the use of the editorial and reportorial staff employed upon the paper. Seven rooms, running along the Fulton street side of the building, are occupied by the editors, while two spacious apartments are devoted to the use of the very large staff of reporters employed on the paper. Adjoining are rooms reserved for the proof readers, etc. The rear half of this floor is occupied by the compositors, who "set up" the paper. This room is believed to be one of the best arranged and best ventilated composing rooms in the country. It is lighted from the roof and from the windows which look out from three sides of it.

On the fourth floor are the rooms occupied by the stereotypers. It also contains the bookbindery, the ruling, the folding, and the drying rooms, and other apartments needed in the conduct of the job office.

POLITICAL VIEWS.

The BROOKLYN EAGLE has long ago repudiated such distinction as is to be secured by mere party organship. In its reportorial columns equal favor is shown to all, the main object of the paper being to daguerreotype life in Brooklyn, with perfect impartiality and accuracy. The EAGLE has consistently advocated and upheld those principles of government with which the name of Thomas Jefferson will be associated as long as our Federal system of Republican government continues to exist. Entirely independent of party, it is enabled to maintain a tone of courtesy, candor and independence in its editorial columns, which commends it alike to the honest masses of both parties.

BUSINESS MANAGEMENT.

The BROOKLYN EAGLE, has been published for several years past by an incorporated association. Its stock, however, is concentrated in very few hands. Outside of the family of its founder, Mr. Van Anden, there are but three stockholders—one of them the gentleman who has filled for many years the position of editor-in-chief of the paper. William C. Kingsley and Abner C. Keeney, very well known citizens of Brooklyn, are the only other stockholders. The business interest of the EAGLE is represented by Mr. William Hester, nephew of its founder, Mr. Van Anden.

THE EDITOR-IN-CHIEF.

In the formation of political and public sentiment, the EAGLE takes a leading place in the ranks of American newspapers. Its editorial conduct is under the full control of Mr. Thomas Kinsella, who has grown up with the paper, having served it in nearly every capacity—compositor, contributor, reporter, assistant editor, and editor-in-chief. Mr. Kinsella takes an active part in the public affairs of his city and State. He has held various offices of trust under the local government of Brooklyn. In 1864 he was a member of the Democratic National convention; in 1866 he was a delegate to the Union Convention, held in Philadelphia, to sustain President Johnson's administration; in 1872, as a zealous advocate of the election of the then head of his profession—Horace Greeley—to the Presidency of the United States, he presided over the Rochester Democratic State convention, and was one of the delegates to the National Democratic convention, which was held at Baltimore, and through whose action Greeley secured the support of the Democratic party. Mr. Kinsella was a member of the House of Representatives during the Forty-second Congress.

SECRETS OF SUCCESS.

The marvelous success of the BROOKLYN EAGLE is due in part to the fact that it has identified itself in all things with Brooklyn and her people, but mainly to this: It is run as a newspaper, and finds its own interest in upholding that of the great public, whose favor alone insures journalistic success.

THE "SCIENTIFIC AMERICAN."

THEN AND NOW.

A SKETCH FOR THE BOOK OF THE CENTENNIAL NEWSPAPER EXHIBITION.

It was in the year 1845 that the first number of that popular illustrated newspaper, THE SCIENTIFIC AMERICAN, was issued to the public. its circulation for the first few months averaging barely 300 copies per week; and it was then the

only scientific and mechanical journal in the United States. Now, in the centennial year, 1876, 50,000 copies hardly suffice the weekly demand, this number being largely in excess of the combined circulation of all the other papers of its class published on this continent.

In the 31 years thus passed, the history of this well known weekly paper is contemporaneous with and largely illustrates the astonishing progress of this country in the mechanical arts and in industrial science; and it is with feelings of satisfaction that the proprietors refer to the public sentiment which universally prevails: that THE SCIENTIFIC AMERICAN has done more to foster improvements and promote the progress of invention and the mechanical arts in this country during the last quarter of a century than all other publications; and although the publishers continue to regard the promulgation of practical information, on the industrial arts and mechanical progress generally, as the legitimate aim of the paper, they are glad to know that their paper is a welcome guest in the home and at the fireside, as well as in the library, workshop, and laboratory. To fulfil all these requirements, a journal must record all the discoveries in the arts at home and abroad, report all important patents as fast as they are issued, and leave nothing that pertains to the prosperity of the manufacturer or the comfort of the home unnoticed. With pride the publishers refer the reading public to the past volumes of their journal, to be found in the most important libraries at home and abroad, where they are constantly referred to for data in all matters pertaining to discoveries and inventions.

The large subscription list and sale of the SCIENTIFIC AMERICAN enables its proprietors to give out weekly the handsomest and most useful illustrated periodical extant. It is one of the most popular weekly journals in the world, and the cheapest periodical devoted to science, art, mechanics, and all their branches now published in either hemisphere. For engravings of mechanical subjects, the SCIENTIFIC AMERICAN has always stood at the head of all publications of its kind in the world, and the same artist who won a name for himself for the good quality of his engravings on this paper a quarter of a century ago, still executes the superb cuts which now grace its pages; and for the superiority of such work, none has ever excelled him. The cost for a good engraving and its publication in the editorial column is but trifling compared with the benefit derived, if one wishes to negotiate sales of territorial rights, or the manufactured article. The advantage of placing a picture and description of a new invention before the eyes of fifty thousand persons, most of which are of the class interested in new discoveries and new devices, cannot fail of attracting the attention of all of this vast number, and of being of special interest to some. The receipt of a model, photograph, good drawing, or a copy of the Letters Patent, is sufficient to estimate the cost for engraving, and we would recommend parties to this course in advance of giving the order for the execution of the work.

There is not a country or a large city on the face of the globe where the paper does not circulate. We have the best authority for stating that some of the largest orders for machinery and patented articles from abroad have come to our manufacturers through the medium of the SCIENTIFIC AMERICAN, the parties ordering having seen the article illustrated or advertised in these columns Small models, as well as photographs and drawings, may be sent by mail.

Messrs. Munn & Co., finding that their endeavors were so widely appreciated by the public, commenced on January 1, 1876, the publication of an additional paper, entitled the SCIENTIFIC AMERICAN SUPPLEMENT. The success of the new enterprise was ensured as soon as the first number was issued; and within three months of its first appearance, it attained a circulation of 15,000 copies weekly, making it, with the single exception of the SCIENTIFIC AMERICAN, the most widely spread and valuable advertising medium in the country. It is, like the SCIENTIFIC AMERICAN, illustrated with a constant succession of excellent engravings of new engineering enterprises and mechanical subjects.

In 1846 Messrs. Munn & Co. established, in connection with the publication of the SCIENTIFIC AMERICAN, the business of soliciting patents, and soon afterwards established branch offices at Washington, London, Paris, Brussels, and Vienna. In the past thirty years this concern has grown till it has become the largest patent-soliciting establishment in the world, having been honored with the confidence of more than 60,000 clients, and prosecuted to a successful issue no less than 40,000 applications for letters patent in this and other countries. This vast number is not much less than one fourth of the whole patent business of the United States, and has been acquired by lengthened experience and unrivaled facilities for transacting all business connected with patents and the Patent Office. The principal or home office in which this large amount of business is conducted is represented in the engraving at the commencement of this article; and the large number of experts constantly employed have been selected mostly from the ranks of the Patent Office at Washington, and they comprise men of unusual ability for the execution of the duties of their peculiar profession. Inventors who visit this great establishment, or communicate their inventions by writing, will find that the best professional advice and instructions are freely given, and that all such communications are kept strictly confidential. Daily access to the records of the Patent Office, through the branch office of the SCIENTIFIC AMERICAN in Washington, renders it possible for Munn & Co. to conduct their immense business of soliciting patents in the United States and all foreign countries in the quickest, cheapest, and most satisfactory manner. The principal office of the SCIENTIFIC AMERICAN and the patent department is located at 37 Park Row, New York City.

THE NEW YORK LEDGER.

A SKETCH FOR THE BOOK OF THE CENTENNIAL NEWSPAPER EXHIBITION.

It was in the latter part of the year 1854 that ROBERT BONNER set himself the task of making the NEW YORK LEDGER the best and the best-known family paper in America. Mr. BONNER was then thirty years old, and had already had several years' experience as a publisher and an editor. He did not enter upon his new undertaking without much and well-considered deliberation. He possessed unusual advantages for the enterprise. He was not only an experienced publisher and editor, but he was also a practical printer, and a thorough master of his business in every department and phase of it.

LEDGER BUILDING.

During the year 1855 Mr. BONNER got his plans well in hand, and though limited in means, he accomplished most gratifying results. The sale of the LEDGER ran rapidly up to a high figure, and the profits soon became large. But

Mr. BONNER was not content with a measure of success that might have satisfied an ordinary ambition. He turned his profits into his business, and pushed the LEDGER with unexampled enterprise and liberality. He, and his paper, and his energy, and his novel modes of procedure became matters of general public discussion.

The circulation of the LEDGER continued to increase, and before the close of the year 1856 it far exceeded two hundred thousand copies a week. From that time it has constantly grown in prosperity, in reputation, and in power, until, in its commanding influence, in the extent and character of its circulation, and in the vastness of the fortune which it has yielded to its proprietor, the NEW YORK LEDGER has become the most successful literary and family paper of which we have any knowledge. Its circulation at times has reached over three hundred and fifty thousand copies.

In truth, the success of the LEDGER is looked upon as one of those marvels of the times which nobody expects to comprehend. The general impression is that the LEDGER has been pushed with almost superhuman energy, and conducted with almost superhuman sagacity; but of course the public at large cannot be expected to understand or even to remember just what this energy and sagacity have done, or how they have done it. It is doubtful even if the most assiduous readers of the LEDGER for the last twenty years could name a tenth of the illustrious statesmen, editors, educationists, divines, scholars, essayists and poets who have in that time written for it.

We must confess that until we recently examined the files of the LEDGER we ourselves had no idea what an astounding list of contributors it has had. We cannot give the names of all these contributors—it would be too much like publishing a dictionary of authors; but must content ourselves with mentioning some of the more eminent ones.

Prominent among the names of statesmen who have written for the LEDGER are those of Edward Everett, James Buchanan, President of the United States; Henry Wilson, Vice-President of the United States; George Bancroft, and General N. P. Banks. Also, United States Senators Anthony and Sprague of Rhode Island, Edmunds of Vermont, Ferry of Connecticut, Stockton of New Jersey, Sherman of Ohio, Morton of Indiana, and Cameron of Pennsylvania.

Many of the greatest journalists we have ever had in America have been contributors to the LEDGER; among others, James Gordon Bennett (senior), Horace Greeley, Henry J. Raymond, George Ripley, Charles A. Dana, and George D Prentice and William Cullen Bryant, also eminent as poets as well as distinguished as editors. In addition to these, in the list of poets, we find the names of N. P. Willis, George P. Morris, Mrs. Sigourney, Phebe Cary, Alice Cary, Emma Alice Brown, Ethel Lynn, Nathan D. Urner, John G. Saxe, Henry W. Longfellow and Alfred Tennyson.

On the list of prose contributors to the LEDGER we find the names of Charles Dickens, Fred. S. Cozzens, Paul Morphy, James Parton, Fanny Fern, Mrs. Horace Greeley, Mrs. Southworth, Mrs. Harriet Lewis, Miss Eliza A. Dupuy, Mary Kyle Dallas, Sylvanus Cobb, Jr., Leon Lewis, Prof. William Henry Peck, Judge Clark, Miss L. M. Alcott, Mrs. Elizabeth Blackwell, Lydia Maria Child, Mrs. Horace Mann, Mrs. N. P. Willis, Madame Le Vert, Mrs. General Banks, Mrs. President Barnard, Mrs. Howard Crosby, Mrs. Chancellor Ferris and Mrs. Jessie Benton Fremont.

The presidents of many of the leading colleges in America have also been contributors to the columns of the LEDGER. Among these eminent scholars were Rev. Thomas Hill, D.D., LL. D., President of Harvard College; Rev. Theodore D. Woolsey, D.D., President of Yale College; Rev. John Maclean, D.D., President of the College of New Jersey; Rev. D. R. Goodwin, D.D., President of the University of Pennsylvania; Rev. Asa D. Smith, D.D., President of Dartmouth College; Rev. W. A. Stearns, D.D., President of Amherst College; Rev. Mark Hopkins, D.D., LL. D., President of Williams College; Rev. Laurens P. Hickok, D.D., LL.D., President of Union College; Rev. E. O. Haven, D.D., LL. D., President of the University of Michigan; Rev. Joseph Cummings, D.D., LL. D., President of the Wesleyan University; Rev. S. G. Brown, D.D., President of Hamilton College, and Rev. M. B. Anderson, LL. D., President of the University of Rochester.

In addition to these eminent scholars and divines, we also find the following names on the list of writers for the LEDGER: Rev. Stephen H. Tyng, D.D., Rev. Francis Vinton, D.D., Rev. Edward Everett Hale, Rev. J. Hyatt Smith, Rev. Tryon Edwards, D.D., Rev. John McClintock, D.D., Rev. Thomas Armitage, D.D., Rev. Samuel Osgood, D.D., Rev. Thomas H. Skinner, D.D., Rev. Leonard Bacon, D.D., Rev. Howard Crosby, D.D., Bishop Simpson of the Methodist Episcopal Church, Rev. J. Williams, D.D., LL. D., Bishop of Connecticut, Rev. John Hall, D.D., of New York, and Rev. Thomas M. Clark, D.D., LL. D., Bishop of Rhode Island.

What other paper can show such a list of illustrious contributors? History, biography, statesmanship, theology, poetry, art, science, philosophy, literature, and whatever relates to the educational interests and the social and domestic well-being of the people, have their representatives and advocates here. If we properly grasp this great fact it will enable us to get some notion of the means by which the LEDGER has gained the commanding position which it now holds. It always has the largest number of great and distinguished contributors writing for it. It appeals to and gratifies every wholesome literary and educational taste. It is always a *live* paper, and perpetually keeps pace with the genius and spirit of American progress. It contains the purest, sweetest and most delightful stories, striking narratives and instructive biographical and historical sketches; also, a popular and carefully-prepared collection of scientific facts, forming a weekly register of the latest scientific discoveries.

All kinds of questions which interest the great family of man are also answered in the columns of the LEDGER; and a great amount of information on matters of law, business, marriage, love, housekeeping, the relations of friends, personal differences, etiquette, plans of life, &c., is thus communicated.

As the LEDGER is largely the oracle of the young people of the country, one of its great guiding principles is to inculcate the sentiments of self-respect and self-reliance in its readers, and thus to strengthen and render more manly the characters which are just assuming form, to endure through all their days. Thus, while the LEDGER is read with the warmest and most intense interest by hundreds of thousands of persons, it is doing much to inculcate sound principles wherever it goes, and to make better men and women of the rising generation. This is one reason why the LEDGER is such a general favorite, and why the educationists of the country like to write for it. A College President, or a Doctor of Divinity, who addresses the public through the columns of the LEDGER reaches every city, town, village and hamlet in the United States, and speaks to hundreds of thousands of intelligent people.

One of the most striking facts in connection with the LEDGER is the continuous vitality of Mr. BONNER'S personal energy and business enterprise. He is as wide awake now as he was twenty years ago. He is always on the alert for any new feature that he thinks will render his paper more useful and attractive, and he never allows the cost to stand in the way of his securing a good thing for the LEDGER.

The grand result of all this enterprise and sagacity—of this vast array of eminent and popular contributors—of these deep, pure streams of literature which have been flowing through the columns of the LEDGER for so many years—is, that the popularity of the NEW YORK LEDGER is now unbounded; its circulation covers the whole land; the young, the middle-aged, and the old, the rich and the poor, the learned and the unlearned alike find entertainment and instruction in its pages; it enlivens and brightens thousands upon thousands of homes; it is firmly fixed in the confidence and the affection of the American people, and its influence—which is always on the side of virtue, morality and religion—is immeasurable.

"THE EVENING NEWS," DETROIT, MICH.

A GREAT JOURNALISTIC SUCCESS IN THE WEST.

A SKETCH FOR THE BOOK OF THE CENTENNIAL NEWSPAPER EXHIBITION.

For several years Mr. James E. Scripps, then manager of the Detroit *Tribune*, had entertained a growing conviction that a cheap, popular newspaper, somewhat similar to the Boston *Herald*, the New York *Sun*, and the Philadelphia *Public Ledger*, might be made as great a success in the West as in the Eastern cities, although all attempts of the kind had previously proven failures. From a long practical acquaintance with journalism, and an attentive study of it as a science, he believed that the rocks and shoals upon which so many newspapers had been wrecked might be avoided, and publishing be made as safe and certain as any other business enterprise. It was in pursuance of this theory that, on August 23, 1873, THE EVENING NEWS was launched in Detroit, the chief city of Michigan. The new venture was thoroughly advertised beforehand, an able corps of assistants was secured, embracing the very best men that could be had, and a four cylinder Hoe press was purchased, with a capacity of 10,000 copies per hour. Within five months THE EVENING NEWS had reached a paying basis, and was printing regularly over 5,000 copies each afternoon. By the close of its first year its circulation exceeded 10,000 copies; its second year closed with a regular average issue of 17,025 copies, and by May 1, 1876, it had risen to over 18,000 copies each day. The success of THE EVENING NEWS is owing to several causes.

1st. The paper is cheap and readily within the reach of the masses, being sold to the public at two cents per copy, or at fifty cents per month.

2d. It is of such a size (22x32 inches) that it is kept constantly crowded, either with advertising at good, fair prices, or with choice reading matter—nothing dull, prosy or carelessly prepared being permitted in its columns.

3d. It has a large staff of capable writers, and aims to maintain as high a standard of excellence in the character of work done upon it as any newspaper in the country.

4th. It is independent in all things, and neither fears a foe nor shields a friend.

5th. It is emphatically a *news*paper, and is looked to by the people of Michigan both for the *earliest* tidings of current events and the *most trustworthy* accounts of them.

Between 7,000 and 8,000 copies are circulated throughout the State of Michigan, while the remainder are taken in and around the city of Detroit, which, with its suburbs, exceeds 150,000 inhabitants.

What the *Herald* is to Massachusetts, the *Sun* to New York, and the *Public Ledger* to Pennsylvania, THE EVENING NEWS is to the prosperous and growing State of Michigan, and the border counties of Ohio, Indiana and Ontario.

The actual number of papers printed and sold in the first year of THE EVENING NEWS history was 2,063,950. In the second year the number rose to 4,097,460, and for the first eight months of the third year to 3,489,190, indicating a total for the full year (which does not close till August 23d) of 5,233,785.

THE EVENING NEWS is one of the very few newspapers in the United States which can afford to publish from week to week its exact circulation. This it has conscientiously done from the first.

"THE MORNING NEWS," SAVANNAH, GA.

A SKETCH FOR THE BOOK OF THE CENTENNIAL NEWSPAPER EXHIBITION.

In point of rapid growth and prosperity, the ranking paper of the Southern States is the Savannah (Ga.) MORNING NEWS, of which Mr. J. H. Estill is proprietor. He has just moved into a new building of his own, which, in its finish and appointments, has no equal in any of the more Southern States, and is the first building of the kind south of Maryland and Kentucky.

Its erection was commenced on the 6th of July, 1875, and its occupation took place on the 15th of January, 1876, the 26th anniversary of the paper. It presents an attractive and imposing exterior, is four stories on a basement, with neat front of Georgia granite, and from the street to the top of the cupola is eighty-eight feet high. The arrangements of the building are admirable, and afford ample facilities for the various departments of the newspaper publication office, the extensive job printing establishment, and the blank book manufactory and bindery. Communication is had with the various floors by means of speaking tubes, dumb waiters and one of Bates' patent elevators; and the entire building is supplied with all the modern conveniences and comforts, with thorough ventilation and protection against fire, and, in brief, is a model newspaper edifice, an ornament to the city, and a practical evidence of the prosperity of the influential and able journal whose home it is.

"NEWS" BUILDING.

From a little bantling, one-third its present size, the MORNING NEWS launched upon the uncertain seas of journalism in 1850, with three formidable competitors already occupying the field, and at a time when public feeling ran high in consequence of the diversity of interests and political opinions in the South, by its persistent and fearless advocacy of constitutional liberty, steadily progressed in the good will of the community. During the first decade of its existence it had written the obituaries of two of its original competitors and four subsequent journalistic rivals, and at the commencement of the war, the MORNING NEWS and the old *Republican* were in sole possession of the field, and were undisturbed during the continuance of the struggle.

The career of the MORNING NEWS during the war was similar to that of most papers in Southern cities, with the difference that it never suspended, save for a few days, consequent upon the occupation of the city by the Federal forces.

From that time until 1867, when the present proprietor took charge, the MORNING NEWS had a very precarious existence. From that period onward, however, there was a marked change in the paper; energy, good management, with the expenditure of every dollar that could be spared, soon placed the MORNING NEWS far in advance of its contemporaries, several new papers having been started after the close of the war. One by one these journalistic enterprises drooped and died, and in the summer of 1875, the MORNING NEWS, by absorbing the *Advertiser*, became the only daily paper in Savannah, and is so to this day, with little prospect of having any competition, as the experiences of the past ten years have demonstrated the fact that in the South, where there is almost entire unanimity of political views among the whites, one live, progressive journal fills the public demand. Such a journal is the MORNING NEWS, the acknowledged head of the Georgia press, from its large circulation and great influence.

Particular attention is given to Georgia and Florida affairs, as also to South Carolina news, in which States the NEWS circulates largely, especially in Florida, where its circulation almost equals the combined circulation of the entire press of the State. Hence, to those desirous of obtaining correct information in regard to Southwest Georgia and Florida, the MORNING NEWS is invaluable. In all its departments the paper is fully up with the spirit of the age, and is a credit to Southern journalism.

The NEWS, however, does not confine its efforts to the section in which it is published, but stands prominent among Southern journals as a first-class medium for general intelligence, and as a bold and fearless exponent of the principles of the democratic party. It publishes three editions—a daily, tri-weekly and weekly.

The rank which the NEWS has attained among the newspapers of the South is somewhat remarkable when it is taken into consideration that Savannah was outranked by a number of other cities in population before the war.

"THE NEW YORK WEEKLY."

A SKETCH FOR THE BOOK OF THE CENTENNIAL NEWSPAPER EXHIBITION.

The NEW YORK WEEKLY, which is universally recognized as "the greatest story and sketch paper of the age," came into the possession of its present proprietors, Messrs. STREET & SMITH, in March, 1859. At that time its circulation was about 28,000 copies, and outside of the metropolis it was little known. Now the name of the NEW YORK WEEKLY has a familiar ring in every habitation within the boundaries of American civilization. Its constituency is numbered by millions, and its circulation is greater than that of any other paper in the world.

The remarkable prosperity of the NEW YORK WEEKLY cannot be attributed to chance or luck. The tact, judgment, industry and enterprise of STREET & SMITH have commanded success where men of less pluck and energy would have ingloriously failed.

Many publishers who have tried the experiment are aware that it is no child's play to compete with the numerous literary papers now established. But the NEW YORK WEEKLY, in its competition for popular favor, long since stepped far in advance of all opposition, and is now considered the leading literary paper in the world.

"THE NEW YORK WEEKLY" ESTABLISHMENT.

A brief reference to the NEW YORK WEEKLY establishment, with a description of its various departments, may prove interesting to the reader. The NEW YORK WEEKLY buildings are located at NOS. 27, 29 & 31 ROSE STREET, within sight of the City Hall and the Post-office.

THE PUBLICATION OFFICE.

The private offices of Messrs. STREET & SMITH and the publication department are on the second story of No. 31. The office of Mr. FRANCIS S. STREET fronts on Rose street; and here the contributors and visitors who call for the first time are amazed on beholding piles of unpublished manuscripts, some in safes and some on shelves.

The aggregate value of manuscripts now on hand, we have learned, is over two hundred thousand dollars. Fancy for a moment the anxiety with which these manuscripts are contemplated by the hundreds of writers whose busy brains and nimble fingers produced them. For years many of the authors have impatiently awaited the appearance of their works in print, and with keen eyes scanned each number of the NEW YORK WEEKLY, with the hope of finding the announcement that at last a definate day has been named for the appearance of the story which, it is hoped, is to bring fame, and consequently fortune, to the author.

At the rear of the second floor is the sanctum of Mr. FRANCIS S. SMITH, which is tastefully decorated with paintings of a high order of merit. Here Mr. SMITH'S pleasant face may be seen in a cloud of blue smoke, for he is an inveterate smoker, and seems to derive poetic inspiration from a cigar. Here the voluminous correspondence received each day is glanced over by Mr. SMITH after the business letters have been selected therefrom by Mr. STREET, who is the business manager and attends to all the financial matters. Mr. SMITH devotes his attention exclusively to the literary management of the paper, and while each partner is in a measure independent in his own sphere, perfect harmony prevails.

The Publication Department is between the two offices just mentioned. The cashier and the receiving and mail clerks occupy this portion of the building The sides of the room are faced with boxes containing *back numbers* of the NEW YORK WEEKLY, for which there is a constant demand.

THE MAILING ROOM.

The mailing room is on the second floor of No. 29. Numerous clerks are here kept busy putting the names of new subscribers in the mail books, writing wrappers, and preparing for the post-office the immense edition which each week is forwarded to mail subscribers.

EDITORIAL ROOMS.

The editorial rooms are directly over the publication department. On one side of the room is the library—a collection of useful works of reference. The great variety of information supplied by this library may be inferred by glancing over the correspondence column of the NEW YORK WEEKLY. Authors cannot object to our terming the editorial department "the council chamber of a literary grand jury." Here a jury of four experienced journalists sit in judgment upon the various manuscripts received. Upon their decision rests the hopes and fears of thousands of writers who have sought the NEW YORK WEEKLY as a medium to spread their productions broadcast throughout the land.

THE ENGRAVING DEPARTMENT.

The engraving department is on the same floor with the editorial rooms. The blocks from which the illustrations are printed are here engraved by a corps of competent artists. The subjects for illustration are usually selected by the editors, but sometimes by the draughtsmen.

THE COMPOSITION ROOM.

The composition room is on the fourth floor, over the editorial rooms. Here are arranged in proper order the multitudinous types which each week impart to the world instruction, entertainment, and amusement. Here the interesting stories, the suggestive essays, the stirring poems, and mirth-arousing anecdotes are converted from manuscripts, letter by letter, and word by word, into square "forms" of type, ready for the electrotyper. So large is the circulation of the NEW YORK WEEKLY that nine sets of plates are taken by the electrotyper. These duplicates are absolutely necessary, as nine presses, working night and day, are required to print the immense edition of the NEW YORK WEEKY.

THE PRESS-ROOM.

The press-room is in the building No. 27 Rose street. In this department the nine presses, moved by an engine of 160 horse-power, may be seen at work, night and day, throwing off the printed sheets, ready for the counter, who counts and arranges the papers in bundles of fifty. One man is constantly employed counting the NEW YORK WEEKLY, and performs no other duty, his entire time being occupied in this work. When the edition is all printed, it is conveyed in wagons to the establishment of the American News Company, the wholesale agents, by whom it is distributed to the various retail agents throughout the country.

The BOYS OF THE WORLD, a paper intended for the instruction and entertainment of the rising generation, is also published by STREET & SMITH. This paper, although but seven months established, has a circulation of over 60,000 copies, and is greatly admired by the young folks.

The MAMMOTH MONTHLY READER is another publication issued by STREET & SMITH. This, also, has a wide circulation, chiefly among mail subscribers, to whom it is sent at the low price of seventy-five cents per year.

THE NEW YORK "CLIPPER."

A SKETCH FOR THE BOOK OF THE CENTENNIAL NEWSPAPER EXHIBITION.

Issued originally on April 30, 1853, this is the oldest sporting paper in America. Its editor at the beginning is its editor to-day, and this enables the paper to be consistent with itself. Its reports are the work of trained minds, who have seen years of associated service; its summaries are compiled with care, so as to be a reference for all time; its comparative reliability has passed into a proverb, and its decisions upon mooted points are solicited from almost every known quarter. Recognized for more than twenty years as the favored organ of the sporting community in America, since 1855 it has steadily grown in popular regard as the leading amusement journal of America. It is a reflex of every phase of show life; its correspondents, almost ubiquitous, are numerous; its reports of amusements are fuller than those of any other journal published on this continent, while covering a greater area of country; and its constant aim is to furnish facts, which are unchangeable and endure, rather than opinions, which fluctuate and perish. Its many and well-stored columns regularly devoted to the movements of established performers, to the erection and opening of new theatres and halls and the closing of old ones, to the production of new plays upon the legitimate stage and of new acts in the variety, minstrel or circus line, and to the *debut* of new performers and the whereabouts of temporarily retired ones, have of late years been supplemented by an old-bill department, to which many of our leading actors, minstrels and circus people are occasional contributors. These old playbills, while recalling pleasant memories, serve to brush away the cobwebs of time, and in many instances of error.

THE N. Y. "CLIPPER" BUILDING.

THE NEW YORK CLIPPER is a paper for everybody—a daily and a weekly combined. In it are original serials, bright tales, humorous sketches and dialogues, songs, glees and poems, News of the Week, Record of the Deaths of Prominent Individuals, CLIPPER Post-office List, and, finally, the department known as Answers to Correspondents, which, although from time to time treating of almost every known subject, are especially serviceable to persons seeking information concerning amusements or sports, the most trustworthy and complete record of both of which are the files of the paper. The questions thus answered weekly have the supreme merit of being *bona fide*; and, apart from the instruction they afford, the answers are invaluable as determining disputes alike in the social circle and among professional people.

THE NEW YORK CLIPPER is essentially a journal of record and of reference. It is to be expected that a newspaper possessing so many features, and in its fifty-six long columns of compact type covering so vast a field, should be in demand in the business community. The extent of this demand is attested weekly by advertisements filling several pages, making public proclamation of manifold industries, and representing a thousand different interests. It has created a special class of advertisers, and yet all classes avail themselves of its columns, for its moderate tariff places it within reach of all. Its rates of advertising are:

For cards coming under the head of Amusements, *fifteen cents* per line for each insertion; for cards of a Miscellaneous or Sporting character, *twenty cents* per line; for Notices, such as extracts from other papers and incorporated in News Departments (not to be inserted more than once), *thirty cents* per line. The terms are cash, with a reduction of twenty per cent. on all advertisements paid for three months in advance. The paper has no advertising agents, and has never solicited an advertisement. The subscription prices are $5 per annum, $2.50 for six months, and $1.25 for three months; single copies, 10 cents. To clubs of four or more a reduction of fifty cents is made on each single subscription; but subscribers in Canada and the British Provinces are charged $1 per annum extra, to cover postage. No subscriptions in New York City are taken. All business letters or communications must be addressed to FRANK QUEEN, Editor and Proprietor NEW YORK CLIPPER, corner of Centre and Leonard streets, New York, where the paper occupies an elegant building expressly erected for it in 1869.

"TIMES," TROY, N. Y.

A SKETCH FOR THE BOOK OF THE CENTENNIAL NEWSPAPER EXHIBITION.

The TROY TIMES was founded in 1851 by Francis & Thompson. The latter retired in about one year, and John M. Francis continued the paper alone as editor and publisher until 1863, when Henry O'R. Tucker became his partner and the business manager of the concern. The TIMES is one of the most succcessful journals in New York State, and enjoys a larger advertising patronage than any other paper in the State outside of the cities of New York and Brooklyn. Its circulation is nearly double that of any daily in the State not metropolitan, and it is the favorite journal, not only in the city of Troy, but also in Northern New York and the adjacent portions of Vermont and Massachusetts. Its area of circulation and influence extends from Troy northward along both shores of Lake Champlain to the very borders of Canada.

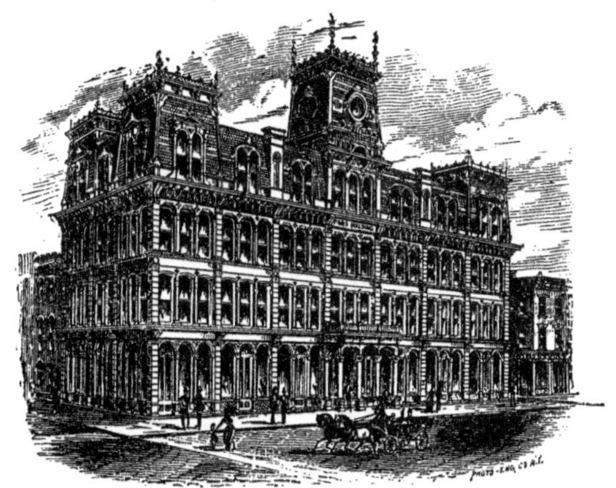

"TIMES" BUILDING.

The TIMES has an influence commensurate with its business success, and its opinions and sentiments on all subjects are widely quoted, and command general attention. Its editor, Hon. John M. Francis, has achieved almost a national reputation in his profession; while as a diplomatic representative of our government at the court of Greece from 1872 to 1874, when he resigned the position, and as a traveler his name is well known in distinguished and educated circles in Europe. The TIMES is published in an elegant iron building costing upwards of $150,000, and its office appointments are unusually complete in detail and perfect in arrangement. The building occupies one of the most valuable sites in the city of Troy. It is four stories high, surmounted by a French roof with towers, and presents a very imposing architectural appearance. Its dimensions are 130 feet in length by 50 in width. The paper is printed upon a four-cylinder Hoe rotary press, but its proprietors are now contemplating the purchase of a web perfecting machine, with which to lay its large and constantly-increasing edition more quickly and satisfactorily before its readers. The TIMES is Republican in its political convictions, and an earnest advocate of the principles of that party. During the war, so heartily had it espoused the cause of the government, that in the draft riot in the city of Troy, July, 1863, its office was mobbed, and all its type and material destroyed. The TIMES is a folio 29x41 inches in size, and contains eight columns upon each page. On Saturdays the size of the paper is increased by the addition of one column per page, in order to accommodate the pressure upon its advertising department. The system which prevails in the management of its business departments—especially in the arrangement and classification of its advertisements—is perfect in detail and admirably carried out. This, together with the large circulation of the paper, and the relative cheapness of its advertising rates compared with those of journals of inferior circulation, makes its columns so attractive and valuable to all who desire to reach the public through the press. The TIMES is admirably printed, and typographically is excelled in appearance by no daily journal anywhere. It is a representative newspaper every way—in the clearness and freshness of its editorial discussions, in the unrivalled excellence of its news department and miscellaneous selections and in the fullness and intelligence of its correspondence from all parts of the world. As a newspaper simply, it ranks with the best in this country; while as an advertising medium it has no equal (in fact no single journal approaches it) in the territorial limits to which its circulation is confined.

"THE EVENING BULLETIN," SAN FRANCISCO.

A SKETCH FOR THE BOOK OF THE CENTENNIAL NEWSPAPER EXHIBITION.

This journal was founded in 1855, at a time when corruption in public affairs at San Francisco had become the rule, and all the avenues of justice were so completely in possession of the vicious classes, that virtue scarcely dared to raise its head There was slight exaggeration in the assertion often made in those days, that a ruffian thirsting for the blood of an enemy, or desiring to remove some human obstacle from his own path, could bargain in advance, with sheriffs and courts, and definitely arrange the sum for which he should be put through the forms of a bogus trial, and acquitted of the murder which he contemplated. Gamblers, thieves and ballot-box stuffers were the terror of the cities. The great majority of the people silently mourned this condition of affairs, but seemed powerless. The desperadoes were organized, and therefore formidable. The honest masses were without organization, and so their sentiments were not consolidated and embodied in action. It was in this condition of society that the EVENING BULLETIN came into existence. Its aim was, first, to interest the people by providing the fullest and most reliable news; and when its audience was thus secured, its second effort was addressed to the task of arousing public indignation against the vicious classes, and to concentrate a sound sentiment for aggressive warfare upon them. It not only exposed the criminal acts which were sapping the foundations of society, but boldly named the men who perpetrated or were responsible for them. From its first hour it was a success, morally and financially. The masses rallied to the support of its utterance of truths which were already in the heads and hearts of all good citizens, and which now found voice and expression through a fearless and independent journal. Its founder lost his life at the hands of one whose iniquities it had exposed. Then the people arose *en masse*, in the vigilance committee of 1856, visited swift and sure justice upon assassins, drove ballot-box stuffers, corrupt officials and criminals of every grade beyond the borders of the State, and initiated the reform movement which has freed San Francisco from debt and kept it free, and which has given it, ever since, the best average municipal government to be found upon the continent.

The BULLETIN'S existence has been somewhat stormy. It is ever the foe of jobbers against public interest, and of corporations and monopolies when they abuse their power to oppress the people. Necessarily it has challenged the ill will of the selfish and corrupt; but it has constantly won the approval of all who set the true interests of the masses above the greed of the few. Sometimes it has, for a few days, been thought to be in error, when it pointed out some public wrong and persistently warned the people against its consummation. But invariably the result has vindicated its wise foresight, and the cavils of doubters have been turned into pæons of praise. Subsidized journals have been started, time and again, to draw off its business, limit its power and cripple its influence; but the people, to whom it was ever faithful, have adhered to it with as singular fidelity, and "the gates of hell" have not prevailed against it. A memorable instance of its faithfulness against powerful and threatening influences, and of the defeat of those who, whether ignorantly or maliciously, sought its destruction, is fresh in the memory of all. During the autumn of last year it persistently opposed a job, secretly engineered by the then President of the Bank of California, to saddle the city of San Francisco with a debt of many milions, ostensibly for the purchase of city water works, but really in order that the bank President might reap for himself over $3,000,000 of profit, out of more than double that sum which was to be taken from the city in excess of the true value of the property to be sold. To this end he had corrupted and controlled political conventions and demoralized political parties to an alarming degree. Day by day he denied the facts, and vicious journalists were subsidized to lavish falsehood and abuse upon the BULLETIN'S conductors, in the hope of silencing its batteries or impairing their effectiveness. Just then the Bank of California suspended, and, simultaneously, its president met his tragic end. The panic and wild confusion which followed were terrible and severe. For a brief time a part of the public was made to believe that the BULLETIN had done injustice to the bank President, and had precipitated or created the evils associated with his failure and death. But soon the truth came out; his leading connection with the water job stood confessed; his responsibility for squandered millions and his betrayal of his old and best friends and most sacred trusts were all revealed. Then the BULLETIN was vindicated once more, and its influence, circulation, power and patronage became greater than ever before.

The BULLETIN is in all respects a first-class journal. Nothing is admitted to its editorial, news or advertising columns that can offend the most fastidious sentiment or taste. Thus it is essentially a family paper. Its financial articles and market reports are carefully prepared, and kept scrupulously free from all speculative influence. For these reasons it is found in every banking institution and all first-class mercantile establishments. It presents a rare instance in which an evening journal is recognized as the financial authority in a great mart of commerce and trade. Independent in all things, but neutral in nothing, its opinions upon public topics are as freely and explicitly declared as they are carefully considered and adopted. Thus its influence upon public affairs is deep and strong; and seldom has an unfaithful public servant been able to stand up under its criticism, or has any unjust measure survived its earnest assault. There are few journals in the country which can present such a record; but it is one which every well-informed and truthful Californian will accord it without hesitation.

As a literary journal it has no superior on the Pacific, and its very large weekly as well as daily circulation supplies the reading community with a great variety of miscellaneous matter, embracing the whole field of public affairs, current events throughout the world, agriculture, manufactures, practical philosophy as applied to popular wants, and whatever else it is the office of good journalism to supply. A glance at its columns will attest the high estimation in which it is held by advertisers who desire to reach the intelligent and cultivated classes; it attests also the fact that the BULLETIN affords its proprietors an adequate reward for the intelligence, energy and enterprise which mark its conduct in every department. The BULLETIN Company consists of Messrs. LORING PICKERING and GEORGE K. FITCH, who have been prominent in California journalism from its earliest date, and J. W. SIMONTON, long known in connection with the New York *Daily Times*, and during the last ten years as general agent and executive officer of the Associated Press.

"THE MORNING CALL," SAN FRANCISCO.

A SKETCH FOR THE BOOK OF THE CENTENNIAL NEWSPAPER EXHIBITION.

This journal was established in 1856. It was then little larger than a letter sheet, but was eagerly sought by the multitude who could not afford to buy other newspapers at the high prices then general in the Golden State. Gradually its dimensions increased with its growing prosperity, until in 1869, when it came into the hands of its present proprietors, with a daily circulation of about 11,000 copies. At this time it was about the present size of the New York *Sun*. The new proprietors put into the concern abundant capital, and, what was of more importance, the experience of a lifetime employed in successful journalism. Having procured an eight-cylinder Hoe Lightning Press and other machinery for its use, its dimensions were again increased, until it became the largest paper in America published at its price, or in the world, with the possible exception of the London *Telegraph*. The subscription rate is 12½ cents weekly, per six issues, or 15 cents including the Sunday edition. Now, the pressure upon its advertising columns compels the printing of a full-sized double sheet on Sundays and a half sheet supplement twice per week.

The circulation of the MORNING CALL is most remarkable when we consider that the population of the entire State, excluding 100,000 Chinese, does not exceed 700,000, and that 250,000 is a liberal estimate for San Francisco itself. For more than two years the CALL'S circulation has exceeded an average of 30,000 daily. At this time it is above 33,500 per day, and still rising. When one reflects that this is equal to one copy for every seven and a half men, women, and children in the city, it will be seen to be a marvellous evidence of success. A similar per centage to the 1,500,000 population (a low estimate) of New York and its immediate suburbs, would give the journal enjoying it a circulation of more than 200,000 copies daily. That there is no exaggeration in the CALL'S claim on this score is readily established, because its proprietors freely admit to their press-room any respectable party, at any time, to inspect its work and satisfy himself. Its regular shipment from New York City of 2,600 reams of printing paper per month, for use of the CALL, will also attest its wonderful circulation to parties at the East who, naturally enough, can scarcely understand the possibility of such a patronage.

It follows that the MORNING CALL is in the hands of all classes. No matter what other newspaper he takes, the intelligent reader adds the CALL. The poor, the rich, the merchant, banker, farmer, trader, mechanic, artisan—all, from the highest to the humblest, buy and read it. Advertisers crowd to it, because they have learned that no other journal can give such wide publicity to their wants or wares. The journal is pre-eminently a newspaper. Entirely independent in politics, while it gives all parties fair and equal representation, it avoids partisan discussion of any question in such manner as to offend honest differences of opinion among honest men. But, like the *Evening Bulletin*, it has a heavy hand for rogues, and is swift to expose and oppose public abuses or wrongs, no matter how powerful the influences or combinations by which they are attempted. To this steady support of the best interests of poor and rich alike is to be attributed much of the CALL'S success.

"THE BEE," OMAHA, NEB.

A SKETCH FOR THE BOOK OF THE CENTENNIAL NEWSPAPER EXHIBITION.

The BEE, a Republican journal published at Omaha City, Nebraska, is one of a few newspapers in the West that has attained prominence in American journalism.

It was first launched into existence by its present proprietor, Mr. Edward Rosewater, in June, 1871. Though bitterly opposed at the outset by the then established Omaha journals, both Republican and Democratic, through fear of competition and jealousy, its fearless and honest course, coupled with the varied and spicy character of its news matter, gained for it the approbation of the general public, and made it a popular journal among the masses. Its circulation has from its incipiency had a steady growth, both at home and abroad. Recognizing the want of a Western journal in the Western country, and the facilities which Omaha as a railway center affords for news gathering, its founder and present publisher has made it his aim to study Western interests and develop the agricultural and mineral resources of the West by bringing them forcibly before the public. In this endeavor every effort to gather and place before the public in an interesting form items of passing events and facts bearing upon the undeveloped resources of the West has been made. The price of the DAILY BEE has been fixed at $8 per annum, and the WEEKLY at $2, rates which from their reasonable nature have made the BEE of easy access to all.

The BEE is the first newspaper in the Trans-Missouri country that has issued regularly a series of illustrated editions setting forth in a very striking form the events and improvements of each year. It is the only journal in the West that maintains a regular corps of travelling and local correspondents.

ITS CIRCULATION, owing to this wide scope of its news, has become general, extending through nearly every town for eleven hundred miles west of Omaha. The DAILY BEE is now a 36-column journal, and is the only daily west of the Mississippi that issues two editions daily, one in the evening and one in the morning. The morning issue is expressly prepared for its Western readers, to supply them with news almost up to the hour of the departure of the mails. Although over one thousand miles away, the DAILY BEE has a very extensive circulation in Salt Lake City and other Utah towns. In Wyoming, a territory only developed in the past few years, the DAILY BEE circulates over 400 copies. In Omaha City its daily circulation is nearly 2,000. It is delivered to the city subscribers by eleven carrier boys, six of whom are mounted on horseback.

THE WEEKLY BEE.

In the past two years the demand for the WEEKLY BEE has become so great that it has been deemed advisable to enlarge it to an eight-page, 56 column journal. This enables the publisher to furnish its readers with a large portion of the varied and interesting correspondence which appears in the daily during the week. Its circulation extends through Western Iowa, Nebraska, Dakota, Wyoming, Utah, and the other Territories, and is rapidly increasing.

EDITORIAL DEPARTMENT.

This is presided over by Mr. Edward Rosewater, who is also the publisher. His literary acquirements and terseness have made him well known throughout the West. Mr. Rosewater speaks four languages with fluency. On the occasion of Rochefort's tour through the United States, after his romantic escape from imprisonment, Mr. Rosewater secured the first successful interview with that individual, and received creditable notices for this effort by the Chicago and New York metropolitan journals. The local news department is managed by the city editor, Mr. Alfred Sorensen, a former student of Harvard College, who is a practical printer as well as a stenographic reporter.

The BEE also keeps three regular travelling correspondents, who visit every section of Nebraska and the Territories each year. Aside from these, special local correspondents are maintained by the BEE at San Francisco, Salt Lake City, Custer City, Lincoln, Neb., and also a special correspondent at Philadelphia during the Centennial.

THE BUSINESS DEPARTMENT.

This is in charge of Andrew Rosewater, manager, and consists of an accountant, mailing clerk, superintendent of city circulation, and messenger. The number of employes in the entire establishment are forty-two. There has been an average of three tons per month of news paper consumed in the past year. Thirty-five newsboys sell the paper daily upon the streets.

The enterprise of the BEE has been acknowledged by the Western press generally. It lately issued a finely-illustrated supplement, showing the city of Cheyenne in detail. It now has in hand a supplement of the scenery of the Black Hills and mining districts, which will be issued in the early part of May.

THE NASHVILLE (TENN.) AMERICAN.

A SKETCH FOR THE BOOK OF THE CENTENNIAL NEWSPAPER EXHIBITION.

This paper and its predecessors in regular line have existed for more than fifty years in this city. There were the *National Banner* and the Nashville *Republican*. These were united under the name of *Republican Banner*, which itself had an existence of more than half a century. Then there was the *Union*, established in 1835, under the auspices of Jackson in his contest against nullification. Afterwards, in 1849, the *Centre State American* was established as a Democratic paper, which, in 1850, was merged into the *Union* under the name of *Union and American*. These two papers, the *Republican Banner* and the *Union and American*, were the representatives of the party sentiment of Tennessee during all the exciting periods of its political history—the former being Whig and the latter Democrat. The great names of Jackson, White, Bell, Polk, Johnson and others who have impressed their names on the country's history, have fought their glorious battles of principle through these columns. On the 1st of September, 1875, the *Union and American* and the *Republican Banner* were consolidated under the name of THE AMERICAN, and its proprietors trust that in this name it will be printed for all time to come The last fusion and change of name was no more a matter of business than a matter of patriotism. The general unanimity in the sentiments of the people of the State suggested the change on political and patriotic considerations, and the business view conceded it. It now wields the leading influence in the State.

THE AMERICAN

Has now a positive circulation much greater than that *claimed* by any newspaper published in the States of the South, except Kentucky, Missouri and Louisiana. Its united editions exceed several which claim the greater number. It has a firm hold on the confidence of the people, because it has never deceived them; and we are gratified to say that in spite of the "hard times" its subscription lists are greater than those of both its immediate predecessors, and greater than any paper ever had in Tennessee. Address THE AMERICAN, Nashville.

"THE SHOE AND LEATHER REPORTER."

A SKETCH FOR THE BOOK OF THE CENTENNIAL NEWSPAPER EXHIBITION.

The SHOE AND LEATHER REPORTER is the oldest industrial newspaper published in this country—the pioneer of its class—leading the van of the great army of "Trade papers" which register the progress of nearly every branch of business conducted in the United States at the present time.

The REPORTER was founded in August, 1857, and made its first appearance as a semi-monthly. Its circulation and business increased, and it was issued weekly at the end of the first six months. It has since been enlarged, until it is now almost ten times the size of the original sheet.

To the casual observer there might seem to be little of importance to chronicle in the lines of shoes and leather, unless it might be records of prices or dry statistical figures; such, however, is not the case. There is no product in which the chemical change is more intricate and interesting than in that of the manufacture of leather from hides and skins; no industry is pursued where the aid of a greater or more varied amount of machinery is required than in the production of boots and shoes, and, with the single exception of agriculture, no branch of business in this country employs so large a capital or requires a greater exercise of skill. So much for the mechanical part. As a mercantile interest it stretches to every quarter of the globe. The work of collecting and disseminating information in every branch of these great industries, and of defining the relations they bear to each other, is immense, and the publisher employs the best capacity obtainable for a thorough and careful compilation of the market reports, as well as the most intelligent criticism of the various inventions and theories introduced to the trades.

The circulation extends throughout all the States of the Union, and it has a considerable list of subscribers in Europe, and in the East and West Indies, South America, and in fact every country where hides and skins are a product, or shoes and leather a necessity. It is under the editorial charge of a gentleman who has pursued from boyhood the business of making and dealing in leather, and has an extensive acquaintance with men engaged in all the various branches of the trade at home and abroad. Experience and knowledge combine to qualify him to represent the views and express the sentiments of his co-laborers in the great industry to which the paper is exclusively devoted. He is supported by able assistants in the three cities; by capable correspondents in the West, the South and the chief foreign marts. Mr. Jackson S. Schultz, who is thoroughly well versed in the practice and theory of the tanning trade, is a regular contributor to its columns. He is at present engaged upon a serial work, defining and illustrating all the details and mechanical processes of the art of tanning, the initial chapter of which was published in the first issue of the current year.

A supplementary pattern sheet is published quarterly, containing the latest styles of boots and shoes, giving exact directions for reproducing the various styles. It is artistic in execution, and is a prominent feature of the paper, being looked for and preserved.

The compilation of the statistics of the trade necessitates an amount of care and labor which can only be appreciated by those who have occasion to refer to the semi-annual tables; they are accepted by the trade as a valuable aid in their transactions.

The SHOE AND LEATHER REPORTER is published simultaneously in New York, Boston and Philadelphia by Isaac H. Bailey. The subscription price is $3.50 a year. The New York office is at 17 Spruce street, the Boston office at 114 High street, and the Philadelphia office at 149 South Fourth street.

THE "ILLINOIS STAATS ZEITUNG."

A SKETCH FOR THE BOOK OF THE CENTENNIAL NEWSPAPER EXHIBITION.

Of those German newspapers published in the United States, which have for a number of years exerted a positive and decisive influence upon public opinion, there is, in the great Northwest, none that could claim to excel or even to equal the ILLINOIS STAATS ZEITUNG of Chicago. The ILLINOIS STAATS ZEITUNG, established at a time when the great metropolis of the Lake region was a town of barely 20,000 inhabitants, has grown, both in its value as a newspaper and in the influence wielded by it upon many thousands of readers, in proportion with the wonderful development of its place of publication. It is, and has been for almost half a generation, a recognized political power, perhaps so to a greater extent than any other German daily paper in the country. In this respect not only does the ILLINOIS STAATS ZEITUNG fully rank with its Chicago contemporaries published in the English language, but it has on several occasions successfully defied and actually defeated in some of the hottest political contests a combination of the entire English press of Chicago, without any exception. In Germany it is probably better known and more widely quoted than any other German-American daily paper, except its New York namesake. There must be good reasons for such success other than mere good luck or the importance of the city where the ZEITUNG is issued. Such reasons may be found in the intense positiveness of mind, the perfect independence of opinion, and the trenchant keenness of judgment displayed in the discussion of all questions of public interest in the columns of the ILLINOIS STAATS ZEITUNG; and also in the completeness, variety, and freshness of its news; in its careful selection of the gist of foreign newspapers; and in the excellence of its correspondence. The remark has frequently been made by German-Americans, temporarily residing in their native country, that they found a greater amount of interesting and important news from Germany in the columns of the ILLINOIS STAATS ZEITUNG than in the great papers easily accessible to them in Germany itself. The comments of the ILLINOIS STAATS ZEITUNG upon the public affairs of Germany have often, on account of their thoroughly American independence of thought and directness of expression, been quoted, and been either highly commended or angrily discussed by leading newspapers of Germany. As an evidence of the position generally accorded to the ILLINOIS STAATS ZEITUNG abroad, the fact may be mentioned here, that, beside Mr. Smalley of the *N. Y. Tribune*, the chief editor of the ILLINOIS STAATS ZEITUNG is the only American editor to whom the Chancellor of the German Empire, Prince Bismarck, has accorded an extended interview, the record of which was, at the

"ILLINIOS STAATS ZEITUNG" BUILDING.

time, translated and copied from the ILLINOIS STAATS ZEITUNG into many hundreds of newspapers in this country, in England, Germany, and even in France.

In the quality of its reading matter the ILLINOIS STAATS ZEITUNG is the second German-American newspaper, ranking immediately next to its New York namesake. Its circulation is the largest of all German dailies, excepting only the New York *Staats Zeitung* and, perhaps, one daily published in the West. Its weekly issue is widely circulated all over the Northwestern States, and in its efficiency as an advertising medium is superior to almost any other weekly publication in the Northwest.

When, in October, 1871, the city of Chicago seemed to be wiped out from the face of the earth by the great fire, the ILLINOIS STAATS ZEITUNG was a greater sufferer than any other paper published in Chicago, for this reason: that not only its entire establishment (including files and safes with books) was utterly destroyed, but all its editors, reportors, clerks, compositors, pressmen, with the exception of barely half a dozen were "burned out" of their homes and personal property. It took two or three days to gather up a mere handful of the employees of the paper and to provide a temporary abode. Then there arose the further difficulty that, while English type could be had in abundance within call, it took weeks to procure the required quantity of German type. In fact, the struggle against the effects of that terrible calamity to many would have appeared utterly hopeless. And yet, after having been printed in Milwaukee for a few weeks, twenty days after the great fire the ILLINOIS STAATS ZEITUNG was issued again in its old size from its own press, and fifty days after the fire it enlarged its size and the amount of reading matter by one-sixth over what it had been before the fire. The hackneyed metaphor of the Phœnix rising from its ashes would not seem out of place in this connection.

In rebuilding Chicago the ILLINOIS STAATS ZEITUNG would not be found behindhand. A site for a permanent home was selected within one square from the heart of the business center of the city, the Board of Trade building, the new Court House, the W. U. Telegraph, and Military Headquarters building. Fronting Washington street (40 feet) and extending 110 feet on Fifth avenue, the ILLINOIS STAATS ZEITUNG block covers an area of 4,400 square feet. Its height from the floor of the basement to the roof is 100 feet, making it the tallest building but one within five squares in each direction. The architecture is of that chaste and massive style of modern renaissance to which the new portions of the great cities of Europe owe their proudly dignified, monumental aspect. The ornamentation is in excellent taste and superior to that of any other public or private building in Chicago. For, while the statues of Franklin and Gutenberg, raised over the porticoes of the two main entrances, happily denote the character and purposes of the building, the top of the house is beautifully and appropriately ornamented by five life-size statues, representing Science, Industry, Agriculture, Commerce, and Justice. These were cast in Paris, while a very characteristic and expressive center piece, representing the reclining figures of Columbia and Germania, is the conception of a French artist who has made Chicago his home.

The ILLINOIS STAATS ZEITUNG enjoys a prosperity which it may justly be proud of, since it may see in it a hearty recognition by the people of its unceasing efforts, not only to satisfy, but to anticipate the wants of its readers. Its circulation since the great fire has so increased, that in order to issue its large edition in proper time for early distribution, it has to stereotype its forms and print them from a Bullock press capable of turning off 14,000 copies in an hour.

Standing upon the firm foundation of established success, shaken as little by the financial crisis of 1873 as by the great fire of 1871, the ILLINOIS STAATS ZEITUNG may, without fear of being charged with self-conceit, lay just claim to the designation as one of *the* representative newspapers of this country.

"WESTLICHE POST," ST. LOUIS, MO.

„Die größte und verbreitetste deutsche Zeitung im Westen."

A SKETCH FOR THE BOOK OF THE CENTENNIAL NEWSPAPER EXHIBITION.

It has been pronounced that "*The progress of a country is best indicated by the growth of its newspapers;*" and the present position of the WESTLICHE POST —foremost in rank among the daily journals of the Western States of America—clearly proves this assertion.

The career of this paper during the comparatively few years of its history, marks the success which hardly ever fails when industry, perseverance and able and faithful management are united in conducting a newspaper in this country. The WESTLICHE POST has fairly kept even step with the development of the West, and in clear and cloudy days foremost stood up for general progress at home and abroad and for the interest of the German element, which for ever has represented this position in the history of the United States.

"WESTLICHE POST" BUILDING.

Established September 27, 1857, it was then a small paper of little influence and of small circulation, while it now ranks among the leading journals of this country, with an average circulation of more than fifteen thousand copies, and since April, 1874, is fairly established in its own fine building SOUTHWEST CORNER OF FIFTH AND MARKET STREETS, ST. LOUIS, MO., on the most prominent thoroughfare of the Queen City of the Mississippi Valley, right opposite the court-house, and in the most prominent and central location within the city.

The WESTLICHE POST is published in folio size, and has a daily, weekly and Sunday edition, each of four pages, the pages of the daily and Sunday having nine columns, and those of the weekly ten. The Sunday edition is accompanied by an eight-page supplement, the MISSISSIPPI BLAETTER. The WESTLICHE POST circulates in every State and Territory of the great West and South, from Ohio to the Pacific shore, and from the far Northwest to the Gulf. It has a larger circulation than any other German daily paper published west of New York, and as an advertising medium is surpassed by none.

It is incorporated according to the laws of the State of Missouri. Arthur Olshausen, Esq., is the president, Messrs. E. Preetorius and Carl Schurz are the editors, and Gustavus A. Olshausen, Esq., is the treasurer and secretary. It is not strange that with the co-operation in its management of gentlemen possessing the exceptional ability of Mr. Carl Schurz, it should have acquired its great moral influence, as well as its commercial value, in respect to the German population of the West. Its always-crowded advertising columns show peculiarly that its excellence is acknowledged and realized by the public in general, and not only by a fragmentary class or nationality. Its serried advertisements remind a person of every branch of commerce, finance, and trade, of things domestic and foreign, and in short, of every department of human life. The names of its local advertisers do not merely consist of those betokening a Germanic origin, but savor of nativities quite distant from the Rhine. This would of itself be very favorable evidence. Men of moderate or ordinary trade or business are not apt to resort to publications in foreign languages for the advertising of that which they have, unless they are imbued with a decided belief in the standing and merits as an advertising medium, if not as a general newspaper, of a publication of this character selected by them. No one can deny that the WESTLICHE POST possesses this standing and these merits to an unusual degree, both as a general newspaper and as an advertising medium. It has no superior in the West, and perhaps not elswhere, in regard to celerity and enterprise in laying before its readers that which is "news" in the strictest sense. Everything not out of place in a daily newspaper appears in its diurnal editions, while its Sunday issues are models of well-chosen literature. The weekly is a judicious and succinct history of the occurences of each week. The circulation which the WESTLICHE POST enjoys represents a far greater influence than an equal circulation of an English paper. In the large and ordinarily prosperous American cities, it is not at all unusual for an individual to daily pass through the labor or diversion—in which ever way he may regard it—of perusing two or three, and sometimes even four or five, of the newspapers that circulate in his locality. He reads them all with equal attention or inattention, as his humor may lead him, and seldom allows either one of them to have the special honor of arousing his most profound reflections. A great number of the American people, indeed, appear to regard their newspapers as something which it is their duty to criticise and to pick fault with if they can. They are capable of finding considerable amusement in seeking to invent transitory theories which shall be utterly at variance with those advocated by the newspaper they may happen to read, and are seldom so complacent as when some opinion which they have expressed proves to be more correct than that of the newspaper. Among the Germans, however, the case is different. They look up to respectable newspapers as a species of paternal guides and instructors, and the feeling with which they regard the most worthy of German publications can hardly be appreciated by a critical, fault-finding, captious American mind. Though a German may not be reluctant to express his disapprobation of the course of a particular paper, he never does it with the same invectives and fierceness so frequent in America. The influence of German newspapers, indeed, is comparatively extreme; and the influence of the WESTLICHE POST, with its great circulation, may be conceived. That it *worthily* possesses and wields this influence is very plain. It is a paper in which the German populace of the Western States are not and need not be ashamed to trust, and is the best existing fulfilment of their ideal of a newspaper. In every respect, the WESTLICHE POST of St. Louis may be pointed out as a proper representative of the Germans in our country —an element which bravely sustains the claim of industry and practical progress, and has given Americans the least reason to regret that America is cosmopolitan.

THE MIRROR, MANCHESTER, N. H.

A SKETCH FOR THE BOOK OF THE CENTENNIAL NEWSPAPER EXHIBITION.

The Manchester DAILY MIRROR was founded in 1850, and the WEEKLY MIRROR in 1851, by Joseph C. Emerson. In October, 1852, both papers were purchased by John B. Clark, who has owned, edited, and published them ever since. As the MIRROR grew in strength and influence, its owner purchased and his establishment absorbed the *Daily American*, the *Weekly American*, and the *New Hampshire Journal of Agriculture*, all of which are now comprised and published under the MIRROR headings. The MIRROR AND AMERICAN and the WEEKLY MIRROR AND FARMER are the most successful journals in New Hampshire. From the start money has been spent upon them with a free hand in every department, which, with liberal dealings with friends and patrons, has put them far in advance of all rivals, and given them a circulation, influence, and advertising patronage which no other even claims.

Manchester, New Hampshire, is the fifty-fifth city in population in the United States, according to the last census—larger than any two other cities in New Hampshire. It is fifty-two miles from Boston, and is devoted to manufacturing. Its corporations employ nine thousand persons, and have a monthly pay-roll of THREE HUNDRED AND ELEVEN THOUSAND DOLLARS. They use every year twenty-six thousand and one hundred tons of coal, eight thousand cords of wood, and about thirty million feet of gas. The mills have about three hundred thousand spindles, and make *one hundred and forty-three miles of cloth a day*. The Manchester Locomotive Works can turn out fourteen locomotives a month, and the Amoskeag Manufacturing Company fifty steam fire-engines a year.

To make a paper worthy of such a city, and one which should find its way into nearly every family, and be authorized to speak for and to the substantial and intelligant citizens has been the aim of the publisher of the MIRROR, and that he has succeeded the subscription books and daily sales of the paper fully prove. The DAILY MIRROR AND AMERICAN is an evening paper, issuing three editions each afternoon, and has a larger circulation than any other two dailies in the State.

The WEEKLY MIRROR AND FARMER is an eight-page sheet, of forty-eight columns, and is a general news and agricultural paper. Its first and second pages are devoted to farming interests, and are filled with live and readable matter, which gives it a welcome, and makes it authority in a large proportion of the farm-houses of New Hampshire and Vermont.

The other six pages are devoted to news, editorials, selections, and advertisements, so written and arranged as to give timely and bold expression to the convictions and opinions of honest people, and to present a complete and reliable record of the world's work, wisdom, worry, and wickedness during each week.

The paper owns no man as master, and is the slave of no sect or party. It speaks for its readers openly, freely, and without fear or favor. Its system of news gathering is nearly complete, and in the department of State news particularly, its numerous correspondents and reporters, and a free use of the telegraph enable it to keep far in advance of its rivals. These features have introduced the MIRROR, and make it a household word among all who are interested in New Hampshire news and have a liking for an independent and outspoken organ of public opinion.

It reaches, in large clubs, nearly every town in the State, and many in Vermont and Maine, and has not only an aggregate circulation larger than any other paper in the State, but larger than any other one of its class published in New England, out of Boston. Its circulation is a natural and healthy one. It employs no agents to crowd it into places where it is not welcome, and is not sent to any man who has not paid for it. Its friends are such of their own volition, because it meets their wants and approves itself to their judgment; and they are friends who, when once they come, are sure to stay. The MIRROR is by far the best advertising medium to be found in New Hampshire. Its rates are less than three-fourths of a cent a line for each thousand circulation.

THE CLEVELAND HERALD.

A SKETCH FOR THE BOOK OF THE CENTENNIAL NEWSPAPER EXHIBITION.

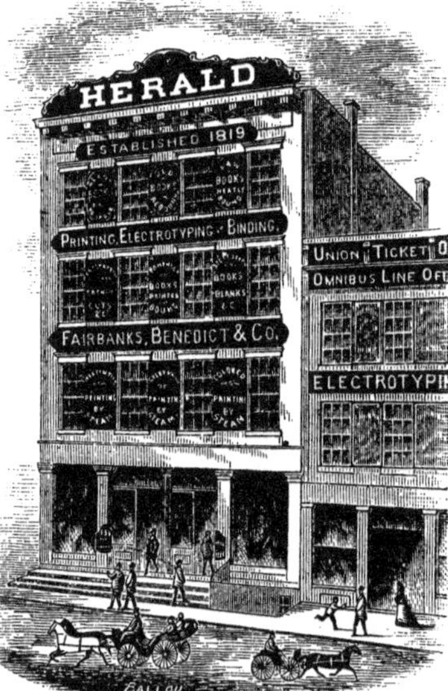

The prosperity and growth of a country can be estimated very fairly by its newspapers. The growth of the West, or what was a few years ago known as the West, has been beyond belief. Cleveland has increased since 1830 to the present time, from a small village to a city of 175,000 inhabitants. The HERALD, the oldest paper here, was established in 1819, and has done much to forward the progress of this section of Ohio, and has steadily kept pace with that increase. It was started as a weekly, on a small sheet, and continued so until 1837, when it was issued daily. It has been since that time a prosperous paper, until now its aggregate circulation exceeds that of any paper in Northern Ohio, and is printed on one of Hoe's Rotary Presses, eight pages, the size of the New York *Herald*. The engraving represents the office, built and occupied by the proprietors some twenty years since, and is divided and conveniently arranged for the various departments of its large business. The counting room and stock room are on the first floor. The press and engine rooms are in the basement, which contain besides the newspaper presses, folding machines, and duplicate boilers and engines, almost precluding the possibility of a delay of our publications from accident to our machinery. The editorial rooms and composing rooms are on the second floor. The three stories above are used for jobbing, book binding, electrotyping, &c. There are thirteen presses used in job printing, besides a large number of machines for paper cutting, card cutting, perforating, embossing, &c. In fact, it is one of the most complete offices of its size in the country.

THE STATE REGISTER, DES MOINES.

THE LEADING PAPER IN IOWA.

A SKETCH FOR THE BOOK OF THE CENTENNIAL NEWSPAPER EXHIBITION.

Iowa, the young giant of a State which rose almost into instant greatness, springing from an Indian hunting ground in 1840 into a rich State of nearly a million and a half of people in 1876, has found always its most potential adjutant in its press. The good story sent out to the world by the Iowa press of the fair fortune there awaiting honest industry, drew to the fertile prairies an emigration of reading, cultured, enterprising people, who naturally became, in turn, the stimulating patrons of the press. In keeping pace with the bounding energies and wonderfully rapid development of the State, the press was fairly forced into early prominence, influence, and wealth. At the head of the vigorous papers of the vigorous young State has stood for ten years the STATE REGISTER, published at Des Moines, the capital—which stirring young city, an Indian camping ground in 1848, is now a place of 20,000 people, with all the modern appointments of civilization, gas, water works, many and large manufactories, and five railways. Located at the geographical, political, and business centre of the State, the REGISTER enjoys the benefit of commanding position and superior advantages—and, with double the circulation of any of its Iowa contemporaries, circulates largely in every county in the State, and goes abroad in the Union and to other countries as the representative Iowa paper. It has no competitor in Iowa as a newspaper or as an advertising medium. The daily edition is a large thirty-six column, four-page sheet, the largest paper and giving the largest amount of news and reading matter of any paper in the world, published in a city of 20,000 inhabitants. The weekly edition is a mammoth forty-column sheet of four pages; it sustains, in addition to its other features, an agricultural department, edited by C. F. Clarkson, a practical farmer, and an old-time editor—who makes his department an authority with Iowa farmers, and a necessity to them, thus giving it an immense circulation among that especial class.

The REGISTER is known in newspaper circles to be the most valuable press property in the Northwest, outside of Chicago. It occupies a home—and as its own home—a fine brick building 22x100 feet in size, with three stories besides basement, all of which the establishment occupies. There is maintained with the paper the largest book and job printing offices in the State, which for years have done and are now doing the State printing. The REGISTER, its machinery, and building are estimated at a total value of $150,000, and that money would not buy them, cash down. The paper is now printed on a double cylinder Hoe press, made expressly for it, but which will soon have to be superseded by one of double its capacity. The first aim of the STATE REGISTER is to be a paper of news, next of politics, third of business, then of literature—always of life and vivacity. It is conducted on the live idea of never being found dull. Its proprietors—both young men, just turned into the thirties—are enthusiasts in their profession, and enamored of their paper. They were both raised in a printing office, and their lives and ambition are in their work. This inspiration is the working motto of their subordinates, and every editor and every reporter has as much pride in the paper and its success as the proprietors have. The paper has but two owners, R. P. Clarkson, the business manager, and J. S. Clarkson, the chief editor. The money they have invested in this now valuable property is of their own gaining, earned by hard work and sheer business tact. The young proprietors of an old, fairly-established, popular, and profitable paper, they will keep the property permanently and improve it daily.

The pride of the paper is in its State and city. To the upbuilding, advancement, and progress of both it lends every effort and every energy. In politics the paper is radical republican. But it has been guilty frequently of bolting bad nominations which its party has made. In all things the REGISTER, as a constant and long-time reader of it would judge, proposes to have the independence and vigor of the prairie—to be always worth the money paid for it by anybody—to hold unrivalled excellence in its own State as a paper of news—to be the best possible advertising medium within the territory of its circulation--and, generally, to be the best and best paying paper of its size and field in the country.

INDEPENDENT STATESMAN, CONCORD, N.H.

A SKETCH FOR THE BOOK OF THE CENTENNIAL NEWSPAPER EXHIBITION.

STATESMAN BUILDING.

The INDEPENDENT STATESMAN is a large eight-page paper, Republican in politics, and fearless in the advocacy of its principles. It pleads earnesly for reform, in its truest sense, and for the restoration of the government to the purity of the fathers. In its own State it occupies the foremost position as to all the elements that combine to make a desirable country newspaper, and in the ability shown in its editorial columns. Its agricultural and miscellaneous departments are especially attractive, and its full State news makes it widely sought for both in and out of the State. In short, its fine qualities have steadily advanced it in the estimation of the people, so that it has reached a circulation (10,000) almost unequalled for a country newspaper. It was established in the year 1823. REPUBLICAN PRESS ASSOCIATION, Publishers. EDWARD A. JENKS, Manager.

The DAILY MONITOR, established in 1863, is one-half the size of the weekly. It finds a generous circulation in the city of Concord and the county of Merrimack.

THE NEW YORK EVANGELIST.

A SKETCH FOR THE BOOK OF THE CENTENNIAL NEWSPAPER EXHIBITION.

The NEW YORK EVANGELIST is in the forty-seventh year ot its publication. Its career has been a prominent one. It sprang at once into conspicuity as the champion of the rising cause of the slave and of temperance reform, and especially as the advocate of revivals and of a greater tolerance of new methods of aggression on the part of the Churches.

Its early years were marked by great movements of population, as well as by the earnest discussion of social and religious questions. The Erie Canal was then a new and gigantic improvement—the wonder and pride of the whole North. It was the chief channel of our Western trade. It brought wheat and corn and furs to tide-water, and returned their equivalent. It also served as an highway and outlet for the enterprising young families of New England. They crowded its jaunty packets and settled along its borders; while many of the older residents of the region, feeling the general impulse of our westward-moving empire, covered their stout wagons with canvass and took up the long march to Ohio or remoter Michigan. (It was in the growing villages and cities of this new theatre of commercial activity that the late President Finney won his greatest successes and most enduring fruits as a preacher of the Gospel. It is also worthy of mention here that his celebrated Lectures on Revivals were reported for and published exclusively in this paper.)

Sprung of fathers who had borne the burden and heat of the day in revolutionary times, and in the later war with the mother country, these thrifty sons of freedom had, for the most part, the consciousness of a responsibility for the moral and intellectual culture of their growing communities beyond their own well-ordered families; and material and moral progress followed in their track as they came from New England, Eastern New York, New Jersey, and Pennsylvania. Churches and schools sprang up where lately only the dense and silent forests stood.

Religiously of several denominations, the Presbyterian and Congregational elements predominated, and these, under the then "Plan of the Union," made common cause, and the NEW YORK EVANGELIST, under the able conduct of the late Dr. Joshua Lavitt, became their great mouthpiece.

Recognized and sustained by such a people—the first and best of their communities—at a time when men's minds were beginning to be deeply stirred in view of the wrongs of slavery, and by other questions already hinted, and standing firmly to these councils of charity and humanity, and of progress as well, in later years, when the "war of words" gave place to the more terrible "arbitrament of the sword;" and withal never abating one jot of heart and hope in all the long struggle which followed—the NEW YORK EVANGELIST is enabled to look back from the vantage ground of this Centennial Year with devout thanks to God, and sincere congratulations to its many readers. It has no reason to be ashamed of its record.

Since the war and the auspicious reunion of the two Assemblies of the Presbyterian Church—which reunion this paper promoted with all its power—the great Evangelical Churches, as well as the Nation, seem to be entering upon a new era—one that betokens their enlargement and a corresponding increase of moral influence. And surely the remaining problems to be solved ere the prayer of our risen Lord shall be brought to pass, are such as can be best, yea, only successfully dealt with by the more general reception of the Gospel itself. It is the only real solvent and unifyer of the nations that are now for the first time, by reason of swift-flying ships and trains, face to face with each other. The EVANGELIST, in common with an increasing number in all the Churches, looks to see the great wealth and material resources which have originated quite within the span of its own life, not selfishly hoarded, but more and more freely given to the furtherance of the Gospel and kingdom of Jesus Christ.

Identified with a particular corps of our Lord's militant host, the EVANGELIST is quite content with these relations. It loves the order and strength of the Presbyterian Church, and seeks the things that make for her peace and progress. Mindful of its name and origin, it will continue to labor for and welcome the return of such ingatherings as marked the time of Edwards, Whitefield, and Finney—such as shall purifiy the social, commercial, and political relations of the whole nation. It is taken chiefly by ministers and the more intelligent and reliable Church members. It has lost many old subscribers by reason of death, but the children's names have taken the place of the fathers. They have carried it from their early Eastern homes to the Rocky Mountains, and beyond. It seeks to extend its circulation everywhere throughout the Presbyterian Church. No longer shut out of the South, it asks for new friends there as well as at the North and West.

Any complete catalogue of the names of those who have from time to time become recognized as contributors to this paper would require several pages of this publication. They are, or were, our best known ministers and laymen. It is hardly necessary to add that the best and ablest pens will continue to be employed in its columns, and all the features of a first-class religious and family paper will be maintained. It comments upon a wide range of topics, from its proper point of view, and will include, as heretofore, a large variety of miscellaneous and literary reading, and its special departments for the children, the Sunday school, and readers interested in rural and scientific information. Its subscription price is three dollars a year.

An especially attractive feature of the EVANGELIST for coming months (as for a full year past) will be the letters of its editor-in-chief, Rev. Henry M. Field, on his way around the world. It is seldom that a series of letters have been so generally quoted by the press of the country, and so constantly referred to as a source of instruction and delight, both in the editorial and business correspondence of the paper. We may add that it is probable, in response to the wishes thus expressed, that their author will issue them in a more permanent form on his return home.

When last heard from, Dr. Field was just quitting India. And we cannot better close this brief and inadequate sketch of the journal which he has managed now for more than twenty years (with the assistance of his partners, the Rev. Wm. Bradford a short and Dr. J. G. Craighead a longer time), than by quoting the closing paragraph of the last letter to hand from that remote quarter. Dr. Field writes:

"And here I take leave of the readers of the EVANGELIST for several weeks, as we are just 'launching off' from this part of Asia into what seems almost like boundless space. On Monday morning, the 13th of March, we leave India for Burmah. Crossing the Bay of Bengal we shall proceed first to Rangoon, and then down the coast to Maulmain, Malacca, Penange, and Singapore, stopping a day or two at each point, and thus taking in the whole voyage seventeen days—twice as long as it took us to cross the Atlantic. From Singapore we may go up the Gulf of Siam to Bangkok, or proceed direct to Hong Kong. At Singapore we are almost exactly on the opposite side of the globe from the longitude of New York. In due time we hope to emerge from this wilderness of islands and oceans, and come around on 'the right side' of the planet, which is, of course, the American side. Our letters will hereafter go East across the Pacific, instead of West across India, and Egypt, and Europe, and the Atlantic.

"THE WATCHMAN," BOSTON, MASS.

A SKETCH FOR THE BOOK OF THE CENTENNIAL NEWSPAPER EXHIBITION.

The WATCHMAN is, with a single exception, the oldest religious weekly newspaper in the United States. In character and in reputation, in quality as in age, it is the first journal of its denomination. It was founded in 1819, and is, therefore, now in its fifty-seventh year.

The *Christian Watchman*, the original paper, was the only Baptist journal in New England until 1840. In that year the *Christian Reflector* was established. The two papers were united in 1848, under the double name of *Watchman and Reflector*. The new journal grew in popularity, under the editorship of Rev. John W. Olmstead, D.D., and the efficient business management of Mr. D. S. Ford, now of the *Youth's Companion*, until in 1867 its circulation was more than 20,000 copies. In that year a new departure was taken. The paper was doubled in size and became the first to assume the eight-page form now so common with the religious weeklies. The *Christian Era*, another Baptist paper, which was moved from Lowell to Boston in 1856, being more radical than its older brother, divided with him the patronage of New England until the close of 1875, when both papers were purchased by a corporation of laymen and united under the present new, yet good old name—the WATCHMAN. The combined lists of the two papers gives the new journal a circulation larger, with one exception, than that of any other Baptist organ in the world. The WATCHMAN, though its special field is New England, goes largely into every State and Territory of the Union. It has readers in every civilized country on the globe.

"THE WATCHMAN" BUILDING.

Our space will not allow us even to mention the men, good and true, who either by their editorial or business services have contributed to the stability and prosperity of the paper. At present its editorial staff consists of Rev. John W. Olmstead, D. D., who has been connected with the paper for thirty years; Rev. Franklin Johnson, D. D., of Cambridge; Rev. George C. Lorimer, D. D., pastor of Fremont Temple, Boston; Prof. Heman Lincoln, D. D., of Newton Theological Institution; Rev. W. N. Clarke; Mr. J. B. Houser; and Mr. Thomas L. Rogers. Rev. Granville S. Abbott has charge of the Sunday School Department, and the Family Department is under the supervision of the well-known authoress, Mrs. Jane Dunbar Chaplin. Mr. T. L. Rogers is the business manager, and the office of the WATCHMAN is at the "Headquarters of New England Baptists," Tremont Temple, a cut of which building accompanies this sketch.

THE KANSAS CITY TIMES.

THE REPRESENTATIVE JOURNAL OF THE "NEW WEST."

A SKETCH FOR THE BOOK OF THE CENTENNIAL NEWSPAPER EXHIBITION.

The New York "Herald of the West."—The Kansas City TIMES' *fast newspaper train, carrying early copies of that paper between Kansas City and Topeka during the session of the Legislature, January,* 1876.

It has required decades and the lives of many men to establish the reputation now enjoyed by the metropolitan papers of this country. Until within a very few years no journal west of the city of St. Louis, Mo., has come in for a position in the catalogue of newspapers now occupying prominent places. And so many are the obstacles in the way of accomplishing this that there is but one instance where it has been done. This exception is the Kansas City TIMES. Other newspapers in its section are older, but beyond their naturally legitimate section they are unknown and have achieved nothing beyond local influence and reputation. That the Kansas City TIMES has leaped beyond the ordinary groove and become something greater may seem marvelous to the average reader of remote sections, but the fact can be attested by leading journals of the country, by the official figures given of its circulation by what is recognized authority in journalistic circles, and by the immense advertising patronage from abroad which has sought its columns.

THE SPIRIT OF ITS PRESENT MANAGEMENT.

In 1871 the TIMES was purchased by the present management and organized as a corporation into what is now known as the Kansas City Times Company, with M. Munford as business manager. Prior to that the paper had been nothing beyond what its contemporaries were. The new management saw the field which was presented. In the whole domain of a country that is fertile and populous —a country that has excited the curiosity and admiration of the most distinguished tourists—which occupies the scope that stretches from the western bank of the Mississippi up into the range of the Rocky mountains—there was not a single paper which had a metropolitan feature. By nature Kansas City seemed to be the gateway of the western continent, and from the summit of one of its hills the statesman Benton had prophesied that here one day the commerce of the East would meet the trade of the wide West and that of India. What was then considered a poetic fancy has been almost literally verified. Here the railways of the East and West have centered. From here they have branched out in every direction, and all along the innumberable lines are towns, villages and cities that are daily opening up the fertile lands adjacent, which are being occupied by a class equal in intelligence and refinement to the older sections of the Union. Kansas City being the chief entre-port of the immense trade coming from all of these, the capitalist has established himself here, and immense elevators have become necessary for the accommodation of the almost fabulous cereals of a country the most productive and progressive under the sun. Texas and the Indian Territory being the chief grazing grounds of the land, and being in direct communication by rail with Kansas City, here are established the largest beef and pork packing establishments in the United States, from which are yearly exported direct to Liverpool immense quantities of bulk meats. These facts, in addition to the mercantile houses which have to supply to a great extent the wants of the towns and minor cities on the various railroads leading here, made the point one of the most favorable in the West for the establishment of a first-class daily paper that would be metropolitan in all its appointments. From 1871 to the present time such a strict and rigid adherence to this idea has been kept up that the intended results has already been achieved, until the TIMES is invariably alluded to by its many contemporaries as the "New York *Herald* of the West." Upon assuming control of the paper the new management put in steam-power presses to supply on time the increase which commenced at once to its subscription lists. The TIMES became recognized at this point as the leading morning paper of the city. Its make up, its resume of daily news from neighboring vicinities, its special telegrams, which were first introduced by it in the West, made it the very foremost in the ranks of Western journalism. When this was established the ultimate result was attempted, and the success was not only attained but so suddenly did the paper leap to that station that its political opponents of their own accord pronounced it a marvel of enterprise, carrying with it a dash which caused it to make inroads upon the circulations of its St. Louis contemporaries.

ITS POLITICAL INFLUENCE AND STANDING.

At the State capital it became the recognized organ of its—the Democratic—party of the State, and its opinions and views were quoted by the law-makers of the commonwealth. As wonderful as this appeared to the larger and older papers of Western cities, it was eclipsed by the TIMES crossing the border and entering the State of Kansas, where it at once surpassed in circulation and influence every daily paper there, and to-day it is delivered in the leading cities of that State, by carriers, almost as early as the morning papers of those cities. Its general circulation in that State exceeds the combined circulation of all the dailies of Kansas. This is a step in advance of any newspaper west of the Alleghany mountains. It stands out as especially creditable to the TIMES, in consideration of the fact that while the paper is fearlessly and ably Democratic the State of Kansas is overwhelmingly Republican in sentiment. To gain a foothold under such circumstances as these is a triumph which the oldest and ablest paper of the seaboard might well wish to achieve and wear with pride. In accomplishing this the TIMES has won the confidence of the people of Kansas, because its policy has never been adverse to the interests of that State, because it contains the latest and freshest news, and because it has stood by the reform movement there in all of its endeavors to root out a nest of political corruptionists that took possession of its State affairs only to plunder. Every *expose* of fraud and corruption that has been made is credited to the vigilance and ability of the TIMES.

THE TIMES' ANNUAL REVIEW.

Another feature which was introduced by the TIMES, and has been steadily kept up, is its mammoth yearly review of the commerce, trade, and growth of its city and the circle of country tributary to it. So popular has this feature become, that on the first of the present year its review was the largest ever issued—surpassing those of St. Louis—covering twenty pages of closely-printed matter, accompanied by fifty-two distinctive cuts of public buildings, a mammoth view of the Great Union Stock Yards, all printed on the finest paper. The circulation of this review was over and above that of anything similar ever issued from a Western press. So complete was it, and so gigantic an undertaking that the columns of the papers of the West, South, and even many of the metropolitan papers teemed with encomiums, which have been collected and are now issued in a neat volume.

THE TIMES' FAST NEWSPAPER TRAIN.

When all of these features had been perfected, and the TIMES had achieved that which its management had foreshadowed upon their accession to it, the public seemed to be content, and as the TIMES had become a visitor in every hamlet and metropolitan in all of its workings, there appeared to be nothing beyond except a maintainance of what its energy had wrought. It was at this juncture that the managers conceived another feature which, when it was announced would have been discredited had not the public become convinced that every advance made by the paper had been carried to the front. This was none other than the starting of a daily fast newspaper train of its own between Kansas City and Topeka, the capital of Kansas, the same to be continued during the legislative session at the latter city. This was a dash in advance of any paper in the United States. The New York *Herald* had its fast Sunday newspaper train, and the Chicago *Times* had one which it run between that city and Milwaukee once a week. But the Kansas City TIMES, a paper which had come into existence years after the reputation of both the former had been established, conceived the idea of running a fast newspaper train of its own, at its own expense, daily, between its city and the capital of Kansas. The illustration which is embodied in this article will probably convey a more accurate idea of this train than language can do. The first trip was made January 11, 1876, and it continued to run consecutively for fifty-five successive days. The time card was so arranged that the TIMES arrived in Topeka and was delivered there—as it was at all intermediate points—by early breakfast and many hours in advance of the regular mail. Returning, the train brought back the full legislative proceedings of the day, thus giving the readers of the section where the TIMES circulated on the following morning a full and carefully prepared account of the proceedings of the Legislature.

This extraordinary movement on the part of the managers of the TIMES eclipsed every former attempt at enterprise by the papers of the country, and proved conclusively, if the fact had ever been doubted, that the TIMES was so successfully established that it had moved far beyond the line which bounds the existence of ordinary journalism. If the manmoth review had caused a flutter, the fast newspaper train had created a furore, and for weeks after the train had commenced its runs the press of the entire West and many of the papers of the East and South were munificent in their awards of praise to the enterprise of the Kansas City TIMES. This was continued until the encomiums reached a bulk equal to ten columns of leaded minion type of the paper. During the entire session of the Legislature not a delay or accident occured, and on the day of adjournment a free excursion, consisting of ten coaches, to the Kansas Capitol, was given by the managers of the TIMES. To this were invited the city officials of Kansas City, prominent citizens, and the press of Missouri and Kansas.

The expense of the newspaper train was borne by the TIMES alone, and amounted in the aggregate to more than the value of an ordinary Western newspaper.

RESULTS OF ITS ENTERPRISE.

To show how the enterprise was appreciated, and the additional interest taken in a paper of such energy elsewhere, the circulation was argumented to such an enormous extent that the press facilities were unable to supply the demand in time for the various out-going trains. There was no delay in meeting this emergency. The want was seen and felt, and in due time a new two-cylinder Hoe press was purchased and placed in position, being the first and only one used by any newspaper between St. Louis and San Francisco. This enterprise was again heralded by the press of the country, and another laurel was twined about the most enterprising newspaper west of Chicago.

THE LEADING JOURNAL OF THE "NEW WEST."

Thus in five years, with capital, determination, unexampled spirit and appreciated ability, the Kansas City TIMES has become a newspaper of national reputation, a mark—with due deference to the press of its section—not achieved by any between St. Louis and San Francisco. Having reached this point, there can be no retrograde. In its course there has been no failure. Every adventure thus far has been attended with all of the elements of increase. It stands to-day the only recognized first-class daily in its city, with a working force on the same plan as those of the great dailies of the larger cities. The leading Democratic organ of its own State, though not published in the State's metropolis. The great newspaper of the State of Kansas, and of that vast fertile region known as the "New West," and the first in every respect beyond the Mississippi river, its circulation extending into the Territories and penetrating the leading sections of Texas.

This brief review of the Kansas City TIMES makes its own showing. It has not a parallel in the annals of journalism, and establishes the reputation, and rivets it securely, that it is the only great newspaper conducted on a metropolitan plan west of the metropolis of its own State.

THE PORTLAND TRANSCRIPT.

A SKETCH FOR THE BOOK OF THE CENTENNIAL NEWSPAPER EXHIBITION.

The Portland (Me.) TRANSCRIPT, a weekly literary and family journal, was started in April, 1836, by Charles P. Isley, who had the editorial management of it for about ten years. In 1848 it came into the hands of Erastus E. Gould and Edward H. Elwell, the latter assuming its editorial management. In consequence of ill health Mr. Gould retired from the firm in 1856, and the paper has since been published by Mr. Elwell and Messrs. Samuel T. and Charles W. Pickard, under the firm name of Elwell, Pickard & Co. Mr. Elwell has had an unbroken editorial connection with it for nearly twenty-eight years, Mr. Samuel T. Pickard has been connected with its management for twenty-three years, and Mr. Charles W. Pickard for sixteen years. From the first the TRANSCRIPT has maintained a high position as a first-class literary weekly. Among its contributors are many who have made a name in the literary world, and are now valued contributors to the first periodicals of the day. It has reached a well-deserved rank among family papers, as much by its high moral tone as by the excellence of its original and carefully selected matter. In addition to its original stories, sketches, essays, poems and reviews, it gives a condensed summary of the news of the State and the county, as well as market reports and commercial reviews. Faithful to good principles and the best interests of the State, it is received and appreciated by thousands of families, to whom it is a most valuable auxiliary in the education of the rising generation; giving tone and vigor to the essential elements which are the bulwarks of the country. In the course of its history of forty years it has absorbed a considerable number of other journals which ran well for a season, and now stands upon a consolidated basis as wide as the limits of our country. Its subscribers are found in every State in the Union, and its subscription list has reached a point surpassing any other in the State by thousands. It has a limited space devoted to advertisements, and its great circulation makes it the best possible medium for business men desiring to attract attention. It has the best and most convenient newspaper office in the city, where its publishers are always pleased to receive their friends.

THE ARGUS, ALBANY, N. Y.

A SKETCH FOR THE BOOK OF THE CENTENNIAL NEWSPAPER EXHIBITION.

For more than sixty years the Albany ARGUS has held a prominent place among the most eminent and leading journals of the country. It was founded January 26, 1813, by Jesse Buel, a man of culture and practical business training. Although Albany was then, as now, the capital of New York, its population was less than the last census gives to the smallest of the twenty-four cities of the State. The paper, however, was from the start a recognized power in the country. It gave a vigorous and cordial support to the war then raging between the United States and Great Britain, and did all in its power to strengthen and uphold the Administration of President Madison. Its patriotic course in this and other respects secured for it a strong hold upon the public confidence.

Mr. Buel conducted the paper until 1820, when it passed into the hands of Moses I. Cantine (a brother-in-law of Martin Van Buren) and Isaac Q. Leake. Three years afterwards Mr. Cantine died, and its proprietorship experienced another change. It was this circumstance that brought Edwin Croswell to Albany. He had for some years conducted a weekly paper in Catskill, Greene county, and being a former neighbor of Mr. Cantine he came to Albany to attend his funeral. Before returning home he was offered the editorship of the ARGUS. He accepted, purchased the interest held by the Cantine estate, and the ARGUS was launched upon a career of increased prosperity. This was in the winter of 1823. Mr. Leake soon afterwards retired, leaving Mr. Croswell the sole owner. Like his predecessors, Messrs. Buel and Cantine, Mr. Croswell was made State printer. The ARGUS was started as a semi-weekly, and was so published until October 18, 1825, when it made its appearance as a daily morning paper—a stretch of enterprise at that time, but a step which was warranted by the subsequent success it secured. From this time the ARGUS assumed a character and position not before accorded to it. Martin Van Buren, Silas Wright, William L. Marcy, and other statesmen, who afterwards wielded great power in the country, were just forcing their way to the front rank of national politics. The ARGUS was the organ of this new element of political power, and when it spoke there was meaning and significance in every line and sentence. This combination soon became known far and wide as the "Albany Regency." In the course of a few years the men composing it reached the highest places in the National and State governments.

In those days the three pre-eminently great Democratic newspapers of the country were the Albany ARGUS, the Washington *Globe* and the Richmond *Enquirer*—Croswell, Blair, and Ritchie. Whatever party programme was agreed upon by this triumvirate, it were needless to oppose. They were strong with their party and with the country. Years of continued success and prosperity furnished evidence of their wisdom and ability. During all those years the ARGUS made a record for itself which can be contemplated with unvarying satisfaction. It advocated and supported the leading measures of the Administrations of the government to which men now of all parties revert with pride—the Administrations of Madison, Monroe, Jackson, Van Buren, and Polk.

On the 19th of April, 1854, Mr. Croswell retired from the paper, having had the editorial management of it for a period of thirty years. He was succeeded by Sherman Croswell. In 1855 this gentleman was succeeded by Calvert Comstock, and in 1856 the *Atlas* and ARGUS were united, and Calvert Comstock and William Cassidy became editors and proprietors. In 1865 Mr. Comstock retired on account of impaired health, and the ARGUS COMPANY was organized, William Cassidy being President and editor-in-chief, and Daniel Manning and J. Wesley Smith associates. In January, 1873, Mr. Cassidy died in the midst of his editorial labors. His career is fresh in the minds of the thousands who were accustomed to watch for his brilliant articles. His style was peculiarly his own—eloquent, original, and sparkling. Mr. Manning succeeded Mr. Cassidy. The present owners of the ARGUS are Daniel Manning, Mrs. William Cassidy, J. Wesley Smith, and William H. Johnson.

At no time in its history has the circulation of the ARGUS been so large as at present, or its prospects brighter for a long and prosperous career. As in its past history, so it is now the recognized exponent of democratic principles and democratic policy.

The ARGUS has three editions—Daily, Semi-Weekly, and Weekly. Its patrons are to be found in every section of the country, and are rapidly increasing, thus inviting the patronage of advertisers and business men. Its market reports are made a specialty, and are unsurpassed for completeness and accuracy.

THE ARGUS BUILDING.

The ARGUS building is located on the corner of Broadway and Beaver street. The structure has a front of forty-five feet on Broadway, eighty-five feet on Beaver street, and is five stories high. The entire building is occupied by the extensive printing establishment of the ARGUS COMPANY. The building is supplied with elevators operated by steam, and possesses all the accommodations for conducting a great newspaper. It has recently been greatly enlarged and improved. It occupies a site which is one of the most attractive in the city. Located on Broadway, just below its junction with State street, it commands a complete view of Broadway to the Delavan House on the north, and to the steamboat landing on the south. The new post-office in course of erection by the Federal Government is located within twenty rods, and in full view of the ARGUS building.

The terms of the ARGUS are: Daily, $10 per annum; Semi-Weekly, $3 per annum; Weekly, $1 50 per annum. The usual reduction made to clubs.

"THE WORLD," NEW YORK.

A SKETCH FOR THE BOOK OF THE CENTENNIAL NEWSPAPER EXHIBITION.

"THE WORLD" BUILDING.

THE WORLD building is on the site of the old brick church, and its proximity to the new Post-office and its situation at the angle of Park Row and Beekman street, with entrances to the publication office on both streets, give it the most eligible newspaper location on Printing House square.

This great journal was established June 14, 1860, and announced in its first issue that it would be "independent in politics." In July, 1861, it united with itself the New York *Courier and Enquirer*, one of the oldest and most respectable journals in the city. Enormous sums of money were expended, but THE WORLD was not a success till it was purchased, April 12, 1862, by Mr. Manton Marble who had been connected with it since its establishment. He at once made it a Democratic journal, devoted to the time-honored principles of "Hard money, free trade, and home rule." He parted with a portion of the stock of the paper to influential Democratic associates, retaining, however, a controlling interest and always having exclusive management, with no interference, of every department. In January, 1864, he bought back the shares he had sold, and so became the sole proprietor and editor of the paper.

Manton Marble is a born journalist. Almost immediately after his graduation at Rochester University, in 1855, he went to Boston, where he joined the staff of the *Journal*, and soon afterward became the responsible editor of the Boston *Traveller*. In 1858 he joined the staff of the New York

Evening Post, to which he was attracted by its free-trade principles, and remained in that position till THE WORLD was established. He was but twenty-seven years old when he assumed the entire control of THE WORLD, which, under his management, at once became a powerful journal, and has long since been generally conceded to be "the leading Democratic journal in the Union."

Mr. Marble's high standard of professional duty and professional accomplishments enabled him from the first to draw around him a staff surpassed by that of no other journal in the country. When he assumed the management of the WORLD large sums had been sunk in the enterprise, and it was regarded by many persons as past redemption. He inspired his associates with his confidence in its future, boldly increased its outlays for news, enlarged and reorganized its working force in all departments, poured into it all the resources of scholarship and ability at his command, and in a very short time compelled the public to recognize its power and authority, both as an organ of opinion and a vehicle of information on all subjects of real and vital interest to the community. The verdict of the press and public of the United States has long ago been recorded, and is but echoed by the latest foreign critic of our metropolitan journalism, who has recently said of the WORLD in the columns of the leading conservative journal of Great Britain that "it has the ablest, wittiest and most scholarly editorial writers in the city of New York. Its money article," adds the same observer, "is confessedly the ablest in any of the city journals. It wants free trade, hard money and home rule; and is the organ of the Northern Democrats, with principles broad enough for all sections."

In addition to its daily, semi-weekly, and weekly editions, THE WORLD publishes a special Sunday paper. The first number was issued April 5, 1868, and it at once attained great popularity from its introduction of features which the pressure of news and advertisements on week days did not admit. It is, of course, a regular continuance of the daily issue; but the Sunday issue is greater by some thousands than that of any other day, from the fact that there are thousands who buy and read a paper on no other day, and the SUNDAY WORLD is the most popular of all the Sunday papers. Among its salient specialties are always delightful dramatic feuilletons and entertaining communications from regular contributors. The Sunday editorials, too, are generally non-political and devoted to social topics; and with all, there is a vast amount of most interesting miscellaneous matter.

The WEEKLY WORLD, at the astonishing low price of one dollar a year, with extra inducements to clubs, is unquestionably the best and cheapest newspaper in the United States. Instead of being, like many weekly issues of the metropolitan dailies, a hastily pitched-together jumble of matter standing on the galleys, it is a carefully and specially prepared journal, with its special editor and assistants, under supervision of the Chief, and is, in fact, totally distinct from the daily, in these respects—that the news of the week is largely rewritten and condensed so as to give all that is important from all parts of the world, and special articles, agricultural and industrial, together with elaborate market reports, prepared expressly for this issue, are presented in the WEEKLY, which do not appear in the daily at all. There is always a "good story" for family reading, either orginal or selected from the best English, or translated from French or German magazines, the publication of which, of course, would be impossible in the daily, with much miscellany, giving the family days of reading till the next issue arrives, thus making the always welcome Weekly, as used to be said of Sherman's poor man's plaster, "good for a week back." Of course, the very latest news, including all the important telegrams and cablegrams of the day of publication are given, with the latest markets and quotations. The most salient editorials of the week, presenting THE WORLD'S views on all important political issues, are also presented, thus widely extending its influence in the effort to break down corruption and to unite the Democrats and Conservatives in the coming Presidential struggle, which is to decide the future destinies of the Republic. Its admirably edited Grange department makes it an especial favorite with the farmers of the West. As long ago as June, 1868, and apropos of the arrival of delegates from all parts of the country to the National Democratic convention in New York, the New York correspondent of the Boston *Courier* thus described the mere mechanical processes necessary to produce the issue of the WEEKLY WORLD.

* * * "The city casually 'done,' that is surfacewise, in a day or two, the curiosity of the newly-arrived delegate centers upon Tammany Hall, now rapidly completing, Central Park, which never will be finished so long as grass grows and water runs, and the office of the 'great daily' which has furnished the political pabulum and literary and news record for himself and his family far away. Of the daily he knows and sees little. It is the peculiarity of the rural regions to be content with a good weekly paper, and the weekly issues of the great dailies in the city are generally more widely known, and are more a force necessarily from their larger circulation, than the daily issues of the same journals. Down to Printing House square comes our inquisitive Delegate to see how the paper that comes to him once a week as a guide, philosopher and friend is manufactured. Not specially to see how the brain work is done in the top stories of those lofty buildings, but how the paper is printed, folded, mailed, and forwarded, Let us push by the cords upon cords of bundled paper that always block the sidewalk here and there on the square, the assumed right of the publishers tacitly admitted, even by policemen, to be superior to the right of way, and push down into the bowels of THE WORLD. It is six o'clock on Tuesday night. At this hour the counting room above is almost deserted, and the cars centering at City Hall Park are rapidly depleting that part of the city, for business men and clerks are going home to dinner. But from the comparatively quiet street, down, deep down in the basement of THE WORLD building, two stories underground, we come upon a busy scene indeed. The WEEKLY WORLD is just going to press. The steam engine is doing a driving business—that is, it is driving a ten-cylinder Hoe press, which, in turn, is driving at the rate of from thirty-two to thirty-six revolutions a minute, each revolution printing ten papers, or from three hundred and twenty to three hundred and sixty papers every minute. A foreman, assistant, ten feeders, oilers, lifters, and sundry other workers make this a lively corner in the huge cavern. But the engine drives also six folding machines, a man at each, each machine folding from 2,000 to 3,000 copies an hour, or an average say of 2,500 copies to each. From 6 p. m. till 12 m. runs press and folders, when the weekly rests and the daily goes to press. At 6½ o'clock next morning begins work on the weekly again, and press and folders run till 1 p. m., or about thirteen hours on this one issue. From the press room to the quite as busy bundling room, and here we find another foreman and twenty-four men who act as supplementary folders to the machines, folding an average of 600 copies each in an hour; and these with the bundlers, packers and baggers put up in packages of all sizes and in bags for the mail during the night and morning 135 bags, averaging 1,000 copies to the bag, or 135,000 copies for the twelve or thirteen hours' work. Delegate is astonished when he is told that the white paper for this single issue weighs about seven tons, would fill a room twenty feet square, and if pieced out sheet by sheet would extend a distance of about ninety-four miles."

This was written seven years ago, and is by no means an adequate description of the department at present. The largely increased circulation of all issues of THE WORLD, especially of the daily, have long ago necessitated the introduction of another gigantic Hoe press, so that both sides of the paper can now be printed simultaneously. Another and important advantage is that the paper can be put to press at a later hour, with later news, and yet catch the earliest mails, which is of especial importance to the daily morning issue. What is lost in the employment of a necessarily larger force is gained in time. All the latest machines for folding and mailing have been freely introduced, regardless of cost, and in all its appointments in this department THE WORLD office is thoroughly complete.

Since 1868 this establishment has annually issued the "THE WORLD ALMANAC," which is simply the most complete, concise, correct, and best Political Manual published in the United States.

THE EVENING STAR, WASHINGTON CITY.

A SKETCH FOR THE BOOK OF THE CENTENNIAL NEWSPAPER EXHIBITION.

In a greater degree perhaps than any newspaper in the country, THE WASHINGTON EVENING STAR is the exponent and representative of the interests of the city in which it is published. This has been its character from the beginning, and to this distinctive feature is largely due its present wide circulation and its high character as an advertising medium. Founded in 1852, it is by many years the oldest, as it is also the most popular and influential, of the many news papers published at the National Capital. The policy of giving the closest attention to local interests which was adopted by its founders has not only been adhered to, but still farther developed by its present management, into whose hands the paper came, by purchase, in 1867. Not only this, however. Immediately on assuming control they determined to solve the problem of publishing a daily news and business journal, strongly local in character, so cheap as to be within the means of the poorest citizen. yet so wide in its scope, so high in its aims, and so full and complete in all its departments as to meet the exacting demands of those wishing to keep posted in the daily doings of the whole world. To this end the largest and best attainable force of editors, reporters and correspondents is constantly employed, the telegraph is freely and liberally used, and the fastest and most powerful printing machinery is called into service. The result is a daily newspaper which literally goes into every household in the District of Columbia. It has indeed been conclusively established that THE STAR has more than three times as many subscribers and more than five times as many readers as any other daily paper published in Washington. And not this alone. Its regular permanent subscription list is believed to be larger than that of any evening paper in the United States, no matter where published, while its circulation is, in proportion to the population of the city where printed and circulated, the largest and fullest possessed by any newspaper in the world. It follows, therefore, that within the territory covered by its circulation it has no rival, nor anything approaching an equal, as a means of reaching the public. It has, in fact, passed into a maxim that "Every body in the District of Columbia who can read, reads THE STAR, and every one who advertises at all advertises in its columns." Yet it must not be thought that its circulation and influence are only local. It has a wide distribution through the mails, and in addition to this every issue of the paper is carefully read by the throngs of strangers constantly visiting the National Capital on business or for pleasure, and who constitute in a very large degree the wealthy and purchasing population of the different States and Territories; so that, while its field is in a marked degree local. it is nevertheless in the best sense cosmopolitan and uncircumscribed in its sphere.

But perhaps the history of this remarkably successful and popular journal can best be epitomized by stating the suggestive facts that it commenced its career in 1852 with less than $500 capital, was sold to its present proprietors for $100,000 cash in 1867, and is now held to be worth not less than a quarter of a million dollars. These figures tell the story of patience, of sound judgment, of well-directed energy and enterprise, of independent action, of fair dealing, of defence of popular rights, and of strong hold in public esteem, more plainly than a whole volume of words. It is doubtful, indeed, whether the history of journalism anywhere in the world can show, in all respects, a parallel to it.

THE HOUSEHOLD, BRATTLEBORO, VT.

A SKETCH FOR THE BOOK OF THE CENTENNIAL NEWSPAPER EXHIBITION.

The HOUSEHOLD has the honor of being the pioneer in its class of periodicals, it having been the first, and, for several years, the only journal published in the country entirely devoted to domestic affairs. It was founded in the belief that the literature previously furnished by the various "ladies magazines" and kindred publications, though occupying its appropriate sphere, and well-adapted to the needs of a large portion of its readers, was not such as to meet the requirements of those earnest working women who constitute so large a portion of the wives and daughters of our land, but that they needed something more practical in its nature, whose tendency should be to elevate that peculiar labor of caring for and managing the family, known by the general term of "housework," from a mere drudgery to a science, and at the same time extend the sympathizing hand to those who have a longing to make their home an index, as it were, of their characters—a reaching out for an attractiveness of surroundings which, with much or little expenditure, according to their means, shall attract and retain their husbands and friends, educate and refine the boys growing from youth to manhood, and cultivate a love for the good, the beautiful and the true in the daughters of the household, and in this way to make home, however humble, the dearest place and the family the happiest people.

Such is the aim and purpose of the HOUSEHOLD, and the generous and appreciative patronage it has received may be taken as good evidence that the faith of its projectors was well founded, especially in view of the fact that unlike many, if not all of the successful journals of the present day, it was in no sense a child of fortune, either by birth or adoption. It is a well-known saying that "it takes a fortune to establish a paper," and the history of nearly every prominent periodical bears witness to its truth, they having been founded or assisted by capitalists who were enabled to bring to their aid all the resources that wealth can supply, and thus command success from the outset. On the other hand, the HOUSEHOLD was of humble origin, reared in penury and schooled in the hardships and privations incident to the life of a country printer, and it has won its way from obscurity to its present position solely by hard labor and indomitable perseverance. Starting in January, 1868, with a subscription list of *thirteen*, with no capital to sustain it, and but little experience in newspaper life to guide and direct its hazardous course, amid doubts and fears, gaining a little firmer foothold every year, it has fully solved the problem of success, has established itself upon a firm financial basis, and has to-day the largest circulation of any monthly published in New England. During this time it has twice been enlarged, four pages having been added to its original sixteen in the early part of 1869, the publisher having offered to make such an enlargement when the circulation of the journal should reach 12,000, and at the same time promised to make another and equal enlargement when the subscription list should number 20,000. The latter promise he was able to redeem with the commencement of the third volume, just two years from the time the first number of the paper was issued, and since that time it has contained twenty-four large and well-filled pages, making it considerably the largest dollar monthly issued from an American press.

Instead of being disposed of through newsdealers, as a large portion of most of the monthly publications are, the large edition of the HOUSEHOLD is mailed almost entirely from the publishing office, and fills nearly a hundred of Uncle Sam's large mail sacks per month. These are mailed from the middle to the last of the month preceeding the date of issue, according to their destination, those having the farthest to go taking the earliest trains, which enables the whole edition to reach its readers on time and with the regularity of clock work. From the mailing table the sacks, weighed by the post-office clerks and duly labelled, are delivered to the mail agents and by them forwarded to every State and Territory in the Union, besides a large number sent to foreign countries, from which it will be seen that the HOUSEHOLD is not a local paper with a circumscribed field and influence, but a cosmopolitan journal, adapted to all sections of the country, and is pretty generally found wherever there is a representative of the class to whose interests it is devoted. Its subscribers are found in nearly every county in the Northern and Western States, while in the far South and on the Pacific Coast its patrons are already numbered by the thousands. It has a large and efficient corps of agents, numbering many hundreds, scattered throughout the country, many of whom have canvassed for it from its commencement, and it is a remarkable fact, and one, it is believed, unparalleled in the history of journalism, that since the first number was issued not a week-day has passed without bringing some addition to its subscription list.

A good idea of the character and scope of the HOUSEHOLD may be derived from a brief review of the special departments into which it is arranged. There are ten in number, corresponding to the apartments of a dwelling, as follows: The Veranda, the Drawing Room. the Conservatory, the Dressing Room, the Nursery, the Dining Room, the Dispensary, the Library, the Kitchen, and the Parlor.

In the Veranda are given the architectural notes, hints for out-door work, while a lookout is kept upon the surroundings of the dwelling, and assistance given toward beautifying the premises. The Drawing Room has articles on the art of furnishing the house, care of furniture, etiquette, and interior decorations. In the Conservatory are gathered the pets of the family in pots, cages and aquarium, and information given upon all matters pertaining to their treatment, The Dressing Room contains a brief review of the fashions, toilet recipes and practical suggestions upon needle-work and kindred topics. The Nursery is devoted to the care and management of infants and children, and furnishes the little folks with an assortment of entertaining reading and puzzle work. The Dining Room is furnished with hints upon table etiquette, the analysis of food, table talk, and a column of jokes and funnygraphs as a "dessert." The sanitary articles of the Dispensary are from some of the best writers in the country, and abound in valuable information concerning the care of the sick and the preservation of health. In the Library literary and educational topics are freely discussed, and there are also notices and reviews of books and current publications, and a page of original music in every issue; as the kitchen is generally the most important room in the house, so here the Kitchen is a large and well filled department, where contributions are received each month from many of tee most successful housekeepers in all sections of the country upon the various subjects that please or perplex their younger and less experienced sisters, with a large number of original and well-tried cooking recipes, a column of "Questions and Answers" upon all subjects pertaining to home life and domestic economy, a fund of practical information under the title of "Chats in the Kitchen," and a page of "Letters" from the Household Board. which is not surpassed in interest by any other feature of the paper; last, but not least, is the Parlor, in which is a choice collection of original and selected stories, miscellaneous reading, poetry, etc. In short, the HOUSEHOLD is designed to give aid and sympathy to the housekeeper in every department of labor to which she may be called, and especially in her efforts to make home beautiful and attractive. It shows how this may be done by the simple taste and skill of the house wife in a thousand devices and products of domestic ingenuity for the comfort of the family and the adornment of the dwelling, while it labors to promote the sweetness and grace of true womanhood in its presiding genius.

As an advertising medium the HOUSEHOLD ranks among the first, being especially valuable to all who desire to attract the attention of housekeepers and heads of families. Manufacturers and dealers in articles of domestic use, who have used its columns for years, frequently say that but few papers equal and none excel it as a means of extending their business. As an illustration of the estimation in which it is held by advertisers who have given it a trial, the following extract from a business letter from Messrs. I. L. Cragin & Co., of Philadelphia, the well-known manufacturers of Dobbin's Electric Soaps, may be appropriately given here: "We are hearing from the HOUSEHOLD from all parts of the United States, and don't think we shall ever cease to patronize its advertising columns. We are in 1,500 papers, and it seems as though half of the letters we get speak of the HOUSEHOLD." Many others of like import might be given. One reason of its popularity among advertisers is to be found in the fact that the limited number of advertisements admitted—not exceeding four pages—enables the publisher to sift out all the doubtful ones, and so virtually endorse such as appear in its columns, and this being well known to the readers, they feel safe in giving their patronage to any firm whose responsibility is thus vouched for, which makes the space occupied highly profitable to its advertising patrons. The utmost care is taken to exclude everything of a questionable character, and nothing but what is believed to be in every respect entirely unexceptionable is permitted to appear in its columns. The fine quality of the paper upon which it is printed, its clear type and good press-work, give to the advertisements that peculiar prominence characteristic of a well-printed page, causing them to be easily seen and read. Then, too, unlike the majority of *newspapers*, which are hastily read and soon forgotten, it is generally preserved through the entire month for family reading, and then quite frequently laid away to be bound at the close of the volume and kept for future reference, so that it often occurs that advertisements are replied to several years after their first appearance. The subscription price of the HOUSEHOLD is one dollar per year, to which has recently been added ten cents to cover the postage now prepaid by the publisher.

THE IRON AGE, NEW YORK.

THE LARGEST NEWSPAPER IN THE WORLD.

A SKETCH FOR THE BOOK OF THE CENTENNIAL NEWSPAPER EXHIBITION.

During the past twelve or fifteen years trade journalism has experienced a marked and beneficial change. Previous to that time the commercial journal was expected to be in itself the representative of all departments of commerce and industry. When business men were content with a few brief words of comment on the condition of the markets which interested them, and were satisfied if they found them after searching through column after column of matter which had for them only a remote and general interest, the commercial newspaper of the olden time filled a want. When business became more speculative, profits smaller, and competition so close that early and exact information on all subjects of interest was of value to merchants and business men, the general commercial journals were unable to meet the demand. Their field was so extensive that they could only cover it in a superficial way; their reporters and editors, having to divide their attention among a number of markets, could not closely follow all the changes in, or familiarize themselves with all the conditions affecting each. The necessity for fuller and more exact information led to the establishment of trade journals devoted to some special business or industry, and while there are still some general commercial journals, there are few trades or industries which are not represented by class journals, whose columns are devoted exclusively to the literature, statistics and prices current of the trades and markets which constitute their special fields.

Among the first of the special trade journals was THE IRON AGE. Established in 1855, it is the oldest newspaper in the world devoted to Iron, Hardware and the Metal Trades. Its original title was the *Hardwareman's Newspaper*, but in 1859 it was changed to THE IRON AGE. The next oldest journal of its class is the *Ironmonger* of London, established in 1859.

THE IRON AGE early assumed, and has since maintained, a first position in American trade journalism, and for several years has been the largest newspaper published in this or any country. It consists of forty pages, 11½x17 inches, well printed on good paper. Each number is carefully indexed for reading matter and advertisements; and each copy is folded, stitched and cut. The area of printed surface in each weekly number measures 54 11-36 square feet, being considerably larger than any of the popular monthly magazines. Beside the weekly edition, there are semi-monthly and monthly editions.

The policy of the editorial management of THE IRON AGE has always been to give each issue an interest and value for all classes of its readers. As a trade journal it was the first to give thorough, exhaustive and exact reports of the markets it represented, and in carrying out this plan it has practically revolutionized commercial journalism. To obtain the information needed was at first very difficult and always very costly. To make its reports complete and accurate it was necessary to employ as reporters men of business experience, who could at any time command large salaries as salesmen; correspondents had to be secured at home and abroad, and branch offices, under the management of accomplished journalists, have been established in Philadelph a and Pittsburgh

Among the features of THE IRON AGE trade report may be mentioned, weekly telegrams from London, a thorough and exhaustive report on the condition and changes of price in the American Hardware market, careful and accurate reports of the Iron and Metal market in the principal cities of the United States, and condensed translations from the latest exchanges, trade circulars and private advices from the principal metal markets of all countries of the world

These are features never before combined in a newspaper trade report, and there are few commercial journals in the world which could afford the large annual expenditure involved in the maintenance of such a system.

In its editorial and reading columns THE IRON AGE possesses a character which is distinctively national. It is valuable as a record of current progress in metallurgy, mechanics, engineering and the useful arts, and is conspicuous for the extent, variety, and interest of its reading matter. In its editorial columns all questions of current interest to the iron, steel, metal and hardware trades are calmly and intelligently discussed, and no space is wasted in acrimonious and unprofitable disputation with other journals. Its acknowledged position at the head of American commercial and technical journals has been gained and retained by an unwavering adherence to the policy to making a paper as valuable and useful as possible, without regard to cost or trouble. The result has been the growth of a circulation larger than that of any other trade journal in this country, or, we believe, in the world, and a large and firmly-established prosperity, which the commercial and financial troubles of the past three years have not even menaced.

In the amount of its advertising TLE IRON AGE is a curiosity in journalism. This averages from 130 to 150 columns, and in a number containing 48 pages it has reached very nearly 200 columns. Its advertising pages are an illustrated trade directory of exceptional interest. This great amount of advertising is due to the extensive circulation of the paper and the fact that its rates of advertising have always been exceptionally low, considering its circulation and influence. In consequence of this policy, THE IRON AGE has gained a constituency of advertisers who find it to their interest to keep their advertisements in the paper without interruption.

THE IRON AGE is published every Thursday at 10 Warren street, New York, by David Williams, publisher and proprietor. James C. Bayles has been its editor since 1871, aided by a well-selected staff of assistants and contributors. The Western office, established at No. 14 Fifth avenue, Pittsburgh, is under the management of Joseph M. Weeks, formerly editor of the *American Manufacturer* of that city, who is also associate editor, with especial charge of Western iron trade news. The Philadelphia office is at No. 220 South Fourth street, under the management of Thomas Hobson.

THE COURIER-JOURNAL, LOUISVILLE.

A REPRESENTATIVE, INDEPENDENT NEWSPAPER OF THE SOUTH AND SOUTHWEST.

A SKETCH FOR THE BOOK OF THE CENTENNIAL NEWSPAPER EXHIBITION

COURIER-JOURNAL BUILDING.

The COURIER-JOURNAL of Louisville, Ky., is an anomaly in American journalism. Issued from a city of the sixth class, it is a journal of the first class. No newspaper in the country has so extended a range of circulation; no other is so generally and widely quoted. It is both cosmopolitan and provincial, showing in its make-up an unusual versatility of editing. Its news is collated in the most minute and painstaking way, whilst its humor, paragraphic, and otherwise, is celebrated and popular. It is thoroughly representative of the South and Southwest, and has come to be considered a tolerably sure indicator of public opinion in those sections.

The COURIER-JOURNAL is the offspring of three newspapers which flourished in Louisville from 1830 to 1868, to wit: the *Journal*, established by George D. Prentice on the 24th of November, 1830; the *Courier*, established by Walter N Haldeman June 3, 1844, and the *Democrat*, established by John H. Harney about the same time. These three newspapers, competing with each other for nearly twenty-five years, experienced the varying fortunes of the city and the time; but were in the main successful. On the 8th of November, 1868, Henry Watterson having succeeded George D. Prentice in the management of the *Journal*, made an arrangement with Mr. Haldeman for a consolidation. The union effected, the two journalists purchased the *Democrat*, throwing the three into one under the title of the COURIER-JOURNAL.

In this way they secured the exclusive telegraphic franchise for the city of Louisville, embracing a population of a hundred and fifty thousand. This is the only instance of the kind on record, and will partly account for the unexampled prosperity of the enterprise so inaugurated; for it enabled Messrs. Haldeman and Watterson to compete with the journals of Chicago, St. Louis, and Cincinnati, cities very much larger than Louisville. They improved their opportunity with energy and vigor. The COURIER-JOURNAL has now a larger circulation in Kentucky, Indiana, Tennessee, Mississippi, Alabama, Georgia, Arkansas, and Texas than any of the journals of those States. It is sent into every State and Territory of the Union, and may be found upon the files of more libraries, boards of trade, literary societies, mercantile exchanges, chambers of commerce, Young Men's Christian Associations, hotels and club houses than any of its contemporaries in the Southwest.

The COURIER-JOURNAL has just erected, and now occupies, a newspaper building in all respects the handsomest and most commodious in the world. This building, which stands upon the corner of Fourth avenue and Green street, the most conspicuous corner in the city of Louisville, has a Fourth avenue front of 165 feet by a depth of 95 feet, is five stories high, with a Mansard roof, and is furnished throughout in a style of great magnificence. It is constructed of stone and pressed brick, and is of rare architectural beauty. Its principal facade is ornamented by a marble statue of George D. Prentice, the founder of the *Journal*. The composing, editorial, and press rooms are capacious and elegant, whilst its business is transacted in a counting-room unsurpassed in size and beauty.

In politics the COURIER-JOURNAL has always been Democratic, but has led the liberal and advanced elements of that party, and is at all times thoroughly independent.

The COURIER-JOURNAL is a folio sheet 30x48 inches in size. Its forms are stereotyped, and the paper is printed on a double Bullock press, capable of throwing off upwards of 20,000 perfect papers per hour.

The new building and office is supplied with all modern conveniences and improvements, such as freight and passenger elevators, steam engines, steam pumps, extinguishers, fire protectors and folding machines. Indeed, everything has been provided to render the COURIER-JOURNAL the finest, most complete, and convenient printing establishment not only in the United States, but in the world.

TERMS:

DAILY COURIER-JOURNAL..................................	$12 00 a year.
SUNDAY COURIER-JOURNAL................................	2 00 a year.
WEEKLY COURIER-JOURNAL...........	2 00 a year.
WEEKLY COURIER-JOURNAL, to clubs, $1 70, $1 60, and	1 50 a year.

Advertising in daily paper, 10 and 12½ cents per line, and in weekly 40 cents per line, each insertion.

The COURIER-JOURNAL has a special office in New York, No. 37 *Tribune* Building, under the management of Mr. E. B. MACK, for the convenience and accommodation of advertisers.

THE INTER-OCEAN, CHICAGO.

A SKETCH FOR THE BOOK OF THE CENTENNIAL NEWSPAPER EXHIBITION.

Westward the course of journalism as well as empire takes its way. Yesterday the great dailies of the country belonged to New York alone. To-day Chicago contests and divides the honor, and crowds its rival over the Eastern slope of the Alleghanies.

It is about six years since Chicago began a newspaper rivalry with New York, but it was not until THE INTER OCEAN was founded, in 1872, that a serious attempt was made to establish in the West a

HIGH-TONED POLITICAL AND LITERARY NEWSPAPER.

Before that the journals of Chicago were exclusively *news*papers. Their opinions were little regarded, and their literary character partook much of the frontier order; the rough and sensational, instead of the refined and æsthetic, were sought after.

It was doubted whether a newspaper of a better character could prosper in the West; but that doubt is removed. From its inception THE INTER-OCEAN appealed to the loftier instincts of the people, and from the start met with generous encouragement. It has never been found in the slums, nor is it hawked about in the disreputable quarters of the Western metropolis, but goes to the homes of more reading and thinking people than any other journal in America.

IN CITY AND COUNTRY ALIKE

it is recognized as the organ of respectability *par excellence*. To read THE INTER-OCEAN is *prima facie* proof of intelligence, and no surer sign of cultivation can be given than to be known as a regular subscriber to the great literary monitor of the Northwest.

The circulation of THE INTER-OCEAN has increased with a steady rapidity, astonishing even its most sanguine friends. Its printing facilities, large at first, have been from time to time increased, and in March of the present year its presses, including one immense eight-cylinder Hoe, were still found inadequate, and contracts were closed with the Bullock Printing Press Company for two of their new perfecting presses of the latest pattern, each capable of printing 13,000 perfect sheets per hour.

As an indication of the magnitude of the present circulation of the paper, it is only necessary to refer to the indubitable evidence furnished by the post-office returns. Postage, by law, must be paid in advance at the office of publication, and from this official source the actual facts regarding the circulation of any newspaper through the mails can be obtained. The evidence thus on file shows that during the year 1875 THE INTER-OCEAN

PAID IN POSTAGE $13,029.84—

a sum equal to that paid by all the other political journals in Chicago combined, and absolutely unapproached, with one exception, by any other newspaper in the United States.

This enormous circulation grows less wonderful when we take into account the character of the people who look to Chicago for their newspaper literature. Outside of a narrow strip of New England, there is not in the Union, according to population, so large a percentage of reading and thinking people as inhabit the nine States having Chicago for a commercial and financial centre. That among so many millions of thoughtful, industrious, and prosperous people THE INTER-OCEAN should gain an extended foothold is not strange. The paper is but the reflex of their own thoughts and sentiments, and has become endeared to the people of the West as a part of themselves.

Though Republican in politics,

THE INTER-OCEAN IS FRANK AND OUTSPOKEN

on questions of public policy, and its bold course in this respect has made its name familiar throughout the country. On the Southern reconstruction, the railway problem, and the currency question, it has been a law unto itself. Beginning the discussion of each of these subjects alone, it built them up into great living national issues, commanding the attention of the entire people and press of the country.

The flow of subscribers that set in alone from the West, ere long had its counterpart from the East and South also, until now the tide has swept the whole continent and THE INTER-OCEAN embraces a constituency national in extent and first in wealth and culture.

A year or so ago a distinguished bishop of the Methodist Episcopal Church, writing to the New York *Independent*, said: "THE INTER-OCEAN is the clearest wisest, and strongest of American dailies. It is the true and almost only successor of the great New York *Tribune* of ante-bellum fame and power. When it circulates Eastward, as the Greeley journal of yesterday went Westward, we shall feel and follow our way out of the lowness and guiltiness and cowardice and crime that now nationally envelop and fester us."

The growing strength of THE INTER-OCEAN in the East shows that the day hoped for by the Bishop may not be far away.

A PROMINENT AND EXCELLENT FEATURE

of the INTER-OCEAN is its *reliability*. This is so marked as to be frequently observable in an amusing way. The past year has been full of surprises and scandalous exposures. When any of these have been made public the demand for THE INTER-OCEAN has been most marked and extensive. The readers of other newspapers have seemed to turn with one accord to its columns for a verification of such reports. The inquiry on all sides has been, "What does THE INTER-OCEAN say?" and by its silence, contradiction, or confirmation has the reliability or untrustworthy character of such rumors been generally judged.

CHICAGO IS A NATURAL ENTREPOT OF NEWS.

More than 21,000 miles of railroad connect it with the surrounding territory, and "Chicago" appears in the corporate name of fifty railways. Twenty lines radiate from the city, and more than one-half of the entire population of the Union can be reached in twenty-four hours from this great INTER-OCEANIC metropolis.

Gradually but surely the newspapers of the Atlantic seaboard are being driven back into their natural local boundries, while the great central organs of the West push their way North, and South, and East in simultaneous accord.

The star that shines ever so brilliantly on the verge of a cycloid pales when the centre is reached, and fades away entirely at the antipodean boundary; but the centric sun distributes its radiance equally, and sheds light upon the East and the West alike.

The West, so-called, is now the center of the Union and, with its vast population, controls the destinies of the Republic. There is but one West, and Chicago is its capital. There is only one Chicago, and THE INTER-OCEAN is its prophet.

THE CONGREGATIONALIST, BOSTON.

REPRESENTING THE OLDEST RELIGIOUS NEWSPAPER IN THE WORLD.

A SKETCH FOR THE BOOK OF THE CENTENNIAL NEWSPAPER EXHIBITION.

In January of the year 1816, Nathaniel Willis, after long labor to prepare the way, published the first number of the Boston *Recorder*. He always claimed

THE CONGREGATIONALIST BUILDING.

that it was the first effort ever successfully made to establish a weekly newspaper upon a distinctively religious basis, and the claim has been allowed by impartial history. In May, 1849, Deacon Galen James started the CONGREGATIONALIST in Boston, to meet the views of a school of Congregationalists who were not satisfied with then existing journals. In 1867—following the spirit of the Boston Council of 1865, and falling in with the tendency to harmonize into one all members of the great family of the spiritual descendants of the Pilgrims—the *Recorder* and CONGREGATIONALIST were united under the editorship of Rev. Henry M. Dexter, D. D.; and from that time to the present the resultant journal has had a recognized standing at the head of Congregational newspapers, not merely in point of circulation, but of general ability.

Its proprietors, while holding it steadily to the doctrinal standards of the Congregational Churches, and while aiming to give it a special value in all its relations to polity and to practical Christianity, have sought also to make it, what it is conceded to be—

A FAVORITE FAMILY PAPER.

By a liberal expenditure it has attached to itself, as a staff of regular contributors, a large number of the best religious writers, while the learning, force, aptness, and general value of its editorials, the marked candor and ability of its book reviews, and the unsurpassed variety and freshness of its religious news, entitle it to hold and increase the wide popularity which it has gained. W. L. Greene, C. A. Richardson and H. M. Dexter, proprietors. Terms, $3 a year, in advance. Address W. L. Greene & Co., Congregational Building, No. 1 Somerset street, Boston, Mass.

"THE YOUTH'S COMPANION," BOSTON.

A SKETCH FOR THE BOOK OF THE CENTENNIAL NEWSPAPER EXHIBITION.

FIRST YOUTH'S PAPER.

The YOUTH'S COMPANION is the pioneer paper in the juvenile literature of our own country, and the oldest weekly paper for young people in the world. It is now forty-nine years of age, and in a few months will celebrate its semi-centennial anniversary. It was commenced in May, 1827, by NATHANIEL WILLIS, of Boston, the father of N. P. Willis, the poet, who also founded the *Eastern Argus* and the Boston *Recorder*.

ORIGIN.

The early history of the paper is novel and interesting, and illustrates the growth of an idea. Mr. Willis having been accustomed to relate stories to his own children, as a reward for committing to memory the lessons he assigned them, was led to see the value of such literature in developing the thought and character of the young. It suggested to him the plan of having a Children's Department in the Boston *Recorder*. He acted upon the suggestion, the new feature of the paper became popular and successful, and it has been since adopted by nearly all religious journals.

The stories for young people in the *Recorder* were so eagerly sought for, that Mr. Willis determined to start what at that time seemed a very novel enterprise —a paper exclusively for the young. A specimen number was issued in May, 1827, a sufficient number of subscribers was obtained to warrant its continuance, and, in the month of June following the first weekly paper for young people began its successful career.

The sheet was a very small one, hardly larger than an old-fashioned pane of glass, the type was large and coarse, and the single picture it contained would now bring a smile to the face of the most inartistic reader. But, though coarse in appearance, its literary material, like the old *N. E. Family Magazine*, was usually of a high order, indicating excellent taste and judgment. It attained a circulation of about 5,000 copies.

FORD & OLMSTEAD.

For many years the COMPANION published under its name the information, in one long line, that it was issued "by Nathaniel Willis, weekly, at No. 11 Cornhill, office of the Boston *Recorder*, at one dollar a year." In 1857 Mr. WILLIS' health having become impaired by advanced age, the paper was purchased by Messrs. Ford and Olmstead, proprietors of the *Watchman and Reflector*, and published under the firm of Olmstead & Co. The editing of it passed into the hands of Mr. D. S. Ford, who is now its editor, and since the year 1867 has been its sole proprietor. Mr. Willis, its founder, died in 1870, in the 91st year of his age.

ENLARGEMENT AND GROWTH.

The little paper had made for itself a good reputation and character. Its new editor enlarged it in size, and aimed to give it a higher literary value. Its articles took a wider range, very engaging writers were secured, and the circulation under this impetus began to rapidly increase. In a few years its subscription list grew from 5,000 to 40,000 names.

RAPID INCREASE.

The increase in resources was followed by a corresponding increase in the literary value of its contents. It became the aim of its editor, after the model of *Chambers' Journal*, to furnish the best reading at a comparatively small cost. The paper was again enlarged, new literary departments were formed, emnent contributors were secured, and its editorials were prepared by the most capable city editors. In 1870 its subscription list reached 70,000.

A FAMILY PAPER.

From about this time the character of the paper underwent a change, and it became both a literary journal for the young and for the family. Its stories adapted themselves to the tastes of a larger audience of readers; its articles on current topics were so prepared as to be interesting to the cultivated and critical as well as to the young. The wants of the family from the youngest to the oldest were considered, and the purest and the most entertaining writers were employed to meet these wants.

ONE HUNDRED AND FORTY THOUSAND SUBSCRIBERS.

Nothing is so successful as success, or more trustworthy than success gained by a well-directed purpose and a generous and liberal aim.

is now a thirty-two column paper, and has a circulation of 140,000 copies weekly. Many of the parents who subscribe for it for their families to-day were readers of it when they themselves were boys and girls. The paper holds from year to year the great body of its old subscribers, and adds to these a yearly list of new names which many publishers would consider a liberal subscription list.

ITS ARTICLES AND WRITERS.

The COMPANION publishes three or four serial stories, some two hundred shorter stories, more than two hundred editorials, and more than fifteen hundred shorter articles, selections, poems, etc., each year. It employs some fifty contributors. Among these are the well-known names of J. T. Trowbridge, Edward Eggleston, Rev. E. E. Hale, Rev. Wm. M. Baker, Hon. C. C. Hazewell, Geo. M. Towle, Esq., Mrs. Leonowens, Miss L. M. Alcott, Mrs. H. P. Spofford, Mrs. Rebecca Harding Davis, Celia Thaxter, Mrs. Moulton, and Mrs. Diaz. Among occasional or promised writers are Wm. Cullen Bryant, Dr. Hayes, Hon. Schuyler Colfax, etc. Its editorial department is managed in a very careful and critical manner, the articles on literature, science, and politics being prepared by gentlemen who have special and exceptional fitness for the work.

1827—1877.

Nearly fifty years of its history have passed, and one generation has already handed the paper to another. To give the faces at the fireside a warmer glow; to create character and intelligence; to publish nothing of which the influence will not be good; to honor God, and to bring stainless and hallowed memories out of all the relations of the family and daily life, will be its aim in 1877, as it was in its origin fifty years ago.

THE REPUBLICAN, SPRINGFIELD, MASS.

A SKETCH FOR THE BOOK OF THE CENTENNIAL NEWSPAPER EXHIBITION.

The Springfield (Mass.) REPUBLICAN, established in 1824, has become the leading and representative paper of New England, and the first provincial paper in America.

A Whig journal in the days of the old Whig party, it was first and conspicuous in the formation of the republican party; but since that party's great work was completed, the paper has grown steadily into a position of entire political independency, and made itself a leader in the press of the country for sectional reconciliation and administrative reform.

The REPUBLICAN now ranks, practically, as the independent journal of New England; the advocate of honesty and reform in government, honor and purity in politics, economy and simplicity in public and private life; the slave of no party, the organ of no politician; an honest paper for honest people.

As a newspaper, the REPUBLICAN cherishes the qualities which have made it popular and powerful—promptness, clearness, brevity, and comprehensiveness, regarding the development of thought, the difference of opinion and the discoveries of science, equally as news with current accidents and crimes, and giving especial attention to the record of events and the progress of life in New England. As a public journal, it is all-embracing in its field of discussion and selection, and independent and thoughtful in its treatment of all current topics, and aiming to make for itself both a welcome and useful place as an instructor, a critic, and a stimulant in every family that adopts it.

Published both daily and weekly, the WEEKLY REPUBLICAN is made up with especial care for a general circulation, and may fairly claim to be the best eclectic weekly newspaper in the country. It offers itself especially to politicians and scholars, to New Englanders at home or in distant parts of the country, and to Americans abroad, as giving, in a single sheet, a more comprehensive and impartial summary of general New England and American news, and fuller and more independent discussions of all prominent topics of American life, and a more varied picture of our literary, art and social progress than can be found anywhere else.

The REPUBLICAN is printed on a large double sheet of eight pages, forty eight columns. The daily is three cents a copy, seventy-five cents a month, and $9 a year; the weekly is five cents a copy, $2 a year, and $1.50 in clubs of five or more.

As an advertising medium, the REPUBLICAN presents peculiar advantages in the amount, character and field of its circulation and the low rates charged. The DAILY REPUBLICAN has a firm circulation of 11,000 copies, which is as many or more than is printed by any daily paper in Boston save two; two or three times as many as by any other paper in Massachusetts out of Boston, or in Connecticut; and larger than by any other provincial paper in the country. In all western Massachusetts and up and down the Connecticut valley, it circulates more largely than all other daily papers together; while in more distant parts of New England, in Vermont and Connecticut especially, both the daily and weekly have exceptionally numerous readers among the most intelligent and influential members of society.

The terms of advertising—low, uniform and for cash—are five cents a line of eight words, each insertion, in the daily, and twelve cents a line in the weekly. Special or displayed notices, ten cents a line of space in the daily and twenty cents in the weekly. Address the REPUBLICAN, Springfield, Mass.

THE PHILADELPHIA PRESS.

A SKETCH FOR THE BOOK OF THE CENTENNIAL NEWSPAPER EXHIBITION.

The Philadelphia PRESS was founded on the 1st of August, 1857. It was the creation of John W. Forney, who has figuered for more than thirty years in public life, and who is the last member of the great quartette that once dominated American journalism—Greeley, Bennett, Raymond and Forney, and who, with a single exception, have surrendered their pens and lives. The history of THE PRESS is nearly that of Mr. Forney. He was its originator, and he has been its guiding spirit. In 1857 Mr. Forney, who had already achieved national distinction as a journalist, and as an earnest worker in the ranks of the Democratic party, who had edited its national organs and led its army of voters to victory in the doubtful and Keystone State, became disgusted with its management and distrustful of its purposes. A Democrat by conviction, but of the old and better school, and a disciplinarian by habit, he sought in the establishment of THE PRESS to reform his party within its own lines, to win it back to its original principles, and to save it from its enemies in its own household. The sequel of that determined struggle is well remembered. The fight was a gallant one, but the results were not those for which the editor hoped. He builded better, however, than he knew and it was through his efforts and those of the brave Douglass Democrats who co-oporated with him, that the Republican party was consolidated for victory, Abraham Lincoln elected, and the nation newly born and baptized in the blood which has purified it from the great sin of slavery. The subsequent history of the newspaper of which he was the founder, and is still the active editor and proprietor, is well known. It is as it has been since 1860, an ardent and consistent advocate of Republican principles, but its party fidelity has never been subordinated to its personal sense of duty, and while its loyalty to the party and principles it prefers is not questioned, THE PRESS has never hesitated to speak out boldly against the mistakes and corruptions of its political friends.

As a newspaper THE PRESS is without a rival in Pennsylvania. In the extent of its correspondence, the multiplicity of its genius and the amplitude of its resources, it has no competitor. Its founder, John W. Forney, is at its head, and its ability is unquestioned. It is dignified in its discussions, but where denunciation is merited and necessary, it is unsparing. Sensationalism is a stranger to its columns, even while it prints all the news of the day, while it does not mince matters as a rule, it always supplies the knife where it deems it necessary.

THE PRESS enjoys a large circulation and extensive business patronage from the very best circle of readers—people of intelligence and means—who find it the only medium which supplies their wants and the best guide to their purchases. It was never more prosperous than at present, and its circulation is constantly increasing. It is recognized as the Journal of the Centennial Exposition as clearly as if the Commission had issued a proclamation to that effect, and the influence of this upon its growth is attested by its rapid rise in circulation since that great enterprise became a fixture.

For the centennial year THE PRESS has been completely reorganized, and with its founder at its head, has a staff of writers and contributors unequaled by that of any Philadelphia journal. Mr. Forney's vigorous pen is daily seen in its columns, and among his associate editors are Dr. R. Shelton Mackenzie, who has a literary reputation second to that of no other journalist in the country, Mr. Thomas Meehan, the scholar and scientist, Mr. John W. Forney, Jr., well known as dramatic critic, Mr. Audubon Davis, who has been connected in various capacites with many of the leading journals of the country, and Messrs.

Thomas F. Logan and Thomas A. Egan, well-known writers. It has a large and well-trained corps of reporters, the chief of whom is Robert M. McWade, able and regular correspondents at London, Washington, and Harrisburg, the capital of Pennsylvania, and occasional correspondents in nearly every town and hamlet in the State, who keep it informed of every important and interesting event that occurs.

THE PRESS occupies a large and convenient building at the Southwest corner of Seventh and Chestnut streets, in Philadelphia, the largest building, with one exception, occupied by a Philadelphia newspaper, and in the excellence of its appointments is unexcelled by any of its contemporaries. During the continuance of the Centennial Exposition it will have a branch office at the Globe Hotel, adjoining the Exposition and grounds, and in 1876 it will be conspicuous as *the* newspaper of Pennsylvania. It also prints Weekly and Tri-weekly editions, which also have large and well-deserved circulations.

The terms of THE PRESS are: Daily, single copies, 3 cents. Mailed to subscribers, including pre-paid postage, at $8.75 per annum; $4.40 for six months; $2.20 for three months. Served to city subscribers at 18 cents per week.

THE TRI-WEEKLY PRESS is published every Tuesday, Thursday, and Saturday. Mailed to subscribers, including pre-paid postage, at $4.40 per annum; $2.20 for six months, and $1.10 for three months.

THE WEEKLY PRESS, $2 per annum; five copies, including pre-paid postage $9.50; ten copies, including pre-paid postage, $16; twenty copies, including pre-paid postage, $29; fifty copies, including pre-paid postage, $60. Larger clubs than fifty will be charged in the same proportion per copy. To the getter-up of clubs of ten or more an extra copy will be given.

All business letters for this office should be addressed to JOHN W. FORNEY, Editor and Proprietor of THE PRESS, Southwest corner Seventh and Chestnut streets, Philadelphia.

THE CHRISTIAN UNION, NEW YORK.

HENRY WARD BEECHER, EDITOR.

A SKETCH FOR THE BOOK OF THE CENTENNIAL NEWSPAPER EXHIBITION.

The CHRISTIAN UNION was established in September, 1869, and is therefore one of the youngest of the religious weeklies.

From its commencement the association of Rev. Henry Ward Beecher with it as editor gave it a strong impetus, and it sprang rapidly into favor. In a very few years it attained a circulation of thirty thousand subscribers, when by the introduction of chromo premiums, then a novelty (but since discontinued by the paper), the circulation was increased in a few months to the unprecedented number of one hundred and thirty-two thousand, extending to every State and Territory in the Union, to the Canadas, and indeed to every quarter of the globe.

As the medium of Mr. Beecher's "Lecture Room Talks," editorials and articles of a general nature, the paper was warmly received by all classes, and still maintains its strong hold upon the Christian public. Its has been neither sectarian nor actively controversial. Its past and present position can best be described in Mr. Beecher's own language. He wrote:

"The CHRISTIAN UNION will seek the *Union* of all Christians, not by chasing the phantom of an organic unity, but by promoting such dispositions of charity and kindly sympathy as shall bring men of whatever mode of worship into a real sympathetic relation with each other.

It will recognize the existence and importance of Christian doctrine, but it will not admit any human statement of doctrine to be inspired or authoritative, but to be always open to new thought, criticism and reconstruction. It will regard no doctrine as *fundamental* unless it is indispensable to the formation of Christian character. Doctrines may be fundamental to the structure of a given system of theology, which are quite unimportant in the formation of Christian habits and dispositions.

Believing that the Sacred Scriptures represent the Gospel, not simply as an accomplished and external history, but as the Disclosure of Divine Power, forever active, and unfolding itself in the experience of God's people, through all generations, we shall interpret the spirit and text of Scripture not alone by the laws of language, but by the experiences of the Church, and by all the disclosures of Divine Providence in human society.

Whatever throws light upon the structure of the body, the nature of human faculties, the divine method of creation and development of human life and society, we shall believe to be included in Christianity, as trees are included in the seeds from which they grow. Whatever in the whole range of science, and in the results of art, promotes the welfare of mankind; whatever in political economy augments the productive forces of society; whatever in politics tends to purify the State, destroy its enemies, exalt the government in wisdom, fidelity, and benignity, we shall regard as a part of that great development to which the name of Christ will be forever joined, who is the divine fountain from whence flows the vital influence by which mankind are to be exalted from animalism to Christian manhood. Above all material laws, and behind all sensuous instruments, is a Living Soul. We receive devoutly records and revelations of the truth wrought out in human life and experience by that Soul in the past, and with a quick sensibility we shall listen to every disclosure of God's truth which he is making through all avenues in our own day.

It is the purpose of the CHRISTIAN UNION, 'as much as lieth in it,' to avoid controversy But when it is unavoidable it will 'do with its might what its hands shall find to do.' But its chief endeavor will be to secure good, in the household, the Church, and the State, by the genial and kindly forces of Christianity. Conscience, without benignant sympathies, is unchristian. A high ideal of human life and society, enforced by a cold and severe criticism which disdains all human weaknesses and infirmities, is less vulgar than ribald scoffing, but is none the less tyrannic and Satanic.

While generous criticism of the views and practices of all sects, parties and persons will not be disallowed, it is the purpose of this paper, in all ways, to bring men's hearts together. It will earnestly strive to encourage good works in all sects, to rejoice in the prosperity of each denomination; to cover their faults rather than to proclaim them; to be generously just; to avoid all spite and malice toward enemies; to resist all influences which tend to separate men from each other; to promote kindness and sympathy between unlike men; not to disown severity of rebuke, and yet mainly to overcome evil with good; to promote cheerfulness and innocent mirth; to give to conscience an atmosphere of benevolence; to inspire hope, courage, and love in every household. It will, in short, seek to diffuse that Gospel, whose annunciation was, 'Good Will to Men,' whose Author and Hero sacrificed his own life to save mankind, and whose God and Father is named Love."

The following is a partial list of the present contributors to the CHRISTIAN UNION: Edward Abbott, Lyman Abbott, John S. C. Abbott, Augustus Blauvelt, Elihu Burritt, Leonard Bacon, Edward Beecher, Chas. L. Brace, Leonard Woolsey Bacon, Amelia E. Barr, Thos. N. Beecher, Joel Benton, Mrs J. G. Burnett, Henry A. Beers, Anna C. Brackett, Hezekiah Butterworth, Mrs. M. E. Bradley, Mrs. M. L. B. Branch, Mrs. F. Barrow, Mryon H. Benton, R. R. Bowker, Rose Terry Cooke, J. Leonard Corning, "Henry Churton" Prof. Timothy Dwight (Yale), Mary B. Dodge, Edward Eggleston, Prof. Geo. P. Fisher (Yale), Edgar Faucett, Kate Foote, Rev. W. L. Gage, Howard Glyndon, Mrs. S. C. Hallowell, Paul Hayne, Lucretia P. Hale, Amanda B. Harris, Edward Everett Hale, Gail Hamilton, Horatio King, Augusta Larned, Mrs. H. W. Beecher, Geo. S. Merriam, Kate Putnam Osgood, Pres't Noah Porter (Yale), Mrs. L. G. Runkle, R. W. Raymond, B. G. Northrup, Rachel Pomeroy, Sarah J. Pritchard, James Richardson, Margaret E. Sangster, Harriet Beecher Stowe, Homer B. Sprague, Isabella Grant Meredith, T. Harwood Pattison, Carl Spencer, Joseph P. Thompson (Berlin), Olive Thorne, H. Clay Trumbull, Geo. M. Towle, Sophy Winthrop, and Sarah C. Woolsey.

The pages of the CHRISTIAN UNION are never soiled by advertisements of a doubtful character. Neither does it knowingly admit *blind* advertisements intended to decoy, mislead, and defraud the innocent. No advertisement is received which cannot be read aloud in the household without invidious comment. All advertisements are carefully examined, and their character known to the publisher before insertion. Its value as an advertising medium has been very fully tested by the most prominent advertisers in this country. Their statements have frequently appeared in its columns; but a better attestation of its merit is the fact that it has retained many of them during all the financial distress of the past two years, and is still receiving their constant patronage. The fact, too, that its columns are continually employed by the best-known and most influential *advertising agencies and advertisers* in the land, is additional evidence of the excellent and remunerative character of the circulation.

The present publisher is HORATIO C. KING, and the office of the company is at No. 27 Park Place, New York.

THE CINCINNATI GAZETTE, CINCINNATI, O.

ESTABLISHED 1793.

A SKETCH FOR THE BOOK OF THE CENTENNIAL NEWSPAPER EXHIBITION.

The CINCINNATI GAZETTE has been in existence eighty-three years. Cincinnati was at that time merely a frontier village of a few hundred inhabitants. Now it is one of the important and prosperous cities of the country—the centre of its population, and the heart of the continent.

The GAZETTE'S growth aptly illustrates the general growth of American journalism, for no paper of equal age has attained a similar circulation and celebrity. The most material change thus denoted is that in the cost and revenues of leading papers. As lately as 1850 the entire yearly receipts of the GAZETTE for subscriptions would not have equalized the present expenditure for correspondence by telegraph and mail. The labor of half a dozen persons then sufficed for the editorial work, while the expense of correspondents was seldom incurred. Now the editors, reporters, and correspondents of the GAZETTE are numbered by hundreds, and it has a representative in every leading city of either hemisphere. Its other disbursements have augmented in the same degree, being measured by the public demands and expectations, and compensated by its ever-increasing patronage. A long and firmly-established paper's expenses are regulated by its circulation, and the latter is effected only by the matter of brains, business enterprise, and density of population. The city of Cincinnati is notably superior in its intelligence, and exacting in newspaper requirements, while the contiguous country upon all sides is thickly populated. Its newspaper standard is, therefore, above the average, and confers upon the paper that acceptably fills its requirements a superior character and circulation.

The changes in the publication department of the GAZETTE are worthy of notice. The first "power press" used West of the Allegheny mountains was bought by it. It cost twelve hundred dollars—a very large outlay for the purpose in that early day. The wheel that moved the machinery was turned by a single man. Its hourly capacity was 800 sheets, printed on one side, and to furnish that number of complete papers required two hours. The same person who turned the wheel of that press is still employed in the office on the new Hoe Perfecting Double Press, which has a self-feeding capacity of 28,000 sheets per hour, printed on both sides. It is the fastest press in the world. In sixty minutes it does as much and better work than the first power press could do in seventy hours. The machinery and appliances in existence thirty years ago could not have accomplished in a week the work now done in a single day in any large newspaper office. A century ago it could not have been accomplished at all.

The GAZETTE has three editions—daily, semi-weekly, and weekly—printed from stereotype plates. There are printed weekly an aggregate of 160,000 papers, which are read by a half million of people distributed throughout Ohio, Indiana, Michigan, Kentucky, Tennessee, and West Virginia. The annual issues of the paper aggregate about 8,000,000, and the paper thus used, if in a continuous sheet, would reach over 5,000 miles. The vast business thus indicated has mainly grown up within a third of a century, for prior to 1840, Cincinnati's newspaper traffic was trifling. In 1835 the GAZETTE'S aggregate circulation did not exceed 1,200 copies, while at the present time these figures barely cover the mere occasional fluctuations, within a few days, in its circulation. The bed of the old stream is but the margin of the new.

As a complete American newspaper the CINCINNATI GAZETTE has no superior. Its ability and its integrity are recognized and unquestioned. It has a national reputation for its fearlessness no less than for its fairness in the discussion of matters of political and public policy. As a commercial paper it has been regarded as a standard for over twenty-five years. It has aimed for over half a century to fully satisfy the demand for a paper wholly acceptable to the cultured and active business classes of its section, and it has succeeded. In a population older, more advanced and denser than can be found in any other part of the West, it is undeniably the leading paper in character, in influence and in circulation.

The weekly edition of the GAZETTE is one of the most widely-circulated family and agricultural papers. Its agricultural value is seen in its abundant correspondence from practical farmers, who make it their medium for the exchange of views and intelligence. Of literature it is not unmindful. Great prominence is given to reviews of new publications, and to scientific, social and religious movements. It contains more reading matter than any other Cincinnati paper, and the character of its contents precludes a comparison with the pretentious but worthless and transitory mushrooms of the journalistic field. It has more than 3,000 regular club agents, and is sent to subscribers at over 4,000 post-offices throughout the land.

The GAZETTE'S publication building, on the northeast corner of Fourth and Vine streets, was bought by its proprietors fifteen years ago, and is now the most valuable corner in the city. Except a small part of the first floor, the entire edifice is devoted to the business of the GAZETTE, and recently the latter was obliged to secure additional space in a contiguous building. The Eastern office of the paper is at No. 37 Tribune Building, New York city.

In proportion to its circulation, and to the manifest value of the latter to advertisers, the GAZETTE rates are the lowest in Cincinnati. Its columns have uniformly been preferred by foreign advertisers to those of any neighboring cotemporary, and for a long time no other Cincinnati paper has enjoyed an equal revenue from distant sources.

THE PHILADELPHIA DEMOCRAT.

A SKETCH FOR THE BOOK OF THE CENTENNIAL NEWSPAPER EXHIBITION

PHILADELPHIA DEMOCRAT BUILDING.

The PHILADELPHIA DEMOCRAT was established 1838 as a daily German newspaper by Mr. L. A. Wottenweber. Like all its contemporaries of that time, it was of humble origin, and made but slow progress until the events of 1848 brought about that great tidal-wave of German immigration to our shores, which continued with undiminished force till the beginning of our civil war, and greatly changed the character and the status of the German element in the United States, making it much more influential, not only by more than trebling it in numbers, but by adding to it by thousands highly-educated Germans, who, having joined the revolutionary movement, had, after its defeat, to seek refuge abroad, which most of them sought and found in the United States. At the beginning of that period the DEMOCRAT came by purchase under the control and management of Messrs. John S. Hoffman and Dr. E. Morwitz, who, under the firm name of Hoffman & Morwitz, at once infused new life into it and made it one of the leading and most influential newspapers in the United States. When the PHILADELPHIA DEMOCRAT was established it was located in the then centre of the German population of the city, but after the year 1848 the German element was spreading over the whole city, and besides, it became of more importance to be located in the business centre of the city. With this view the proprietors purchased a most eligible site on Chestnut street—the old Jones hotel—and by extensive alterations, amounting almost to rebuilding, made it one of the best-arranged newspaper establishments and printing houses in the country.

The building is five stories high, and has a front of fifty-five feet on Chestnut street and a depth of 245 feet to Sansom street.

From the removal of the PHILADELPHIA DEMOCRAT to its new office building, 612 and 614 Chestnut street, may be dated a new era for it, so rapidly were extended its circulation and its business patronage. Mr. Hoffman leaving for Europe in 1873, the proprietor, Dr. Morwitz, changed the name of the firm to Morwitz & Co.

The DEMOCRAT is the leading German organ in Pennsylvania, one of the oldest and largest eastern States, and the one which, from the beginning, was settled and influenced by Germans, from whose settlements most of the Western States have received and are still receiving, year by year, their solid native immigration, whereby the circulation and business of the DEMOCRAT have been constantly, naturally, and largely increased, until now the circulation and influence of the PHILADELPHIA DEMOCRAT, in its various publications—daily, weekly, Sunday and others—are by the great public regarded and appreciated as the largest and most important of the German newspapers in the United States.

THE PIONEER-PRESS AND TRIBUNE.

ST. PAUL AND MINNEAPOLIS, MINNESOTA.

THE ONLY MORNING PAPER IN MINNESOTA—THE GREAT NEWSPAPER OF THE UPPER MISSISSIPPI VALLEY.

A SKETCH FOR THE BOOK OF THE CENTENNIAL NEWSPAPER EXHIBITION.

THE PIONEER-PRESS AND TRIBUNE BUILDING.

In no direction has the marvellous progress of the West in the last fifteen years been more distinctly marked than in its journalism; but not even the marvellous growth of the Chicago newspapers, which equal if they do not surpass those of New York in all the characteristics of the first-class metropolitan newspaper, affords a more striking illustration of the journalistic development of the West than the newspaper which has recently assumed the title at the head of this article. As its name indicates, it is the product of the consolidation of the three old morning dailies of St. Paul and Minneapolis. The St. Paul *Pioneer*, established in 1849, and whose history dated back to the organization of the Territory of Minnesota, was consolidated in the Spring of 1875 with the St. Paul *Press*, which since 1861 has been the leading Republican journal of the State. In May last the *Pioneer-Press* was again consolidated with the Minneapolis *Tribune*, which was founded in 1865—and these three journals had previously swallowed up or supplanted in the course of their career some dozen rival or antecedent journals, so that the PIONEER-PRESS AND TRIBUNE represents and embodies the mature results of nearly all the labors, the enterprise, the capital, and the brains which have been devoted for the last twenty-seven years to the building up of journalism in these two flourishing cities. The practical result of this consolidation of the three rival morning newspapers of Minnesota is to give the PIONEER-PRESS AND TRIBUNE a *bona fide* daily circulation of nearly 10,000 copies. No other daily newspaper in the Northwest, outside of Chicago, has half so large a circulation, and it is five or six times as large as that of any other paper in Minnesota. Nor does any other newspaper in the Northwest, outside of Chicago, enjoy so extensive a field of circulation, or so commanding a position and so exclusive an ascendency within that field. It is the only morning newspaper published in the two adjacent cities of St. Paul and Minneapolis, the commercial and manufacturing centres of Minnesota and the upper Mississippi Valley, with an aggregate population of 75,000 souls, and it is the only morning newspaper published in the State of Minnesota with a population of 650,000 souls. It is the only important morning journal published west of Chicago and Milwaukee, from which St. Paul is separated by a breadth of 500 miles, or north of St. Louis, which is 900 miles distant. Its actual field of circulation embraces the whole of Minnesota, Northern Iowa, Northwestern Wisconsin and Dakota, and within this field, with an aggregate population of 850,000 souls it has no competitor.

As a newspaper the PIONEER-PRESS AND TRIBUNE is every way worthy of its great constituency. It is an eight-page paper of the size of the great Chicago and New York dailies, and publishes daily more reading matter than any Philadelphia, Cincinnati or Boston daily. Among the western journals the greatest of the Chicago and the St. Louis newspapers can alone compare in standing, influence or circulation with the PIONEER-PRESS. But these newspapers, which overshadow and supplant all rivals in Illinois, Central and Southern Iowa, and Eastern and Southern Wisconsin, are published at points too remote from the great northwestern territory of the PIONEER-PRESS to compete with it in this, its own exclusive field, where it distributes the news of the day from twelve to thirty-six hours ahead of the Chicago dailies, and it is the unrestricted possession of so large a field which has permitted the building up of a first-class newspaper like this in a region so comparatively new. The same conditions which have promoted the marvellous growth of the PIONEER-PRESS in the past afford an ample guarantee that its future growth in circulation and character will be commensurate with the rapid grogress of this great and fertile region, which constitutes the wheat belt of the continent, and is now advancing more rapidly in wealth and population than any other part of the Union.

The DAILY PIONEER-PRESS is universally taken by all classes of readers in Minnesota and the adjacent districts of the neighboring States who take any daily newspaper at all. The WEEKLY PIONEER-PRESS, a magnificent quarto, circulates as universally among the intelligent rural population of Minnesota. Its weekly edition is 14,000, and is rapidly increasing.

The Pioneer-Press Company are also the publishers of the Minneapolis EVENING TRIBUNE, the best evening paper in the State, and the only one in Minneapolis, with a large local circulation.

The Pioneer-Press Company own one of the largest and finest structures devoted to the newspaper and printing business in the West. It was built a few years ago for the St. Paul *Press*, on the corner of Minnesota and Third streets, St. Paul. It is 50 feet front by 150 feet deep, being four stories heigh, with a mansard roof, and two-thirds of its whole area is occupied by the newspaper, printing, binding and lithographic business of the Pioneer-Press Company. It is undoubtedly in all its departments the best equipped printing and newspaper office in the Northwest, outside of Chicago.

THE SACRAMENTO

DAILY AND SEMI-WEEKLY RECORD-UNION.

A LEADING CALIFORNIA NEWSPAPER.

A SKETCH FOR THE BOOK OF THE CENTENNIAL NEWSPAPER EXHIBITION.

Sacramento is the capital of the State of California, centrally located, and the chief city of the interior of the State. The only morning paper published at the capital of the State is the Sacramento RECORD-UNION. Its history is co-equal with that of the State, and closely interwoven with the historical, social and political progress of California. No paper on the Pacific Coast is more widely known, or enjoys a more general circulation. The Sacramento DAILY AND WEEKLY UNION was established in the year 1851. Its progress was one unprecedented in newspaper annals, and during a quarter of a century it justly gained the reputation of being the best newspaper on the Western slope. Its influence was commensurate with its great reputation, and it was the acknowledged leader of independent thought, progress and all material movements looking to the advancement of the State, the upholding of purity in politics and social and business life, and as the most thorough and reliable of newspapers. It was the tocsin for years of all popular movements, the unflinching friend of sobriety, permanency and real merits in all those early years when the society of the Pacific Coast was receiving the impress which should fix its future standing. Its proprietors grew gray in the service, and in 1875 they retired from its management, and it became consolidated with the Sacramento *Daily and Semi-Weekly Record.* The *Record* was established *in facto* in the year 1867. It had for its business rival the *Union*, it moved in the same circle, and sought the same patronage. From the outset it was a prosperous paper. Its conduct was that of energy, refinement and independence. It grew in popular favor day by day and finally stood side by side with its competitor in rank, standing and extended influence. In the height of its career, enjoying an enviable reputation, and recognized as an honor to the State, it was consolidated with the *Union*, and in February, 1875, the RECORD-UNION was issued. Since that date the current of these two papers, flowing in the same channel, has been one of force, independence and broad influence more than equal to that of any newspaper on the Pacific slope. Two marked features distinguish the RECORD-UNION, a total absence of sensationalism, in place of which is a perfect news reliability and energetic spirit; and second, an elevated tone not equalled in the history of journalism. Its departments are seven in number: Editorial, News, Literary, Agricultural, Commercial, Statistical and Local.

In the Editorial Department the RECORD-UNION has no compeer west of the Mississippi for vigor, scholarly ability, clearness of perceptions, nicity of diction or independence and originality of thought. In its News Department its facilities are those afforded by the Associated Press dipsatches, a thorough private system of coast telegraphic news gathering, an extended and able corps of local correspondents and special reporters, and a systematic departmentized arrangement of selected news from an unlimited exchange with the papers of the world. Its Agricultural Department leads all efforts of this kind in newspapers in the United States, and is under the management of a pioneer-experienced and thorough agriculturist. Its Literary Department is ably managed and conducted with an eye-single to presenting the choicest and most varied selections from American, English, German and French literature, and a total exclusion—as, indeed, is done in all the departments—of all matter which can offend the most refined taste, or shock the keenest sensibility. Its Commercial Department is prompt and constantly up to the business standard of the Coast. Its Local Department is controlled in the interest of purely local news, and is acknowledged to be most thorough, correct and dignified of the Coast. The Statistical Department is a marked feature of the paper, and presents constantly all progressive results of State industries and growth, culminating on New Years' day of each year in a mammoth holiday statistical sheet combined with the usual issue of the paper, which on that occasion is marked by enlargement and annual review in all the departments upon topics congenial to them.

In addition, the RECORD-UNION has a large corps of regular Eastern, English German and home correspondents, whose writings partake of the same free, energetic, independent and scholarly character which characterizes the entire paper.

The RECORD-UNION on the Pacific Coast and throughout the Union is acknowledged as the leader in journalistic thought and expression in California. It is thoroughly independent in tone, bound to no party, the organ of no sect or interest, and the tried champion of Republican institutions. Its tendencies are strongly those which are reflected in the principles of the National Republican party, and its constant voice is for the integrity of the government, the perpetuation of free institutions, purity in all govermental branches, and honesty in all things. It enjoys the largest and most extended circulation, daily, of any interior paper, and its semi-weekly edition surpases in extended circulation that of any journal circulating west of the Mississippi.

Its building is one of the most prominent in the capital city, and all its interior arrangements are those usual to a first-class newspaper. The RECORD-UNION as an advertising medium for the Pacific Coast, attests its value by the constantly-crowded condition of the columns set apart for that purpose, and which are availed of with avidity by the business men of the Coast and the great East.

In conclusion, the paper has no equal on the Pacific slope, has no compeer there in influence, intelligence and energy, and no rival in the esteem of the people.

It is published by the Sacramento Publishing Company, of which William H. Mills is general and sole manager. It is issued each morning, except Sunday, and the semi-weekly appears on Wednesdays and Saturdays of each week.

THE PRESBYTERIAN, PHILADELPHIA.

A SKETCH FOR THE BOOK OF THE CENTENNIAL NEWSPAPER EXHIBITION.

The PRESBYTERIAN was established as a weekly journal in the year 1831, and has long been regarded one of the best religious family papers in the country. Its corps of correspondents embrace able writers in all parts of the world. Its editorial columns are presided over by Rev. M. B. Grier, D. D., and Rev. J. A. Mutchmore, D. D. It is an excellent advertising medium, reaching a most substantial and intelligent class of people. The office of publication is at 1512 Chestnut street, Philadelphia.

"JOURNAL," ALBANY, N. Y.

A SKETCH FOR THE BOOK OF THE CENTENNIAL NEWSPAPER EXHIBITION.

THE EVENING JOURNAL was established by Thurlow Weed in 1830. It was in the height of the Anti-Masonic excitement which swept over the State like a wave, and THE JOURNAL was founded as the organ of the very able group of young and aspiring leaders who stood in the front of that public feeling. Mr. Weed was at the time a member of Assembly, and among those who co-operated with him in the enterprise were William H. Seward—with whom Mr. Weed formed an historic friendship—Francis Granger, Albert H. Tracy, and other men of similar stamp, all of whom achieved distinction. The Masonic question soon passed out of politics, and THE JOURNAL at once became the chief Whig organ, and has ever since been the recognized representative in the State of New York, and one of the leading representatives in the country of that party, and of the Republican party which succeeded it.

Mr. Weed speedily developed into one of the most remarkable journalists and politicians the country has ever known. He combined a rare power of terse expression with extraordinary sagacity and skill in management, and for more than thirty-years remained the unquestioned leader of his party in New York—still surviving at an advanced age, though in a retirement from which his wise counsels are often sought and given to the public. THE JOURNAL, as the representative of its party at the capital of the foremost State, has been closely identified with its successes, and has a brilliant political history. It was recently described by the chief newspaper of the opposition as one of the two most nfluential organs of its party in the country. It is now the official State paper, and is one of the few newspapers outside of metropolitan cities which have more than a local circulation. In its several editions—daily, semi-weekly, and weekly—it goes throughout the State, and its aggregate circulation is much larger than that of any other newspaper in New York outside of the metropolis. In the last political campaign its weekly edition reached nearly 50,000, and exceeded in the State even that of any New York paper.

This political prominence and wide circulation make THE JOURNAL a representative paper, and an excellent medium for advertisers. It is enterprising and vigorous in al respects. The feature of a page of choice miscellany, now so general and popular, was first introduced by THE JOURNAL, and it has led the way in other advancements. Its mechanical facilities are superior to those of any other State paper outside of New York. The job office in connection with it is one of the most extensive and best appointed in the United States, and does book and other classes of work for all parts of the country. In a word, THE JOURNAL is very complete in all its departments, and ranks among the most successful and prosperous papers in the land.

It is published by Dawson & Co., George Dawson, the senior proprietor, having been connected with it, except for a brief period, during its whole history. Messrs. Philip Ten Eyck, the business manager, John Ten Eyck, the commercial editor, and John D. Parsons, have also been members of the firm many years, and in 1870 Charles E. Smith joined it, and became one of the editors.

"THE HERALD," BOSTON, MASS.

A SKETCH FOR THE BOOK OF THE CENTENNIAL NEWSPAPER EXHIBITION.

The Centennial year finds the Boston Daily and Sunday HERALD at the head of New England newspapers. For nearly forty years the DAILY HERALD has been established, but the surprising success which now attends it, and which lifts it into association with those journals which admittedly stand foremost in popularity at the present day, was won under the direct management of its present conductors. Long ago it discarded the traditions and forms of the old school of journalism and sought to identify itself with the aims and fully meet the exacting requirements of the generation of to-day. It is progressive. It understands that a journal, like an empire, can never stand still —that for it is inevitable growth or inevitable decay. So it endeavors to be not merely the historian of the hour—chronicling to-day what occurred yesterday—but also to reach out into the future, to deal with the "coming events which cast their shadows before." Editorially it is independent. It refuses to pay slavish court to any party. Its strength is with the people—not with politicians, and therefore nothing which should be reprobated is condoned in order to leave political organizations unshorn of power. It holds itself bound to praise or blame with unrestricted freedom, firmly beieving that the perpetuity of republican government in this country depends, in part, at least, upon a fearless and independent press. But its chief field is New England, and its specialty news. It reaches into every State in that section. It is found in the villages of Maine, and is read more extensively than any other journal on the hillsides of New Hampshire and Vermont. To the people of Rhode Island and Connecticut, as well as to the citizens of western Massachusetts, its name is as familiar as a household word. It has also a wide metropolitan constituency, and with the inhabitants of Boston and its suburbs it is unquestionably the favorite newspaper of the time. As it addresses itself to all of the New England States, so does it address itself to all classes. It visits rich and poor alike. It is purchased by merchant and mechanic, by farmer and laborer. Of course its daily edition is enormous. For years it has not printed less than 100,000 daily. More frequently the number has reached 125,000, while editions of 150,000, and on exceptional occasions 175,000 and 200,000, are produced. Last year 35,612,208 copies were printed and sold. This circulation, so enormous, so various, so widespread, is far beyond that of any of its contemporaries. It daily exceeds that of most of them by nearly 100,000 copies. Its most enterprising rival claims a distribution of but 33,000 copies per day, thereby surrendering to THE HERALD a daily superiority in circulation of nearly 100,000 copies. And if the editions of all the other newspapers published daily in Boston be combined, it still is indisputable that to THE HERALD remains the distinction of printing 30,000 copies more than the public demand calls upon its contemporaries to produce. The paper which it daily consumes weighs near y six tons, and if stretched in a continuous line would reach almost from Boston to Portland. To supply this marvelous demand the mechanical departments are simply perfect. To this end one Mayall and three perfecting Bullock presses are used, and each of these splendid specimens of mechanism, with seemingly more than human ingenuity, cast forth the paper, printed upon both sides from stereotype plates, at the rate of 20,000 impressions per hour. Upon advertisers the knowledge of these facts is not without effect. Their demands are imperative and constant. Space is alike in request by merchants who advertise at an expense of thousands of dollars annually, and by individuals who simply solicit employment or assistance for themselves, who lease or sell, who buy or hire dwellings and estates. In brief, the wish to secure admission to its advertising columns and profit by its unbounded circulation is general among all trades.

THE SUNDAY HERALD was established in 1861. It is a handsome quarto sheet of 64 columns, conducted upon the same principles as THE DAILY HERALD, and has attained a circulation of 60,000, being recognized as the best paper issued in New England. Both of these journals are conducted under the business and editorial supervision of R. M. Pulsifer & Co.

"THE EVENING WISCONSIN," MILWAUKEE.

EDITED FOR THIRTY YEARS BY WM. E. CRAMER.

A SKETCH FOR THE BOOK OF THE CENTENNIAL NEWSPAPER EXHIBITION.

THE EVENING WISCONSIN, of Milwaukee, was founded in 1847 by Wm. E. Cramer, who for nearly thirty years has been the head and directing power of its editorial staff. Mr. Cramer served his apprenticeship under Edwin Croswell, of the Albany *Argus*, and took with him to his new home in the West the practical experience which at once demanded attention for his journal, which has not only kept pace with the marked and rapid progress of the West, but has become the acknowledged leading newspaper of the city and State.

Mr. Cramer is a close observer, a shrewd critic of men and their work, and a ready and pleasing writer; and under his guidance the paper has secured a great measure of success. He spent three years in Europe, and made other visits of length to Mexico, to Cuba and other points, and his letters to THE WISCONSIN were not only largely read at home, but largely copied and favorably commented upon by metropolitan journals in all sections. THE EVENING WISCONSIN has a well earned reputation as a family newspaper, and is the only evening paper that has been able to establish itself permanently in Milwaukee. Republican in politics, it is bound by no party trammels. The weekly edition of THE WISCONSIN is known throughout the West as a complete family paper, and, like the daily, enjoys a very large circulation.

THE EVENING WISCONSIN was the first daily paper in the Northwest to adopt the system of making up news on the outside of the paper, and the first to adopt cash in advance for subscriptions.

It was in THE WISCONSIN office that the system of co-operative newspaper printing was first developed by one of the publishers. The Milwaukee Newspaper Union is a part of the printing department of THE WISCONSIN office, and the proprietors have seen the work set afloat by them in a decade grow so wonderfully, that to-day *two thousand newspapers*, or one-half of all the county journals of the United States, are so printed.

THE EVENING WISCONSIN office has unquestionably the most complete printing department of any paper in the State, and the proprietors have spared no expense to keep it up. They have completed arrangements for the erection of a new building in Milwaukee, and it will be ready for occupancy next season. Built and fitted for the large business of the office, it will be one of the most notable printing houses in the Northwest. THE EVENING WISCONSIN is published and the business conducted by Cramer, Aikens & Cramer, experienced newspaper men, as the success of their various enterprises testifies.

THE CO-OPERATIVE NEWSPAPERS.

A SKETCH FOR THE BOOK OF THE CENTENNIAL NEWSPAPER EXHIBITION.

A most remarkable peculiarity of American journalism is the combination or system of so-called "Co-operative Newspapers," a system originated about fourteen years ago, and which has had a wonderful growth, until it now embraces over 2,000 of the weekly journals of the United States—and the number is still increasing.

Comparatively few people are aware of the existence of this important element of journalism. Unless the reader is connected with the press or is a general advertiser, he probably is unacquainted with the meaning of the term "Co-operative Newspaper." If, during a visit to the Newspaper Pavilion, you should take up for perusal some newspaper published, for instance, in one of the interior towns of New York, and should afterwards take up a newspaper published in some town in Pennsylvania, you might be very much surprised to find that there was apparently a striking coincidence in the articles appearing in the two papers. It would lead you to compare them. You would notice that there were two pieces of poetry in the first column of one of the papers, and on turning to the other paper you would observe the same two poems in the same corner of that paper. Following the poetry in one paper there would be a story occupying several columns; you look into the other paper and find the same story there. You think it a very strange coincidence that two editors, one hundred miles apart, should have made the same selections to that extent the same week, and that the articles should be placed in the same position in both papers. You compare the papers further, and notice a summary of the news of the week. Both papers have the same summary, word for word. Then the advertisements are examined and found to be precisely alike in both papers and placed in the same order. A further examination reveals the fact that the outside pages of both papers are exactly alike throughout, with the exception of the heading which gives the name of the papers. Your curiosity is aroused, and you determine to solve the mystery. If you inquire of one of the attendants at the Pavilion you will obtain the information sought for. You will be informed that the two papers were both printed at an establishment in New York city, which also prints over 300 other newspapers. It prints but one side of the sheet, however, the matter selected for this purpose consisting of general news, literature, poetry, agricultural and other subjects of general interest. The other side of the sheet is printed subsequently at the office of publication, and is filled with editorials, and local news and advertisements. The papers printed at the New York establishment are not all exactly alike, however, nor of the same size. Nine different sizes of folio and quarto sheets are printed, and when two or more papers are supplied which are published in the same or near-by counties, the matter furnished is entirely different. Similar establishments exist in Chicago, Milwaukee, Cincinnati, Memphis, St. Paul, and other cities, and altogether they save to the country press over $2,000,000 annually. There is also a further great saving to advertisers. Formerly, if a general advertiser wished to insert an advertisement in these 2,000 papers, the expense of correspondence and the time involved in making contracts was necessarily very great. This time and expense are saved to the advertiser under the co-operative method, and he also secures a lower rate for the advertising than he could obtain from the papers direct, for the reason that an advertisement does not require to be set up 2,000 times, or once for each paper, but only forty times, and it frequently happens that the price charged for an advertisement is less than the actual cost of setting up the type, if it were set up once for each newspaper. The leading advertisers of the country patronize these lists very extensively, and it is not uncommon for the annual bills of an advertiser to amount to from $10,000 to $20,000, and sometimes to even $30,000 to $40,000. The Chicago *Daily Times* of March 11, 1876, thus alludes to the American Newspaper Union, which includes 1,200 of the co-operative papers:

Within the past twelve years there has been a vast improvement made in the country newspaper—particularly in respect to the care in which all the news of the day is gathered and edited, and the literary ability displayed in its columns, which relieves the provincial press from the few objections that have been heretofore urged against it, and has accorded to it higher dignity, extended its influence, and greatly augmented its power for good. The typographical appearance of the country journal of to-day is perfect; the display and classification of its advertisements tasty; the quality of the paper used and the printing far superior to that of its city contemporaries.

This has been chiefly due to the American Newspaper Union, which practically shapes the literary tone of some 1,200 different newspapers scattered through the Eastern, Middle, Western, and Southwestern States; collates their foreign and national news, selects their miscellany from the best sources, and infuses a vigor into their columns such as they never knew before. The work of the American Newspaper Union is as curious and interesting as it is valuable. We doubt if many of our city readers understand the peculiar field in journalism that it occupies, and we therefore devote a little space to the subject for the purpose of conveying the information.

The idea on which the Union is founded originated with Mr. A. J. Aikens some twelve years ago. He was then engaged in the publishing business at Milwaukee, and being a practical printer and a thorough business man, the thought occurred to him that a number of country papers might co-operate and have the inside, *i. e.*, the news and literary portion of their sheets, printed at one general city office, where the opportunity for having the work well done is superior to that enjoyed by most country newspaper offices. The idea was put into practical operation at the office of Cramer, Aikens & Cramer, proprietors of the *Evening Wisconsin*, Milwaukee, and it worked so admirably as to attract the attention of newspaper men all over the country, and met with universal approval.

The cost of advertising in these lists is ridiculously cheap. *One cent per line* in each paper covers the expense. We are not aware of any kind of newspaper advertising, good, bad, or indifferent, that will compare in point of cheapness with this. But when we take into consideration the character of the papers, the class of intelligent readers whom they reach, their power and influence, their general diffusion over the whole country, and the manner in which the advertisement is printed, it must be admitted that the American Newspaper Union has reached the desideratum long sought for by advertisers, viz.: "The largest amount of benefit for the least possible sum of money."

The economy of advertising in these lists is apparent for another reason, viz.: If the advertiser desires to use a cut in his advertisement, but one cut is necessary for the whole 1,200 papers. If he were to advertise direct with 1,200 different papers it would require an equal number of cuts, and the cost for the cuts and for postage would equal or exceed the cost of the advertising, as many advertisers have found to their sorrow heretofore. And they found, too, to their disgust, that their advertisements were not always inserted as directed, being frequently left out and often disfigured by the dropping out of type. With the Union the advertiser is relieved of all trouble, all expense for extra cuts and postage; the advertisement is neatly set up and stereotyped, and the advertiser may rely on its going in the whole edition of 1,200, for if the officers of the Union were disposed to leave it out of a part of their edition, it would cost them more than to print it.

The distribution of the papers is as follows:

New England	78	Indiana	81	Iowa	85
New York	101	Illinois	117	Nebraska	15
New Jersey	27	Michigan	86	Missouri	17
Pennsylvania	65	Wisconsin	98	Georgia	10
Virginia	24	Tennessee	29	Alabama	32
No. and So. Carolina	24	Kentucky	29	Louisiana	11
Ohio	122	Minnesota	79	Mississippi	29

Other States, 46.

Persons wishing to learn more of this subject, or to make arrangements for advertising in the lists, should send for a catalogue to either of the establishments, as follows:

New York Newspaper Union............150 Worth street, New York.
Chicago Newspaper Union............114 Monroe street, Chicago.
Aikens Newspaper Union............143 Race street, Cincinnati.
Milwaukee Newspaper Union............365 East Water street, Milwaukee.
Southern Newspaper Union............227 Second street, Memphis.
St. Paul Newspaper Union............17 Wabashaw street, St. Paul

Bound volumes of the various sizes of newspapers of the different lists may be seen in the Newspaper Pavilion, Fairmount Park, during the Centennial Exhibition. An inspection of these volumes will be found an interesting eature of the exhibition.

G. P. ROWELL & CO.--ADVERTISING AGENCY.

A SKETCH FOR THE BOOK OF THE CENTENNIAL NEWSPAPER EXHIBITION.

WHAT IS AN ADVERTISING AGENCY?

A gentleman lately stepped into the office of the New York *Times* for the purpose of inserting a notice of "Situation Wanted" for a cook, who had lived in his family and for whom he was desirous of obtaining a place before closing up housekeeping, as he then contemplated. The girl had, at a former period, lived in Brooklyn, and, having friends there, it was thought best to insert the advertisement in the Brooklyn *Eagle*. Intending to give the matter his personal attention, he inquired the location, in Brooklyn, of the office of the *Eagle*. He was informed that if he was going there for the purpose of causing this advertisement to appear in that paper, he could save himself the trouble by leaving the order in the advertising agency in the *Times* building, up stairs.

GEO. P. ROWELL & CO'S COUNTING ROOM.

The gentleman thereupon came to the agency with the order—six lines, one insertion—for which he paid sixty cents, being informed that that was the amount required according to the rates of the Brooklyn paper. Never having heard of an advertising agency before, the advertiser wished to know how much additional he must pay for being saved the journey, ferry fares and time. In answer to this he was informed that, upon making settlement with the *Eagle*, the sum of twelve cents would be allowed to the agency as a commission or payment for the service rendered in taking and forwarding the order.

This incident conveys nearly all that can be told to explain the uses of a Newspaper Advertising Agency. Had the notice been intended for a San Fráncisco paper, for one in Montreal, New Orleans, or any of the New York city journals, it would have been received on the same terms. The Advertising Agency is a convenience; it is nothing more.

The advertising agent, from the knowledge gained by experience, becomes an expert. He learns from papers the lowest prices which they say they will accept for advertisements. He learns from advertisers the rebates and favors which they have obtained. He knows the strong points and the weak points of the publishers; what papers will take advertisements low and what class of advertisements they will take lowest.

To nine persons in every ten the words Newspaper Advertising Agency convey no idea. They never heard of such a thing, or, if they have, wondered what it was all about. Of the forty millions of people in the United States not more than one in five hundred pays a penny in a year for an advertisement in a newspaper. Of those who do, barely one in ten advertises beyond his own immediate neighborhood, and consequently has no occasion to consult or advise with any agent or middle man.

The above calculations give 10,000 persons, distributed throughout the Union, but mainly in the larger cities, who advertise or desire to advertise in papers issued at a distance from their homes, about the character, appearance, value, circulation and prices of which they have no reliable information. An Advertising Agency is the source from which such information may be obtained.

Inasmuch as no more than one person in five thousand has any personal interest in them, and that the existence of such institutions dates back hardly forty years, no cause exists for wonder that, to the general public, their uses are not well known.

To many persons who have some knoweledge of Advertising Agencies, the scope of their business is still unknown. We write with a hope of making the matter better understood and to answer some of the questions which are so frequently propounded by interested inquirers.

A Newspaper Advertising Agency doing a general business is an institution where are received and kept on file copies of newspapers issued in various parts of the country, which are mailed to the agency, that they may be there accessible to persons who desire to use their advertising columns. Schedules or tables of rates, and special information about the cost of advertising in each separate paper are also a necessary part of the paraphernalia of the agency.

Some Agencies make a speciality of a certain class of publications, as for instance: in New York one takes advertising for magazines, another for papers printed in the German language, several confine their operations almost exclusively to publications issued in the city, while in various parts of the country are those who make a leading specialty of the religious press; others, again, represent only country papers, while a few act for every class, shade, and denomination of the entire press of the country.

As the files of papers which are found at the agency are furnished by publishers gratuitously, they are taken as establishing the authority of the agency to represent such as are regularly received, and for which a schedule of advertising rates has been furnished.

The cost of the yearly subscription upon his publication is a tax which the publisher pays for the support of the agency. As the payment of this tax is voluntary, the regular receipt of the paper is, with reason, taken to be the sufficient authorization of the agency to represent it. By this rule may be tested the comparative hold possessed by the various establishments of this kind upon the confidence and esteem of newspaper publishers.

WHO ARE THE PATRONS OF ADVERTISING AGENCIES?

Few persons have any conception of the amount of money paid for newspaper advertising. The number of papers printed in the various States exceeds eight thousand; while the advertising patronage of a single New York daily is said to exceed $750,000 per annum! To insert a single column on the last page of the principal illustrated weekly costs no less than $720 a week—$4 a line! If every paper averages an annual receipt of $1,000 per annum from advertisements, we have $8,000,000 in the aggregate; while, if every paper printed received the magnificent patronage of the daily above referred to, it would amount to sufficient to pay the national debt in four months!

Only advertisers in the largest cities have occasion to apply to an agency concerning advertising in their own vicinity. The principal patrons of the Advertising Agency are those who wish to reach distant points. Of these, first in importance are the patent medicine men; next comes that class whose announcements commences with the words, "Agents Wanted," which includes dealers in subscription books, sewing machines, patent rights, and the thousand and one articles which may be sold by hawkers or pedlers; then come the Bond advertisements, "For I vestment," Land Companies, "All Wanting Farms," Gift Concerts, Newspaper Prospectuses, Business Cards, &c., &c. Advertisements of "Information Wanted," are also among those most frequently brought to the agency, but as they go into few papers, and for no more than one or two issues, their cost is inconsiderable.

Several individual advertisers, known to the writer, are in the habit of investing yearly upward of $100,000 per annum, but their number will not exceed ten. Perhaps fifty or more spend as much as $20,000; while those who pay sums ranging from $1,000 to $10,000 may be counted by hundreds. The amounts expended by those remaining, to make up the ten thousand who send advertisements beyond their immediate neighborhood, range from one dollar upward, according as hope, caprice, their desire to experiment, or their means of paying may dictate.

WHAT THE ADVERTISER GAINS BY EMPLOYING THE AGENCY.

"What do I gain by going to the Advertising Agency in preference to appealing to the paper direct?" is the question most frequently propounded by the novice in advertising. To this the true answer can only be, Convenience and the benefit of experience.

The old advertiser, of undoubted responsibility, who knows what he it about, knows the value of papers, their prices; knows how to set up his advertisement to secure the best display in the smallest space, and how to order its insertion that the publisher will not extract a justification for an extra or increased charge, has nothing to gain by transacting his business through an agency except the convenience of making one transaction, verifying one account at one place, at one time, and paying one bill instead of many. Yes the old advertiser deals mainly through agencies for this reason, and the saving of time, stationery and postage.

It is not fair to suppose that the reputable agent will underbid his principal; his duty does not lie in that direction. It is his province to arrange that his advertiser shall not pay for more space than he requires, that he get a good position without an unnecessary extra charge. The advertiser who deals through a reputable agency knows beforehand that the cost is not to exceed a given sum. If more must be paid the matter is submitted for his reconsideration. How many advertisers have received from publishers bills amounting to dollars when they expected to pay dimes only—to hundreds of dollars when they supposed tens would be all that would be required? How many have ordered the insertion of cards by word of mouth, believing that advertising was cheap, and learned when too late how erroneous was any such supposition?

It is a notorious fact that as soon as advertisers begin to do business through agencies their bills decrease in individual papers, and the amount saved is devoted to extending the announcement in other journals, procuring thereby a wider circulation. It is in recognition of this fact that some publishers decline allowing any commission to an agency on advertisements from those who have previously dealt with the paper direct. So thoroughly is it understood that no advertiser now deals direct who understands his interests, pays his advertising bills, and makes them pay him, that it is often considered an evidence of irresponsibility or incapacity for an advertiser to apply direct for terms of advertising. There are exceptions to this rule among the largest and oldest advertisers, who commenced business before the agency system was perfected; but it requires good credit and a well-known name to bring specific answers from publishers to applications for rates or even orders for insertion, as many an advertiser has found out to his chagrin, although classed in the mercantile books as of first-rate standing.

As the advertising agent is paid for his services, and for assuming to become responsible to the publisher for the payment of all bills for advertising ordered through the agency, it becomes common for the advertisers to demand the same allowance on their own business when they deal direct. To this demand publishers who are in the habit of sustaining their rates rarely respond, but inasmuch as the making of the request supported by such questions as, "Isn't my money as good as that of the agent's," etc., etc., expose the advertiser to the imputation of being deficient in sense or moral rectitude, or that he believes the publisher to be so, the latter sometimes forgets himself and the duty he owes his agent, and makes a reduction equivalent to the agent's commission, as the easiest way of satisfying the advertiser and putting an end to further talk or correspondence. The advertiser not infrequently finds, by after experience, that the agent is able to procure for him even a greater reduction, and at the same time retain his own commission intact.

A moment's careful consideration will convince an advertiser of good sense that although a publisher would prefer the order direct, when sure of his pay, for the sake of saving the reduction taken by the agency for a commission, yet if the reduction *must* be made in one shape or another, leaving him nothing to gain, he will prefer to give it to the agent, to whom it can be allowed without seeming to break down his rates or violating his self-respect.

The advantages of the Newspaper Advertising Agency to the advertiser then are these:—Experience without cost; one contract instead of many; guarded against unnecessary extra charges, and knowing in advance the price, beyond which an order will not be carried without his full knowledge and consent.

Of those advertisers who believe that they can obtain the same net terms direct as would be accorded to the agency, we ask, is it reasonable that publishers should extend as good rates to an advertiser who expends $5,000 a year as to an agent who forwards $50,000 a month? If any one is to be pleased or catered to, is it not, under the circumstances, more likely to be the agent? Would eight thousand publishers contribute free their periodicals from year to year, the subscriptions upon which, taking dailies, weeklies, and all, amounts to more than $20,000 per annum, and then set about undermining the institution for the support of which they have paid so much? Is such a supposition reasonable? The truth is that between the best class of agencies and the publishers there is no competition. On any considerable order, the agent, by taking advantage of every point in the advertiser's favor, is *always* below the aggregate price obtained by application to publishers.

Before entrusting his work to an agency an advertiser should first satisfy himself of its ability to secure for him the best advantages, after which his business should be placed in the hands of the agent selected, and kept there as long as he is faithfully served. When confidence is no longer had in the agent, let the advertiser resort to no half-way measure, but withdraw his patronage altogether.

THE BEST ADVERTISING AGENCY.

The best advertising agency is one that secures so much business from a good class of advertisers as to enable it to command from the greatest number of publishers the most favorable rates ever accorded.

The American Newspaper Advertising Agency of Geo. P. Rowell & Co., No. 41 Park Row, New York, is the principal one in the United States, and by far the most complete establishment of the kind in the world, for in no other country are these institutions conducted with anything like the system which obtains here. Messrs. Geo. P. Rowell & Co. established their agency in 1865, and in 1870 consolidated with and succeeded to the business of the advertising agency conducted till that time, since 1840, by Mr. John Hooper, who was the first advertising agent who did business in the city of New York.

The Advertising Agency of Messrs. Geo. P. Rowell & Co. controls by far the largest amount of advertising patronage ever secured by any institution of the kind. From their office is forwarded an amount not short of that emanating from all the other agencies in the United States combined. They receive and have on file all newspapers published in the United States and Canadas, with scarcely an exception of importance. They receive the best terms and largest reductions allowed to any advertising agency.

They are the source from which all other advertising agencies, without any exception, derive their information about newspapers. Let an advertiser step into any agency and ask the name of the publisher of a paper at any distant point; let him ask how many papers are issued in such and such a city, how many are daily, how many weekly, what is the politics, character, or circulation. To any or all of these questions he will receive no reply until a reference has been made to Geo. P. Rowell & Co's Annual Newspaper Directory. No account is kept in any other agency of the new papers which are started; now averaging five every day; or of the old ones, which die or change hands. For all information of this kind all the agencies depend upon Geo. P. Rowell & Co's Weekly NEWSPAPER REPORTER.

Besides the advantage of their position at the head of their business, they have special contracts which give them an unequaled advantage in more than two thousand of the newspapers of the country.

WHAT IS DONE WITH THE NEWSPAPERS?

Messrs. Geo. P. Rowell & Co. receive more than one hundred and forty thousand newspapers every three months, or more than seventeen hundred and fifty every day. On occasions in the winter, when the snows interfere with the regular running of the trains, as soon as the blockade is removed it not unfrequently happens that as many as twenty-five bushels will come in of a single morning, counting possibly as many as ten thousand papers in one mail delivery.

What *becomes* of all the papers? What do you do with them? are questions which are often asked The papers coming from every quarter are assorted throughout the day and night by the Post-office employes. Those addressed to Geo. P. Rowell & Co's Advertising Agency are thrown into large mail bags, arranged on a rack or frame made to support them, with the mouth held open, and these, when filled, are tied at the top and set aside to wait until called for. The bags are brought to the office, after which the papers are taken out, and heaped upon a table. Then the wrappers are taken off and the papers smoothed out, uniformly folded and arranged

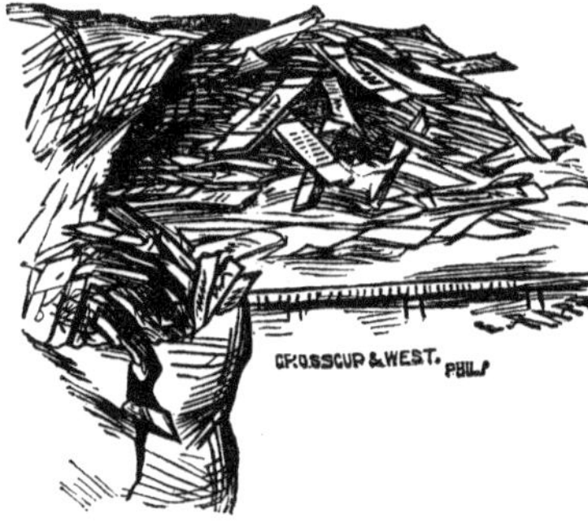

by States, after which the various piles are handed over to the men who have in charge the business of examining each separate paper to make sure that advertisements ordered from the Agency are being inserted according to specifications of contract.

The country is divided into sections and apportioned out. One person attends to papers issued in

the city of New York; another checks those in States near by; one has Canada, one the South, and another the Territories and Pacific Coast.

With his book spread out before him the work of examination and checking proceeds.

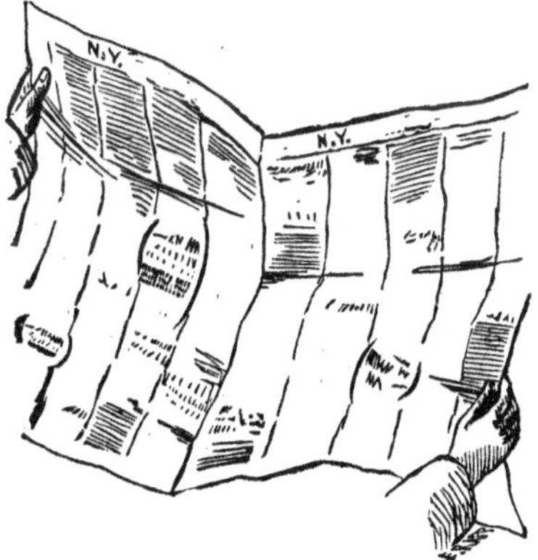

546 Chicago (Ill) Prairie Farmer.

ORDER BOOK	ADVERTISEMENTS.	SPACE	POSITION	TIME	DATE OF ORDER		JANUARY				FEBRUARY				MARCH					APRIL				MAY				
							4	11	18	25	1	8	15	22	1	8	15	22	29	5	12	19	26	3	10	17	24	&c
3K10	Geo. Stinson & Co.	5 l.	Ord.	1 year	Jan	3/73		/\	//	//	//	//	X	//	//	//		//	//	//	//	//	//	//	//		//	
3N28	D. M. Ferry & Co.	35 l.	"	1 time	Feb	19 "										/\												
3N42	S. T. Sanford & Sons	6 l.	S.N.	1y E.O.W.	"	22 "													/\	X	//	X	/'	X	/'		//	
3P28	Dr. O. Phelps Brown	3 in	Ord	4 times	Mch	4 "												/\	//	//	//							
3R40	C. H. Drake & Co.	13 "	5th pg	1 year	"	20 "														/\	//	/,	/,	//	//		/'	
3S92	Claverack College	5 l.	R.N.	4 times	Apl	10 "																/\	//	//	X		//	

Every paper in which an advertisement is running is opened out and the advertisements, one or more, are marked with a crayon so as to be easily found or seen at a glance when the advertiser comes to make *his* examination before paying his bill.

The checking books are arranged to show the actual number of insertions which every advertisement is to receive. Special marks are used to designate special things, and the checking clerk, guided by instructions, produces a page which will show the advertiser at a glance whether his insertions have been truly and correctly rendered, or otherwise.

- /\ **first insertion.**
- // **correct insertion.**
- /' **wrong position.**
- /, **short space.**
- X **omission.**

By the accompanying diagram the plan is made plain, as in use for a weekly paper. The name of the advertiser, the space, position, style and length of time an advertisement must appear are all indicated. The various marks have their meaning—all easily understood and not readily mistaken

If a paper fails to come to hand, the checking book reveals the fact, and it is sent for. It may not be of much importance, but the clerk in charge is instructed not to consider that, but to GET THE PAPER *and keep files complete.*

If an advertisement is materially wrong, is out of position, has important typographical errors, or for any reason is not what the advertiser is entitled to expect, notice is dispatched to the publisher at once, and the error is made good by another insertion or a reduction from the bill.

This system is carried to great perfection.

The checking books are kept permanently for inspection by advertisers. The papers themselves are kept three months from date of issue, after that time the Agency does not guarantee to exhibit them.

After the examination and marking, the paper is again folded, and receives a heavy mark on its upper right hand corner to indicate that it has passed through the requisite examination, and is ready to be placed upon file. It is then taken and placed in the space accorded to it. Every weekly paper is assigned a pigeonhole, 8 inches by 10 1-2, and one foot deep, while to a daily is accorded three such. These spaces are all designated by a label, having printed upon it the name of the paper to which the space is accorded.

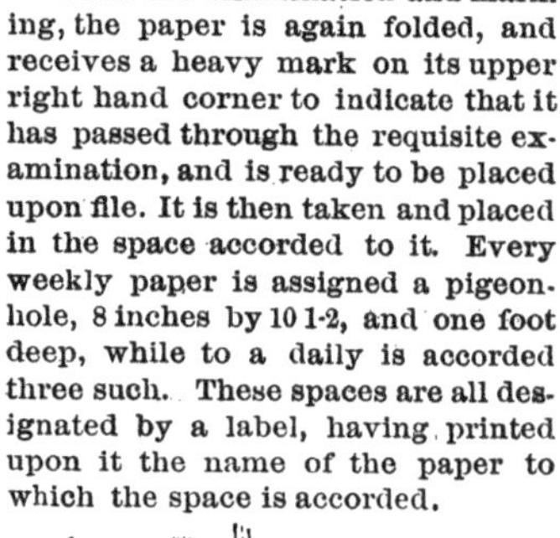

These being placed in tiers or cases placed back to back and set up to form galleries, so as to permit of the whole being arranged alphabetically by States, the name of each State being designated on the cases and again over the entrance to each separate gallery.

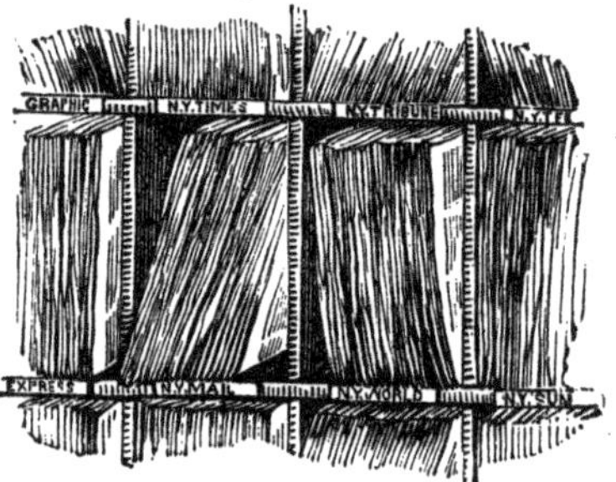

A stranger is thus enabled to search out the depository for his own local paper, or any other that he may desire to see, with as much readiness as he finds a word in a dictionary or a name in a directory.

These galleries being arranged one story above another and as compactly as possible, occupying portions of the same rooms where all the work upon the papers is performed, leave nothing to be desired in the way of convenience.

An advertiser whose rule it is to pay no bills until he sees *all the papers* can here be accommodated, and a business amounting to $20,000 per annum in cheap country papers can be looked after (every copy of every paper examined) by the advertiser, or his representative, who will devote three days' time to the examination four times a year.

The time required for examining papers is mainly used in looking after the advertisement which is *not* there. This work has all been done beforehand, and each advertisement marked plainly with a black crayon. If it is so marked the examiner takes in its appearance, style, position, everything in an instant, and if it is *not* marked he need go no farther; it is not there, and he is entitled to one other insertion or an allowance.

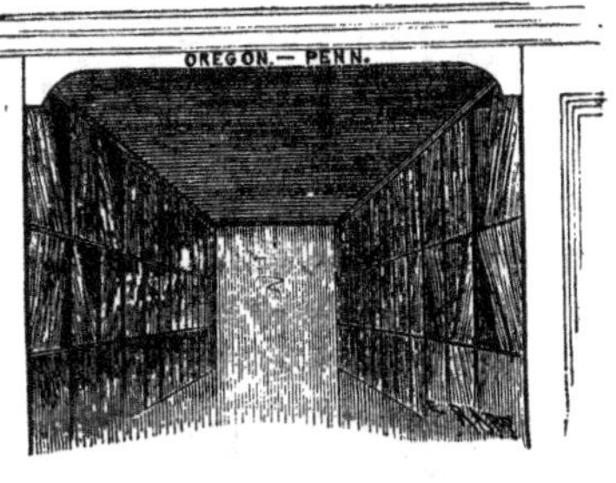

An important use of having complete files of papers so conveniently arranged consists in being able to produce for large advertisers samples of all the papers in which they wish to insert their announcements, that they may *see* for themselves what each paper looks like, and judge what style of advertising will be most effective in each.

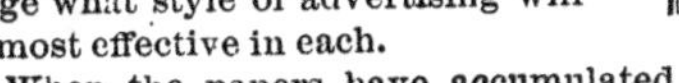

When the papers have accumulated until their alloted spaces assume a crowded appearance, then comes the final solution of the problem of "What do you do with them?" Boys go through the galleries, extract the superfluous papers from each of the spaces (being careful to leave a complete file for at least three months), throw them into one great heap; after which a dealer in paper stock sends men who cart them all away, and in another month they may be found in the store of the paper dealer, made into new bundles, upon which may again be printed other papers to repeat the same round of experiences.

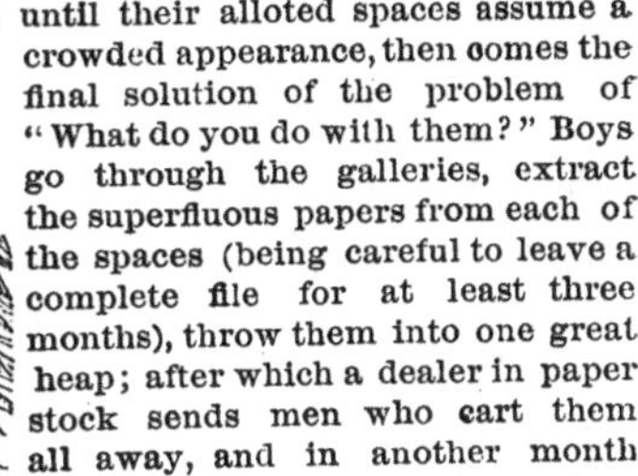

As a display of sample copies of eight thousand newspapers, the Centennial Exhibition in the Newspaper Pavilion at Fairmount Park, Philadelphia, attracts well-merited attention. It is substantially a reproduction of Geo. P. Rowell & Co's Advertising Agency in the city of New York, except that as the latter has been established many years, and conducted upon a carefully-arranged system, it is more complete in its arrangements than would be possible to make such an exhibition elsewhere in a few weeks or months.

THE BURLINGTON, IOWA, "HAWK-EYE."

A METROPOLITAN EIGHT-PAGE DAILY. HAWK-EYE PUBLISHING COMPANY, PUBLISHERS.

This bright Western paper, under the able management of its young chief, Mr. Frank Hatton, hardly yet thirty years of age, has, within the two years of his proprietorship, earned a national reputation for its terse and vigorous handling of all live topics, and for its sparkling and original humor. It is quoted and circulated from ocean to ocean, from Maine to Texas and the mountains, being universally acknowledged one of the best of its class. THE HAWK-EYE occupies the ground floor, 30x130 feet, and five floors 30x80 feet—undoubtedly one of the finest newspaper buildings in the West. On the great transcontinental line, well known as the "Burlington Route," in the very centre of the richest portion of the country, in a town of 30,000 people, why should it not grow and prosper? The first paper in Iowa to require and use for its circulation a double cylinder press, it leads in all things and follows in nothing. Republican and Radical in politics, it fearlessly and independently criticises Republicans as it sees their errors.

While its daily has a general circulation unequaled by any other daily, in a territory at least 350 miles in diameter, it also has a large and growing weekly circulation unparalleled in its immediate locality, and a very warm and admiring support in city and country round. Besides a regular city and mail circulation of 2,500 copies daily it has a metropolitan circulation, by news-dealers and train dealers, reaching often 1,000 and frequently 1,500 copies per day. Dealers declare that within 100 miles east and 150 miles west of Burlington they sell more of HAWK-EYES than any other except Chicago papers, and ten to twenty times as many as of all other Iowa papers. Jealous of its supremacy as a newspaper, welcome to people of all parties for its editorials, literature, and wit, and the fullness of its press and market reports, it does not wish to make itself a cheap circulating advertiser; but to those who choose to pay its rates it offers one of the best mediums in the country for reaching a large and excellent portion of the people. The local patronage of THE HAWK-EYE is the best we have ever seen, and shows the faith the people of the Hawk-Eye State have in THE HAWK-EYE newspaper.

www.ingramcontent.com/pod-product-compliance
Lightning Source LLC
LaVergne TN
LVHW020242110826
845151LV00003B/1003

* 9 7 8 1 4 2 5 5 2 8 8 8 1 *